CULTURALLY COMPETENT PRACTICE

A Framework for Understanding Diverse Groups and Justice Issues

FOURTH EDITION

Doman Lum, Editor
California State University, Sacramento

BROOKS/COLE
CENGAGE Learning

Australia • Brazil • Japan • Korea • Mexico • Singapore • Spain • United Kingdom • United States

BROOKS/COLE
CENGAGE Learning

Culturally Competent Practice: A Framework for Understanding Diverse Groups and Justice Issues, Fourth Edition
Doman Lum

Acquisition Editor: Seth Dobrin

Assistant Editor: Nicolas Albert

Editorial Assistant: Rachel McDonald

Media Editor: Dennis Fitzgerald

Marketing Manager: Trent Whatcott

Marketing Assistant: Darlene Macanan

Marketing Communications Manager:
Tami Strang

Content Project Manager: Sathyabama Kumaran,
Pre-PressPMG

Creative Director: Rob Hugel

Art Director: Caryl Gorska

Print Buyer: Linda Hsu

Rights Acquisitions Account Manager, Text:
Bob Kauser

Rights Acquisitions Account Manager, Image:
Don Schlotman

Production Service: Pre-PressPMG

Text Designer: Pre-PressPMG

Photo Researcher: Pre-PressPMG

Illustrator: Pre-PressPMG

Cover Designer: Caryl Gorska

Cover Image: ML Harris/Iconica/Getty Images

Compositor: Pre-PressPMG

For product information and technology assistance, contact us at
Cengage Learning Customer & Sales Support, 1-800-354-9706.

For permission to use material from this text or product, submit all requests online at **www.cengage.com/permissions**.
Further permissions questions can be e-mailed to
permissionrequest@cengage.com.

Library of Congress Control Number: 2010922530

ISBN-13: 978-0-8400-3443-4

ISBN-10: 0-8400-3443-1

Brooks/Cole
20 Davis Drive
Belmont, CA 94002-3098
USA

Cengage Learning is a leading provider of customized learning solutions with office locations around the globe, including Singapore, the United Kingdom, Australia, Mexico, Brazil, and Japan. Locate your local office at **www.cengage.com/global**.

Cengage Learning products are represented in Canada by Nelson Education, Ltd.

To learn more about Brooks/Cole, visit **www.cengage.com/brookscole**

Purchase any of our products at your local college store or at our preferred online store **www.cengagebrain.com**.

Printed in the United States of America
4 5 6 7 8   21 20 19 18 17

To my wife, Joyce, children and their spouses, and grandchildren: Lori and her husband Noel and children Riley and Alyssa; Jonathan and his wife Lisa and child Evan; Amy and her husband Ross and children Jack and Joel; and Matthew, my youngest son.

This book is dedicated to my growing family who have been a blessing, joy, and challenge for over 38 years. May you all celebrate your diversity, culture, and ethnicity and strive to be good to each other and do good to others.

BRIEF CONTENTS

CONTENTS

FOREWORD

Lorraine Gutierriez

I am honored and delighted to write a brief foreword to this new edition of *Culturally Competent Practice: A Framework for Understanding Diverse Groups and Justice Issues*. In this book, one of our foremost scholars in the field of culture in social work practice moves our field forward to address the complex challenges of social work practice in the 21st century. This new edition presents a thorough reconceptualization of how we need to incorporate and address cultural understanding into our practice.

When Dr. Lum and others began their work on cultural competence and culturally sensitive practice over 25 years ago, they were concerned with the rapid demographic changes in our society. Since that time, the changes have accelerated and we will soon live in a country in which people of color will comprise the majority of the population. This demographic growth takes place in an era in which economic and educational opportunities have contracted and racial, gender, and ethnic inequalities have persisted. It is now imperative for our field to develop ways to work effectively with communities of color. Our society demands that social workers learn ways to effectively build human capital and reduce or eliminate these social inequalities.

The civil rights struggles and liberation movements in the late 20th century contributed to our focus on race, gender, ethnicity, and culture. Our profession was strongly influenced by social workers and community members who questioned a practice paradigm that encouraged us to be culture free and universal. These internal and external critiques led us to consider how gender, culture, sexual orientation, race, and other social identities play in the experiences, problems, and solutions of the communities with which we work. These early critics and advocates placed equal importance on developing methods that were culturally relevant *and* focused on advocacy and social development and change. Since these early years, models for culturally relevant methods, programs, policies, and services have been developed. However, during these decades, we have sometimes lost this integrated focus on services and change. In this volume, Dr. Lum addresses this gap and provides a creative vision of how these priorities can be integrated.

This book contributes to our literature on cultural competence in significant ways. It presents a view of cultural competence that focuses on process, dialogue, and interaction rather than a specific outcome. It recognizes that much of our work on culture may have provided a superficial or cursory view of different groups. This book identifies cultural competence as an essential practice skill for social workers that involves lifelong learning, a perspective on practice, and a dialogue with community members. This interactional perspective directly addresses previous critiques of more linear and essentializing views.

A second contribution is the extension of the concept of cultural competence to include a larger number of groups, including European Americans, older people, and gay men and lesbians. This extension of the model underscores the centrality of cultural understanding to all social work relationships. It asks us to recognize how we are all shaped by culture and how culture can provide insights for practice.

A final significant contribution is both the depth and breadth of the model. In Parts One and Two the authors provide the basic perspectives and methods for culturally competent practice. Each of these chapters provides the vision and techniques needed for this work. Part Three adds to this knowledge by describing how a culturally competent approach can be used with ten distinct cultural groups. These chapters were written by some of the finest scholars in our field. These chapters provide exemplars of how abstract concepts such as empowerment, dialogue, or context can be brought into practice.

As I read through this manuscript, I was struck by how central culture is to our profession and practice. It is impossible to be a social worker today without confronting and addressing these issues of diversity and social justice. I am grateful to Dr. Lum for the significant contributions he has made to this work and look forward to his future work. I am sure he shares my hope to see a time when cultural competence is seamlessly integrated and infused into what we call *social work practice.*

Lorraine M. Gutierrez, PhD
Arthur F. Thurnau Professor of Psychology and Professor of Social Work
University of Michigan
Ann Arbor, Michigan

PREFACE

Doman Lum

FROM START TO FINISH

When I received a telephone call at my office in Fall 1996 (you never know who is going to call or what that person is going to ask you) from Dr. Larry Ortiz, who is now the program director of the social work department of California State University, Dominguez Hills, to give a workshop on cultural competence at the 1997 Annual Program Meeting (APM) of the Council on Social Work Education in Chicago from Dr. Larry Ortiz who is now the program director of the social work department of California State University Dominguez Hills with a MSW program focus on cultural competence, to give a workshop on cultural competence at the 1997 Annual Program Meeting (APM) of the Council on Social Work Education in Chicago, I readily agreed, knowing that I knew little or nothing about the subject.

When in such a situation it is best to call a colleague for collaborative help. I turned to Dr. Eva Lu who was then a post doctoral social welfare fellow at the University of California, Berkeley, and who later joined the social work faculty at New York University. We met many times at the Black Oak Restaurant by the Nut Tree, a half way point between Berkeley and Sacramento, to discuss, read, and conceptualize a cultural competence framework for social work education.

At the Chicago workshop we presented our framework model to a packed audience of 60 curious and excited social work educators and students and were amazed at the enthusiasm that was generated in the room. I have never since drawn that size of an audience to a workshop with the same electric charged atmosphere. The 1999 first edition of this book was based on the framework and later the 2003 second edition was expanded to include important chapters on social and economic justice and six cultural and ethnic diverse groups. The 2007 third edition refined the scope and content of the previous edition. This 2011 book marks my fourteenth text publications of books and editions that I have been privileged to write as a social work educator. I am pleased and excited for these opportunities to share my findings and writings with you.

The 2011 fourth edition makes great strides by including four new groups (European Americans, Muslim Americans, Persons with Disabilities, and the Older Adult) and expanded chapters on Human Rights and Social and Economic Justice; Women; and Gay, Lesbian, Bisexual, and Transgender Persons. I have also included a series of journal articles reflecting the heated and lively debate over the nature of cultural competence by social work educators and multicultural counseling psychology professors across the country. Several recent books have been written by social work and counseling psychology authors. These new sources of knowledge have forced me to scrap much of the material of the previous three editions and to write many new sections in the book to capture the intensity and passion of many authors who have strong views about cultural competence issues. Along with the major revisions of this edition is the addition of an instructor's manual and test bank and chapter PowerPoint slides which are available on the Cengage Learning Web site. Social work readers, both faculty who teach a course on diversity and students who are required to matriculate through such a course, will hopefully become excited to read these chapters and work on the exercises, view the PowerPoint slides, and take the tests and grade them.

The original and current purpose and mission of *Culturally Competent Practice: A Framework for Understanding Diverse Groups and Justice Issues* was and still is to present and foster a culturally competent social work practice approach that supports the social work professional efforts in cultural competence indicators for social workers (NASW) and core competencies in social work education accreditation standards (CSWE). A secondary purpose is to offer a social work cultural competence perspective which will build a bridge to the books generated by many multicultural counseling psychology authors, such as Dr. Derald Wing Sue of Columbia University Teachers College and Dr. David Sue of Western Washington University.

As we pass the first decade of the 21st century I am glad to be alive and in good health in my early seventies. I am pleased to be living in California with my growing family who are in the state of California nearby to visit children and grandchildren. When I wrote the first edition of *Culturally Competent Practice: A Framework for Growth and Action* in 1999 the concept of cultural competence was familiar to multicultural psychologists but rather unfamiliar to multicultural and culturally diverse social workers. I coined the phrase, culturally competent practice, after consulting a faculty colleague in the English department of California State University, Sacramento for correct grammar phrasing. I wanted to transfer cultural competence and cultural competencies from psychology to social work and give it a social work practice context. At the same time I knew that the cultural competence movement was already underway in several other disciplines (medicine, psychology) and professions (health care and mental health) and on the national and state levels. However I wanted to "ride the wave" of cultural competence with *a social work surfboard* and was warmly and richly supported by my social work educator colleagues who were teaching and still are pursuing professional writing and research interests in culturally competent practice.

I want to thank Dr. Lorraine Gutierrez and Dr. Maria Zuniga who along with me planned and cochaired the 1998 University of Michigan, Ann Arbor National Conference which brought together 50 outstanding social work educators across the country to spend time together with the University of Michigan social work faculty integrating cultural competence into eight social work curriculum areas and producing a book of proceedings as a finished product, *Education for Multicultural Social Work Practice: Critical Viewpoints and Future Directions* (Council on Social Work Education publications, 2004). Dr. Moses Newsome, Jr. was president and Dr. Donald W. Beless was executive director of the Council on Social Work Education at the time and gave their moral and financial support to bring the delegates to Ann Arbor for the conference. This event gave a group of social work educators direction and purpose and later encouraged the writings of Dr. Rowena Fong who with Dr. Sharlene Furuto edited *Culturally Competent Practice: Skills, Intervention, and Evaluation* (Allyn & Bacon, 2001) and by herself edited *Culturally Competent Practice with Immigrant Children and Families* (Guilford Publications, 2004).

Soon afterwards Dr. Hilary N. Weaver wrote *Explorations in Cultural Competence: Journeys to the Four Directions* (Brooks/Cole Thomson Learning, 2005) and brought a Native American perspective to cultural competence. What a wonderful contribution by a culturally sensitive social work educator who wrote the entire book by herself, surveying eight selected cultural groups. Dr. Juliet Rothman has also written *Cultural Competence in Process and Practice: Building Bridges* (Pearson Allyn & Bacon, 2008) which has kept the momentum in culturally competent practice publications. Working on the fourth edition of *Culturally Competent Practice: A Framework for Understanding Diverse Groups and Justice Issues* has provided an opportunity for me to catch up on the literature (books and journal articles) and to activate my mind and writing skills after three years of full retirement. I am pleased to report that as a retired professor I can still read the material, take notes on the articles, evaluate the quality of publications, and write sections of the book in a coherent and thoughtful manner.

NEW FEATURES OF THIS EDITION

This book represents *a major paradigm (model) shift* of cultural competence by responding to the criticisms of the critics who are concerned about the emphasis on worker competence, the lack of agreement on defining cultural competence, and research and epistemology (theory of knowledge) issues.

It proposes alternative definitions of cultural competence and culturally competent practice based on dialogue (the dialogic self and process) which rediscovers the historic nature of the social work client and worker relationship and consistently carries out this concept throughout the text. Readers are asked to rethink how to interpret cultural competence and how to practice culturally competent practice. Moreover it reformulates the major concepts in the previous three editions of this book and challenges those who are part of the cultural competence movement to reassesses how to implement cultural competence in practice terms.

The new features of *Culturally Competent Practice: A Framework for Understanding Diverse Groups and Justice Issues* (fourth edition) reflect a major revision of this book. There are a number of reasons for these changes in content, writing, and scope of cultural competence and culturally competent practice in social work:

- The National Association of Social Workers (NASW) offers a detailed blueprint of cultural competence standards: *Indicators for the Achievement of the NASW Standards for Cultural Competence in Social Work Practice* (NASW, 2007). Various sections of chapters cover Standard 1 Ethics and Values (Chapter One: Culturally Competent Practice) , Standard 2 Self-Awareness (Chapter Five: Cultural Awareness), Standard 3 Cross-Cultural Knowledge (Chapter Six: Knowledge Acquisition), Standard 4 Cross-Cultural Skills (Chapter Seven: Skill Development), Standard 5 Service Delivery (Chapter Seven: Skill Development), and Standard 6 Empowerment and Advocacy (Chapter Seven: Skill Development, Chapters Eight to Seventeen on various culturally diverse groups). In most instances the authors of this text sought to address the interpretation and indicators of these standards in sections of relevant chapters. The editor endeavored to follow the spirit and letter of the standards and indicators as he revised his five chapters and gave to each contributor a detailed outline of chapter headings citing the NASW document.

- The Council on Social Work Education (CSWE) has adopted the 2008 Educational Policy and Accreditation Standards with an emphasis on ten core competencies. Six competencies are operationalized in terms of the text content of this book. Educational Policy 2.1.2 on ethical principles is addressed in Chapter One: Culturally Competent Practice, and values and ethical dilemmas are parts of sections in Chapters Eight to Seventeen on culturally diverse groups. Educational Policy 2.1.3 on critical thinking is covered in Chapter Six: Knowledge Acquisition, while Educational Policy 2.1.4 on diversity and difference is found in Chapter Two: Social Context. Chapter Three: Human Rights and Social and Economic Justice is solely devoted to Educational Policy 2.1.5 on human rights and social and economic justice, while Chapter Two: Social Context addresses Educational Policy 2.1.9 on contexts shaping practice. In each of the chapters on culturally diverse groups (Chapters Eight to Seventeen) there is a skill development section on engagement, assessment, and empowerment and advocacy which discusses Educational Policy 2.1.10 on engage, assess, intervene, and evaluate. Moreover, Chapter Seven: Skill Development was revised to follow Educational Policy 2.1.10 on practice process.

- There are four new chapters on culturally diverse groups which are long overdue: Chapter Nine: Cultural Competence with European Americans, Chapter Thirteen: Cultural Competence with Muslim Americans, Chapter Sixteen: Cultural Competence with Persons with Disabilities, and Chapter Seventeen: Cultural Competence with the Older Adult. There are two chapters which have been rewritten to be more inclusive than their previous counterparts: Chapter Fourteen: Cultural Competence with Women and Chapter Fifteen: Cultural Competence with Gay, Lesbian, Bisexual and Transgender Persons

- There are a number of new sections in this book. Chapters Eight to Seventeen have a new format featuring sections such as Cultural Competence with Client Group(s), Historical Oppression and Current Social Issues, Values and Ethical Dilemmas, Cultural Awareness, Knowledge Acquisition, Skill Development, Social and Economic Justice Resolution, and a Concluding Case Study. Chapter One: Culturally Competent Practice has undergone major revision with new sections on the Pew Research Center U.S. Population Projections from 2005 to 2050, Connecting Building Blocks of Cultural Competence, My Beliefs and Aspirations About Cultural Competence, and Cultural Competence and Constructive Criticisms. Chapter Two: Social Context has been reshaped and refocused to cover 13 concepts related to Contextual Realities and to present social justice, empowerment, diversity and difference, the lenses of the client, and the transcendent person. Chapter Five: Cultural Awareness has been formatted to offer students an opportunity to develop an experiential approach to cultural awareness with a new section on the dialogic self. Chapter Six: Knowledge Acquisition contains a new detailed section, Historically Oppressed Groups. Chapter Seven: Skill Development has been revised to incorporate material on inductive learning into the engagement stage and to include engagement, assessment, intervention, and evaluation (CSWE Educational Policy 2.l.10—Engage, assess, intervene, and evaluate)
- Writing style has been simplified to the extent that sentence construction is conversational and there are selected references and quotations which are placed in strategic sections of the text. The text is less academic and less complicated than the previous edition. The reader should not feel overwhelmed by the complicacy of the text and should be able to follow the train of thought with ease and enjoyment.

A GROUP OF OUTSTANDING CONTRIBUTORS

The strengths of a good text lay in the talents of its writers. I am pleased to welcome back a number of contributors who wrote chapters in the third edition and readily agreed to revise their previous chapters according to a new format for this edition. They are indeed a noteworthy group of authors who are outstanding teaching and research professors and practitioners who have written in their fields, lectured nationally, and are well known and respected by their social work colleagues and students:

- Dr. Dorothy Van Soest, Professor of Social Work, University of Washington, Seattle, Chapter Three: Human Rights and Social and Economic Justice
- Dr. Francis Yuen, Professor of Social Work, California State University, Sacramento, Chapter Seven: Skills Development
- Dr. Hilary N. Weaver, Professor of Social Work, State University of New York at Buffalo Chapter Eight: Cultural Competence with First Nations Peoples
- Dr. Ruth G. McRoy, Donahue and DeFelice Endowed Professor, Boston College Graduate School of Social Work and Ruby Lee Piester Centennial

Professor Emerita, University of Texas at Austin, Chapter Ten: Cultural Competence with African Americans
- Dr. Betty Garcia, Professor of Social Work, California State University, Fresno, Chapter Eleven: Cultural Competence with Latino Americans
- Dr. Rowena Fong, Ruby Lee Piester Centennial Professor, University of Texas at Austin, Chapter Twelve: Cultural Competence with Asian Americans
- Dr. Christine T. Lowery, Associate Professor of Social Work, University of Wisconsin, Milwaukee, Chapter Fourteen: Cultural Competence with Women

I also feel that it is important to introduce fresh ideas and perspectives by inviting new authors who are equally talented and distinguished in their teaching, practice, writing, and research. I want to welcome to this writing venture a number of well-known professors and practitioners:

- Dr. Nacona L. Pewewardy, Assistant Professor of Social Work, Portland State University; Dr. Rhea V. Almeida, founder of The Institute for Family Services, Somerset, NJ; Ms. Lisa Dressner, staff member of the Affinity Counseling Group, North Brunswick, NJ; and Ms. Caroline Hann, Director of the Children and Adolescent Program, The Institute for Family Services, Somerset, NJ, Chapter Nine: Cultural Competence with European Americans
- Dr. Margaret Lombe, Assistant Professor of Social Work, Boston College, Chapter Ten: Cultural Competence with African Americans
- Dr. Fariyal Ross-Sheriff, Professor of Social Work, and Dr. Altaf Husain, Executive Assistant for Academic Affairs, Howard University Chapter Thirteen: Cultural Competence with Muslim Americans
- Dr. Carol Tully, Professor Emerita of Social Work, University of Louisville Chapter Fifteen: Cultural Competence with Gay, Lesbian, Bisexual, and Transgender Persons
- Dr. Romel Mackelprang, Program Director and Professor of Social Work, Eastern Washington University, Chapter Sixteen: Cultural Competence with Persons with Disabilities
- Dr. Donna L. Yee, Chief Executive Officer, and Dr. Linda A. Revilla, Program/Grants Developer, Asian Community Center, Sacramento, California, Chapter Seventeen: Cultural Competence with the Older Adult

ACKNOWLEDGMENTS

Dr. Lorraine Gutierrez, Arthur F. Thurnau Professor of Psychology and Professor of Social Work, University of Michigan, Ann Arbor, has graciously written the foreword to the fourth edition of this book. Dr. Gutierrez grew up in South Pasadena, California near the neighborhood of my wife's relatives and went to South Pasadena High School. She is a graduate of Stanford University, University of Chicago School of Social Services Administration, and University of Michigan where she received her Ph.D. in social work and psychology. After teaching at the University of Washington, Seattle, she returned to join the social work and psychology faculties at the University of Michigan. She recently completed a term as chair of the joint doctoral program and has published in the areas of macro practice, community organization, empowerment, and ethnic minorities. Dr. Gutierrez and I served on the board of directors of the Council on Social Work Education where she provided leadership as chair of the cultural diversity committee. She has been approachable, honest, and forthright in her interactions with me and has my deepest respect.

Special thanks go to Seth Dobrin, editor of social work and counseling at Cengage Learning, who saw the need for a fourth edition of this book and recruited a group of helpful reviewers who provided excellent suggestions for revision. His thoughtful recommendations, relative calm, and steady hand have seen this project grow from revision to reality. Without Seth's leadership this book would not have been a quality product. Also I appreciate the technical and nuts-and-bolts support of Nicolas Albert, assistant editor of *Social Work and Counseling* particularly his numerous suggestions on how to strengthen the manuscript and his perspectives on the dialogic process and Rachel McDonald, editorial assistant for Social Work and Counseling, who assisted me with numerous tasks from the start to finish of this book. I also want to acknowledge the contributions and recommendations of the six manuscript reviewers who offered honest and helpful suggestions:

Najma N. Adam, Governors State University
Tommy E. Turner, Jacksonville State University
Linda Anderson Smith, Springfield College
Jose M. Maldonado, Monmouth University
Patty Gibbs Wahlberg, East Tennessee State University
Mary Kay Houston-Vega, University of Texas at San Antonio

I would also like to acknowledge Sathyabama Kumaran of Pre-PressPMG and the Cengage Learning Brooks/Cole staff who supported this project in the acquisition and production phase: Matt Ballantyne, Caryl Gorska, Don Schlotman, Linda Hsu, and Bob Kauser.

Above all, a special word of recognition and thanks goes to my growing family who surround me with their love and care: my wife, Joyce, who is a retired first-grade teacher with the Elk Grove School District and who keeps me busy and honest every day; my daughter, Lori, and her husband Noel, a computer consultant with AE.Com, who are raising Riley and Alyssa; my son, Jonathan, who is an occupational therapist with the University of Southern California-Los Angeles County Medical Center, and his wife Lisa, senior benefits specialist for AHMC Health Care Inc., San Gabriel, California, and their child Evan; my daughter, Amy, and her husband Ross, co-founder of Pediatric Motor Playground, who are parents of Jack and Joel; and my son, Matthew, who is an urban planner with the California State Department of Transportation (Cal Tran). Every member of my family brightens my day as I interact with them.

Doman Lum, Ph.D., Th.D,
Professor Emeritus of Social Work,
California State University, Sacramento

CONTRIBUTORS

Rhea V. Almeida. Dr. Rhea V. Almeida is the founder of The Institute for Family Services (IFS), a family therapist and received her Ph.D. from Columbia University School of Social Work. She is the creator of the Cultural Context Model, coauthor and editor of *Expansions of Feminist Theory Through Diversity and Transformations in Gender and Race: Family and Developmental Perspectives*, and coauthor of *Transformative Family Therapy: Just Families in a Just Society*. She has also written numerous journal articles. She received the American Family Therapy Innovative Contributions to Family Therapy award and is annually honored by the Domestic Violence Hotline for her work with women and families with domestic violence. She has been on the editorial boards of the *Journal of Cultural Diversity and Mental Health*, *Journal of Marital and Family Therapy*, and *Journal of Feminist Family Therapy* and currently serves on the advisory board of Department of Counseling and Human Services, Johns Hopkins University and the cultural diversity committee of the National Association of Social Workers (NASW), New Jersey chapter.

Lisa Dressner. Ms. Lisa Dressner is a founding member of Affinity Counseling Group and received her MSW degree from Rutgers University. She completed post-graduate training programs in family systems therapy at the Multicultural Family Institute and in domestic violence and cultural context at the Institute for Family Services. She serves on the Middlesex County Council for Children's Services and on the Middlesex County Vicinage Committee. She has written and received grants providing clinical and case management services to youth and families in the juvenile justice system and has trained mental health professionals through graduate student internships and national and international workshops.

Rowena Fong. Dr. Rowena Fong is the Ruby Lee Piester centennial professor in services to children and families, University of Texas at Austin. She received her MSW from the University of California, Berkeley, and her Ed.D. from Harvard University School of Graduate Education. Her teaching, research, and scholarship have focused on Asian American children and families, international and transracial adoption, child welfare disproportionality, victims of human trafficking, and culturally competent practice. Her numerous publications and books include *Intersecting Child Welfare, Substance Abuse, and Family Violence: Culturally Competent Approaches* (with Ruth McRoy and Carmen Ortiz Hendricks); *Culturally Competent Practice with Immigrant and Refugee Children and Families* and *Children of Neglect: When No One Cares* (with Margaret Smith); *Culturally Competent Practice: Skills, Interventions, and Evaluation* (with Sharlene Furuto); and *Multisystem Skills and Interventions in School Social Work Practice* (with E. Freeman, C. Franklin, G. Shaffer, and E. Timberlake.) Currently she is writing *The Church Leader's Resource Book for Pastoral Counseling: Everything You Ever Wanted to Know about Mental Health and Social Problems* (with Cynthia Franklin). She received the 2008 Distinguished Recent Contributions in Social Work Education Award from the Council on Social Work Education; the 2007 Texas Exes Teaching Award from the University of Texas at Austin; the 2001 Regent's Teaching Award from the University of Hawaii at Manoa; and the 2001 Social Worker of the Year in Education and Training from the National Association of Social Workers, Honolulu Chapter. She currently serves as president of the Society of Social Work and Research (SSWR).

Betty Garcia. Dr. Betty Garcia is professor of social work in the Department of Social Work Education at California State University, Fresno. She received her MSW degree from San Diego State University and her Ph.D. in social psychology from Boston University. Dr. Garcia has worked in numerous mental health settings (prison and community clinics) conducting individual treatment, sexual abuse evaluation and treatment with children, and group work. Her teaching areas are practice with individuals, couples, groups, and families and public mental health. She has developed certificate programs in cultural competency and interprofessional collaboration. Her research and publication subjects include Latinos and higher education, empowerment issues for Latinas, child welfare and incarcerated mothers, and the social service needs of the elderly. Dr. Garcia is vice president/secretary of the Council on Social Work Education (CSWE) and has been on the national board of directors for the National Association of Social Workers (NASW), the *Affilia* corporate board, and chair of the NASW National Committee on Racism and Ethnic Diversity (NCORED). She has written two books with a fellow contributor, Dorothy Van Soest (*Social Work Practice for Social Justice: Cultural Competence in Action, A Guide for Students* and *Diversity Education for Social Justice: Mastering Teaching Skills* [CSWE Publications])

Caroline Hann. Ms Caroline Hann is director of the children and adolescent program at The Institute for Family Services (Somerset, NJ) and a team member of Affinity Counseling Group (North Brunswick, New Jersey). She received her MSW from Hunter College, City University of New York and completed a post graduate program in transformative family therapy at the Institute for Family Services. Ms. Hann is a member of the Alliance for Racial and Social Justice and has authored an article (Remembering children within a social justice landscape: Therapeutic strategies of intervening with children).

Altaf Husain. Dr. Altaf Husain serves as the executive assistant for academic affairs in the office of the provost and chief academic officer at Howard University, Washington, DC. He received his Master of Science in Social Administration from Case Western Reserve University, the Mandel School of Applied Social Sciences and his Ph.D. in social work from Howard University. His research interests include displaced populations (the homeless, victims of disaster, immigrants and refugees), mental health and psychosocial well-being of adolescent immigrants and refugees of color in the United States; immigration policy and its impact on the family; cultural competence; and the development of social service agencies in the Muslim community. Dr. Husain coedited a thematic issue for the *Journal of Muslim Mental Health* on refugees and forced migrants. He also coauthored two chapters on culturally competent social work practice with children of South Asian Muslim descent and is an invited lecturer in North America and Europe on the integration of Muslims in the United States. He has written and researched on Islam and Muslims and recently completed a quantitative study on Somali youth in the United States. He has been invited by the Department of Homeland Security, Office of Civil Rights and Civil Liberties to provide insights on Islam and the Somali Diaspora as well as by the U.S. Department of State, Bureau of Democracy, Human Rights & Labor, Office of International Religious Freedom to participate in Muslim American Roundtables.

Margaret Lombe. Dr. Margaret Lombe is assistant professor of social work at Boston College Graduate School of Social Work. She received her Ph.D. in social work from Washington University, St. Louis George Warren Brown Graduate School of Social Work. She is also a faculty associate at Washington University, St. Louis Center for Social Development. Her area of expertise is in international social development with an emphasis on social inclusion/exclusion and capacity building. She has been a consultant with the United Nations and has participated in a number of Experts Group Meetings (EGM) to develop indicators to assess inclusion/exclusion for the United Nations. She has published book chapters and articles on poverty and social inclusion which have appeared in the *Journal of Human Behavior in the Social Environment; Social Work Research; Journal of Community Practice;* and the *Journal of Sociology and Social Work* and has presented papers at national and international conferences in this field.

Christine T. Lowery. Dr. Christine Lowery is associate professor of social work and the undergraduate coordinator for the Helen Bader School of Social Work, University of Wisconsin-Milwaukee. She received her Ph.D. in social work from the

University of Washington, Seattle. Since 1994 she has been teaching direct practice and cultural diversity courses at the undergraduate and graduate levels and received a UWM Distinguished Undergraduate Teaching Award in 2009. Dr. Lowery is a member of the Hopi and Laguna pueblos in Arizona and New Mexico, respectively. She is in the ninth year of a ten-year ethnographic study of elders and cultural change on the Pueblo of Laguna. With her coeditor, Dr. Lowery has produced an advance social work foundation textbook specifically for master-level students without a bachelor degree in social work. Dr. Lowery is currently the book editor for the journal, *Families in Society,* and is a founding member of the Commission on Diversity and Social and Economic Justice for the Council on Social Work Education.

Doman Lum. Dr. Doman Lum is professor emeritus of social work at the California State University, Sacramento. He received his Ph.D. in social welfare from Case Western Reserve University and his Th.D in pastoral counseling and psychology from Claremont School of Theology. He has been clinical instructor of psychiatry (religion) at the University of Hawaii School of Medicine. His previous books have been in the areas of cultural competence and practice and client systems, multidimensional contextual practice, social work practice and people of color, health care policy and social work, and suicidal crisis intervention. He has written articles on culturally competent practice, Asian Americans, health care delivery and health maintenance organizations, culturally diverse social work practice, suicide prevention, and pastoral counseling. He has been on the board of directors of the Council on Social Work Education and a member of the CSWE Commission on Accreditation. Dr. Lum received the 2000 Distinguished Recent Contributions in Social Work Education award from CSWE and the 2004 Lifetime Achievement award from the Asian Pacific Islanders Social Work Educators of the Council on Social Work Education and He was the keynote speaker for the Korean Academy of Family Social Work, Seoul, Korea in April 2008. Dr. Lum is an ordained minister of the United Church of Christ, Northern California Conference, a docent for the California State Railroad Museum, and a golf marshall for the Bing Maloney Golf Course, Sacramento.

Romel W. Mackelprang. Dr. Romel W. Mackelprang is the director of the Center for Disability Studies and Universal Access at Eastern Washington University where he has been a social work professor since 1987. He received his DSW degree from the University of Utah. He has coauthored two books: *Sexuality and Disabilities: A Guide for Human Service Practitioners* (a special issue appearing in the *Journal of Social Work and Human Sexuality,* 1993, 8 (2)) as coeditor with D. Valentine which was later reprinted as a textbook by Haworth Press and *Disability: A Diversity Model in Human Service Practice* (second edition) (Chicago: Lyceum Books, 2009) with R. O. Salsgiver. Since 1980 he has been active in disability rights and continues to be involved in the independent living movement. He has served on the Council of Social Work Education Commission on Disability and Persons with Disabilities and the Commission on Curriculum and Educational Innovation. In recent years he has been invited to present his work and to consult with disability rights organizations in Canada, Europe, Australia, and Africa. He is currently working with multiple organizations to promote accessibility and disability rights in East Africa. He is also writing a human behavior and the social environment text that uses the social-ecological framework consisting of biosocial, psychosocial, and social-structural domains.

Ruth G. McRoy. Dr. Ruth G. McRoy is Donahue and DiFelice endowed professor at Boston College Graduate School of Social Work and a Research Professor and Ruby Lee Piester centennial professor emerita at the University of Texas at Austin School of Social Work. Her teaching, research, and writing interests have been in cultural competency, adoption disproportionality, foster and adoptive family recruitment, kinship care, minority adoptions, transracial adoptions, family reunification, family preservation, adoptive family dynamics, birthparent outcomes, sibling placement issues, open adoptions, older child adoptions, and postadoption services. Her books include *Transracial and Inracial Adoptees: The Adolescent Years* (with L. Zurcher), *Special Needs Adoptions: Practice Issues, Openness in Adoption: Family Connections* (with H. Grotevant), *Intersecting Child Welfare, Substance Abuse, and Family Violence: Culturally Competent Approaches* (with R. Fong and C. Ortiz-Hendricks), and numerous articles and book chapters on child welfare issues.

Nocona L. Pewewardy. Dr. Nocona L. Pewewardy is assistant professor of social work at Portland State University School of Social Work. She received her BA in social work and her MSW from the University of Oklahoma and her Ph.D. in social welfare from the University of Kansas. Her research interests are critical approaches to social work education, critical race theory, structural social work, cultural pluralism, strategies for challenging and deconstructing white privileges, and other catalysts of structural inequalities. She is the author of the highly acclaimed book, *Challenging White Privilege: A Critical Approach to Social Work Education* (Council on Social Work Education publications, 2007).

Linda A. Revilla. Dr. Linda A. Revilla, programs/grants developer at the Asian Community Center of Sacramento Valley, California, received for Ph.D degree in psychology from the University of California, Los Angeles where she studied with Dr. Stanley Sue, a well-known Asian American psychologist who has made major contributions in Asian American studies. Dr. Revilla has taught at the University of Washington, the University of Hawaii, and California State University, Sacramento. She has coauthored three books (*Counseling Families Across the Stages of Life: A Handbook for Pastors and Other Helping Professionals; Bearing Dreams, Shaping Visions: Asian Pacific American Perspective;* and *Ethnic Studies Anthology*). She has written on Filipino American history and has been on the staff of the Veterans Affairs Pacific Center for PTSD.

Fariyal Ross-Sheriff. Dr. Fariyal Ross-Sheriff is a graduate professor of social work and the director of the Ph.D. degree program in social work at Howard University, Washington, DC. She earned her Ph.D. from the University of Michigan. Her area of specialization is displaced populations: internationally with refugees, immigrants, and undocumented migrants; and within the United States with the homeless and disaster victims. Within displaced populations, Dr. Ross-Sheriff's work emphasizes women, children, and the elderly. She has worked extensively with Muslim refugees in Pakistan examining the challenges facing them and service providers and in Afghanistan to facilitate the repatriation and resettlement of refugees. In addition, she has conducted research on the role of women in the repatriation process. Among her many publications are several articles and chapters on Muslims in America, two coedited books (*Mental Health and People of Color: Curriculum Development and Change* Howard University Press, 1983; *Social Work Practice with Asian Americans*, Sage Publications, 1992); and a co-authored 2003 monograph entitled *Muslim Refugees in the United States: A Guide for Service Providers.*

Carol T. Tully. Dr. Carol T. Tully is professor emerita of social work at the University of Louisville. She received her Ph.D. in social policy and social work with a focus on gerontology from Virginia Commonwealth University and taught at West Virginia University, University of Georgia, and Tulane University. She has written numerous journal articles and authored the renowned *Lesbians, Gays, and the Empowerment Perspective* (Columbia University Press), coedited with G. G. Wood *The Structural Approach to Social Work* (Columbia University Press), and edited *Lesbian Social Services: Research Issues* (Harrington Park Press). Dr. Tully is chair of the CSWE Council on Publications and an editorial reviewer for the *Journal of Social Work Education.* She has retired to New Orleans, Louisiana, where she is a volunteer with the American Red Cross and the Central City Partnership.

Dorothy Van Soest. Dr. Dorothy Van Soest is professor of social work and former dean of the University of Washington Seattle School of Social Work. Prior to this she was Associate Dean at the University of Texas at Austin School of Social Work and taught at the University of Minnesota, St. Thomas University, St. Catherine College, and Smith College. She has written several books: *Diversity Education for Social Justice: Mastering Teaching Skills* and *Social Work Practice for Social Justice* (both with Dr. Betty Garcia); *The Global Crisis of Violence: Common Problems, Universal Causes, Shared Solutions; The Global Crisis of Violence: A Curriculum Module* (with Jane Crosby); and *Incorporating Peace and Social Justice into the Social Work Curriculum.* Her research and teaching interest cover student learning about cultural diversity and societal oppression, peace and social justice, and violence prevention.

Hilary N. Weaver. Dr. Hilary N. Weaver is professor of social work at the University of Buffalo (State University of New York), School of Social Work. She has her Doctor of Social Welfare (DSW) degree from Columbia University School of Social Work and currently serves as president of the American

Indian Alaska Native Social Work Educators Association and vice president of the board of directors of Native American Community Services of Erie and Niagara Counties. Her teaching, research, and service focus on cultural issues in the helping process with a particular focus on indigenous populations. She has presented her work regionally, nationally, and internationally including the Permanent Forum on Indigenous Issues at the United Nations in 2005–2008. Dr. Weaver has written numerous books including *Explorations in Cultural Competence: Journey to the Four Directions* (2005) and edited numerous books including *Voices of First Nations Peoples* (1999) and *The American Indian* (1999) with Priscilla Day. She has received funding from the National Cancer Institute to develop and test a culturally grounded wellness curriculum for urban Native American youth, called the Healthy Living in Two Worlds program.

Donna L. Yee. Dr. Donna L. Yee is executive director of the Asian Community Center of the Sacramento Valley, California. She administers a consortium of services and facilities which includes a senior day care program, a residential apartment facility, and a long-time nursing home for older adults. She received her MSW degree from the University of Washington and her Ph.D. in social policy from Brandeis University, the Heller School where she specialized in ethnic gerontology. She has served as director of policy and research for the National Asian Pacific Center on Aging, Seattle, and as chief executive officer for the Harry and Jeanette Weinburg Foundation in Maryland. She has coauthored several chapters on the quality of life for communities of color, diversity, and cultural competence; care for persons with dementia; and resident-centered assisted living care. She is a board member of the American Society on Aging and the Coming Home Program National Advisory Committee.

Francis. K. O. Yuen. Dr. Francis K. O. Yuen is professor of social work at California State University, Sacramento Division of Social Work. He received his MSW and DSW from the University of Alabama, Tuscaloosa. His practice and research interests are in the areas of family health social work practice, children and families, disability, high-risk behaviors, refugees and immigrants, grant writing, and program evaluation. He has published widely including numerous journal articles, book chapters, and books. His latest book is *Effective Grant Writing and Program Evaluation for Human Service Professionals* (2009, John Wiley & Sons). He is the chief editor for the *Journal of Social Work in Disability & Rehabilitation* (Taylor & Francis). Dr. Yuen was an agency and university administrator working with diverse populations on health, mental health, and social issues. Since 1995 he has also been an evaluation coach and trainer for AmeriCorps and Senior Corps programs funded by the U.S. Corporation for National and Community Services.

CULTURALLY COMPETENT PERSPECTIVES

Part One lays the foundation for understanding culturally competent practice perspectives. Chapter One provides the necessary background on cultural competence in its evolution as a practice approach. It begins with the history of the cultural competence movement to give the reader a sense of the journey cultural competence has taken. Next the chapter addresses the present by explaining the current context, particularly the demographic shifts in population in the last 40 years (the steady growth and surge of ethnic and cultural immigrants into the United States with rapid birth rates, unique social problems, and existing cultural and ethnic groups with multiple needs) and how cultural competence and culturally competent practice need to be ready to meet the challenges of these trends.

We then move to the present state of the art in cultural competence studies: the current definitions of cultural competence and current criticisms particularly about the methodology and operationalization of the concept, measurement, instrumentation, and epistemology. The chapter sets forth several remedies for the immediate future: the construction and connection of the building blocks of cultural competence, which include a *research-informed practice approach* on *definition, levels and dimensions* of cultural competence, *ethical and professional standards and competencies* (the National Association of Social Workers [NASW] Code of Ethics and Indicators of Cultural Competence, and the Council on Social Work Education [CSWE] Educational Policy Core Competencies), my *beliefs and aspirations* about cultural competence, and *measuring beginning competence*.

Chapter Two presents a framework for understanding the social, economic, and political forces that create the societal environment of the United States, as culturally competent practice impacts the lives of clients. It explains the meaning of social context, presents a contextual realities framework that covers social stratification issues, ideological beliefs, affective expression, and behavioral reactions and

1

suggests a number of strategies to cope with these contextual realities. Chapter Three covers the theory and practice of human rights and social justice and economic justice and reminds us that in the midst of helping clients to cope with problem situations we must assert our human rights and strive for social justice and economic justice.

CULTURALLY COMPETENT PRACTICE

CHAPTER I

Doman Lum

This book is an introduction to cultural competence, which is now firmly a part of the helping profession as we pass the first decade of the 21st century. There are some interesting signs of cultural competence in social work education. The Master of Social Work program at California State University, Dominguez Hills, is organized around culturally and contextually competent practice. There is a graduate certificate program in Latino Cultural Competency in Social Work at Arizona State University School of Social Work. The University of Maryland Baltimore School of Social Work sponsored a conference on Culturally Competent Evidence Based Practice in Child Welfare in July 2007. Such academic programs and meetings are expressions of the development of cultural competence, which is having an effect on social work educators, students, and practitioners and their clients.

Throughout this book we will refer constantly to two documents, which have set the standards for cultural competence in social work: *Indicators for the Achievement of the NASW Standards for Cultural Competence in Social Work Practice* (NASW, 2007) (see Simmons, Diaz, Jackson, & Takahashi, 2008 for details on the development of the indicators) and *Educational Policy and Accreditation Standards (EPAS)* (Council on Social Work Education [CSWE], 2008). The concepts of cultural competence and competencies will be examined in various chapters of this text.

The *thesis* of this book is that *cultural competence is a relational, dialogical process (a dialogue rather than* an emphasis on *worker's competence)* between the worker and the client, between cultures, and between people and context. Dialogue means conversation, interchange, discussion, and mutual understanding involving an egalitarian relationship of equal status and rights. This appears to be a missing link of current cultural competence: *the present emphasis is on building the cultural competence of the worker rather than emphasizing that the client and the worker together must learn to be competent and proficient in cultural ways of coping with the problems of living.* We hope to remedy this situation and move culturally competent practice toward this *participatory relationship* between the worker and the client.

In other words, we are calling for *a major paradigm (model) shift* from an exclusive focus on the cultural competence of the worker to an inclusive relationship between the worker and the client based on the development of cultural competence and proficiency of both parties in the helping process. This stems from the historical emphasis of social work practice on the worker and the client, the search for a common, agreed-upon definition of cultural competence, and the trend toward dialogue (the dialogic self and process) from current criticisms of social worker educators and practitioners. As such we want to offer a constructive response as we *review the past achievements* of the cultural competence movement, *critique the present problems* confronting cultural competence as a practice approach, and *propose where we need to move the movement in the immediate future which is now.*

This chapter discusses the history of the cultural competence movement, the current context for cultural competence, current definitions and criticisms, the construction of building blocks for cultural competence, levels and dimensions of cultural competence, the ethical standards and professional/educational competencies of cultural competence, beliefs about cultural competence, and measuring beginning competence. We want to provide an essential background on culturally competent practice. We hope that you will, as a part of your social work education, prepare yourself to be a competent and effective professional who is able to integrate the knowledge, values, and skills for competent practice, particularly with culturally and ethnically diverse clients. In turn we hope that these clients will understand and learn about cultural strengths. The emphasis is on *mutual consent and participation of the worker and the client* to become *culturally proficient* in the *exploration and learning* process.

THE HISTORY OF THE CULTURAL COMPETENCE MOVEMENT

We need to review the past of the cultural competence movement in order to understanding its journey, where it came from, where it is today, and what changes it needs to make in order for its momentum as a practice approach to continue and thrive in the immediate future. As you will see, there are firm foundations for cultural competence rooted in social work and psychology and supported by federal and state programs in health care and mental health. We want to answer where the notion of cultural competence began, the major changes it has undergone, and the major actors who have influenced its directions in its brief past and its present.

THE INVOLVEMENT OF SOCIAL WORK AND PSYCHOLOGY

The Civil Rights Act of 1964 set in motion *legal protection based on nondiscrimination* of persons on the basis of race, sex, color, national origin, disability, age, and religion. (It is interesting to note that *sexual orientation* does not exist as a category in the 1964 civil rights legislation.) In the early 1970s, when social work educators began to study a number of ethnic groups, Solomon (1976) published her landmark book on African American powerlessness and empowerment. Green (1982) and Pinderhughes (1989) introduced the concept of cultural competence to social work. Pinderhughes (1989) explained,

> "Cultural competence" demands that clinicians develop flexibility in thinking and behavior, because they must learn to adapt professional tasks and work styles to the values, expectations, and preferences of specific clients. This means that practitioners must choose from a variety of strategies that are useful for the range of cultural groups and social classes, levels of education, and levels of acculturation that exist among clients. (p. 163)

These social work educators pioneered the theme of cultural competence and laid a foundation on which we have built more dimensions related to culturally competent practice.

The field of psychology also has shown concern in the area of cultural competence. The American Psychological Association (APA) in 1980 adopted a professional competence practice requirement and recognized cultural competence as an essential element of competent practice (APA, 1980). In 1982, a major position paper on cross-cultural counseling competencies asked that there be specified multicultural knowledge, awareness, and skill areas in counseling psychology (Casas, Ponterotto, & Gutierrez, 1986; Ibrahim & Arredondo, 1986).

In 1989, Terry Cross, a First Nations Peoples social worker, took the leadership in composing a monograph (Cross et al., 1989) and formulated six anchor points along a cultural competence continuum regarding an organizational system of care (see the discussion on meso-level cultural competence later in this chapter). Those of us who write about cultural competence point to this publication as the first systematic treatment of this topic.

In April 1992, the Association for Multicultural Counseling and Development (AMCD), a group of counseling psychologists who were committed to infusing the profession with multicultural content, approved a document that emphasized the need and the rationale for a multicultural perspective in counseling. This document covered such areas as counseling psychology doctoral education and training internships, professional standards and practices, and research and publication. As a result of this effort, the Professional Standards Committee of the American Association for Counseling and Development proposed 31 multicultural counseling competencies to the APA and recommended that the APA adopt these competencies in its accreditation criteria (Sue, Arredondo, & McDavis, 1992).

In 1992, a paradigm model of the characteristics of a culturally competent counselor and the dimensions of cultural competence was constructed. This model gave the movement a conceptual framework. According to this model, a culturally competent counselor is aware of his or her own values, understands the worldview of his or her culturally different clients, and uses sensitive intervention strategies and skills with clients. Dimensions of cultural competence entail beliefs and attitudes about racial and ethnic minorities, knowledge and understanding of the counselor's own worldview, and intervention strategy skills that can be used with minority groups (Sue et al., 1992). By 1993, the APA had committed itself to multicultural competence with ethnically, linguistically, and culturally diverse populations (APA, 1993).

Another useful description of cultural competence has been provided by Zayas, Evans, Mejia, and Rodriguez (1997). According to these authors, cultural competence includes knowledge and interpersonal skills to understand, appreciate, and work with individuals and families from cultures other than one's own; the use of knowledge and skills effectively to employ therapeutic techniques in achieving behavioral and emotional change; the awareness of critical cultural values, beliefs, behaviors, and interactions that structure social and family life and psychological functioning; and self-awareness, acceptance of differences, knowledge of a client's culture, and adaptation of helping skills to the client's culture (Zayas et al., 1997).

The cultural competence movement has grown in two related directions. First, on the clinical level, it has provided the helping professions (psychiatry, psychology, and social work) with a culturally focused theme. LaFromboise et al. (1993) described the client from a culturally competent perspective. Second, cultural competence has provided an education and training perspective by which to develop academic and professional expertise and skills in working with culturally diverse clients.

Social work education has fostered cultural competence in child welfare and social work practice. The Title IV-E child welfare training grant under the auspices of the California Social Work Education Center at the University of California at Berkeley (1996) identified 14 cultural competencies according to population groups, child welfare knowledge, and practice skills. Population groups competencies recognized cultural and ethnic differences, ethnic group dynamics, cultural influence on behavior, socioeconomic and psychosocial issues facing immigrants and refugees, and the importance of client language. Child welfare knowledge competencies involved knowledge of child welfare services to cultural and ethnic populations and knowledge of relevant ethnic child welfare legislation. Practice skills competencies dealt with relationship information and communication development, ethnic sensitivity assessment, evaluation of intervention models, community outreach collaboration, and resource and service advocacy.

THE INVOLVEMENT OF THE FEDERAL AND STATE GOVERNMENTS

On the community level, efforts have been made to place cultural competence on the national public health and mental health agendas. The U.S. Public Health Service's Office for Substance Abuse Prevention launched a series of monographs that integrated cultural competence, alcohol and drug abuse treatment programs, and ethnic groups and community (Orlandi et al., 1992)—a match between ethnic target groups, major problem areas, and cultural competence for treatment workers that illustrated how macro cultural competence can be expressed. By 1997, cultural competence guidelines for managed care and mental health were identified for Asian and Pacific Islanders and Native Americans (Substance Abuse and Mental Health Services Administration [SAMHSA], 1997a & b). The guidelines for Asian and Pacific Islander populations (1997a) offered a provider network plan for public and private sectors that set the standards for cultural competence and service delivery, including overall system standards and guidelines specifying cultural competence planning, ongoing program development, governance, benefit design, quality monitoring and improvement, decision support and management information systems, and human resource development; provider competencies addressing knowledge and understanding, skills, and attitudes as well as prevention, education, and outreach; and clinical standards and guidelines covering access and service authorization, triage and assessment, care planning, plan of treatment, treatment services, case management, communication styles and cross-cultural communication support, communication styles and linguistic support, self help, and discharge planning.

In the 1990s, states such as California (in 1997) and New York (in 1998) were in the midst of articulating cultural competence plans on the state and county levels. California was concerned about planning culturally competent mental health services, particularly through population assessment of county geographic and socio-economic profiles, demographics (ethnicity, age and gender, primary language), and Medi-Cal mental health services utilization (ethnicity, age and gender, primary language), as well as through organizational and service provider assessment of mental health plans, policy, and administrative direction; human resources; location; quality of care and competency; and quality assurance. New York developed cultural competence performance measures for managed behavioral health care programs to identify methodology and data collection strategies. It formulated a conceptual framework for domains of cultural competence in mental health service delivery. Domain areas were needs assessment, information exchange, services, human resources, policies and plans, and cultural competencies outcomes. Related areas in which to implement these domains were the administrative managed care organization and state mental health authority, provider network, and individual staff members.

South Carolina had a cultural competence plan for 2003–2005 (Office of Multicultural Services, 2005), which addressed governance and administration (the support of the leadership of the South Carolina Department of Mental Health [SCDMH] to develop a system of culturally and linguistically competent care), human resources (the workforce of SCDMH to reflect the diversity of their communities), education and training (programs to promote and assure cultural competence among staff), clinical services (culturally and linguistically appropriate clinical care and services), consumers' families, the community (the involvement of advocacy groups, consumers and their families in participatory, collaborative partnerships to design and implement cultural and linguistically appropriate services) and outcomes, data, and information management (statewide performance indicators reflecting cultural competence in the care of children and adults).

New Jersey (Adams, 2005) passed a law in 2005 requiring physicians to take cultural competency training as part of licensure. It is the first state to require physicians to learn how to culturally attune to patients in order to practice medicine. The intent of this law is to help reduce health care disparities among racial and ethnic minorities and to ensure that physicians become more responsive to cultural and language differences among their patients. Approximately 30,000 physicians who already had a license had to complete cultural competency training to renew their licenses every two years.

INTERDISCIPLINARY PARTICIPATION IN CULTURAL COMPETENCE

Cultural competence as a movement has made major strides. Medicine, psychology, and social work have established national cultural competence standards in their academic and professional disciplines. For example, in 2003 the APA adopted Guidelines on Multicultural Education, Training, Research, Practice, and Organizational Psychology (Constantine & Sue, 2005). Sue & Sue (2003, pp. 18–23) developed three major competency sets involving therapists' awareness of their own assumptions, values, and biases; understanding the worldview of culturally diverse clients, and the development of appropriate intervention strategies and techniques. Social work education has begun to apply this theme to its curriculum structure (ten core competencies, on identity as a professional social worker, ethical principles, critical thinking, diversity and difference, human rights and social and economic justice, research-informed practice and practice-informed research, human behavior and the social environment, policy practice, contexts, and practice process). The Title IV-E child welfare training grants have incorporated mental health competencies into graduate level Master of Social Work child welfare curriculum. The California Social Work Education Center (CalSWEC) at the University of California at Berkeley has generalist foundation and advanced practice levels where competencies are identified. Each competency statement is related to the practice of mental health and reflects a comprehensive understanding and social work diversity content. These competencies cover the broad range of practice concerns and skills that are necessary in working with ethnic population groups who are in socioeconomic need. The foundational competencies emphasize knowledge and understanding, whereas the advanced competencies focus on knowledge application and the development of skills.

Cultural competence needs to be applied to such social problem areas as family violence and substance abuse, mental health and health care practice, and related issues. Cultural competence is the theme of a movement that can be carried in multiple directions as social work educators continue to apply the concept to the client populations confronting them. We move from the history of cultural movement to an understanding of the present context facing cultural competence in the second decade of the 21st century.

THE CONTEXT FOR CULTURAL COMPETENCE

In the 21st century, we are faced with a rich ethnic and cultural diversity context. Between 1980 and 2000, there was a marked increase in minority populations as compared to the White non-Hispanic population. In 1980, out of a total population of 226.5 million, the minority population was 45.6 million. By 1990, the total population of 248.7 million was composed of 60.6 million of the minority population and 188.1 million of the White non-Hispanic population. In 2000, however, the total population reached 281.5 million with a minority population of 86.9 million and a White non-Hispanic population of 194.6 million.

The significance of this 20-year growth was the doubling of the minority population, which increased by 41.3 million, whereas the White non-Hispanic population in the same period increased by only 13.7 million persons ("A Rapid Move to Diversity," 2001). Moreover, two groups emerged as the most rapid growth groups in the United States: Hispanic or Latino, and Asian. Hispanics or Latinos moved from 22,354,059 in 1990 to 35,305,818 in 2000, an increase of 12,951,759 persons or a 57.2 percent growth. Asians went from 6,908,638 in 1990 to 10,242,998 (race alone, a 3,334,360 increase or a 48.3 percent growth) or to 11,898,828 (race alone or in combination, a 4,990,190 increase or a 72.2 percent growth). The 2000 U.S. Census allowed persons to indicate a single ethnic group (race alone) or combinations of ethnic groups (in combination). By 2004 the total population of the United States was 319.9 million, with Whites (236 million), Hispanics or Latinos (41.3 million), Blacks (37.5 million), Asians (12.3 million), and American Indian and Alaska Natives (2.8 million) (U.S. Census Bureau, 2004). The Latino population exceeded the Black population and was over three times that of Asians.

The demographic profile of ethnically diverse and age-diverse people in the United States will constantly change due to significant growth in the projected population in the next 40 years. The Pew Research Center in an important study projecting U.S. population trends from 2005 to 2050 (Passel & Cohn, 2008) has some interesting findings based on ethnicity and age:

The non-Hispanic White population, which was 199 million (67% of the population), in 2005 will increase more slowly than other ethnic groups (207 million in 2050) and will be a minority (47%) in 2050. Slow growth will be due to low fertility rates and relatively low immigration (increase of only 8 million or 4%).

The Black population was 38 million (12.8% of the population) in 2005 and will be 59 million (13.4%) in 2050, an increase of 56%. However, *the major projected increases are from the Hispanic and Asian populations.*

The Hispanic population (42 million in 2005 or 14% of the population) will grow to 128 million in 2050 (29% of the population), tripling in size. Latinos will account for 60% of the population growth between 2005 and 2050. Latino growth is mainly due to birth rate with a relatively young Latino population and a higher-than-average fertility rate that is twice the number of new Latino immigrants entering the United States.

The Asian population was 14 million (5% of the population) in 2005 and will increase to 41 million (9% of the population) in 2050. Most Asians were foreign born in 2005 (58%) but fewer than half (47%) will be so in 2050. Asian population growth will be due to new immigrants arriving after 2005 and their descendants (94% of the Asian growth increase).

Working-age adults (ages 18–64) were 186 million in 2005 and will be 255 million (37% increase) in 2050. However, working adults (63% of the population in 2005) will slightly decrease to 58% of the population in 2050. Immigrants are projected to be an important part of the working-age population, particularly foreign-born residents, whose number will increase from 15% in 2005 to 23% in 2050. Hispanic working adults will go from 14% in 2005 to 31% in 2050, while non-Hispanic Whites will decline from 68% in 2005 to 45% in 2050.

Children will grow from 73 million in 2005 (23% of the population) to 102 million in 2050 (25% of the population), a 39% increase. This will be due to the arrival of new immigrants after 2005 who will have 36 million children by 2050, combining first and second generations of immigrants. This group on average will have more children (one child in three or 34%) in 2050 compared with native-born U.S. residents. Hispanic children will increase markedly from 20% in 2005 to 35% in 2050, while non-Hispanic Whites, who had 59% of the children in 2005, will have 40% of the children in 2050.

The elderly is projected to grow from 37 million in 2005 to 81 million in 2050 (19% of the population), mainly because the last of the post–World War II baby boomers will turn 65 in 2029. Hispanic elderly will nearly triple from 6% in 2005 to 17% in 2050. Non-Hispanic Whites will remain the majority of the elderly but will experience a decline from 82% in 2005 to 63% in 2050. Black elderly will grow from 8% in 2005 to 12% in 2050, while Asian elderly will increase from 3% in 2005 to 8% in 2050.

The dependency ratio between combined nonworking age groups, mainly children and the elderly, and the working-age population will increase from 59 elderly and children per 100 working-age Americans in 2005 to 72 per 100 in 2050. The elderly dependency ratio was 20 per 100 in 2005 and will be 32 per 100 in 2050, while the child dependency ratio will remain constant at 40 per 100. Regardless, this will mean a greater tax burden for working-age adults (ages 17–64) to pay for elderly programs such as Social Security and children programs such as local education.

The demographic shifts toward a significant increase of *Latino and Asian new immigrants with high birth rates* challenge cultural competence not only to maintain historic relevance but also to increase its relevance given these trends. From a training and service planning perspective new immigrants mean the development of a culturally competent worker cadre who can speak Spanish and a variety of Asian languages; understand the cultural beliefs, mores, and behavior patterns of these target groups; and plan with clients new services to meet their problems of living needs. These demographic trends have implications for health care, housing, education, employment, social services, and related human service areas. Such data points to new arrivals and growing groups in the United States. It increases Americans' understanding of new immigrant adjustment patterns, customs, family structure, and related data, which challenges them *to evaluate the nature of cultural competence.* Demographics generate research and result in knowledge of various population trends, which has implications for practice, human behavior, and diversity and for planning of policies, legislation, and programs to meet the social needs of diverse populations.

CURRENT ISSUES FACING CULTURAL COMPETENCE

The cultural competence movement has experienced significant growth in the last 20 years in scope, influence, and size. However, cultural competence is involved in *an ideological struggle* involving the methodology and operationalization of the conceptual meaning of the term, research issues concerning measurement outcomes and instrumentation, and epistemology (theory of knowledge). Cultural competence could be likened to the rapid growth and development of a metropolitan city that partially realized that it was built below sea (or river) level and flooded periodically, like New Orleans, Louisiana, and Sacramento, California (the latter is my home town). As cultural competence shores up its theoretical conceptualization and methodology foundation, we are confident that it will move forward with new horizons and carry out unfinished agendas in its future as a major practice approach for the human services.

However, we turn to a number of pressing issues that we face in the present. We want to sketch them out for you and ask what we need to do to answer the criticisms of the critics. We need to exercise *clear thinking that pinpoints the issues, propose answers borne from critical thinking and research-oriented reflection, and move the movement* along the journey toward cultural competence and proficiency of the client and the worker.

CURRENT DEFINITIONS

There are multiple definitions of culture and cultural competence that have been conceptualized and taught in texts and classrooms across the United States. As you may find in the previous edition of this book, this author counted four different definitions of cultural competence cited by various authors and federal and state governments, each with a varied emphasis and slight difference. It is precisely this lack of focus and agreement about a common definition of cultural competence that is clouding the theory conceptualization of this practice approach. Without a clear, specific, and precise meaning of cultural competence, one has difficulty operationalizing the concept in a research-informed sense. Without adequate operationalization how can we conduct significant research on cultural competence and client effectiveness or conceptualize culturally competent oriented policies or design social planning of culturally competent components in social legislation or programs? This fuzziness cannot be allowed to continue to blur the clear nature and meaning of cultural competence. This book therefore intends on providing clarity from a research methodological approach.

As of this writing, there is lack of agreement about the definition and meaning of cultural competence on a number of levels. The field of social work has defined cultural competence in an attitudinal and ethical sense as "the process by which individuals and systems respond respectfully and effectively to people of all cultures, languages, classes, races, ethnic backgrounds, religions, and other diversity factors in a manner that recognizes, affirms, and values the worth of individuals, families, and communities and protects and prescribes the dignity of each." (NASW, 2007, p. 4). SAMHSA defines cultural competence on micro and meso levels as a set of congruent practice skills, behaviors, attitudes, and policies that come together in a system, agency, or among professionals and enables that system, agency, or those professionals to work effectively in cross-cultural situations. It is the ability to demonstrate skills and knowledge that enables a person to work effectively across cultures; the person should also possess the ability to provide mental health treatment within the cultural framework of the consumer and effective services to people of a specific cultural background, including one different from that of the provider (SAMHSA, 1997a).

Recently Rothman (2008, p. 7) explains cultural competence as process and practice: "a process, which can be learned, through which a social worker attains the necessary knowledge and skills needed to practice competently and sensitively across cultures...[and] the content, a social worker's knowledge and skills in working with a specific population...." However, the NASW defines cultural competence as an attitudinal process that communicates ethical values, while the SAMHSA focuses on micro skills, behaviors, and attitudes and meso system policies skills. The Rothman definition focuses on the functional levels of cultural competence and uses the adverb *competently*, which reflects the need to operationalize the concept rather than to repeat the concept word in formal and operational definitions. These varying definitional emphases are examples of the confusion reflected in the criticisms of Ridley, Baker, and Hill (2001) and Davis (2007).

CURRENT CRITICISMS

Cultural competence has evolved during the last two decades as a concept, a set of principles, knowledge theory, practice framework, and ethical and ethnic/cultural standards. There is no question that the cultural competence movement is an integral part of the disciplines of medicine, nursing, psychology, and social work as well as the professional fields of health care and mental health. Along the way in its growth and development there has been criticism—both constructive and critical—that points out the shortcomings and the need for further development of cultural competence. Is cultural competence a rallying cry, a concept, a system of helping, a professional standard and benchmark, a theory that can be operationalized so that it can be quantifiably and qualitatively measured, or a new field for those interested in working with the ethnically and culturally diverse? The answer is that cultural competence and culturally competent practice are inclusively all of the aforementioned and yet has many miles to go to reach maturity as a scientifically respectable social science helping system approach.

We want to share with our readers a sample of the current criticisms that have been written in the last ten years. It reflects the fact that most social work educators and practitioners as well as applied social science thinkers in related disciplines accept the reality that cultural competent practice has arrived on the scene. But at the same time it underscores the reality that cultural competence as a theory and practice system has a long way ahead. The focus of the criticisms is pointed and telling, but the spirit of the criticism is helpful and needed. Reading the critiques on the issues confronting cultural competence hopefully may inspire some social work students to conduct social work practice research in this area, write an MSW research paper or thesis with a cultural competent practice theme aspect, or produce a noteworthy article that will contribute toward clarifying an issue related to culturally competent practice.

MEASUREMENT AND INSTRUMENTATION

Boyle and Springer (2001) express concern about the lack of systematic measurement of educational outcomes for cultural competence, due in part to the fact that instrumentation is in its infancy in the field. The goal is to provide a measurable outcome based on consistent and effective ethnic minority content. Part of the task is to operationalize specific practitioner proficiencies in terms of clarifying and specifying competences as "the link between the concepts of cultural competence and measureable outcomes with empirical indicators for use in the evaluation of educational objectives" (p. 55). Boyle and Springer (2001) overview four existing instruments that measure cultural competence skill development: The Cross-Cultural Counseling Inventory—revised (1985, 1991), The Multicultural Counseling Awareness Scale—Form B (1991), The Multicultural Awareness-Knowledge-and-Skills Survey (1991), and The Multicultural Counseling Inventory (1994). While they do not offer an alternative new instrument, they suggest that we start by designing a culture-specific instrument for a specific population (e.g., for Latino clients) and then move toward the development of a general instrument that measures general cultural competence. The main thrust is empirical instrument development for cultural competence.

Likewise Davis (2007) points out that the majority of cultural competence measurement instruments were developed to assess individual provider competence during provider–consumer interaction. More recently measures have been developed to assess cultural competence at the organizational level for accreditation and managed care, child welfare organizations, and children's mental health care systems. (For a discussion of the current definition and measurement scales of cultural competence from a social work education viewpoint, see Krentz & Townsend, 2008).

EPISTEMOLOGY (THEORY OF KNOWLEDGE)

There has also been recent criticism regarding the epistemology (theory of knowledge) of cultural competence in social work education, which parallels former critical reviews of cultural competence in multicultural psychology (Marsella & Yamada, 2000). Kwong (2009) points out,

> However, it has been documented in the literature that the concept of cultural competency and competency-based training, practice, and research require further investigations to refine concepts and conceptual frameworks, training objectives and process; integration of values, knowledge and skills; and operationalization for research outcomes. Thus, further studies are needed to refine its definition, from broad to specific; its constructs, from conceptualization to operationalization; and its practice framework, from general to culture-specific. (p. 147)

Kwong specifically underscores the need to clarify and refine the definition of culture from a psychological perspective, the need to measure cultural competency and to move away from conceptual, cognitive, and behavioral constructs, the need to operationalize awareness, knowledge, and skills as abstract indicators in concrete and behavioral terms, the lack of clear theoretical models for multicultural counseling and insufficient broad-based empirical support, the absence of a link between specific cultural elements and particular processes (e.g., the problem of transforming knowledge into concrete operations and strategies), and the lack of clinical and cultural integration that causes cultural bias and two different conceptual assumptions and worldviews are some of the issues that are needed to refine culturally competent practice. In brief, Kwong (2009, p. 119) states, "Many issues—e.g. definitional variance, theoretical construct obscurity, unspecific clinical and cultural integration in practice, and unclear competency educational goals and evaluative methods—need to be dealt with as research proceeds."

Likewise, Johnson, and Munch (2009) are concerned about the conceptual tensions that are at the center of cultural competence, specifically the epistemological foundations, the rights and dignity of the individual, and the question of whether a social worker can ever be culturally competent. From their perspective they focus on four major criticisms of cultural competence: 1) the epistemological (questions of knowledge and the manner in which knowledge is obtained) emphasis on a priori knowledge of cultural difference (i.e., prior assumptions about cultural differences among and between cultural and ethnic groups) contrary to the social work practice principle of learning from the client; 2) the stereotypical classification systems used to describe cultural differences and away from the uniqueness of the individual; 3) the oversensitivity to cultural group differences that may lead to a privileging of group rights that is at odds with individual self-determination; and 4) the ill-defined and less achievability of cultural competence. In short, Johnson and Munch (2009, p. 223) argue "that the major tenets of CC are self-contradictory or in contradiction with other social work values." They raise four contradictions:

1. Contradiction 1 (knowing about cultures) reminds us that we should practice an inductive learning approach (learning from the client) rather than a deductive assumption stance (knowing about the client), be aware of social constructionism versus a priori knowledge, utilize self-awareness to the extent of changing attitude and behavior at the expense of increasing knowledge, be leery of the generalizations and inaccuracies over descriptions of cultures which can be reductionistic and stereotypic and affirm the dynamic, ever-changing nature of cultures.

2. Contradiction 2 (collective identities) reaffirms the opportunity to discover one's own identity (individual identity as a part of group identity), the importance of self-determination and reaching our full potential, the emphasis of commonality (respect for all humanity) and the danger of overprivileging difference and diversity which may be at odds with autonomy and expected modes of belief and behavior, the reality of a mixing of cultures rather than cultural autonomy, the reality of intersectionality and intra group differences and diversity within diversity or multiple identities, the danger of accepting grand generalizations of ethnic and racial groups, the affirmation of the ever-changing nature of cultures and the danger of external maintenance of a culture and the learning of culture through honest and sincere communication.

3. Contradiction 3 (group rights) poses the dilemma of the protection of group rights while denying an individual's right to self-determination when group mores and practices may be contradictory, the affirmation of self-determination and social justice in the midst of harmful and oppressive cultural group practices.

4. Contradiction 4 (cultural competence is achievable) warns us to consider whether cultural competence is humanly possible, encourages us to think levels of cultural competence rather than ultimate attainment of cultural competence, poses whether cultural competence is linear development or nonlinear, the need for empirical research validation based on a clear definition and a coherent theory base and models of cultural competence, and the need for cultural humility which favors openness, respect, sensitivity, and life-long self-critique.

Such observations ought to soften a dogmatic view of cultural competence and encourage a resolve to address these issues, knowing that the cultural competency movement is still in its infancy and is still coping with growth development. Johnson and Munch's (2009) criticisms of cultural competence are justified and call for further reflection and research.

This book is based on an inductive learning, not-knowing social construction theory base; a striving for knowledge theory that is operationalized in two sets of pretests and posttests in order to reach quantitative research results; and a deep concern that social work educators and practitioners who have dedicated their professional careers to building a culturally diverse practice base have not been given due credit for the knowledge theory and practice skills contributions that they have made during the past 40 years, from the early days of ethnic minority social work practice. At the same time I am encouraged by the warm words of the opening sentences of Harper-Dorton and Lantz (2007):

> Culturally competent social workers, counselors and other human service professionals are critically important in the multicultural world of the twenty-first century. The ability to interact professionally with clients who are culturally different requires great cultural awareness, sensitivity, and empathy for the human experience of living in the world. (p. 1)

Cultural competence is a new and alternative practice orientation, which is striving to gain maturity and should welcome constructive criticism for its development.

CONNECTING THE BUILDING BLOCKS OF CULTURAL COMPETENCE

In light of the current context of significant demographic shifts toward immigrant groups, lack of current agreement regarding the definition of cultural competence, and research and knowledge theory concerns, we believe that we need to launch a major effort to address these issues. The metaphor *connecting the building blocks* conjures up a construction process of identifying and placing together the essential elements of an edifice. The task is prompted by the definition and methodology issue.

There has been a debate over definition and methodology on cultural competence inside and outside the multicultural competence community. Ridley, Baker, and Hill (2001) raise concerns about the nature of cultural competence as a conceptual construct, the need for a solid agreed-upon definition of cultural competence that operationalizes the construct, the connection of the definition to the purpose of cultural competence, and desired outcomes and steps that include theory, practice principles, and the evaluation of cultural competence. They question whether the current methodology of cultural competence is adequate. Davis (2007) similarly points out the variety and evolving meanings of cultural competence, the historical lack of clarity around the conceptual meaning of cultural competence, which has had an effect on the constructs underlying the models and the evaluative measures based on those models, and the lack of clarity around the construct's meaning. These are some of the problems that beset advocates of cultural competence.

In light of these critical observations, it is important that readers receive a clear and consistent presentation of culturally competent practice. Figure 1.1 identifies eight connecting building blocks of the cultural competence process for the reader to gain an understanding of the interdependent relationships of major variables related to culturally competent practice. Each of the eight variables are building blocks that are presented in various sections of chapters throughout this book and endeavors to address the concerns of Ridley, Baker, and Hill (2001) and Davis (2007) as they strove to bring methodological clarity to multicultural competence.

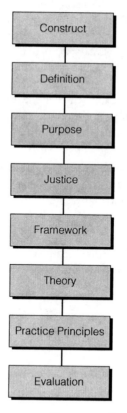

FIGURE I.I   THE BUILDING BLOCKS OF CULTURAL COMPETENCE

THE CONSTRUCT: CULTURAL COMPETENCE

A construct is a building concept that integrates in an orderly way the diverse data on a phenomenon that could be a set of facts, circumstances, or experience. A construct is an organizing concept from which various supporting components are derived. For example, the construct *birthday party* conjures up a series of components essential to a successful event: the person who is the honoree of the party, the age of the person, a surprise element, a list of invitees, location, food, birthday cake, gifts, and other celebrative elements. We have the concept (the idea) of a birthday party. We have defined what it means for a particular person who is celebrating his or her birthday. We have a methodological procedure of how we will execute the party. We then proceed with its operationalization. The party turns out to be a successful occasion because it was well thought out and planned. However, unlike this familiar analogy, we are now in the midst of rethinking the methodology and operationalization of cultural competence.

If we take the criticisms of the critics seriously, we must realize that there is an alternative way of reconceptualizing and articulating the nature and meaning of cultural competence. We must develop a new language syntax or systematic arrangement concerning cultural competence. Ridley, Baker, and Hill (2001) have given us some major clues on reordering the etiology (causes and origin) of cultural competence. The construct *cultural competence* is a concept that is preliminary to a working definition of cultural competence. What is the meaning of the construct *cultural competence*? How is the construct then operationalized into a working definition? How does the definition then translate into a purpose? Does the construct create an integrative environment so that major variables fall into place and provide logic and connection? Ridley, Baker, and Hill (2001) raise these questions because of the lack of clarity and preciseness in current cultural competence studies.

Dean (2001) is critical regarding the use of the construct *cultural competence*. According to her, cultural competence is a myth and flawed. Rather she argues for the need to be aware of one's lack of competence in a helping relationship. Dean (2001, p. 624) states her argument:

> I believe it [cultural competence] to be a myth that is typically American and located in the metaphor of American "know-how." It is consistent with the belief that knowledge brings control and effectiveness, and that this is an ideal to be achieved above all else. I question the notion that one could become "competent" at the culture of another. I would instead propose a model in which maintaining an awareness of one's lack of competence is the goal rather than the establishment of competence. With "lack of competence" as the focus, a different view of practicing across cultures emerges. The client is the "expert" and the clinician is in a position of seeking knowledge and trying to understand what life is like for the client. There is no thought of competence—instead one thinks of gaining understanding (always partial) of a phenomenon that is evolving and changing.

We ask you to suspend your judgment on cultural competence for now. Dean is reacting to the construct and a stereotypic definition and is proposing a model and a particular practice approach based on a theory simultaneously. We ask you to set aside these criticisms as we explain each variable separately and then interconnect the variables in a process approach.

The construct *cultural competence* is best understood by examining two sub-variables: culture and competence.

CULTURE AS A SUB-VARIABLE

What is culture? Culture is the integrated pattern of human behavior that includes thoughts, communications, actions, customs, beliefs, values, and institutions of a racial, ethnic, religious, or social group (NASW, 2000). It has been broadened to be inclusive of many groups. Culture also refers to "the totality of ways being passed on from generation to generation," and "includes ways in which people with disabilities or people from various religious backgrounds or people who are gay, lesbian, or transgender experience the world around them" (NASW, 2001, p. 4). However, there is a changing dynamic aspect of culture, which must be understood in order to recognize that culture is not a fixed static entity. Marsella and Yamada (2000, p.12) speak of

> Shared learned meanings and behaviors that are transmitted from within a social activity context for purposes of promoting individual/societal adjustment, growth, and

development. Culture has both external (i.e., artifacts, roles, activity contexts, institutions) and internal (i.e., values, beliefs, attitudes, activity contexts, patterns of consciousness, personality styles, epistemology) representations. The shared meanings and behaviors are subject to continuous change and modification in response to changing internal and external circumstances.

In brief, culture involves shared meanings and behaviors in a social activity setting with external and internal learning patterns that are constantly changing.

COMPETENCE AS A SUB-VARIABLE

The word *competence* means sufficiency, adequacy, and capability. Competence may vary from person to person. The concept implies a striving toward mastery of a particular ability or area of expertise. Competence "implies having the capacity to function effectively within the context of culturally integrated patterns of human behavior defined by the group" (NASW, 2001, p. 4). The NASW Code of Ethics (1996) views competence in terms of a value of the social work profession that develops and enhances professional expertise through knowledge and skills applied to practice. The code also understands that competence is an ethical standard under which social workers are to provide competent services within the boundaries of their professional education, licensing, and certification—with appropriate study, training, consultation, and supervision from competent persons—and to take responsible steps to ensure the competence of their work and to protect clients from harm. Competencies are also understood from a social work education viewpoint as measurable practice behaviors that comprise knowledge, values, and skills that are demonstrated in practice with individuals, families, groups, organizations, and communities (*EPAS,* CSWE, 2008, Educational Policy 2.1).

CONSTRUCT MEANING

In light of the preceding discussion the construct *cultural competence* literally means "being capable of adequate understanding and sufficient learning of shared meanings and behaviors in a social activity setting with external and internal learning patterns that are constantly changing." The construct *cultural competence* provides the raw data information to operationalize the definition of cultural competence in a social work practice context.

THE DEFINITION OF CULTURAL COMPETENCE

THE USE OF THE TERM   As a part of clarifying the issues surrounding the definition of cultural competence, Whaley (2008) focuses on the usage of the term, observing that misinterpretation of the term (he cites White colleagues who advocate using the term *culturally relevant*) is symptomatic of the lack of definitional clarity. Using descriptive analyses (i.e., the electronic reference database PsycINFU) and multivariate analysis (multidimensional scaling and cluster analyses), Whaley (2008) found that in a search parameter there were 2,520 hits for "cultural sensitivity" and 473 hits for "cultural competence." Furthermore, the term *cultural competence* was most prevalent in the clinical psychology literature—the social work literature would yield probably a similar result—and multicultural competence was found in the counseling psychology literature.

The implications of the Whaley (2008) findings reveal the need to differentiate the distinctiveness of the two terms, avoiding their interchangeable use (Rothman, 2008). It also underscores the task of interpreting the meaning of cultural competence rather than misinterpreting and misappropriating its usage. These issues surround the effort to bring more conceptual and research clarity to the use of the term.

PROPOSED DEFINITION   From our perspective an adequate definition of cultural competence must include the concept of cultural proficiency as an operational variable for cultural competence involving both the worker and the client and mutual participatory understanding and learning in a practice growth process. Cultural proficiency involves becoming adept, skilled and to a certain degree competent in a helping relationship where cultural and ethnic diverse issues are involved along with other multidimensional relevant areas. In research methodology the selection of a like or similar concept variable is used to operationalize a major term. We operationalize *competent* in terms of *proficient* in order to specify the activities or *operations* necessary to measure it (Kerlinger, 1973, p. 31). The term *proficiency* is a more realistic goal than the term *competence,* which may be more difficult to attain. We all want to be proficient, but we may not all be able to be competent.

Nevertheless, LaFromboise, Coleman, and Gerton (1993) suggest that a culturally competent individual possesses a strong personal identity, has knowledge of the beliefs and values of the culture, and displays sensitivity to the affective processes of the culture. In a cultural setting, this person communicates clearly in the language of the cultural group, performs socially sanctioned behavior, maintains active social relations within the cultural group, and negotiates the institutional structures of that culture. Cultural competence is part of a continuum of social skill and personality development. This concept addresses an individual's sense of self-sufficiency and ego strength; cultural identity related to culture of origin and cultural context; and knowledge, appreciation, and internalization of basic beliefs of a culture. Externally this translates into positive attitudes about a cultural group; bicultural efficacy, or the ability to live effectively within two groups without compromising one's sense of cultural identity; the ability to communicate, verbally and nonverbally, ideas and feelings to members of one's own or another culture; possession of a role repertoire or range of culturally appropriate behaviors or roles; and belonging to stable social networks in more than one culture. This description may fit a *strongly oriented cultural client* and to a lesser extent some personal and professional traits of *a culturally proficient worker.*

From an education and training perspective, cultural competence may also be understood as the development of academic and professional expertise and skills in the area of working with culturally diverse clients. (For a discussion on the academic and scholarly orientation of cultural competence education and training, see Lonner, 1997.) The *three functions of cultural competence* begin with the fostering of *cultural awareness.* The social worker becomes culturally effective with the client when the worker develops cultural awareness through an exploration of his or her own ethnic identity, cultural background, and contact with ethnic others. Next, the social worker must develop a knowledge acquisition perspective and a set of skills in order to work with multicultural clients. *Knowledge acquisition* provides a body of facts and principles that serve as boundary guidelines. *Skill development* applies knowledge acquisition to actual practice with clients from a culturally competent perspective. It also addresses inductively learning from the client and establishing the service delivery structure that ought to be in place for client services.

WORKING DEFINITION   In brief, *our working definition of cultural competence* in a social work practice context involves the *mutual consent* of the worker and the client to become *culturally proficient by participating together* in the *exploration and learning* of cultural and ethnic history, values, and behavioral issues which are relevant to *understanding particular problems* in the helping relationship as part of the *micro practice process* and to work toward the development of *meso and macro policies and programs* which benefit clients who are culturally and ethnically diverse.

DEFINITIONAL IMPLICATIONS   Such a working definition places the worker and the client in an egalitarian relationship. It transcends "the worker is competent, while the client is not competent" trap door. Rather it endorses a mutual and joint relationship of consent, respect, and participation where both the worker and the client are helping themselves and each other as they strive toward cultural proficiency through the study of cultural elements impacting the problem situation. They focus on *culture as a primary base* and *practice process as an understanding and a learning experience*, which initiates *a problem-solving continuum* familiar to social work.

Whaley and Davis (2007) have a similar definition of cultural competence, which highlights culture, heritage adaptation, and cultural problem solving. They conceptualize cultural competence

> As a set of problem-solving skills that include (a) the ability to recognize and understand the dynamic interplay between the heritage and adaptation dimensions of culture in shaping human behavior; (b) the ability to use the knowledge acquired about an individual's heritage and adaptational challenges to maximize the effectiveness of assessment, diagnosis, and treatment; and (c) internalization (i.e. incorporation into one's clinical problem-solving repertoire) of this process of recognition, acquisition, and use of cultural dynamics so that it can be routinely applied to diverse groups. (p. 565)

Furthermore Whaley and King (2007) have a treatment approach for cultural competence that is attuned to social work: culturally based problem solving, brief treatment, and task-centered. Whaley and King (2007, p. 565) state, "Treatment is short term; the emphasis is present focused and problem focused; skills training is stressed; the therapeutic relationship is considered to be important; and homework is assigned." Moreover, they recognize the need for cultural competence empirical effectiveness.

Whaley and King (2007) also propose *a relationship between cultural competence and evidence-based practice*. They advocate the *cultural adaptation of evidence-based practice* as a means of increasing the *empirical effectiveness of cultural competence and modifying the scientific nature of evidence-based practice* through an integration of both. The implementation of such a proposal undoubtedly might influence the course of current practice approaches and strengthen the collaboration of practices on both sides. This is an example of the dynamic and creative dialogue taking place between the cultural competence movement and other practice perspectives.

THE PURPOSE OF CULTURAL COMPETENCE

Ridley, Baker, and Hill (2001, p. 824) advocate "therapeutic gain" as the purposeful and positive change elicited by the therapeutic process and the purpose of cultural competence. However, their orientation is from a multicultural counseling perspective as counseling psychologists. Consistent with our construct and definition of cultural competence, the purpose of cultural competence for a social work practice is "*culturally based empowerment and advocacy.*" The competence and proficiency of the worker and the client are means to an end. The purpose is to empower the client and advocate for the client through cultural and related resources.

A major indicator of empowerment and advocacy is to "use practice methods and approaches that help the client facilitate a connection with their own power in a manner appropriate for their cultural context" and "provide support to diverse cultural groups who are advocating on their own behalf" (NASW, 2007, Standard 6, Nos. 3 and 4). Empowerment and advocacy involve micro, meso, and macro levels of intervention where cultural resources are available. The culture base uses such resources as cultural beliefs, cultural life narratives for insight-oriented solutions, natural support systems such as kinship and extended families, cultural and ethnic social services, culturally based faith groups, and other bases that can be focused on the person, the problem, and the immediate social environment from a broad cultural perspective. In the following brief explanations of subsequent variables, the reader will learn how we operationalize cultural competence as cultural proficiency in justice, framework, theory, practice principles, and evaluation.

JUSTICE

Multicultural competence has recognized the importance of incorporating social justice as part of the concerns when working with culturally and diverse clients. Sue and Sue (2008) define social justice as providing equal access and opportunity to all groups; being inclusive; removing individual and systemic barriers to fair mental health treatment; and ensuring that counseling/therapy services are directed at the micro, meso, and macro levels of our society. Social work has a broader and more inclusive perspective on justice than this viewpoint. Social work and particularly culturally competent social work practice encompass the scope of human rights and social justice and economic justice. The social work standard is

> Each person, regardless of position in society, has basic human rights, such as freedom, safety, privacy, an adequate standard of living, health care, and education. Social

workers recognize the global interconnections of oppression and are knowledgeable about theories of justice and strategies to promote human and civil rights. Social work incorporates social justice practices in organizations, institutions, and society to ensure that these basic human rights are distributed equitably and without prejudice. (CSWE, 2008, Educational Policy 2.1.5)

To be *culturally proficient* in culturally competent practice means that the worker and the client have applied the parameters of these concerns to the problem situation in the helping relationship.

THE FRAMEWORK FOR CULTURAL COMPETENCE

Chapter Four presents a framework for cultural competence that emphasizes *cultural proficiency based on generalist and advanced social work cultural competencies*. Cultural competencies are based on two levels of the social work curriculum and cover statements related to proficiencies on cultural awareness, knowledge acquisition, and skill development. The development of a framework is essential to demonstrating how cultural proficiencies can be operationalized in a system. Ridley, Baker, and Hill (2001) have pointed out the paucity of frameworks in multicultural competence psychology.

THEORIES FOR CULTURAL COMPETENCE

Williams (2006) has set forth four theories (postpositivism, constructivism, critical theory, and postmodernism) with applications to cultural competence. Chapter Six (Knowledge Acquisition) features these *macro knowledge theories* along with several *micro knowledge theories*. Consistent with our working definition of cultural competence the emphasis on worker and client *mutual consent and participation* on the learning and understanding of culture are some of underlying characteristics of social constructionism theory, which we shall cover in Chapter Six.

PRACTICE PRINCIPLES FOR CULTURAL COMPETENCE

Rothman (2008) identifies seven culturally competent practice skills: engagement, trust, and relationship-building; assessment; need definition and contracting; intervention; evaluation and termination; utilization of cultural resources; and advocacy. Chapter Seven (Skill Development) focuses on *culturally proficient skills* involving process, conceptualization, and personalization skills clusters with the stages of engagement (involving contact, inductive learning, and problem identification), assessment, intervention (emphasizing empowerment), and evaluation. Culturally diverse service delivery is also covered in the chapter.

EVALUATION OF CULTURAL COMPETENCE

Ridley, Baker, and Hill (2001) call for the need to develop research instruments that strengthen research validation of cultural competence clearly defined in our discussions on construct, definition, and purpose. There has been a survey of cultural competence research instruments and the need to link the concepts of cultural competence and measurable outcomes (Boyle & Springer, 2001; Davis, 2007). Our text contains two tests: pretests and posttests (Social Work Cultural Competencies Self-Assessment and Social Work Cultural Competencies with Culturally Diverse Groups and Social and Economic Justice), based on the contents of various chapters and designed to operationalize *cultural proficiency* in text content.

This overview of the connective building blocks of the cultural competence process presents the major variables that are essential to culturally competent and proficient social work practice. We now turn to understanding the levels and dimensions of cultural competence, which describes how we put together the various stories of the building itself.

THE LEVELS AND DIMENSIONS OF CULTURAL COMPETENCE

There are numerous ways to describe how we put together cultural competence. The current literature has two major divisions: practitioner, agency, and community levels, which are various functions of cultural competence, and micro, meso, and macro dimensions, represent a systematic arrangement.

PRACTITIONER, AGENCY, AND COMMUNITY LEVELS

Miley, O'Melia, and DuBois (1998) view cultural competence on three levels: practitioner, agency, and community. On the *practitioner level,* the worker must know about self-awareness in terms of his or her own personal values and cultural heritage, values differences and conflicts regarding assimilation and cultural pluralism, and awareness of the cultures of others, especially clients. The authors suggest that the social worker take a cultural self-inventory on personal identity, spiritual beliefs, knowledge of others, and cross-cultural skills, and study cultural groups through observational community research. They state:

> In summary, learning to be a competent cross-cultural practitioner is an evolutionary process that begins with awareness and increases with each interaction with clients. Workers first attempt to understand their own cultural filters. Next, they build a knowledge base of other perspectives through literature reviews and field research. Third, workers analyze the impact of cultural identities on the power dynamics of the worker–client partnership. Finally, practitioners continue to fine tune their cultural sensitivity through their ongoing practice experiences with unique client systems. (Miley et al., 1998, pp. 72–73)

In terms of *agency-level* cultural competence, workers are trained in the skills necessary for diversity-sensitive practice, and multicultural awareness and functioning are promoted in organizational structure and program delivery. Cultural competence permeates agency policies on hiring and training staff, program evaluation, and criteria for eligibility, and it involves programs and procedures that focus on client strengths; culturally sensitive assessment instruments; culture as a resource; and ethnically oriented indigenous helping networks. Structures are designed for multicultural interchanges between agency, worker, and client; worker control over practice; and client influence on services. For example, in the field of health care, Kaiser Permanente (2004) has published an educational monograph on cultural competence and has established Centers of Excellence in Cultural Competence targeting specific populations. BlueCross BlueShield of Florida (2004) has instituted internal diversity training and cultural competence education for providers. These health care agency efforts have created a favorable atmosphere for cultural competence to flourish as providers consider how best to deliver services. The desired physical environment is an accessible neighborhood location, outreach services, and cultural decor and setting. Culturally competent agencies have resource networks that include institutions and individuals in the ethnic community, such as churches, schools, clubs, local healers, neighborhood leaders, and culturally oriented media.

The third level of cultural competence discussed by Miley et al. (1998) is the *community level,* which replaces the context for discrimination, segregation, and distinct boundaries with a context of pluralism, celebration of diversity, promotion of cross-cultural interaction, and social justice. The model for practitioner, agency, and community cultural competence sets a new benchmark for this field. An increasing area of cultural competence has been the health care of persons with chronic conditions and medical care in general.

The Center on an Aging Society (2004) reports,

> If the providers, organizations, and systems are not working together to provide culturally competent care, patients are at higher risk of having negative health consequences, receiving poor quality care, or being dissatisfied with their care. African Americans and other ethnic minorities report less partnership with physicians, less participation in medical decisions, and lower levels of satisfaction with care. The quality of patient–physician interaction is lower among non-White patients, particularly Latinos and Asian Americans. Lower quality patient–physician interactions are associated with lower overall satisfaction with health care. African Americans are more likely than other minority groups to feel that they were treated disrespectfully during a health care visit (e.g., they were spoken to rudely, talked down to, or ignored). Compared to other minority groups, Asian Americans are least likely to feel that their doctor understood their background and values and are most likely to report that their doctor looked down on them. (p. 5)

As a result on the community level, cultural competence in health care services has sought to provide interpreter services; recruit and retain minority staff; provide training to increase cultural awareness, knowledge, and skills; coordinate with traditional healers; use community health workers; incorporate culture-specific attitudes and values into health promotion tools; include family and community members in health care decision making; locate clinics in geographic areas that are easily accessible for certain populations; expand hours of operation; and provide linguistic competency beyond the clinical encounter to the appointment desk, advice lines, medical billing, and other written materials.

The Liaison Committee on Medical Education (LCME), the accreditation body for medical schools in the United States and Canada, has mandated higher standards for curriculum material on cultural competence. Medical schools must provide students with skills to understand how people of diverse cultures and belief systems perceive health and illness and respond to various symptoms, diseases, and treatment, as well as explore the racial and gender biases in themselves, others, and in the delivery of health care. Harvard Medical School (2005) reported on the use of the Association of American Medical Colleges (AAMC) Tool for Assessing Cultural Competence Training (TACCT), which has created a map of the knowledge, skills, and attitudes of students and faculty for the Harvard medical curriculum. It depicts current cultural competence training efforts and identifies gaps where further integration of cultural issues is needed. The Harvard Medical School has sponsored a session on Developing Culturally Competent Care Faculty and offers an elective course called "Emerging a Culturally Competent Physician," using case-based learning to teach cultural competence. In addition, there is a coordinator for the Harvard Medical School Culturally Competent Care Education Committee. These community thrusts in cultural competence and health care are encouraging signs of growth and development.

MICRO, MESO, AND MACRO DIMENSIONS

Likewise, we can view cultural competence on the micro, meso, and macro dimensions. *Micro cultural competence* involves the client and the social worker. The client acquires cultural competence from personal background and development. The client has the task of sorting his or her culture of origin and elements of the dominant culture to achieve bicultural integration and bicultural competence. Likewise, the worker develops expertise and skills through education and through working with culturally diverse clients. It is

> The process by which individuals and systems respond respectfully and effectively to people of all cultures, languages, classes, races, ethnic backgrounds, religions, and other diversity factors in a manner that recognizes, affirms, and values the worth of individuals, families, and communities and protects and preserves the dignity of each. (NASW, 2001, p. 5)

This client system is broad and comprehensive in scope and outreach.

Meso cultural competence addresses the organizational dimension to determine whether an institution has a culturally competent system of care. Cross, Bazron, Dennis, and Isaacs (1989) explain six anchor points along a cultural competence continuum with regard to an organizational system of care:

1. Cultural destructiveness describes attitudes, practices, and policies that promote the superiority of the dominant culture and attempts to eradicate the inferior and different culture.
2. Cultural incapacity refers to attitudes, practices, and policies that adhere to separate but equal treatment and tend toward segregated institutional practices.
3. Cultural blindness refers to attitudes, practices, and policies that have an unbiased view of undifferentiated elements of culture and people and treat all people as assimilated.
4. The culturally open organization has attitudes, practices, and policies that are receptive to the improvement of cultural services through staff hiring practices, training on cultural sensitivity, and minority board representation.

5. The culturally competent agency has attitudes, practices, and policies that demonstrate respect for different cultures and people by seeking advice and consultation from ethnic and racial communities and by being committed to incorporating these practices into the organization.

6. Cultural proficiency describes attitudes, practices, and policies that are sensitive to cultural differences and diversity, improve cultural quality of services through cultural research, disseminate research findings, and promote diverse group cultural relations.

On the meso dimension, cultural competence is "a set of congruent behaviors, attitudes, and policies that come together in a system or agency or among professionals and enable the system, agency, or professionals to work effectively in cross-cultural situations" (NASW, 2001, p. 5). A culturally competent service delivery system should value diversity, have the capacity for cultural self-assessment, be conscious of the dynamics of cultural interaction, institutionalize cultural knowledge, and develop programs and services that promote diversity between and within cultures.

However, Nybell, and Gray (2004) underscore the conflictual nature of organizational change rather than a unified, linear development continuum as previously depicted by Cross et al. (1989). In terms of cultural competence and multicultural organizational development, in an organizational case study of three child and family agencies, Nybell and Gray found that "achieving cultural competence in a predominantly White social services agency requires redistributing power toward clients, toward programs that disproportionately serve the most disenfranchised clients, to workers of color, and to representatives of communities of color" (p. 25). Nybell and Gray emphasize the conflictual nature of cultural competence change and redistribution of power in organizations and communities as realities that we must confront.

Macro cultural competence refers to large system efforts to address cultural competence issues and programs. On the national level, the National Center for Cultural Competence (NCCC) has been a leadership force at the Georgetown University Child Development Center. The mission of the NCCC is to increase the capacity of health care programs to design, implement, and evaluate culturally competent service delivery systems. It is a funded project of the Health Resources and Services Administration (HRSA), Department of Health and Human Services (DHHS). The center serves as the clearinghouse for planning, policy, and programs related to cultural competence (see http://gucchd.georgetown.edu/nccc/pa.html).

A number of major texts address cultural competence issues on a macro professional level (see Constantine & Sue, 2005b; Fong, 2004; Fong & Furuto, 2001; Ponterotto, Casas, Suzuki, & Alexander, 1995; Pope-Davis & Coleman, 1997). The U.S. Public Health Service's Office for Substance Abuse Prevention launched a series of monographs that integrated cultural competence, alcohol and drug abuse treatment programs, and ethnic groups and community (Orlandi, Weston, & Epstein, 1992). This interface between ethnic target groups, major problem areas, and cultural competence for treatment workers further illustrates how macro cultural competency can be expressed. Macro-level efforts have resulted in statewide cultural competence programs in mental health and health care in such states as California, New York, and South Carolina.

Having described levels and dimensions, we move to the application of cultural competence in terms of current ethics and standards for social workers. In a real sense we are witnessing how cultural competence as a concept is adopted and professionalized for such a helping profession as social work at the present time.

THE ETHICAL STANDARDS AND COMPETENCIES OF CULTURAL COMPETENCE

NASW CODE OF ETHICS AND STANDARDS FOR CULTURAL COMPETENCE

Social work ethics has a connection to cultural competence. Part of the NASW Code of Ethics relates to sensitivity to cultural and ethnic diversity. There are a number of ethical issues such as how individuals cope with problems from a cultural perspective based on traditions and norms, culturally sensitive social service planning and delivery, worker respect for the dignity and worth of the cultural person, ethical dilemmas regarding the special needs and value conflicts of cultural clients, strengths of cultures, and related ethical areas (NASW, 2007).

Ethics are based on the values that we have as individuals and as professionals, which guide our choices based on our sense of right and wrong and on ideals such as the highest good, the promotion of fairness, or the moral duty and obligation that we have to ourselves, others, our profession, our community, and to a higher being. At times, our ethical guidelines force us to make a tragic moral choice where we must choose the lesser of the two evils because the two or more available selections are less than ideal. Social work has a tradition of a professional code of ethics.

The NASW's 1999 Code of Ethics has a section on cultural competence:

1.05(a) Social workers should understand culture and its function in human behavior and society, recognizing the strengths that exist in all cultures.

1.05(b) Social workers should have a knowledge base of their clients' cultures and be able to demonstrate competence in the provision of services that are sensitive to clients' culture and to differences among people and cultural groups.

1.05(c) Social workers should obtain education about and seek to understand the nature of social diversity and oppression with respect to race, ethnicity, national origin, sex, sexual orientation, age, marital status, political belief, religion and mental or physical development.

Interestingly, the *Standards for Cultural Competence in Social Work Practice* and the NASW Code of Ethics charge the social worker with the ethical responsibility to be culturally competent. Both go hand in hand to delineate ethical and professional standards for culturally competent social work practice. Our task in this section is to blend this understanding of culture with the values, beliefs, and guidelines of ethics in order to address the ethics of cultural competence.

There has been increasing interest in the ethics of cultural competence. Among the ethical moral guidelines and the cultural beliefs and practices are the following principles that comprise an ethical notion of cultural competence (Cross et al., 1989; Paasche-Orlow, 2004):

- The acknowledgment of the importance of culture in people's lives
- The respect for cultural differences
- The minimization of any negative consequences of cultural differences, which has a discriminatory effect on persons and/or groups
- The assessment of personal cultural values, acknowledging the existence of a cultural lens that shapes our interpretations of the world
- The understanding and acknowledgment of the historical relationship between your own culture and other cultural groups
- The creation and dissemination of institutional culture knowledge, which recognizes and honors diversity
- The development of policies and ethical guidelines, which implements service delivery reflecting an understanding of cultural diversity

The ethics of cultural competence ought to sensitize social workers, clients, and community to cultural similarities and differences that are the essence of diversity. It should allow us the freedom to use cultural symbols and practices in communication and daily living. It should guide us in the development of policies and practices that seek the input of community members of various cultures. It should encourage agencies and professional bodies to develop written ethical guidelines and practices that guide the infusion of cultural competence into staff selection and development, as well as strategies, policies, procedures, and practices for cultural competence. In short, it is the underpinning for evaluating the relationship between the ethics of cultural competence and the ethics of social work.

The NASW (2001) issued the *Standards for Cultural Competence in Social Work Practice.* Ten standards provide guidelines, goals, and objectives of cultural competence; these standard statements are considered cultural competencies:

Standard 1. Ethics and Values: *Social workers shall function in accordance with the values, ethics, and standards of the profession, recognizing how personal and professional values may conflict with or accommodate the needs of diverse clients.*

Among the major ethical and value areas is a sensitivity to cultural and ethnic diversity. Cultural and ethnic sensitivity extends to behavior appropriate to a culture based on cultural traditions and norms, client cultural background, the planning of social services, a recognition of cultural strengths, and ethnical and cultural value conflict dilemmas.

Standard 2. Self-Awareness: *Social workers shall develop an understanding of their own personal and cultural values and beliefs as a first step in appreciating the importance of multicultural identities in the lives of people.*

Social workers should examine their own cultural backgrounds and identities, become culturally aware of their own heritage as well as those of others, and move from cultural awareness through cultural sensitivity to cultural competence.

Standard 3. Cross-Cultural Knowledge: *Social workers shall have and continue to develop specialized knowledge and understanding about the history, traditions, values, family systems, and artistic expression of major client groups served.*

Social workers are challenged to expand their knowledge about culture, behavior, language, social service policy impacts, resources, and power relationships; particular providers and client groups; social, cultural, and political systems in the United States; and the limitations and strengths of current and relevant theories and principles.

Standard 4. Cross-Cultural Skills: *Social workers shall use appropriate methodological approaches, skills, and techniques that reflect the workers' understanding of the role of culture in the helping process.*

Among the personal attributes and qualities of a culturally competent social worker is an acceptance and openness to differences among people, an understanding of the role of language in the client's culture, an assessment of cultural norms and behaviors as strengths rather than problematic or symptomatic behaviors, and advocacy and empowerment skills.

Standard 5. Service Delivery: *Social workers shall be knowledgeable about and skillful in the use of services available in the community and broader society and be able to make appropriate referrals for their diverse clients.*

Among the specific ways of implementing culturally competent service delivery are recruiting multiethnic staff and including cultural competence job requirements, reviewing demographic trends to determine interpretation and translation services, having program décor and design that reflect the cultural heritage of clients, and developing culturally competent performance measures.

Standard 6. Empowerment and Advocacy: *Social workers shall be aware of the effect of social policies and programs on diverse client populations, advocating for and with clients whenever appropriate.*

Empowerment involves consciousness raising, the development of personal power, and skills for social change. Advocacy involves a client's understanding of what it means to advocate based on respectful collaboration and mutually agreed-on goals for change.

Standard 7. Diverse Workforce: *Social workers shall support and advocate for recruitment, admissions and hiring, and retention efforts in social work programs and agencies that ensure diversity within the profession.*

This standard implies the recruitment and retention of a diverse cadre of social workers who have some indigenous sense of cultural competence and make efforts to increase culturally competent skills.

Standard 8. Professional Education: *Social workers shall advocate for and participate in educational and training programs that help advance cultural competence within the profession.*

Social work needs to keep up with the changing needs of diverse client populations. There should be continuing education offers in culturally competent practice. Above all, it is important to provide culturally sensitive supervision and field instruction.

Standard 9. Language Diversity: *Social workers shall seek to provide and advocate for the provision of information, referrals, and services in the language appropriate to the client, which may include the use of interpreters.*

Agencies and providers should take reasonable steps to provide services and information in appropriate languages for clients who speak limited English. Language interpreters and translation are important, and persons engaging in these services should be trained in the ethics and linguistics of interpreting in an effective and confidential manner.

Standard 10. Cross-Cultural Leadership: *Social workers shall be able to communicate information about diverse client groups to other professionals.*

Leadership entails empowering diverse client populations, disseminating information about these groups, and advocating for fair and equitable treatment at the interpersonal and institutional levels.

NASW cultural competence standards are the benchmarks for the social work profession. But how does one turn these standards into culturally competent statements or cultural competencies and measure them to determine to what extent a social worker has accomplished them? The NASW *Standards for Cultural Competence in Social Work Practice* (2001) states, "As the social work profession develops cultural competencies, then the profession must have the ability to measure those competencies. The development of outcome measures needs to go hand in hand with the development of those standards" (p. 14).

Social work has begun to apply cultural competence to various populations at risk. Teasley (2005) presents cultural competence research regarding school social workers and African American children. In a sample of 247 school social workers in Atlanta, Philadelphia, Cleveland, and Baltimore, Teasley found that perceived levels of cultural competence were associated with postgraduate professional development and that African American school social workers scored higher on overall perceived levels of cultural competence in urban schools than their White counterparts. He suggested that many practitioners gain advanced knowledge of their service population after completing their formal education and that school systems may require and design professional development programs relevant to such populations as urban African American youth. Van Den Bergh and Crisp (2004) make the case for cultural competence with gay, lesbian, bisexual, and transgendered clients and conceptualize around attitudes, knowledge, and skills. At the same time, there is increasing concern about adequate assessment instruments to measure cultural competence. Teasley (2005) advocates the development of reliable and valid measures of assessing levels of cultural competence, and Green et al. (2005) share extensive research on the Multicultural Counseling Inventory surveying 344 social workers on their multicultural awareness, multicultural relationships, knowledge, and counseling skill. Cultural competence and social work practice and research are currently of great interest. In the diverse group chapters of this text we deal with values and ethical dilemmas and a case study to illustrate these issues. We hope that these will serve as "teaching moments" in your classroom. Now let me share with you some personal beliefs and aspirations that I have for culturally competent practice.

MY BELIEFS AND ASPIRATIONS ABOUT CULTURAL COMPETENCE

I hope that as you read this book you will formulate some strong convictions and beliefs about cultural competence as part of your knowledge and skill base as a practitioner. This approach is part of a vast repertoire of theory and skill that you can call upon when working with a client. No one approach is indispensable. One should draw upon many practice approaches. Here I share some of my beliefs and aspirations about cultural competence in the hope that they will prompt creative discussions among social work students, educators, and practitioners in both the classrooms and agencies.

Belief 1: Culturally competent practice is a major subject area for culturally diverse social work practice and a tool for working with cultural and ethnic clients.

Cultural competence is a concept that involves a *developmental goal* of preparing the social work student with the necessary knowledge theory and skill development to deal with a variety of clients who have cultural and ethnic concerns. In this book there are three functions of culturally competent social work practice: 1) cultural self awareness of the cultural and ethnic backgrounds of the worker and cultural other awareness of the background of culturally and ethnically diverse clients whom we seek to help; 2) knowledge acquisition related to essential theory and practical information necessary for understanding and assisting culturally and ethnically diverse clients; and 3) skill development related to engagement, assessment, intervention, and evaluation of culturally and ethnically diverse clients, particularly from an inductively learning process of listening to the life stories of clients.

This reaffirms the work of the AMCD, which adopted the awareness, knowledge, and skills categories (Arredondo et al., 1996). Smith et al. (2004) explain these concepts:

> *Awareness* refers to therapists' personal self-awareness: awareness of their worldview, values, assumptions, expectations, privileges, biases, theoretical orientation, and so on. *Knowledge* refers to therapists' understanding and knowledge of human diversity in all its form: racial, cultural religious, gender, sexual orientation, and so on. *Skills* refers to therapists' ability to use their personal awareness and knowledge of client culture and diversity in a therapeutic manner during the treatment process. (p. 11)

Although this perspective is from multicultural psychology, these variables have been recognized as *culturally competent practice functions* for the helping professions.

Belief 2: We recognize a historical progression of related multicultural themes such as ethnic sensitivity, cultural awareness, cultural diversity, and now cultural competence. These concepts are not mutually exclusive. Rather, cultural competence serves as a rubric that recognizes that there is a sufficient body of knowledge and skills related to culturally and ethnically diverse clients that must be learned and mastered to the extent of development and refinement.

Social workers (Rothman, 2008) often use such terms as *cultural sensitivity, cultural awareness,* and *cultural diversity* interchangeably when they discuss cultural competence. It is a misnomer to do so. Rather these terms should be explored in their historical development and form a progression of where the field has moved since the early 1980s until the late 1990s. In social work practice Devore and Schlesinger (1981) began to talk about ethnic sensitive social work practice, popularized the term *ethclass,* which focused on ethnicity and social class, and provided a practice structure for working with all ethnic groups. Green et al. (1982) introduced cultural awareness with an ethnographic approach to offering help. Green was a cultural anthropologist who taught in a graduate school of social work. His text wrote about the common and specific patterns of four major ethnic minority groups.

By the middle of the 1990s, multiculturalism and diversity were key concepts in the ethnic studies literature. Schlesinger was a major influence for social work education to adopt these two terms. I (Lum, 1996) conceptualized culturally diverse social work practice. About the same time, the CSWE revised its evaluative standards to include the emphasis on outcome measurements and began to use *competencies as operational variables* for social work education. Social work educators influenced by the cultural competence movement in multicultural psychology in the middle 1990s began to speak about cultural competence in their own discipline. At the 1997 annual program meeting of the CSWE Lu and I (Lum and Lu, 1997) presented a social work cultural competence framework, which was enthusiastically received by the social work educator audience. Culturally competent social work practice was on its way as a practice approach.

Belief 3: There has been widespread interest about evaluating the competence of students through measurement instruments. While cultural competence is a practice approach, cultural competencies are outcome statements that can be stated and measured to determine the extent to which social work students have attained teaching/ learning objectives as well as educational content areas pertaining to cultural diversity.

The 2008 *EPAS* of the CSWE has ten core competencies. Educational Policy 2.1—Core Competencies state, "Competency-based education is an outcome performance approach to curriculum design. Competencies are measurable practice behaviors that are comprised of knowledge, values, and skills. The goal of the outcome approach is to demonstrate the integration and application of the competencies in practice with individuals, families, groups, organizations, and communities." Of the ten competencies, *six competencies touch on content areas in this book.*

The following competencies contain specific outcome goal statements that are major behavioral and learning variables with a series of supportive sub-variables operationalizing how the major variables can be achieved. The *six competencies pertaining to our study* are

Educational Policy 2.1.2 Apply social work ethical principles to guide professional practice

Educational Policy 2.1.3 Apply critical thinking to inform and communicate professional judgments

Educational Policy 2.1.4 Engage diversity and difference in practice

Educational Policy 2.1.5 Advance human rights and social and economic justice

Educational Policy 2.1.9 Respond to contexts that shape practice

Educational Policy 2.1.10 Engage, assess, intervene, and evaluate with individuals, families, groups, organizations, and communities

Belief 4: The question of who comprises the culturally and ethnically diverse and the coverage of who is included or excluded in the range of groups relevant to culturally competent practice has been answered by a broad diversity of clients.

I started as a social work educator in the early 1970s teaching in a graduate MSW problem area and target population concentration called "Poverty and Minorities." In those days there was a paucity of material on poverty and poor people and ethnic minorities from a social work practice and policy perspective.

Over the years concerns about women, gays and lesbians, the elderly, the disabled, and other groups were voiced and we as researchers enlarged our perspectives as we moved from a focus on strictly ethnic minorities to the broadening of many groups comprising the culturally diverse. As late as 2005 there was still a vigorous debate about how broad and inclusive should we apply the term *culture* and what are the groups who embrace and possess culture. Does culture extend beyond ethnicity to encompass the culture of women, the poor, and gays and lesbians? (Ridley, 2005, pp. 183–184). Now this is a moot point. Culture is a broad and inclusive term that encompasses multiple populations. As long as there are advocates for groups, there will be a broad application of cultural competence for these peoples. In this edition, we have added European Americans, Muslim Americans, Persons with Disabilities, and the Elderly Persons and have broadened chapters on Women and Gay, Lesbian, Bisexual, and Transgender Persons.

Belief 5: The application of culturally competent practice to subject areas and target populations reminds us how fast this approach has grown in the last two decades.

It is common place to discuss cultural competence on the federal, state, and county health care and mental health levels; to go to national conferences and workshops on cultural competence; to see programs and courses on cultural competence in medicine, nursing, psychology, social work, physical education, and related health and human services fields; and to read journal articles and textbooks on cultural competence in family therapy, with populations such as Latinos, and the applied social sciences.

The application of cultural competence to various settings should be a priority for us. In social work education the core competencies emphasis naturally goes hand in hand with a culturally competent practice approach. On the one hand, we must revisit the constructive criticism of the cultural competence critics, who have raised legitimate questions and issues pertaining to the articulation, development, and operationalization of cultural competence. We must creatively work to refine concepts, principles, research design and instrumentation, and related theory and practice applications. Perhaps we need to bring together the advocates and critics of cultural competence and define common areas of interest and concern, and collaboratively work together. On the other hand, we need to evaluate where we are as a culturally competent movement and where we ought to head in the coming decade. Much of the direction may come from the findings of the 2010 U.S. Census, which provides leading social, cultural, and ethnic indicators of where the United States has come in the last ten years. Now we turn to measuring your beginning cultural competence as you use this text in a social work diversity course.

MEASURING YOUR BEGINNING CULTURAL COMPETENCE

You should now understand the importance of translating cultural competence standards into cultural competencies that can be measured in a questionnaire. We have operationalized a series of cultural competencies based on the content of this text into pretest and posttest instruments. The instruments included here are the Social Work Cultural Competencies Self-Assessment instrument and the Social Work Cultural Competencies with Culturally Diverse Groups and Social and Economic Justice instrument.

The Social Work Cultural Competencies Self-Assessment instrument is a 36-item Likert-type scale that measures your level of cultural competence. It is based on the framework in Chapter Four and covers three competence areas (cultural awareness, knowledge acquisition, and skill development) and two levels (generalist and advanced). It is designed to support the Core Competencies (Educational Policy 2.1) of CSWE's *EPAS*. You are invited to take the self-assessment instrument as a pretest now. At this point, you should be familiar with the idea of cultural competence, although you may have minimal comprehension of this field.

Your score on the self-assessment instrument is determined by counting the numbers you have circled and adding them together (see scoring information at end of instrument). You will score the instrument yourself and need not disclose the results to anyone else. Your scores at the beginning and at the end of the course will not affect your grade. There are four possible levels; you are expected to score in the Level 1 or 2 range on the pretest unless you have had a strong multicultural life experience or extensive course work in ethnic studies, or both. It is normal to score at the lower levels when you are just beginning the course. You will master knowledge and skills during the semester. At the last class session, you will be asked to take the test again as a posttest outcome measurement and to score yourself. There should be a significant difference between your pretest and posttest scores. You should move into the Level 3 or 4 categories.

I suggest that you write a two-page analysis comparing the results of the test before and after the course and sharing areas of growth and inquiry. The results provide excellent feedback for your instructor, who is concerned about teaching effectiveness in a culturally diverse practice course. These results will help your instructor determine which themes require more explanation in the next class.

A companion instrument is the Social Work Cultural Competencies with Culturally Diverse Groups and Social and Economic Justice instrument, which measures the knowledge and skills of students concerning ten diverse groups and the theme of human rights and social and economic justice. Whereas the first pretest measures generalist cultural competence, this pretest covers cultural competence with diverse groups and justice themes. You are invited to take this pretest now. As with the first pretest, scoring information is presented at the end of the instrument.

Chapter Eighteen contains some posttests that are related to both of the pretests presented here.

Social Work Cultural Competencies Self-Assessment Pretest

Written by Doman Lum, PhD (all rights reserved)

Introduction

This instrument measures your level of cultural competence at the beginning and end of the semester or quarter. The results of this self-assessment will be evaluated by your social work instructor. Strict confidentiality is observed regarding the results of the self-assessment.

Rate yourself on your level of competency on a scale of 1–4: 1 = Unlikely; 2 = Not very likely; 3 = Likely; and 4 = Definitely. Circle the appropriate number.

Social Security # (last four digits):   Course: Instructor: Campus:

Background Information

1. Age: ____

2. Sex: Male ____ Female ____

3. Ethnicity (please check all that apply):
   African American _____   Asian American _____   European American _____
   Jewish American _____   Latino American _____   Middle Eastern _____
   First Nations Peoples ____ Other (please specify) —————————————————————

4. Years of education (e.g., 12 = high school graduate) (circle correct number):
   12   13   14   15   16   17   18   19   20   21 or more

5. Highest degree earned/major:

6. Years of previous social service volunteer experience:
   None ____ 1–3 years ____ 4–6 years ____ 7–9 years ____ 10 years or more ____

7. Years of previous social work employment:
   None ____ 1–3 years ____ 4–6 years ____ 7–9 years ____ 10 years or more ____

8. Prior courses on cultural diversity:
   None ____ 1 course ____ 2 courses ____ 3 or more courses ____

Cultural Awareness

1. I am aware of my life experiences as a person related to a culture (e.g., family heritage, household and community events, beliefs, and practices).

   1–Unlikely   2–Not very likely   3–Likely   4–Definitely

2. I have contact with other cultural and ethnic individuals, families, and groups.

   1–Unlikely   2–Not very likely   3–Likely   4–Definitely

3. I am aware of positive and negative experiences with cultural and ethnic persons and events.

   1–Unlikely   2–Not very likely   3–Likely   4–Definitely

4. I know how to evaluate my cognitive, affective, and behavioral experiences and reactions to racism, prejudice, and discrimination.

   1–Unlikely   2–Not very likely   3–Likely   4–Definitely

5. I have assessed my involvement with cultural and ethnic people of color in childhood, adolescence, young adulthood, and adulthood.

   1–Unlikely   2–Not very likely   3–Likely   4–Definitely

6. I understand such terms as positionality, intersectionality, and the dialogic self.

   1–Unlikely   *2–Not very likely*   *3–Likely*   *4–Definitely*

7. I have had or plan to have professional employment experiences with culturally diverse clients and programs.

   1–Unlikely   *2–Not very likely*   *3–Likely*   *4–Definitely*

8. I have assessed or plan to assess my academic and professional work experiences with cultural diversity and culturally diverse client.

   1–Unlikely   *2–Not very likely*   *3–Likely*   *4–Definitely*

Knowledge Acquisition

9. I understand the following terms: critical thinking, identity development, social constructionism, and marginalization.

   1–Unlikely   *2–Not very likely*   *3–Likely*   *4–Definitely*

10. I have developed a critical thinking perspective on cultural diversity.

    1–Unlikely   *2–Not very likely*   *3–Likely*   *4–Definitely*

11. I know information about knowledge theories related to cultural competence.

    1–Unlikely   *2–Not very likely*   *3–Likely*   *4–Definitely*

12. I understand the history of oppression and multicultural social group history.

    1–Unlikely   *2–Not very likely*   *3–Likely*   *4–Definitely*

13. I know about culturally diverse values.

    1–Unlikely   *2–Not very likely*   *3–Likely*   *4–Definitely*

Skill Development

14. I understand how to overcome the resistance and lower the communication barriers of a multicultural client.

    1–Unlikely   *2–Not very likely*   *3–Likely*   *4–Definitely*

15. I know how to obtain personal and family background information from a multicultural client and determine the client's ethnic/community sense of identity.

    1–Unlikely   *2–Not very likely*   *3–Likely*   *4–Definitely*

16. I understand the concepts of ethnic community and practice relationship protocols with a multicultural client.

    1–Unlikely   *2–Not very likely*   *3–Likely*   *4–Definitely*

17. I use professional self-disclosure with a multicultural client.

    1–Unlikely   *2–Not very likely*   *3–Likely*   *4–Definitely*

18. I have a positive and open communication style and use open-ended listening responses.

    1–Unlikely   *2–Not very likely*   *3–Likely*   *4–Definitely*

19. I know how to obtain problem information, facilitate problem area disclosure, and promote problem understanding.

    1–Unlikely   *2–Not very likely*   *3–Likely*   *4–Definitely*

20. I view a problem as an unsatisfied want or an unfulfilled need.

    1–Unlikely   *2–Not very likely*   *3–Likely*   *4–Definitely*

21. I know how to explain problems on micro, meso, and macro levels.

    1–Unlikely   *2–Not very likely*   *3–Likely*   *4–Definitely*

22. I know how to explain problem themes (racism, prejudice, discrimination) and expressions (oppression, powerlessness, stereotyping, acculturation, and exploitation).

    1–Unlikely   *2–Not very likely*   *3–Likely*   *4–Definitely*

23. I know how to find out about problem details.

    1–Unlikely   *2–Not very likely*   *3–Likely*   *4–Definitely*

24. I know how to assess socioenvironmental impacts, psychoindividual reactions, and cultural strengths.

    1–Unlikely   *2–Not very likely*   *3–Likely*   *4–Definitely*

25. I know how to assess the biological, psychological, social, cultural, and spiritual dimensions of the multicultural client.

    1–Unlikely   *2–Not very likely*   *3–Likely*   *4–Definitely*

26. I know how to establish joint goals and agreements with the client that are culturally acceptable.

    1–Unlikely   *2–Not very likely*   *3–Likely*   *4–Definitely*

27. I know how to formulate micro, meso, and macro intervention strategies that address the cultural needs of the client and special needs populations such as immigrants and refugees.

    1–Unlikely   *2–Not very likely*   *3–Likely*   *4–Definitely*

28. I know how to begin the evaluation phase which links the client to an ethnic community resource, reviews significant progress and growth development, evaluates goal outcomes, and establishes a follow-up strategy.

    1–Unlikely   *2–Not very likely*   *3–Likely*   *4–Definitely*

29. I know how to design a service delivery and agency linkage and culturally effective social service programs in ethnic communities.

    1–Unlikely   *2–Not very likely*   *3–Likely*   *4–Definitely*

30. I have been involved in services that have been accessible to the ethnic community.

    1–Unlikely   *2–Not very likely*   *3–Likely*   *4–Definitely*

31. I have participated in delivering pragmatic and positive services that meet the tangible needs of the ethnic community.

    1–Unlikely   *2–Not very likely*   *3–Likely*   *4–Definitely*

32. I have observed the effectiveness of bilingual/bicultural workers who reflect the ethnic composition of the clientele.

    1–Unlikely   *2–Not very likely*   *3–Likely*   *4–Definitely*

33. I have participated in community outreach education and prevention that establish visible services, provide culturally sensitive programs, and employ credible staff.

    1–Unlikely   *2–Not very likely*   *3–Likely*   *4–Definitely*

34. I have been involved in a service linkage network to related social agencies that ensures rapid referral and program collaboration.

    1–Unlikely   *2–Not very likely*   *3–Likely*   *4–Definitely*

35. I have participated as a staff member in fostering a conducive agency setting with an atmosphere that is friendly and helpful to multicultural clients.

    1–Unlikely   *2–Not very likely*   *3–Likely*   *4–Definitely*

36. I am involved or plan to be involved with cultural skills development research in areas related to cultural empathy, clinical alliance, goal-obtaining styles, achieving styles, practice skills, and outcome research.

    1–Unlikely   *2–Not very likely*   *3–Likely*   *4–Definitely*

What are your questions and views on cultural competence and cultural competencies?

What are your reactions to this self-assessment instrument?

Please count your scores on the 36 self-assessment items and rate your level of cultural competence. Circle the appropriate level and write your raw score in one of the following levels:

Level 1: Unlikely (scores 36–69)
Level 2: Not very likely (scores 70–94)
Level 3: Likely (scores 95–128)
Level 4: Definitely (scores 129–144)

Thank you for your cooperation on this self-assessment instrument. You have made a significant contribution to our research on culturally competent practice.

Social Work Cultural Competencies with Culturally Diverse Groups and Social and Economic Justice Pretest

Written by Doman Lum, PhD (all rights reserved)

Introduction

This instrument measures your level of cultural competence with culturally diverse groups and social and economic justice at the beginning and end of the semester. The results of this test will be evaluated by your social work instructor. Strict confidentiality is observed regarding the results of this instrument.

Rate yourself on your level of competence on a scale of 1–4: 1 = Unlikely; 2 = Not very likely; 3 = Likely; and 4 = Definitely. Circle the appropriate number.

Social Security # (last four digits):   Course: Instructor: Campus:

First Nations Peoples

1. I know about the diversity of Native nations, which differ in terms of language, religion, social structure, political structure, and many aspects of culture.

    1–Unlikely   2–Not very likely   3–Likely   4–Definitely

2. I understand the concept of Seven Generations, which provides a historical and current perspective on oppression experiences.

    1–Unlikely   2–Not very likely   3–Likely   4–Definitely

3. It is important to choose interventions and design programs that accurately target the needs of First Nations Peoples, which may be different for each community.

    1–Unlikely   2–Not very likely   3–Likely   4–Definitely

4. Knowledge about First Nations Peoples requires an understanding of sovereignty issues and policies that apply to indigenous people.

    1–Unlikely   2–Not very likely   3–Likely   4–Definitely

5. Patience, listening, and silence are important skills to practice when working with First Nations Peoples clients.

    1–Unlikely   2–Not very likely   3–Likely   4–Definitely

6. I know about First Nations Peoples community immersion projects to increase inductive learning.

    1–Unlikely   2–Not very likely   3–Likely   4–Definitely

7. The Supreme Court has consistently ruled against the rights of First Nations Peoples.

    1–Unlikely   2–Not very likely   3–Likely   4–Definitely

European Americans

8. Whiteness determines a privileged social location in the United States.

    1–Unlikely   *2–Not very likely*   *3–Likely*   *4–Definitely*

9. American society is oriented around Eurocentric processes.

    1–Unlikely   *2–Not very likely*   *3–Likely*   *4–Definitely*

10. A lack of white racial identity awareness is a feature of white supremacy.

    1–Unlikely   *2–Not very likely*   *3–Likely*   *4–Definitely*

11. White supremacy culture must be named and dismantled.

    1–Unlikely   *2–Not very likely*   *3–Likely*   *4–Definitely*

12. Jane Addams, an early social worker who won the Nobel Prize for Peace in the early 20th century, was a racist who believed in white supremacy.

    1–Unlikely   *2–Not very likely*   *3–Likely*   *4–Definitely*

13. Peggy McIntosh coined the term, white privilege, and pointed out the ways that white people benefit from structural and institutional racism in the United States.

    1–Unlikely   *2–Not very likely*   *3–Likely*   *4–Definitely*

14. The cultural context model raises white privilege to consciousness and helps to name injustices that whites participate in and benefit from.

    1–Unlikely   *2–Not very likely*   *3–Likely*   *4–Definitely*

African Americans

15. Diversity among African Americans involves such factors as physical characteristics, residential patterns, marital status, education, income, age, social class, and employment.

    1–Unlikely   *2–Not very likely*   *3–Likely*   *4–Definitely*

16. I understand the unique historical background of African Americans regarding involuntary migration, slavery, segregation, and continued oppression.

    1–Unlikely   *2–Not very likely*   *3–Likely*   *4–Definitely*

17. I am able to explain the four stages of the helping process that African American clients may go through with a practitioner.

    1–Unlikely   *2–Not very likely*   *3–Likely*   *4–Definitely*

18. I can identify several knowledge areas about the African American population and about the African American client.

    1–Unlikely   *2–Not very likely*   *3–Likely*   *4–Definitely*

19. I understand Afrocentric practice approaches, which are based on the Nguzo Saba value system.

    1–Unlikely   2–Not very likely   3–Likely   4–Definitely

20. I can explain the inductive learning strengths perspective approach for African American clients.

    1–Unlikely   2–Not very likely   3–Likely   4–Definitely

21. I comprehend the internalization of oppression that leads to disempowerment as a starting point for understanding how to achieve social and economic justice.

    1–Unlikely   2–Not very likely   3–Likely   4–Definitely

Latino Americans

22. I know the distinctions in Latino diversity pertaining to language differences, immigration history and patterns, and traditional and intergenerational acculturation.

    1–Unlikely   2–Not very likely   3–Likely   4–Definitely

23. I understand the historical and current oppression experiences of Mexican, Puerto Rican, Cuban, and Central American Latinos.

    1–Unlikely   2–Not very likely   3–Likely   4–Definitely

24. The religion of a Latino client is important because Catholic and Protestant denominations often establish social service outreach resources for the Latino community.

    1–Unlikely   2–Not very likely   3–Likely   4–Definitely

25. Knowledge of children and youth from war-torn countries such as El Salvador and Nicaragua indicates that exposure to violence may result in suicidal behaviors, serious antisocial acts, insomnia, and other physical, psychological, and social problems.

    1–Unlikely   2–Not very likely   3–Likely   4–Definitely

26. In social work practice with Latinos, it is important to use a "dicho" to create a cultural ambiance.

    1–Unlikely   2–Not very likely   3–Likely   4–Definitely

27. It is important to cover legal documentation with Latino clients in order to seek, in an inductive nonthreatening manner, services that will not endanger them.

    1–Unlikely   2–Not very likely   3–Likely   4–Definitely

28. I understand the dynamics of Latino immigrant exploitation in employment and housing as issues of social and economic justice.

    1–Unlikely   2–Not very likely   3–Likely   4–Definitely

Asian Americans

29. I know about the diversity between Asians and Pacific Islanders, among different ethnic groups of Asian Americans, and between Asian immigrants and refugees.

    1–Unlikely   2–Not very likely   3–Likely   4–Definitely

30. I am aware of the discriminatory experiences of Asian immigrants, the racist attitudes and behaviors toward American-born Asians, and the colonialist practices toward Pacific Islanders, particularly Native Hawaiians.

    1–Unlikely   2–Not very likely   3–Likely   4–Definitely

31. I understand the broad and varied social service needs of specific Asian American and Pacific Islander groups.

    1–Unlikely   2–Not very likely   3–Likely   4–Definitely

32. I know that Asian American and Pacific Islander knowledge acquisition consists of knowing the ethnic culture and using the cultural values to explain ways of thinking and behaving.

    1–Unlikely   2–Not very likely   3–Likely   4–Definitely

33. I understand that in developing treatment planning with Asian and Pacific Islanders, traditional ways of healing should be matched with Western interventions, and Western interventions should be evaluated to determine whether they foster the cultural values of the ethnic community.

    1–Unlikely   2–Not very likely   3–Likely   4–Definitely

34. I am aware of the need to discuss Asian Americans and Pacific Islanders by lifespan development, gender, and sexual orientation issues and needs in order to create an intersection of inductive learning themes.

    1–Unlikely   2–Not very likely   3–Likely   4–Definitely

35. I understand the social and economic issues of land rights and welfare reform for Asian and Pacific Islander immigrants.

    1–Unlikely   2–Not very likely   3–Likely   4–Definitely

Muslim Americans

36. I know about the increasing Muslim population in the United States due to natural births, immigration and conversion and that the Muslim presence dates back to the arrival of slaves, many of whom were Muslims, from West Africa.

    1–Unlikely   2–Not very likely   3–Likely   4–Definitely

37. I know about the diversity among Muslim Americans, many of whom differ in terms of language, ethnicity, culture, and religious beliefs and schools of thought.

    1–Unlikely   2–Not very likely   3–Likely   4–Definitely

38. I understand the impact of the September 11, 2001 terrorist attacks on the mental health and psychosocial well-being of Muslim Americans, especially when examined through the lens of historical and current perspectives on oppression experiences.

    1–Unlikely   2–Not very likely   3–Likely   4–Definitely

39. I appreciate that developing cultural competence with Muslim Americans is challenging at best due to the fact that the increase in Muslim Americans' help-seeking from outside one's family and relatives and close friends is a relatively recent phenomenon.

    1–Unlikely   2–Not very likely   3–Likely   4–Definitely

40. I understand that unlike the dominant secular worldview in which most practitioners are being trained, Islam promotes a harmonious co-existence between the private and the public, the sacred and the secular, and the present life and the afterlife.

    1–Unlikely   2–Not very likely   3–Likely   4–Definitely

41. I know about the role of faith in the lives of Muslim Americans especially as it relates to divine help-seeking, the concept of Divine forgiveness for sins; and the concept of life challenges and problems, as tests from Allah.

    1–Unlikely   2–Not very likely   3–Likely   4–Definitely

42. I understand that as I prepare to establish contact in person with a Muslim American client, it is important that I put the client at ease by demonstrating knowledge and awareness of and respect for the client's value-informed worldview.

    1–Unlikely   2–Not very likely   3–Likely   4–Definitely

Women

43. In Haiti women have a major responsibility for feeding and ensuring the health of their families.

    1–Unlikely   2–Not very likely   3–Likely   4–Definitely

44. In Haitian informal economy women have skills in cooperation and leadership.

    1–Unlikely   2–Not very likely   3–Likely   4–Definitely

45. Aid to poor women will increase poor women's decision-making power.

    1–Unlikely   2–Not very likely   3–Likely   4–Definitely

46. Women in the National Congress of Rural Workers in Honduras played a major role in agrarian land reform.

    1–Unlikely   2–Not very likely   3–Likely   4–Definitely

47. The Campesino or Farmers' Movement in Latin American illustrates people, particularly women, working together and growing food under chaotic circumstances.

    1–Unlikely   *2–Not very likely*   *3–Likely*   *4–Definitely*

48. Women in the Campesino Movement used Paulo Freire's problem-solving education with political consciousness-raising.

    1–Unlikely   *2–Not very likely*   *3–Likely*   *4–Definitely*

49. The Campesino Movement is a model for socio-cultural social work.

    1–Unlikely   *2–Not very likely*   *3–Likely*   *4–Definitely*

Gay, Lesbian, Bisexual, and Transgender Persons

50. I understand the different meanings of the terms: gay, lesbian, bisexuality, and transgender.

    1–Unlikely   *2–Not very likely*   *3–Likely*   *4–Definitely*

51. I am aware of the distinctions between life and culture of gay/lesbian, transgender, and bisexual persons.

    1–Unlikely   *2–Not very likely*   *3–Likely*   *4–Definitely*

52. I am aware of the religious intolerance, societal discrimination, and denial of rights confronting sexual minorities in the United States.

    1–Unlikely   *2–Not very likely*   *3–Likely*   *4–Definitely*

53. I am aware of the ethical dilemmas facing sexual minorities and their families in the coming-out process

    1–Unlikely   *2–Not very likely*   *3–Likely*   *4–Definitely*

54. I am familiar with the organization Parents, Families, and Friends of Lesbians and Gays (PFLAG).

    1–Unlikely   *2–Not very likely*   *3–Likely*   *4–Definitely*

55. When working with lesbian, gay, transgender, and bisexual people in helping relationships, I endeavor to keep an open mind, not assume that all persons are heterosexual, and let the client determine the pace of revealing sexual and gender orientation.

    1–Unlikely   *2–Not very likely*   *3–Likely*   *4–Definitely*

56. I am in the process of educating myself about sexual minorities and am working through lingering and damaging stereotypes about this population group.

    1–Unlikely   *2–Not very likely*   *3–Likely*   *4–Definitely*

Persons with Disabilities

57. I understand that disability is an element of diversity rather than pathology.

    1–Unlikely   *2–Not very likely*   *3–Likely*   *4–Definitely*

58. I am aware that social policies, environmental barriers, and discrimination are the primary employment obstacles faced by disabled persons.

    1–Unlikely   *2–Not very likely*   *3–Likely*   *4–Definitely*

59. I can explain the moral model of disability, the medical model of disability, and the social/minority model of disability.

    1–Unlikely   *2–Not very likely*   *3–Likely*   *4–Definitely*

60. I agree that the older a person is at the offset of an acquired disability, the less likely the individual is to adopt a disability identity.

    1–Unlikely   *2–Not very likely*   *3–Likely*   *4–Definitely*

61. I agree that disabled people are much more likely than nondisabled people to receive charity services and control services.

    1–Unlikely   *2–Not very likely*   *3–Likely*   *4–Definitely*

62. I agree that nondisabled people are more likely to receive investment services and benefit services.

    1–Unlikely   *2–Not very likely*   *3–Likely*   *4–Definitely*

63. I agree that solutions to the problems disabled persons and groups face are primarily located in changing social environments and societal policies, not in changing individuals.

    1–Unlikely   *2–Not very likely*   *3–Likely*   *4–Definitely*

The Older Adult

64. In 2008 the number of older adults was 506 million and by 2040 it will be 1.3 billion globally.

    1–Unlikely   *2–Not very likely*   *3–Likely*   *4–Definitely*

65. The leading country in the 2008 rank order of the world's largest older populations was China (106.1 million).

    1–Unlikely   *2–Not very likely*   *3–Likely*   *4–Definitely*

66. The growth of persons ages 80 and above is the fastest growing segment of the population of many countries.

    1–Unlikely   *2–Not very likely*   *3–Likely*   *4–Definitely*

67. Increasing numbers of older adults have higher incomes with decreasing numbers in poverty and in low income groups may be attributed to more older persons, especially older women, in the work force.

   1–Unlikely   *2–Not very likely*   *3–Likely*   *4–Definitely*

68. Almost 75 percent of Latino elderly living alone and about 50 percent of Latinos residing with their spouse are unable to meet basic needs.

   1–Unlikely   *2–Not very likely*   *3–Likely*   *4–Definitely*

69. Ageism is a process of systematic stereotyping and discrimination against people because they are old.

   1–Unlikely   *2–Not very likely*   *3–Likely*   *4–Definitely*

70. The two leading causes of death among adults aged 65 and older in 2007 were heart disease and cancer.

   1–Unlikely   *2–Not very likely*   *3–Likely*   *4–Definitely*

Social and Economic Justice

71. I understand the relationship between cultural diversity and social justice in terms of historical and ongoing oppression and privilege that different social identity groups experience in our society.

   1–Unlikely   *2–Not very likely*   *3–Likely*   *4–Definitely*

72. I understand the meaning of economic class as a prime indicator of oppression and the creation of a class system based on difference as a function of oppression.

   1–Unlikely   *2–Not very likely*   *3–Likely*   *4–Definitely*

73. I can explain the concept and perspectives of distributive justice and their implications for social and economic justice.

   1–Unlikely   *2–Not very likely*   *3–Likely*   *4–Definitely*

74. I can connect the concepts of moral exclusion and fairness.

   1–Unlikely   *2–Not very likely*   *3–Likely*   *4–Definitely*

75. I understand the human rights and oppression concepts of the United Nations Universal Declaration of Human Rights.

   1–Unlikely   *2–Not very likely*   *3–Likely*   *4–Definitely*

76. I am aware of the United Nations materials on human rights for social work.

   1–Unlikely   *2–Not very likely*   *3–Likely*   *4–Definitely*

77. I understand the meaning of and the connection between empowerment and social and economic justice.

    1–Unlikely   2–Not very likely   3–Likely   4–Definitely

78. I understand how the grieving cycle is related to how a person feels about oppression and injustice.

    1–Unlikely   2–Not very likely   3–Likely   4–Definitely

Please count your scores on the 78 items and rate your level of cultural competency. Circle the appropriate level and write your raw score in one of the following levels:

Level 1: Unlikely (scores 78–155)
Level 2: Not very likely (scores 156–233)
Level 3: Likely (scores 234–254)
Level 4: Definitely (scores 255–272)

Thank you for your cooperation on this self-assessment instrument. You have made a significant contribution to our research on social work cultural competence.

SUMMARY

This chapter has presented the case for cultural competence for social work students, educators, and practitioners who work with culturally and ethnically diverse clients. We have underscored the growing development of this emerging area. We have traced the *history* of the cultural competence movement; focused on *present and current* context, definitions, and criticisms; and have proposed an *immediate future*—which is *now*—where we have an opportunity to connect the building blocks of cultural competence, lay levels and dimensions, affirm ethical standards and competencies, and share beliefs and aspirations about this topic.

Central to this book are the Social Work Cultural Competencies Self-Assessment and the Social Work Cultural Competencies with Culturally Diverse Groups and Human Rights and Social and Economic Justice Test instruments. These self-assessment tools, which are unique features of this text, aid the social work student in the measurement of competencies at the beginning and the end of the semester. In the next chapter, the social contexts of societal forces and a responsive strategy will be covered with the understanding that social workers must grapple with these issues in order to maintain cultural competence with self and others.

CHAPTER 2

SOCIAL CONTEXT

Doman Lum

Social context is an important topic for social work because it acknowledges that the individual as part of a group or community is *constantly interacting with the social environment*. Context or setting influences how persons act, react, and interact in many ways. Social context has a psychosocial dimension attached to it. That is, socio-environmental impacts affect psychoindividual reactions of the person. Behind every action in the environment is the action, reaction, and interaction of the individual, group, neighborhood, and community. A person is a product of his or her community and a community is the byproduct of persons and groups who live in it. Social work education affirms that we must respond to contextual organizations, communities, and society and that context shapes all levels of practice This means that we must shape the way we practice with clients according to *the dynamics of the contextual setting* and use knowledge and skill to respond proactively. We must read and respond to the changes in locales, populations, technological developments, and emerging societal trends to provide, change, and improve social services (Council on Social Work Education, 2008, Educational Policy 2.1.9).

In this chapter we are concerned about the social context that affects much of the country and its history in terms of reactions to diverse peoples. We want to cover a number of contextual realities, such as power and privilege, socioeconomic status, majority status, and acculturation, which are termed *structural status*. We also want to discuss such *ideological beliefs* as racism, ethnocentrism, sexism, homophobia, and ageism. We plan to relate these ideological beliefs to the *affective expression* of prejudice that results in *behavioral reactions* of discrimination, oppression, and violence. We admit that there are no final answers to these isms but there is a constant need to be aware of them, cope with them, and work toward resolution. Finally we want to cover social justice, empowerment, diversity, the client's lenses, and transcendence as *strategies for coping with the contextual realities* that confront us on a daily basis and as part of the social context of the United States of America.

THE MEANING OF SOCIAL CONTEXT

The term *context* implies the "joining and weaving together" of textures that are surrounding or immediately next to parts that create how a situation, background, or environment is structured or put together. In social work we discuss the social context in terms of the person and the environment or the psychosocial perspective. That is, we are concerned about understanding the important characteristics of the person and the environment as well as the interaction between the person and the environment. This is the *core meaning of social context.*

In order to fully understand a person, one must take into account the total context of how the texture of the person has been woven together to form a unique being. What pieces or ingredients have been put together to form a mosaic or detailed pattern? What is the total context that transcends the person and the environment and must be understood for helping to proceed? Why has there been racism, sexism, homophobia, and other isms? Are these expressions of human depravity? Are they universal in all peoples throughout the world? Are these *social contextual realities*? By this we are referring to societal aspects of social context.

However, there are aspects of social context applicable to the helping relationship. Social context is increasingly a crucial theme in the worker–client relationship. A number of social science clinicians view the context as the overarching theme— as a major part of the sum total of the scope of understanding the client and the situation. Context has a broad inclusive meaning. Rose (1990) speaks of context in terms of *contextualization.* For Rose, this involves a focus on the client's own understanding of himself or herself that allows a dialogue between the worker and client to occur based on the client's reality. In the dialogue, the client is enabled to express, elaborate, and reflect upon his or her feelings and understanding about life. This reaching into the client and for the client's context is an important conception in comprehending a contextual practice perspective. Ragg (2001, pp. 13–18) identifies a number of contextual environmental influences that encompass the family and the broader social environment: family rules; family problem solving; emotional expression; family roles; and relating to others, neighborhood, culture, and institutions.

In particular, the life stories of the person are the basis for comprehending *contextual behavior.* The assumption is that life stories are recollections of the important behavioral events that have occurred in the human context of living. Murphy and Dillon (1998) articulate a pragmatic understanding of the context of behavior. By context, they mean "when, with whom, and under what circumstances the target behaviors occur" (p. 183). Furthermore, Murphy and Dillon (1998, p. 68) explain that context is important for understanding the client's stories. The *immediate context* refers to the client's personal circumstances where there are happenings pertaining to current living arrangements, family and social relationships, economic status, personal history, health, and the particulars of daily life. However, the immediate context is often embedded in a larger system context where economic, social, political, and religious forces and institutions affect global relationships and developments. Often, connective and mutual influences relate to immediate and larger contexts. These *spheres of context* are broad ranging and get at the dimensions of context that are a part of our perspectives. In this sense we can never understand the context of an individual without comprehending the context of the larger system that forms the playing field of human interaction and drama.

We may also move social context into the areas of assessment and intervention. *Contextual assessment* focuses on the construction of both personal and environmental interaction; issues of concern and available resources; personal social networks for active consultation, collective exchanges, and empowerment; and the partnership of worker and client in the process of knowledge development. *Contextual intervention* should critically analyze the impact of environmental conditions, particularly power relationships; offer effective action to oppressive social and environmental conditions; and make connections between individual experiences and collective issues, such as linking different communities of interest and larger coalitions and efforts.

Kemp, Whittaker, and Tracy (2002) bring together the themes of *environment and empowerment*. They point out that social life is spatial and contextual; that empowerment practice is contextualized in the sense that there is an emphasis on the importance of external circumstances and conditions in client concerns; and that changes in personal and interpersonal resources and aspirations must be supported and reinforced in external contexts. For them, contextual social work practice involves *person–environment practice*. There are links between people's issues and the challenges and resources in daily life contexts. Among the dimensions of environment are the physical environment (natural and built), the social/interactional environment, the institutional/organizational environment, the cultural and sociopolitical environment, the experienced environment, and environmental strengths and resources. These person and environment transactions are apparent in the areas of contextual assessment and contextual intervention.

When we apply the preceding discussion of social context to cultural competence, there are at least three issues confronting us: definition, outcome studies, and culture. Sue (2003, p. 969) explains the issues of definition and outcome research studies: "Cultural competency is difficult to define because it is contextually based rather than technique specific, and outcome studies should also examine the context." That is, how we conceptually define cultural competence is dependent on understanding this definition in terms of the social context realities of social stratification (structural status), ideological beliefs, affective attitude, and behavioral reactions. How do we take into account these contextual realities in our definition of cultural competence? At the same time, outcome research measurements of cultural competence are influenced by social context. For example, how do we measure the social context aspects of racism as we seek to determine the degree of cultural competence of the worker and the client as they cope with experiences of racism in the helping situation? Furthermore culture as a reality and cultural context as an environmental factor play an important part in defining and understanding cultural competence. Sue (2003, p. 968) comments, "Cultural competency involves the client, therapist, and context, as well as the therapeutic technique, because context and culture are so important." Here again we are struck with the importance of understanding social context and cultural dynamics in the helping process.

With these issues in mind it is important to lay out the essential ingredients of the social context. Our concern in the following sections is a basic understanding of social context in terms of the conflicts that we experience in society, which we call *contextual realities* and *the reality of diversity or difference* in society, which is increasing in the United States. Our premise is that although we will constantly fight the contextual realities of racism, sexism, homophobia, and the rest of the isms, we must also counter with a number of strategies for coping: social justice, empowerment, diversity and difference, the lenses of the client, and transcendence.

CONTEXTUAL REALITIES

In order to understand the relationships between societal forces that impact individual and group behavior, we use the term *contextual realities* to describe the interactions of the person and the environment, particularly the societal forces of the social context that are a part of the history of social stratification, negative ideology and beliefs, affective attitudes, and behavioral reactions. Can social change occur in the United States that brings life, liberty, and the pursuit of happiness to every American? Are there overwhelming societal structural forces that impede us and divide us into the wealthy and the poor, the haves and the have nots, the oppressors and the oppressed? Are racism, ethnocentrism, sexism, homophobia, and ageism alive and flourishing in the minds and behaviors of people who prey on others and in the policies and practices of institutions that interact with us? Or do these isms naturally flare up when Dr. Henry Louis Gates Jr. enters his home or Taylor Swift receives an award? Are these societal givens or can there be *a different set of responses* that we can communicate to each other? Do the practicing of social justice make a difference to reducing these contextual realities? Does the reality of growing diversity and the presence of difference serve as counter forces for the common good? What is the role of the client to cope with these contextual realities according to a culturally competent practice approach? Figure 2.1 organizes these

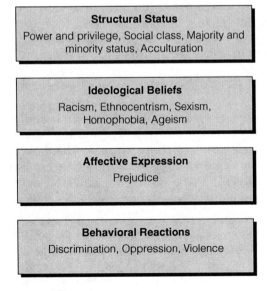

FIGURE 2.1 | CONTEXTUAL REALITIES

contextual realities into four major categories (structural status, ideological beliefs, affective expression, and behavioral reactions), and thirteen subcategories that are the basis for social conflict. Then in a later section we talk about teachable moments and coping strategies.

THE CONTEXTUAL REALITIES FRAMEWORK

STRUCTURAL STATUS

We are part of a social structure that separates people into various categories and classifications. We assign a particular social status based on a social and economic class order. We use the term *structural status* to emphasize that there are a series of related givens in the fabric of American society. *Social stratification* holds that society is stratified or separated into groups according to social class, birth, education, income, and other socioeconomic factors. Popular terms alluding to social stratification include the haves and the have nots, White privilege, the majority and the minority, the wealthy and the poor, and other social class distinctions. Beeghley (2008, p. 1) alludes to a structural status view of social stratification: "The structure of social stratification can be defined as the distribution of resources in society, such as income, wealth, occupation, education, and power. In every society, these resources are allocated unequally. Unequal possession of resources affects people's life chances: their ability to share in the available goods and services." Structure has the idea of building, organization, and arrangement, while status means position, rank, and standing.

Iceland (2009) illustrates the reality of social stratification in his focus on immigration and race in the United States. His concern is *residential segregation* as an expression of housing patterns, which reflect structural status: where I live compared to where you live. Iceland (2009, p. 8) observes, "People are residentially segregated across a number of socioeconomic and demographic characteristics, including age, income, and [the focus here] race, ethnicity, and nativity. It is commonly thought that differences in residential patterns across racial and ethnic groups reflect social distance." In short, we are describing fixed societal organizational arrangements, which are givens. In this section we cover power and privilege, social class, majority and majority status, and acculturation.

POWER AND PRIVILEGE   Whiteness, White supremacy, White privilege, and racism involve a discussion on power and privilege. Sue (2006) argues that *whiteness* is a default standard from which racial/ethnic minorities are evaluated, judged, and often found lacking, inferior, deviant, or abnormal. In other words, whiteness is considered to be normative and ideal and automatically confers dominance on fair-skinned people in our society. Sue (2006, p. 15) states,

> Whiteness is an invisible veil that cloaks its racist deleterious effects through individuals, organizations, and society. The result is that White people are allowed to enjoy the benefits that accrue to them by virtue of their skin color. Thus, whiteness, white supremacy, and white privilege are three interlocking forces that disguise racism so it may allow [W]hite people to oppress and harm persons of color, maintaining their individual and collective advantage and innocence. (p. 15)

He further describes the dynamics behind White privilege, which is a form of invisible power. Sue (2006, pp. 15–16) explains,

> Racism hides in the background of Whiteness and is protected through a conspiracy of silence that aids in making it invisible. As long as it is an unacknowledged secret, it allows White people to accept the unearned advantages of their skin color while allowing them to deny responsibility for how it disadvantages other groups....Whiteness becomes transparent when White people are taught to think of their lives as morally neutral, average, or ideal. The result is that both White supremacy and racism become culturally conditioned into the lives of White people....

In short, there are interlocks between power, privilege, and whiteness.

What are the solutions to these issues? Nylund (2006) advocates a critical multiculturalism that recognizes the power and the privilege of whiteness and being white and opens up space for whites to formulate an oppositional white identity, which is antiracism, and advocates for racial and social justice. Sue (2006) suggests,

> Make whiteness visible. Explore yourself as a racial/cultural being. Take responsibility for defining whiteness in a nondefensive and nonracist manner. Take antiracist actions aimed at the individual, institutional, and cultural levels. Look at yourself honestly. Confront the truth about yourself and the world. Liberate yourself from the invisible cultural conditioning of a racialized society.

In other words become aware and conscious that these dynamics, assumptions, mind-set, and practices do exist and begin to *deconstruct whiteness* at the individual, institutional, and cultural levels. Do not allow it to be *the main point of reference* which guides your life, organizational participation, and cultural interactions with others. Instead have *an alternative mind-set* which reconstructs and reorients yourself around the realities of people who are different and diverse from you. Be conscious and aware of *differences in others*. Learn from them and *celebrate your life* in light of these new experiences.

SOCIAL CLASS AND CLASSISM   *Social class* addresses social stratification or the social hierarchical arrangement of people based on economic, power, and status differences. People of color tend to be class bound due to racial discrimination and socioeconomic constraints. Aguirre and Baker (2008, p. 4) state,

> From our perspective, social inequality is both the means and the ends of a racially stratified society. *Race and gender stratification* establish a graded hierarchy of superior and inferior ranks in society. Society allocates access to valued resources and opportunities according to one's placement in the social hierarchy. For example, those at the top of the social hierarchy (*whites* and *males*) have access to a larger share of social opportunity and resources than those near the bottom of the social hierarchy (*non-whites* and *females*). The resources valued in a society are usually those that allocate privilege: material wealth, social status or social prestige, and political power.

The dynamics of a stratified system are rooted in a disproportionate distribution of valued resources and result in two culturally distinct groups of people: a culturally dominant group and a culturally subordinate group. The dominant group maintains its social position by controlling the production of valued resources, which they are able to do because they have better access to a larger share of opportunities and resources. For example, by means of property ownership, the dominant group can decide who will have access to valued resources such as jobs and home mortgages. In contrast, members of the subordinate group are unable to improve their rank within the social hierarchy because they lack access to the necessary resources (p. 4). This is a description of classic social stratification theory and social class and classism.

Aguirre and Baker (2008) identify four issues that amplify their discussion: structured social inequality, structured discrimination, racial and ethnic oppression, and the persistence of inequality. These are givens in society that one must become aware of and cope with in terms of fighting for human rights and social justice and economic justice inspite of overwhelming forces that comprise the nature of American society. It is the tension between the idealism of American values and the reality of American societal makeup.

Social class affects our perspective on life. Devore and Schlesinger (1999) observe,

> ✳Social class is about inequality. It refers to the fact that some people have more income, find themselves in more highly valued and rewarded occupations, and have more prestige than others. This in turn affects well-being in such respects as health and illness, the ability to exert power and influence to achieve desired ends, the sense of self-respect, and the degree of dignity conferred by others. Differences related to wealth, occupation, and education are generally referred to as social class differences. (p. 44)

Social class distinctions reflect degrees of social inequality based on economic (wealth, income, consumption, occupation), social (influence, community power, group identification), and family status. These social boundaries reinforce the belief that ethnic groups are class bound. Classism is where social class is used to assert unearned privilege, dominance, and power over others in the same class or other classes (Lott, 2002).

Liu, Soleck, Hopps, Dunston, and Pickett (2004) have joined *social class* and *classism* and have constructed a social class worldview model, which posits that people live in economic cultures that place demands and expectations on all individuals. These expectations produce values and norms to which individuals must adhere to remain congruent with others in a particular economic culture. In fact there are multiple middle-class cultures in the United States, which vary in their focus on materialism, lifestyle considerations, and social class behaviors. Individuals living in Chicago, Illinois, may differ from those in Los Angeles, California, although both may consider themselves and the other middle class. Moving from one city to another may require adjusting to the pace, values, and particular patterns of living that each city adheres according to the residents of a similar socioeconomic class. A popular example is Bravo's Real Housewives series about middle and upper middle class women in Orange County (California), New York City, New Jersey, and Atlanta. Comparing and contrasting them from within and between these locational groupings illustrate the varying ways that classism plays out in different parts of the United States. Viewers of this series see similarities and differences in the personalities and behavioral actions of these women in four distinct places. Classism may vary according to specific ways and functions of particular economic cultures.

There are four forms of classism (Liu et al., 2004) that operate in terms of fostering prejudice and marginalization and creating macro- and micro- level aggressions toward people, resulting in perpetuating marginalization and oppression. The first form involves *downward classism*, where those who are in perceived higher classes marginalize those in perceived lower classes. An example of downward classism is upward mobility bias, where it is assumed that people are always motivated toward upward social mobility (higher levels of education, income, and occupation) and that rejecting these values are considered deviant. The second form is *upward classism*, where those in perceived lower classes regard those in perceived higher classes as snobs and elitists. The third form is *lateral classism*, where individuals experience classism from those in a similar social class. Keeping up with those in the same social group or excelling beyond them is an example of how lateral classism operates in a "dog eat dog" environment. Finally, the fourth form is *internalized classism*, where an individual feels that he or she is unable to maintain his or her social class, resulting in anxiety, frustration, anger, or depression, which may be due to the loss of employment or other forms of economic reversals. New dimensions of social class and classism help us to understand the dynamics of change, challenge, and variation in these two concepts.

MAJORITY AND MINORITY STATUS   *Majority status* relates to the power and control of socioeconomic resources by the numerical majority of people, although a powerful minority may constitute a majority through the possession of force, wealth, status, and family connections. *Minority status* relates to the inferior and unequal rank in power and access to resources of a subordinate and disadvantaged group in relation to the superiority in power and resources of the dominant majority. Racial myths and stereotypes, prejudice, and discrimination are invented and practiced by the majority group. An example was the myth of the Yellow Peril (Asian immigration), which was invading the United States in the latter part of the 19th century, causing economic panic and racism to occur among the masses of white blue-collar workers who feared that Chinese labor might take away their jobs. Legislation that favor the majority and the control of civilian and military force are used to maintain the status quo. However, throughout the history of the United States, the courts and the legal system have been utilized to overturn unjust laws and practices on behalf of people of color, women, and gays and lesbians.

Shifts in population, political representation, and social policies and programs are occurring that have implications for minorities. People of color, specifically Latino Americans, are projected to be the numerical majority of the population in the 21st century. Political power, social policies, legislation, and programs have yet to shift in favor of the needs of ethnic minorities. With the White majority in control of political and economic power, it is doubtful that there can be major changes away from the status quo.

ACCULTURATION   *Acculturation* involves the adjustment and adaptation of the individual from the culture of origin to the dominant culture. The danger is that the person acculturating or adjusting/adapting to the majority culture may reject previous cultural ties. However, there is a growing consensus on a *multidimensional approach* to defining acculturation. That is, acculturation is a *balancing of learning* about the dominant culture *and maintaining* the culture of origin. The goal is *an equilibrium* between these two poles. According to Pedersen (2005,

p. 208) acculturation is "the individual's process of learning about and adopting White cultural values, beliefs, attitudes, and behaviors into his or hers self-concept and the degree to which the person maintains his or her own ethnic culture (or other ethnic cultures) through adherence to cultural values, beliefs, attitudes, and behaviors." This is a *both/and* rather than an either/or perspective.

A 2009 episode of the CNN series *Latino in America* depicts the case of Francisca, a 14-year-old girl, who comes to America to be with her mother after a four-year separation from her in the Dominican Republic. In New York City Francisca falls into a depression because she is torn by her mother's strictness and demands that her daughter maintain her Latino culture and her American friends who pull her in another direction. The dilemma of whether to adhere to a strict Latino way of life, which includes obeying her mother and her ways, or to maintain her independence with her American friends is too much for Francisca, who makes a mild suicide attempt by taking her mother's pills. Eventually her school teachers and counselor realize that Francisca is in a depression and alert her mother, who is instructed by the school to admit her daughter to a psychiatric hospital for brief stabilization and follow-up therapy. She falls in love with a teenage Latino boy in school and becomes pregnant. A baby girl named Destiny is born and Francisca and her mother are drawn close to each other because of the child. Gradually there is a sorting out process (bicultural integration), where Francisca realizes that being in America for her means finding out and choosing the helpful aspects of American culture as well as the learning and accepting aspects of her Latino culture, which will assist her as a daughter of a Latino immigrant mother and the mother of a Latino baby who needs nurturing and caring. Francisca and her mother have moved *from an either/or* (American or Latino cultural ways) *conflict to a both/and selection* of meaningful (idiosyncratic to the involved individuals) American and Latino values and behavior patterns that balance their lives and promote harmony in the family. The story of Francisca illustrates the multidimensional approach to acculturation mentioned by Pedersen.

Paniagua (2005) examines four models of acculturation: 1) *the assimilation model*, where a highly acculturated client strongly identifies only with the dominant or host culture; 2) *the separation model*, where the client values only the behaviors and beliefs of his/her own culture; 3) *the integration model*, where the client displays behaviors and beliefs of both the traditional and host or dominant cultures; and 4) *the marginalization model*, where the client rejects the behaviors and beliefs of the traditional and host (dominant) culture (pp. 13–14). Depending on the particular acculturation of the person, acculturation may or may not involve rejection of the culture of origin. *Bicultural integration* occurs where an individual evaluates aspects of both cultures and connects them in a functional way. Cultural barriers are societal and exist along a continuum from *segregation* (geographic, social, educational, and marital separation of races and socioeconomic classes) to *assimilation* (acceptance and adaptation into the dominant society, particularly in terms of social and marital inclusion).

When individuals, families, and ethnic and cultural groups and communities experience acculturation over many generations, *intergenerational acculturation* relates to how the acculturation process affects each succeeding generation, from grandparents to parents to children and their offspring. Over the generations, one witnesses degrees of transformation toward the new culture as well as preservation of traditional cultural practices, beliefs, customs, and values. An intricate pattern of weaving together a bicultural integration of American and country-of-origin perspectives makes sense and becomes functional for each individual who is in this process. I (Lum, 2004) discuss *the paracultural perspective*, which depicts and explains three related intergenerational stages (recent immigrants who are confronted with two distinct cultures; first generation, American-born who undergo acculturation; second generation, American-born who experience Americanization; and third generation, American-born who are often drawn toward the rediscovery of culture-of-origin elements). Portes and Rumbaut (2001) have created intergenerational models of acculturation to understand parent–child dynamics in immigrant families. These dynamics interact with such contextual factors as racial discrimination, urban subcultures, and labor market opportunities. In turn, these elements can affect the child's social, academic, and economic outcomes.

The 2009 CNN series *Latino in America* also features the Garcia family. The Garcias live in Charlotte, North Carolina. Mr. Garcia is Puerto Rican, while Mrs. Garcia is from the Dominican Republic. They met as young adults in the Latino section of New York City and eventually married and raised two sons who are now teenagers. Mrs. Garcia berates herself for not teaching her boys the Spanish language. She believes that when you speak the language, you learn the culture. One of her sons is in a Spanish language class in high school but is failing the course because he is not motivated to learn the language. Mrs. Garcia is patient but very frustrated with her sons over their indifference to being Latino, while Mr. Garcia is understanding and supports his wife's efforts. Every year the Garcias drive to their old neighborhood in New York City to reconnect with relatives and friends and to relive their lives as they were growing up. Mr. and Mrs. Garcia hope that their sons will learn and accept the Latino culture as they interact with uncles, aunties, and cousins from both sides of the family. CNN documents their last trip to New York City and shows how the Garcia sons bond and connect with their uncle, who is a well-known Latino radio dj and an excellent street basketball player, and with cousins at family gatherings with the extended Latino family (la familia). This segment of the series underscores the playing out of intergenerational acculturation and the paracultural perspective of culture.

Three ideal-type relationships exist between parents and child and form the basis for consonant acculturation, dissonant acculturation, and selective acculturation:

- *Consonant acculturation* describes the situation where both the parent and the child abandon their native culture and assimilate to the dominant American culture. A variation of this is the situation where parents and the child resist acculturation and remain rooted within their ethnic community. These families are most likely to return to their home countries.
- *Dissonant acculturation* occurs when the child abandons his or her native culture of origin in favor of integration into the American mainstream while parents lag behind. This situation may lead to intergenerational conflict. Moreover, if the parents do not have ties to the ethnic community as a support system, role reversal may occur where the parents rely on their child to interact with institutions and others in society because the child has learned the language and is able to communicate and broker services for the parents.

- *Selective acculturation* occurs when both parents and the child maintain ties to their native culture while also learning the English language and American customs. This seems to be the most desirable form of acculturation because there have been strong associations among continued contact with ethnic communities and academic achievement (Bankston & Zhou, 1995; Portes & Hao, 2002) and little intergenerational conflict between parents and the child and fluent bilingualism for the child when there is a mutual acculturation transition made by both parents and child (Portes & Rumbaut, 2001).

Portes and Rumbaut (2001) tested this model using data from the Children of Immigrants Longitudinal Study (CILS), a national sample of Asian and Latin American second-generation youth. They measured dissonant acculturation by limited bilingualism (fluency in one language and poor command of another) and parent–child cultural conflict, which measured the difference in viewpoints and frequency of arguments between parents and child. They found a strong negative influence of dissonant acculturation on middle school grade-point averages that continued through high school. Selective acculturation was operationalized by fluent bilingualism and the presence of co-ethnic friendships (friends of the child from both the culture of origin and the dominant culture), which had a strong positive effect on middle school grades but was not significant for high school grades. Nevertheless, strong empirical research evidence bolstered these models of intergenerational acculturation.

In light of this research, it is important to work with immigrant and refugee families to ensure that selective acculturation is achieved. This means selectively identifying useful elements from the culture of origin and simultaneously providing resources that will help both parents and child learn the English language (English as a second language for school children and adults) and American customs as a family unit. This family interaction pattern based on language ability, socioeconomic resources, and sociocultural supports contributes to educational, social, and cultural achievement of immigrant and refugee groups and serves as a basis for understanding other ethnic groups. At the same time it is crucial to monitor immigrant families in order to assess the extent to which there is acculturation stress and tension between parents and teenage children. The two case studies from the CNN series *Latino in America* are reminders of how acculturation unfolds in the lives of real persons and how social workers are required to be culturally competent and proficient as they work with immigrant families.

IDEOLOGICAL BELIEFS

People learn racism, sexism, homophobia, and the rest of the isms from parents, neighborhood, friends, church, and related sources. Many internalize these biases so that they become a way of thinking and eventually a belief system that is confirmed and reaffirmed by the interaction with persons who are the objects and targets of racists, sexists, homophobic persons, and other parties.

RACISM   *Racism* is the cognitive belief that one ethnic group is superior to and dominant over another inferior and subjugated group, supposedly because of genetic composition, intelligence, skin color, character, or related rationale. Racism is a bias that is learned from individuals, the family, groups, and/or society and is perpetuated through the negative affective feelings of prejudice and the behavioral action/reaction of discrimination on the personal, institutional or organizational, and cultural and societal levels. There are a number of facets of racism, which several authors discuss. Sue (2006, p. 17) defines racism as "the individual, institutional and cultural expression of the superiority of one group's cultural heritage over another and the power to impose and enforce that worldview upon the general populace." Ridley (2005, p. 29) states, "Racism is any behavior or pattern of behavior that tends to systematically deny access to opportunities or privileges to members of one racial group while allowing members of another racial group to enjoy those opportunities or privileges." Carter and Jones (1996, p. 2) underscore the inferiority and majority themes of racism when they state, "Racism results from the transformation of race prejudice and/or ethnocentrism through the exercise of power against a racial group defined as inferior, by individuals and institutions with the intentional or unintentional support of the entire (race or) culture." In particular, institutional forms of racism erect structural barriers that exclude certain groups from social resource access and power.

Drawing from a number of sources Constantine (2006) has structured racism into four dimensions, which intersect with each other, and has reminded us that racism is a complex interaction:

Dimension 1: *Types of racism. Individual racism* refers to any discriminatory attitude or act that serves to subordinate a person or persons based on their color. *Institutional racism* refers to policies, practices, or structure of any institution that supports or enforces decisions that oppress people of color and simultaneously benefit the majority group. *Cultural racism* refers to the majority group assuming cultural heritage superiority and imposing this superiority onto other groups.

Dimension 2: *General contexts of racism. Interpersonal context* refers to racism as it is manifested during exchanges or interactions between individuals. *Collective context* refers to racism in large groups of people where there is the combined effect of racial disparities. *Cultural-symbolic context* refers to racism expressed through vehicles of cultural knowledge where people of color are portrayed as inferior, criminal, lazy, or terrorists in efforts to perpetuate notions of White racial superiority and to maintain White racial dominance. *Sociopolitical context* refers to racism displayed in political debates, public discourses on race, institutional policies, and legislative processes where any message about race is created by these sources.

Dimension 3: *Acts of racism. Overt or intentional racism* refers to explicit acts of oppression toward people of color and unconcealed attitudes of racial superiority. *Covert or unintentional racism* refers to subconscious racist beliefs that manifest as attitudes or actions that subordinate people of color.

Dimension 4: *Racial harassment* refers to biased, oppressive, and *differential treatment* based on race in the context of work or social environment involving verbal harassment, *exclusionary practices* from work-related or social events, and *physical forms* of harassment directed at a particular person or group because of race or ethnicity.

These dimensions of racism are helpful handles to analyze the multiple dynamics involved in any encounter where racism is expressed or implied. Ridley (2005) talks about *unintentional racism*, where a person denies his or her racism overtly but covertly exhibits racist behavior: "Unintentional racists perpetuate racism not because they are prejudiced but because they deny that they are racists. Denial—the refusal to recognize the reality of external threats—is the essence of the unintentional racist's mind-set. For an unintentional racist, admitting to racism is a threat to the individual's conception of him- or herself as a nonracist person" (p. 161). Ridley is concerned about *covert racism* that is unacknowledged by the person.

ETHNOCENTRISM   *Ethnocentrism* is the view of an individual or group whose perspective focuses on his, her, or their own ethnic-cultural group and believes that this is the central point of reference for making judgments on situations that are encountered. Marsella and Yamada (2000, p. 12) define the term:

> "Ethnocentrism refers to the natural tendency or inclination among all people to view reality from their own cultural experience and perspective. In the course of doing so, the traditions, behaviors, and practices of people from other cultures are often considered inferior, strange, abnormal, and/or deviant."

Weaver (2005) explains,

> "Ethnocentrism is the natural tendency of people to view reality from their own cultural perspective and to believe that perspective is the most appropriate. This belief—that the way they see the world is "normal," and that others are abnormal, strange, or inferior—can create oppressive situations. Prejudice is closely related to ethnocentrism. When people hold negative attitudes toward members of other cultural groups, this creates a psychological distance between the prejudiced person and the target of prejudice. This distance makes it difficult to overcome biases and develop understandings between diverse people. (pp. 49–50)"

Ethnocentrism often develops when a person or group is so oriented to and involved with his, her, or their ethnic grouping that there is no regard, knowledge, or awareness for other ethnic and social entities. Weaver (2005) recommends that people need to shift their thinking and orientation and begin to increase their empathy for different types of people through learning about others beyond their own group viewpoint. Inductive learning or learning about another person without assumptions by asking questions and seeking answers is a next step toward moving away from ethnocentrism and toward ethno awareness. Weaver (2005) is cognizant that social workers are often professionally ethnocentric when they superimpose their beliefs about the nature and treatment of problems on their clients, emphasize talking to resolve problems, interpret problems from intrapsychic causes, and push for separation and autonomy from the family without regard to discovering cultural and social values of the individual client or the group values of which the person may be a part. Social workers may have to relearn practice assumptions and assume a not-knowing, constantly asking, and continuous discovery stance in order to short-circuit professional ethnocentrism.

SEXISM   According to Longres (1995), sexism is "those norms and expectations existing in law, in religious dogma, or in kinship relations that assign women a subordinate place with regard to men (p. 57)." *Sexism* is the ideological belief that one gender, generally male, is superior to and dominant over the other gender, female, because of intelligence, physical strength, education and career status, and related factors.

Related to sexism are the concepts of gender stratification and male dominance. Stockard and Johnson (1992, pp. 3, 4) define *gender stratification* as "hierarchical ranking of the sex groups that involves their differential access to both resources and rewards," while *male dominance* is "the beliefs and cultural meanings that give higher value and prestige to masculinity than to femininity, and that value males over females, men over women." These conceptual dynamics express how sexism is played out in society. Worden (2001) argues that gender difference is a social construct of a society that perpetuates sexism.

> Social constructionism views people as active participants in perceiving and making sense of their surrounding environments. In this perspective, there are no universal truths about innate differences, which are socially constructed, consensually held, and reinforced. These beliefs become our definitions of reality. (p. 71)

If a social constructionist view of gender differences is correct, we must deconstruct this concept and in its place reconstruct a reality where men and women are equal persons in rights, privilege, and opportunities.

From a conceptual perspective, sexism along with racism is a form of *colonization*. It reiterates the subjugation and exploitation of one party over another. Comas-Diaz (1994) states,

> For women of color, the status of being colonized involves the added negation of their individuality by their being subjected to sexual-racial objectification. Women of color are stripped of their humanity, denied their individuality, and devalued. As female colonized entities, women of color are often perceived as part of the bounty conquered by the colonizer. Historically, conquered males have been killed while conquered females have been raped, enslaved, and sexually subjugated. (pp. 289–290)

The colonization motif illustrates the historical oppression of women as sexual objects. As a result, women of color experience low social status and limited access to power (Gutierrez & Lewis, 1999) due to racism, sexism, and classism.

Uncovering the dynamics of sexism means interconnecting the specific factors that comprise the sexist experience of a particular client. Therefore, it is important to delineate an accurate and detailed statement of what constitutes sexism as part of the problem dynamics. Sexism is a systemic institutional problem that is played out in *labeling of and blaming the victim*. Greene (1994) states,

> Additionally, racism and sexism come together in attempts to present African American women as the cause of failures in family functioning, suggesting that a lack of male dominance and female subordination has prevented African Americans from being truly emancipated. Males in the culture are encouraged to believe that strong women are responsible for their oppression, and not racist institutions. Many African American women, including those who are lesbians, have internalized these myths. (p. 389)

Ethnic gender blaming is a trap that people want to avoid as not being healthy and helpful.

There is a growing realization that sexism must not only include women but also it must involve a discussion of *how sexism affects men*. Miville and Ferguson (2006) have balanced out this dual emphasis by summarizing such *male sexism* themes as men of color having power differentials (few resources available and compensating by being tough or cool); a reluctance to ask for help; aggression and control, which may lead to developing dependencies such as addictions; and the invisibility of positive gender role models, such as the care and nurturing of grandmothers or the lack of a fathering figure in early childhood. Canales (2000) observes that African American men have tried to meet the requirements of the traditional male role of protector, provider, and breadwinner. However, racism, the economic downturn, and related negative societal forces have interrupted these expectations for many African American men who cope with a façade called *cool pose* to hide feelings of fear, hurt, and rage. Canales (2000) describes this demeanor,

> Cool Pose is the appearance of being emotionless, calm, and detached in the face of pain and atrocities. Cool Pose is beneficial to Black men in that it provides them with dignity, self-worth, and strength. However, it is not without costs. To the extent that Cool Pose becomes deeply internalized, it can be difficult to discard when necessary, for example, in relationships with women. Routinely having to hide their feelings, their needs, and their weaknesses may prevent them from letting down the façade in order to achieve intimacy with women. (p. 66)

External persona and *internal feelings* are social role dilemmas affecting men in general and minority men in particular. *Social role expectations* imposed on men may be a form of sexism and racism that needs to be acknowledged and dealt with in a helping way.

HOMOPHOBIA   Weinberg (1972) first used the term *homophobia* to describe prejudice against homosexuality. Appleby and Anastas (1998) assert that one must understand homophobia as the result of heterosexism. That is, *heterosexism* is an ideological system that denies, denigrates, and stigmatizes any nonheterosexual form of behavior, identity, relationship, or community, whereas *homophobia* is the fear and hatred of those who love and sexually desire those of the same sex. The implication is that heterosexuals have the responsibility to change their sexual orientation perspective to include the acceptance of same-sex persons as equal members of society. Or as Miville and Ferguson (2006, p. 93) point out, "Heterosexual activities, beliefs, attitudes, and behaviors are considered the standard or norm against which nonheterosexual forms of behavior are denigrated, denied, and rejected." Tully (2000) explains that homophobia has three components: institutional, individual, and internalized. *Institutional homophobia* refers to the heterosexual macro-cultural structural barriers against gays and lesbians that are manifested in public policy initiatives (e.g., the U.S. armed forces policy of "don't ask; don't tell" and the ban on gay and lesbian marriage). Tully (2000) cites the following examples:

> [T]he criminalization of same-sex sexual activities; the refusal by most businesses, communities, and states to acknowledge same-sex partners; the lack of support for same-sex marriage; the difficulty faced by gays and lesbians who want to have or adopt children; and the generalized lack of support in the nongay community for gay families. (p. 157)

The equal rights of gays and lesbians were excluded from the Civil Rights Act of 1964, which does not include sexual orientation in its nondiscrimination policy statement. Recent attempts to reverse institutional homophobia include protection of gay and lesbian students against sexual harassment in schools and the inclusion of civil and legal rights of gay and lesbian partners.

Individual homophobia manifests itself in singular acts of overt and covert hostility and violence against gay and lesbian persons on a continuum ranging from hate crimes, such as murder, rape, and physical assaults, to threats, ridicule, and related forms of verbal harassment. The murder of Matthew Shepherd in Laramie, Wyoming, and the murders of a gay couple in Redding, California, by the Williams brothers are examples of individual homophobic homicidal responses. Institutionalized and structural homophobia are manifested in public law on the state or federal level, excluding gay and lesbian persons from legally recognized marriages (although several states such as Massachusetts, New Hampshire, and Vermont recognize same-sex marriage) and where institutional policies exclude gay and lesbian persons from institutional recognition, as in the case of the ordination of seminary-trained ministers. Generally, gay and lesbian marriages are prohibited in the Roman Catholic Church and major Protestant denominations (with the exception of the United Church of Christ and the American Episcopal Church and other individual instances of Protestant clergy performing such ceremonies). Many major Protestant denominations such as the Presbyterian Church in the United States, the United Methodist Church, and the Southern Baptist Convention have rejected or are deeply divided over clergy ordination of homosexual individuals and gay and lesbian church marriages.

Internalized homophobia is where the gay or lesbian person introjects society's view or his or her own negative feelings about his or her sexuality. It results in self-hatred and loathing and a learned fear of his or her sexual orientation, which may result in a personal and unhealthy crisis situation. Greene (1994) observes,

> When passing is accompanied by the belief that being gay or lesbian is a sign of inferiority or pathology, it represents an expression of internalized homophobia. Lesbians and gay men who pass, particularly when it is dangerous not to do so, are confronted with stressors that can leave them at risk for negative psychological outcomes. (p. 5)

Undoing the psychological damage is a major task for a person who has suffered internalized homophobia. We may add to these categories professional homophobia. Health and mental health providers may have to cope with medical psychopathology biases learned before 1973, when the category of homosexuality was removed from the list of mental disorders recognized by the American Psychiatric Association. Appleby (2001) observes,

> Health and mental health professionals, including social workers, are not immune from the negative attitudes toward gay, lesbian, and bisexual people that other Americans share. Their attitudes are especially significant in that these are the professionals who have responsibility for assisting gay, lesbian, and bisexual clients to cope with the personal and social consequences of homophobia, to work through the shame and guilt imposed by a homophobic and heterosexist society, to develop a positive lesbian or gay identity, and to help with the management of stigma and stress. Nonjudgmental attitudes are necessary to support social change and to end individual and organizational prejudice. Gay men and lesbians have not always been well served by the health, mental health, and social service professions. (pp. 163–164)

Messinger (2004) conducted an exploratory study of the experiences of lesbian and gay social work students in field placement and identified problems as well as supports and resources. There were 11 sexual orientation issues: managing disclosure of sexual orientation, homophobic attitudes and behaviors, heterosexist attitudes and behaviors, absence and dismissal of gay and lesbian issues, unfriendly climate of placement, professionalism as a gay or lesbian person, identity development concerns, conflicts in intimate relationships, pressures associated with hiding one's sexual orientation, conflicts with field instructors, and general feelings of lack of safety or anxiety. A number of interpersonal supports and institutional resources were suggested: faculty support and mentoring, supportive field education staff, gay and lesbian social work professionals as mentors, field instructors educated about sexual orientation issues, out gay and lesbian agency staff, educated and supportive heterosexual coworkers, resource information for lesbian and gay students, information about sexual orientation issues in placement, a list of gay-friendly agencies, gay and lesbian agencies as placement sites, and resources for gay and lesbian clients.

AGEISM   The term *ageism* originated with Butler (1969) and describes negative attitudes and stereotypes experienced by older persons as a form of bigotry and prejudice. Yet, according to Friedman (2004), older adults are the fastest-growing population group in the United States and will increase from 35 million to 70 million between 2000 and 2030, or from 13 percent to 20 percent during this time period. The areas of mental health and health care are of most concern regarding the elderly. The number of older adults with mental illnesses will grow from 7 million to 14 million between 2000 and 2030. Adequate health care for the minority elderly is a major national concern. It is estimated that older minority adults are more likely to be living in poverty: White elderly (10 percent), Native American elderly (20 percent), Latino American elderly (25 percent), and African American elderly (30–50 percent).

There is a growing body of literature on ageism and cultural competence, particularly in the fields of health care and mental health. Fain (2005) observes that our health care system remains largely separate and unequal in the field of minority geriatrics. There is unequal treatment for racial and ethnic minority elderly, where minorities are less likely than Whites to receive needed services even when controlling for access to care. Black patients in the United States generally receive lower quality health care than White patients. To a large extent, Black and White patients are treated by different physicians. The physicians treating Black patients may be clinically less well trained and may have less access to important clinical resources than do physicians treating White patients. Specifically, ageism in medical practice occurs to minority elderly in the following ways:

- Five minutes less time per visit
- Fewer tests
- Fewer treatment responses
- Fewer referrals
- Fewer responses to pain symptoms
- Less effort to save life
- Negative response to caregiver

Fain (2005) advocates cultural competence in geriatrics, where physicians and other providers will provide health care in ways that are acceptable and useful to elders and congruent with their cultural background and expectations. Health providers need to be aware of their personal biases and their impact on professional behavior. They should have knowledge of health-related cultural values, beliefs, and behaviors; disease incidence, prevalence and mortality rates; population-specific treatment outcomes; and skills in working with culturally diverse populations.

AFFECTIVE EXPRESSION

PREJUDICE   *Prejudice* is an attitudinal response that expresses racist, sexist, homophobic, or similar beliefs in an unfavorable feeling—such as hatred, anger, or hostility—toward an excluded group or individual members. It is a negative affective attitude and a learned condition. Allport's (1954) classic definition of prejudice notes that it is the expression of either *affirmative or negative bias* toward persons of a particular group or who fit into a certain category. Prejudice is a negative attitude, distinct from discrimination, which is a negative action resulting from prejudiced attitudes (Ponterotto, Utsey, & Pedersen, 2006, p. 195).

There are three components related to the definition of prejudice: 1) prejudice is *negative* in nature and can be focused on the individual or the group; 2) prejudice is based on *faulty or unsubstantiated data* (e.g., rumor and hearsay, bias and stereotype, folk beliefs, misinterpreted research data); and 3) prejudice is rooted in *an inflexible generalization about a group* that does not take into account that there are exceptions that must be considered (Ponterotto, Utsey, & Pedersen, p. 12).

How can prejudice be reduced? Allport (1954) sets forth *the social contact principle* of reducing prejudice. The contact hypothesis of Allport proposes that contact between individuals of different groups can lead to positive outcomes (lowering prejudice). These conditions include cooperative interdependence, acquaintance potential, equal status, and institutional support for positive intergroup interaction. Molina and Wittig (2006) observe that Allport's specification of the conditions that intergroup contact could likely reduce prejudice is one of the most influential approaches in social psychology to understand how intergroup relations could have a positive effect.

On a practical level Haberman (1994) offers a number of *concrete steps to reduce prejudice*, which involves rational thinking and concrete implementation. They are as follows: 1) analyze prejudices as they relate to beliefs about the inferiority or superiority of others who are different so that you acknowledge and own your particular set of prejudices; 2) seek the sources of beliefs that are related to attitudes of prejudice (e.g., examining the experiences, people, environments, and events that shaped our current thinking; your world views and lens perception of how you view the world and others in the world; your earliest memories and messages received from people who were sources of socialization, such as parents, grandparents, and significant others; and other sources of ideas such as stereotypes and myths and ethnic, cultural, gender, religious, or social class background); 3) examine the unintentional benefits of prejudice (e.g., the unearned privileges granted by group membership from prejudice, the liabilities and negative effects of my prejudice); and 4) plan to eliminate prejudice (e.g., an intentional and specific plan to acknowledge, unlearn, counteract, and get beyond prejudice with realistic, time-oriented goals and with the support and help of others who can assist you in the execution of your plan).

BEHAVIORAL REACTIONS

DISCRIMINATION   *Discrimination* is a behavioral response that is unfavorable to members of an ethnic, gender, sexual-orientation, or related out-group. A person discriminates against others because of an ideological belief (e.g., racism, sexism, homophobia, ageism) and an affective attitude (e.g., prejudice). There are several theories related to discrimination. First, discrimination occurs because of *situational pressures*. For example, a person may not associate with another person because of peer reaction in a wider group that pressures the person not to relate to another and because of the social sanctions that may occur as a result of the relationship. Situational peer pressure that goes against the majority population or against the will of an influential group is a strong force reinforcing discrimination. A specific example might be a situation in which associating with a gay or lesbian person would provoke a strong reprimand from a person's family, church, or community that is extremely homophobic. Second, discrimination may occur as *a reaction to group gain*. That is, competition for scarce resources and ethnocentrism may result in ethnic domination and subordination, particularly when there is the possibility for loss of jobs or a downturn in the economy. A scapegoat group may be blamed when jobs are scarce or there is a threat of losing employment to a group that will work for lower wages. Third, institutional discrimination occurs in employment, education, housing, and other life-sustaining areas, where marginal and fringe out-groups are unable to secure resources due to *dominant social majority locks* on unionized jobs, schools and housing in desirable neighborhoods, and other amenities.

Bonacich and Goodman (1972) identify a number of *social conditions that heighten discrimination* in a community:

1. Biologically, culturally, and socially distinct populations that are present in a social system and do not allow other groups outside these perimeters to enter their geographical location
2. A segment of the population that is threatened by another group over competition for scarce resources and that believes these resources will be lost as a result of the entrance of the outside group
3. A group that is stereotyped and perceived as the common enemy of other groups so that the label of enemy unifies the other groups regardless of whether the group in question is a threat or whether there is an irrational reaction formation on the part of the majority population
4. Unequal degrees of power in populations so that the haves with power over access to resources react against the have-nots without power, goods, and services
5. Institutional discriminatory actions that are legitimated in social structures and cultural beliefs such as religious institutional sanctions, ethnic exclusion, and negative community practices

McAleavy (2002) reports on a national survey study of 1,003 workers interviewed between September 28 and October 18, 2000, by Rutgers University and the University of Connecticut under the auspices of the John J. Heldrich Center for Workforce Development. The study, on what minority and White employees experience on the job, reported that 28 percent of African Americans and 22 percent of Latinos stated that they had personally experienced unfair treatment at work, compared with 6 percent of White employees. Fifty percent of African American employees believe that they are the most likely racial group to be treated unfairly at work compared with 10 percent of Whites and 13 percent of other races. When discrimination was reported, 57 percent of minorities said that their employer did not respond promptly or satisfactorily to complaints (e.g., being passed over for promotion, being assigned undesirable tasks, or hearing racist remarks). Ethnic discrimination on the job remains a primary issue.

OPPRESSION   *Oppression* is a form of discrimination and occurs when a segment of the population, systematically and over a period of time, prevents another segment from attaining access to scarce and valued resources. Oppression is a process whereby specific acts are designed to place others in the lower ranks of society and is also a structure that creates a bottom rank in a hierarchical system of ranks. There are interlocking systems of oppression—that is, institutions and systems in society interrelate and interconnect with each other to form oppression. An interplay of oppression exists among different systems (Collins, 1990). Schriver (2001) states,

> We...recognize that oppression in any institution directed toward any individual or group is connected with and results in oppression in other institutions and of many other individuals and groups. This interrelated or interlocking quality gives oppression its systemic nature. (p. 97)

The emphasis should be to focus on the links among the systems of oppression. In this sense, the discussion is on the structural nature of oppression. Young (1990) explains,

> Oppression in this sense is structural, rather than the result of a few people's choices or policies. Its causes are embedded in unquestioned norms, habits, and symbols, in the assumptions underlying institutional rules and the collective consequences of following those rules. (p. 41)

Institutional oppression results in the oppression of groups and individuals. This is why we must understand *the history of oppression.*

History, which chronicles past achievements, mistakes, and failures, provides valuable lessons for the present and the future. It is a chronological narrative of a series of events that reflect cause and effect or circular repetition. We should not be sentenced to repeat the mistakes of the past but should strive to overcome present and future challenges with a historical perspective by asking critical questions about people, events, and happenings in order to gain an accurate picture of the circumstances. In short, history is a record of the past that has implications for the present and future. The history of African, Latino, and Asian Americans and First Nations Peoples reaches into the oldest existing civilizations in the world. The history of these groups in the United States represents only a fraction (about 400 years) of their cultural past.

The theme of oppression features prominently in the American experience with ethnic minority groups. *Oppression* occurs when one segment of the population keeps another segment from obtaining social, economic, political, and related human rights through institutional practices and social stratification. The dynamics of oppression involve the oppressor, with presumed power and control, and the oppressed, who is powerless. The *victimization of the oppressed* by the oppressor or oppressive forces occurs in a social and political context. Oppression began in the United States with the concept of *Republicanism* (Takaki, 1990), which advocated the virtuous self-control of the American population during colonial times. Morality, education, and virtue were the hallmarks of the White American male. Women were the bearers of children, the property of their husbands, and the teachers of their male offspring. African American slaves were inferior, and American Indians were savage (a term used by the English to describe the Irish in their country before the settlement of the Americas).

The history in America of African, Latino, and Asian Americans and First Nations Peoples reveals a number of common themes:

- African, Latino, and Asian Americans and First Nations Peoples were exploited for their land and cheap labor and became subservient to White Americans from social, economic, and political perspectives.
- Treaties and laws were enacted that either removed these groups from land or barred them from immigration into the United States.
- African, Latino, and Asian Americans and First Nations Peoples lived in segregated, isolated communities—such as reservations, Harlem, or Chinatown—and were barred from equal education, employment, and housing opportunities.
- Ethnic minority groups used the legal court system in their struggle for civil rights and equal justice under the law.
- Poverty, family fragmentation, and social dysfunction are major symptoms of class stratification affecting the Black underclass, reservation Indians, Mexican farm workers, and recent waves of Southeast Asian refugees.

A case could be made for women of color. I (Lum, 2004) have traced the historical relationship between White feminism and African American women, beginning with the abolition of slavery movement and the suffrage movement, where there was racism in women's suffrage and a historical parting of the ways between White and African American women due to the Fifteenth Amendment (right to vote to African American males rather than to women in general) of the U.S. Constitution. Not only has *White male-dominated society oppressed women* but also *White women have historically discriminated against women of color.*

I (Lum, 2004) have also documented the history of oppression of gays and lesbian people in terms of the struggle for open and affirming church acceptance and marriage, the civil rights of gays and lesbians, and the exclusion of gay and lesbian people of color from the White gay and lesbian community and their own cultural and ethnic communities. There is major concern about sexual minorities who have experienced oppression in the dominant heterosexual culture and society. Van Den Bergh and Crisp (2004) address oppression in "a nonsupportive sociocultural environment that engenders a variety of forms of prejudice" (p. 230). They list such incidents as social repercussions for showing affection to a partner in public, intolerant reactions of family, friends, and coworkers when GLBT (gay, lesbian, bisexual, transgender) clients disclose their sexual orientation, pressure to censor details about their experiences as a GLBT person, and hate crimes where at least 14 percent are based on the victim's sexual orientation.

Single histories of oppression could be written about multiethnic/multiracial people, the elderly of color, poor people, the homeless, and other groups. However, a person has *multiple identities* that transcend solely one category. For example, we could be focusing on an African American–Irish American multiethnic lesbian woman of color who is 65 years old, living alone in substandard housing, and solely dependent on Social Security. No longer are single ethnic, gender, sexual orientation, or social class groups and populations-at-risk important, but the person who is a composite of these identities emerges as a real individual who has experienced oppression and needs liberation.

Young (1990) discusses five *faces of historical oppression*: exploitation, marginalization, powerlessness, cultural imperialism, and violence. These types of oppression are played out in the social and economic order of society and are directed against vulnerable populations-at-risk.

Exploitation   This form of oppression occurs when the results of the labor of one social group are transferred to benefit another group. The energies of the have-nots are expended to maintain the power, status, and wealth of the haves. Gender oppression is a case in point. Not only is there an inequality of status, power, and wealth between women and men but also women are excluded from privileged activities. Women work in jobs that enhance the pleasure and comfort of others, usually men. Solutions to economic and status oppression involve the reorganization of institutions, the revamping of existing practices of decision making, and alteration of the division of labor.

Marginalization   This is the most dangerous form of oppression because it sets aside people that the labor system cannot and will not use as workers. This results in severe material deprivation and social dependency. A major concern is to restructure productivity to address the right of participation and to include marginalized people in a public works or self-employed economic effort.

Powerlessness   This form of oppression involves persons who are powerless or who lack the authority to develop and exercise skills in work. Young (1990) observes, "The powerless have little or no work autonomy, exercise little creativity or judgment in their work, have no technical expertise or authority, express themselves awkwardly, especially in public or bureaucratic settings, and do not command respect" (pp. 56–57). They are inhibited in the development of their capacities, lack decision making in their work life, and are exposed to disrespectful treatment due to their lack of status.

Cultural Imperialism   This involves the establishment of a dominant group's experience and culture as the norm to the exclusion of other groups that are rendered invisible and stereotyped. Women, Jews, First Nations Peoples, African Americans, and gays and lesbians are prime examples of excluded groups. Cultural imperialism results in the experience of *double consciousness*, a term coined by Du Bois (1903/1969). Young (1990) explains,

> Double consciousness arises when the oppressed subject refuses to coincide with these devalued, objectified, stereotyped visions of herself or himself. While the subject desires

recognition as human, capable of activity, full of hope and possibility, she receives from the dominant culture only the judgment that she is different, marked, or inferior. (p. 60)

Such a person experiences a sense of worthlessness and subjugation.

Violence   Violence is directed at certain persons because they are members of vulnerable groups that are liable to suffer violation. Violence against others is perpetual, tolerated, and irrational and is based on fear and hatred of these groups. Violence may be an expression of the will to power, marked by the insecurities of the violators, and is a form of injustice (humans' inhumanity to humans).

Freire has done the pioneer thinking about the nature and dynamics of oppression. He has reflected on his experiences while working with poor peasant people in South America in the 1960s and 1970s. Freire (1970), in *Pedagogy of the Oppressed*, defines *oppression* in the following terms:

Any situation in which "A" objectively exploits "B" or hinders his pursuit of self-affirmation as a responsible person is one of oppression. Such a situation in itself constitutes violence, even when sweetened by false generosity, because it interferes with man's ontological and historical vocation to be more fully human. With the establishment of a relationship of oppression, violence has already begun. (pp. 40–41)

An oppressive situation leads to *the act of violence* and *the state of dehumanization* as a historical reality. Freire (1970) teaches,

As the oppressors dehumanize others and violate their rights, they themselves also become dehumanized. As the oppressed, fighting to be human, take away the oppressors' power to dominate and suppress, they restore to the oppressors the humanity they had lost in the exercise of oppression. (p. 42)

Dehumanization is a distortion of what it means to be fully human.

The historical task of the oppressed is *to liberate themselves and their oppressors*. According to Freire, to restore the humanity of the oppressed and the oppressors is to restore true generosity. However, the oppressed, instead of striving for liberation, find in their oppressor their model of manhood because the oppressed have internalized the image of the oppressor and are fearful of freedom, which includes autonomy and responsibility. The oppressed must not fall into this trap. They must liberate themselves from becoming the oppressors. To be free is human completion.

Oppression is dehumanization. The oppressed have been unjustly dealt with, deprived of their voice, and cheated in the sale of their labor. The oppressed must develop *the pedagogy of their liberation*. They must affirm that they are persons and, as persons, they should be free. Liberating education carries out the pedagogy of the oppressed through educational projects to organize the oppressed and systematic education that can be changed by political power. There are two stages of the pedagogy of the oppressed, according to Freire: The first stage is where the oppressed unveil the world of oppression and commit themselves to its *transformation*, while the second stage is the reality of the oppressed transformed and the pedagogy becomes a pedagogy of all in the process of *permanent liberation*. The oppressed go from self-depreciation ("we don't know anything") to realization ("we were exploited"). The oppressed must engage in critical and liberating dialogue and reflection on their concrete situation. The oppressed have the ability to reason. Libertarian action must transform dependence into independence. The oppressed must intervene critically in the situation that surrounds them and must be subjects, not objects, and fight in the revolutionary process. The oppressed must learn this perspective, which serves as a guideline.

Freire (1970) provides solutions that involve community organizing based on *dialogical action and education*. Action to overcome oppression begins with the oppressed and the leaders dialoguing and communicating with each other. People in communion liberate each other, according to Freire. *Antidialogical action* consists of conquest, divide and rule, manipulation, and cultural invasion. First Nations Peoples identify with this pattern, as leaders often took such actions against them. *Dialogical cultural action* consists of cooperation based on a critical analysis of a problematic reality, unity for liberation growing out of communion with the united people from a consciousness of being an oppressed class, organization based on authentic and critical witness (consistency between words and actions, boldness to confront existence, radicalization leading to increasing action, courage to love, and faith in the people), and cultural synthesis from the oppressed people's own values and world ideology, which are guidelines for mutual support and action.

Gil (1998) broadens the discussion on oppression to the concerns of social work. *Oppression* is "a mode of human relations involving domination and exploitation—economic, social, and psychologic—between individuals; between social groups and classes within and beyond societies; and, globally, between entire societies" (p. 10). *Dominion, exploitation*, and *oppression* are related, according to Gil (1998), as follows: "Domination is the means to enforce exploitation toward the end of attaining and maintaining privileged conditions of living for certain social groups relative to some other groups" (p. 10). Gil also observes that oppression is fluid and changing in a society: Societies whose internal and external relations involve oppressive tendencies are usually not divided simply into oppressors and oppressed people. Rather, people in such societies tend to be oppressed in some relations and oppressors in others, while some relations may involve mutual oppression. Oppression is not a static context but a dynamic process. At the same time, a nonoppressive society is one in which people are treated as equals, have equal rights and responsibilities, and are subject to the same level of expectations and constraints about work and other aspects of life. Gil advocates that social workers follow these radical practice principles of social change:

- Reject political neutrality and affirm politics of social justice and human liberation.
- Affirm values of equality, liberty, cooperation, and affirmation of individual and social development.
- Transcend technical/professional approaches in favor of helping people trace the links between their problems and ways of life.
- Facilitate critical consciousness through dialogue leading to insights into human nature, shaping social realities, and changing and reshaping these realities.

- Advocate human rights to which people are entitled, such as equal rights, responsibilities, and opportunities.
- Confront obstacles to needs fulfillment of human needs and people's capacities for a just and free society.
- Gain insight into personal oppression that will transcend divisions and identify with human liberation and social equality.
- Prefigure future possibilities toward participatory democratic egalitarian forms of human liberation.
- Spread critical consciousness and build social movements that promote political action.

Gil follows in the tradition of Freire and makes a case for social work involvement in dealing with oppression and liberation on a political societal level.

Violence as an Expression of Discrimination and Oppression   A current concern is violence against women. Lee (2008) observes about the expansion of violence:

> Violence has continued to plague our society and hurt our citizens and families. After more than 30 years of work by feminist activists, scholars, and practitioners who have been the force behind the Battered Women's Movement, the issue of domestic violence has gained enough public prominence that it can now be considered mainstream in North America. Dating violence also becomes another issue that has attracted increasing attention in our society because of its prevalence among the youth population. The proliferation of our collective knowledge and understanding of violence and its prevention and treatment has still neglected the experience of people from diverse ethno-racial backgrounds. Research regarding the impact of race and ethnicity upon violence will have significant implications for developing culturally relevant, appropriate, and viable prevention and treatment programs. (p. 105)

Women as victims, the battered woman syndrome, and women's experience of domestic violence are major concerns that relate violence and oppression. Mahoney (1994) explains the interrelationship between violence and oppression:

> The long struggle to reveal the prevalence and harm of domestic violence often emphasized incidents of violence, however, rather than placing the woman's experience in the context of her life in an oppressive society, or emphasizing the abusive patterns of the batterer's quest for control. Inquiry focuses on particular incidents of violence and the woman's response to them. When battering is seen only as discrete episodes of physical assault, this facilitates the position that leaving the relationship is the sole appropriate form of self-assertion. But battering reflects a quest for control that goes beyond separate incidents of physical violence and that does not stop when the woman attempts to leave. A focus on control reveals the danger that violence will continue as part of the attempt to reassert power over the woman. (p. 75)

In other words, unless we move beyond the acts of physical violence against women to focus on the issues of power and control in an oppressive society, we miss the whole point, namely, that *violence is an expression of societal oppression.*

The power and control wheel developed by Ellen Pence (n.d.) and the Duluth Domestic Abuse Intervention Project illustrates oppression as physical and sexual violence. Power and control are at the hub of the wheel, with spokes emphasizing the use of economic abuse, coercion and threats, intimidation, emotional abuse, male privilege, children, isolation, and minimizing, denying, and blaming. Under each of these headings are details of oppressive behavior:

- *Economic abuse*: preventing her from getting or keeping a job; making her ask for money; giving her an allowance; taking her money; not letting her know about or have access to family income
- *Coercion and threats*: making and/or carrying out threats to do something to hurt her; threatening to leave her, to commit suicide, or to report her to welfare; making her drop charges; making her do illegal things
- *Intimidation*: making her afraid by using looks, actions, gestures; smashing things; destroying her property; abusing pets; displaying weapons
- *Emotional abuse*: putting her down; making her feel bad about herself; calling her names; making her think she's crazy; playing mind games; humiliating her; making her feel guilty
- *Male privilege*: treating her like a servant; making all the big decisions; acting like the "master of the castle"; being the one to define men's and women's roles
- *Children*: making her feel guilty about the children; using the children to relay messages; using visitation to harass her; threatening to take the children away
- *Isolation*: controlling what she does, who she sees and talks to, what she reads, and where she goes; limiting her outside involvement; using jealousy to justify actions
- *Minimizing, denying, and blaming*: making light of the abuse and not taking her concerns about it seriously; saying the abuse does not happen; shifting responsibility for abusive behavior; saying she caused it

These categories are areas of assessment that can be used to determine the specific incidents of violent oppression against women.

COPING WITH CONTEXTUAL REALITIES

CONTEXTUAL REALITIES AND TEACHABLE MOMENTS

On Friday July 31, 2009 Harvard scholar Henry Louis Gates Jr. and Cambridge police sergeant James Crowley met with President Barack Obama and Vice President Joe Biden for beer and conversation in the Rose Garden of the White House. Gates and Crowley agreed to disagree over an incident that happened on July 16th prior when Gates was arrested at his home after a neighbor saw two men breaking into Gates's home and called the Cambridge police to report the incident. Dr. Gates reported that he showed Sergeant Crowley his identification, but Sergeant Crowley claimed that Dr. Gates became enraged and consequently arrested him for disorderly conduct and booked him at the police station, where he was released after several hours. Dr. Gates charged the officer with racism, although Sergeant Crowley called for back-up and there were several other police officers present. Among them was Sergeant Leon Lashley, an African American Cambridge police officer, who was at Gates's home and who stood up for his fellow officer and was later assailed as an Uncle Tom. Lucia Whalen was the woman who reported the presumed break-in to police and said that she has been living in fear for her safety after being labelled a racist for describing "the possible burglars as black men with backpacks." 911 tapes record no such conversation between Ms. Whalen and the 911 operator. Later Officer Justin Barrett of the Boston Police Department used a crude racial slur to describe Gates in an e-mail to *The Boston Globe* and later forwarded to fellow National Guardsmen and police officers. Barrett apologized but is facing a termination hearing after being placed on administrative leave. A New York City political aide resigned after her Facebook posts called Gates "a racist" and Obama "dumb" because President Obama said at a presidential news conference that police "acted stupidly" for arresting Gates. This caused an uproar among officers in the Cambridge police department and at a news conference several of them spoke out against the criticisms of the president. Obama quickly declared that his first reaction was "unhelpful," professed his appreciation for the police, and allowed that Gates bore responsibility for escalating the situation. The president called this a "teachable moment" and set up the White House meeting with Gates, Crowley, Biden, and himself.

On Sunday September 13, 2009 Taylor Swift, a 19-year-old country and pop sensation, received an award at the MTV Video Music Awards for the best female video, "You Belong With Me." She was interrupted in the midst of her acceptance speech by Kanye West, who has been known for his awards show outbursts when he did not win. West jumped on stage and protested this time for Beyonce Knowles. West said to Swift: "Taylor, I'm really happy for you, and I'm gonna let you finish, but Beyonce had one of the best videos of all time." A shocked Beyonce looked on and the crowd began to boo West. Swift did not finish her speech but later when Beyonce won the video of the year award for Single Ladies ("Put a Ring on It"), she invited Swift to the stage so she could "have her moment." A smiling but nervous Swift thanked the audience. West later apologized on his blog to Taylor but it took several days for him to call her personally on the phone and apologize to her after Swift and West appeared separately on various talk news shows where commentators interviewed them about the incident.

These contextual realities are microcosms of the life dilemmas that we face on a daily basis as ordinary and high profile people face situations that trigger outrage, embarrassment, confrontation, regret, and apology. Was Dr. Henry Louis Gates Jr., a Harvard professor, a victim of racism? Was Sergeant James Crowley a racist or was he objective and within his legal rights to arrest Dr. Gates on disorderly conduct? Did Gates's anger and rage consume him so that he was beyond rational reasoning and discourse with the police officer? Was Sergeant Leon Lashley really an Uncle Tom practicing a code of silence and sticking up for a fellow officer or did he witness another African American cross the line with a police officer? Was Ms. Lucia Whalen a victim of racism from non-Whites who maligned her with false information about "black men with backpacks"? Why did Officer Justin Barrett use a racial slur that cost him his police job? Was it permissible for the New York City political aide to use the terms "racist" and "dumb" to describe Dr. Gates and President Obama? Should the president have used the incident to raise the civility of the nation and to make this a "teachable moment" for respect and tolerance? Was Taylor Swift a victim of racism and sexism when Kanye West interrupted her? Was Kanye West an ethnocentricist in his admiration for Beyonce, a fellow African American, at the exclusion of allowing a White woman, Taylor

Swift, to finish her acceptance speech? Perhaps the only gracious and sensitive person in these two incidents was Beyonce, who allowed Swift her time to have "her moment."

How does a client *cope with* the preceding *contextual realities* and the *teachable moments* incidents that have been covered in this chapter? We want to offer you a number of strategies that pose alternative ways of coping with these contextual realities. Some of them are micro and personal, while others are macro and action oriented. Some strategies are useful in your interactions with others. Others are relevant in social change efforts.

STRATEGY ONE: PRACTICE SOCIAL JUSTICE

Social justice is a CSWE (Council on Social Work Education) accreditation standard that is taught in accredited social work programs and is an integral part of the National Association of Social Workers (NASW) Code of Ethics. Social workers practice the principles of human rights and social and economic justice in their interactions with individuals, families, groups, and communities and in the formulation of policy, legislation, program, and administration. Distributive justice and resource allocation and related theories and principles of justice are covered in an entire chapter of this text. Social work prides itself in teaching and practicing social justice.

In cultural competence studies there is a movement toward social justice as a strategy and cultural competence as a practice approach. Social workers are moving from social justice to cultural competence, whereas counseling psychologists are moving from cultural competence to social justice. Both groups acknowledge the values of social justice and cultural competence. For example, Weaver and Congress (2009) are social workers who are moving from social justice to cultural competence and making the directional link between social justice and cultural competence. Weaver and Congress (2009) state, "This concept of social justice in social work practice can be operationalized as cultural competence, the ability to work with diverse populations in respectful and effective ways within clients' cultural contexts" (p. 166). This is an amazing step to take in the rapprochement between the two areas.

From the counseling psychology side there is a wide discussion about social justice and cultural competence. The content of the discussion resembles the core content of a social work course on social justice. Social justice issues, content, and methodology are concerns for those in the field of multicultural competence counseling psychology, which reflects an expansion beyond individual one-to-one counseling (Vera & Speight, 2003). Past concerns about ways to cope with oppression and racism in established competencies are the basis for formulating a conceptualization of social justice for counseling psychology. Oppression, privilege, social inequities, and communitarian justice based on collective decision making and community empowerment are content areas for practice, training, and societal involvement, which synthesizes social justice and professional practice. This proposal (Vera & Speight, 2003) has raised a debate of whether counseling psychology has been committed to social justice in the history of their profession. Arredondo and Perez (2003) indicate prior involvement of ethnic psychologists, counselors, and psychiatrists in social justice issues involving racism and genetic inferiority of Blacks, cultural deprivation of minorities, and a commitment to social justice in their professional organization. They point out several inaccuracies and misinterpretations cited by Vera and Speight (2003) and urge actual involvement in local social justice struggles. Ivey and Collins (2003) reach back to Freire's concept of critical consciousness, concerns over oppression and social justice in the counseling session, and the integration of liberation in clinical practice. They assert that the adoption of the multicultural competencies by the American Psychological Association (APA) represents social justice in action. Both social work and counseling psychology should collaborate on the teaching of social justice content for their discipline and joint projects, where common social justice programs can be devised along with a social justice training and research center. Both fields would profit, especially when there is a link to cultural competence.

STRATEGY TWO: PRACTICE EMPOWERMENT OF SELF, OTHERS, AND COMMUNITY

Gutierrez and Lewis (1999) offer an empowerment strategy in situations involving racism and sexism:

- Developing a specific focus on the details of how individual women have been affected by racism, ethnocentrism, and sexism and on which particular social structures might be challenged
- Assisting the client to gain a sense of personal, interpersonal, and political empowerment with the ultimate goal of changing oppressive structures
- Tracing the strengths of ethnic women in history and in contemporary society to forge ahead in the face of obstacles and using these stories as a road map for similar journeys
- Recognizing that ethnic women have worked with their male counterparts to foster change because racism and sexism have affected both equally in terms of acts of violence against people
- Breaking the cycle of male domination and the gender division of labor to free men and women to participate equally in their ethnic community

Implementing these principles helps the client to combat sexism and racism by analyzing the situation, devising an empowerment plan, drawing on the strengths of role models, and freeing men and women so that they are able to work on these problems together. Moreover, Stockard, and Johnson (1992) argue for economic, legislative, and social egalitarianism on behalf of women:

> Women's greater participation in the labor force, the passing of legislation that requires equality in the economy, and the increasing acceptance of egalitarian roles for men and women are certainly important steps toward a more egalitarian society. As feminists work toward additional changes that focus not just on increasing women's representation at all levels of the occupational world, but also on support for families and children and the specific concerns of working class and poor women, we may be able to move closer to a society in which greater equity exists for women and men in all areas of society. (p. 255)

Working toward eliminating sexism frees both men and women in the end.

How does one bring an empowerment perspective to working with gays and lesbians? Tully (2000) offers some excellent suggestions:

- Establish an egalitarian relationship where the worker demonstrates concern for the client and creates a safe, homosocial environment where a relationship can develop and flourish.
- Assume a nonjudgmental approach where the client is able to disclose his or her own particular situation, sort through available resources, master the immediate crisis, and make a positive resolution of the issues.
- Start with the client's narrative of what has happened and evolve in a non-threatening way through a respect for the client's rights and responsibilities.
- Strengthen adaptive potentials (internalized and environmental resources), work for gradual social and economic justice for gays and lesbians (equal rights, protection, nondiscrimination in all aspects of living), and believe that all disenfranchised groups should be permitted the opportunity to succeed.

Hopefully these practical suggestions will provide modest answers to individual, institutional, and cultural social realities that have faced us. We turn to a discussion on diversity, which is a part of our social context and a growing reality as our country recognizes the multicultural and multiethnic composition of its people.

STRATEGY THREE: AFFIRM THE REALITY OF DIVERSITY

Diversity or the reality of difference is the antidote to racism, sexism, homophobia and the other isms because diversity confirms that the real world is a multicultural United States of America. We are no longer separate and divided. We are united, free, and diverse. Viva la difference! The unique diversity of people is our focus in this section. *Human diversity* involves the recognition of differences and similarities in the experiences, needs, and beliefs of people. Diversity focuses on the differences that make a person distinct and unique from another person. It offers an opportunity for a person to name these distinctions and invites another person to discover those particular qualities about that particular individual. It is an inclusive term that encompasses groups distinguished by race, ethnicity, culture, class, gender, sexual orientation, religion, physical or mental ability, age, and national origin. Diversity tends toward these distinctive categorical differences (Greene, Watkins, McNutt, & Lopez, 1998).

Yet diversity recognizes that there are similarities between persons that bind people together as part of our common humanity. There may be common and uncommon experiences, needs, and beliefs that cause bonding and distinctiveness. Human diversity calls for discovery, learning, and understanding of each other.

Schriver (2001) covers four categories of diversity that contribute to our understanding:

1. *Diversities and worldviews*: the values and perspectives that shape the worldview of a person who is part of an ethnic/cultural group; emphasis varies from collective and corporate family and society to values as a response to

oppression over a period of time; biculturality may be a part of functioning in two related societies such as the heterosexual and gay/lesbian worlds; alternative cultures offer a strength perspective in diversity such as the acceptance of gay and lesbian members in some Native American communities as seers, shamans, full of wisdom; belief systems about the harmony of humans and the natural world; and the role of the elders and their contributions to the common good.

2. *Diversity within diversity*: the movement away from viewing the world in terms of binary White and Black people and toward multiple racial realities of many diverse groups with diverse characteristics and qualities within and between the ethnic categories and subcategories.

3. *Multiple diversities*: considerable variability of an individual who may simultaneously have membership in multiple diverse groups in terms of ethnicity, genetics, gender, sexual orientation; emphasis is upon the need to understand the full background and perception of identities of the client; multidimensionality stresses multiple fluid identities with various groups that offer differing and rich understanding of individuals.

4. *Interrelatedness and interconnectedness of human beings*: a holistic perspective that shares a sense of interrelatedness of humans with all elements of environment; mutuality or partnership in a process of seeking meaning and understanding that results in mutual help to reach our potentials as persons; sharing of our personal experiences with those around us in order to recognize similarities and differences about ourselves and others, which helps in joining together.

Schriver makes the case that diversity means inclusion of worldviews and mutual perspectives and interrelatedness and interconnectedness, which reiterates the concept of similarities. At the same time diversity reminds us that differences and distinctions are important in terms of diversity within diversity (intergroup and intragroup diversity) and multiple diversities (often called multiple identities). In a real sense diversity means recognizing that every person that you meet is different from you in many ways but also similar to you in some ways. Part of the zest for life is to meet and discover the other person's similarities and differences and enjoy them. This is experiencing diversity in the fullest sense of the word.

Gender and diversity are obvious realities. Gender includes male and female but the majority of the social science literature concentrates gender on women. Women's studies have been historically neglected and so the focus is on women. We provide this development of gender and diversity studies for your understanding of where the field has gone in the last three decades. Multicultural feminist theory is concerned with women of color (African, Latino, and Asian Americans, and First Nations Peoples) in the United States. Major contributions to studies on women of color have been made in texts by Mirkin (1994), Comas-Diaz (1994), and Greene (1994). Along with the development of texts on women of color, an alternative knowledge base (social constructionism) has emerged that relies on personal narratives of experiences of individual women of color and lays the basis for establishing some common themes (Holland, Gallant, & Colosetti, 1994; McNamee & Gergen, 1992; Radtke & Stam, 1994). Moreover, White feminist therapy has recognized that racial, ethnic, social class, and related issues need to be addressed along with gender opposition (Greene, 1994; Kliman, 1994; Kopacsi & Faulkner, 1988).

During the 1970s and 1980s, limited research existed on ethnically related gender differences and feminist issues in culturally diverse populations due to the domination of feminist therapy by White women writers. Gender oppression and therapeutic solutions dominated the scene at the expense of recognizing the problem of ethnic/racial oppression and its resulting consequences in the lives of women of color. During the 1990s, there was a gradual dawning of awareness that racial, ethnic, and cultural factors are just as important as gender oppression for women. Moreover, women of color practitioners (Aguilar & Williams, 1993; Collins, 1990; Comas-Diaz & Greene, 1994; Greene, 1994; Kliman, 1994) began to reflect and write on the unique problems and issues facing multiethnic and culturally diverse female clients. These contributions represent crucial components of the women of color mosaic that delineates particular helping approaches. For example, Congress and Kung (2005) point out the conflict between traditional and American gender roles and role reversals that produce conflict and domestic violence. They state:

> Traditional gendered roles within the family also exert significant impact on the family, especially when circumstances change after migration. For example, in some cultures women are expected to take care of internal familial affairs, including household chores and child care, while men are expected to work outside and be income earners. However, changes in socioeconomic status of the family after migration may necessitate both spouses to work outside of home. If the role of domestic caretaker continues to be rigidly assigned only to women, they may become overburdened. In situations in which the woman is able to find a job while the man is unemployed, if the family lacks flexibility in their role adaptation, conflict, blame, and burden within the family may become so enormous that it may threaten the survival of the family unit. (p. 14)

Working with both spouses to ensure the socioeconomic transitions of marriage, family, and economic survival is a major task.

Regarding the etiology of a multicultural feminist perspective, Brown (1990) analyzed the limitations of existing feminist therapy and the need for multicultural theory building. On the one hand, feminist therapy and feminist therapy theory were developed by White women, who excluded diversity issues that were the concerns of women of color, poor or working-class women, and non–North American women. Past feminist therapy theory was based on a sociological description of the external reality and social context (i.e., gender and societal oppression) and a phenomenological recollection of the lived and inner reality of women's life experiences. Both approaches describe the interactive relationships of internal and external realities of predominantly White working-class and middle-class women.

Brown (1990), on the other hand, advocated the development of an alternative culturally diverse gender knowledge. There are four goals of multicultural feminist therapy theory:

1. The creation of a multicultural, non-White, and non-Western feminist database reflecting the varieties of female experiences, connected with research questions and data gathering that are guided by a feminist consciousness

2. The de-emphasis of gender oppression as the primary central issue for women of color, poor women, and women from non-Western cultures, and the inclusion of multicultural female socialization experiences, which may vary according to ethnic and cultural factors

3. The search for how internal reality is shaped by diverse external experiences utilizing phenomenology (observable reported experiences) and introspection (personal sharing of an ethnic-cultural perspective in relationship to one's culture of origin and participation in the dominant society) as tools for theory development

4. The acknowledgment of cultural factors outside the control of particular group members that shape the internal experiences of individual women related to a particular ethnic group and become symbolic representations of how women accept culturally defined roles and yet transcend them to become liberated people in their cultural society

Yet Brown (1990) warns educators and practitioners concerned with cultural diversity:

> If we do not soon undertake the process of making feminist theory a multicultural theory, we may lose our chance and become yet another White, exclusionary system. Some therapists who are women of color and feminist in their theoretical perspectives have refused to take on an identification with feminist therapy in part because of its overly White bias, and in part because feminist political theory has seemed to deny to women of color the importance of their racial and cultural identities. (p. 17)

We must move beyond refusal and criticism of past feminist theory and forge ahead with the development of systematic multicultural knowledge that addresses understanding and helping women of color in their personal growth and life development. Most feminist groups in the 1990s recognized the need for a multicultural emphasis that addresses racism, social class inequality, and homophobia along with sexism. Renzetti and Curran (1995) state,

> If the movement is to remain strong and make up ground lost as a result of the conservative backlash of the 1980s, then the needs and experiences of diverse groups of women must not just be taken into account by the powers that be within feminism, they must reshape the focus and course of the movement itself. (p. 566)

As mainstream feminists incorporate multicultural concerns, there must be adequate principles on working with women of color. Nonsexist resocialization involves enacting liberating changes in family, education, religion, economy, and politics while preserving the best of traditional social values. To this end, we hope that gender barriers will be removed and that the potentials of women and men as respected and genuine people will be realized in significant ways.

STRATEGY FOUR: FOCUS ON THE LENSES OF THE CLIENT

There has been a shift of focus from counselors' multicultural competence to the interface between the counselor and the client. Client perspectives on what constitutes effective multicultural counseling, perceptions of the counseling services received and what constitutes cultural competence from the client's vantage point, perceived and actual client need for cultural issue concerns, the cultural competence or incompetence of the counselor experienced by the client, how cultural issues were discussed and explored, and changing clients' perceptions during the counseling sessions have been reported by research in a qualitative research study with a sample size of ten consisting of undergraduate university students (Pope-Davis et al., 2002). Strengths, potential concerns, and implications for future directions have been expressed, which reflect a movement of multicultural competence counseling to focus on the effectiveness of cultural competence on clients.

Davis (2009) concurs in a research study based on relational competence theory, that is, objectives related to communication are perceived to be fulfilled through interaction appropriate to the interpersonal context based on four personal relational components (motivation, knowledge, skills and outcomes, and a complex contextual component) and four models of social work diversity practice. Davis (2009) observes,

> Practitioners often believe that if they perform behaviors they learn as culturally appropriate with diverse populations, then they are responding in a culturally competent manner. Relational competence theory, however, conceptualizes competence as perceived appropriateness and effectiveness viewed through lenses of the interactants. (p. 62)

As we see the contextual realities through the eyes of the client and respond to the client's directions and perceptions of problems, experiences, and significant others, we will develop cultural competent knowledge and practice solutions from the client.

STRATEGY FIVE: BE THE TRANSCENDENT PERSON

Lee and Ramirez (2000) talk about *the transcendent person* who is able to rise above the contextual realities and move to higher ground. They state, "The transcendent person encourages individuals, groups and/or cultures to break from the bonds of racism, sexism, and prejudice in general and to move toward greater openness, inclusiveness, and acceptance of diversity" (p. 296). It is changing direction and celebrating diversity that is the turning point in this chapter for the reader to recognize as vitally important. Of course there are no easy answers and solutions to these social problems, which have plagued Americans through their history. However in practical terms, one might take the following steps toward transcending negative situations.

First, gain a perspective on the structural status, ideological beliefs, affective expression, and behavioral reactions. Look at yourself, uncover what needs to be worked on, and begin the journey toward resolution. Second, be aware of these realities as you interact personally and professionally with other people in general and with clients in particular. Put persons, places, and problems in their social context. Examine what dynamics are present and active in these settings and how do they affect the person with the problems. Third, ask yourself what can be changed, what will probably remain the same, and what new directions you can point to your client. Fourth, recognize that power and privilege, racism, sexism, homophobia, and other isms can be quite debilitating and overwhelming for the client and the worker. *Modest and gradual movement toward making realistic social changes in the person and in the contextual environment* may be the reality that is most plausible in the situation. Finally there are some practical principles that relate to empowerment and empowering the client in the midst of racism, sexism, homophobia, and other isms.

SUMMARY

This chapter on social context has covered a contextual realities framework consisting of 13 subcomponents and has offered 5 micro and macro strategies to cope with these contextual realities. In order to become culturally proficient the culturally competent worker should become aware of the issues surrounding structural status, ideological belief, affective expression, and behavioral reaction. Revisiting the Henry Gates Jr. and Taylor Swift incidents and analyzing them according to the 4 major categories and 13 subcomponents is a helping exercise to identify how and why people act, interact, and react against a structural status backdrop of social stratification. Likewise applying several of the strategies to cope with contextual realities to the Gates and Swift case studies helps to develop how to respond in similar or different circumstances.

The social context of diversity, racism, sexism, homophobia, discrimination, and oppression is with us as we help people with problems. This chapter has presented these themes along with solutions and strategies for immediate action. The message is that these social contextual factors must be confronted and dealt with on a constant basis. It is hoped that the reader will return to these sections with possible answers to these perennial problems.

In the subsequent chapters of this book, we make the case for a culturally competent framework and for the culturally competent themes of cultural awareness, knowledge acquisition, skill development, and inductive learning. Being a culturally competent practitioner in the midst of the social context described in this chapter is the way that we must point to social work students and practice providers.

Human Rights and Social and Economic Justice

CHAPTER 3

Dorothy Van Soest

Considerable attention has been paid during the past decade to the increasingly diverse appearance of the United States. Much of the attention has focused on the significant increase in non-White populations and projections of increasing numbers of "minority majority" cities, regions, and states. Two prevailing responses exist. First, dominant White America clearly shows signs of being threatened, as evidenced by increased use of institutional and individual violence to maintain dominance and oppression over people of color. Some examples are widespread anti-immigrant and anti-affirmative action sentiment and political action, growing numbers of hate crimes, and a proliferation of White hate groups and on-campus accusations of balkanization of student bodies. The intensity of the anti-immigrant sentiment has even spilled over to include immigrants with European backgrounds. The election of President Obama in 2008 as the first African American to lead our country has resulted in increased hate speech and actions on the one hand and the myth that we have achieved a post-racial society on the other.

The second predominant response is an attempt to successfully prepare for a significantly more diverse workplace. A proliferation of education and training efforts aimed at cultural awareness and multicultural competence in the workplace characterizes this response. For social work and other helping professions, this translates into a focus on preparing professionals to effectively serve clients from diverse cultures. The notion of cultural competence has become the center of this response; it is defined by Cross, Bazron, Dennis, and Isaacs (1989) as a "set of congruent behaviors, attitudes, and policies that come together in a system, agency, or among professionals and enable that system, agency, or those professionals to work effectively in cross-cultural situations" (p. 13).

Although the two predominant responses to changing demographics represent either a stance of resistance or a stance of working together to strengthen the economy, this chapter proposes a third response. The fundamental premise of this chapter is that, in order to be truly culturally competent, it is necessary to understand that the experience of difference means both culture as a source of strength (i.e., capacity to overcome life circumstances and mobilize social movements) and group membership as a basis of inequity, injustice, and oppression. This means it is important to understand that the threat many people feel in the face of an increasingly diverse U.S. society is related to fear of losing their position of dominance and privilege over those who are assigned a subordinate status primarily because they are perceived as "different."

Thus, successfully navigating the new multicultural terrain not only requires an understanding and appreciation of diverse cultures but also requires an equal understanding of the sources and dynamics of injustice and oppression that are inextricably connected with cultural difference. Although social workers, in particular, have professional responsibilities to provide culturally competent services, they have additional mandates to challenge social injustice and to promote social and economic justice. These mandates are expressed in the National Association of Social Workers (NASW, 2008) Code of Ethics, the *International Declaration of Ethical Principles of Social Work* of the International Federation of Social Workers (IFSW, 2004), and the *Educational Policy and Accreditation Standards* of the Council on Social Work Education (CSWE, 2008).

For almost three decades, social work education has increasingly addressed the need to develop social justice practitioners who are culturally competent. Beginning in the early 1970s, the inclusion of diversity has been mandated by social work curriculum standards for purposes of accrediting educational programs. In 1992, the CSWE's curriculum requirements for accreditation specifically mandated content on women, people of color, gay men, and lesbian women; on the patterns, dynamics, and consequences of oppression related to these and other vulnerable groups; and on skills to promote change for social and economic justice. The CSWE's *Educational Policy and Accreditation Standards* (2008) delineated that the foundation curriculum content in all social work education programs must integrate content on diversity and cultural competence; social and economic justice content grounded in an understanding of distributive justice, human and civil rights, and the global interconnections of oppression; and implementation strategies for combating discrimination, oppression, and economic deprivation and for promoting social and economic justice so that students are prepared to advocate for nondiscriminatory social and economic systems.

This chapter connects the themes of the other chapters in this book with the concepts of social and economic justice and operationalizes CSWE's (2008) most recent accreditation standard that requires the advancement of human rights and social and economic justice and recognition of the global interconnections of oppression. It is based on the following premises: that dimensions of cultural competence must be understood within the social context of an environment of social and economic injustice that is inextricably interconnected with discrimination and oppression based on race, ethnicity, gender, sexual orientation, age, ability, and so on; that one's own determination of who is entitled to social justice rests in understanding one's own personal and professional cultural awareness as well as one's acquisition of knowledge about diverse populations and how they are subjected to social injustice and the development of skills necessary for restoring social and economic justice; and, finally, that learning to advance human rights and social and economic justice in one's social work practice requires a learning process characterized by empowerment.

The first section of this chapter briefly discusses definitions of social justice, economic justice, social injustice, and economic injustice. The second section argues that culturally competent practice insists on a commitment to promoting social and economic justice. Since the role of social justice advocate requires that social workers engage in critical thinking that begins with serious reflection, awareness, and analysis of their own personal beliefs about what is fair and just, the third section suggests some exercises as a place to begin that work. This is followed by a section on social justice theory that presents perspectives against which one's personal perspectives can be critically assessed. The fifth section defines and proposes global human rights as the cornerstone of social and economic justice. The sixth section presents the connections between social justice and oppression. The last three sections—empowerment of social workers, values and principles to guide action, and a case study—are aimed at helping social workers translate knowledge and understanding of social and economic justice into effective strategies for social change.

DEFINING SOCIAL AND ECONOMIC JUSTICE AND INJUSTICE

The roots of social justice can be traced from the Settlement House Movement to the Rank and Film Movement, Civil Rights Movement, and contemporary struggles in the context of globalization (Finn & Jacobson, 2008). Yet throughout history, social justice as an idea has been highly contested, and it has taken on various meanings. As will be discussed later in this chapter, social justice is often seen through the eye of the beholder, based on his or her position in society. As Reisch (2002) points out, people march under the banner of social justice while promoting radically different ideas of what it is, with "liberals and conservatives, religious fundamentalists, and radical secularists all regard[ing] their causes as socially just" (p. 343).

While NASW clearly mandates in its Code of Ethics that, based on the profession's core value of social justice, "social workers promote social justice," it leaves social workers to face the immediate difficulty of understanding what social justice and social injustice mean. Although there is not yet one common, universally accepted definition of social justice and social workers are challenged to engage in their best critical thinking in order to determine its meaning in practice, several related definitions in the social work literature guide our thinking. The same is true for the concepts of economic justice and economic injustice.

Our immediate task is to define the following concepts that are essential in understanding the scope of this chapter: social justice, economic justice, social injustice, and economic injustice. With regard to the concepts of *social justice* and *economic justice* there are at least three dimensions inherent in these terms: 1) *an ideal and a real comparison*; 2) *an expressive value or a set of interrelated values*; and 3) *the institutional implementation of social justice and economic justice*. An example of *the ideal and the real* aspect of social justice and economic justice is the following definition:

> An ideal condition in which all members of a society have the same basic rights, protection, opportunities, obligations, and social [and economic] benefits. Implicit in this

concept is the notion that historical inequalities should be acknowledged and remedied through specific measures. A key social work value, social [economic] justice, entails advocacy to confront discrimination, oppression, and institutional inequities. (Barker, 2003, pp. 404–405)

That is, an ideal condition of basic rights for all but with the reality of historical inequalities. The real and the ideal is the basis for *the tragic moral choice* that we must make, recognizing that we believe in the ideal (similar rights) but must act against the real (historical inequalities). Aspects alluding to *an expressive value or a set of interrelated values* are found in defining social justice as the embodiment of fairness (reasonable treatment), equity (similar situations are dealt with similarly), and equality in the distribution of societal resources (Flynn, 1995). Economic justice parallels social justice in the economic sphere of society and social and economic obligations. One could argue that social justice and economic justice interface and complement each other and are one or more of these value aspects. Still the institutional implementation feature of social justice and economic justice underscores that social justice and economic justice go hand in hand but that they impact socioeconomic institutions and their settings in their own distinctive ways on behalf of the social and economic needs of people. A side-by-side institutional definition of social justice and economic justice says:

Social justice governs how social institutions deal fairly or justly with the social needs of people as far as opening access to what is good for individuals and groups. It also secures social rights and benefits in terms of such social provisions of well-being such as nutrition, housing, employment, education, and health care. Social justice also addresses historical and current forms of oppression and seeks legal and societal means to correct such abuses and establish an equal playing field for all regardless of ethnicity, gender, sexual orientation, social and economic class, age, and other related areas.

Economic justice encompasses moral principles of how to design economic institutions so that a person can earn a living, enter into social and economic contracts (monetary agreements to buy a car, house; obtain assets; e.g., stocks), exchange goods and services in order to produce an independent material foundation for economic sustenance. It also ensures education and employment to nurture people in learning and career development and, when a person is unable to provide for him/herself, economic justice fosters temporary welfare assistance until a person can function in a work environment. (Lum, personal communication, May 9, 2005)

In a real sense you might want to explain social justice and economic justice as separate but related concepts that embody the ideal state of what society ought to ensure for all people and the real situation of how society often tragically fails to meet these standards. We as social workers never stop to fight for the ideal but recognize and cope with the real. Basic to the struggle for social justice and economic justice are the core values that the social work profession believes and embodies such as fairness, equity, and equality. Through social policy, planning, legislation, and program implementation, social justice and economic justice reach social and economic institutions that are the vehicles for the delivery of just and fair programs for people in need.

Davis (2004) combines the elements of social and economic justice (rather than considering social justice and economic justice as separate but related concepts) into a global definition of social justice. He emphasizes the concepts of access as the independent variable and equity and fairness as the dependent variables. He states,

> Social justice is a basic value and desired goal in democratic societies and includes equitable and fair access to all social institutions, laws, resources, opportunities, rights, goods, and services for all groups and individuals without arbitrary limitations or barriers based on observations or interpretations of the value of differences in age, color, culture, physical or mental disability, education, gender, income, language, national origin, race, religion, or sexual orientation. (p. 236)

Such a comprehensive definition underscores the importance of recurring efforts to define and redefine social justice and economic justice periodically depending on the changing nature of the social context of our times as well as diversity and difference as inclusive factors in social justice.

However, in our definitions of social justice and economic justice we must touch on the concepts of *social injustice* and *economic injustice*. Parallel to the previously addressed complementary features of social justice and economic justice, definitions of social injustice and economic injustice have three common characteristics from the root word *injustice*: 1) *unfairness or biased and not impartial (favoring one side)*; 2) *injury or a violation of rights*; and 3) *wrong or a violation of legal rights*. A prime example of social injustice and economic injustice is the lack of civil acts afforded gays and lesbians in the United States, a population excluded from the 1964 Civil Rights Act. Since the great civil rights legislation of the 1960s passed over gay, lesbian, bisexual, and transgender people, the Stonewall riots of 1969 can be seen as the formal beginning of the civil rights movement for that population. A landmark victory for the movement was the elimination of homosexuality as a clinical pathology in the American Psychiatric Association's *Diagnostic and Statistical Manual of Mental Disorders* (1973). The gay civil rights movement has been visible and active for over 40 years as it struggled against social injustice and economic injustice.

A particular instance of social injustice and economic injustice against gays and lesbians is the don't ask, don't tell policy instituted by former President Bill Clinton, which prohibits gays and lesbians from serving openly in the U.S. armed forces. The policy illustrates how a partial attempt to bring about social and economic justice—a covert strategy to allow gays and lesbians to serve in the military—actually resulted in grave injustice. "Don't ask" meant that the military chain of command would avoid sexual orientation inquiry, but if sexual orientation were to be somehow disclosed by the particular gay or lesbian person or by other military peers, the military command would institute procedures to release that particular person from military service based on sexual orientation. Such military exclusion due to disclosure is a classic example of social injustice and economic injustice, because it is *unfair, biased, and not impartial* (favoring the military establishment rather than the particular person), *injurious or a violation of first amendment rights* under the U.S. Constitution, and *wrong or a violation of legal rights* to work on a job without discrimination. Moreover, the military don't ask, don't tell policy could have been challenged in the U.S. Supreme Court, but political, legal, and social forces were not in place for that to happen. President Barack Obama in the fall of 2009 was poised to work with the joint chiefs of staff and the U.S. Congress to rescind don't ask, don't tell policy and to allow gays and lesbians to serve openly in the U.S. military similar to the current policies of armed forces in the United Kingdom, France, Germany, and Israel. You may note that we were formal in our definitions of social justice and economic justice but more illustrative in our explanation of social injustice and economic injustice. However, we hope that you understand these four concepts and feel at home in your reading and discussion of the rest of this chapter.

In this chapter, three types of social justice are recognized—distributive, legal, and commutative—with distributive justice having been a long-standing concern of social work. Wakefield (1988) favors it as the organizing value of social work, a position that is taken in this chapter as well. However, if we are to connect the dots between social work's traditional notion that citizens have a right to have their needs met and the issues of multiculturalism, cultural competence, and oppression—a main contention of this chapter—then the distributive paradigm is not sufficient to encapsulate the complexities of injustice (Young, 1990). The concept of social justice needs to be about more than the distribution of income and other goods and services; "a concept of justice should begin with the concepts of domination and oppression" and should seek institutional remedies for "cultural sources of oppression, the manifestations of which are seen in racism, sexism, homophobia, ableism, etc." (van Wormer, 2004, p. 12).

CULTURAL COMPETENCE MEANS PROMOTING SOCIAL AND ECONOMIC JUSTICE

The definition of *cultural diversity*, as that term is used in this chapter, refers to differences between groups with distinctive characteristics and social identities based on culture, ethnicity, gender, age, sexual orientation, religion, ability, and class. Diversity is seen as inseparable from issues of oppression and social and economic justice. The integration of cultural diversity and social justice recognizes the historical and ongoing oppression and privilege that different social identity groups experience in the United States. It recognizes economic class as a prime indicator of oppression and, in fact, sees the creation of a class system based on difference as a function of oppression. It further recognizes the intersection and complex interaction of multiple social identities and a continuum of harm and privilege that these identities confer.

Multiculturalism thus refers to issues of representation and democratic inclusiveness with its roots in the relationship between politics and power, within the context of a historical past and a living present where racist exclusions were "calculated, brutally rational, and profitable" (Goldberg, 1993, p. 105). Thus, in order to be culturally competent, social workers need to learn how to "interrogate, challenge, and transform those cultural practices that sustain racism" and to "link the struggle for inclusion with relations of power in the broader society" (Giroux, 2000, p. 499). In sum, the definition of *culturally competent social work*, as that term is used in this chapter, begins with Lum's (1999) definition as "the set of knowledge and skills that a social worker must develop in order to be effective with multicultural clients" (p. 3) and includes as a requirement a commitment to promote social justice arising from a clear understanding of the impact of oppressive systems on individuals and families. Ultimately, the goal of culturally competent practice is to transform oppressive and unjust systems into nonoppressive and just alternatives (Gil, 1998). This means that, in an increasingly diverse and inequitable society, social workers face the challenge of not only understanding societal oppression but also translating that understanding into actions designed to facilitate social change for social justice. The challenges are daunting and require careful study, reflection, and action.

In the book *Teaching/Learning Anti-Racism: A Developmental Approach* (1997), the authors, Louise Derman-Sparks and Carol Brunson Phillips, provide the following parable:

> Once upon a time a woman, strolling along a riverbank, hears a cry for help and, seeing a drowning person, rescues him. She no sooner finishes administering artificial respiration when another cry requires another rescue. Again, she has only just helped the second person when a third call for help is heard. After a number of rescues, she begins to realize that she is pulling some people out of the river more than once. By this time the rescuer is exhausted and resentful, feeling that if people are stupid or careless enough to keep landing in the river, they can rescue themselves. She is too annoyed, tired, and frustrated to look around her.
>
> Shortly after, another woman walking along the river hears the cries for help and begins rescuing people. She, however, wonders why so many people are drowning in this river. Looking around her, she sees a hill where something seems to be pushing people off. Realizing this as the source of the drowning problem, she is faced with a difficult dilemma: If she rushes uphill, people presently in the river will drown; if she stays at the river pulling them out, more people will be pushed in. What can she do? (pp. 1–2)

The second woman's thoughts suggest that she may be questioning why people in the river share particular characteristics and if a selection process is underway. Consider that both women who witnessed people drowning in the river are social workers who want to help. If we define racism, sexism, heterosexism, classism, and other forms of oppression as the force on the hill, then this metaphor suggests three alternative solutions for social workers: 1) rescue people in trouble and return them to the oppressive conditions that caused the problem; 2) after rescuing people, teach them how to manage their problems so that if they "get pushed into the river again," they at least will not drown; and 3) organize with people to destroy the source of the problem (Derman-Sparks & Phillips, 1997, p. 2).

As stated in the introduction to this chapter, there is an inextricable connection between diversity and social justice. Thus, culturally competent practice requires choosing the third position. Social workers need to do more than just respond to the symptoms or consequences of oppressive conditions. They need to develop strategies for responding to the sources of oppression. Further, they must be willing to reevaluate their own role, on both personal and professional levels, in the continuation of that oppression. Social work must ultimately be about recognizing the problem and learning to understand and to eliminate it.

The metaphor presented in the story of the two women at the river raises several questions:

- If the river represents a situation of oppression or disadvantage, what is it like to be in the river? In other words, what are the conditions and processes of oppression, and how do they affect people's lives and life chances?

- Who are the people being pushed into the river? What characteristics do they have in common? What is the singular facet of their experience that puts them at risk?
- What people are *not* being pushed into the river? What are their common characteristics? How do they benefit from having others pushed into the river?
- If the force on the hill that is pushing people into the river represents racism, sexism, classism, heterosexism, ageism, and other systems of disadvantage, how does the force operate? How much of this is to be understood in individual, psychological terms, and how much as a "business-as-usual" patterning of institutional practices? What is the mix of factors that keep the force on the hill operating?
- What happens so that people who used to be in the river get out and then go up the hill to push people who look like them into the river?
- What role can social workers learn to take in helping the people pushed into the river?
- What organizational, collaborative, and advocative skills can social workers develop in order to eliminate the force that is pushing them into the river? How can social workers differentiate business-as-usual discrimination from behavior motivated out of personal bias?

In order to address these questions, social workers need to understand the centrality of race and racism as "a mode of human relations involving domination and exploitation" that, on an economic level, creates a class system (Gil, 1998, p. 103). They must further understand the complex interaction of racism with the systemic dynamics of oppressions based on gender, class, sexual orientation, age, ability, and the concept of multiple identities. Striving for such understandings is not easy. Gil also asserts the following:

> Understanding injustice and oppression and their sources—domination and exploitation—tends to be fraught with multidimensional existential dilemmas and emotional stress, for it implies the need for people to make significant changes in their ways of life, work, and patterns of social relations. It means therefore exchanging the "bliss of ignorance" for the burden of holistic social knowledge along with difficult new choices, conflicts, and fears. (p. 130)

A PLACE TO BEGIN: AWARENESS, REFLECTION, CRITICAL THINKING

In our efforts to understand diversity and social justice issues and to develop cultural competence aimed at social change, we must start with ourselves. We as social workers need to conscientiously engage in a process of becoming aware of our personal values and beliefs about social justice, reflect on where those values and beliefs originated, and engage in critical thinking about the implications of our current perspective.

We often hear the expression *life is not fair*, especially when something bad has happened to us or to someone we care about. The expression is perhaps a manifestation of a belief that life is, indeed, not fair. Is it fair that our destinies are often shaped and determined by accident of birth (i.e., by race, gender, class, abilities, country of origin, etc.)? A more relevant question, when considering issues of social justice, might be: Is life *just*? The following exercises are aimed at individual and small-group exploration of issues related to those questions.

Reflection Exercises

Take some time to answer the following questions. Write down your thoughts so you can look at them later and also discuss them with others.

1. What are rights? What do people have a right to (i.e., what should people get just because they are human beings)?

2. What are privileges (i.e., what do people deserve because they have earned it)?

   Now consider the following more focused questions.

3. Is it fair to take (e.g., through taxes) from one group and give to another group? When is it fair and when is it not fair? Does it have to do with rights or privileges? When is it a form of justice, and when is it an infringement on people's freedom?

4. If there is a situation in which the goods and services produced are inadequate to satisfy everyone's desire for them, on what basis or according to what principles can they be distributed justly? For example, if you believe that everyone has a right to food and there is an inadequate supply, how do you distribute it? If you believe that having food is a privilege, then what do people have to do to earn it? And what should be done when people who have not earned it get it and those who earn it do not get it?

5. If there is a situation in which the goods and services produced are adequate to satisfy everyone's desire for them, on what basis or according to what principles can they be distributed justly?

Reflection and Discussion

Now take a moment to read your responses and reflect on them. Do any themes emerge? Are you surprised by any of your responses? What beliefs do you think underlie your answers? Where do those beliefs come from? How comfortable are you with your responses?

In a small group of three to four of your peers, discuss each of the questions. Hear how others respond, and compare their responses with yours. Be sure to talk about where your beliefs come from.

Classroom Exercises

After reflecting on and discussing the previous questions, use the following two exercises to help you think further about your perspectives on justice and to identify the principles upon which you judge whether a situation is fair.

Exercise 1. Provide a bag of small candy bars such as those you can buy at Halloween (or you might just imagine that you have a bag of candy bars) to the students of a class. Allow small groups of four to six students, depending on class size, to discuss how to distribute the candy to the class according to what they think is just. Each group will present their proposal (if the candy is imaginary) or actually distribute the candy according to the distributive system they have developed. If the candy is actually distributed, it will need to be collected for the next group to implement their distribution plan. After each group has presented their method of distribution, discuss the following questions:

1. On what was your distribution system based (e.g., everyone should get an equal amount)? Should distribution be based on need (e.g., who did not eat breakfast this morning)? Should distribution be based on what people deserve according to a merit system?

2. Which system would you consider to be the most fair?

3. Which system would you consider to be the most just?

4. Might there be a situation when one system would be more fair and just than in another situation? How do you decide?

Exercise 2. Read the following case scenario and then discuss the questions that follow.

A staff association at a major university is calling for a "sick out" to call attention to a number of their demands. One of the demands is that all staff getting salaries up to $60,000 should get an increase of $321 per month.

1. Would you consider this to be a just (fair) demand? Why or why not?

2. Would it be just (fair) to give the same amount to a person who has been working at the university for a short time (say 1 year) at a salary of $59,500 as to a person who has been working there for more than 10 years and still only makes $15,000 a year?

3. On what basis do you think the cutoff point (in this case, $60,000) should be set? Why not set it at $30,000 or $35,000? On what basis would you make such a decision?

4. What do you think about demanding a monthly increase for workers earning salaries in the bottom quintile?

The intent of the discussion exercises is to stimulate awareness of your own perspective and the diverse meanings of social justice. The point is that, when discussing issues and strategies related to promoting social and economic justice, it is important to understand how the term *justice* is being used and to have guiding principles from which to make decisions about justice claims. We need to struggle with the question of justice. What is it? Is justice equality? Is justice having freedom? Whether we are aware of them or not, each of us believes in certain principles about and theories of justice. And, as Figure 3.1 illustrates, our perspective on what is just and fair is often related to our own position in society.

SOCIAL JUSTICE THEORY

As the previous section aimed to illustrate, we need to be rigorous in our thinking about what social justice means and how to go about achieving it if we are to take the social work mission seriously. Many of us have experienced the phenomenon of finger-pointing, both within the profession and with our student peers, with some

FIGURE 3.1 | FAIRNESS FROM DIFFERENT PERSPECTIVES

people claiming to be for social justice while others accuse them of not being for social justice. A misperception or myth exists among social workers that we all mean the same thing when we use the term *social justice*. We as social workers need to develop a knowledge base and framework for understanding social justice as an organizing value of our profession. We must begin by examining and critically challenging our personal perspectives about justice, developing a knowledge base about social justice perspectives and principles that are coherent and congruent with social work values, and translating these understandings into effective strategies and actions to promote justice and fairness.

What follows is a brief review of a few principles and contemporary social justice theories that are prevalent in the literature, with a focus on the different types of social justice and different perspectives about the type of justice called *distributive justice*. This section aims to highlight the complexities of social justice issues that point to the need for critical thinking and continuous knowledge development as professionals.

TYPES OF SOCIAL JUSTICE

When we speak about social justice, it is important to recognize that conceptually there are different types of justice: distributive, legal, and commutative. The types are based on the social contract tradition that has prevailed among political philosophers from Hobbes, Locke, Kant, and Rousseau to John Rawls and Robert Nozick. The three types of justice are illustrated in Figure 3.2. When looking at the contract involving what society owes the person, we are talking about distributive justice. When looking at the contract involving what the person owes to society, we are talking about legal justice. When looking at the contract between persons—what we owe each other—we are talking about commutative justice.

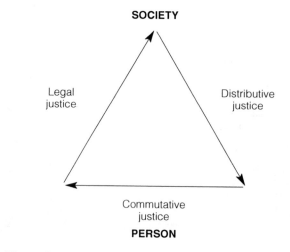

FIGURE 3.2 | THREE TYPES OF JUSTICE

DISTRIBUTIVE JUSTICE AS AN ORGANIZING FRAMEWORK FOR SOCIAL WORK

Although social work is concerned about all three types of social justice, Wakefield (1988) argues that the organizing value of social work is distributive justice and that Rawls's particular perspective (described later in this section) on distributive justice provides the most coherent framework for the social work profession. Distributive justice has particular relevance for the professional role of advocating for social and economic justice. The following definition of justice for social work, proposed by Beverly and McSweeney (1987), emphasizes its distributive quality:

> Justice ... means fairness in the relationships between people as these relate to the possession and/or acquisition of resources based on some kind of valid claim to a share of those resources.... the justice or injustice of a particular policy or situation is determined by looking at the fairness of the distribution of resources in relation to the claims or demands made for those resources. (p. 5)

For social workers, the distribution of goods other than political or economic resources, such as health services, education, and leisure, is within the realm of social justice. To begin thinking about distributive justice, do the following exercise.

A Beginning Exercise

Read the following statistics and then reflect on the questions that follow. It is suggested that you write your reactions on paper before engaging in classroom discussion.

Imagine a society in which the top fifth of the population owned 50.4% of the income and the lowest fifth owned only 3.4% of the income[1] and a society in which the top 10% of the population owned 80% of the wealth while 80% scrambled over the remaining 20% of the wealth.[2]

1. Is such disparity just or unjust?
2. Can you think of any situation or condition in which this kind of disparity might be just?
3. What principles would be used to conclude that such disparities are, in fact, just?

Whereas most social workers would jump to the quick conclusion that the disparities given in the exercise are definitely unjust, others might consider that their justness or unjustness could depend on certain qualifying conditions, and still others might even say that they are actually just. How do we account for such differences of perspectives, even among social workers? The following brief overview of four theories of distributive justice will illustrate how each would judge the justness of disparities in wealth differently. The first three—utilitarian, libertarian, and egalitarian—are prescriptive, not descriptive; that is, they present a case for what social justice should be or how each theorist would want us to define social justice. They do not describe the situation as it is now; that is, they do not discuss what the state of their society and the rest of the world is in relation to achieving any semblance of social justice as they define it. The fourth theory, the racial contract, is critical in understanding social work's role of promoting social justice and economic justice. The racial contract perspective of distributive justice is descriptive, in that it explains the inequities of the actual social contract, and normative, in that analysis of the way things actually are is used normatively to point to reform.

UTILITARIAN PERSPECTIVE

The major proponent of the utilitarian theory was John Stuart Mill (1863, as reprinted in Sterba, 1992). The key question from the utilitarian perspective is, "What distribution of goods, what principles of justice, what ascription of rights are such that their acceptance is in the general interest?" Justice is arrived at by weighing the relative benefits and harms of a situation or condition and determining what maximizes the greatest good for the greatest number of people.

So, from a utilitarian perspective, it may be determined that social justice exists even if some people have no rights met while others have all their rights met as long as it is determined that it is for the common good. Utilitarian justice would tend to produce a distribution of goods and services similar to a Bell curve (Figure 3.3).

The "common good," however, is open to varied definitions, and the definition determines whether one believes a situation is just or not. For example, some people believe that it would not serve the common good if some people are provided for when they can provide for themselves; on the other hand, others argue that when some people are not provided for, the common good is not served because there may be unrest or because it harms us morally as individuals and as a society.

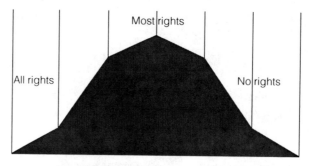

FIGURE 3.3 | DISTRIBUTION OF GOODS BASED ON UTILITARIAN JUSTICE

LIBERTARIAN PERSPECTIVE

In contrast to the utilitarian perspective, the libertarian position advanced by Robert Nozick (1974) is based on the principle that the distribution of resources occurs by means of a natural and social lottery. Thus, this theory is considered to be basically amoral and based on a description of the social contract as it occurs naturally. According to the libertarian perspective, people hold certain rights by entitlement, and justice consists in the widest possible latitude of freedom from coercion in what they accumulate and what they dispose of and when. From this perspective, it is good to give to others, and charity is considered a virtue. However, in a just society each person has total freedom to determine how much, to whom, and when to give. No institution or person should interfere with that freedom.

When a segment of the population appears to be unjustly treated and lacking in access to goods and services, the libertarian perspective argues that we are only looking at one slice of history and that the long-term historical picture would reveal that that same population, at another point in time, may have occupied a privileged position. In other words, the natural social lottery is at work, and there is an inherent justice to it over the long term.

EGALITARIAN PERSPECTIVE

Egalitarianism, developed by John Rawls (1971) and based on Locke's theory of social contract, maintains that designing a just society needs to be done under a veil of ignorance—that is, with the sense that none of us would know in advance what our position in that society would be, and thus we would all have a stake in avoiding extreme inequalities at the outset.

Rawls developed two egalitarian principles upon which a just society would be based. His principles rule out justifying inequalities in order to achieve a greater common good (utilitarianism) or to maintain individual freedom (libertarianism). The first principle requires that basic liberties must be equal because citizens of a just society have the same basic rights to freedom, to fair equality of opportunity, to access to goods and services, and to self-respect. The second principle asserts that although the distribution of income and wealth need not be equal, any inequalities in power, wealth, and other resources must not exist unless they work to the absolute benefit of the worst-off members of society.

Thus, from an egalitarian perspective, in contrast to the libertarian view, redistribution of resources is a moral obligation. The unmet needs that should be redressed first are those of the least-well-off people. This means that, in order to provide genuine equality of opportunity, society must give more attention to those with fewer native assets and to those born into the less favorable social positions. According to egalitarian principles, then, greater resources might be spent, for example, on the education of the less- rather than the more-intelligent students in our schools, at least in the earlier years, in order to ensure equality of opportunity in life.

THE RACIAL CONTRACT

Although the three contemporary distributive justice theories discussed so far serve as useful tools for social work, they have serious limitations in terms of explaining why certain groups of people consistently get less justice, and they do not explain the phenomenon of oppression. The racial contract (Mills, 1997) is a perspective that provides a way of making a connection between contemporary mainstream theories and the injustices prevalent in the United States and the rest of the world. The racial contract perspective is based on the social contract tradition, as are the others. However, Mills's viewpoint is different in that he sees the notion of the social contract as being the basis of Western democratic societies as, in fact, a myth. He contends that the real basis of Western societies is a "racial contract." The basic difference between Mills's perspective of social justice and other perspectives is that the peculiar social contract to which he refers is not a contract between everybody (as in "we the people"), but a contract between just the people who count and the people who really are people (i.e., were considered to be fully human when the United States was founded—"we the White people," "justice for 'just us'").

Utilitarians, libertarians, and egalitarians use the social contract as a normative tool—to present an ideal social contract that explains how a just society would be formed, ruled by a moral government, and regulated by a defensible moral code. Mills's usage of the social contract is again different: he uses it not merely normatively but descriptively to explain the actual genesis of the society, how government functions, and people's moral psychology. The racial contract thus explains how an unjust, exploitative society, ruled by an oppressive government and regulated by an immoral code, came into existence.

According to this perspective, it is crucial to understand what the original and continuing social contract actually was and is, so that we can correct for it in constructing the ideal contract toward which social work can then strive. Mills points out that the social contract has always consisted of formal and informal agreements between the members of one subset of humans who are designated as White and are thus considered to be full persons. The remaining subset of humans who are designated as "non-White" and of a different and inferior moral status of subpersons are not a consenting party to the contract but the objects rather than the subjects of the agreement. The moral and legal rules normally regulating the behavior of Whites in their dealings with one another do not apply in dealings with non-Whites or apply only in a qualified form. Mills's main point is that the general purpose of the social contract, as it has been and is, is always the differential privileging of Whites as a group with respect to non-Whites as a group. From the beginning, then, race is in no way an "afterthought" or a "deviation" from ostensibly raceless Western ideals of the social contract but rather a central shaping constituent of those ideals.

The racial contract makes a strong claim to being an actual historical fact as Mills describes specific subsidiary contracts designed for different modes of exploiting the resources and peoples of the rest of the world for Europe, including the expropriation contract (which granted Europeans dominion over all territories of the world, not by virtue of any conquest of them, but as a right acquired simply by "discovery"), the slavery contract, and the colonial contract.

The racial contract is a conceptual bridge between two areas now largely segregated from each other. On the one hand, there is the world of mainstream philosophy (including the utilitarian, libertarian, and egalitarian theories of social justice) that focuses discussions of justice and rights in the abstract. On the other hand, there is the world of First Nations Peoples, African Americans, and political thought of the global South that has historically focused on issues of conquest, imperialism, colonialism, race and racism, slavery, jim crow, reparations, apartheid, Afrocentrism, and so on.

In order to endorse or emulate an ideal social contract, the nonideal contract as it exists needs to be demystified and condemned. So, the point of analyzing the injustices as they exist both in the past and in the present—predominantly along race and gender lines—is to explain and expose the inequities of the social contract as it actually is in order to see through the theories and moral justifications offered in defense of them. Just as Mills's *The Racial Contract* (1997) provides a framework for analyzing the social contract related to race, Carole Pateman's *The Sexual Contract* (1988) provides a similar analysis of how the social contract has been based on gender. The point is that analysis of the way things are does normative work for us by enabling us to understand the social contract's actual history and how its values and concepts have functioned to rationalize oppression, in order to reform them.

DIFFERING PERSPECTIVES AND SOCIAL WORK

Differing popular perspectives exist about what social justice is or should be. So, when we say that social workers need to see social problems and individual troubles through a social justice lens, it is important to recognize that there are different lenses that provide differing views on what is just. It is often proposed that the egalitarian theory of justice is closest to traditional values and ethics of social work. Wakefield (1988) supports that view by arguing that "social work strives to ensure that no person is deprived of a fair minimum level of those basic social goods to which everyone is entitled" (p. 187) and supports Rawls's inclusion of self-respect in the list of social goods. Yet, there is some empirical evidence that social workers, perhaps holding to egalitarian principles as the ideal, may tend to operate from a utilitarian perspective (Conrad, 1988; Reisch & Taylor, 1983).

Terms such as *cost-benefit analysis* and "triage" strategies related to managed care realities might point to a utilitarian approach in practice. The racial contract perspective provides a conceptual tool for the integration of diversity, social and economic justice, and the impact of oppression.

The social work profession continues to struggle with the following questions: Which perspectives are compatible with what social work is about? Which justice principles should be adopted to provide guidance for our profession? The combination of the racial contract and the egalitarian perspective merits serious consideration for the profession. Whereas the racial contract explains and describes injustice, the egalitarian perspective can point the way for reform.

HUMAN RIGHTS: THE BEDROCK OF SOCIAL JUSTICE

Human rights are universal guarantees to basic individual and group obligatory life issues that transcend national and international boundaries. Human rights encompass rights in general as well as rights related to particular protections and humane treatment. They are a major concern of the United Nations and a particular passionate interest of former President Jimmy Carter who championed human rights during and after his presidency in the late 1970s. The United Nations (1987) defines human rights as those rights that are inherent in our nature and without which we cannot live as human beings. Human rights are basic for a life in which the inherent dignity and work of each person receives respect and protection. Human rights are universal and apply to every person without discrimination. Rights corresponding to human needs have to be upheld and fostered.

A human rights perspective provides a universal and in several ways less ambiguous approach than the other constructions of social justice in that it provides the legal mandate for fulfilling human needs, a conceptual frame for social work practice, and a more comprehensive and defined set of guidelines for promoting social and economic justice (Finn & Jacobson, 2008; Ife, 1997, 2001; Reichert, 2003; Witkin, 1998; Wronka, 2007). Support for the human rights perspective can be found in the joint statement of the International Federation of Social Workers and the International Association of Schools of Social Work, *Ethics in Social Work, Statement of Principles,* which states that "the principles of human rights and social justice are fundamental to social work" (IFSW, 2004). In addition, as stated at the beginning of this chapter, CSWE (2008) requires schools of social work to advance human rights and social and economic justice and to recognize the global interconnections of oppression.

Social work as a profession is grounded on humanitarian and democratic ideals with a focus on meeting human needs and developing human potential and resources. This focus on human needs shapes a professional conviction that the fundamental nature of these needs means that their being met is not a matter of choice but an imperative of basic justice. This imperative of basic justice applies to all humanity. A 1992 United Nations publication, *Teaching and Learning about Human Rights: A Manual for Schools of Social Work and the Social Work Profession,* moves the discussion of diversity and social justice to a consideration of human rights as the organizing principle for professional practice (p. 9). A transition from an orientation of meeting human needs to one of affirming human rights is necessary because substantive needs must be met, making the idea of human rights a powerful social construct to fulfill human needs (Wronka, 1998). The discussion that follows revolves around the connections between affirming human rights and promoting social and economic justice from a global perspective.

From a human rights perspective the social work profession's focus on meeting substantive human needs is inseparable from the search for and realization of positive rights and entitlements and, in fact, the IFSW has called social work a *human rights profession* (Wronka, 2007, p. 8). Working within different political systems, social workers around the globe uphold and defend the rights of their clients while attempting to meet their needs. Because social workers are often employed as agents of powerful institutions or agencies, many are placed in a precarious role due to their duty to be a loyal employee and to serve their clients. Culturally competent social workers, as they strive to eliminate oppression and promote social justice, are often required

> [T]o mediate between the people and state and other authorities, to champion particular causes, and to provide protection when state action for the public good threatens the rights and freedoms of particular persons or groups.... as a bridging profession, social work has to be conscious of its values and possess a solid knowledge base, not least in the field of human rights, to guide it in many conflicting situations throughout its practice. While social workers through their actions may well reinforce the rights of clients, faulty judgment can lead them to jeopardize those rights. Viewing its work from a global human rights perspective helps the profession by providing a sense of unity and solidarity, without losing sight of the local perspectives, conditions and needs which constitute the framework within which social workers operate. (United Nations, 1992, p. 9)

Human rights and social and economic justice have been linked together in social work education curriculum core competencies. The competency on advance human rights and social and economic justice states,

> Each person, regardless of position in society, has basic human rights, such as freedom, safety, privacy, an adequate standard of living, health care, and education. Social workers recognize the global interconnections of oppression and are knowledgeable about theories of justice and strategies to promote human and civil rights. (CSWE, 2008, Educational Policy 2.1.5)

Human rights are inseparable from social work theory, values and ethics, and practice. They are inseparable from culturally competent practice. Advocacy for such rights must therefore be an integral part of social work. In countries under authoritative regimes, such advocacy can have serious consequences for social work professionals.

The direct knowledge that social workers have of the conditions of vulnerable populations makes them more conscious than other professionals that their concerns are closely linked to respect for human rights. Social workers understand that the full realization of civil and political rights is not possible without enjoyment of economic, social, and cultural rights. And, in order to achieve lasting progress in the implementation of human rights, there must be effective national and international policies of economic and social development.

WHAT RIGHTS ARE HUMAN RIGHTS?

Three generations of human rights are set forth in the Universal Declaration of Human Rights, which was adopted and proclaimed by the United Nations General Assembly in December 1948. The first generation, *negative rights*, represents civil and political rights as set forth in articles 2–21. These are rights devised to ensure freedom from any curtailment of individual liberty. The second generation, *positive rights*, is aimed at ensuring social justice, freedom from want, and participation in the social, economic, and cultural aspects of life as set forth in articles 22–27. The third generation, *collective rights* (article 28), expounds that everyone is entitled to a social and international order in which the rights and freedoms set forth in the Declaration can be fully realized. The Declaration, with its three generations, combines the antioppression social work imperative with its calling to promote social and economic justice. In an increasingly interdependent world, recognition of the interdependence of the three human rights generations is increasing, and the struggle for social and economic justice is being seen as one of international solidarity. The 1992 United Nations manual for social workers advises the following:

> The evolution from a defensive stand against oppression to an affirmation of the right to satisfaction of material and non-material human needs and equitable participation in the production and distribution of resources is the logical outcome of an increasing socio-political consciousness and economic development mainly, but not exclusively, in industrialized nations. In developing countries the sheer proportion of need, and possibly of exploitation, lead to the collective vision of the right to social and economic development beyond the personal level to the national and regional levels, with a system of international solidarity for development as its ultimate aim. (p. 6)

THE GLOBAL CONTEXT IN WHICH SOCIAL WORKERS ADVOCATE FOR HUMAN RIGHTS AND SOCIAL JUSTICE

The 1992 United Nations manual for social workers emphasizes that human rights and social work have to be considered within the context faced by the majority of people in the world. The manual offers the following poignant contextual conditions:

- It is estimated that in the 1980s alone, more human beings lost their lives as a result of economic and social deprivation than those who perished in World War II.
- Countless people have been killed and tortured or have disappeared in a world subjected to domination and oppression. Exploitative and oppressive systems and structures give rise to dictatorships and authoritarian regimes under which millions become victims of human rights violations as the price of their struggle for freedom and survival.
- Each day, 40,000 children die from malnutrition and diseases including AIDS, lack of clean water, and inadequate sanitation.[3]
- Of a population of about 6 billion, 900 million adults are illiterate, 10 million are homeless, and 15 million are refugees. Of the 15 million refugees, at least 75% are women and children. In some developing countries, women and children constitute 90% of the refugee population.[4]

- Women are prominent in the statistics of poverty and deprivation. Two-thirds of the world's illiterate people are women.[5] Maternal mortality rates are high in most developing countries. An African woman, for example, has 1 chance in 21 of dying in childbirth; an Asian woman, 1 chance in 51; and a South American woman, 1 chance in 73. In contrast, a North American woman has 1 chance in over 6,000.[6]
- The crisis is deepening. Military spending is about 15% of gross national product in industrial as well as developing countries. In the early 1990s, the World Bank estimated that the staggering debt burden of the developing countries (including the debts of Eastern Europe) amounting to $1.3 trillion would increase substantially in the near future.[7] (pp. 10–11)

Hope exists for improvement in the implementation of the human rights instruments that guide global human rights and an ever-growing international consciousness and solidarity. Social workers have a role to play in strengthening such solidarity and ensuring that the principles preserved in the international human rights instruments are "gradually translated into reality, paving the way for a world in which people's most urgent and legitimate needs are satisfied" (United Nations, 1992, p. 11).

It has been argued that social work has been a human rights profession from its conception due to its basic tenet that every human being has intrinsic value and its mission to promote equitable social structures. Yet, the IFSW and the IASSW believe that greater knowledge and understanding of human rights is needed to improve the actions and interventions of social work professionals in advancing social and economic justice and eliminating oppression. As these two bodies state,

> [S]ocial workers work with their clients on a variety of levels: the micro level of individual and family; the meso level of community; and the macro level of society—nationally and internationally. Concern for human rights must be manifested by social workers at all levels and at all times. (United Nations, 1992, p. 3)

Wronka (2007) maintains that human rights documents are the "tools that can help create a human rights culture, which is a lived awareness of human rights principles from the global to the local" (p. 24). A short summary of the basic instruments concerning human rights, with the dates of adoption by the United Nations General Assembly, is included here. It illustrates the connection between culturally competent social work practice and its requisite commitment to promote social justice and human rights.[8] Social workers need to become familiar with the documents and the specialized agencies, United Nations bodies, and mechanisms for implementing the human rights mandates.

Instruments Providing General Protection:

- The Universal Declaration of Human Rights (1948)
- The Covenants on Human Rights (1966)
- The International Covenant on Civil and Political Rights
- Right to life, liberty, and security
- Right not to be subjected to torture and cruel, inhuman, or degrading treatment or punishment
- Prohibition of slavery
- Right not to be arbitrarily detained

- Right to freedom of expression, religion, assembly, and association, including trade union membership
- Right to freedom of movement and residence
- Right to vote through universal suffrage
- Right to a fair trial
- Rights of minorities to protection
- The International Covenant on Economic, Social, and Cultural Rights
- Right to work
- Right to social security
- Right to protection of the family
- Right to an adequate standard of living
- Right to education
- Right to health
- Right to join trade unions

Instruments Providing Particular Protection

- International Convention on the Elimination of All Forms of Racial Discrimination (1965)
- Convention on the Elimination of All Forms of Discrimination against Women (1979)
- Convention against Torture and Other Cruel, Inhuman, and Degrading Treatment or Punishment (1987)
- Convention on the Rights of the Child (1989)
- International Convention on the Protection of the Rights of All Migrant Workers and Members of Their Families (1990)

Rules Regarding Detention and Treatment of Offenders

- Standard Minimum Rules for the Treatment of Prisoners (1955)
- Principles of Medical Ethics (1982)
- Standard Minimum Rules for the Administration of Juvenile Justice (1985)

Other Human Rights Instruments

- Declaration on the Rights of Mentally Retarded Persons (1971)
- Declaration on the Protection of Women and Children in Armed Conflicts (1974)
- Declaration on the Elimination of All Forms of Religious Intolerance (1981)
- Declaration on the Right to Development (1986)

SOCIAL JUSTICE AND OPPRESSION: MAKING THE CONNECTIONS

The social justice theories briefly described in the previous section provide a foundation for understanding the complexity of our notions about what social justice is and what social justice should be. Analysis of notions about social justice point to their race- and gender-based nature. The questions posed about social justice at the beginning of this chapter were, "Is life fair?" "Is life just?" In this section, we turn to the related question: Justice and fairness … for whom? While a human rights perspective would answer that justice and fairness should be for all, in reality that is not the case. In this section, we discuss how the struggle for social and economic justice must be explicitly connected with an understanding of oppression.

WHO IS ENTITLED TO JUSTICE? THE CONCEPT OF MORAL EXCLUSION

At the beginning of this chapter, some exercises were suggested to promote self-reflection and examination of our personal beliefs about social justice and a critical assessment of them within the context of contemporary theories. Grounded in the notion of racial (and sexual) exclusion as the basis of Western society's social contract, we can now look at how we also have beliefs about which people should be treated justly. The concept of moral exclusion (Opotow, 1990; Schwartz, 2007) provides a useful framework for understanding personal beliefs in relation to different groups in society.

Moral exclusion occurs when persons or groups are perceived as being outside the boundary in which values, rules, and considerations of fairness apply—that is, outside the boundaries of social justice. Persons outside our moral boundaries appear expendable or undeserving, and thus harming them appears acceptable, appropriate, or just. The process of categorizing groups negatively and excluding them from the realm of acceptable norms or values is linked to stereotypes and prejudicial attitudes related to ethnocentrism. It is linked to the notion that the social contract has always been and is an exclusionary one.

Although seldom conscious of them, we all have beliefs about which people should be treated justly, and the broadness or narrowness of our moral boundaries is influenced by prevailing cultural norms (e.g., it is no longer considered acceptable in the United States to own people as slaves or to make interracial marriages illegal, but it is generally considered acceptable to exclude gays and lesbians from certain benefits such as partner benefits and the right to marry).

The exclusion of an out-group from the norms of fairness is a cognitive, affective, and behavioral phenomenon that enables otherwise considerate people to engage in self-serving behavior or inaction in everyday situations in order to gain benefits to themselves even though at injurious costs to others. We live in a world where certain groups of people benefit from an implicit and explicit contract that disadvantages other groups. At the same time, most people who benefit from the contract do not think about it or, if they do think about it, consider it to be just the way things are rather than as the outcome of a history of political oppression (Mills, 1997).

The concept of moral exclusion provides a tool for making obvious one's own personal processes of excluding certain people from the boundaries of fairness. A considerable body of research exists on moral exclusion, disengagement practices that make it possible to justify exclusion, and antidotes to exclusion (Keetsm, 2001; Opotow, Gerson, & Woodside, 2005). Analyzing one's own moral boundaries within the context of oppression theory, along with research evidence of antidotes to marginalization, suggests strategies for change.

OPPRESSION AND ITS COMMON ELEMENTS

The racial contract perspective discussed earlier reveals that some people are seen as expendable or undeserving and are thus excluded from the realm of social justice. The process of categorizing groups negatively, and thus justifying their exclusion, is linked to stereotypes and prejudicial attitudes related to ethnocentrism. The result is a condition of oppression. Oppression is defined as a situation in which one segment of the population acts to prevent another segment of the population from attaining access to resources or that acts to inhibit or make them less than in some way in order to dominate them (Bulhan, 1985). It is generally understood as "the domination of subordinate groups in society by a powerful (politically, economically, socially and culturally) group" (Mullaly, 2002, p. 27). Oppression is a multidimensional social phenomenon, a dynamic and relational group-based concept that is not accidental—though usually unintentional—and that, once integrated into societal institutions and individual consciousness, comes to permeate almost all relations and, depending on the circumstances, involves all individuals in the role of both oppressor and oppressed at one time or another (Gil, 1998; Mullaly, 2002).

Persons who have been and are excluded from the realm of the norms and values of social justice include people of color; women; gay, lesbian, bisexual, and transgendered persons; elderly people; and people with disabilities, among others. Although the conditions and manifestations of oppression may vary, as well as each person's unique experiences of its effects, common elements characterize all oppression. The definition in the previous paragraph, for example, is one that fits all oppressions. In addition, the condition of oppression always involves power and advantage, which are granted to certain people and denied to others based on the notion of the "other" that is different from what is considered to be the norm. The defined norm (White, male, heterosexual) is the standard of rightness wherein all others are judged in relation to it. The "other" is not only different from the norm but also believed to be inferior and deviant, which justifies advantage for those who fit the norm and disadvantage for the "other."

Power is an essential factor in all oppression. Racism, sexism, and heterosexism are not personal prejudices based on stereotypes; they include social and economic power as an essential part of the equation that makes the difference between talking about prejudices and discrimination (which we all engage in) and a system of advantage that confers economic, social, judicial, and political power on people who fit the "norm." To understand oppression, we can look at indicators in any of those areas. For example, in the political arena, how many senators are black, women, or openly homosexual?

Another common element of oppression is that all oppressions are held in place by ideology and the use or threat of violence. The ideology on which Mills (1997) contends that the racial contract, a contract of oppression, is based is that of racial superiority (i.e., White supremacy); the ideology on which sexual oppression is based is that of gender superiority; and the ideology on which homosexual oppression is based is that of heterosexual superiority and morality. With an ideology of superiority as its foundation, violence is used to enforce and maintain all oppressions. The violence may be physical and direct (lynching, rape and battering, gay bashing), or it may be personal and psychological, such as name-calling. It may be indirect, or it may be institutionalized and characterized by indicators such as differential poverty rates, the predominance of men of color in the criminal justice system and on death row, and the reality of police brutality.

Another element that is common to all oppressions is that they are institutionalized, which means that racism, sexism, and heterosexism are built into the norms, traditions, laws, and policies of a society so that even those who have nonracist, nonsexist, and nonheterosexist beliefs are compelled to act otherwise. Institutionalized racism ensures that Whites, males, and heterosexuals benefit regardless of the intentions of individuals in those institutions. Pinderhughes (1989) writes about how institutional racism ensures that Whites benefit and exonerates them from responsibility while at the same time blaming people of color. She points out that there is considerable resistance against comprehending the institutional aspect of racism and that the process of understanding its systemic nature can be very painful, especially for Whites who have seen themselves as different from Whites whom they view as racists. She further writes about how it is particularly devastating for White people who have been involved in civil rights activities to face the implication that they, along with other Whites, could be the beneficiaries of racism. There is a sense of injury that stems not only from the recognition of themselves as trapped in the systemic process of racism that benefits them and exploits people of color but also from the realization that, although for many people of color this reality has been obvious, for them it has heretofore been obscure.

IMPLICATIONS FOR SOCIAL WORKERS

If the mission of social work is truly to promote social and economic justice, we must translate that commitment into culturally relevant and nonoppressive social work practice. Social workers need to do their own work in relation to understanding their own boundaries of moral exclusion and developing a stance of inclusion, in which all people are entitled to the same values, rules, and considerations of fairness. Further, social workers need to understand the elements of oppression and how they operate and translate that understanding into antioppression practice. Van Voorhis (1998) suggests that practitioners need to integrate the following elements into their direct practice with clients: knowledge about oppression; self-awareness and acceptance of one's own multiple identities and position in relation to power and privilege; knowledge about the psychosocial effects of oppression for people in all marginalized groups; and skills in listening to clients' stories, assessing the psychosocial effects of oppression on clients, intervening to enhance identity and change oppressive social conditions, and evaluating practice interventions by monitoring client progress related to empowerment outcomes.

BECOMING EMPOWERED TO UNDERSTAND AND PRACTICE CHANGE STRATEGIES AND SKILLS

Any meaningful incorporation of social justice principles into social work practice requires an ongoing examination of the questions of difference, power, and oppression (Saleebey, 2006). It is necessary but not sufficient for social work practice with social justice as its primary goal to recognize cultural differences; it must also recognize and address both difference and dominance dimensions of life experience (Reed, Newman, Suarez, & Lewis, 1997). This means that translating the value of social justice into practice requires that social workers align themselves with those who have experienced the world from positions of oppression and challenge the practices and conditions that reproduce inequality (Finn & Jacobson, 2008). The journey to becoming culturally competent, which means working for social justice, is a daunting task and the journey toward employing effective strategies for social change not for the faint of heart. Empowerment theory and empowerment process help us work with clients who have been marginalized and excluded from the boundaries of fairness and justice. Social workers need equally to engage in an empowerment journey for themselves as well.

EMPOWERMENT PROCESS[9]

Dictionary definitions of *empowerment* include phrases such as "to give power or authority to," "to authorize," "to enable or permit," and "to license." When social workers become empowered to advocate for social justice, they affirm the authority that already belongs to them as human beings and as citizens. This power is both internal, in terms of how they experience their own efficacy, and external, in terms of the power they have to persuade others in interpersonal encounters and relationships. This power enables them to protest injustice and to seek alternatives to oppression at the levels of organization, community, country, and world.

The theoretical foundation of empowerment is *transformation* from inside oneself, between oneself and others, and in political liberation. It rests upon the connection of the personal and the political and from the notion of learned hopefulness (Parsons, 2008). Empowerment is thus seen as a process of discovering within oneself and in others the capacity to bring about change. Empowerment means accepting personal responsibility to act. As social workers realize their power, they become free to transform themselves and to discover untapped strengths. Their individual actions of protest and creativity create a ripple effect that empowers others. At the heart of the empowerment process is the phenomenon of helping someone to see something that he or she has not seen before and, subsequently, to act upon that insight. It is a power to help others see new things as possible and to help them respond to oppression and injustice with resilience, enhanced self-awareness, increased efficacy, and a greater sense of responsibility to self and society.

In the model proposed in this section, social workers are encouraged to see the empowerment process as beginning with the smallest of individual actions. When joined with others, these efforts create a chain reaction that releases human energy. Over time, this energy can build to become a critical mass that results in social change. Each person's awareness and actions will increase the likelihood that a critical mass will accumulate and that ultimately change will take place.

Creating a just society and world is a global issue of overwhelming proportion. A transformation from injustice and oppression to just alternatives will not come about easily or quickly. Giving birth to social justice will be a long and painful process. It requires personal commitment and social transformation on a massive scale. Despite the magnitude of the problem, if social change for social justice is to take place, it will grow from the grassroots—at the level of the individual, the small group, local organizations, and communities. By starting at this level, the empowerment process provides a bridge that connects the person and the smaller group with the larger social change movement. This bridge becomes a vehicle for change as students join with others in crossing over to yet uncharted terrain. If we trust the process, empowerment will provide the energy needed for creating a just society.

PERSONAL TRANSFORMATION AND CONNECTIONS

In the 1980s it became clear that if social movements were to grow, organizations needed to focus on the individual. Individual needs must be met if the larger cause is to flourish. In *The Aquarian Conspiracy*, Marilyn Ferguson (1980) describes how social activism stems from personal transformation. In the empowerment process, first steps toward such personal transformation take place when social workers acknowledge their deep feelings about injustice and oppression and the role they play as privileged or oppressed based on their social identities. Personal connections are critical, and they can be painful. However, once we begin to accept feelings of shame, guilt, anger, and other feelings of distress as normal human reactions to the horrors of injustice, we can become free to see ways in which we are all personally connected to the issue.

Personal connections can be many and varied. Awareness and acknowledgment of their own feelings about racism in the United States begins the change process for many people, who may begin to feel personally involved with racism in a variety of ways. Perhaps the most basic connection comes from personal fears about being victimized by racism and other forms of oppression. For those who have benefited from an oppressive system based on race, concerns about being viewed as a racist can cause some people to take action. Although some of those actions might take the form of defensiveness and attempts to prove they are not racist, connecting with the issue of racism in such a personal way opens the door to exploring new ways of thinking. Some people become enraged when they learn about historical events of which they had previously been unaware, and they make new connections through those feelings of anger at not having been taught all aspects of their country's history. Some become outraged at the lack of vital human service programs for certain populations in the United States. Others make a connection to the issue of social justice in a more direct, political way through an analysis of how economic and political interests operate to ensure inequities. Some people begin to question laws that sanction and create oppressive conditions and realize that horrors can be unleashed legally as, for example, when slavery in the United States was legal. They realize that everything done by the Nazis in Germany, based on creating a superior race, was done legally and with the approval of citizens and the establishment. Such questioning compels some people to begin to respond to higher principles. Some people feel a deep sense of commitment based on a moral or philosophical principle regarding the value of human life, a perspective that transcends traditional differences between people based on race, ethnicity, religion, and so on.

Educating ourselves about cultural diversity for social justice calls upon us to look within to identify connections such as those described earlier. By making connections between injustice and oppression and our personal lives, we begin to consider ways to respond. Thus, the empowerment process starts with where each of us stands on the issues and the personal connections that create feelings of conflict and distress.

During the process of exploring diversity and oppression, some people make a profoundly personal connection when they discover a gap between what they want to see in themselves and what they actually find in themselves. We may experience a loss of or threat to self-respect and question the self-image we want to hold as we struggle to come to terms with effects that privilege and oppression have had in our own lives (Pinderhughes, 1989). Marris (1974) proposes that such a sense of loss is triggered by a "discrediting of familiar assumptions" that creates a "crisis of discontinuity" (p. 21). Thus, learning about social justice and injustice often involves a process similar to the grieving process. By understanding the grieving process and appreciating it as a normal response, we can support and validate each person's personal journey toward change. The following discussion demonstrates how the process of transformative learning to become social change advocates relates to issues of loss and grief.

THE GRIEVING CYCLE

As we begin to share our experiences and reactions to injustice and oppression, we may experience a process that is similar to the grieving cycle described by Elisabeth Kubler-Ross (1975) and others in relation to death and other losses. The following summaries of the five stages of grieving contain examples of how each may be experienced in relation to racism and other forms of oppression.

1. Denial.   Although many social workers believe there is injustice in the United States and the rest of the world, they deal with their feelings by denying that a problem exists at this stage of the process. This protects them from making personal connections that thus do not need to be felt. It is a state of *psychic numbness*. In this state, we are protected against a feeling of being out of control and against feeling responsible. The denial stage helps cushion the impact of the horrors of injustice and oppression under which we all live. We are resistant to information about injustice. Our response is automatic and unemotional. For example, upon hearing about racism as an institutionalized phenomenon, some people may experience confusion and be incapable of comprehending what that means. They may consider such ideas to be propaganda. There is a desire to hold on to a belief that the world as they perceive it is a just place and to maintain faith in our "experts" and leaders to uphold justice.

2. Anger or rage.   In reaction to loss—whether it is loss of innocence, of belief that the world is just, or of self-image—denial is often followed by anger or rage. At this stage, we react with intense feelings, for instance, as we share stories about a racial profiling incident, a hate crime, an innocent black man living on death row for decades before his innocence is proved, or any number of stories of oppression. As one social worker expressed,

> I am angry when I realize that I have always lived in a racist and sexist society and that everyone lied to me about it.... I am furious when I discover that our country was founded on violence, slavery, and annihilation of indigenous people when I have always been taught that it was founded on truth and justice.... I am angry when I consider that some people are considered to be expendable by the powers that be.

A student of color in a social work class expressed his anger when he wrote,

> I could strangle some of the privileged white students in this program and in this class! They don't know about police brutality? What in the world do they think slavery was about? Are they stupid or do they just choose to put their heads in the sand? I am so sick of hearing them be shocked about injustice that I want to scream!

This stage of the grieving cycle is perhaps the most uncomfortable for many, especially those of us who have been taught that it is not polite to be angry and who may cringe at the expression of anger by others.

3. Bargaining.   In the bargaining stage, we may be aware of the seriousness of injustice and oppression and at the same time try to protect ourselves from understanding the full impact on both ourselves and other people. A desire to strike a bargain to minimize pain and sense of responsibility might be expressed in words such as the following:

> I understand that the world is unjust and that there is work to do. Yet, it is important that we understand that things are not anywhere near as serious now as they used to be. We no longer enslave people, for example, and everyone has the right to vote. While there are still problems with some people accessing what they need, there are laws that now protect people from unfair and unequal treatment.

4. Depression.   The magnitude and ramifications of oppression, when truly faced directly, can be so overwhelming that thinking about it can produce feelings of extreme helplessness and even despair. Social workers sometimes describe their dismay at recognizing the disparity between the personal anguish over the realities of oppression and injustice and the social reality of "business as usual." Some people express feelings of self-blame, suggesting that it is they who are insane and overreacting rather than society perpetuating and allowing such injustices. When we begin to experience such feelings, we often retreat to a state of denial in which we may refuse to acknowledge the problems and resist becoming involved in change actions.

Apathy characterizes the depression stage of the grieving cycle. Social workers who observe the consequences of oppression on a regular basis may report withdrawal symptoms and feel that they have no energy left to hear anything else about injustice. They feel hopeless, helpless, and alone. It is a state of despair. Optimism vanishes, and all that remains are pain, separation between all human beings, and ignorance and prejudice. There is little or no hope for changing conditions.

5. Acceptance and reorganization.   At this stage, social workers refuse to accept the inevitability of injustice. Instead, they accept responsibility to act and are able to reorganize their behavior and purposefully work toward finding solutions. They have an increased awareness of reality. They are empowered to bring about change. They have hope in the possibility of change.

The grieving cycle, as described here, can provide a useful guide for understanding what we may go through as we face the realities of racism, injustice, and oppression. The cycle is not absolute—not everyone goes through every stage in the exact sequence or at the same predictable pace. Yet the model can help us comprehend our own feelings and behavior and those of others. It is also important to recognize that the cycle, as applied to our reactions to learning about cultural diversity and oppression, differs from other types of grieving in that we cannot foresee a final resolution of the problem, nor of our grieving, in the immediate future. As long as problems of injustice are ongoing, we may find ourselves repeating stages. In other words, the feelings of denial, apathy, despair, anger, and helplessness may return when we learn of a new situation of injustice. Social workers need to be prepared for that eventuality and to understand that, although feelings of grief can be overwhelming at times, hope cannot be bought with a refusal to feel.

GRIEF WORK TASKS

The empowerment process helps us to accept the fact that experiencing the feelings in the grieving cycle is a sane reaction to facing the realities of an unjust world. It helps us to know that we are not alone in our feelings. Whether in the classroom or in a social service agency, social workers can help each other by acknowledging their mutual feelings and by talking about the problems. It is important to discover that we are all in this together. The fact that our situation is a collective one, bearing on us all, albeit in different ways depending on the status conferred by our social identities, has tremendous implications. It means that in facing oppression together, openly and deeply, people can rediscover their interconnectedness in the web of life, and this brings personal power and resilience (Macy, 1983).

Specific tasks involved in grief work help move us through the stages to acceptance of responsibility for social change and a place of empowerment to take action. As with the stages of grief, the tasks may occur in varied sequence and even simultaneously when the work of one task moves us along the work of other tasks. Four tasks developed in regard to bereavement (Morrow, 2008; Slap-Shelton, 1998) are described as steps we can take to work through the process of grieving as a reaction to injustice and oppression.

1. Recognize the reality of the situation. Facing the reality of injustice and oppression, both our own and that of others, is the first task that needs to be completed. Accepting reality is difficult work. Initially, we may want to deny or minimize it.

2. Release your emotions. Weep, express anger, feel the pain. The pain experienced at the loss of your former perceptions of the world involves many intense emotions including sadness, despair, anger, guilt, fear, loneliness, and shame. Being able to weep over the loss of one's self-concept may be necessary. When first facing issues of injustice, painful feelings may be omnipresent, and it can feel like being on an emotional roller coaster. The task is to experience the feelings, not suppress them.

3. Develop new skills. Accepting responsibility for bringing about social change means taking on new roles and making new kinds of contacts in the world. Making new friends and colleagues, finding a support network, taking on new roles in the community may all be part of the process. The opportunity for personal growth and development may be most obvious in this part of the work.

4. Reinvest emotional energy in a new commitment.   As grief work tasks are achieved, more energy is available to create ways to work for social justice and to invest in new activities and actions for change.

The phases of grief and the grief work tasks are meant to serve only as compasses to normalize the process of coming to terms with injustice and oppression and accepting responsibility as a change agent. They are not prescriptive for there are no rights or wrongs on our empowerment journeys but can provide useful insights into the process you may be experiencing.

The Necessity of Actions

Actions give social workers the energy to work through the grieving cycle, and they are the backbone of grief work tasks. Callahan (1982) writes about the effectiveness of actions:

> New and different actions can change thought and feeling just as new and different thoughts can change behavior. Taking even one small step on a journey changes one's perspective on the landscape, as well as changing one's self definition to that of a person who is able to move out toward new goals. Action, either practical or symbolic, overcomes the learned helplessness, inertia and apathy correlated with the absence of hope. (p. 1)

By taking action, commitment to effecting change is strengthened, and so are the chances for making social change possible. Actions become the steps on the empowerment journey. Often the first steps are the most difficult. To act in response to social injustice is an evolutionary process. What we are able to do today may be radically different from what we may be doing next month or next year. It is important to learn that small steps lead to larger actions in a natural progression. As a first step, we may think more about racism and other forms of oppression and begin to talk about it with our families, friends, and others in our immediate circles. Gradually, we may move to reading more about the subject on our own, to speaking out at public gatherings, to writing letters, to educating others, to wearing a button, to circulating and signing petitions, to lobbying our political representatives, to advocating for agency policy changes, to peaceful demonstrations, to organizing actions with others. It is important that all efforts are acknowledged, including the smallest effort, because social justice is accomplished by laying one brick at a time, taking one step at a time.

In order to be advocates for social justice, we can weave the issues into our daily lives and work. We can be most effective by bringing our advocacy work with us wherever we go—in our own families, neighborhoods, workplaces, social gatherings, and agencies. Everyone has a skill or talent that can be used in the empowerment process. By focusing on the present, asking ourselves what it is we do in our clients' daily lives, and then doing it for social justice, our lives are changed but not rearranged.

Each action becomes the impetus for growth. The more we do, the greater our desire to learn and to share what we have learned. Because we choose our actions, we can set our own limits and control our rate of change. In order to get started, all that is needed is a strong commitment to work for an end to racism and other forms of oppression and injustice. We learn from the examples of others. When we begin to act, our actions join with the actions of others to provide the energy for the journey.

BARRIERS TO CHANGE

Part of the process of change involves looking at the barriers that keep us from being advocates for social justice. A common block for many is personal fear: of taking risks, of standing out by making a personal statement, of being embarrassed in public, of losing security or the respect of people they had thought were friends, of being alienated from family or friends or peers.

Social workers are often deterred from social justice advocacy actions by a fear of stepping outside their personal safety zones. We all have spheres of operation in which we feel safe. Stepping outside this area is risky, for when we confront issues in a public way, we may be subjected to the ridicule, misunderstanding, and anger of others. For example, interrupting a racist joke or challenging an oppressive agency policy can be a terrifying and thus courageous action to take when the response could quite possibly be ostracism from others for doing so. The empowerment process, however, generates confidence and courage. As we become more involved and are sustained by the support of others, we discover that our safety zones expand.

Another significant barrier for many is the fear of creating communication gaps, tensions, and conflict within our own agencies if we identify the prejudice and discrimination within that system. Applying the process of empowerment to that of agency change can be helpful in this regard. Students can be encouraged to be sensitive to each person's attitude toward the issues. Unrealistic expectations about the others' responses usually increase the tension. Communicating consideration for others while respecting one's own stage of involvement can help reduce resistance to open discussion about the issues and help one stay in the struggle.

Some people speak quite honestly about another barrier: that of losing the privileges conferred on them based on their own social identities in an oppressive system. As one social work student wrote in his journal:

> I feel terrible about the inequities I am learning about and I want to work to change the system. I must admit, though, that I am quite ambivalent about what I might have to give up in terms of the privileges and benefits I currently get from the system as it is since I am a white, heterosexual male. It is easy to think theoretically about social justice but when I think in practical terms—like maybe I wouldn't get preferential treatment in a job application situation if there were truly equal opportunity—I am ashamed to say that I have to think twice.

We need to acknowledge the courage it takes to be honest about this and challenge each other to face our cognitive dissonance rather than slipping back into denial. Positive role models of people throughout history who were advocates for social justice can help in this regard as well.

Two additional barriers frequently impede progress in becoming social justice advocates: the fear of speaking out in public and the fear of not being sufficiently informed. By encouraging small steps, the empowerment process can be used to overcome these fears.

Speaking out in public will seem less frightening if we first talk to those with whom we feel most comfortable. Then, when we are ready, we can begin to speak to other people in small groups and at public meetings. It can be very rewarding to find that acquaintances and even strangers are willing to talk about issues of racism, poverty, and oppression of other kinds. Often the message on a pin or button (e.g., "Stop Racism," "A Social Worker for Justice") will help begin a conversation. Speaking out is a natural outgrowth of increased commitment and involvement.

To reduce the fear of being uninformed, it is helpful to understand that we can never have enough information or remember all the facts. Statistics change, and one fact can counteract another. What is most important is an understanding of underlying concepts. If we develop a point of view as a framework for our own thinking, the facts will fall into place. A preponderance of information exists in books, articles, and videotapes. To make sense out of the facts, it is helpful to absorb only small amounts of information at one time and take time to process it. We will soon be surprised by how much we know.

Benefits of Empowerment

As advocates for social justice, social workers are enriched and strengthened by the friendships that are made with others who share common goals. We get to know and appreciate others whose backgrounds and lifestyles may be quite different from our own. People who work for social justice are old and young, are rich and poor, are religious and nonreligious, are heterosexual and homosexual and bisexual and transsexual, and come from a variety of cultural and ethnic backgrounds. Our strength grows as we celebrate this diversity and face our differences honestly. In the process, we learn to trust each other enough to live justly on a personal level.

Throughout the empowerment process, our actions become seeds that germinate best within a supportive environment. As the seeds grow, we discover that we have developed previously untapped strengths and talents. We find ourselves taking actions that we thought we could never take when the opportunity to act presented itself. Like wildflowers, our actions spread, affecting those in the world around us. Thus, the circle continues to grow. As personal transformations become interwoven with social change, lives take on new meaning and deeper purpose.

What sustains us in our social justice advocacy work is the belief that our actions can and will make a difference. Although individual acts may seem insignificant, they have tremendous power when joined with the efforts of countless others. Historically, we know that social and political changes have always stemmed from the grassroots. The abolition of slavery, the right to unionize, women's rights, and civil rights, to name a few, all came about as a result of grassroots efforts. If social justice is to become a reality, a collective commitment to change must be made at the local level. As more and more people unite, we gain the strength to change both the world and ourselves.

> Actions are clearly effective when those involved in them experience their capabilities and their strength. That exciting feeling of empowerment is something that cannot be taken away. It becomes part of how we think about ourselves, as purposeful, effective people who can express ourselves clearly on an issue of vital importance.[10]

SOCIAL AND ECONOMIC JUSTICE VALUES
AND PRINCIPLES TO GUIDE ACTIONS

Many problems that social workers encounter at the micro, meso, and macro levels stem from injustices that are grounded in an underlying crisis of values. Social workers need to ground their empowerment strategies and actions in values and principles that hold out hope for remedying such underlying crises of values. Psychosocial and economic explanations for problems social workers encounter need to be reinforced by an understanding of different and deeper dimensions and by understanding the interrelation of the personal and socioeconomic and value structures and processes. Possible actions aimed at promoting social and economic justice are many, and as the empowerment model illustrates, all are important.

VALUES

Social workers are faced with complex decisions about which actions to take given each particular situation, and values provide a road map. In order to guide their thinking, the following eight values are identified as being central to social workers' decision-making process as they determine how to promote social justice. They are intended to be illustrative rather than exhaustive.[11]

1. Life. Value for life is essential for all social and economic justice and human rights work. The worth of life, human and nonhuman existence, is the fountainhead for all other ideas and values that follow. Social workers are called to actively support positive and life-affirming aspects of all situations. Life is intrinsically connected and interdependent in all its parts and forms. Disruption of any aspect affects the social fabric or threatens life, thereby injuring humankind. Thus, value of life implies that suffering and death are not just individual phenomena but that they touch others. Physical health is an important aspect of the value and quality of life. Environmental deterioration, the water crisis including pollution, and the nonexistence and curtailment of health programs are some of the major life-threatening factors.

2. Freedom and liberty. All human beings are born free and have the right to liberty. This presupposes that each human being has the freedom of choice in the conduct of his or her life. The enjoyment of this freedom is, however, frequently curtailed by material and other constraints. Freedom is likewise restricted by the principle of not infringing on the freedom of others. Yet, freedom, next to life itself, is viewed as the most precious human value, closely linked to human dignity and to the worth of human life. The quest for freedom and liberty has inspired many people to seek release from territorial or geographical domination. The quest for spiritual and intellectual freedom has inspired heroic acts of resistance. Social workers are often in the forefront of the struggle for freedom. In parts of the world where freedom does not exist, social workers pay a heavy price in oppression for pursuing their principles.

3. Equality and nondiscrimination. The fundamental principle of equality of all human beings is imperfectly applied in everyday life, not least in the manifold aspects of interpersonal relations. For social workers it is a crucial concept related to personal and professional attitudes. It is also the cornerstone for the all-important principle of justice, requiring serious consideration of just and unjust equality and inequality based on biological factors; on psychic, social, cultural, and spiritual needs; and on individual contributions to the welfare of others. Once the principle of equality is accepted, it becomes impossible to discriminate against any person or group of persons.

4. Justice. Various aspects of justice have to be taken into consideration, including the legal, judicial, social, economic, and other aspects that constitute the basis by which a society upholds the dignity of its members and ensures the security and integrity of persons. Social workers have long promoted such principles and are conscious of the fact that human rights are best upheld by a law-abiding state. Impartiality in the administration of justice is an important tool to safeguard the rights of the vulnerable members of society who make up the majority of social work clients. The pursuit of justice, however, has wider implications that are less easily codified. Social justice encompasses satisfaction of basic human needs and the equitable sharing of material resources. It aims at universal access to fundamental services in health, education, equal opportunities at the start, protection for disadvantaged persons or groups, and a degree of moderation in the areas of retribution, consumption, and profit.

5. Solidarity. This is a fundamental intrinsic value that implies not only understanding and empathy toward humankind's pain and suffering but also identifying and taking a stand with the sufferers and their cause. Social workers are expected not only to stand by people who are struggling but also to express their solidarity in words and in deeds in the face of any form of denial of people's political, civil, social, economic, cultural, and spiritual rights. The social work profession must identify itself with victims of violence, torture, expulsion, and curtailment of freedom anywhere in the world.

6. Social responsibility. This is action undertaken on behalf of sufferers and victims: standing for them, championing their cause, and helping them. Social responsibility is the implementation corollary of solidarity. The principle of social responsibility is crucial for a profession such as social work because service and commitment to the poor and the needy are its *raison d'être*.

7. Evolution, peace, and nonviolence. The values mentioned so far are determining factors for the quality of interpersonal relations. Peace as a distinct value, and not simply as the absence of organized conflict, is one additional value. It is to be nurtured and striven for, with the ultimate goal of achieving harmony with the self, with others, and with the environment. Although conflicts in human relations are unavoidable, ways to solve them can be either peaceful or violent, constructive or destructive. The revolutionary "raze all and build anew" approach has held fascination for people over the centuries, producing untold human suffering. An evolutionary approach is slower, often less immediately rewarding, but in the end longer-lasting and therefore more effective. It is an approach often chosen by social workers in relation to conflicts. Confrontation and resistance in the quest for freedom are not eschewed. Neither are justice and social justice. Violence is. Although the world is not ready to abandon the use of arms, and just causes for revolutions clearly exist, it should be recognized that arbitration and conciliation are effective tools to overcome seemingly irreconcilable differences provided they are practiced consistently and with respect, understanding, and knowledge.

8. Relations between human beings and nature. Respect for other species and a quest for harmony with nature are more often permeating human consciousness in the 21st century. Environmental degradation cannot be ignored. The world economic order, faulty development models, inequality with regard to all resources, consumption patterns, and nuclear, industrial, and other pollution in industrialized as well as developing countries are recognized as causes of the earth's serious plight. Excessive consumerism and extreme poverty endanger nature as well as vulnerable groups of people through greed, lack of information, and need for survival. Comprehensive policies to halt and, where possible, repair damage to the environment need to be complemented by comprehensive environmental education programs and advocacy campaigns. Social workers have an important role to play in this process by linking with other groups.

PRINCIPLES

Empowerment strategies and actions, grounded in the eight values set out previously, can be guided by the following five principles (NASW, 1996, pp. 6–8).

1. Development. Community development is based on tapping into and building the integrity and leadership of the members of the community. Breaking the cycle of violence and injustice and promoting social and economic justice are development processes that local people must direct and ultimately sustain. No imported scheme can substitute for bottom-up ingenuity.

2. Participation. Participatory community development is needed to counter the powerlessness, isolation, and exclusion that are the result of oppression and injustice and that are often expressed through violence. Sustainable development must have the participation of community members. Successful participation calls for engaging people, unleashing their creativity, building their capacities, and giving them a sense of ownership.

3. Reciprocity. Successful development calls for an equitable relationship between "the givers of help" and "the recipients of help" and a blurring of who receives from whom. Assisting a community requires one to become involved with it, to learn from it, to be influenced and changed by it—in a sense, to join it. Homegrown strategies to address injustice must be retrieved and exchanged, and new methods must be devised to share learning about what works and why.

4. Innovation. As budget cuts and managed care change the face of social service delivery, U.S. social workers must become innovative. As in resource-poor developing countries, accomplishing more with less and pooling resources to achieve otherwise impossible goals is becoming increasingly important. The infusion of more community-wide approaches to treating societal issues must become part of the day-to-day jobs of social workers. Innovation demands that social workers review the root causes of problems so that they can begin to institute positive change for more people at less cost.

5. Global learning.   The gap between home and abroad, between "us and them," is rapidly shrinking. Not only do so-called Third World conditions exist in neighborhoods across America, but the globalization of the economy, immigrant flows, environmental degradation, and a host of other factors all combine to make interdependency a fact of life. Armed with a more sophisticated knowledge base by which to analyze and understand current situations and policies, social workers can enhance their effectiveness. The search for solutions to societal problems should not be limited to U.S. communities and policies.

CONCLUSION: IDENTIFYING, ANALYZING, AND RESPONDING TO SOCIAL INJUSTICES

Social workers work with clients on a variety of levels—micro, meso, and macro—nationally and internationally. Concerns about human rights, social inequities, oppression, and other forms of injustice need to be identified on all levels. Social workers can be guided by the values and principles suggested in the previous section. They can also be assisted by tools for analyzing situations and making decisions about strategies and actions.

The following case example illustrates how two individuals in two different countries are connected by the bonds of exploitation, oppression, and poverty. In both situations, industrial initiatives that are motivated solely by the desire for profits and that confer value on individuals only to the extent that they produce profits exploit the very people who should benefit from the economic development in their communities. A framework for analyzing and responding to the social justice issues inherent in their life circumstances is provided as a tool for thinking about their situation and other client situations.

Case Study: Randy Conway and Angelica Hernandez

Randy Conway is 44 years old and lives with his wife and three children in the small town of Mount Vernon, Missouri. He worked 20 years in a Zenith factory making televisions. Zenith had moved from the northern United States to Missouri in search of workers who were willing to toil for lower wages and without the benefit of trade unions. By 1992, Randy was making $11 per hour, but when Zenith moved 20,000 of its U.S. jobs to Mexico, including most of the jobs in Missouri, Randy was out of work. Zenith spokesperson John Taylor admitted that "the wage structure in Mexico is a primary reason for our relocation there."

Angelica Hernandez now works in Zenith's Reynosa, Mexico, factory. She works in a noisy plant with hazardous chemicals all around and takes home $35 for a 48-hour week. Angelica, her husband, and their seven children live in a shack with a dirt floor that measures 12 feet by 18 feet and has no electricity or running water (*GATT and NAFTA*, n.d.).

An Analytical Framework[12]

In order to fully understand the social justice and human rights issues and determine possible responses in the case example as well as other client situations, an analysis of the causes, symptoms, shortfalls, and the potential of the population (or clients) for action and solutions needs to be undertaken. The overriding justice theme inherent in Randy's and Angelica's situations is poverty. The following framework can be used to guide your thinking about the role of social workers in advocating for social and economic justice. The framework can be used in relation to other overriding justice themes (e.g., racism, gender discrimination, environment and development, religion) and vulnerable populations (e.g., children, women, people of color, refugees, people with disabilities).

I. *Aspects of the Situation*
A. Quality of life
B. Food
C. Employment
D. Housing
E. Health
F. Education
G. Environment/pollution
H. Access to property (land, housing)
I. Other aspects:

II. *Analysis*
A. Causes (e.g., inequality in global resource distribution, industrial exploitation, nonunionization)
B. Symptoms (e.g., powerlessness, unemployment, hunger, health)
C. Shortfalls (e.g., lack of social security provisions and legislation protecting workers, lack of trade unions)
D. Potential of the population for solutions (e.g., self-help groups, bulk purchases of products, political mobilization, union organizing efforts)

III. *Social Work Intervention*
A. Social work intervention has a long tradition and has spearheaded innovative action through cooperation with poor people themselves, nongovernmental organizations, and other partners that reinforce advocacy and a concerted thrust to combat poverty situations such as these.
B. Consider here the following question: What is the scope and what are the limits of social work interventions at different levels (micro, meso, macro)?

IV. *International Human Rights Instruments*
A. Consider the main international instruments addressing the theme of poverty and how they might be used to advocate for change (e.g., the Universal

Declaration of Human Rights—1948, the International Covenants on Economic, Social, and Cultural Rights and on Civil and Political Rights—1966, and the Declaration on the Right to Development—1986).

Questions for Social Workers and Social Work Students

1. What particular human rights issues (e.g., rights to life, to work, to an adequate standard of living) that are linked to the issues of poverty are illustrated in the case example?

2. What attitudes of social discrimination, marginalization, stigmatization, and injustice need to be combated?

3. In what way can clients—individuals, families, communities—become empowered to bring about change in their own situation and in the attitudes of others toward them?

4. In what ways can social workers become empowered to alleviate or eliminate poverty and facilitate empowerment of people in the face of industrial and global exploitation? What are the barriers to their own empowerment, and how can they overcome those barriers?

NOTES

1. These statistics were taken from Joel Blau (2008), Income distribution, in *Encyclopedia of Social Work*, Terry Mizrahi and Larry E. Davis (eds.), National Association of Social Workers and Oxford University Press.

2. These statistics were taken from V. Quadrini and J.-V. Rios-Rull (1997, Spring), Understanding the U.S. distribution of wealth, *Federal Reserve Bank of Minneapolis Quarterly Review*, 21(2), 22–36.

3. World Declaration on the Survival, Protection and Development of Children, World Summit for Children, United Nations, September 30, 1990.

4. *U.N. Focus, Refugee Women: In the Spirit of Survival*, March 1991, p. 1.

5. Preamble of the World Declaration on Education for All, World Conference on Education for All, Jomtien, Thailand, 1990.

6. *From Crisis to Consensus: The United Nations and the Challenge to Development*, p. 1. Keynote speech delivered by Mme Therese Sevigny, United Nations Undersecretary-General for Public Information, at the 1990/1991 inaugural conference, University of Ottawa, Institute for International Development, November 14, 1990.

7. The World Bank, *World Development Report 1991*, New York: Oxford University Press, p. 25; United Nations Department of Public Information, Development Forum, 19(6)/20(1), November 1991–February 1992.

8. These instruments are described in more detail in United Nations (1992), *Teaching and Learning about Human Rights: A Manual for Schools of Social Work and the Social Work Profession*, New York: United Nations.

9. This section is adapted with permission from M. S. White and D. Van Soest (1984), *Empowerment of People for Peace*, Minneapolis, MN: Women Against Military Madness.

10. From A. Cook and G. Kirk (1983), *Greenham Women Everywhere* (Boston), as quoted in M. S. White and D. Van Soest (1984), *Empowerment of People for Peace*, Minneapolis, MN: Women Against Military Madness, p. 18.

11. The values are drawn from United Nations (1992), *Teaching and Learning about Human Rights: A Manual for Schools of Social Work and the Social Human Rights Work Profession*, New York: United Nations, pp. 14–19.

12. Adapted from United Nations (1992), *Teaching and Learning about Human Rights: A Manual for Schools of Social Work and the Social Work Profession*, New York: United Nations, pp. 52–53.

A Cultural Competence Framework

Part Two introduces the reader to a cultural competence framework that consists of two levels (generalist and advanced) and three functions of cultural competent practice (cultural awareness, knowledge acquisition, and skill development) based on generalist and advanced practice social work curriculum (Council on Social Work Education [CSWE], 2008, Educational Policy B2.2 & M2.2). The framework is a structural road map that plots the route that we take in this book. We visit cultural self-awareness of the worker and cultural other awareness of the client. Next we explore theories, the history of oppressed groups, values, and behavior patterns related to knowledge acquisition. Finally we investigate the practice process stages of skill development (engagement, assessment, intervention, and evaluation).

A FRAMEWORK FOR CULTURAL COMPETENCE

CHAPTER 4

Doman Lum

The first three chapters lay the groundwork for understanding the range of issues surrounding culturally competent practice, the realities of social context, and the scope of human rights and social and economic justice. As we move into the cultural competence structure part of the text we focus on presenting a road map for understanding cultural awareness, knowledge acquisition, and skill development, which are the major functions for practicing culturally competent practice. A framework is like a house. Building a framework gives you a place to hang out with three rooms (*an awareness room* for you to look at yourself and others; *a knowledge study and office room* full of theory books with a desk for you to study, read, and write; and *a skills work room* with practical tools for you to build various interesting projects and work with people). If you were without such a house, you would be homeless and exposed to the elements, wind, rain, and cold. With a framework you have an orientation to the parameters of cultural competence and proficiency. We built this house with social work materials consisting of generalist and advance curriculum levels, two sets of competencies, and three areas of functions. We hope that you will enjoy living in the house, become familiar with every nook and cranny, and know it from top to bottom.

DEFINITION AND CHARACTERISTICS OF A FRAMEWORK

A *framework* is a structure that serves to hold the parts of a system together. For example, in the construction of a house, the framework establishes the room layout and the roofline and holds together the various components of the house. Likewise, the frame of an automobile is the basic structure that determines the essence of the car. A good course outline is also a framework, holding together a set of ideas and/ or facts. An effective instructor generally teaches from a theoretical framework, and a good textbook is usually built around a framework.

The term *framework* is derived from three Latin root words that illuminate its meaning: (1) *framen*, which means a structure, frame, or problem; (2) *frami*, which connotes profit or benefit; and (3) *frama*, which denotes "to further." These root words describe a structure that provides a benefit or furthers some aim. A framework gives shape, establishes an operational perimeter, identifies procedural principles, and provides flexible application.

The framework for cultural competence has these basic characteristics:

- The framework is a helpful point of reference in social work cultural competence discussions.
- The framework sets an operational perimeter, identifies characteristics of cultural competence, and offers procedural, culturally competent practice principles.
- The framework teaches assumptions, principles, and skills, and provides a road map for social work practice.
- The framework supports the development of social work outcome measures relating to cultural competence.
- The framework brings together the two levels of social work education curriculum design (generalist and advanced practices), the three functions of the culturally competent practitioner (cultural awareness, knowledge acquisition, and skill development), and core competencies for each function.
- The framework advances the state of the art of culturally competent practice by evaluating the existing multicultural counseling competencies model and proposing a social work cultural competencies framework.

SOCIAL WORK CULTURAL COMPETENCIES: GENERALIST AND ADVANCED

Cultural competencies are outcome measurement statements that reflect a set of culturally competent practice functions. The Association for Multicultural Counseling and Development (AMCD) is the first professional group to adopt and operationalize multicultural counseling competence standards and 31 competencies to establish outcome measures (Arredondo et al., 1996). The functions of cultural competence consist of awareness, knowledge, and skills, which are still recognized in the field of multicultural competence. Smith et al. (2004) explain,

> Awareness refers to therapists' personal self-awareness: awareness of their worldview, values, assumptions, expectations, privileges, biases, theoretical orientation, and so on. Knowledge refers to therapists' understanding and knowledge of human diversity in all its forms: racial, cultural, religious, gender, sexual orientation, and so on. Skills refers to therapists' ability to use their personal awareness and knowledge of client culture and diversity in a therapeutic manner during the treatment process. (p. 11)

Sue and Sue (2008) have constructed a three-dimensional model of cultural competence in counseling consisting of worldviews, competence components, and therapeutic interventions:

- Dimension I: Group-Specific Worldviews, which includes human differences associated with race, gender, sexual orientation, physical ability, age, and other reference groups

- Dimension II: Components of Cultural Competence, which focuses on awareness, knowledge, and skills, particularly one's own biases and assumptions of human behavior, knowledge of particular groups, and culturally appropriate intervention strategies
- Dimension III: Foci of Therapeutic Interventions, which critically evaluates biases at the individual, professional, organizational, and societal levels

In contrast our cultural competence social work practice framework is built on a social work curriculum foundation, which consists of two levels (generalist and advanced). The framework has extensive support because as a social work student matriculates through a generalist undergraduate social work curriculum and a graduate MSW program, there is a consistent reinforcement of core competencies in practice, behavior, diversity, policy, research, and field. Core competencies, cultural competencies, and cultural competence go hand in hand throughout both curriculum areas. Moreover there is a focus on developing generalist and advanced competencies in cultural awareness, knowledge acquisition, and skill development. The framework has a concise, tight, and systematic fit and is built on a social work curriculum and cultural competence and competencies base.

Generalist practice is grounded in the liberal arts and the person and environment construct. To promote human and social well-being, generalist practitioners use a range of prevention and intervention methods in their practice with individuals, families, groups, organizations, and communities (Council on Social Work Education [CSWE], 2008, Educational Policy B2.2). *Advanced practice* requires practitioners to refine and advance the quality of social work practice and that of the larger social work profession. Advanced practitioners synthesize and apply a broad range of interdisciplinary and multidisciplinary knowledge and skills. In areas of specialization, advanced practitioners assess, intervene, and evaluate to promote human and social well-being (CSWE, Educational Policy M2.2). The social work cultural competence model is supported by the generalist and advanced levels and has three functions: (1) *cultural self-awareness* of the worker's own culture and cultural other awareness of the client's culture; (2) *knowledge acquisition* consisting of theory orientation and a history of oppressed groups, values, and behavior patterns; and (3) *skill development* related to a practice process with a culturally diverse client. Table 4.1 provides an overview of the social work cultural competencies framework.

CULTURAL AWARENESS

The first cultural competence area is cultural awareness, which focuses on the cultural self-awareness of the worker and the cultural other awareness of the client.

GENERALIST LEVEL   The following paragraphs describe competencies related to cultural awareness at the generalist level.

The social worker is aware of life experiences as a person related to a culture (e.g., family heritage, household and community events, beliefs, and practices). Everyone has a set of unique life experiences related to family, community, beliefs, and practices that are embedded in culture. However, many persons in the United States have blended ethnic backgrounds as a result of intermarriage over many

TABLE 4.1 | SOCIAL WORK CULTURAL COMPETENCIES: GENERALIST AND ADVANCED

Cultural Awareness

Generalist Level:

- Awareness of own life experiences related to culture
- Contact with other cultures and ethnicities
- Awareness of positive and negative experiences with other cultures and ethnicities
- Awareness of own racism, prejudice, and discrimination

Advanced level:

- Assessment of involvement with people of color throughout various life stages
- Completion of course work, fieldwork, and research focused on cultural diversity
- Participation in employment experiences with culturally diverse clients and programs
- Academic and employment evaluation on the progress toward attaining focused cultural awareness of academic material and professional career experiences with cultural diversity

Knowledge Acquisition

Generalist Level:

- Understanding of terms related to cultural diversity
- Knowledge of demographics of culturally diverse populations
- Development of a critical thinking perspective on cultural diversity
- Understanding of the history of oppression and of social groups
- Knowledge of culturally diverse values

Advanced level:

- Knowledge of theories on postpositivism, constructionism, critical knowledge, and postmodernism
- Mastery of social science theory

Skill Development

Generalist level:

- Understanding of how to overcome client resistance
- Knowledge of how to obtain client background
- Understanding of the concept of ethnic community
- Use of self-disclosure
- Use of a positive and open communication style
- Problem identification
- View of the problem in terms of wants or needs
- View of the problem in terms of levels
- Explanation of problem themes
- Excavation of problem details
- Assessment of stressors and strengths
- Assessment of all client dimensions
- Establishment of culturally acceptable goals
- Formulation of multilevel intervention strategies
- Evaluation

Advanced level:

- Design of social service programs in ethnic communities
- Understanding that services must be accessible
- Understanding that services must be pragmatic and positive
- Belief in the importance of recruiting bilingual/bicultural workers
- Participation in community outreach programs
- Establishment of linkages with other social agencies
- Fostering a conducive agency setting
- Involvement with cultural skill development research

generations and are unable to point to a predominant ethnic and cultural heritage. They see themselves simply as Americans. But, on closer examination, the experiences of these people may reflect regional and sectional culture (southern culture, New England culture, Midwestern culture, California culture) or residual traces of recognizable Irish, German, or English cultural behavior patterns. It is important for the social worker to recognize and become aware of his or her cultural life experiences. It is the beginning of cultural awareness for the social worker and prepares the worker for discussing cultural recognition with clients.

The social worker has contact with individuals, families, and groups of other cultures and ethnicities. As a person of culture, everyone knows another person, family, or group who is either like or unlike him or her. As the social worker widens the range of contact, patterns emerge regarding cultural groups and communities. In some cities and rural areas, ethnic communities are still intact as functioning groups. Newly arrived cultural and ethnic groups have thriving neighborhoods. Some small ethnic communities are homogeneous and have minimal contact with individuals or families of different cultural and ethnic backgrounds. It is important to talk about the degree of contact a person has with other persons of distinct and blended cultures and ethnicities. Contact is established through school, work, sports activities, clubs, church, festivals, and other events. Contact could be sporadic or constant, superficial or intimate, short-lived or for a lifetime.

The social worker is aware of positive and negative experiences with persons and events of other cultures and ethnicities. Contact causes a set of positive and/or negative experiences to occur in the life and mind of a person. A positive or negative experience either dispels or confirms a stereotype. A positive experience with an individual of another culture or ethnicity may dispel a previous negative stereotype about this group. A negative experience may confirm an already held negative stereotype. Based on a series of such experiences, our stereotypes about other groups are deeply rooted in our psyches. Positive and negative experiences with persons and events of other cultures and ethnicities should be discussed, shared, and examined. A cultural awareness session is an opportunity to investigate stereotypes and beliefs based on our unique experiences and biases.

The social worker evaluates the cognitive, affective, and behavioral components of his or her racism, sexism, homophobia, ageism, and other isms, prejudice, and discrimination. These isms, prejudice, and discrimination are related to the cognitive, affective, and behavioral dimensions of an individual. For example, *racism* is the cognitive belief in the superiority of one group over another. *Prejudice* is negative feelings toward a group or its individual members. *Discrimination* is an unfavorable behavioral response or reaction to members of an ethnic or racial group. Racism and other isms, prejudice, and discrimination are universal; we are the oppressed recipients and the oppressive agents. The social worker must become aware of his or her own isms, prejudice, and discrimination. Uncovering and dealing with these inherent tendencies helps the worker be effective with a culturally diverse client.

Advanced Level   The following paragraphs describe competencies related to cultural awareness at the advanced level.

The social worker assesses his or her involvement with culturally diverse clients in childhood, adolescence, young adulthood, and adulthood. It is important to take a longitudinal view of one's involvement with the cultural and ethnical diverse client in the various developmental stages of life. Childhood and adolescence represent the formative years of living and learning, when incidents of racism, prejudice, and discrimination have a lasting effect upon the mind. Further contacts in young adulthood and adulthood may confirm or change attitudes from earlier developmental periods. Conducting a self-study of involvement uncovers an understanding of how past and present perceptions, attitudes, and beliefs about people of color affect the worker–client relationship. The social worker internalizes positive and negative experiences based on a series of developmental encounters during various life stages.

The social worker does academic course work, fieldwork, and research on culturally diverse clients and groups. Social work education requires course work on diversity that may include consideration of groups distinguished by race, ethnicity, culture, class, gender, sexual orientation, religion, physical or mental ability, age, and national origin. A social work student is expected to have taken a course on racial, ethnic, or cultural diversity. A field practicum or a research project involving people of color as clients or subjects may or may not be a part of social work education. This does not mean that a social work student must intern at an ethnic field placement or conduct research with a primary focus on an ethnic population. Though ideally a social work student has seen several culturally diverse clients in a field agency or interviewed culturally diverse human subjects in the course of conducting social work research, there is no guarantee that every social work student has been exposed to this range of experiences. To ensure cultural competence might mean that a social work program provides every student with a planned series of course work, fieldwork, and ethnic social research focusing on cultural diversity.

The social worker has professional employment experiences with culturally diverse clients and programs. A social work career takes a person through a meaningful set of program and client experiences in the social service sector. Along the way it is crucial to have employment experiences with a wide range of culturally diverse clients and to be responsible for program services that impact this population. Career employment experiences with culturally diverse clients and programs will help the social worker to grow—in his or her general competence, as an effective professional, and in his or her specific competence, as a culturally sensitive person.

The social worker evaluates academic material and professional experiences related to cultural awareness and cultural diversity. The beginning social worker relies initially on the body of academic knowledge and field experience on cultural diversity gleaned in school. Increasingly, the social worker reads new books and studies reports on racial, ethnic, and cultural factors that affect programs and services of his or her agency. Culturally diverse clients may be sources of new insights for the social worker. Interaction with ethnic colleagues and collaborative ethnic service agencies may broaden the understanding and perspective of the worker. Ideally, the social worker grows in his or her career through such contacts with cultural diversity and culturally diverse clients.

KNOWLEDGE ACQUISITION

Knowledge acquisition involves the acquisition of a body of information that organizes material about a topic into sets of facts that plausibly explain phenomena. Social work has been sensitive to the need for a theoretical foundation ever since the Flexner Report (Flexner, 1961), which criticized that *social work was not a profession because it had no theory base.*

GENERALIST LEVEL The following paragraphs describe competencies related to knowledge acquisition at the generalist level.

The social worker understands the following terms: ethnic minority, multiculturalism, diversity, and people of color. The social worker understands and can explain a number of basic terms that are essential to culturally diverse social work. *Ethnic minority* denotes a numerically smaller or politically powerless group in relation to a larger, controlling, and dominating majority and was used during the civil rights struggle for political, economic, legal, and social opportunities for African, Latino, and Asian Americans and First Nations Peoples. *Multiculturalism* recognizes the pluralistic nature of cultures and societies and has been associated with academic and political movements. The term has been used in a positive sense to denote the collective movement of people who are committed to the realities of cultural differences, and in a negative sense by detractors who associate the term with being merely politically correct. *Diversity* emphasizes the similarity and dissimilarity between numerous groups in society that have distinguishing characteristics. There is diversity in the United States in terms of ethnicity, culture, gender, sexual orientation, age, religion, and related areas. *People of color* is a collective term that refers to the major groups of African, Latino, and Asian Americans, and First Nations Peoples who have been distinguished from the dominant society by color.

The social worker has a knowledge of demographic profiles of culturally diverse populations. The 2005 Pew Research Center Study reflects a major influx of immigrants, refugees, and aliens into the United States, mainly from Asia, Central and South America, and eastern Europe. Accordingly, it is important to study shifting area population trends to determine how new ethnic groups have changed the face of the local community. What are the emerging social problems that have resulted from this influx? Have communities changed as a result? Have there been adverse or positive reactions to the socioeconomic situation of a locale? What new social service programs are needed to respond to these changes? These questions are crucial to the discussion of changing cultural profiles.

The social worker develops a critical thinking perspective on cultural diversity. Kurfiss (1989) defines *critical thinking*:

> [T]he process of figuring out what to believe or not about a situation, phenomenon, problem or controversy for which no single definitive answer or solution exists. The term implies a diligent, open-minded search for understanding, rather than for discovery of a necessary conclusion. (p. 42)

Critical thinking is an assessment of the nature of a problem or issue and an open-ended search for understanding of the cause-and-effect relationship. It is a mind-set that is applied to a number of different situations.

Alter and Egan (1997) identify five social work critical thinking skills: (1) the ability to understand social work theories, (2) the ability to divide a theory into its components (assumptions, concepts, propositions, hypotheses), (3) the ability to assess the practice implications of a theory, (4) the ability to develop and apply criteria for evaluating a theory, and (5) the ability to identify common errors in reasoning. These skills are explained further in this book (Chapter Six).

The social worker understands the history of oppression and of multicultural social groups. People of color share a common history of oppression, although there is variation in the histories of multicultural social groups. First Nations Peoples and African, Latino, and Asian Americans attest to a history of domination by the European–American majority society. Oppression occurs when one segment of the population systematically prevents another segment from obtaining access to resources or denies a fair and equal playing field. First Nations Peoples were victims of genocide and were forced to relinquish their lands, their children, and their freedom of movement on reservations. African Americans were victims of slavery and have fought racism, prejudice, and discrimination in employment, housing, and related forms of segregation. Latino Americans have been the victims of political, social, and economic discrimination and have been the sources of cheap labor. Asian Americans were historically used as cheap labor, have been underrepresented in their political and legal rights, and have been the objects of hostility from the dominant society.

The social worker has knowledge about culturally diverse values. Multicultural values revolve around collective structures such as family, spirituality, and group identity. These values are the source of group solidarity, cultural networks, and hierarchical authority. People of color have internal and external values that are a part of their own being and existence as cultural and ethnic persons. Cultural consciousness, personality, attitudes, emotions, and perceptions are internal processes that are manifested in the external behavior of people of color who persist in the struggle for dignity and equality.

Advanced Level   The following paragraphs describe competencies related to knowledge acquisition at the advanced level.

The social worker has knowledge of theories on postpositivism, constructionism, critical knowledge, and postmodernism. Theories on *ethnicity* deal with the racial heritage that is passed on from generation to generation. Theories of *culture* focus on the way of life of a particular group and encompass language, norms of behavior, values, religion, beliefs, customs, practices, food, music, and the arts. Theories on *minority identity* address an individual's or group's status in the dominant society and how it affects the response of and interaction with members of the whole society. Theories on *social class* involve social, economic, and political arrangements that affect power and social status.

The social worker draws on a range of social science theories from cross-cultural psychology, multicultural counseling and therapy, and cultural anthropology. Cross-cultural psychology has focused on East–West comparisons of group characteristics and has spread to other parts of the world. Multicultural counseling and therapy has been termed a fourth force in the field of counseling psychology (Pedersen, 1991) in view of the fact that it has its own standards, theory base, and academic visibility. (The other three forces are the psychodynamic, behavioral, and humanistic movements.) Cultural anthropology has been the forerunner of cultural studies and has sought to understand various cultures by interviewing members of a particular culture. Social work draws on applied cross-cultural social science theories and disciplines to construct relevant knowledge systems.

SKILL DEVELOPMENT

Skill development is the professional application of practice principles based on knowledge theory and research to working with a client. In social work education there is practice-informed research and research-informed practice (*Educational Policy and Accreditation Standards [EPAS]*, CSWE, 2008, Educational Policy 2.1.6). Skills range consists of engagement (contact, inductive learning, and problem identification), assessment, intervention, and evaluation. Concerning inductive learning of client and problem situation data, Van Den Bergh and Crisp (2004, p. 2) affirm the need for this culturally competent component:

> "The addition of an ongoing learning perspective is consonant with an empowerment approach to practice, which includes the idea of praxis. The latter term refers to the continual evaluation of one's practice by processes of action, reflection, evaluation, potential modification of practice approaches, and a reemergence into action. Inductive learning is the heuristic outreach and investigation of new cultural groups that emerge on the scene, such as recent migrant and refugee groups coming to America."

On the whole, skill development is where the worker and the client deal with and resolve the problem(s).

GENERALIST LEVEL   The following paragraphs describe competencies related to skill development at the generalist level.

The social worker understands how to overcome the resistance and lower the communication barriers of a multicultural client. At the outset of the helping relationship, it is important to minimize resistance and to maximize motivation *(the mini–maxi principle).* Overcoming resistance involves the willingness of the worker to reveal background and to build structure in the relationship with the client, to be a good person who is worthy of trust, and to be a part of the client's life situation. At the same time, lowering communication barriers is initiated by polite conversation, inquiry about the cultural story of the client, and decreasing language, stereotype, and stress barriers.

The social worker obtains personal and family background information from a multicultural client and determines the extent of his or her ethnic/community sense of identity. The worker should discover the personal and family background of the client to understand the person and to build a psychosocial profile. It is important to determine whether the client relates to his or her ethnic community. Being a part of an ethnic community means that the client has a degree of support from significant others such as family and community members. Being isolated from one's ethnic community may have an adverse effect on the client.

The social worker understands the concept of ethnic community and practices relationship protocols with a multicultural client. The social worker should understand the demographics of the ethnic community served by the agency. An ethnic community has a unique history, set of problems, and needs that influence the life of a person who is part of the community. It is crucial for the worker to study these facts. Relationship protocols involve the expression of respect toward the client and/or the client's family. Parents, grandparents, and related significant others should be consulted about the problem situation. Rather than telling the client what to do, it is important to ask the client about his or her perspectives.

The social worker uses professional self-disclosure with a multicultural client. The worker takes the initiative in building a relationship with the client by disclosing an area of interest they have in common. The purpose of professional self-disclosure is to humanize and deprofessionalize the helping relationship and to model the sharing of meaningful information. This relaxes the client and encourages him or her to disclose vital personal problem material in return.

The social worker develops a positive and open communication style and uses open-ended listening responses. The communication style of the worker is important in eliciting responses from the client. Many years ago when I was a young doctoral graduate in my first community mental health center job, I encountered a professor of psychiatry who conducted teaching interview sessions before large numbers of mental health professionals. Whenever it was his turn to preside over grand rounds (a session where various patients are examined before a teaching/learning audience in a hospital setting), I could anticipate his line of questioning. Indeed, the professor of psychiatry was schooled by a famous classical psychiatrist who taught his students to conduct extensive probing. In the interview process, the poor client/patient was asked question upon question based on his or her answers. This single line of probing responses underscored to me as a young clinician the need for the worker to vary his or her responses by asking open-ended questions that offered an opportunity for the client to take the worker through a number of locked mental doors. At the same time, the worker's follow-up responses to open-ended questions should involve reflecting, summary, and directive expressions.

The social worker obtains problem information, facilitates problem area disclosure, and promotes problem understanding. Problem identification entails gathering the essential facts of the person and the social environment surrounding the problem by facilitating a positive process so that the client willingly discloses the problem area. The result is that both the client and the worker understand the problem from their different perspectives. Succeeding in uncovering the problem in a concise and careful way takes skill on the part of the worker, who has laid the groundwork since the initial contact.

The social worker views a problem as an unsatisfied want or an unfulfilled need. Reid (1978) described *a problem as an unsatisfied want or an unfulfilled need.* This perspective gets behind the pathology of a problem by understanding that a problem has a positive aspect. That is, a problem exists because of a lack of satisfaction (unsatisfied want) or a lack of fulfillment (unfulfilled need). If the worker can help the client to reframe the problem around this perspective, the client can be redirected in a positive direction, toward ways in which to achieve need satisfaction and fulfillment.

The social worker classifies problems on micro, meso, and macro levels. From the social work practice vantage point, problems are multidimensional. The micro (individual, family, and small group), meso (community and organization), and macro (complex organization, geographical population) levels of a problem persist and interact with each other. For example, problems resulting from welfare reform involve a macro-level federal law that mandates the restructuring of welfare and employment, meso-level state and county mandates to implement the law, and micro-level effects on single women, dependent children, and legal immigrants.

The social worker explains problem themes of racism, prejudice, and discrimination, and their expressions. Part of problem identification is uncovering the dynamics of racism, prejudice, and discrimination that may be present in the problems of the multicultural client. It is important to rule these themes in or out. *Racism* is a cognitive belief about superiority and inferiority, dominance and subordination learned from parents, neighborhood, and community. *Prejudice* is the negative attitude or emotional result of racism, whereas *discrimination* is the behavioral expression of racism and prejudice through a negative action taken against a person of color. Problems may be infected with racism, prejudice, and discrimination.

The social worker finds out problem details. Multicultural problems encompass a wide spectrum, ranging from psychosocial dysfunction during transitional adjustment for immigrants to persons who have indirect ways of expressing problems such as storytelling. The worker must be patient and assess the situation, often piecing together aspects of who is involved, when and where the problem occurs, and what the major issues are.

The social worker assesses socioenvironmental stressors, psychoindividual reactions, and cultural strengths. *Psychosocial assessment* takes into account both the socioenvironmental stressors and the psychological reaction to these stressors experienced by the client. The client generally has coping skills to process environmental stress and conflict. However, these resources may temporarily fail and the client may experience psychosomatic reactions that are symptomatic of internalized stress. The worker should also assess cultural strengths and both internal and external resources for change.

The social worker assesses the biological, psychological, social, cultural, and spiritual dimensions of a multicultural client. Social work practice normatively speaks about *biopsychosocial assessment.* However, from a multicultural viewpoint, assessment must address the cultural and spiritual aspects along with the physical, psychological, and social dimensions. A person is mind, body, and spirit in an environmental system. As such, a full assessment of the assets of the person considers the interaction and exchange between and among the biological/physical, psychological/mental, social/environmental, cultural/ethnic, and spiritual/religious aspects of the person.

The social worker establishes joint goals and agreements with the client that are culturally acceptable. Contracting with the client around mutually agreeable and culturally sensitive goals is the initial intervention step. In a cultural context, the agreement may be verbal rather than written because in many cultures verbal agreements are binding. Goals provide an opportunity to structure the course of the change strategy.

The social worker formulates micro, meso, and macro intervention strategies that address the cultural and special needs of the client. Multicultural clients operate in interdependent spheres involving the individual as part of the family; the family and extended family as part of an association, clan, or tribe; and the group as part of a neighborhood, community, or organization. As a result, micro, meso, and macro intervention strategies should be devised to address these multiple levels. Individual and group empowerment, family and network casework, and use of church and community social services are examples of these three levels of intervention.

The social worker initiates evaluation in a way that links the client to an ethnic community resource, reviews significant progress and growth, evaluates goal outcomes, and establishes a follow-up strategy. Evaluation is the end of a beginning. New linkages to a sense of identity and helping persons in the ethnic community, recital of past progress, evaluation of goals that have been achieved, and follow-up on emerging problems are part of a continuing pattern.

ADVANCED LEVEL   The following paragraphs describe competencies related to skill development at the advanced level.

The social worker designs a service delivery and agency linkage and culturally effective social service programs in ethnic communities. Service delivery design involves identifying workable program principles for agencies that wish to adopt and implement culturally sound programs for multicultural clients. Organizing a service program structure provides a vehicle for an agency to deliver a unit of service to a client in an effective manner.

The social worker understands that services must be accessible to the ethnic community. Location is basic to service delivery. An agency program must be located near the target population. It should be within walking distance or near main transportation routes, in community storefronts, recreation centers, and churches. Locating programs should be a joint decision between the agency and community leaders.

The social worker understands the importance of pragmatic and positive services that meet the tangible needs of the ethnic community. Pragmatic and positive services mean useful and stigma-free services arising from a survey of community needs. A mental illness connotation should be avoided. Family education, child-care, and parenting themes should be promoted. The community can be asked for a list of its needs.

The social worker believes that it is important to recruit bilingual/bicultural workers who reflect the ethnic composition of the clientele. The *staffing pattern* of an agency program should reflect the ethnic, gender, and age composition of its constituencies. Staff should be able to speak another language in rudimentary and fluent levels and should know another culture. In this sense, the entire staff has some bilingual and bicultural skills and knowledge.

The social worker should advocate for community outreach education and prevention with visible services, culturally sensitive programs, and credible staff. The ethnic community should be exposed to the staff of an agency through extensive community outreach programs that reach the home, the church, the school, and related community institutions. *Community outreach* builds the visibility, credibility, and integrity of the program and staff, and is an effective way to build referrals to the agency.

The social worker establishes linkages with related social agencies, which ensures rapid referral and program collaboration. It is important to build *working relationships* with colleagues in other social agencies who can refer cases. When there is an emergency same-day referral, collaborative colleagues can help each other.

The social worker fosters a conducive agency setting with a friendly and help-ful atmosphere. The *agency setting* establishes a tone for the worker–client interaction. The most important person in the office is the receptionist because that person is the first program contact for the client. A friendly, helpful, and bilingual person is a necessary ingredient. The decor of the office, staff tempo, and morale should convey a sense of nurture and caring.

The social worker is involved in cultural skill development research to gain new insights on new principles. The importance of *relationship protocols* and skills such as *professional self-disclosure* was recognized more than 25 years ago when I began to write a social work practice text on people of color (Lum, 1986). New skills are needed to keep up with ways of working with people from diverse cultures. Culturally competent practice offers a helping approach that is oriented in a cultural base and is concerned with measuring behavioral action competencies to determine outcome performance and worker–client proficiency.

SUMMARY

This chapter has presented a framework that addresses cultural competence and competencies from the perspective of culturally competent practice. The cultural competence social work model addresses the core competencies of culturally competent practice, cultural awareness, knowledge acquisition, and skill development as essential components at the generalist and advanced levels. I hope that you will read and use this framework, which contains a practical road map for working with culturally and ethnically diverse clients.

CHAPTER 5

CULTURAL AWARENESS

Doman Lum

The road to cultural competence begins with an understanding of your own personal and professional cultural awareness. Understanding your own cultural heritage, beliefs, and behavior provides cultural sensitivity about the cultures of others, involving cultural group experiences and contacts with people of various diverse backgrounds. In turn, personal cultural awareness has a direct effect on how you as a social work professional will interact with a variety of diverse clients. These principles are covered in "Standard 2. Self-Awareness" (National Association of Social Workers [NASW], 2007, pp. 19–21) for cultural competence in social work practice. It asks social workers to develop an understanding of their own personal and cultural values and beliefs, especially to examine their own cultural backgrounds and to increase awareness of personal assumptions, values, and biases, which influences their practice and relationships with clients. This is termed *cultural identity formation*. It also encourages social workers to become culturally aware of the heritage of others, particularly to value differences in others. As a result, social workers are asked to develop diversity in their own group so that they can be more open to the diversity of other groups. In a real sense cultural awareness is the first step that leads to cultural sensitivity and ultimately to achieving cultural competence.

The purpose of this chapter is to help the reader with a series of cultural awareness principles and exercises to increase both personal and professional perspectives. First, we define cultural awareness in a contextual setting, explore the nature of cultural identity and the need for a cultural search, rediscovery, and formulation, and explain some theories of cultural awareness. We use a case study to heighten individual, family, group, and community dimensions of cultural self-awareness and other awareness. These entities shape who we are and how we see ourselves. As a result, we learn cognitive, affective, and behavioral responses. Hopefully the chapter reinforces and illumines the NASW's Standard 2 on self-awareness.

Reynolds (1995) points out that "cultural self-awareness is a vital first step toward cultural sensitivity" (p. 320). We encourage you to be open, to explore your beliefs and values, and to practice introspection and reflective self-evaluation in an environment of trust and openness. In your own private study of this chapter and in the classroom we hope that you explore your thoughts and feelings in a non-threatening manner. We also believe that along with cultural self-awareness of the worker is the task of developing cultural other awareness of the client. (For a discussion on the importance of cultural self-awareness and awareness of the cultures of others, see Whaley & Davis, 2007.) These two components constitute cultural awareness in general.

DEFINITION OF CULTURAL AWARENESS

The term *cultural awareness* has several levels of meaning for our discussion. Awareness deals with conscious attention and knowledge through the mind and the senses. In other words, a person's awareness has both cognitive and sensory dimensions. Culture involves the transmission of beliefs, values, traditions, customs, and practices from one generation to the next. Cultural awareness involves the self in a cultural context. Hardy and Laszloffy (1995) describe cultural awareness as *the learning of cultural background, issues, and relationships in a contextual sense*. The emphasis on cultural context is important to our understanding of cultural awareness.

Sanday (1976) categorizes individuals as relating to cultural contexts in one of four different ways that affect cultural awareness and involvement:

- *Mainstream individuals* have assimilated the values of the dominant society and attempt to emulate these values in their behavior. In the United States, the Americanization of people involves individualism, freedom of expression, casual and fashionable dress, youthful appearance, patriotism, and mergence into the predominant thinking and behavior.
- *Bicultural individuals* move in two distinct cultural worlds: the mainstream, dominant culture of work and society; and their culture of origin, which may have traces of old world traditions, beliefs, and practices. They have a dual commitment to survive and maintain themselves in both spheres, which have meaning and purpose for them.
- The *culturally different* have been exposed to the mainstream culture but have chosen to affiliate and focus their activities in a culturally different and distinct structure. They have made a conscious choice to remain in their cultural and ethnic enclave. They become self-contained residents of Chinatown, Little Italy, Little Havana, or Little Saigon, where they are able to function in an autonomous ethnic setting where language, customs, food, and business exchanges occur.
- The *culturally marginal* have detached themselves from an identified cultural and ethnic identity and live their lives apart from distinct groups. They may be people who were raised away from their ethnic group and now feel neither a part of that group nor a member of their adopted group. American Indian children who were removed and placed in White foster care may now feel a part of neither the tribe nor the White culture. Due to limited acceptance and lack of a sense of belonging to either party, they are marginal people caught outside their ethnicity and the dominant society. The same may be true of the

person who rejects his or her own ethnic group, marries and seeks to identify with another racial group, alters physical appearance for assimilation purposes, and realizes there is limited acceptance in both the original and the alternative ethnic group.

These descriptions may or may not fit your situation or context. As you review them, do you fit into any category or would you describe yourself in a different way? How has your individual, family, neighborhood, and community contextual background and life history affected your cultural self-awareness and your awareness of other people's cultures? How has your cultural self-awareness affected how you might understand and interact with a multicultural client?

Think about these questions and review Sanday's contextual descriptions. Talk with your instructor and classmates about contextual cultural awareness. Personal and class discussions may help you realize the importance of cultural self-awareness and other awareness.

THE CASE OF TABITHA

Tabitha, a 16-year-old Caribbean American, is a client of a large residential facility for girls. She was born and raised in Trinidad, an island in the Caribbean, and still has family there. She was sent by her single mother to be raised by her relatives who settled in Miami, Florida. She has a number of strengths: her enjoyment of reading, her leadership quality, her verbal communication with other residents and with staff, and her survival knowledge. She was raised by her extended family, which has a chronic history of unstable relationships. Her grandmother has been her point of reference and is a spiritual woman.

Tabitha missed high school for a year and a half and was a runaway selling drugs on the streets, but she claims that she did not use drugs. She was involved in physical assault toward her mother and verbal threats and vandalism with her aunt. There is a history of child abuse and neglect on the part of her family. She is now in a nonpublic school, and her academic performance has been inconsistent. She goes to school at the residential facility, is currently employed in a part-time job after school, and would like to transition and finish her education in a nearby public high school.

Imagine you are a social work intern in her residential facility and are working with Tabitha on a one-to-one basis. In the following sections our task is to introduce various steps of cultural awareness and to link them to the case of Tabitha as you work toward increasing cultural self-awareness and other awareness in your helping relationship with her.

STEP 1: KNOW WHERE YOU ARE IN YOUR LIFE

Why did you choose to become a social work major? Was it because you enjoy listening to people and helping them with their problems? Where are you in your life? Where have you come from and where do you see yourself going in the next few years? Before you enter the helping profession of social work it is best to take stock of your life. *Positionality* is a concept that helps you in your personal assessment and is fundamental to our discussion of cultural awareness. It looks at the similarities and differences of people that foster uniqueness to assist us in the sorting out of our multiple identities and establish our position as a person in relations to others. There is a connection between *positionality* and *multiple identities*, which is important to understand as you evaluate yourself. Suarez, Newman, and Reed (2008) explain,

> Positionality refers to our location along the various axes of social group identities, which are interrelated, interconnected, and intersecting. Further, both our internal and external identities interact and influence each other and vary according to changing contexts. The intersections of identities may be external and visible, or internal and invisible, selectively carrying intrinsic privileges of which we may be unaware while others may simultaneously limit our choices in life. Under this conception, since people's identities are so influenced by context, we do not have one identity, but multiple identities that may be contradictory and changeable. (p. 44)

Reed, Newman, Suarez, and Lewis (1997) explain the characteristics of positionality as:

- An inward process of self-examination and self-exploration and an outward process of understanding and situating one's self in the world
- A dialogue between thinking and action, knowledge and experience, where there is a joining of critical reflection and an engagement that leads to involvement and commitment
- A different position involving a different standpoint from which one develops a level of awareness about one's social location
- A connection between positionality and worldview

In one sense, positionality is self-reflection on who you are, where you have come from, and where you are heading as a diverse person. It is the continuous discovery and rediscovery of your place in life and how you want to position yourself in relation to self and significant others. Weaver (2005) reminds us that when we work with a client, we must be aware that there is a cultural distance between the worker and the client that must be bridged. Cultural awareness and positionality (where you are at the present time) are crucial ingredients to work through in order to lessen the distance and bridge the gap. Weaver (2005) states,

> Cultural differences between social workers and their clients can have a major impact on the helping relationship. A client's cultural background may influence what is defined as a problem, how he or she goes about seeking help, and what interventions and solutions are seen as desirable. Likewise, social workers bring their own cultural backgrounds as well as their professional backgrounds to the helping relationship, and this may influence how they approach their clients. (p. 2)

Keenan (2004) encourages us to take an informed not-knowing stance in the worker–client relationship: "This stance is based on an assumption in critical theories that knowledge is always partial, perspectival, and constructed through the lens of understanding, meaning, and interests of one's social position" (p. 543). Later she explains,

> A stance of informed not-knowing assumes a perspectival relation with knowledge, focusing on skills of questioning and listening to obtain understanding and knowledge (otherwise experienced as "how to function in a rapidly changing global world where it is impossible to know everything"). (p. 544)

It is an existential journey into yourself to find out who you are, and a simple declaration of your emerging self to others. It involves self-appraisal and reflection that bring the strength of becoming involved with other persons and issues.

The psychological and social location of a person is constantly changing based on the interactions occurring in life. One must constantly take *a social location contextual reading of the situation.* Keenan (2004) points out,

> Social workers can move out of a center-margin dichotomy by shifting to a description of social location that provides greater complexity (i.e., naming the context in which services are being provided, describing relations between the groups of people present in that context, describing culture–power relations between people and the social structures, and describing the meanings these relations have for the client and the worker. (p. 542)

There is a constant reinventing of self that results in positioning and repositioning. Where is an individual as a growing, emerging person who is changing according to the new experiences encountered in life? How does one explain and interpret what happens in the past, present, and future of a person? Positionality further recognizes the need to understand where the client and the worker are coming from as well as the complex intersections of the past, present, and future positions that influence what positions and postures a person takes in life interactions.

Tabitha as your client and you as her social worker have positions that you both are constantly taking in the dynamic changes that are occurring in your lives together and apart from each other. Understand this fluidity and know your own positionality. Help her find her positions in her life.

STEP 2: WORKING THROUGH THE DILEMMA OF AMERICANIZATION

You may be familiar with the Caribbean American community and have Caribbean American friends. So working with Tabitha may not be a new experience for you. However, you may come from a cultural background where you have had minimal contact with Caribbean Americans. So relating and working with Tabitha is a wholly new experience. We are talking about cultural diversity, particularly cultural differences. Social work education encourages social work students and professions to engage diversity and difference in practice. Diversity characterizes and shapes the human experience and is critical in the formation of identity. Social work education asks social workers to gain sufficient self-awareness to eliminate personal biases and values in working with diverse groups. It encourages us to recognize and communicate our understanding of the importance of difference in shaping life experiences and to become learners and engage others as our informants (Council on Social Work Education, 2008, Educational Policy 2.1.4).

Before meeting Tabitha and beginning the first session with her, you might want to think about "Step 2." In this section, we explain the dynamics of the dilemma and ask you to think about your contextual situation. The dilemma of Americanization is everyone's dilemma of finding out about their ethnic background and culture of origin. The term *Americanization* involves being American in character, manners, methods, and ideas and the assimilation of U.S. customs, speech, and other characteristics to the point of excluding your culture of origin. Americanization should not be confused with *Americanism*. The latter term refers to the devotion or loyalty to the United States or to its traditions, customs, and institutions. The dilemma involves the loss of one's culture of origin to the point of being unable to connect it to one's present American culture. This may or may not be an important factor in cultural awareness, but we hope that you will consider it.

Some people are first-generation American born and have parents who come from other countries and still speak their native language. Their culture of origin is fairly well intact because of language, customs, and traditions still practiced in the family. Others come from an ethnic community in either rural or urban America where generations have preserved language and customs from the Scandinavian countries, or from Southern or Eastern Europe. Little Italy sections, Norwegian communities, and Finnish enclaves exist and have maintained strong cultural and ethnic ties.

Many Americans are many generations removed from great-grandparents who immigrated to the United States and are the products of multiple ethnic European groups blending with other non-White ethnic groups. These people have a difficult time reconstructing their ethnic and cultural origins. All of us contact our cultural and ethnic roots in varying ways.

Giordano and McGoldrick (1996) start their discussion of European Americans with the comment of a colleague who said, "Come on, White ethnics today don't have ethnic issues; they're totally American" (p. 427). They point out the following interesting facts about European Americans:

* They are the majority population (80%) and involve 53 categories. The largest groups are German Americans (58 million), English Americans (41 million), and Irish Americans (39 million). This is because U.S. immigration policy favored Western and Central Europeans until the 1965 McCarran Immigration Act, which opened immigration from countries in Asia and Central and South America.
* They are multigenerational in the history of the United States. Most families from European American groups have been in the United States for three or more generations. This would mean that an American descendant of the Jamestown colony of 1608 would be 20 generations removed from Europe. In the nearly 400 years since the first colony, most traces of European culture and ethnicity have been reduced to residual fragments. Cultural awareness of European roots has simply faded over time.
* Anglo Protestant culture, religion, and values have been dominant due to the presence of Western European settlers in the United States. We know from the history of social welfare that the founding fathers of this country represented the White English American privileged class of the time. The first Irish Catholic president of the United States was John F. Kennedy, who was elected in 1960. Until that point, there had been strong resistance to a non-Protestant in the White House. The English (Anglo-Saxon) brought with them their racism, prejudice, and discrimination. In England, the Irish were termed *savages* by

the British. This label was transferred to the American Indians in the New World. The Protestant work ethic influenced the dominant negative social attitude toward welfare recipients. The moral virtue of the society affected social attitudes toward gays and lesbians.

- They display ambivalence about particular ethnic identity and achievement of success in the dominant society. Giordano and McGoldrick (1996) observe,

> Ethnicity persists in the consciousness of European Americans, in their perceptions, preferences, and behavior, even while mass production and mass communication homogenize their outward appearances. Psychologically, European Americans are often ambivalent about their identities, and are constantly trying to balance the pull of their family histories and experiences with their individual desires to be accepted and successful in the larger society. (p. 439)

It is difficult to build cultural awareness in European Americans who have become so blended into the American culture. Many simply respond with "I am an American" when asked to trace their ethnic and cultural background and distinctive traditions, values, and practices. However, this may be a dilemma of Americanization for the majority of us. Green (1995) observes,

> White Americans often view the matter differently for ... many of them have difficulty in thinking of themselves as "ethnic." Typically they resort to national labels when asked to describe themselves culturally, and their idiom of ethnic affiliation is more geographical. As the dominant group, whites hear the claims of shared substance ... made by Latinos, Asian Americans, and others whose ethnicity they can easily see, but they do not find anything like that in themselves. That is because for them ethnicity is perceived only in the surface features.... From the point of view of whites, that is a convenient perspective to have, especially in a political sense. It locates ethnicity exclusively in others and excuses them from having to consider their own participation in the management and enforcement of separateness. (p. 21)

One can recall one's life-span development and focus on specific incidents where there was significant contact with a diverse person. Childhood incidents are often formative building blocks that shape later beliefs and attitudes about and behavioral responses to diverse people. Did you have meaningful contact with European, African, Latino, Asian American, and First Nations Peoples individuals and families in your childhood years? Did you live in a homogeneous White neighborhood or in a heterogeneous, diverse neighborhood? Who were your neighborhood and school friends? Did you attend an integrated school system? Do you recall positive and/or negative incidents involving you and a diverse person of color that made a lasting impression on your life? These are significant questions to ask from a life-development perspective.

Based on the past and present contact with diverse people, it is crucial to ask about the degree of tolerance and/or acceptance of cultural differences that you have felt. Tolerance is the degree of acceptance of views, beliefs, and practices that differ from one's own. It also denotes the degree of freedom one has from internalized bigotry or prejudice. Finally, it includes the willingness to allow, permit, and respect the divergent beliefs and practices of others. In sum, tolerance is the willingness to accept another person and to allow him or her to be what he or she wants to be, as long as the individual does not harm someone else.

If this dilemma of Americanization is a part of your background, it is important to bring it to your consciousness and begin to work through it. Green (1995) has some practical suggestion to deal with the dilemma and to increase our cultural awareness:

- Adopt a systematic learning style and develop a supportive agency environment that recognizes culturally distinctive modes of behavior with appropriate responses.
- Acknowledge the cultural characteristics of client communities, the realities of power and systematic inequality, and the need for staff and administration commitment to follow through on training initiatives in order for cultural awareness to penetrate the social work profession.
- Participate in discovery of the beliefs and thinking of the client, comparing these to the life and experiences of the worker, and try to understand the meaning of differences between the two.

Thinking about whether this dilemma is a part of what you need to work through at this stage of your life.

STEP 3: EXPLORE YOUR FAMILY CULTURE

As part of your social work education even before you enter your social work major as an undergraduate or graduate student, you should know your family culture. You may have done this on your own at home, in school, or at church. You may have taken ethnic studies courses where this would have been covered by the instructor. However, this may be a new experience for some or not adequately covered for others. Potocky-Tripodi (2002) focuses on family culture background:

> [A] first step in developing culturally competent practice is to be aware of one's own racial, cultural, and ethnic backgrounds, and how these have influenced one's life experiences and outlooks. By doing so one also becomes aware that the decisions one makes may be ethnocentric. (p. 131)

Later, she discusses developing self-knowledge and recommends,

> Social workers' awareness of their own ethnicity may be limited to what they have personally experienced in their lives. Self-knowledge requires workers to actively learn about their ethnic backgrounds. This learning can include such methods as reading about their ethnic groups, interviewing family or other ethnic group members, and participating in traditional activities. (p. 142)

Individual and family experiences are central to an understanding of cultural self-awareness. The discovery of family of origin uncovers family heritage or cultural history. Past family events influence present family attitudes and cultural life experiences. Beliefs and practices from parents and grandparents have a major effect on an individual. Weaver (2005) observes,

> Children learn from their parents and others around them what it means to be a member of a particular cultural group. The way that parents feel about themselves is transmitted to children as they gain a sense of self-worth and their own identities. Likewise, the ways that family, community, and society feel about a particular cultural group are learned and often internalized by children. (p. 31)

The family is the individual's primary group, representing the familiar, the intimate, the positive, the similar, the in-group. Family life experiences and practices shape the worker's beliefs, attitudes, behavior, and view of life and the surrounding world.

Family and culture fulfill our needs. They are the source of our self-perception and worldview. From our family, we view, interpret, and respond to the outside world. The family provides protection, comfort, and care throughout our lives, particularly during times of transition and major change. We derive strength for coping and survival from our family who become our natural support system. In brief, family and culture help the individual become a fully functioning person. Every family has a keeper of the culture, that is, someone who knows the history of the family generations, practices past family customs and traditions, and can provide you with family keepsakes that have been passed down. Spend some time with your family's keeper of the culture. Take a trip to where your ancestors came from. Rediscover family birthplace, long-lost relatives, and family pictures and records. Your sense of family culture will be enhanced and your heightened interest in discussing the family culture of your clients will be increased to the point of recognizing that exploring family culture in the helping relationship may provide the client with a strength to cope with life's problems.

To enhance your understanding of family culture, you can take up the "Cultural Awareness Assessment" that covers various aspects of your family background and culture. It is hoped that you may uncover helpful information about you and your family.

The Cultural Awareness Assessment (Source: From The Social Work Interview: A Guide for Human Service Professionals, by Alfred and Goldie Kadushin. Copyright © 1997 by Columbia University Press. Reprinted with permission of the publisher.)

This is a self-assessment of your family cultural life experiences and your significant contacts with members of other cultural and ethnic groups in your neighborhood and community. You are asked to provide the following information and to bring it to class for group discussion.

1. My ethnic family background is: (circle those that apply)
    a. European origin

1. Amish	6. Greek	11. Scandinavian
2. English	7. Hungarian	12. other (please
3. Dutch	8. Irish	explain)
4. French Canadian	9. Italian	13. combination of the
5. German	10. Portuguese	following:

    b. Slavic

1. Polish	4. Czech
2. Slovak	5. other (please explain)
3. Russian	6. combination of the following:

    c. Jewish

       1. American   4. European

       2. Soviet   5. other (please explain)

       3. Israeli   6. combination of the following:

    d. First Nations Peoples

       1. tribe   3. combination of the following:

       2. other (please explain)

    e. African origin

       1. African American   5. Nigerian

       2. Jamaican   6. other (please explain)

       3. Haitian   7. combination of the following:

       4. African American Muslim

    f. Latino

       1. Cuban   5. Central American

       2. Mexican   6. other (please explain)

       3. Puerto Rican   7. combination of the following:

       4. Brazilian

    g. Asian American

       1. Chinese   6. Indonesian

       2. Japanese   7. Filipino

       3. Korean   8. other (please explain)

       4. Vietnamese   9. combination of the following:

       5. Cambodian

    h. Asian Indian

       1. Hindu   4. other (please explain)

       2. Christian   5. combination of the following:

       3. Muslim

    i. Middle Eastern

       1. Arab   6. Lebanese

       2. Afghan   7. Armenian

       3. Iraqi   8. other (please explain)

       4. Iranian   9. combination of the following:

       5. Israeli

2. My level of acculturation is: (circle one)

    a. very Americanized   d. traditional culture of origin

    b. somewhat Americanized   e. other (please explain)

    c. bicultural

3. My regional culture (circle one) does/does not influence me. If it does, my regional culture is: (circle one)

   a. Southern

   b. Midwestern

   c. Eastern

   d. Northern

   e. Western

   f. New England

   g. New York

   h. California

   i. Texas

   j. other (please explain)

4. The keeper of culture in my family is: (circle one)

   a. my mother

   b. my father

   c. my mother and father

   d. my sister

   e. my brother

   f. my grandmother

   g. my grandfather

   h. my grandmother and grandfather

   i. other (please explain)

   j. no one (please explain)

5. My family observes the following cultural practices: (circle relevant ones)

   a. ethnic holidays

   b. ethnic religious worship

   c. ethnic and cultural food

   d. ethnic conversational language

   e. ethnic marriage traditions

   f. ethnic birthday traditions

   g. ethnic funeral traditions

   h. other (please explain)

   i. none (please explain)

   j. all of the above

6. My best friends in my neighborhood were from: (check one)

   a. the same race

   b. different races (please specify)

   c. other (please explain)

7. My best friends in school were from: (check one)

   a. the same race

   b. different races (please specify)

   c. other (please explain)

8. My closest friends are from: (check one)

   a. the same race

   b. different races (please specify)

   c. other (please explain)

9. I have a partner or will probably have a partner who is: (check one)

   a. a person of my specific ethnic subgroup

   b. a person of my general ethnic background

   c. a person of another race

   d. uncertain

   e. other (please explain) (e.g., European–European, Latino–Latino)

10. My levels of contact with individuals, families, and groups outside my own cultural and ethnic group in the following settings are: (check relevant ones)

Level of Contact	Setting			
	Neighborhood	School	Social Activities	Work
minimal				
moderate				
frequent				

11. My experiences with people of other cultures and ethnicities have been: (circle relevant ones)

positive   negative   mixed

   a. Describe a positive experience: c. Describe a mixed experience:

   b. Describe a negative experience:

12. I have a number of stereotypes about the following groups: (circle relevant ones)

   a. European Americans

   b. African Americans

   c. Latino Americans

   d. Asian Americans

   e. First Nations Peoples

Give an example of a group stereotype that you have:

13. People have a stereotype about me due to: (circle relevant ones)

   a. my ethnic background   f. my income

   b. my gender   g. my place of residence

   c. my appearance   h. the make of my car

   d. my student status   i. other (please explain)

   e. my career choice

14. I (circle one) would/would not like to increase my cultural awareness. If so, I am interested in the following areas: (circle relevant ones)

   a. studying my ethnic/cultural family roots   e. working with multicultural clients in social service agencies

   b. visiting my country of origin   f. learning a multicultural language

   c. learning my ethnic language   g. working in my country of origin

   d. learning about other ethnic and cultural history, beliefs, and interaction patterns   h. working in a Third World country

                                i. other (please explain)

STEP 4: PRACTICE CULTURAL OTHER AWARENESS

As part of beginning a relationship with a client, it is important to explore the other's culture and ethnic background. After all it is part of engaging the client in an understanding of his or her personhood. Perez and colleagues (2005) observe,

> [I]t is important that therapists gain cultural awareness and understanding of their clients' experiences and the way presenting concerns or difficulties may be influenced by racial and ethnic variables as well as the intersection of those variables with issues of racism or other forms of societal oppression. (p. 163)

To uncover elements of cultural other awareness, the "Cultural Other Awareness Inventory" asks for background information on your experiences with other diverse individuals and groups. This may indicate the extent to which you have developed your cultural other awareness.

The Cultural Other Awareness Inventory (Source: From The Social Work Interview: A Guide for Human Service Professionals, by Alfred and Goldie Kadushin. Copyright © 1997 by Columbia University Press. Reprinted with permission of the publisher.)

This questionnaire surveys your involvement with persons of other cultures in childhood, adolescence, young adulthood, and adulthood. You are asked to provide the following information and to share it in class discussion.

1. I was born in: (name of city, population)

2. My ethnic group is: (circle one)
   a. European American
   b. African American
   c. Latino American
   d. Asian American
   e. First Nations Peoples
   f. other (please explain)

3. My childhood years were spent in: (name of city or cities)

4. When I was a child, my neighborhood was predominantly: (circle one)
   a. European American
   b. African American
   c. Latino American
   d. Asian American
   e. First Nations Peoples
   f. multiracial (list ethnic groups)

5. When I was a child, my contact with people of different ethnic groups was as indicated. (circle one in each category)
   a. African Americans: rare / somewhat frequent / frequent
   b. Mexican Americans: rare / somewhat frequent / frequent
   c. Puerto Rican Americans: rare / somewhat frequent / frequent
   d. Cuban Americans: rare / somewhat frequent / frequent
   e. Chinese Americans: rare / somewhat frequent / frequent
   f. Japanese Americans: rare / somewhat frequent / frequent
   g. Korean Americans: rare / somewhat frequent / frequent
   h. Vietnamese Americans: rare / somewhat frequent / frequent
   i. First Nations Peoples: rare / somewhat frequent / frequent

6. When I was a child, my impressions about people of different ethnic groups were as indicated. (circle one in each category)
   a. African Americans: favorable / somewhat favorable / unfavorable
   b. Latino Americans: favorable / somewhat favorable / unfavorable
   c. Asian Americans: favorable / somewhat favorable / unfavorable
   d. First Nations Peoples: favorable / somewhat favorable / unfavorable

7. As a child, I formulated my impression about people of color from: (circle relevant ones)
   a. my parents' attitudes   c. my neighbors' attitudes
   b. my experiences with ethnic   d. my peer group
      individuals   e. other (please explain)

8. My adolescent years were spent in: (name of city or cities)

9. When I was a teenager, my neighborhood was predominantly: (circle one)
   a. European American   d. Asian American
   b. African American   e. First Nations Peoples
   c. Latino American   f. multiracial (list ethnic groups)

10. When I was a teenager, my close friends were predominantly: (circle one)
   a. Whites   d. Asian American
   b. African Americans   e. First Nations Peoples
   c. Latino Americans   f. multiracial (list ethnic groups)

11. As a teenager, I dated predominantly: (circle one)
   a. Whites   d. Asian American
   b. African Americans   e. American Indians
   c. Latino Americans   f. multiracial (list ethnic groups)

12. When I was a teenager, my impressions from childhood about people of different ethnic groups changed (or not) as indicated. (circle one in each category)
   a. African Americans:
      remained the same / changed more favorably / changed less favorably
   b. Latino Americans:
      remained the same / changed more favorably / changed less favorably
   c. Asian Americans:
      remained the same / changed more favorably / changed less favorably
   d. First Nations Peoples:
      remained the same / changed more favorably / changed less favorably
   Explain the reasons for your change in impressions about specific ethnic groups.

13. As a young adult, I lived in: (name of city or cities)

14. I went to the following colleges and universities:

15. My undergraduate college major was:

16. My college degrees are: (circle relevant ones)

    baccalaureate   master   doctorate

17. When I was a young adult, my close friends were predominantly: (circle one)

    a. Whites   d. Asian Americans
    b. African Americans   e. First Nations Peoples
    c. Latino Americans   f. multiracial (list ethnic groups)

18. When I was a young adult, my serious romantic relationships were predominantly with: (circle one)

    a. Whites   d. Asian Americans
    b. African Americans   e. First Nations Peoples
    c. Latino Americans   f. multiracial (list ethnic groups)

19. When I was a young adult, my first full-time job after graduation from college was with an organization whose employees were predominantly: (circle one)

    a. Whites   d. Asian Americans
    b. African Americans   e. First Nations Peoples
    c. Latino Americans   f. multiracial (list ethnic groups)

20. As an adult, I have lived in: (name of city or cities)

    I am now living in: (name of city)

21. As an adult, I married or am living with a partner whose ethnic background is: (circle one)

    a. the same as mine
    b. different from mine (please explain)

22. As an adult, I live in a neighborhood that is predominantly: (circle one)

    a. White   d. Asian American
    b. African American   e. First Nations Peoples
    c. Latino American   f. multiracial (list ethnic groups)

23. My present employer is: (name of the company)

24. My fellow employees are predominantly: (circle one)

    a. White   d. Asian American
    b. African American   e. First Nations Peoples
    c. Latino American   f. multiracial (list ethnic groups)

25. Throughout my life, the degree of contact and involvement with people of color that I have had has been: (circle one)

    a. minimal   b. somewhat frequent   c. frequent   d. other (please explain)

Take some time in class to share this information and to discuss the degree to which you have experienced and presently practice cultural other awareness. If we have done our homework, we have worked somewhat through our biases toward other ethnic groups. Thus, it is mandatory to revisit the range of previous contact experiences—both positive and negative—in order to become aware of feelings toward culturally different others. Cultural other awareness challenges us to look beyond a White–Black dichotomy society. Our country is so diverse and multicultural/multiethnic in certain parts that there has been an explosion of different peoples in our communities.

Delgado, Jones, and Rohani (2005) make the point that immigration and its accompanying changing ethnic demographics move us beyond a mindset of a dominant White majority and an oppressed Black minority. They observe,

> Many people would argue that this nation's view of the world was greatly shaped and influenced by the centrality of slavery in the nation's social fabric. As a result, race relations have historically been viewed from a Black–White perspective. However, the shift in demographic composition has largely been fueled by immigration. The number of newcomers from Latino countries in the Western Hemisphere ... has been so pronounced that this trend, combined with high fertility and low death rates, have converged to make Latinos the largest "minority" in the United States. (p. 233)

A similar case could be made for Asians, which is the fastest growing ethnic group in the United States. All this reminds us to think of cultural other awareness in terms of multiple cultural individuals and groups.

Increasingly, with the population explosion of immigrants and refugees, we need to find out about this dimension of cultural other awareness. Potocky-Tripodi (2002) explains,

> The population of immigrants and refugees in the United States is growing rapidly. Within the next four to five decades, immigrants and refugees will account for 65 percent of the country's population growth, and first- and second-generation immigrants and refugees will make up more than 25 percent of the population. Thus, all social workers are likely to encounter refugee and immigrant clients in their practice. (p. 479)

We need to gear up for this trend in social work education.

Segal (2002) has a helpful framework for immigration that is useful for uncovering the important aspects of the journey from one's home country to the receiving country, which is a crucial part of cultural other awareness. Her model includes eight aspects:

Conditions in Home Country
- Economic, political/legal, social, cultural/religious

Status in Home Country
- Economic, social, political

Experience in Home Country
- Education, vocation, class/caste

Reasons for Leaving Home Country

- Push: Lack of opportunity, persecution (political/legal/religious), natural disasters, adventure
- Pull: Increased opportunity, freedom/safety, family reunification, adventure

Transition to Country of Immigration

- Emigration: planned/unplanned, voluntary/forced, legal/illegal, safe/dangerous, easy/difficult
- Immigration: easy/difficulty, pleasant/traumatic, direct/indirect, legal/undocumented

Response to the Immigration Process

- Immigrant's resources for immigration: psychological strengths, language competence, social supports, professional/vocational skills, economic resources, color of skin
- Readiness of receiving country for acceptance of immigrant: immigration policies, opportunities, obstacles, programs and services, language facility, skin color

Adjustment to the Receiving Country Lifestyle and Culture

- Acculturation and assimilation, segmented assimilation, integration, accommodation, separation, marginalization, rejection

Implications for the Human Services

- Public policy and law, health and mental health, social welfare, housing and urban issues, education, vocational training, social and economic development, social/cultural/emotional adjustment, private and public services. (pp. 4–37)

(For more details, see Segal's "Introduction: A Framework for the Immigration Experience" in *A Framework for Immigration: Asians in the United States* [2002].)

How would you engage Tabitha as you discover her cultural other awareness? Would you be more effective with her if you did your homework and explored your own cultural self-awareness? How would you deal with her immigration into the United States?

STEP 5: CONSTRUCT A CLIENT–WORKER INTERSECTIONALITY SYSTEM

Intersectionality is those multiple intersections and crossroads in our lives that are replete with multiple social group memberships that are interconnected and interrelated. Collins (1990) introduced the concept of intersections of race, class, and gender and coined the term, *a matrix of domination*, based on the societal configuration of race, class, and gender relations. For Collins, this structural pattern affected individual consciousness, group interaction, and group access to institutional power and privileges. However, others used the concept of intersectionality to describe the various connecting points that converge in their lives.

According to Spencer, Lewis, and Gutierrez (2000), intersectionality involves three factors: (1) we all have multiple group memberships and identities, (2) the impact of these factors on our daily lives is not simply additive, and (3) each social group membership cannot be completely extracted from all others. Intersectionality is concerned with the uniqueness of the individual's family and groups and with types of social group memberships such as age, physical or mental ability, and economic class, as well as larger constructs of ethnicity, gender, and sexual orientation. These various combinations affect the allocation of resources and power for individuals, families, and groups.

Multiculturalism and social justice issues are related to intersectionality in terms of target groups influencing change, structural changes in organizations, and a greater participation of people of color in agency governance. Three forces are at work resulting in change: 1) *ethnoconsciousness* based on an appreciation and celebration of the strengths existing in communities of color; 2) *ethnic sensitivity* fostering partnership, participation, and advocacy where people of color are active agents in individual and social transformation; and 3) *empowerment* or the process of gaining personal, interpersonal, and political power where social and individual changes occur through active engagement of community members in change efforts at all levels. Intersectionality begins with an understanding of diversity, particularly multiple identities, and utilizes various intersecting combinations to mobilize people of color toward empowerment and social change in their communities.

The concept of critical consciousness highlights multiple identities. The idea of multiple identities and cultural diversity go hand in hand. In order to connect these ideas, we start with the background of critical consciousness. Critical consciousness is a concept that was introduced by Freire (1970) in his book *Pedagogy of the Oppressed*. Freire speaks of *conscientizacao*, or the awakening of critical consciousness. Developing *critical consciousness* is a two-step process that involves learning to perceive social, political, and economic contradictions and taking action against oppressive elements. It is a process through which people come to an understanding of power, empowerment, and oppression. One develops greater critical consciousness through approaching, equalizing, and finding out about situations. It is developed through *praxis* (the exercise or practice of a skill) or a combination of action and reflection.

Reed et al. (1997) use the concept of critical consciousness to apply the concept of power to relationships and multiple identities. This does not distort the reflective nature of Freire's insights on oppression but further advances the discussion on critical consciousness to include the concept of micro and macro aspects of multiple identities. They explain and start with the commonalities and differences idea, which is the essence of diversity:

> Critical consciousness incorporates and gives us a greater understanding of power relationships and commonalities and differences among and within people. People create multiple identities based on their life experiences that are shaped by these forces. We need to work to understand people through their construction and enactment of their multiple identities. That is, people must be understood in terms of the social/political/ historical macro forces influencing their lives and the meaning they as individuals make of these forces. We can also apply our critical skills to understand the social environments around us—our families, organizations, communities, and governments. (pp. 46–47)

That is, the various identities of people (gender, age, ethnicity, social class, and other primary ways of self-definition) are socially constructed or built as people interact with various larger macro systems that affect their lives.

Ridley (2005) observes,

The notion that any given person has only one racial or cultural identity overlooks the fact that each unique person has multiple identities. A minority client is not merely a representative of a single racial or ethnic group. He or she is a member of a variety of groups, with group identities overlapping to create a blend that is unique and special to that individual. (p. 88)

Or as Keenan (2004) explains,

These multiple cultural group memberships and one's relations in those groups provide the lens of beliefs, expectations, and meanings as well as specific types of status and material resources. People, therefore, are composed of varying combinations of privileged and oppressed social statuses that operate in a fluid manner, changing over time and with various contexts. (p. 542)

An example might be that in the Midwestern United States, a White male may feel a sense of privilege and access in the dominant majority, whereas the same person may feel like an oppressed minority in some parts of Hawaii where there is a majority Asian and Pacific Islander population.

Finding out about these multiple identities that shape the critical consciousness of an individual is part of understanding the unique diversity of a person. The implications for understanding diversity and shaping culturally competent practice according to a critical consciousness are applicable to the social worker. Among the guidelines for developing a sense of critical consciousness in a helping relationship are the following:

- Approach every interpersonal helping practice relationship with an awareness of who you are as a cultural self and what you have to offer as a helping person.
- Equalize the power relationship between you as the professional worker and the client as the vulnerable individual so that you both become persons in the eyes of the other.
- Find out what is similar and common between you as the worker and the person as the client and affirm the similarities and commonalities.
- Explore the differences between the worker and the client, respecting and learning from them, and incorporate these unique features in the relationship.
- Address the multiple identities of the client and relate them to your multiple identities as the worker, understanding where they came from and how they are formed in the beings of two people.
- Understand and respect how each of you constructed and shaped your multiple identities and how this sense of self works for each of you.
- Draw a time line showing how social, political, and historical forces have had an impact on your ethnic group, your family, and yourself and have caused you to be who you are today.
- Critically examine the client's social environment (family, friends, school/work, community) and its effect on the person and on the helping relationship.

Notice that there are critical consciousness areas of concern for the worker and the client. Critical consciousness is an attitudinal approach that you consciously take regarding yourself and others, particularly clients. Implementing these recommendations based on a critical consciousness perspective into a helping relationship translates the concept of diversity into practical action steps. This leads us naturally to a brief discussion on culturally diverse practice.

What are the multiple identities that are a part of our life? How do these identities intersect? I offer two terms to help us in understanding our diversity on external and internal levels. *External intersections* are outward and external characteristics of a person that we can readily observe, whereas *internal intersections* are those that are not readily observable and must be shared, discovered, and appreciated. At a particular point in time, a number of external and internal intersections may converge and mark a crucial crossroad for a person.

For example, three weeks after my 60th birthday (age/life span), I suddenly had pain in my chest and underwent a quadruple heart bypass operation that incapacitated me for six weeks (temporary disability). I was worried that I would not be able to fully resume my teaching and writing at the university (career). I focused on the scars on my chest, arm, and leg from the open-heart surgery and felt self-conscious about showing them (personal appearance). I was so weak that I could hardly walk outdoors or drive a car and laid on the family room couch watching TV (residence), unable to concentrate and read a book. During this time, I felt the support of my wife who nursed me back to health (partnership status), of my family who called and cheered me (family background), and of my friends and colleagues around the country who showed their care for me through visits and get-well cards. These external and internal intersections marked a significant crossroad in my life at a crucial time.

EXTERNAL INTERSECTIONS

AGE/LIFE SPAN   Age is a particular factor in a larger understanding of life-span development. *Life-span development* is concerned about the "behaviors, dispositions, skills, and traits over a substantial period of the life span" and "age-related biological, psychological, and behavioral changes from birth to death" (Ashford, LeCroy, & Lortie, 2001, p. 24). The *life-span perspective* is concerned about growth in every period of life, the interrelationships of the parts of the whole person, and contextual behavior in settings and relationships. *Ageism* should not be confused with age. The former involves *prejudices and stereotypes applied to older persons on the basis of their age*, whereas the latter is seen as chronological age in the midst of life-span interaction and change.

ETHNICITY   *Ethnicity* is identity based on ancestry and nationality (a group's sense of commonality) that is transmitted from one generation to another by the family, which is part of a larger community of similar persons. In the present there is interaction between family and community ethnic groups as well as interaction with other ethnically diverse people. Ethnicity is passed on in future generations in terms of historical continuity. Language, customs, traditions, beliefs, food, and other related ethnic traits are useful indicators of ethnicity.

LANGUAGE   *Language* is related to ethnicity. It is *the primary means of communication*. We often notice the regional accents of English and the accents of people speaking foreign languages.

Gender   *Gender* refers to the social structural relationships of male and female. It is a social construct and includes the social processes of how men and women are to behave in their social life. Behind the gender sex roles of men and women are the power differentials and conflict associated with change when these role expectations are challenged. Gender must be differentiated from biological sexual differences of male and female.

Social Class   *Social class* involves the relative wealth and access to power that differentiate people into socioeconomic classes and social stratification. The term, *social stratification*, refers to a hierarchy of prestige ranking based on money earned or otherwise acquired, level of occupation, and prestige of occupation. *Social classism* pits the privileged wealthy with high status against the poor and working class who are stigmatized and disadvantaged based on relative wealth. *Power and domination* due to social and economic resources become the basis for social class conflict.

Disability   A *disability* involves a physical and/or mental impairment that hinders the major activities of an individual. A *functional disability* deals with the inability to perform certain tasks and the impairment of mobile functions such as walking, eating, sight, and hearing. A *socially imposed disability* refers to the person's perception of his or her interaction with and adaptation to an environment in which society may impose discrimination and isolation on the person.

Size   Height, weight, and body proportion are important to the self-image of a person. The average height of a person is often determined by genetics of the parents. Women generally prefer men to be taller than them. For some, height is an important factor in the selection of a mate or partner. Taller persons have a more commanding effect over an audience compared to shorter persons. Height, weight, and body size are an integral part of a person's persona.

Personal Appearance   Personal appearance is often an indicator of social acceptance. Our hairstyle, selection of clothes for the occasion, jewelry, and demeanor communicate a message about our external persona. Well-dressed people with a current hairstyle and a confident and friendly demeanor make a positive and lasting impression on others.

Others   Think about other primary external characteristics that you would consider important that are not included in this list.

INTERNAL INTERSECTIONS

Culture   *Culture* is the way of life of a society and life patterns related to conduct or ways of behavior, beliefs, traditions, values, art, skills, and social relationships. Culture perpetuates the sharing of ideas, attitudes, values, and beliefs among individuals of that culture.

Sexual Orientation   *Sexual orientation* "refers to a characteristic of an individual that describes the people he or she is drawn to for satisfying intimate affectional and sexual needs—people of the same gender, the opposite gender or of both genders" (Appleby & Anastas, 1998, p. 49). Sexual orientation, that is, sexual identity, is an important part of one's personal self.

EDUCATION   The extent of education (high school, undergraduate, and/or graduate) and the major field of study are important aspects for every individual. Education provides the academic background that prepares one for a professional career.

CAREER   Employment and professional lifetime work may change as we move through our adult years. We may make a series of career choices, or we may pursue multiple careers at the same time. Our sense of self-worth as adult workers is wrapped up in our career.

FAMILY BACKGROUND   Our father, mother, brothers, and sisters are important persons in our lives. The family is our first group and a constant point of reference as we move through the stages of life. Losses of family members, the changing nature of our family, and other family issues affect us.

PARTNERSHIP STATUS   Our partner (the person with whom we share intimate contact and relationship) is the major social being in our lives. Partnership status involves being single, living with another person(s), being married, or other relationship arrangements.

RESIDENCY   Our home is a source of familiarity and comfort. Where we live in terms of geographic region or section of the city/town may be an indicator of socioeconomic class, personal preference, and employment proximity.

FAITH AND RELIGION   Our sense of *spirituality* may be expressed in terms of a personal philosophy of life or faith as well as participation or nonparticipation with a religious community (church, synagogue, or mosque).

Figure 5.1 is a chart that has external and internal intersections. In your work with Tabitha, identify between her and you as her social worker the similarities (use a +), differences (use a −), and neutral areas (use a 0).

Use the exercise to demonstrate how it is important to intersect the client–worker relationship backgrounds that help to enhance cultural self and other awareness and open the door to explore values, beliefs, and biases. The exercise also promotes life-long learning, student and professional development, and self-reflection and self-correction.

STEP 6: WRITE YOUR OWN CULTURAL BIOGRAPHY

All of us have a unique story about our multicultural involvement at different stages of our life. Throughout our lives, the extent of our contact with people of color may vary. Most Americans are a part of the predominant European American culture that forms the majority society. Many Americans are of English, Irish, French, and German ancestry. Most Americans have singular contacts with various people of color. Neighborhoods are still segregated communities, whereas multicultural contact

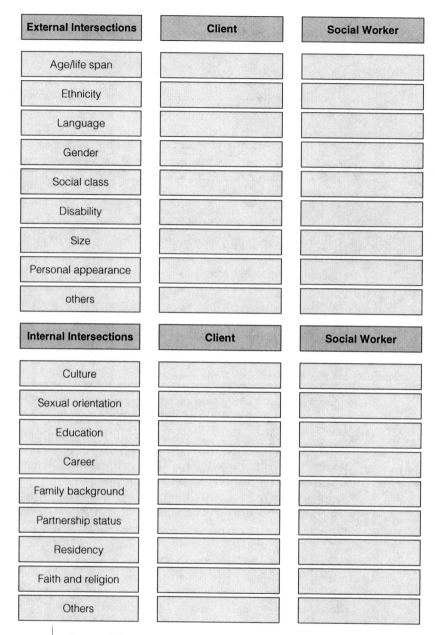

Figure 5.1 | Client–Worker Intersectionality System

is prevalent at school and in the workplace. But even in these settings, people are selective in their choice of school friends and work colleagues. As an assignment and exercise to understand yourself, write down your own cultural biography. Try to recall as many ethnic and cultural incidents that you can remember, particularly in your childhood and adolescent years that may have shaped you today. Here is my attempt to remember my cultural roots.

My life story begins with World War II, the year before England and France declared war on Nazi Germany over the invasion of Poland. I was born on September 23, 1938, in Hamilton, Ohio (population 60,000). Situated on the Miami River in southwestern Ohio between Cincinnati and Dayton, the city was a small industrial center for two quality paper manufacturing companies, Champion Paper and Beckett Paper, and an internationally known manufacturer of safes, Mosler Safes. My parents were both from Honolulu, Hawaii. My father was a 1923 graduate in chemistry from the University of Chicago and the only one of seven children to graduate from college. He settled with my mother in Hamilton in the late 1920s to learn the paper-making business. He was the chief chemist of the Beckett Paper. His dream was to return to China to help the new Republic of China under Sun Yat-Sen, its first president, with a paper factory. Unfortunately, the Sino-Japanese War in the early 1930s ended his vision.

During the 1940s and 1950s, Hamilton was a Republican, conservative, and segregated town. The Miami River divided the city into the west and east sides. The west side was all White; in fact, we were the sole minority family on that side of town. The east side consisted of the downtown; residences of low-income White families; and an isolated, segregated section by the river for African Americans, who in those days were called *Negroes, colored people,* or *the colors.* This area contained a public housing project called Bamboo Harris.

My elementary and junior high schoolmates were all White. I was the only minority child in my schools. I grew up during World War II and the postwar era. I remember going to the Saturday afternoon movies (two cowboy Western features, cartoons, and a thriller serial for a dime) and being threatened by older children during intermission. They were about to beat me up because they thought that I was "a Jap." I remember telling them: "I am Chinese—one of your allies."

My mother attended the local United Presbyterian church and took her children to Sunday school. It was an all-White church but the members readily accepted us. Her social life centered on a few church-women friends. Many years later, my father remarked that he was never invited to his friends' homes because he was Chinese.

During my childhood and early adolescence, I experienced racial slurs and stares. As a child, I was invited to neighborhood birthday parties, but as I attended junior high, invitations to private parties and dates with White girls ceased. About that time, my older sister, a beautiful teenager, was seriously involved with a White boyfriend, and my parents decided that it was time to move back to Honolulu.

It was a difficult transition. My father did not have a job and was in his middle 50s. He struggled financially for several years until he finally got a position as a safety engineer with the State of Hawaii. Moving from a small, all-White culture to a large, island, multicultural environment took years of adjustment for me. I was a "banana": yellow outside but White inside. Island teenage boys were mean to this Oriental "haole" (White foreigner). Most of my junior high and high school classmates were Japanese, Chinese, and Filipino, with some White, Hawaiian, and Portuguese. There were no Blacks in my high school in Hawaii. Most of my teachers during high school and university were White. We lived in a predominantly Asian neighborhood, and I attended a Chinese Protestant church where I became accepted and active in the youth group. I never lost my mainland English accent, but

I adopted the island culture and lifestyle. My dates were mainly Asians, although there were no serious romantic relationships in my adolescence. I never learned to speak Chinese, although this was my ethnic background. I knew little Chinese cultural history and few of the beliefs and practices. I was an American Chinese rather than a Chinese American.

I left to attend graduate school in southern California at two institutions in Pasadena and Claremont. My classmates and professors were predominantly White, with a few Asian and some Black students. I attended several Chinese churches to maintain my ethnic contact and lived in dorms on campus. Several Chinese students who got together on occasion for dinner and conversation served as a support system.

My first romantic relationship was with a Chinese girl in her late teens, but her father did not like me and ended the relationship. However, several years later I met a Chinese woman at church who had come to Los Angeles to teach elementary school. She became my wife after a year and a half of courtship. Years earlier, my mother had taken me aside and said, "I want you to marry a nice Chinese girl." Those words had become a part of my subconscious. Although I dated many ethnic women, I remembered my mother's words and obeyed her wishes. I was able to pass on my ethnic heritage and culture and my family name to the next generation. We have two sons and two daughters.

As a young married couple, we spent five years in Honolulu. We attended a Japanese church, built close relationships with three Asian couples, and maintained contact with them over the years. We lived in a small apartment complex surrounded by young adult Asian singles and married couples.

I returned to graduate school in Cleveland, Ohio. My doctoral graduate class consisted of eight Whites, two Jews, one African American, and me. I was able to complete classes in a calendar year and wrote my doctoral dissertation during my second year. We lived in a suburban community (Euclid, Ohio) in a large apartment complex that was predominantly White. My wife attended a large state university in Cleveland. Her education classes were composed of White and Black students who sat in their separate groups. As an Asian, she was baffled about where to sit and sat next to a young Black woman who became her friend. After the first year, my wife worked in several elementary schools in a school district outside Cleveland, where she was the only minority teacher. During a beginning-of-the-year open house, several parents criticized my wife about being Asian and not being able to speak English correctly. They were forbidden to trespass on the school campus during the year by the principal, who stood up for her, as did several teacher friends. This is the only racial incident I can remember from our two years in the greater Cleveland area. I was treated well by my university professors and classmates. Our oldest daughter was born in Taiwan and adopted by us during our last year in Cleveland.

Our 37 years in Sacramento have been filled with my teaching and writing at California State University, Sacramento. There have been racial tensions on our faculty and at the university and community levels. However, one-third of the social work faculty are people of color. I have had an opportunity to grow and to develop multicultural theory and practice in social work. We live in south Sacramento in an area called Greenhaven, which has been a wonderful place to raise four children. We live in a predominantly White and Asian community on a double cul-de-sac and have friendly neighbors. Our children's friends are multiracial and predominantly Asian.

My oldest daughter is married with two children and lives in Sacramento, whereas my oldest son recently got married and is working in Los Angeles. My younger daughter is married with two children and lives in Novato, California, whereas my youngest son works in Oakland and lives in San Francisco. My wife is a retired first-grade elementary school teacher.

I share these experiences knowing that my life journey as a Chinese American has been limited by living situations, life choices, and educational and career experiences. Each of us sharing our life background will help us understand where we are coming from and where we have to go in our journey with people on this earth.

It is important to share aspects of your life journey with others who will appreciate and understand you.

STEP 7: ENGAGE THE CLIENT USING THE DIALOGIC SELF

Cultural awareness up to this point is a preparatory step to help you develop greater and heighten self and other awareness as you begin with the client. At this juncture the question arises: how do you engage the client in the actual cultural awareness stage of helping? We turn to a recent study encouraging us to rethink the self-awareness principle in cultural competence. Moreover, it advocates the use of the dialogic self where the client and the worker mutually respond to self and others in a learning, feeling, and understanding way. Yan and Wong (2005) help us to avoid the dilemma of being trapped in a self-awareness box and to move toward a liberating way of developing cultural self and other awareness.

Yan and Wong (2005) are critical of a self-awareness stance that is counter to the cultural background of the client. They explain,

> We contend that the cultural competence model's taken-for-granted notion of cultural awareness, which is a form of self-awareness that focuses particularly on one's cultural background, is conceptually incoherent. Its faith in a social worker's capacity to activate a set of techniques in order to suspend their own cultural influences contradicts its postulation of the individual as a cultural being. This conception of social workers' self-awareness also produces a hierarchical subject-object dichotomy in the worker-client relationship, as it assumes that social workers are subjects capable of becoming neutral and impartial culture-free agents, while clients are objects who stay within the limits of their culture, to be regarded as such by social workers. (pp. 181–182)

Rather Yan and Wong propose a conceptualization of *a dialogic self* in cross-cultural practice that is "an ongoing and fluid cocreation through intersubjective dialogue with others" (p. 182). The dilemma posed by Yan and Wong (2005) is that all humans are objects of culture trapped in a cage of culture. Cultural influences, backgrounds, and context control both the worker and the client. Yan and Wong point us toward a dialogic approach:

> Using this notion of a relational self mediated through language, workers are encouraged to consider how their experience of self is constituted in interaction with others, and how together with the clients new meanings are negotiated and created in each social work instance. In other words, the self is an ongoing, fluid construction linked to social context and in dialogue with other people's perceptions of who the self is. (p. 186)

Self-reflexivity, self-reflection process, or intersubjective and reciprocal communication where "new meanings are coconstructed" (p. 186) and "new understandings are reached."

In short, cultural self-awareness is summarized by Yan and Wong (2005, p. 187):

> Instead, self-awareness is a process of reflexive awareness in which social workers are cognizant of how their self may contribute to their perception and experience of their interaction with the client as well as the behavior of the client. Furthermore, reflexive awareness is a process in which social workers are enriched through being open to include the client's worldview into theirs as they seek to understand the client. Cross-cultural social work, like many other human services, thus becomes a site where client and worker from different cultures negotiate and communicate to co-create new meanings and relationships. (p. 187)

Honest, sensitive, and reflective conversation between worker and client about self and others is the essence of the dialogic self. It begins with you and works out to the other person.

Returning to the case of Tabitha, how would you practice and implement the dialogic self in your helping relationship with her? How would you be "open to include her worldview into yours," "co-create new meanings and relationships," and have "honest, sensitive, and reflective conversation" with her? How would you become that dialogic self?

SUMMARY

This chapter has defined cultural awareness from both personal and professional perspectives. It has encouraged you to assess your own cultural background and identity as well as your contacts with groups and individuals of other cultures and ethnicities. It has urged you to explore your beliefs, attitudes, and behavioral responses. It has emphasized the importance of cultivating essential knowledge and skills in social work education and employment experiences. Hopefully, it has increased your cultural self and other awareness so that you can be a competent and proficient social worker.

KNOWLEDGE ACQUISITION

CHAPTER **6**

Doman Lum

Cultural competence is built on knowledge acquisition about demographic information, theories, and group issues, which enhance the understanding of social workers with diverse clients. In specific cross-cultural settings knowledge should include

> the range of historical experiences, resettlement patterns, individual and group oppression, adjustment styles, socioeconomic backgrounds, life processes, learning styles, cognitive skills, worldviews and specific cultural customs and practices, their definition of and beliefs about the causation of wellness and illness or normality and abnormality, and how care and services should be delivered. (National Association of Social Workers, 2007, p. 22)

While it is impossible to cover such a comprehensive listing of specific knowledge areas, we believe that we address knowledge areas for the social work student to master a body of knowledge encompassing basic theories and issues. *Theory* consists of single propositions or of a series of general principles that provide a systemic explanation. Issues relate to specific areas of selective groups that composed the population of the United States.

This chapter surveys the range of knowledge essential to cultural competence. Weaver (2004) points out, "A culturally competent helper must have knowledge about a client's culture, have certain values and attitudes that include respect for diversity and emphasize helper self-awareness, and have the ability to integrate this knowledge and values/attitudes with helping skills" (p. 21). This chapter on knowledge acquisition begins with a focus on critical thinking as a means of analyzing knowledge. It presents social science theory and its application to working with a knowledge orientation. It covers a number of historically oppressed groups weaving in their history and resettlement, current group experiences, values, and cultural behavior patterns.

Gelman (2004) concurs with a similar list of knowledge concerns:

> As this sampling of the social work literature attending to cultural competence with the Latino population illustrates, the importance of possessing knowledge of Latino

demographics, diversity, history, immigration patterns, and the problems facing this population is emphasized. Furthermore, an understanding and respect for cultural values identified as characteristic of many within the Latino population is considered necessary. (p. 86)

We trust that knowledge acquisition may help us to comprehend the extent to which we strive to understand the interaction between the various groups who came from distant shores to the United States and represent diversity and difference. Yet in the midst of conflict, accommodation, and compromise they survived the events that confronted them and struggled to fulfill the pledge of one nation under God indivisible with liberty and justice for all.

CRITICAL THINKING AND EMERGING THEORIES

CRITICAL THINKING

Critical thinking is a mind-set tool that helps the student with a set of criteria for thinking and evaluating the nature of knowledge. Does this particular knowledge theory have potential for a learning approach or is it critically flawed in terms of assumptions, logic, and interpretations about a certain subject area? It is important to develop a critical thinking mind-set, particularly as we approach theories that are compatible with cultural competence. According to Paul (1992, p. 11) critical thinking is a learning process that can help anyone:

- Formulate, analyze, and assess a problem, question, or issue
- Segment an argument or assertion into its components (points of view, major concepts and ideas, theories and underlying assumptions, reasoning, interpretations, and implications and consequences)
- Differentiate theories about culturally diverse social work practice issues
- Build theories of cultural diversity as sources of new knowledge

Critical thinking is required in social work curriculum standards:

Social workers are knowledgeable about the principles of logic, scientific inquiry, and reasoned discernment. They use critical thinking augmented by creativity and curiosity. Critical thinking also requires the synthesis and communication of relevant information. Social workers distinguish, appraise and integrate multiple sources of knowledge, including research-based knowledge, and practice wisdom; analyze models of assessment, prevention, interpretation, and evaluation; and demonstrate effective oral and written communication in working with individuals, families, groups, organizations, communities, and colleagues. (Council on Social Work Education [CSWE], 2008, Educational Policy 2.1.3)

These areas of critical thinking pertain to knowledge and practice skills of applying critical thinking. Mumm and Kerstling (1997) have presented a list of five inter-related skills that promote critical thinking for social workers: (1) the ability to *understand social work theories*; (2) the ability to *divide a theory into its components* (assumptions, concepts, propositions, hypotheses); (3) the ability to *assess the practice implications of a theory*; (4) the ability to *develop and apply criteria for evaluating a theory*; and (5) the ability to *identify common errors in reasoning*. They propose a number of critical thinking ways to evaluate theories:

- *Historical perspective*, refers to a discussion of how and why a theory developed in a historical context
- *Assumptions*, refer to a discussion about the explicit and implicit premises of a theory concerning the client, human nature, the role of the social worker and the client, and the change process
- *Logical flaws*, refer to a discussion about the logic, contradictions among theories, fit with the mission of social work, and errors in reasoning
- *Usefulness in practice*, refers to a discussion about the application of a theory to one's own practice
- *Strengths and weaknesses of a theory* and a comparison of theories and their potential benefit to specific problems, clients, or settings
- *Practice dilemmas*, refer to a discussion of how theories apply to specific problems, clients, or settings

APPLICATIONS TO CULTURAL COMPETENCE

While this is a wide application of critical thinking skills covering knowledge and practice, critical thinking is relevant to culturally competent practice. Our focus is on the application of critical thinking skills to theory concerning cultural competence. As we turn to theory development you are asked to keep these critical thinking principles in mind as we explore a number of theories that are relevant to cultural competence. Cultural competence as a practice approach requires a theory base. *Theory* is an organized set of principles about a subject area. Although space does not allow for a survey of all existing cultural and ethnic theories applicable to social work practice and cultural competence, several recent theories have intriguing possibilities. We offer them here for your understanding and to give you an opportunity to reflect on the possibilities. We have divided knowledge theories into two categories: *macro knowledge theories*, which describe large systems issues related to group and community, and *micro knowledge theories*, which focus on smaller target groups such as the individual and the family. Several knowledge theories are selected in terms of their compatibility with cultural competence.

THE WILLIAMS MODEL OF CULTURAL COMPETENCE EPISTEMOLOGY

Williams (2006) makes a major contribution in her discussion on epistemology (the study of the nature of knowledge) and cultural competence. Based on the theory base work of Guba and Lincoln (1998), Williams (1996), and Sim (1999), Williams explains four theories *(postpositivism, constructivism, critical theory, and postmodernism)* and applies them to cultural competence. These are systematized into four paradigms (models), which make their own distinctive contributions and yet can be combined as theory practice models without becoming mutually exclusive. Knowledge theory explains the etiology of how and why the social worker interacts with the client in a helping relationship. Knowledge theory generates practice approaches and principles that translate into worker–client helping actions.

Williams encourages the use of a single theory or the combination of various theories according to the needs of the client and the nature of the helping situation. Williams states (2006), "Specific choices about which strategy to use will be determined by factors at the professional, organizational, and system levels. Practitioners need to be able to work within various paradigms of cultural competence" (p. 217). Likewise, clients contribute to the choice of paradigms based on their unique set of circumstances. As Williams (2006) observes, "The ultimate definition of cultural competence may be the capacity to collaborate with our clients by recognizing and engaging with these potential entry points and to shift epistemologies to address different needs and different environmental contexts" (p. 218). Williams (2006) further explains

> What each paradigm contributes is different understandings of why the strategies are relevant and are proposed to be effective. Having this lens through which to understand culturally competent practice also lays down the foundation for raising questions about the effectiveness of cultural competence so that we can integrate it into the evidence base for social work. (p. 218)

We now turn to her discussion of four knowledge theories and their application to cultural competence.

Postpositive Knowledge Theory and Cultural Competence

Postpositivism proposes that we can pursue knowledge that is uncontaminated and reasonably stable. Cultural competence understands culture as "part of an identity that is common to members of a group and maintained in a continuous form because of its foundation in their shared experiences" (Williams, 2006, p. 212). Culture is part of a common identity among members of a group with a foundation of shared experiences. For example, drawing on identity development theory is an example of a micro knowledge theory, which is compatible with group member individual identity.

Identity development theory focuses on an understanding of how a culturally diverse person begins to shape a growing sense of what it means to be an ethnic person. Morton and Atkinson (1983) and Helms (1990) have discussed *racial and ethnic identity development* in terms of various stages of growth. Although it is important to recognize that an individual may not necessarily go through all the stages of development, identity development theory does provide an understanding of the range of growth that is possible and may pinpoint a certain critical stage for the worker and the client.

The first stage of identity development may involve the *internalization of the culture's negative imagery*. Often in this stage there is a self-hatred of one's own ethnicity and a strong desire to be accepted by members of the dominant social group. One may intuit the racism, sexism, homophobia, or oppression of society, depending on one's identity, and suffer internalized stress.

The second stage may result in the *expression of anger* as the result of social prejudice and discrimination. The anger is directed outwardly toward the dominant society. The person may become hostile and act upon these emotions. Injustice may be seen through these lenses.

The third state is *immersion*, where the person turns to his or her own culture as a source of strength and support. Rather than reacting to the dominant culture, members of the dominant group become less important and relevant. The person begins to participate in the activities of his or her own ethnic and social group. There is a reevaluation of one's identity and a lessening of anger.

The fourth and final stage is *integration of life* as parts and as a whole. An opposition to prejudice and discrimination may continue, but one is able to distinguish between supportive and unsupportive group members of the dominant society. There are satisfying relations with them and resolution.

Rosenblum and Travis (2000) discuss identity development in terms of stigmatized and nonstigmatized statuses and have various stages for both situations. Tanemura Morelli and Spencer (2000) conducted research on community attitudes toward multicultural and antiracist education in five school districts in Idaho, Montana, Oregon, Washington, and Wyoming. In terms of identity development from the community perspective, they found among 44 school administrators, teachers, and professional services staff the following school and community trends:

- Continuing racist and bigoted attitudes in the form of violent acts, threats, and harassment against minority groups
- Toleration and perpetuation of racism and bigoted behavior in school and community environments
- Reluctance to discuss racism and homosexuality in the classroom due to retribution from the community

In short, a student of color or a gay or lesbian student would be in jeopardy in such an environment in terms of being stuck in the first and second stages of identity development. At the same time, the majority population is a part of community identity development that requires proactive education and supportive policies to end discrimination in the public schools. Tanemura Morelli and Spencer (2000) sum up the mood of their study: "More than 30 years since the zenith of the civil rights movement, the effects of racism and bigotry remain an enduring part of the human landscape in this country. Institutional and tacit racism continue to elude systemic change" (p. 174). Identity development theory leads us to venture forth into immersion and integration that will bring some resolution.

Accurate knowledge about specific cultures can be gathered into cultural information categories in terms of the beliefs, practices, and characteristics of different ethno-cultural groups. Cultural competence in new contexts modify and enhance social work practice by extracting elements from indigenous traditions. At the same time, we must guard against stereotypes based on inaccurate and underrepresentative information and the lack of integration of culture as a core concept in social work practice methodology as well as static descriptions of culture-specific or broad generalizations about traditional cultures versus modern cultures or individualistic orientations versus collective orientations. However, Williams (2006) points out

> Yet the postpositivist iteration of cultural competence offers a tangible method for increasing the capacity to work across cultural differences. It becomes possible for us to evaluate the development of cultural competence by testing the sophistication of our knowledge about different cultures and our capacity to use that knowledge to serve multiple segments of the community. (p. 212)

Postpositivist knowledge theory holds that knowledge of culture, cultural groups, and cultural identity can be readily discovered, drawn from these sources, and made readily available for categorization into helpful patterns of understanding ethnic and cultural groups across the spectrum. We must guard against static stereotypes in dynamic changing cultures or overgeneralizations. But at the same time, cultural competence can be utilized to identify distinctive cultural-common and cultural-specific characteristics, which will increase the data base for cultural competent practice.

CONSTRUCTIVIST KNOWLEDGE THEORY AND CULTURAL COMPETENCE

Constructivist knowledge theory holds that reality is constructed through social interaction and dialogue with participants who are involved in knowledge production. Culture is "a set of group-based experiences and expectations used to make sense of the world" (Williams, 2006, p. 212). Cultural competence "requires readiness to engage with alternative distinctive accounts of what is significant and necessary to gain an accurate understanding of the world" (Williams, 2006, p. 212). Important is the "integration of issues emerging from the specific social context that the group experiences and the individual uses to define identity" (Williams, 2006, p. 212). The culture as the group defines it "must be the core of a helping process that is co-constructed according to emic language, symbols, and social processes" (Williams, 2006, p. 212). The use of life story narratives is how social constructivists formulate information from the client. (For a discussion of cultural competence and storytelling as a form of life narrative, see Carter-Black, 2007.) Williams (2006) observes, "The intra- and intercultural narratives embedded in the helping context affect the helping relationship" (p. 212). The worker takes a listening, not-knowing stance and interacts with the client through open-ended inquiries. Williams (2006) terms these as "professional contributions of expertise based on lived experience and immersion into the contemporary realities of a cultural group and individual" (p. 213).

Social constructionism has an inductive approach that asks open-ended questions about a person's life experiences. Pieper (1994) has moved research-oriented social work practice toward a naturalistic and qualitative compatibility with social constructionism. Pieper's social work practice emphasizes the situational interchanges between people, particularly the historical and cultural influences on how a person's world is constructed. The ways that a person describes his or her experiences and activities are important ingredients in constructing an understanding of an individual. The term *social constructionism* alludes to these aspects of social interaction among and between people. Norton (1993) introduces the social construction of meaning and ecology as an epistemology of social cognition. People use the ecology of their environment to construct meaning for themselves based on their experiences. Relationship stages are part of a person's life development. Norton describes how children construct meaning as a part of their families:

> Children who are immersed in the environment of their families and neighborhoods begin to build on their perceptions about their world and gradually construct what is reality to them. The content of that construction is determined by their personalities in interaction with their social, physical, linguistic, historical, and cultural experiences determined primarily by their families. The children extract information from these experiences at all levels and organize it into schemas that are consistent with their personalities. These schemas help them make sense out of the environment. The process is both interdependent and circular, with the environment and the individual influencing each other. This construction of meaning largely determines the children's behavior. (p. 84)

The individual constructs a worldview from life experiences throughout the life span.

The social construction theory has been applied to people (Gergen & Davis, 1985) in the helping relationship. Anderson and Goolishian (1992) outline the following principles that are important in this process:

- Social construction encourages a therapeutic conversation or dialogue where the therapist and client undergo a mutual search for understanding and exploring problems. It involves a "talking with" rather than a "talking to" one another. There are new narratives, open spaces for conversation, and "not-yet-said" stories.
- In social construction, the therapist adopts a "not-knowing" position or takes on an open, inquiring stance of wanting to know about what has been said, being informed by the client, and joining a mutual exploration of the client's understanding and experience.
- The personal narrative or the story about one's life describes individual problems that provide an opportunity to enter this person's world. Important in the narrative is the client's language and problem metaphors.

Anderson and Goolishian (1992) further explain,

Telling one's story is a re-presentation of experience; it is constructing history in the present. The re-presentation reflects the teller's re-description and re-explanation of the experience in response to what is not known by the therapist. Each evolves together and influences the other, as well as the experience, and thus, the representation of the experience. (p. 37)

Epston, White, and Murray (1992) state,

The "story" or "narrative" provides the dominant frame for live experience and for the organization and patterning of lived experience. Social constructionism leans toward cultural anthropology's approach to discourse and psychology is a product of discourse. Following this proposal, a story is a unit of meaning that provides a frame for lived experience. It is through these stories that lived experience is interpreted. We enter into stories; we are entered into stories by others; and we live our lives through these stories. (p. 97)

This discourse with others is a co-construction of two people and a framework for lived experience and has the following features:

- The focus of helping is an interpersonal construction process and a context for problem solving, evolution, and change. The emphasis is on the interpersonal and social dynamics and processes in the experience between the therapist and the client (Froggeri, 1992).
- Social construction has drawn on cultural assumptions and frameworks to express stories relevant to the individual (Sivan, 1986). The individual may use cultural themes and attributes from relatives and community leaders or interpret events and experiences based on cultural patterns. These cultural influences are housed in the mind of the individual who carries and uses them (Geertz, 1973; Parker & Shotter, 1990).
- The practitioner offers a client alternative themes to make sense of experiences and encourages self-observation, reflections, and developments. The client may

reflect on patterns, explore alternatives, and understand experiences in a self-help approach that is a different response to the past. Both parties help to make sense out of daily experiences with others in relationship. This is the re-storying of life stories (Holland, Gallant, & Colosetti, 1994).

- Social work practice has emphasized the need to focus on client strengths and capacities and to develop meaning and direction to deal with the issues of daily living. This leads to empowerment or mastery of challenges. The client's own strengths, energy, and insights become resources for learning. Holland, Gallant, and Colosetti (1994) observe, "The constructivist approach to teaching social work practice emphasizes the student's strengths, rather than deficits, emphasizes exceptions or times when problems were not overwhelming, and builds upon those times when something the student tried did work effectively" (pp. 49–50).

Social construction theory facilitates several avenues to working with culturally and ethnically diverse people. It highlights the importance of the cultural perspective of clients in terms of their worldview and interactions with other people. Pedersen (2005) explains

A core assumption of social constructionism is that psychology exists as a product of culturally based discourse rather than as the study of internal processes of the individual. All knowledge can be understood only through cultural meanings and practices, rejecting the need for a concept of an "independent self." To this extent, social constructionism is more radical toward anthropology than other versions of cultural psychology. (p. 5)

Cultural anthropology's approach is to investigate and learn from people through inductive discourse. Cultural beliefs, customs, and traditions learned from parents, family, and extended family are crucial connections to understanding how multicultural clients react and respond to normal problems of living and to crisis situations. Cognitive beliefs, affective feelings, and behavioral actions can be traced back to cultural learning from the family as it interacts with a friendly or hostile environment.

Social construction emphasizes the value of narratives or life experience stories, where the practitioner and the client talk with each other. In many cultures, information about the client and the problem situation is communicated indirectly through story. Indeed, the life of a client is a story of the past, present, and future that is unfolding. The story of a diverse person contains ups and downs, joys and concerns, heartbreak and happiness. As the story unfolds, the practitioner and the client endeavor to bring meaning to what has happened in the client's life. It is particularly important to highlight the strengths rather than the pathology of the person. Building on the strengths enables a multicultural client to move forward and to make necessary changes based on affirmation of self and self-empowerment of culture and person. In these ways, social construction theory includes many emerging themes associated with culturally competent practice.

CRITICAL KNOWLEDGE THEORY AND CULTURAL COMPETENCE

Reality is based on "historically based social and political processes" (Williams, 2006, 213), whereas social circumstances are understood as "reflections of a deeply embedded structure that serves the purpose of the powerful" (Williams, 2006, p. 213). People are marginalized in these structures in the relations of domination. Culture is "the outcome of oppressive processes that constrain cultural expression" (Williams, 2006, p. 213). Culture must be negotiated in the problematic context and engagement with culture involves "engagement with the historical, political, and economic structures that have contributed to formulations of ethnic identity, group status, and opportunities for individuals" (Williams, 2006, p. 213). The target of intervention is "discrimination and all types of intercultural domination that result in the decreased opportunities and internalized oppression of individuals in marginalized groups." Culturally competent social work "conceptualize(s) how pervasive inequity affects presenting problems and the capacity to seek help and gain access to services" (Williams, 2006, p. 213). An exclusive focus on deficits and disadvantages must be balanced with "strengths associated with membership in different racial, ethnic, gender, sexual orientation, and other groups" (Williams, 2006, p. 213). Interventions must take place with "the structure that maintains patterns of domination that contribute to individual problems" (Williams, 2006, p. 213). Conscious raising, empowerment practices, mutual support group processes, and challenging institutions by participation and decision making by marginalized groups are some of the ways to promote social work as an anti-oppressive profession (Williams, 2006, p. 213). Cultural competence should "foster positive cultural identity, empower individuals and groups to negotiate oppressive social structures, and promote social change by altering institutional processes that contribute to marginalization" (Williams, 2006, p. 213).

Dean (2001) suggests that cultural competent practice should start with a sociopolitical perspective on oppression and social justice rather than static and fixed beliefs, customs, and historical traditions. Dean (2001) reasons

> If we start with this sociopolitical analysis, we are likely to inquire as to the ways that various forms of oppression have resulted in racial and economic stratification and limited opportunities for our clients and ourselves. This perspective brings in issues of power and the ways that some cultural groups are positioned to control other groups in society. Limiting our focus to studying the beliefs, customs, and historical traditions of individual groups can obscure the oppressive relations between groups. (p. 626)

This is an example of how critical knowledge theory and cultural competence come together from a starting point perspective.

POSTMODERN KNOWLEDGE THEORY AND CULTURAL COMPETENCE

Postmodern knowledge theory throws the baby out with the bathwater when it comes to traditional knowledge and underlying assumptions. Williams (2006) says, "postmodernism urges us to embrace difference, relativism, and the deconstruction of all we have come to accept as true" (p. 214). Williams (2006) explains, "Postmodernism focuses on the inherent indeterminacy of meaning, advocating skepticism of all authority, received wisdom, or claim to cultural norms" (p. 214). According to Williams (2006) culture is in constant change: "all cultural identities are constructed and therefore, changeable in response to different internal and external contingencies" (p. 214). Postmodern cultural competence "explores the collection of identities and experiences that produce continually evolving unique cultural experiences for clients" (Williams, 2006, p. 214). The practitioner takes a "not knowing" stance or "an attitude of complete openness and respect for cultural experience" (Williams, 2006, p. 214). The practice worker casts off expectations and assumptions, centers on the client's experience and ability to educate the professional, and explores client experience without misplaced assumptions of expertise and knowledge. The worker and client develop a common language and use intersubjective space to reveal similarities and differences. They begin a dialogic process building little narratives creating new meanings and dismantling dominant narratives that repress individual creativity and initiative (Williams, 2006, p. 214).

Marsiglia and Kulis (2009) have some hesitation regarding the postmodern knowledge theory approach and its application to ethnic minority individuals and other cultural minority communities. There is a lack of a collective dimension, which is counter to a strong sense of the importance of the group or ethnic community, not the individual. Moreover, postmodernism relies on the transformative power of the spoken word, which constructs the personal narratives (Williams: little narratives) that questions meta-narratives (Williams: dominant narratives). Marsiglia and Kulis (2009) observe that traditional cultures, particularly many Native American and Asian American communities, use alternative forms of communication rather than the spoken word. At the same time postmodern knowledge theory is in line with social work that should be open to marginal alternative viewpoints, accept alternative understandings of society, and be alert to the messages of meta-narrative or dominant narratives.

THEORY SELECTION

Which knowledge theory approach should the culturally competent practitioner select in a helping relationship with a client that might guide the practice principles addressing the problem situation? Williams (2006) reminds us that it depends on *the nature of the problems, the particular problem context, and the client situation.* The definition of culturally competent practice (see Chapter One) emphasizes *mutual consent, cultural proficiency, joint participation,* and *learning and understanding.* That is, the worker and the client ought to agree to select a theory approach that promotes the goal of cultural proficiency, agree to joint participation by both parties, and foster learning and understanding of the problem situation, which may or may not have cultural and ethnic dimensions. Marsiglia and Kulis (2009) similarly concur as they discuss their theory system: "The culturally grounded approach views clients as experts and partners of theorists and helping professionals. Their joint efforts facilitate effective and ethical social work practice and results in the highest levels of client satisfaction" (p. 40). Understanding the knowledge theory alternatives, envisioning which one might be compatible with a worker and a client, and applying a particular theory approach or a combination of two or more is a step toward realizing cultural proficiency, which is the aim of culturally competent practice.

HISTORICALLY OPPRESSED GROUPS

The population of the United States is composed of ethnic groups that have come from different shores into the Americas. If we believe that the Native Americans, who are identified as First Nations Peoples, formerly called American Indians, were the indigenous people of this continent, then we must study the settlement patterns of Europeans, Latinos, Africans, Asians, and other groups who came and how their interactions resulted in oppression, which comprised oppressors and the oppressed.

HISTORY AND RESETTLEMENT

As we celebrate the cultures and histories of each group who came to America, we are aware of the prejudice and hostility that were faced. Part of the triumph over social conflict is due to the strengths of family and culture, which formed bonds of identity and facilitated coping with conflict and adversity. European Americans came to these shores in growing numbers and built cities and towns, established schools and churches, secured land and socioeconomic influence, brought governmental and political structures, and articulated humanistic and religious Western philosophies. White Americans entered the country, moved westward, took land from First Nations Peoples and introduced African Americans as a source of economic agricultural laborers on plantations. Later they employed Asian Americans and Latino Americans as sources of industrial and agricultural labor force. While Anglo Saxon and European groups became the dominant majority forces and later successfully integrated and assimilated into the mainstream of American society and power, the color factor has been a barrier to First Nations Peoples, African Americans, Latino Americans, and Asian Americans. Later heterosexual standards have been sexual orientation barriers to gay, lesbian, bisexual, and transgender persons, while age and ability have been used against elderly and persons with disabilities.

There are a number of recurring themes surrounding the history and resettlement of ethnic, cultural, and related distinguishing characteristics of groups who have historically experienced difficulties in this country.

First, the four major ethnically diverse groups in the United States (First Nations Peoples and African, Latino, and Asian Americans) have *suffered racism, prejudice, and discrimination* inflicted upon them by the dominant society. The history of the relationship between various First Nations Peoples tribes and White settlers is a tale of exploitation and oppression. Tribes were systematically dispossessed of their traditional lands through treaty negotiation, massacre, and removal. The Indian Removal Act of 1830 forcibly removed five tribes (the Cherokee, Choctaw, Chickasaw, Seminole, and Creek) from their lands in the southern states to the Oklahoma Territory. In 1871 Congress decreed that tribes had no independent power and are wards of the federal government. First Nations tribes were then forced onto reservations and into farming. Although the Dawes Act of 1887 gave each First Nations Peoples adult 160 acres and each male child 80 acres, much of the land was unsuitable for agriculture with no funds for its development. Between 1887 and 1932, 90 million of the 138 million acres held by First Nations Peoples were passed to White ownership through deceptive practices. During the early part of the 20th century First

Nations Peoples were confined to isolated rural reservations and their children were sent to distant boarding schools in an effort to Americanize and Christianize them.

African Americans endured exploitation as economic sources of slave labor. They first entered America in 1619 as indentured servants and worked for cheap labor in the second half of the 17th century. African American slaves became part of an economic system dependent on plantation labor. Seized from their western African native villages by White slave traders and fellow Africans and transported by ship to the Americas, these slaves were sold at auction without regard to their families. The abolition of slavery became the moral issue of the first half of the 19th century. The Emancipation Proclamation of 1863 during the Civil War abolished slavery but a series of post–Civil War actions starting with the Jim Crow statutes divided southern society into two segregated classes, culminating with the 1896 *Plessy vs. Ferguson* case before the U.S. Supreme Court that established the principle of "separate but equal," the law of the land until the Supreme Court ruling in *Brown vs. Board of Education* in 1954.

Latino Americans, particularly Mexican Americans, have been victims of political and economic exploitation. Article 8 of the Treaty of Guadalupe Hidalgo, which ended the Mexican American War, granted rights to Mexicans to remain in the United States or withdraw to Mexico in two years, giving them the option of either Mexican or American citizenship and guaranteeing them property rights. However, Mexicans living in the United States eventually lost their land because the burden of proof of land ownership fell on Mexican landowners. Mexican Americans became second-class citizens, deprived of land and social status. During the first two decades of the 20th century economic problems in Mexico forced waves of Mexican migrants to cross the border into the United States. Some became middle-class entrepreneurs and small-business owners, and others worked in agricultural and industrial jobs as railroad laborers, miners, industrial workers, and farm migrant workers. Mexico has provided a source of cheap labor for agriculture and unskilled jobs.

Asian Americans came to the United States in the mid-1800s and early 1900s in search of economic prosperity and to escape economic hardship or political oppression in their countries. The Chinese were the first Asian immigrants. They came to Hawaii as sugar plantation workers and stayed to become businessmen and farmers and later went to California during the Gold Rush of 1849. They became a significant work force in the construction of the transcontinental railroad from 1863 to 1869, worked in the canneries, planted fruit trees, constructed the levees of northern and central California, and planted and harvested rice fields. As the Chinese succeeded in their endeavors, anti-Chinese reactions grew among White miners and farmers. Riots, hangings, and evictions of Chinese from White communities grew along the west coast and segregated Chinatowns in major cities appeared as means of segregation and protection from the White community. A series of legislation effectively barred Asians from entering the United States or having ownership of land: the Chinese Exclusion Act of 1882 barring entry into the United States, the 1907 Gentlemen's Agreement establishing limited quotas, the California Alien Land Bill of 1913 preventing Japanese noncitizens from purchasing farmland, and the Immigration Act of 1924 closing the borders to immigrants from Asia, particularly from China and Japan. Following American entry into World War II after Pearl Harbor, Japanese Americans along the west coast were forced to give up their homes, businesses, and properties under Executive Order 9066 issued by President Franklin Delano Roosevelt on February 12, 1942. They were forcibly removed to rural internment camps for the duration of the war, losing property and income and suffering disruption to family life.

Second, despite the history of exclusion and oppression, people of color groups *organized themselves politically and legally* to overcome racism, prejudice, and discrimination. The history of ethnic minorities in the United States is a history of many people who banded together to fight for equal rights and social and economic justice. Weaver (2005) points out that all people of color cultural groups relied on their ethnic communities for mutual aid, whether it be churches, family associations, tribal assistance, or other forms of support. Historically early social service agencies had more involvement with helping European immigrants and either neglected or avoided working with people of color groups because of racism and segregation.

In 1924 all First Nations Peoples were granted full citizenship. The 1934 Indian Reorganization Act recognized cultural distinctiveness of the tribes in order to preserve them from annihilation, allowed selling of land to tribal members, established tribal councils to manage local affairs, fostered incorporation into self-governing units, permitted the purchase of new lands and the creation of loan funds, extended the trust of First Nations Peoples land, and encouraged the development of constitutions and the functions of local government. The Bureau of Indian Affairs and the U.S. Public Health Service provided assistance for farming, improved local education, and established health and welfare programs. The 1975 Self-Determination and Educational Assistance Act provided tribal leaders the right to allocate federal funds to serve the special needs of their people, fostering greater decentralization and local autonomy. The Indian Child Welfare Act of 1978 protected First Nations Peoples children through placement within the tribe or extended family and provided jurisdiction of tribes in child custody proceedings. It authorized child and family service contracts with tribes and indigenous people's social services organizations to prevent the breakup of families. The principle of sovereignty has played an important part in increasing local tribal autonomy and providing economic revenue from casinos on tribal land. First Nations Peoples and tribes are a political entity and recognized as having a special legal government-to-government relationship with the United States. *Sovereignty* means the recognition of tribes as distinct independent political communities with the power of self-government. There has been a restoration of cultural pride and celebration as well as economic well-being among some tribes. But poverty and lack of an economic stimulus are still problems among many tribes.

The march for social and economic justice among African Americans started during the Civil War and post–Civil War periods with the leadership of Frederick Douglass and George R. Downing. In 1888 the Colored Farmers' Alliance and Cooperative Union was formed to advocate for political rights, while in 1890 the Afro-American League was organized to push for legal and voting rights and school funds. Booker T. Washington sought accommodation with Whites to maintain White support, while W. E. B. Du Bois started the Niagara Movement in 1905, which led to the formation of the National Association for the Advancement of Colored People (NACCP) in 1909. The National Urban League, formerly the Committee on Urban Conditions among Negroes in New York City, was formed during this period. After World War I African Americans migrated from the South to northern industrial cities looking for factory jobs and confronted employment and housing discrimination and segregation. The lynching of African Americans, the Chicago race riot of 1919, and chronic unemployment and poverty were offset by the establishment of historically Black higher education colleges and universities, African American churches, and growing African American middle and blue-collar social classes.

However, the groundwork for civil rights gradually emerged during the forties, fifties, and sixties: Executive Order 9981, by President Harry S. Truman in 1946, integrating the U.S. armed forces; the 1954 U.S. Supreme Court decision that struck down restrictive housing policies and outlawed segregation of interstate bus travel; and the leadership of Martin Luther King Jr. and the Southern Christian Leadership Conference. These events culminated in the Civil Rights Acts of 1964 and 1965 establishing the principles of nondiscrimination and voting rights. Such event patterns continued through the 1980s and 1990s: Jesse Jackson ran for president in 1988 and the Million Man March was held in Washington, D.C., in 1996. Finally, in 2008 Barack Hussein Obama, a native of Hawaii with a Kenyan-born father and a White mother from Kansas, was elected as the president of the United States.

Latino Americans were assisted by the League of United Latin American Citizens in the early 1920s to protect the civil rights of persons of Mexican heritage, while La Alianza provided life insurance and promoted social group events. The rise of the La Raza movement in the 1960s coincided with the Black power and Yellow power movements in ethnic communities and local college campuses. In 1988 the U.S. Immigration Service under President Ronald Reagan and the U.S. Congress offered amnesty to illegal aliens who had lived in the United States for a certain period of time. However, to this day, Mexican Americans are forced to fight for better living conditions, wages, and benefits among farm workers, while Puerto Ricans in large cities on the east coast continue to cope with poverty, substandard housing in inner city neighborhoods, unemployment, drug use, and crime. Cuban exiles from the Castro regime in Miami, Florida, represent a wide spectrum of society, from businesspeople and professionals to the poor and uneducated. With the retirement of Fidel Castro and the open policy of dialogue and engagement by the Obama administration, travel between Cuba and the United States is much more frequent and open. Many Central Americans have come to the United States from Nicaragua, El Salvador, the Dominican Republic, and Honduras due to war and unrest in their countries and economic opportunities in the United States. They need basic assistance due to limited resources: English as a second-language instruction, job training, employment, housing, education, and health care. Latino Americans have been increasingly visible in the movie, television, and entertainment industries and have created role models for young Latinos. In 2009 Judge Sonya Sotomayor was elevated to the U.S. Supreme Court as an associate justice, the first Latino woman to be nominated by President Obama and confirmed by Congress.

Asian Americans have also fought against discrimination. The Japanese American Citizens League was instrumental in advocating for social injustice. In 1944 the U.S. Supreme Court ruled that the relocation of Japanese Americans to internment camps was unconstitutional. After years of petitioning Congress for redress, in 1988 Congress passed a bill granting token remuneration for the property loss sustained as a result of internment. Every Japanese American still living who was in a relocation camp was paid $20,000. During World War II and the Korean War, Chinese, Fillipino, and Koreans immigrated to the United States based on relief and war. The 1965 McCarran Immigration Act opened the United States to all countries. Political unrest and oppression caused many educated businesspeople and professionals from the Philippines and Korea to immigrate to the United States. Later during and at the close of the Vietnam War, Vietnamese, Hmong, Mien, Laotins, and Cambodians came to the United States seeking refugee status. Later former Hong Kong residents and Taiwanese citizens came to the United States due to strained relations between the People's Republic of China, the former British colony of Hong Kong, and the Republic of China on Taiwan. Several Asian Americans have been appointed by President Obama to cabinet positions: Gary Locke, former governor of the state of Washington, was appointed secretary of commerce and David Chang secretary of energy.

Third, the last 40 years have witnessed *the resettlement of America* due to an unprecedented increase in international emigration from every part of the world. This phenomenon could be called *the new resettlement* of the United States, which is becoming a diverse and different country. Potocky-Tripodi (2002) observes,

> The population of immigrants and refugees in the United States is growing rapidly. Within the next four to five decades, immigrants and refugees will account for 65 percent of the country's population growth, and first- and second-generation immigrants and refugees will make up more than 25 percent of the population. (p. 3)

Immigrants tend to have higher educational and occupational levels with a greater proportion of professionals and technicians than the average American labor pool. Even unauthorized immigrants tend to be better educated with a higher level of occupational skills than their counterparts in their countries of origin. Few of these immigrants were unemployed in their own countries but were motivated to come to the United States. Among the main reasons for coming were fulfilling life aspirations and expectations about improved lifestyle and consumption of goods and generally an improved standard of living.

There are at least four types of immigrants to the United States. First, *labor migrants* are the majority of immigrants in search of menial and low-paying jobs. Some cross the border on foot, with the assistance of smugglers who are paid by these migrants, or overstay their tourist visas and blend in with similar ethnic populations. Others enter legally through family reunification policies of the U.S. Immigrant Service as the spouse of a U.S. citizen. Many come as contract laborers as crop field or domestic service workers when there is a shortage of the labor pool. Primary incentives for foreign labor are higher minimum wages for immigrants, savings achieved by urban employers and farm growers, and the willingness of immigrants to perform jobs that American workers are unwilling to handle. Second, *professional immigrants* with technology degrees leave their countries or stay in the United States after graduating from American universities. They represent a drain of talent from their own countries and are motivated by higher salaries and better working conditions. These professionals represent the best in their professions in their countries, must pass difficult entry tests or licensing exams, and still compete with their American counterparts who apply for the same job. They often exceed the educational background and experience of similar American workers. Third, *entrepreneurial immigrants* are self-employed businesspeople who have investment resources and establish their own small businesses or become a part of a business enterprise in their own ethnic enclave. They generally have extensive business experience, access to capital for start-up, and an available labor pool to succeed in their ventures. These immigrants usually hire employees from their own ethnic groups and cater to similar ethnic populations as customers. Fourth, *refugee and asylum status* was formerly granted to those escaping from communist countries in Southeast Asia and eastern Europe. However, the U.S. government's designation of refugee status has been broadened to include a combination of legal guidelines and political expediency based on changing world situations and conditions subject to a case-by-case basis.

The population of the United States is projected to grow to 438 million by 2050 (296 million to 438 million, an increase of 142 million or 48% growth between 2005 and 2050), of which 82% will be immigrants arriving between 2005 and 2050 and their U.S.-born descendants. Of the 117 million added to the population during this period, 67 million will be immigrants and 50 million their U.S.-born children and grandchildren. One of every five Americans (19%) will be an immigrant in 2050 compared with one out of eight (12%) in 2005. Thus, immigration is "the key driver of national population in the coming half century" (Passel & Cohn, 2008, p. 2). There are a number of reasons for the steady increase in immigration during the last 80 years: increasing globalization and population movements, changes in U.S. immigration laws, the linkages of immigrant families in the United States to communities abroad, and labor market factors. The United States is projected to be the third most populous nation in 2050 behind India and China, with a larger foreign-born population than any other country in the world. The U.S. foreign-born population was 36 million in 2005 and is projected to be 81 million in 2050 (a growth of 129%) (Passel & Cohn, 2008).

If immigration is the core factor fueling U.S. population growth, there are enormous implications for human services. Increased housing in ethnic communities, English-as-a-second-language programs in the public schools, educational policies and programs geared to large immigrant groups, public and private social services, health care programs with bilingual staff and maternal and child health clinics, and other related newcomer services are some of the programs that are needed in major metropolitan and rural areas.

CURRENT GROUP EXPERIENCES

Among the numerous current group experiences that help and hinder various people of color groups are four multicultural approaches, which are culturally common to cultural and ethnic diverse clients and are helpful suggestions to cope with social problems. It is useful for the social worker to assume these stances and to focus on these areas, which may reflect group and individual experiences. Lee and Ramirez (2000) identify cultural matching, acculturation and adaptation, ethnic and racial identity, and person-environment.

Cultural matching involves sensitivity to the client's cultural worldview and experiences. Find out as much as is relevant to the person and the problem situation when it comes to cultural worldview and pertinent experiences. As you discover the cultural world of the client, ask yourself if you can identify with the client's cultural perspective as you think about your own cultural background and experiences. Matching the client's and the worker's culture (e.g., noticing parallels or similar experiences) is the start of cultural matching. Lee and Ramirez (2000) point out that culturally different clients may have other worldviews than yours. The worker must use cultural awareness and sensitivity in this matching process. Often times problems are a part of the client's worldview. The worker needs to assist the client to change worldview perspectives and to work collaboratively toward the resolution of problems. The aim is to discover client and worker worldviews (e.g., life perspectives, environmental factors), compare similarities and differences in cultures (e.g., strengths and limitations in the cultures of the client and the worker), and move toward cultural changes (e.g., beliefs and practices about self, family, and significant others).

Acculturation and adaptation involve coping with environmental stressors as one moves to change and adapt to new situations in the environment. Lee and Ramirez (2000) identify such stressors as poverty or discrimination (chronic environmental stressors), a new job or migration to a new country (acute and circumscribed stressors), being a minority person (day-to-day hassle stressor), and related acculturative stress for the culturally different. People generally employ specific coping strategies in order to negotiate living in two or more cultures. They integrate with the majority society, blending positive aspects of their culture of origin and the dominant society, assimilate to the extent of adapting to the majority society in order to survive and strive, separate from the majority society and retain their culture of origin entirely and realistically as possible, and live a marginal life on the edge of society in order to maintain semblances of both cultures. Acculturative stress is most serious when there is a breakdown of maintaining two competing cultures in order to cope with the demands of daily living. The task, according to Lee and Ramirez (2000), is to help the individual, family, or group to overcome acculturative stress and better adjust and adapt to the social environment. The worker should respect the client's worldview, address the immediate problem needs, and assist the client with developing better coping strategies than the ones previously used. This may mean assessing new situational factors that may have arisen recently and formulating new ways of dealing with emerging problems that were not previously a part of the client's life.

Ethnic and racial identity have been impacted by the experience of racism and discrimination, particularly for culturally different persons, according to Lee and Ramirez (2000). Many individuals and institutions view people of color as different and inferior. Often times these experiences, attitudes, and feelings are internalized into the individual and become a part of a person's ethnic and racial identity. This social identity has a marked effect on the person. Lee and Ramirez (2000) conclude, "Sometimes these experiences can produce a significant amount of psychological and interpersonal distress that can impair one's ability to lead a productive life" (p. 291). The worker should help the client to become conscious of his or her ethnic and racial identity and should trace its origin (e.g., early experiences and memories of ethnic and racial events and incidents), development (e.g., ethnic and racial encounters in childhood, adolescence, and young adulthood), and impact on his or her life (recent past and present effects of racism, prejudice, and discrimination). Open and honest discussion is necessary to root out a set of behavior reactions that may be detrimental to the individual. Likewise it is important to affirm the positive contributions that are a part of ethnic and racial identity.

Person-environment emphasizes the importance of the impact of the social environment on the individual and the reactions of the person to his or her surroundings. Person-environment underscores the contextual situation. Lee and Ramirez (2000) remind us that "people live in the context of culture" (p. 291). This cultural context fosters inherent resilience in people embedded within a sense of interdependence among people. In particular they point out such qualities as collective wisdom, shared resources, commitment to community, acceptance of cultural differences in others, cooperative and collaborative work and assistance, a focus on strengths and asset building, the balance of multiple roles and identities in people's lives (e.g., the abilities to multitask and to appreciate the rich diversity among, between, and within people in the community), the belief that persons can be empowered as relational agents of change, greater racial consciousness and a heightened sense of social justice to change unfair conditions and contradictions in life, and a perception of life from multiple perspectives, the contexts of others, and toward the societal good. If a worker can help a client realize this vision of person-environment, the client is on his or her way of achieving change, progress, and healing.

VALUES

A knowledge of values is important because values guide the choices and decisions of individuals, families, and cultural and ethnic communities and are the innate essence of what it means to be a human being. *Values* are beliefs about preferred choices that govern conduct, life decisions, and related normative action by individuals, families, groups, and society. *Social institutional values* are broad in nature and protect and promote social well-being and the public good. *Individual values* are personal idiosyncratic choices based on the orientation of the person and influential significant others such as peers, parents, and family members. *Cultural values* are rooted in ethnic, religious, and generational beliefs, traditions, and practices that influence individual and social values. In strong traditional communities, cultural and religious values are the basis for how community members interact with each other.

Knowledge of culturally diverse values is part of cultural competence. Although there is a range of culturally diverse values, five values are central to our discussion: family, respect, harmony, spirituality, and cooperation.

The multicultural *family* revolves around interdependent collective and/or hierarchical structures. The family is the basic transmitter of cultural values and traditions. It is the source of ethnic identity from biological, psychological, and social perspectives. In many ethnic families, the individual's sense of freedom and choice are subsumed under the good of the family as a whole. The individual family member is interdependent, not independent of or dependent on the family. The family may operate on a collective, extended basis with nuclear/extended family systems or similar social networks. The collective nature of the multicultural family fosters mutual support and may center on a hierarchical authority figure such as a parent, grandparent, or godfather.

Closely related to the value of family is the concept and practice of *respect*. The word *respect* comes from the root word *respicere*, which has a past-tense meaning (to look back on) and a present-tense understanding (to look at). The implied meaning is that one shows honor and regard for those who are held in high esteem in the past and the present. Many cultures express respect for ancestors. Latinos often name children in honor of past and present relatives, and Asians reverently remember their parents and grandparents in ancestor worship. First Nations Peoples have undergone spiritual quests to communicate with the spirits of their ancestors, and African Americans have communed with their deceased loved ones in quiet and prayerful conversations.

Respect is shown toward father and mother, older relatives and adults, and people in general. Polite manners, formal address, and deference of children to the wishes of parents are manifestations of respect in African and Latino American cultures. Respect for the personhood of people communicates a sense of reverence for life, which is an important value for Asian and First Nations Peoples traditional cultures.

Harmony is a sense of congruity and agreement in feelings, actions, ideas, and interests within and between people. Harmony comes from the Greek word *harmos*, which means a fitting or joining. For First Nations Peoples, harmony is essential to maintaining balance in the universe. Illness is the absence of harmony or an imbalance in the body or in relations to self, others, and the world. For Asian Americans, it is important to maintain harmony or peace rather than conflict or disharmony in ethnic group relationships. Harmony is a part of individual and group continuity rather than alienation. As a result, many Asian Americans avoid confrontation and defer argumentation to maintain a higher order: interpersonal harmony.

Spirituality refers to a personal sense of meaning and purpose based on belief in a transcendent cosmic Being or Ultimate Truth. Spirituality may encompass a sense of morality or a personal code of ethical behavior. African, Latino, and Asian Americans traditionally have practiced their spirituality in an institutional religious setting through ethnic churches. First Nations Peoples have combined cultural and spiritual rituals of cleansing and healing through ceremonies presided over by a medicine man.

Cooperation is a value that brings ethnic families and groups together in a common sense of purpose. For African Americans, cooperation or pooling of resources is essential for survival in terms of housing, child care, and related necessities of life. For Latino Americans, cooperation involves helping extended-family members who are immigrant newcomers or working together on church and community projects. Japanese Americans have worked together to support legal, political, and social causes in the Asian community through local churches and legal rights organizations such as the Japanese American Citizenship League. Among First Nations Peoples, there is a sense of purpose when Native people celebrate their cultures in powwows and sweat lodge ceremonies and run Indian gaming casinos for the good of the tribe.

Many more values beyond these five are important to each ethnic group. For example, Manning, Cornelius, and Okundaye (2004) identify an Afro-centric value orientation that underlies a number of clinical principles: assessing the relationship between racism and oppression and mental health and health problems; using empowerment to assess the ego functioning and group consciousness strengths of

African American clients; assessing the level of spirituality and religious involvement, such as value orientation and participation in church activities; considering the value orientation of African Americans in developing Afro-centric, empowerment, and ego psychology intervention strategies; integrating ego functioning and group consciousness from Afro-centric perspective, empowerment, and ego psychology to enhance cultural competence; and advocating for African Americans experiencing stress from racism and oppression. Values reflect a range of cultural beliefs, practices, and behaviors that come from ethnic traditions. Culturally competent social workers must understand and respect these cultural values, which are essential to the well-being of people of color.

CULTURAL BEHAVIOR PATTERNS

A focus on cultural behavior patterns uncovers how cultural and ethnic individuals, families, and groups respond and react to the dominance, oppression, and exploitation of the White societal majority as well as the support, goodwill, and generosity of communities in general and individuals in particular. Historically cultural and ethnic minorities endured the former reactions when they were denied access to land and civil rights and underpaid for their labor. Federal and state laws at the beginning of the 20th century were enacted to force them into compliance with the wishes of the majority society. On the whole, people of color endured these injustices; when they revolted, the police and the military were used to subdue them. However, the 1964 and 1965 Civil Rights Acts were turning points for ethnics of color, women, and other disadvantaged groups except for gays and lesbians. At the same time, when we consider the coming to America of refugee and immigrant groups during the last third of the 20th century, we remember on the whole the generous spirit of Americans expressed to Vietnamese, Hmong, Mien, and Cambodian refugees who were escaping violence and oppression after the fall of Saigon in the Vietnam War.

In this brief section we want to provide brief overviews of three cohort groups of color and examine their cultural behavior patterns: new arrivals of color, women of color, and multiracial persons. We want to offer brief statements on each with the hope that the reader may be motivated to study this topic in depth, knowing that as social workers deal with clients in general and culturally and ethnically diverse clients in particular, the questions surrounding cultural behavior patterns (a topic for cultural human behavior in the social environment) occur in the engagement, assessment, intervention, and evaluation stages of practice process.

NEW ARRIVALS OF COLOR   According to the Pew Research Center the demographics for the first half of the 21st century (2005–2050) show a move toward a significant increase of Latino and Asian immigrants of color in their coming to America. We may want to call this *"the age of the immigrant"* in the first half of the 21st century, since this phenomena will increasingly become a part of the American fabric of peoples and populations. The observation of Portes and Rumbaut (1990) made over 20 years ago still rings true: "Never before has the United States received immigrants from so many countries, from such different social and economic backgrounds, and for so many reasons" (p. 7). There are a variety of reasons why immigrants come to the United States. From a cultural behavior perspective, the major reason is to fulfill life aspirations and expectations in terms of lifestyle and consumption behavior ("to live like the Americans," "to buy like the Americans," and "to enjoy the good life of the Americans" may be stretching this perspective). The primary motivation for immigrants is an improved standard of living that they are unable to find in their country of origin. The drive toward a better standard of living motivates immigrants toward work for the parents and education for the children. Starting your own small business or working for substandard wages are behavior patterns that are experienced by immigrant parents with little education, English language proficiency, and start-up capital. At the same time, with an economic recession bordering on an economic depression, many immigrants of color return to their countries of origin due to lack of work and employment in the United States.

I (Lum, 2004) have identified four types of immigrants who are migrating to the United States: labor migrants, professional immigrants, entrepreneurial immigrants, and refugees/asylum seekers. While there are distinctions to be made about these categories of immigrants, a *strong work ethic*, a *better life* for themselves and their families, and a desire for a *stable and democratic government* are primary themes across the board. If the repatterning of Indo-Chinese refugees in the mid-seventies and early eighties remains true, there will be the maintenance and expansion of ethnic communities clustered in key settlement areas. With the increase of Latino and Asian immigrants there will be a greater urban spiral of Latinos in east Los Angeles, Vietnamese in Little Saigon outside Los Angeles, Chinese in San Francisco and New York Chinatowns, and related immigrant groups who attach themselves to these subcommunities or start small nearby pockets of settlement. The preservation of these ethnic and cultural enclaves helps to ensure continued working capital, protected markets, and labor pools for economic stability and growth as well as mutual support and the survival of cultural practice, which are examples of major social research interest areas for cultural behavior patterns.

From a social work advantage point cultural behavior patterns for new arrivals of color means working with people who experience *acculturative stress* and related *mental health behavioral problems*. On the one hand, high stress is found particularly in women, the elderly, the non–English speaking, the uneducated, and the unemployed. But on the other hand, contributing factors to good mental health include social support systems; high levels of education, professional training, and income; a pervasive sense of cultural heritage; and proficiency in English (Portes & Rumbaut, 1990). From a knowledge theory perspective on cultural behavior patterns these variables are interesting studies that will bear research findings that in turn offer implications for direct practice (such as culturally competent practice), policy formulation, and program delivery and planning.

WOMEN OF COLOR   From a cultural behavior pattern standpoint women of color are in *quadruple jeopardy* as objects of sexist, racist, classism, and sexual orientation biases. This strong statement reminds us that women of color are often, like many women in general, the victims of domestic violence, which is an example of a cultural behavior pattern of aggression. This is particularly true and real for immigrant women of color who are often isolated in domestic violence situations due to lack of English language fluidity and educational background.

Sacramento, California, my hometown, serves as a case in point. Named the most diverse city in the United States by *Time* magazine in 2002, Sacramento has an ethnic balance that is the envy of those who wish to study ethnic profile groups who live and interact with each other. The demographics of Sacramento reflect White European Americans, African Americans, Latino Americans, Asian Americans, and Native Americans proportional to population clusters and balances in the United States. There are also concentrations of White Russians in West Sacramento, Vietnamese in Rancho Cordova, Asians and White ethics in Greenhaven (where I live), African Americans in Meadowview, Latino Americans in Akalai Flats, and Native Americans in nearby Roseville, Lincoln, and Folsom, the sites of two major Indian gambling casinos in the greater Sacramento area. In Sacramento, California, there are at least two domestic violence shelter programs for women in general (WEAVE [Women Escaping a Violent Environment]) and Asian women in specific (My Sister's House). WEAVE has the strong support of the local city and county governments and social services communities in general, while My Sister's House has mobilized the local Asian community with sustaining a relatively new program with modest facilities. The spread of ethnic patterns of living and interaction, the resources for coping with domestic violence against women, and the capital site of California make Sacramento a treasure for studies in cultural behavior patterns. In a real sense Sacramento has been touted as the biggest secret as the most livable city for cultural and ethnic living.

While women in the feminist movement have been united against gender-based social inequality and gender oppression and have been foot soldiers in this battle, women of color have been concerned about integrating race, ethnicity, culture, and multicultural diversity with concerns of family, children, and their ethnic communities. In many instances women of color have been the main breadwinners due to the downturn of the economy, the high unemployment rates, and the need for both spouses to work and care for children in two-parent families as well as increasing single-parent families, where the woman-mother is the sole economic provider (see the 2009 Shriver Report on immigrant women). Cultural behavior patterns revolve around social-cultural issues facing women of color. Women's special mental health problems and socioeconomic needs (problems of overtaxed women of color and women in general who are required to multitask on the job and at home on a schedule that runs 24 hours a day) and the behavior patterns of struggle and survival that are played out daily in the burdens of caring for spouse, children, grandchildren, and elderly parents in need are examples of multiple cultural behavior pattern problems faced by women, something that I observe also in my wife's work schedule.

Yet women of color found strengths from their personal, family, and community traits. The famous and classic social work research study of 164 Latino and 160 African American women (Aguilar & Williams, 1993) is uplifting and revealing in its description of cultural and personal strengths from a behavior patterns perspective. Cultural strengths were pride in culture, family, and ethnic group identity, responsibility at an early age, religious values, the ability to set goals, hard work, dedication, honesty, coping with racism, and belief in education and God. The women's personal strengths were persistence, determination, hard work, assertiveness, faith in God, the desire to succeed, an optimistic point of view, strong self-esteem and self-motivation, a desire to help and to be role models for other women in their ethnic group, a sense of responsibility and independence, resilience, a sense of service, a love for what they do, inner strengths (belief in themselves and a good feeling about life), family support, and being achievement or goal oriented.

MULTIRACIAL PERSONS OF COLOR   Multiracial persons are the products of interracial marriages. Two of the most prominent Americans are multiracial persons of color: President Barack Obama and golfer Tiger Woods. Considered to be high performers in their respective fields of politics and golf, Barack Obama and Woods came from interracial marriages. President Obama's father was a Kenyan scholar studying at the University of Hawaii (my alma mater) when he met his wife, a White woman from Kansas. Woods's father was a career U.S. Army special forces soldier who was part African American and Native American, while his mother was born in Thailand. Both Obama and Woods are well known throughout the world, respected for their skills and demeanor, and highly sought after on the national and international scenes.

However, I (Lum, 2004) observed, "Historically multiracial persons of color were outside the mainstream society; unacknowledged, rejected, and ignored as persons by the dominant ethnic populations; and placed in ambiguous and awkward situations where they were made acutely aware of racial differences" (p. 55). Such is the reality confronting multiracial persons of color in the United States. Persons in regional parts of the country during my generation would often stare and follow the steps of multiracial couples who displayed intimacy and affection in public. People in my generation were prone toward racial segregation in dating and marriage. Multiracial persons were the exception rather than the rule in the mind-set of those of us who grew up in the conservative Midwest.

Dhooper and Moore (2000) identify *marginalization* as the critical problem issue confronting multiracial persons of color. The dilemma is not wanting to disown either side of their heritages and being shunned or ignored by the White society. As a result multiracial persons of color face a confusing and difficult struggle for identity, self-worth, and social acceptance. Because of such a marginalization, multiracial persons may want to "pass" as members of a desired ethnic group. President Barack Obama is a case in point. As a student at the Punahou Academy in Honolulu, Hawaii (a prestigious private school for the local elite and the brightest and best in Hawaii) Barry Obama was considered a local boy who was friendly, athletic, and smart (although his teachers observed that he did not live up to his potential in high school). Barry Obama was identified as a native of Hawaii, although he was not Native Hawaiian. In marriage, he chose a high-profile well-educated and competent African American woman in Michelle. Barack Obama became involved in the African American community of Chicago, Illinois, and rose from a community organizer to a state senator and candidate for the office of President of the United States. He chose "to pass" as an African American by marrying a woman and involving himself in that community although during the 2008 presidential campaign there were early questions of how to identify Barack Obama. Was he a true African American whose ancestors experienced slavery and segregation in the South? Was he rather an American with Kenyan African and European American heritages? Or was he still a native son of Hawaii who long ago left the islands to find his fortune and fame elsewhere on the mainland? These are some aspects of marginalization and multiracial dilemmas that are fascinating discussion points for us to consider around the dinner table at home.

Turning to some crucial issues facing multiracial persons of color, it is important to help multiracial/ethnic families affirm the traditions, rituals, and persons that make up their unique ethnic and cultural heritage and to work particularly with the fear and anger that multiracial children may experience. That is, the fear of rejection (e.g., nonverbal and verbal ridicule, lack of social acceptance) and anger (e.g., internalized due to introjecting the attitudes and behavior of persons in society and the anger of self that emerges from within the person). For many multiracial persons of color it is like riding a roller coaster up (emerging anger of self) and down (internalization of societal anger). These are some interesting observations of cultural behavior patterns for this group, which holds a gold mine for research and practice.

SUMMARY

Knowledge acquisition is a foundational component of cultural competence. This chapter has focused on knowledge theory in terms of critical thinking and alternative theories related to cultural competence, the history of oppressed groups, particularly history and resettlement, current group experiences, values, and cultural behavior patterns. These areas of knowledge are crucial to master in the development of cultural competence in a proficient manner. In the next chapter we will address skill development, which is related to practice process, but we should draw from our knowledge base adequate theories compatible to cultural competence, since we believe there are multiple links between theory and practice.

SKILL DEVELOPMENT

CHAPTER 7

Francis K. O. Yuen and Doman Lum

Skill development is the creation of a repertoire of behaviors for the social worker to use in the helping situation. Skill represents the practical application of cultural awareness and knowledge acquisition. The word *skill* comes from the root word *skel*, which means the ability to separate or discern. In the helping sense, skills are practical tools that have been discerned from knowledge of working with people generally and with culturally and ethnically diverse clients particularly. Helms and Richardson (1997) define skill as "the capacity to use awareness and knowledge to interact effectively with clients and colleagues regardless of their racial classification or cultural origins" (p. 75). Skills are applied at the interface between the social worker and the client and are the heart of social work and culturally competent practice.

Yuen and Terao (2003) discuss the connections between knowledge, skills, and technology.

> [The] many ways of knowing lead to the establishment of certain knowledge, which according to Germain (1983), forms a "recognizable or recognized perspectives entities often called practice model" or approach (p. 31). Method is the specific application of such a model or approach with specific target groups. Germain notes that skill refers to a "particular area of practitioner action, such as observation, engagement, data collection, assessment, contracting, setting goals and planning, and achieving goals. Technique is used to designate a more specific procedure within such an area of skill" (p. 31). Technology is therefore the combination and application of the theories, knowledge, approaches, methods, skills, and techniques that produce the services. (p. 5)

Ridley, Espelage, and Rubinstein (1997, p. 140) speak about "culturally responsive skills" that reflect cultural sensitivity. A wide range of skills is identified: the ability to work with multiple roles and identities and multiple layers of environmental oppression (Comas-Diaz, 1994; Reynolds & Pope, 1991); advocacy and assertiveness training for women; identification of community resources for lesbian, gay, and bisexual clients (Fassinger & Richie, 1997); multicultural assessment, particularly process and outcome assessment (Dana, 1993); varied communication and intervention skills; and development of a therapeutic style (Fassinger & Richie, 1997).

The following sections of this chapter will cover types of skills, process-stage skill clusters, service delivery and agency linkage, design and implementation, and examples of skill development research. It will focus on certain skill principles that help build a repertoire of tools in working with clients.

TYPES OF SKILLS

Skill development is generally process-oriented in social work practice. Social work is seen as a process with a beginning, middle, and end, during which the worker exercises skills having to do with engagement, psychosocial assessment, intervention strategy, implementation of interventions, and evaluation. These skills, applied to individuals, families, groups, organizations, and communities, serve as stepping stones to move the worker and the client through the helping process to a successful conclusion.

Bernard (1979) distinguishes three types of skills in the helping relationship: process skills, conceptualization skills, and personalization skills. These three themes are useful ways of grouping skills and are reminders of essential ways of working with clients and being reflective in the process. The three types of skills are defined as follows:

- Process skills refer to the following therapeutic techniques and strategies: opening the interview smoothly; using reflection, probing, restatement, summary, or interpretation; helping the client say what is on his or her mind; using nonverbal communication to enhance verbal communication; implementing intervention strategies; and achieving closure.
- Conceptualization skills include deliberate thinking and case analysis abilities: understanding what the client is saying; identifying themes of the client's messages; recognizing appropriate and inappropriate goals; choosing strategies that are appropriate to the client's expressed goals; and recognizing subtle client improvement.
- Personalization skills have to do with learning observable and subtle behaviors and with the personal growth of the worker: communicating authority in the helping relationship and taking responsibility for specialized knowledge and skills; hearing client challenges and feedback without becoming overly defensive; being comfortable with the client's feelings and attitudes; and respecting the client.

Process, conceptualization, and personalization skills are developed both in the classroom and in the field placement. These skills provide the worker with tools to move the client through the helping relationship. The process skills are particularly important that they are the core skills for the helping process. Through supervisions, formal training, videotaping or direct observation, case conference, shadowing, or other innovative means, these skills are developed and internalized by social workers. Conceptualization skills include the analysis of verbal and nonverbal communication, processing of problem themes, goal setting, and selection of the intervention strategy.

Likewise, personalization skills focus on the worker's response to the helping situation, including transference and counter-transference. It is important to process how the client affects the worker. "What were you feeling when the client said that she was ready to scream at her mother?" "What was happening to you when the client became angry and said that you were a lousy social worker?" Investigating the worker's feelings of insecurity, threat, fear, and uncertainty are examples of developing personalization skills. The focus is to help the worker realize that the client may be projecting feelings intended for someone else. At the same time, the worker must own up to the feelings of the client who may need to confront the worker. Keeping composure and asking, "What is going on in this exchange?" helps the worker to maintain an objective perspective in the situation.

The development of process, conceptualization, and personalization skills is essential for cultural competence and requires hours of supervision. In the next section, we turn to five process stages: contact, problem identification, assessment, intervention, and evaluation. Each stage encompasses a cluster of process, conceptualization, and personalization skills.

PROCESS, CONCEPTUALIZATION, AND PERSONALIZATION SKILL CLUSTERS

Lum's (2000) framework for social work practice with people of color is built around a systematic process-stage approach, following the classic formula of beginning, middle, and end. The beginning process stages are contact and problem identification; the middle stages include assessment and intervention; and the ending stage is evaluation. This section will discuss several key skill area principles and those process skills necessary to move clients in general and the multicultural client in particular through these five stages, along with essential conceptualization and personalization skills.

CONTACT

CONTACT PROCESS SKILLS   The establishment of the relationship between the social worker and the multicultural client is basic to the contact stage. Relationship building is the primary requisite for engaging and retaining the client. Culturally diverse contact has a skill cluster consisting of understanding the ethnic community, following a relationship protocol, engaging in professional self-disclosure, and developing an effective communication style.

Understanding the ethnic or cultural community means that the social worker has a working knowledge of the client community's profile. U.S. Census reports as well as local government and public interest group study reports could provide useful information on ethnic, social, economic, and related trends and indicators such as unemployment rates, income levels, housing, and related information. A social worker should attempt to become well versed in the history, problems, and profiles of an ethnic or cultural community.

The worker can consult identified community leaders and study reports, but it is important to walk through a community and observe where people congregate and exchange information. This participant observation and thoughtful interaction with the people who live in a community are most helpful. Be sure to patronize businesses and talk with storeowners and customers about the news of the community. Show up at social, cultural, and educational community events and observe how people spend their leisure time. Talking with people living in the community provides valuable knowledge about current issues facing residents. Shadow a staff member of a social service helping agency in the community and get a sense of how one relates effectively with residents. It is important to listen and gain information while also establishing credibility as a reliable and believable person of integrity. Observing, listening, and understanding local ways of relating and conducting business and placing the needs of people first before getting results are some community-understanding guidelines.

The ways in which individuals in a particular cultural community express their gratitude are important to observe and understand as the community interacts. Vasquez (2005) talks about giving and receiving gifts and cites a client's healthy expression of care, which may be a genuine expression of thanks. She observes:

> On the other hand, when a Latina client who works near a restaurant brings me tacos because I squeezed her in during my lunch hour when she was in crisis, we don't need to spend half an hour processing the meaning of the tacos. We know that she felt appreciative, that it was a relatively easy, warm gesture, and that food is a common gift among Latinas. Sometimes a taco is just a taco! (p. 105)

Relationship protocols are cultural ways of relating to a person. A protocol is a code of ceremonial formality and courtesies. Every locale has a particular way of beginning a relationship or a contact with another person. It is important to find out the specific ways in which people relate to each other in initial conversation. In many cultures, a relationship protocol is a prelude to conducting business. It may involve a formal greeting, inquiry about the health and well-being of family, and other friendly topics of conversation. This communicates a message of genuine concern about the well-being of another person and a common exchange of daily activities that are considered important topics of conversation. It may be considered rude to proceed directly to the main order of business or to the presenting problem without proper protocol conversation. Friendly, warm, and thoughtful feelings are important to communicate at the beginning.

Following a relationship protocol involves the communication of respect and recognition to the head of household, grandparents, and other adults. It is important to practice a relationship protocol regarding the father and mother in a family situation, which means supporting their authority and roles rather than undermining their family influence. This may involve relating to and respecting traditional male, female, and age role relationships of a particular cultural and ethnic group. A professional protocol is to assure a client that a level of confidentiality will be maintained in the helping relationship as far as information sharing is concerned. Clients furthermore appreciate structure in the helping relationship to the extent that the worker sets forth flexible and clear guidelines and directions in the sessions.

Professional self-disclosure is an extension of the professional use of self, an important social work principle. Often a client comes to the helping session with distrust, anxiety, and fear of the unknown. Professional self-disclosure is an effort on the part of the worker to reveal a commonality between the worker and the client.

Rather than hiding behind the professionalism of social work, the worker takes the initiative by disclosing an area of interest shared by the client. The intent is to become a real person and to humanize the relationship. On the other hand, proper disclosure of one's professional background and expertise could help establish the practitioner's credibility and the client's confidence in the practitioner's competency.

Finding out about the background of the client may open appropriate topics of self-disclosure, such as travel, children, cars, clothes, shopping, and other areas of common interest. Professional self-disclosure begins to create a sense of community and bonding between the worker and the client. Among the practical suggestions for professional self-disclosure are introducing yourself; sharing pertinent background about your work and role and helping philosophy; and finding a common area of interest with the client that you might reveal in order to build a bridge between the two of you.

The worker should be judicious in the sharing of a professional self-disclosure. Current problems of the worker that are parallel to the client's problems may not be appropriate. Neutral common areas of interests may be more effective to bridge the gap of the unknown between the worker and the client. Professional self-disclosure should put the client at ease, generate rapport, and increase spontaneity and openness.

Lum (2000) suggests three levels of professional self-disclosure:

1. Level One: self-disclosure about common areas of interest to humanize the relationship and to establish a sense of openness with the client, usually at the first session as a point of contact
2. Level Two: self-disclosure of empathy and related warmth from the worker (e.g., how the worker felt as the client was able to express genuine feelings about a problem situation)
3. Level Three: self-disclosure at the problem identification stage when the client is sharing a significant problem and needs support from the worker who may have experienced a similar situation

An effective communication style gives a positive message to the multicultural client. The agency environment sets the tone for the initial contact between the worker and the client. A friendly bilingual receptionist, an accessible location, an attractive facility, a private meeting room, comfortable furniture, a water cooler, and a casual approach create a positive atmosphere. Even a simple display of pictures or posters of people of diverse backgrounds in an agency setting could communicate a tone of cultural and ethnic sensitivity to people who come to the center for services.

Body language, bilingual staff, use of an on-call trained translator or interpreter, and familiarity with cultural mannerisms and gestures make for effective communication. Body language should convey an open and approachable stance. Sitting with the client without a barrier such as a desk, leaning toward the client with arms and open palms of the hand, and legs uncrossed are nonverbal signs of open communication. There should be allowance for personal space between the client and the worker.

Generally, physical contact such as shaking hands is appropriate at the beginning of a session. Further contact such as hugging should be explored with the client in terms of appropriate cultural expressions of support and related behavior patterns. Likewise, the worker should note eye contact of the client. In some cultures, indirect and minimal direct eye contact may denote a respect for the worker as an authority figure. Looking away and the lack of direct eye contact may not connote avoidance or resistance. Talking about sensitive topics in the session may be accompanied by the lack of eye contact because of the serious nature of the conversation. The client may feel uneasy and embarrassed by the topic and may look away or down at the ground as a result. Staffing patterns should mirror the population of the clients served. Allow the behavior of the client to lead and to tell you what an appropriate response is. If a worker has questions about these areas, it would be helpful to get clarification from the client. Likewise, a professional colleague of the same ethnic or cultural group as the client may be a good sounding board to give advice and to orient the worker before the beginning session with a particular client from an unfamiliar cultural and ethnic group.

Bilingual and bicultural staff matching the language and cultural needs of clients conveys a sense of familiarity and expressiveness to clients who are comfortable speaking their culture-of-origin language. Translators should be trained by the staff of the agency to understand and interpret correctly medical and clinical terms and concepts. The worker should address and maintain contact with the client rather than the translator and should continuously ask the client for feedback to determine the level of understanding between the two. On the other hand, in small ethnic or cultural communities, a client may elect to work with someone who is not from his or her own community. Privacy, cultural taboo, cultural norms and power structure, and the nature of the problem may make using a professional from other cultural group more appropriate. For example, a child sexual abuse victim may find it more desirable to work with a female professional of different cultural/ethnic background than with the male cultural staff who also happens to be the elder in the ethnic community.

Active listening responses that vary according to the content of the message and the feelings of the messenger should be used. Strive to offer open-ended questions that will open avenues of information and feelings rather than close-ended questions that trigger brief and dead-end answers. Supportive, understanding, probing, interpretive, and evaluative (SUPIE) responses are examples of varying listening skills. Supportive responses restate the essential thoughts and feelings of the client without using the same words. A paraphrase by the worker reassures the client that he or she has been heard. Understanding responses focus on the client's meaning and the perception of the problem. They verify that significant thoughts have been understood and comprehended. Probing responses seek further information on problem issues that are to be explored or those that are in progress. Open-ended probing may be used to elicit more information, and close-ended probing may help pinpoint a particular detail yet to be uncovered. Interpretive responses seek to bring meaning and organization to the various facts, events, and experiences shared by the client. They order the series of events, provide meaning about what has been going on, and bring a sense of rationality. Finally, evaluative responses offer various alternative directions that the client may take based on his or her readiness to move on the problem situation. They summarize the themes and provide a range of available solutions.

CONTACT CONCEPTUALIZATION SKILLS   Ethnographic skills are important to conceptualization in the contact stage. Ethnography is derived from *ethnos* (people) and *graphics* (writings, drawing) and literally involves the recording (writing and drawing) of the behavioral culture of a person or a group of people. Ethnography is concerned with the words, thoughts, and feelings of the client from a participant observation stance. In the contact stage, we must constantly ask ourselves as workers what clients are saying about themselves, their families, and their primary groups. We must have an ethnographic discipline to record words, thoughts, and feelings and then to translate them as teachable moments for us to learn and uncover new and different ways of understanding and relating to people.

Ethnographic skills could be further utilized in the following areas:

- Qualitative inductive survey research begins by framing a research question and interviewing a sample population without a priori assumptions. Likewise, ethnographic skills in the contact stage encourage open-ended questions about the client's family, work, children, and related background areas.
- Social constructionism focuses on life story or narrative and is interested in how a person has constructed his or her life from various pieces of experience. Again, ethnographic skills include the telling of life story by the person, which is a familiar and nonthreatening way for a multicultural client to open segments of his or her life.
- Emic and etic understanding views the multicultural client from two perspectives. Emic understanding seeks to comprehend the unique particulars of the client in order to understand what sets the person apart from others in his or her culture. Etic understanding is concerned about the link between the client and his or her cultural group. Sobeck, Chapleski, and Fisher (2003) describe the emic perspective in research:

The purpose of emic research is to seek categories of meanings based on how the group being studied defines things. Its research strategy includes conducting interviews in the native language, seeking to discover meaning and relying on the research participant's explanation for their own behavior. (p. 74)

A number of applications have been made to feminist research and to First Nations Peoples communities. Ethnographic contact skills cover these areas and remind us of the importance of open-ended interviewing, finding out about the life story narratives of clients, and determining what is culture-common and culture-specific about individuals, families, and groups.

Green (1995) offers some practical suggestions about ethnographic interviewing:

- The social work interview must have a mutually accepted purpose and must focus on how the client uses language and what language suggests about the client's state of being and thinking.
- Our concern must be on the salient cultural data bearing on the presenting issue or the cultural context of the problem.
- It is important to understand the perspective of the client and how the client explains the veracity (truthfulness) of cultural expressions and communication.
- The client is our teacher who best explains cultural differences.

Green (1995) also explains,

> The intent of ethnographic interviewing is ... to recognize ideas, beliefs, and patterns of behavior in the contexts where they are meaningful—all as an aid to informed understanding of people's problems and appreciation of what one will have to do to effectively help resolve them. (p. 146)

Contact conceptualization skills enable the worker to learn about the client in an inductive manner and assist us with conceptualizing some preliminary notions about the person at the beginning of the helping process. Yuen, Bein, and Lum (2006) describe the utilities of inductive learning in working with clients of diverse backgrounds.

> A researcher doing social survey is constantly asking questions about areas of concern in an inductive manner. A survey researcher uses inductive reasoning in assembling particular facts about a subject or individual cases and then drawing general conclusions based on findings. A good inductive researcher asks open-ended research questions and draws conclusions based on findings. The inductive method is the opposite of the deductive method. Deduction is a process of reasoning from a known principle that serves as a guide or benchmark to a conclusion that confirms the given. The deductive method may go from the general to the specific or from a premise to a logical conclusion.
>
> From an inductive learning perspective, the social worker begins by ascertaining the background and problems of the multicultural client. Based on careful inquiry and investigation, the social worker learns about the unique issues confronting the client. Similarities may exist between multicultural clients. At the same time, unique characteristics may emerge and differ from those found in the existing literature. Inductive learning helps the social worker become a careful and caring practitioner and offers new insights into emerging information that may differ from the body of knowledge on multicultural clients. This may be especially relevant with new immigrant groups from countries where unique cultural knowledge about these people may be lacking (p. 228).

Contact Personalization Skills   What happens to the worker in the contact stage? The range of subjective feelings on the part of the worker may include normal anxiety and curiosity about the reasons for the client coming for help, positive interest in and empathy for the client, or uneasy feelings about the client. The worker should constantly check his or her feelings and ask, "What am I feeling and sensing as I listen to and interact with this client?" "What is the client's message?" "Am I able to help with the client's problems?" The worker needs to process these feelings and reactions including possible transference and counter-transference both internally and with a supervisor or colleague.

Subjective reflection about the first impressions of the client is a part of the personalization skills at the contact stage. Likewise, the client is sizing up the worker and decoding verbal and nonverbal messages and related behavioral responses. Paniagua (2005) discusses attrition, where the client fails to return, and estimates that 50% of clients terminate after one contact with a mental health professional (p. 110). The preceding principles on contact are designed to retain the client. The personalization process involves listening to one's self and becoming curious about how one reacts to the client, the problem situation, and significant others involved. Identifying and checking out these reactions helps with self-learning and provides an opportunity to receive feedback from a third-party source who objectively analyzes the situation. Fieldwork supervisors in social work field education play a vital role as teachers who are able to heighten the personalization skills of social work students in helping situations.

PROBLEM IDENTIFICATION

PROBLEM-IDENTIFICATION PROCESS SKILLS   It is crucial to spend as much time as possible cultivating contact in order to establish a purposive working relationship with the client. For personal or cultural reasons, clients may be reluctant or use various means to mask or to disclose their problems. Problem-identification process skills include problem-area disclosure, problem orientation, and identification of racial/ethnic/cultural themes.

Problem-area disclosure is a skill based on the understanding that a client may have a difficult time expressing a problem directly to the worker. The client may feel shame and hesitation and may have a guarded attitude toward disclosing family secrets to a stranger. The worker should be patient and allow the client to set the pace and format in revealing the problem. It is important not to rush the client prematurely. The client may ask indirect questions ("I have this friend who has a problem. How would you help her?"), make oblique or circular comments that approach a problem in a slanted or peripheral way ("I don't know why I am here, but something is bothering me"), or make similar efforts toward problem disclosure. Rather than spelling out all the negative details and unburdening one's self in humiliation, certain clients have learned to infer and allude to problem issues. In turn, the worker must read between the lines and piece together the inferences. It may be more culturally appropriate for the worker to figure out the problem, spell out the details, and ask for comments from the client, who is excused from disgracing himself or herself. A culturally competent social worker is able to pick up on this approach and decipher these indirect messages from the client within the sociocultural context of the clients.

A natural way to begin problem-area disclosure is through the worker's expressions of genuine interest in learning about the client and his or her families. This is a respectful and nonthreatening way of helping a person talk about himself or herself. Questions such as "How are your parents/children?" "Could you tell me about your family?" "What are they like?" "Where are they living?" help break the barrier and begin conversation about the family unit and the client's membership in the family.

Problem orientation is the core of problem identification. Problems are normally viewed as negative intrusions in our lives. However, problems are opportunities for growth and learning. A problem is viewed as an unsatisfied want or an unfulfilled need (Reid, 1978), which is a way of interpreting the problem in a positive light. That is, behind every problem are wants that have not been satisfied and needs that have not been fulfilled. The task is to restructure the problem so that the worker can reorient the client toward positive growth. This is called *reframing the problem*. The worker and the client reframe the problem and change the point of reference from negative pathology to positive want satisfaction or need fulfillment. As part of the reframing process, one begins to mobilize client strengths and resources to fulfill the want and satisfy the need. Reframing a problem is not denying the problem but empowering the client to start the process of identifying, owning, and addressing the problem with new and productive perspectives. Greene, Lee, and Hoffpauir (2005) explain reframing:

> The reframing process involves offering clients a plausible, alternative positive interpretation for something they have defined as negative and undesirable or unchangeable. Once clients accept the plausibility of the new and more positive reality represented by the new category, they cannot go back to using only their former, more narrow worldview. (p. 272)

Racial/ethnic/cultural themes may be a part of problem identification. Multiple problem levels may occur simultaneously and require analysis and unraveling. Fong (2004) describes the layer-upon-layer problems of immigrants and refugees coming to the United States. She describes them:

> At the macro-level, poverty, discrimination, racism, language, immigration laws, and legal and illegal status characterize many of their experiences. At the meso-level, families often struggle with role reversal, husband–wife tensions, grandparent relations, and questions of abandonment and loyalty. At the micro-level, a father may encounter problems with his traditional role as the head of house and loss of authority, because he lacks command of the host-culture's language. At the micro-level, for the mother, accepting employment may introduce tension about her role as wife and mother. At the micro-level, for the child, tensions may be related to school and language deficiency. Children may also have conflicts due to illiteracy, the necessity to interpret for parents, and pressure to achieve and hurry through childhood. (pp. 12–13)

Yuen (2003) discusses the connections among stereotype, prejudice, discrimination, and oppression. These related concepts have similar dynamics: in-group/out-group, superiority/inferiority, domination/submission, power/powerlessness, and systemic-institutional/individual. Yuen (2003) explains,

> *Stereotype, prejudice, discrimination,* and *oppression* are terms that often used in the social work literature. As a profession, social work commits to social justice and values diversity. Part of the preparation for becoming a professional social worker is to learn to overcome discrimination and to promote social justice. The term *stereotype* is the over-simplification and overgeneralization of a particular group of individuals based on few characteristics. It is an ill-informed knowledge that may include both positive and negative attributes of the group. For example, a stereotype exists that Asian-American students do well in school, excel at math skills, but do not have the capacity to be good managers. *Prejudice* is a negative attitude that is based on stereotypical knowledge. This attitude is a belief that may or may not turn into action. However, when one acts on prejudice and violates the civil or human rights of any individuals, then that is *discrimination*. An employer who has a prejudice against Asian Americans as managers, hurtful as it may seem, simply has a personally held negative attitude. When the employer refuses to hire or to promote any qualified Asian Americans as managers, the discrimination has taken place. When discriminatory behaviors are acted out in an organized manner at the systemwide or societal level, a situation of *oppression* has occurred. The happenings of discrimination and oppression have forced the situation beyond personal virtue and then become legal, social, and civic concerns. (pp. 26–27)

Discrimination and oppression that are based on race, social class, and gender will result in racism, classism, sexism, and alike. Homophobia is a prejudice as well as a form of discrimination that is based on sexual orientation. The culturally competent worker should explore and identify possible problem themes that may be related to the client's situation and problems.

Yuen et al. (2006) advocate the use of inductive approach for problem identification, particularly from ethnic or cultural minority clients:

> Inductive approaches are particularly appropriate for cross-cultural social work practice. Practitioners move beyond cultural stereotypes or etic (universal) categorization of psychosocial dynamics when they listen to and appreciate the client's own story. Clients tell social workers about what events, conditions, behaviors, and decisions mean to them, and social workers understand the client's narrative on the client's own terms. When clients teach social workers about their lives, clients experience having their voice count, being respected, and knowing they are not judged. (p. 231)

Problem-Identification Conceptualization Skills Ethnographic problem-identification skills involve how the multicultural client formulates the problem. Green (1999) explains his help-seeking behavior model that relates four principles to problem identification and resolution: the individual's definition and understanding of an experience as a problem; the client's semantic evaluation of a problem from his or her language explanation; indigenous cultural strategies of problem intervention; and acceptable culturally based problem resolution. That is, rather than defining the problem for the client, it is vital to understand how the client defines and understands his or her problem situation. It may well be that because the client wears another set of cultural and ethnic lenses, his or her perception of the problem is different from the worker's.

Different languages explain the same problem with a different semantic meaning. Finding out how the client and his or her family name a problem from a linguistic perspective may give workers a clue to how the client understands and handles a problem situation. Furthermore, from a bicultural vantage point, one may ask an ethnic caregiver for information and advice on appropriate indigenous ways of intervening and solving a problem. Cultural practices, group support, and medicinal cures may all play a role in problem solving. It is important to determine how traditional a client is and how receptive a person might be to applying a combination of indigenous healing and clinical therapy practices to a problem situation. This is an example of the biculturation of problem-solving practices.

Problem-Identification Personalization Skills The worker has to be cognizant of his or her own reaction to the problem. Does the worker grasp the cultural and ethnic implications of the problem? Has the worker misidentified the problem? Has the worker strived to reframe the problem with the client and thus brought new insights and directions? Does the problem have clinical, ethnic, cultural, gender, social class, and/or sexual orientation implications? Does the problem involve a single dimension or a multiple set of dynamics? Is there a problem or are there problems? Does the problem shock the worker in its sensationalism or taboo nature? Is the problem so overwhelming that the worker privately recognizes that problem resolution is not likely to happen? Is it better to sustain the client through supportive maintenance than to push for a rapid solution? Is the problem a part of a problem cluster that will take time to unravel, and should the worker direct the client toward a series of modest solutions? The culturally competent worker must consider these questions and others in the problem-identification stage.

ASSESSMENT

ASSESSMENT PROCESS SKILLS Assessment process skills involve a psychosocial perspective that analyzes environment and person. Some factors in the social environment are related to maintaining basic survival needs, such as food, housing, clothes, employment, health care, and education. Other related environmental stressors include ethnic identity formation, intergenerational disputes, and related cultural conflicts. These areas are termed *socioenvironmental impacts*.

Assessment is related but different from evaluation. Assessment is usually done with the client to learn the various dimensions of the person. Evaluation is normally done to the services or tasks being performed in relation to the client. Assessment focuses on the clients and evaluation focuses on the service.

The many ways to conduct assessment include 1) use of established instruments such as scales, questionnaires, genogram, and ecomap; 2) application of a set of research-based criteria or classification systems such as *Diagnostic and Statistical Manual of Mental Disorders* (DSM), child abuse risk assessment, or school grade; and 3) agency mandates specific assessment such as domestic violence or drug use assessment. Many agencies use a combination of these assessments and develop their own psychosocial assessment or mental status examination formats.

Throughout the history of social work, there have been many theory-based assessments. For example, Richmond (1917) employs the psychodynamic approach that emphasizes personality, pathology, and the client's insight. Since 1964, Woods and Hollis (1990) advocate psychosocial approach that focuses on biopsychosocial process, developmental and cognitive issues, and stress and coping. Perlman (1957) promotes the problem-solving approach that pays attention to the four Ps: person, problems, place, and process. For the task-centered approach (Epstein, 1992; Reid, 2002; Reid & Epstein, 1972), the goal of assessment is to specify the target problems and their desired outcomes. Similarly, various family therapeutic approaches also have their model-specific assessment focuses and techniques.

The psychosocial perspective views the environment as socioenvironmental impacts and people as psychoindividual reactions. Clients in major transition such as refugees or new immigrants may experience psychosocial stressors such as newcomer acculturation, psychosomatic reactions, psychological identity issues, and related survival adjustment concerns. Newcomer acculturation consists of culture shock and culture dislocation, language barriers, legal and immigration problems, employment/unemployment/welfare, and school adjustment for children. Their psychosomatic reactions may include anxiety and depression with accompanying insomnia, weight loss, and lack of energy; ache and pain; hypertension; and loneliness and isolation. Psychological identity may be impaired due to ethnic identity confusion, conflict, and ambivalence; cultural value conflict; family role conflict; dating, mate selection, and intermarriage; and youth delinquency and gang activities.

Emphasis of the psychosocial assessment is placed on the strengths of the client including cultural and spiritual strengths. Cultural strengths are a focus of social work assessment in line with the asset resource understanding advocated by Saleebey (2002) and Cowger (1994). This assessment emphasis discovers internal strengths of the person and external ethnic group strengths from the culture. Examples of cultural strengths are religious beliefs, historical achievements, ethnic pride, capacities for endurance and hard work in the family, and related areas. Bricker-Jenkins (1997) talks about supporting the life world and strengths of the client from a cultural perspective:

> The workers who engaged networks skillfully had two competencies that were essential: They were "culturally competent," knowing how to get "inside the skin" of a culture not familiar to them; and they used the oral histories of clients to assess their strengths and understand their systems of meaning. Thus they were able to place clients not only in time and situation but in their ethnic and class medium as well. These workers were able to assume, with patience and sensitivity, the "standpoint" of their clients. (p. 141)

The cultural strengths perspective emphasizes the discovery of strengths in the person and the culture, the motivation toward perseverance and change based on inner strength and endurance, and the environment as full of resources at the family, group, and community levels.

The inclusion of cultural and spiritual assessment expands the concept of biopsychosocial assessment beyond the biological, psychological, and social categories to include cultural and spiritual dimensions. Most cultures recognize this interconnectedness. Part of culture is the spiritual and part of spirituality is the culture. In minority communities such as the African American, Latino, and Asian American communities, the ethnic temples and churches are the source of imparting spiritual values and celebrating cultural events. For First Nations Peoples, the cultural and spiritual aspects of life are a part of rituals and group gatherings.

Psychiatric cultural assessment (American Psychiatric Association, 1994) addresses cultural identity, cultural explanations of illness, psychosocial environmental levels of functioning, and cultural elements between the worker and the client. Cultural identity is concerned about the degree of involvement that a person has with both the culture of origin and the host culture including language abilities, use, and preference. Cultural explanations of illness are important to determine in relation to cultural expressions of stress, cultural group norms and perceptions of symptom severity, local perspectives on cultural forms of illness, cultural explanations of dysfunction, and the blending of professional and indigenous helping. Psychosocial environmental levels of functioning involve culturally sensitive interpretations of social stressors, available social supports, and the role of religion and kinship networks. Finally, the relationship between the worker and the client is important in determining the degree of difficulties in language communication, understanding the cultural significance of symptoms, negotiating an appropriate relationship, and determining whether a behavior is normative or pathological.

Regarding spiritual assessment, linking spirituality and social work is a growing movement in social work education and professional practice (Amato-von Hemert, 1994; Bein, 2009; Clark, 1994). Part of the movement recognizes the importance of religion and spirituality in people's life, and another part is active in churches, synagogues, and mosques. From a cultural competence standpoint, it is appropriate to understand and explore past and present spirituality and religious faith in the life of the client. Spiritual assessment is to explore the person's sense of life purpose and views on how one relates to the world and others.

Yuen and Lum (2003) differentiate several related terms: spirituality, faith, and religion, which are often treated interchangeably. However, each is a distinct term. *Spirituality* is "an inner sense of connectedness and meaningfulness in life" (Raines, 1997, p. 8). *Faith* is "an inner system of beliefs which relate one to the transcendent or ultimate reality, for the theistic believer, God" (Joseph, 1997, p. 2). Conversely, *religion* is "the organized, out-ward expression of that connection and meaning" (Raines, p. 8) or "the external expression of one's faith" (Joseph, p. 2). A good possibility exists that someone can be very spiritual but have no affiliation with any religious organizations. Equally, a very religious individual may not be spiritual (Yuen & Lum, 1991, pp. 131–132).

ASSESSMENT CONCEPTUALIZATION SKILLS   Culturally sensitive assessment reinterprets and reconceptualizes psychosocial factors as socioenvironmental impacts and psychoindividual reactions; it also acknowledges cultural strengths and includes both the cultural and the spiritual (Lum, 2000). This extension of the conceptual framework should be included in any meaningful discussion of culturally sensitive assessment.

Inductive learning provides an approach to construct assessment that includes client's own perspectives and to understand the meaning of the situation according to the client. Yuen et al. (2006) explain how the use of social constructivist research could help achieve this goal:

> Social constructivist research is a type of naturalistic inquiry in which the researcher focuses on the "cognitive schemes that construct the subject's experience and action and lead to new interpretive frameworks or structures" (Rodwell, 1998, p. 254). Cognitive schema is the cognitive map or diagram of a person. The term "can also refer to the way individuals categorize to make sense out of complexity" (p. 262). This schema is often the result of one's data analysis processes. This cognitive map informs how one perceives and understands reality. Through linguistic negotiations and other narrative exchanges that are achieved intersubjectively, researchers gain understanding of the development of the new reality and meaning. In other words, through the communication process, new common referent terms and understandings between individuals are achieved, and they shape and construct the new reality. For example, suppose a social worker is working with a newly arrived refugee who is still traumatized by the war and torture he suffered. Through extensive dialogues that include genuine support and direct challenges, the social worker can gain the trust and understanding of the client and can attempt to help him sort out and make sense of his war experience and his life in a new land. The social worker and the client together write a chapter of his history and coauthor a new chapter of his future that is sensible to the client. (p. 231)

Ecological perspectives and systems theories offer an interactive and holistic framework to conceptualize the environment and problems experienced by diverse clients. Pardeck and Yuen (2006) assert that the ecological perspective is "based on the metaphor of biological organisms that live and adapt in complex networks of environmental forces. It is grounded in an evolutionary, adaptive view of human beings in continuous transaction and interaction with their physical and social environment" (p. 7). As the result "both the person and the environment continuously change and accommodate one another. Ecological perspective stresses that people and environments are holistic and transactional" (p. 7). They further describe systems theory as the theoretical underpinning of the ecological approach to practice. It allows the practitioner to "understand how the client system is influenced by and affects the greater social ecology. It is critical of a reductionistic view of human behavior and stresses behavior can best be understood in the context of the various social systems" (p. 8).

The orientations of ecological perspective and systems theory form the ecosystem ways of conceptualizing diverse client populations. Yuen (2003) explains the application of these theoretical frameworks to foster holistic and culturally appropriate understanding. He states,

> Ecologically, individuals and families as habitats occupy and develop their particular niches within their environment; their existence and reciprocal exchanges with others form the relatedness along with the life experience of rewards and growth as well as stress and difficulties. Individuals and families develop particular coping strategies, meaningful to their culture and reality, to deal with various life stresses throughout the different stages of individual and family life courses.

> From a systems theory perspective, if individuals or families behave as open systems that have continuous input, output, and feedback, they will continue to develop and result in the attainment of the state of homeostasis or equilibrium. If the environments in which they reside exist as closed systems, they will eventually become extinct. These environments also interact and network constantly with other ecosystems ... social work practitioners should develop the ability to understand the dynamics within and among these ecosystem networks to form the basis for designing proper interventions. (p. 21)

The worker is to understand the negative and positive niches one occupies such as single motherhood, new immigrants who do not speak English, or the new teacher or medical doctor in town; the stressors and their coping strategies; the interrelatedness and reciprocal exchanges among people and entities; as well as the environment of their communities. The worker could further understand how the client's system is a lively and dynamic system that takes input, processes the input throughout, produces the output, and provides feedbacks as it relates to other equally active ecosystems.

Case Theory The development of a case theory for a client will help move the assessment forward to the formulation of suitable interventions. Bisman (1999) explains the function of the use of a case theory:

> To intervene effectively, social workers need to make sense of clients and their situations. A case theory approach to assessment provides a framework to formulate assessments that are clear and directly related to the real-world problems clients present. Explaining the problem situation, case theory forms the foundation for selection of intervention strategies and methods to achieve change. Building case theory requires practitioner

abilities to form concepts, relate concepts into propositions, develop hypotheses, and organize these into a coherent whole. Including case background information, observations and relevant professional literature, case theory presents an accurate and cogent comprehension of the client. (p. 240)

The development of a case theory for change for a client employs the process, conceptualization, and personalization skills. It allows the social worker to develop a logical approach to understand and to develop intervention that makes sense to the situation, the worker, and the client.

ASSESSMENT PERSONALIZATION SKILLS   Psychosocial assessment provides an opportunity to evaluate the positive potential of the client. One must not be trapped into focusing on negative pathology. Cox and Ephross (1998) point out the need for a balanced assessment. Assessment ought to mobilize positive resources that support change intervention strategies. A client's strengths and weaknesses are a given reality. However, a conscious effort to focus on positive client potentials and strengths helps create intervention strategies that draw on these resources that reframe the problem as an unsatisfied want or an unfulfilled need and the assessment as an evaluation of client potentials and strengths. As a result, intervention builds on these preceding stages in a substantive way. The worker has positive confidence based on these building blocks.

INTERVENTION

INTERVENTION PROCESS SKILLS   The purpose of intervention is to affect a positive change between the person and the problem situation. Among the intervention process skills are goal setting and agreement; the selection of culturally diverse intervention strategies; and micro, meso, and macro levels of intervention. An intervention plan must be based on the needs of the client.

Goal setting and agreement is a cooperative effort between the client and the worker. It involves the detailed formulation of goal outcomes, expected behavioral changes, task objectives, and contracting.

Goal outcomes are terminal achievements accomplished at the end of the intervention stage. They are specific areas that give direction to the client. It is important to write down the exact words of the client as far as a goal outcome is concerned. Begin by asking the client what he or she wishes to accomplish based on resolving the problem. Often, clients may present many interrelated problems and there are many possible strategies for different solutions. The worker should work with the client to compartmentalize and prioritize the presenting problems with special attentions to those that are related to immediate survival, safety, and urgency. Certainly, behind the presenting problems, there are the underlining problems that may be the crux of the presenting problems and the true focus for intervention.

Expected behavioral changes are specific ways the client is willing to alter existing patterns and introduce a positive and alternative way of handling a situation. A workaholic mom may agree, instead of working continuously in her home office, to have family dinners at least three nights a week and to spend at least an hour each night with her children doing homework or just spending time together.

Task objectives are intermediate steps that are taken to move toward the achievement of goal outcomes. This over-working mother may immediately start working biweekly with a counselor to develop effective time management skills for her involvement in her work and her family. Meanwhile, the worker should explore the underlining issues that may have contributed to the nonstop work scheduling of the mother and the possible neglect of the family and the children within the cultural context of this family.

Contracting may involve working with the client individually or bringing relevant client parties (e.g., family members) together to initially discuss the key goal setting (goal outcomes, expected behavioral changes, and task objectives), sketch them on a board or on a piece of paper, then draw up a written or verbal agreement that is realistic and fair for all client parties involved. Contracting is a dynamic, back-and-fro process that may take several attempts to complete.

The culturally competent worker utilizes intervention skills by selecting relevant micro, meso, and macro strategies based on the problem identification and assessment workup of the case. Among the multiple intervention strategies is the empowerment intervention approach. According to Browne and Mills (2001), empowerment is "the gaining of power by an individual, family group of persons, or a community" (p. 23). While empowerment presupposes a state of powerlessness on the part of the client group, it believes in the client's capacity to develop the power or competency to affect change, may be, with proper support and facilitations. Powerlessness is the inability to control self and others, to alter problem situations, or to reduce environmental distress (Leigh, 1984). Empowerment is a unique and useful intervention that employs a range of change strategies (micro, meso, macro) applicable to client problems. Crafting an intervention plan that embodies empowerment and addresses all three levels of concern denotes the holistic nature or this practice skill.

On the micro level, empowerment is the mobilization of the uniqueness and self-determination of the client to take charge and control his or her life, to learn new ways of thinking about the problem situation, and to adopt new behaviors that give more satisfying and rewarding outcomes (Cowger, 1994). In the empowerment process, the client recognizes that social forces have negatively affected his or her life and moves toward an internal locus of control over the outcome of his or her life as well as an external locus of responsibility to improve his or her life. The client is able to mobilize personal and community resources and control and master the environment. The focus is on client strength and responsibility (Gibson, 1993). Pinderhughes (1989) emphasizes the need to help clients with a sense of positive strength:

> Empowerment requires the use of strategies that enable clients to experience themselves as competent, valuable, and worthwhile both as individuals and as members of their cultural group. They no longer feel trapped in the subordinate cultural group status that prevents them from meeting their goals. The process of empowering requires helpers to use their power appropriately to facilitate this shift. (p. 111)

The social worker is a vital resource to nurture the client and to help him or her in this self-discovery. At the same time, a person experiences empowerment as a member of a group. In order to make this empowerment transition, micro individual empowerment is interconnected to meso-group empowerment.

Meso-level empowerment relies on the development of group consciousness and participation. The individual must reach for his or her internal power and at the same time be energized by the group. Group consciousness involves developing an awareness that there is collective power in a group and that political structures affecting individual and group experiences need to be changed (Gutierrez, 1990). Collective action and change take place on the meso-group level. Such collaborative partnerships between clients and social workers, client groups, and constituents focus on program and service changes.

Macro-level empowerment addresses large-scale organizational and institutional change. Group empowerment involves the ability to work with others to change social institutions. Political power and resource allocation for those who are powerless but who have mobilized a group's efforts are a part of rebalancing traditional power and control. Macro-level empowerment involves connecting groups with a number of social, political, and economic advocates and agencies who are sensitive and responsive to disenfranchised and powerless individuals and groups. This networking on the macro level is a demonstration of large-scale empowerment. It involves redistributing resource allocations (distributive justice), initiating class action discrimination suits (corrective justice), and working with state and federal legislators on fair and just social programs (political and social justice). Manning, Cornelius, and Okundaye (2004) have identified strengths as an expression of empowerment theory:

> The client's support system, as a strength, can provide physical resources such as shelter, financial assistance, and emotional comfort. Individual strengths might be certain innate capacities like the ability to communicate, interact with others, or function under difficult circumstances. The role of the social worker is to help the client identify these strengths and then maximize their usefulness by identifying how these supports can be accessed. (p. 231)

Empowerment as an intervention strategy is appropriate to clients of color, in particular. In First Nations Peoples settings, empowerment is useful to support an individual to function as an integral part of creation. Gaining or developing power is seen as "securing help from the spiritual and natural world for a higher purpose than the individual self—to benefit the Oyate (Lakota Nation)," according to Yellow Horse Brave Heart (2001, p. 165). Empowerment and sovereignty have been linked in that there is the protection of power to advocate for rights, beliefs, and values. Traditional American Indian forms of governance are important to maintain in light of internalized oppression and the impact of colonization. Empowerment and resiliency are two critical themes in this circumstance (Weaver, 2001).

With African Americans, the powerlessness and empowerment themes were first used by Solomon (1976) to describe the situation of Black communities. African American spiritual beliefs and churches have been the source of community empowerment. In large urban areas, African American churches provide recreational, social service, housing, and other tangible economic programs (Manning, 2001). Empowerment is grounded in African American principles of self-determination and an equitable distribution of political, economic, and social choices.

Regarding empowerment with Latino Americans, Negroni-Rodriguez and Morales (2001) indicate that Latinos have natural strengths among extended family members, traditional support and healing systems, and levels of biculturalism and bilingualism. At the same time, they caution that it is important to "assess the ability to help Latino clients move from self-blaming and powerless views to being agents of change." This involves working with Latino clients to build a relationship of collaboration and partnership in problem solving and to impart social work knowledge and skills. Client preparation is crucial to launching an empowerment intervention strategy. Like other groups that have a history of being oppressed and discriminated, Latinos may have suffered socioeconomic and sociocultural oppression (racism, colonialism, economic exploitation, and cultural domination) and internal oppression (gender, sexual orientation, race, and class) (Acevedo & Morales, 2001). As a result, it may take longer to sort through these areas as part of the empowerment process.

INTERVENTION CONCEPTUALIZATION SKILLS   Intervention strategies should be based on the unique experience of the multicultural client (Ridley, Espelage, & Rubinstein, 1997) and tailored from a broad repertoire of intervention strategies to apply specifically to the client's problem situation. This involves recognizing the unique factors related to the client, the problem, and the social/cultural environment. Boehm and Staples (2004) identify six essential conceptual characteristics of empowerment:

1. Empowerment is both a process and an outcome. As a process it involves individuals and groups moving from relative powerlessness to increased power and as an outcome it has end products whereby a measure of power is achieved such as access to information or increased economic resources.
2. Empowerment is operative at both the personal and the collective levels. Personal empowerment relates to the way people think about themselves as well as the knowledge, capacities, skills, and mastery that they possess such as increased levels of self-esteem, assertiveness, self-determination, social responsibility, critical consciousness, participatory competencies, and hope. Collective empowerment refers to individuals joining together to break their solitude and silence, to support and help one another, to learn together, and to develop skills for collective action.
3. Empowerment assumes that even when people are in situations of relative powerlessness, they have capacities, skills, qualifications, and assets that serve as resources for individual or collective change.
4. Empowerment cannot be created for another person, but professionals, such as social workers, can help facilitate the empowerment process through consumer self-determination and critical consciousness where people gain understanding of their sociocultural reality and their ability to change social conditions.
5. Empowerment underscores the need for consumers to make decisions and take initiatives as well as establish a partnership between social workers and consumers to share power, joint responsibility, and division of labor.
6. Empowerment focuses on oppressed groups in society, on better understanding of the way inequality and lack of power perpetuate personal and social problems, and a concern for stigmatization and unequal structural relations of power and the means for achieving social and economic justice. (pp. 270–271)

They conducted research on empowerment with 145 respondents (84 consumers, 61 social workers) and reported that mastery and competencies were basic elements of empowerment: physical mastery including the use of equipment and technology; mastery of emotions and behavior; mastery of information and decision making; mastery of social systems; efficient mastery of time and the effective use of time; mastery connected to autonomy and individual freedom; and planning mastery to prevent negative situations and to actualize positive ones. Empowerment intervention presupposes conceptualizing a plan that addresses micro individuals, meso groups, and macro communities and organizations.

Another conceptual skill of empowerment intervention involves using the client's belief system and culture as sources of strength and empowerment. Conceptualization of indigenous interventions identifies natural cultural ways of helping and reconciling differences, such as the family group resolution effort in Hawaiian culture called *ho'oponopono*. There are other ways that ethnic groups and communities introduce intervention change. Ron Lewis, a Native American social work educator, asserts that it is important for an Indian with a drinking problem to attend and participate in powwows in order to contact his or her First Nations Peoples culture and tribe. These elements help an Indian person cope with alcoholism (Ron Lewis, personal communication, March 1985). Conceptualizing an indigenous intervention with a particular client offers indigenous expressions of empowerment.

Greene, Lee, and Hoffpauir (2005) advocate the solution-focused approach, which is based on a strengths and competence orientation:

> The solution-focused approach operates from the assumption that change is occurring much of the time and that there are times when the problem is less frequent, intense, severe, or even not present. The language of solutions facilitates identifying the strengths, resources, and competencies clients use to make these exceptions to the problem occur. (p. 272)

They further explain,

> The language of solutions never attempts to deny the existence of problems; rather, it emphasizes the fact that people have strengths, competencies, resources, potentials, and creativity which they or others are ignoring, forgetting, or underutilizing. By focusing the therapeutic dialogue on solutions and strengths, the power of language can facilitate the client and clinician in co-constructing a view of reality that contains an expanded definition of self that includes competence, skills, power, and personal agency. (pp. 272–273)

Conceptualizing interventions that accent empowerment, strengths, competencies, and solutions to problems are directions that culturally competent practice should take.

INTERVENTION PERSONALIZATION SKILLS The culturally competent worker is concerned about intervention implementation. Is the client motivated to make a change? To what extent will the intervention strategy be successful? How can the worker be a source of encouragement and facilitate the change process?

Yuen (2005) asserts that "social work practice could become merely a time-wasting and meaningless exercise of human interactions" (p. 5), if it does not believe in people and their ability to make change. Social work believes in human potential and the need for holistic interventions. The clients and their environment are the targets for both change and improvement. What motivate people to consider change? Frederick Perls, the founder of Gestalt Therapy, believes that change occurs when one becomes aware of what he or she is, not what he or she is not. Clients seek change as they experience conflicts between who they are and who they should be (Yuen,

2005). Motivation for change often comes from the aspiration for a better future or well-being as well as the pain and suffering experienced by the client as a result of the problem faced. The worker recognizes that the client has the power to make choices. The worker cannot and should not assume this responsibility. If the worker has structured the necessary means for change, the client has choice in determining the process.

Why do people come to social workers seeking help to change? Compton and Galaway (1998) believe that people who come to seek services have encountered life situations that have overwhelmed them and their means of solution. As previously suggested, after the initial contact, a psychosocial assessment is often the first step of the helping process. "The aim (of a biopsychosocial assessment) is to understand the clients and their situations in a manner that is culturally, developmentally, socially, and spiritually appropriate. It is also important to assess 'clients' unique concerns, strengths, and challenges'" (Yuen, 2005, p. 6). In some crisis situations, a thorough assessment is not feasible and the worker should still "strive to understand clients' reasons and needs for change, engage clients in working for change, and take aim at the outcomes of change" (p. 5). Assessment and any other efforts of intervention in facilitating changes have to make sense to the clients in their sociocultural contexts and environments. "Service providers with different theoretical orientations have different views on why and how people change. Behaviorists attempt to change behaviors through behavioral modifications. Psychoanalytic therapists try to identify insights that lead to change" (p. 8).

Yuen (2005) explains, "Clients or service recipients come to social workers' attention voluntary or involuntary. Some are highly motivated, while others are reluctant or unsure about their involvement and the necessity for change" (p. 5). Due to cultural and personal issues, unfamiliarity of the service system, feeling of shame, and history of abandonment and discrimination, many minority clients are hesitant to seek out services or resistant to engage in the helping process by reacting as uncooperative or reluctant. Some have chosen to maintain silence. Culturally competent social workers should be able to recognize these difficulties and respond appropriately.

Resistant Clients Instead of immediately labeling clients as difficult clients, the worker should first look inside and ask how one could make this encounter sensible within the client's cultural and personal contexts. A worker should spend time to build trust, identify common ground, and develop relationship instead of hurrying into an explanation of the agency's bureaucratic requirements and paperwork and setting goals without even knowing what the problem is. Acknowledging the client's unique situations and perspectives is more than relationship building, it is also validating the client's concerns, emotions, and feelings. It lays the foundation for cooperative effort for change. "It must be difficult for you. If it is okay with you, I would like to hear about your experience." "I am amazed by your resiliency and determination!" "How do you feel?" "How is your family?" are examples of some simple but powerful statements that indicate the worker's willingness to give credit to and show respect for the client's perspectives.

Positive framing of the problem, overstating of the problem, or over-praising client's effort to address the problem usually draws the client to attempt to correct or agree with the worker and start describing in his or her view of what really is happening. At that particular point, the client has become more engaging and open to assist the worker to understand the problem and the interventions within the cultural and personal views of the client. In working with children or youth who are not ready to engage, some have suggested to start doing things that would trigger clients' curiosity and cooperative spirit. For example, the worker may start arranging the figurines in the sandbox or drawing a picture of schoolchildren at recess. The client may be curious to figure out what the worker is doing and unknowingly become participating in the story telling. There are clients who do not know why they are seeing a social worker or those who do not see they have the need to seek help. The social worker may draw a circle on a paper and ask the client to write down what is going on in his or her life at the moment within the circle and other nonessential events outside the circle. The client may be amazed by how many they put in the circle and how overwhelmed they are that some assistance may be needed. The list of items in the circle could also become the initial list for prioritizing and identifying focus for intervention.

Silence   Silence may be the social norm for many cultures. Silence is, however, threatening and unbearable for inexperienced workers that they feel like they have to do something. Silence can be seen as an opportunity for reflection, evoking intervention, and building a sense of kinship and union (Elson, 2001). Silence may be the result of the lack of words to describe the feeling, that situation could be true to both native and foreign English speakers. Silence is protective that it guarantees one has said nothing wrong. An empathetic silence is healing that shows the worker is being considerate and respectful of client's need for not using words. The worker should develop the ability, both clinically and culturally, to gauge the appropriate extent of silence. Silence could facilitate deeper reflection for growth; it could also provoke anxiety that drives client away and result in loss opportunities. Workers again have to recognize that clients of diverse cultural backgrounds may have different meanings toward silence. Empathetic communication may not require words that to say nothing does not mean not to do anything. Silence has it sounds and workers just have to listen.

No Show   We all know that it is a fantasy to believe that all our clients are eagerly looking forward to working with us. Some come to see a social worker because they want to; some come because they have to. Moreover, some come without knowing why. Many new social workers have found that they lost more clients than they retained. Many have also been frustrated by doing all the preparations only to find out the clients fail to show up. No show is a common concern and is particularly more frequent among clients of lower socioeconomic status, having substance abuse–related problems, or having been waiting for a long time to receive services (Meyer, 2001). Ethnic and cultural minority clients are also known to have a high dropout rate. Clients of minority backgrounds as well as refugees and immigrants might have too many negative encounters with the systems and authorities that they become skeptical and less hopeful toward working with a social worker who may be perceived as the representative of the authority or the system. Psychologically and practically, it is easier for the client to drop the social worker than to be disappointed or dropped later on by the social worker. Culturally competent social workers will need to first recognize the mistrust and disappointment that have been experienced by the clients.

There are many ways to address the issue of no show. Building a working relationship with a client may require patience and several attempts, because trust takes time to develop. Reputation, words of mouth, and introduction through a respected source certainly would be helpful. Many ethnic and cultural communities use teacher or medical doctor as the first point of contact as well as referral sources for services. As to the use of community leaders, there are true community leaders and there are self-proclaimed so-called community leaders. A social worker is not called to judge who the true leader is and who is not, but has to be cognizant of the political economy within that community. The first phone call or the first culturally appropriate greeting is the all-important opportunity for a positive first impression. Helping clients to achieve tangible, concrete, and immediate results, small as they may be, could help the clients to see the benefits and confidence of continuing working with the worker. For clients who have repeatedly failed to show up for appointments, Meyer (2001) suggests that a social worker should not set up a dynamic that he or she is pursuing the client. He or she could ask the client resolutely on what the client wants to go from that point. If the client cannot be reached in person, he or she may send the client a brief note expressing his or her concern of the client's well-being and informing the client where the services will be available when the client is ready. For clients who are new to the community or from low socioeconomic status, having time off, finding childcare, or having available transportation are common challenges. While there are many ways that an agency or a social worker could accommodate these logistic needs, the service provider should always consider bringing service to the clients' neighborhood rather than requiring clients to come to the agency.

EVALUATION

EVALUATION PROCESS SKILLS   Evaluation, or the ending stage of the social work process, is a critical transition time for the client. On the one hand, a meaningful relationship between the worker and the client is ending, but on the other, the client is making a transition, with the worker's help, to coping with the normal problems of living. Lum (2000) describes four of the process skills:

- Helping the client connect with an ongoing support network: family and friends, ethnic community resources, a referral to another agency for follow-up care
- Conducting retrospective analysis of the problem situation and the growth that has occurred during the helping relationship
- Ascertaining whether the goals and outcomes agreed upon in intervention planning have been achieved
- Establishing a sensible plan for follow-up such as periodic phone calls, visits for checking in, and rechecks that gradually taper off

Evaluation does not start at the end; it begins at the first contact. The end of a working relationship could be the result of the attainment of the expected outcome and the ending is planned and mutual. A client may decide to leave because he or she chooses to do so. Failure to see progress, satisfaction of the progress, conflict between the client and the worker, frustration with the agency policies and procedures, inability to follow agency rules or adhere to the intervention agreement, relocation of the client, or worker leaving the position are all possible reasons for both planned and unplanned termination (Walsh, 2003). Evaluation is an anxiety-laden process. For many clients of vulnerable populations, their earlier holding environments or refugee/immigrant experiences might have encountered many forced or violent separations and many of the transitions have been difficult. These letdowns and disappointments are often mixed with much unresolved grief and loss of property, people, culture, identity, and even dignity. Ragg (2001) challenges workers to help clients address these "rotten good-byes" and provide them the experience of some "good good-byes." He suggests the worker to highlight and acknowledge client's feeling of loss and anxiety, assist clients to review and evaluate the progress made, capture the feeling with token gifts or favorite sayings, draw boundaries for separation, set limits for future contact including return path for necessary reconnection, and visualize success. Approaching the end of a relationship may trigger many mixed responses ranging from denial of the ending or the importance of the helping relationship, regression to old problem or emergence of new problem, anger and lash out on others including the worker, avoidance and flight by not attending the last session or meeting, to celebration of success, trying out new skills, and making plan for future gains.

Worker should expect some type of "doorknob counseling" behavior such as while client's hand is on the doorknob ready to open the door and leave, the client may suddenly turn around and say "one more thing." Although the client has been working with the worker on a particular issue over time and developed some degree of trust, the reality of the end of a relationship create a sense of "now or never" urgency for client to decide whether to seek help for a critical concern. Some may finally decide to tackle the underlining problem of the presenting problems that they have been working on; some may just be a way to prolong the working relationship. Social workers need to use their professional judgment to decide what the appropriateness responses should be.

People of different cultures and backgrounds have different ways to say goodbyes. For some it is the end but for other it is only the beginning. Social workers who work with diverse clients have extra layers of considerations in implementing termination. It is not unusual, particularly for new workers and students, to doubt whether they have provided the best service to the client or hold themselves responsible for some of the failed attempts. Shulman (2006) cautions social workers on this type of thinking:

> First, it's important for students to gain a clear perspective on the interactional nature of their practice. They will never be able to reach all clients, no matter how effective and skillful they become. Second, social workers can only do the best they can at any particular moment in their professional careers. They cannot hold themselves responsible for not being able to give a client more than they had. Instead they should guard against allowing their feelings to cause them to underplay the help they have given-just as big a mistake as overplaying their contribution to the client. (p. 199)

EVALUATION CONCEPTUALIZATION SKILLS   Evaluation is a critical stage, but it is least considered in social work practice. It is important for a worker in an agency to study the termination rates of clients. What is the agency doing to conclude successful client cases? In cases of premature or unsuccessful termination, what are the agency elements that may have contributed to unresolved cases? Follow-up on unsuccessful cases may teach the worker and the agency as much as analyzing successful cases. Exit interview surveys and follow-up on premature termination are important because of the high dropout rate of multicultural clients. Research and reflection on early termination and clients of color are helpful at this stage.

EVALUATION PERSONALIZATION SKILLS Evaluation triggers a range of responses on the part of the worker. The caseload number and intensity, along with the stress of unsuccessful resolution of problems, take their toll on the social worker. The daily demand on staff is apparent in many service agencies. Many agencies are using case management to broker a network of services for their clients, group treatment with crisis intervention on serious cases, brief treatment with community referral, and other strategies to deal with the volume of clients. As a result, intensive casework with single clients is the exception rather than the rule of service. Short-term treatment with reachable, concrete, and practical goals results in frequent evaluation and reliance on social services, the family, indigenous community agencies, and ethnic church and community.

CULTURALLY DIVERSE SERVICE DELIVERY

Developing skills to design culturally diverse service delivery program structures is a prerequisite to working effectively with clients. Service delivery deals with structuring programs, facilities, staff, funding, and administration on behalf of serving the needs of client populations in a geographic area. Service delivery design through an ethnic lens is crucial to culturally diverse services.

Service delivery is based on the philosophy of social services reflected in the administrative unit and the board of directors of an agency. It may change as a series of events occurs or as new policies are made that alter how services are organized and delivered to clients. Iglehart and Becerra (2000) observe, "Service delivery as a system or organizational process continues to be a dynamic process that is altered by technological, ideological, political, and economic factors. The mode of service delivery has varied from specialization to integrated, comprehensive services" (pp. 244–245). These authors offer the following observations about social service delivery:

- Social service delivery systems are changing as the population of the United States becomes more diverse and as there is an increased challenge to provide services to ethnic minority groups.
- The client–worker relationship is important in the delivery of ethnic-sensitive services, because the client experiences the agency through the worker as the worker interprets the policies of the agency and implements its services.
- In service delivery planning and implementation, there is a need to accept and respect the client's ethnicity and culture and to increase sensitivity to the cultures and values of minorities.
- In service delivery arrangements, the client is a member of other systems such as groups, communities, and other service delivery systems that are bounded by ethnicity, culture, and community.
- Effective ethnic-sensitive service delivery utilizes and incorporates the client's community and community services in the service delivery process so that the

ethnic minority agency is a focal organization with minority staff, services, and access to the minority group and community.

• Service delivery occurs in the context of a system that is shaped by the culture, values, and ideologies of groups and individuals who plan and implement services.

• The ethnic agency captures the interface between a social service delivery system and a client system that blends use of services with community and ethnicity.

• The history of social work reveals racism and exclusion in the charity organizations and settlement house movement, which resulted in disregard for the needs, concerns, and rights of ethnic minority groups, and partially explains the current lack of minority clients in these types of agencies.

Lum (2000) has written about the essential characteristics of multicultural service delivery in terms of location and pragmatic services, staffing, community outreach programs, agency setting, and service linkage. The agency should be located in or near areas with a large ethnic population and be accessible to public transportation. It should offer needed and attractive services, such as health care, family services, and/or child care. Mental health services may have a social stigma attached in ethnic communities, and services should not be advertised as such. There should be bilingual/bicultural staff in a ratio that reflects the ethnic and gender composition of the service population. There should be strong community outreach programs to schools, churches, and family associations in order to build agency/staff credibility and integrity. The agency setting should be friendly and informal with a bilingual receptionist, clean and private offices, and an ethnic-friendly decor. There should be service linkage and a working relationship between ethnic agencies and other organizations that serve the same client population base.

Similar assertions are also made by Yuen, Terao, and Schmidt (2009) in explaining the characters needed to achieve cultural competency in program development and agency management.

Yuen and Terao (2003) propose to assess the "five As: accessibility, availability, awareness, appropriateness, and acculturation" (p. 25). Cultural factors could block as well as facilitate services. Yuen (1999) states that "accessibility refers to both geographical and cultural relevance as well as difficulties in service delivery.... Availability refers to the existence, recruitment, and retention of services, clients, and a qualified service provider" (p. 109). Awareness is the knowledge and perspectives of the target population and the community regarding the identified areas of concerns and the services provided. Appropriateness refers to the suitability and acceptability of the services to the recipients both culturally and developmentally. Yuen (1999) further explains: "[A]cculturation refers to the quality and extent of exposure to the dominant American culture and the degree of functioning within the dominant culture" (p. 110).... Ideally, culturally specific service programs are available (Availability) to meet the identified needs in culturally appropriate approaches (Appropriateness) that take into consideration the different degrees of acculturation (Acculturation) of the service recipients. Target populations are aware (Awareness) of the needs/problems and the available services they can access (Accessibility) geographically and culturally. (pp. 114–115)

Yuen et al. (2009) further discuss the issue of ethnic match and cultural match:

It is important for service providers to be sensitive to the issue of cultural match versus ethnic match. Ethnic match certainly increases the likelihood of cultural and linguistic compatibility but is no guarantee of cultural match. A youth may agree with her Asian immigrant parents that they all feel more comfortable working with another experienced Asian American worker, because of the ethnic match. She may also feel more connected to a younger African American worker, because the two of them share more aspects of the same youth and contemporary American cultures. (p. 115)

When planning a new service delivery program, the worker must be aware of a number of interrelated factors that create a "political climate" for the planning group, the host agency, related organizations, and the target population client groups. Iglehart and Becerra (2000) identify seven external and five internal forces of agency change to accommodate an ethnic-sensitive service delivery system. The external catalysts for change are the following:

1. Changing funding policies with funding regulations that stipulate the inclusion of specific ethnic populations as service beneficiaries
2. Shifting funding priorities to seek new client populations (such as ethnic minority senior citizens) as funding for services to these groups becomes available
3. Out-group protests on behalf of underserved ethnic groups that cause some agency change, inclusion of ethnic populations, and increase of ethnic utilization
4. New constituencies resulting from the creation of new minority voting districts that elect minority representation who support ethnic-sensitive services
5. New agency leadership (e.g., new directors or staff with particular skills and political positions) shifting the agency toward the concerns of clients of color
6. The worker as a change catalyst for the client and the agency
7. Routinization of change where special programs for specific ethnic groups are absorbed as a part of permanent agency structure

The internal forces for change include the following:

1. The ideology of the agency in terms of ethnic client perception, situational causes, worker and client roles, and desired outcomes
2. The technology of the agency and worker–client activities in terms of process stages, desired outcomes, and client movement
3. The structure of the agency regarding the rules and ethics governing worker–client interaction, agency contact encounters, and agency hierarchy
4. Client inputs about and assessment of services
5. The accountability of the agency in terms of the recognition of the ethnic community as an agency constituency, procedures for ethnic community input about agency services, and agency accountability to the ethnic community

How would a worker cope with these trends in funding, out-group protests, new constituencies, new agency leadership, existing staff, anticipated changes, the ideology and technology of the host agency, rules and regulations, community inputs, and agency and project accountability? How would a worker plan a process where one would consider and allow a number of constituent groups to participate and interact with the planning group in order to receive input and exchange ideas? How would one incorporate relevant recommendations into the final proposal plan? These external and internal forces offer avenues for introducing change into existing agencies in order to make them more responsive and sensitive to ethnic populations.

AGENCY LINKAGE, DESIGN, AND IMPLEMENTATION

In order to design and implement culturally diverse service delivery, one needs to understand how agency services interrelate. This is called *agency linkage* or *interorganizational relations*. Service delivery cooperation and coordination are crucial as funding shrinks or shifts toward specialized needs, ethnic populations increase with new immigrant influx, and qualified ethnic practitioners become scarce resources.

Iglehart and Becerra (2000) offer 10 propositions about agency linkage:

1. Ethnic agencies are not in competition with mainstream social services for clients, but they do receive funding for specialized services to ethnic groups.
2. In an interorganizational relationship, the ethnic agency does have access to a particular ethnic population because of its presence in the ethnic community and its relationship with specific target populations.
3. Ethnic agencies are participants in alternative service delivery as services are redefined and new interorganizational relations emerge.
4. Ethnic agencies will extend more services to special populations due to privatization (purchase of service contracts, contracting).
5. Interorganizational relationships are likely to develop between public and ethnic agencies because public agencies are mandated to meet the needs of the general population, public agencies provide funding and ethnic agencies use the funds to provide services in an exchange relationship, and ethnic agencies with access to ethnic communities have power and bond with public agencies over funding.
6. Changing federal funding requirements develop partnerships between mainstream agencies and ethnic agencies.
7. The availability of funding governs the interface between mainstream agencies and the ethnic agency in terms of the development of partnerships, reduction in service duplication, and reaching special populations.
8. Ethnic agencies are particularly vulnerable to service contract cuts and grants in terms of financial austerity.
9. Ideological conflict can occur between the ethnic agency and mainstream agencies.
10. The problems of societal race relations may permeate the relations between ethnic and mainstream agencies.

These propositions on service delivery and agency linkage serve as the basis for the design and implementation of culturally diverse service delivery. Service content changes as various ethnic target groups emerge on the scene: the ethnic elderly, legal immigrants, and former welfare recipients. The needs of ethnic and racial groups are defined by public agencies that are the funding source: alcohol and drug abuse, AIDS, gang violence prevention. These trends may be determined by federal and state policies and legislation that cope with social problem areas and include application to ethnic populations. Programs should be derived from the changing needs of the ethnic community, which should influence ethnic-sensitive public social services or ethnic-responsive indigenous community agencies. With decentralization and downsizing of government services, it is politically and fiscally expedient to contract with ethnic agencies that serve ethnic populations.

Agency ideology and philosophy, technology, staffing, and structure may change in light of federal and state funding of ethnic-related programs. Funding requirements and stipulations can transform the service delivery of an agency.

Agency program implementation usually involves a three-year cycle: start-up, initial and full implementation, and periodic program evaluation. Agency implementation starts with federal and state regulatory compliance or the terms of the grant. Regional consortiums may pool resources in a cooperative effort. Cooperative projects are the preferred choice for university program training, research evaluation, and/or community-based agencies.

Iglehart and Becerra (2000) discuss agency linkage between ethnic and mainstream agencies:

> A continuum of services seem to unfold in which the ethnic agency may serve as the first line of defense for filling service gaps, for responding to the needs of marginalized groups, and for helping when no other agency does. It may also substitute for public agencies in delivering uniquely packaged and specially tailored services. In the quest for ethnic-sensitive practice, it seems to be a resource that has been underutilized. Mainstream social services and agencies will continue to vary in the degree to which they adopt ethnic-sensitive practice. The variation is due to agency history, ideologies, structure, and technologies. Mainstream agencies are responding to the needs of a mainstream America, and shifts in paradigms do take years to accomplish. (p. 283)

Specifically, there are a number of helping suggestions to build a multicultural organization with a cultural competence emphasis (GLSEN, 2001):

- Form a cultural competence committee within your organization with representation from policymaking, administration, service delivery, and community levels that serve as a governing body for planning, implementing, and evaluating organizational cultural competence.
- Write a mission statement that commits the organization to cultural competence activities.
- Find out what similar organizations have done and develop partnerships, gathering the processes and information from other groups that are consistent with your organizational needs for cultural competence.
- Use free resources from federally funded technical assistance centers that catalog information on cultural competence.
- Do a comprehensive cultural competence assessment of your organization that will result in a long-term plan with measurable goals and objectives incorporating cultural competent principles, policies, structures, and practices and that will change your mission statement, policies, procedures, administration, staffing patterns, service delivery practices, outreach, telecommunications and information dissemination systems, and professional development activities.
- Find out about cultural groups in the community and the degree to which they access community services.
- Have a brown bag lunch to involve staff in discussion and activities about their attitudes, beliefs, and values concerning cultural competence.
- Ask your staff about their development needs regarding interacting with cultural groups in your area.

- Assign a part of your budget to staff development in cultural competence, particularly conferences, workshops, and seminars.
- Include cultural competency requirements in job descriptions in the hiring process and discuss the importance of cultural awareness and competency with potential employees.
- Be sure your facility's location is accessible and respect of difference, for example, how to show respect to racial and ethnic elders.
- Collect resource materials for staff use such as free online resources, printed material, and library books on culturally diverse groups.
- Build a network of natural helpers, community informants, and other experts who have valuable knowledge of cultural, linguistic, racial, and ethnic groups in the community.

RESEARCH ON SKILL DEVELOPMENT

Research on skill development gives practitioners a fresh perspective on how to develop new skills and confirms or modifies the skill base. Beach et al. (2005) reviewed 34 studies on cultural competence of health professionals from 1980 to 2003:

> There is excellent evidence that cultural competence training improves the knowledge of health professionals (17 of 19 studies demonstrated a beneficial effect), and good evidence that cultural competence training improves the attitudes and skills of health professionals (21 of 25 studies evaluating attitudes demonstrated a beneficial effect and 14 of 14 studies evaluating skills demonstrated a beneficial effect). There is good evidence that cultural competence training impacts patient satisfaction (3 of 3 studies demonstrated a beneficial effect), poor evidence that cultural competence training impacts patient adherence (although the one study designed to do this demonstrated a beneficial effect), and no studies that have evaluated patient health status outcomes. There is poor evidence to determine the costs of cultural competence training (5 studies included incomplete estimates of costs). (p. 356)

Further research is needed to show how cultural competence improves patient adherence to therapy, health outcomes, and equity of services across racial and ethnic groups. Similarly, Stanhope, Solomon, Pernell-Arnold, Sands, and Bourjolly (2005) call for more empirical evaluation of cultural competence. They state,

> Both the training in and evaluation of cultural competence continues to inform the development of good empirical measures for behavioral health providers and their agencies. Ultimately, the key to effective cultural competence training is the extent to which it generates positive outcomes for clients, not merely increased awareness, knowledge, and skills of trainees. (p. 232)

Personal Styles and Clinical Process

Relationship building between the worker and the client results in case effectiveness and client/problem situation change. Research has claimed that psychological characteristics (cultural attitudes, emotional well-being, values, attitudes, beliefs, expectations, clinical relationships) of the clinician and the client, and the style match between the two, affect the clinical efficacy and make significant impacts on client change. The subjective personal style differences between the clinician and the client contribute to the dynamics of the clinical process (Bergin & Garfield, 1996).

These personal styles were researched and named *achieving styles* by Lipman-Blumen, Handley-Isaksen, and Leavitt (1983). Subsequently, the Achieving Styles Inventory (ASI) was revised and standardized to assess both individual and organizational styles. Three major sets of domains (direct, instrumental, and relational) contain three related but distinctive styles. Altogether there are nine achieving styles, each of which is a preference pattern for a particular orientation or situation. The concept of personal achieving styles is discussed in business, education, and counseling. Specifically, an achieving style is an individual preference that reflects the behavior, value system, and strategic reasoning of a person. It refers to various learned ways to accomplish tasks or achieve goals, regardless of the specific nature of these goals (Lipman-Blumen et al., 1983).

An individual's achieving style is shaped by his or her attitudes, norms, values, and cultural boundaries (Spence, 1985). On a practical level, it involves an individual's way of thinking, talking, and feeling, particularly as a person acts and interacts with others. These styles are profoundly influenced by the individual's personal experiences and cultural/social context. Beginning in childhood, we learn different ways or strategies to get what we want. These thinking, feeling, and behaving patterns become personal styles for accomplishing tasks or achieving goals. A person uses his or her unique set of achieving styles to project himself or herself, accomplish life goals, and relate to the world. These personal achieving styles seem adequate for accomplishing tasks until we are confronted by a difference or mismatch of interpersonal styles in cross-cultural encounters. An individual is not conscious of his or her achieving styles without a deliberate and conscious examination of himself or herself.

Social work has been concerned about worker–client effectiveness in the helping process due to interaction relationship patterns. Personal achieving styles research is a way to examine this concern. Clinicians often have little awareness of their own personal achieving styles that closely link and relate to their own clinical practice. Clinicians with direct achieving styles tend to focus their attention on the task and use direct problem-solving approaches. They tend to offer direct advice as a helping authority for clients. Clinicians with instrumental achieving styles frequently use their own credibility, influence, professionalism, or a support system to resolve problems. They rely on clients to assume partial or full responsibility for their actions. Clinicians with relational-cognitive behavioral achieving styles allow clients to select the means and the ends of their goal accomplishments. They use collaborative or contributory approaches to help clients accomplish their own goals through group efforts.

Social work interventions tend to offer a choice of approaches: direct (problem solving or task centered), instrumental (family therapy), and relational-cognitive (functionalism, existentialism). However, what is the personal and idiosyncratic nature of the worker's helping approach? Are there cultural and ethnic differences between practitioners? These are some of the questions answered by skill development research.

Just as the clinician's choice of skills and intervention strategies is shaped by his or her cultural self, the client comes with his or her culturally contained self.

Consequently, an important element of effective cross-cultural clinical practice is the clinician's awareness of this value choice's impact on the clinical process. Recognizing the importance of having styles match is essential for a successful cross-cultural clinical process.

EMPIRICAL RESEARCH ON ACHIEVING STYLES

Research on skill development has used the variables of therapeutic alliance, achieving styles, and practitioner ethnic background. This section reports on European, Asian, Latino, American Indian, and African American helping professions and reveals differences in achieving styles based on ethnicity.

As a part of regional studies of achieving styles related to skill development, Lu, Lum, and Chen (2001) reported on a number of research studies that examined the relationship between linguistic and cultural differences and individual achieving styles among social workers. The ASI instrument (Lipman-Blumen et al., 1983) was used for the following populations.

ASIAN AMERICAN POPULATION   Lu et al. (2001) conducted achieving style research on 146 clinicians in southern California from two groups (64 bilingual/bicultural Asian American clinicians and 82 non–Asian American clinicians). Of the 146 clinicians, 18.2% held BA degrees, 55.5% had MA degrees, 13.1% were PhDs, and 13.1% were MDs. The mean and median for education were both 18 years. There were 36.6% males and 63.4% females. Age consisted of 38.2% (35 years and younger) and 61.8% (36 years and older), with 40 years as the mean and 39 years as the median. Statistical analyses were employed using t-test, correlation, and regression. Findings showed that the language/culture variable was significantly related to the differences between the two groups as far as achieving styles were concerned, controlling for gender, age, and education. Most significant was that Asian bilingual/bicultural clinicians used vicarious-relational and collaborative-relational styles more frequently than non–Asian American clinicians.

LATINO POPULATION   Lu, Organista, Manzo, Wong, and Phung (2002) studied 53 Latino American clinicians who were members of the Bilingual Association of Spanish Speaking Clinicians and Advocates in the San Francisco Bay Area and 47 non–Latino White American clinicians from county mental health agencies in the Bay Area. There were 44 males and 63 females. Thirty-six were less than 39 years old; 33 were between ages 39 and 50; and 35 were 50 years and older. Seventy-three held MAs or MSWs, and 28 were PhDs or MDs. Using multivariate analysis of variance and multiple regression, the researchers found a significant difference between the ASI profiles of the two groups. The non–Latino White American group scored higher on the power-direct style, the self-instrumental style, and the reliant-instrumental style and lower on the relational style, whereas Latino clinicians were more collaborative and relationship-oriented with clients.

AMERICAN INDIAN POPULATION   Lu, DuBray, Chen, and Ahn (2000) surveyed 18 American Indian social workers and social work faculty who were affiliated with the California American Indian Social Work Association and the American Indian

Social Work Faculty Association, as well as 47 European American professionals from the San Francisco Bay Area county mental health agencies. There were 21 males and 43 females, with 29 who were 45 years or younger and 33 who were 46 years or older. Forty had MAs or MSWs, and 22 held PhDs or MDs. Cross-tabulations and *t*-tests were used to determine their ASI scores. The American Indian group scored higher on relational style but lower on the direct styles than the European American group.

AFRICAN AMERICAN POPULATION   Lu et al. (2001) conducted a parallel study of 188 African American clinicians and 181 White non-Hispanic clinicians who were members of the National Association of Social Workers, New York City Chapter. There were 89 males and 279 females, with 189 who were less than 44 years old and 73 who were 44 years and older. MA or MSW degree holders numbered 312, and PhDs or MDs numbered 20. Based on the Wilks's Lambda statistic, significant differences existed based on race/ethnicity. African Americans scored higher on competitive-direct style, intrinsic-direct style, social-instrumental style, contributory-relational style, and vicarious-relational style but lower on power-direct style than their White counterparts.

SUMMARY OF ACHIEVING STYLES RESEARCH   Although this research is preliminary and exploratory, Lu et al. (2001) offer some advice:

- With Asian Americans, use vicarious- and collaborative-relational styles such as empathic listening, joint participatory problem solving and task assignments, and mutually agreed-upon empowerment strategies.
- With Latino Americans, employ nondirective and relational styles that offer self-exploration, relationship building, and nonconfrontational trust.
- Work with First Nations Peoples around relational styles that focus on the search for personal growth experiences and the forming of life stories.
- Focus with African American clients on a direct style that communicates honesty, advice, recommendations for change with an empathic relationship, and a positive contribution to the person's life.

SUMMARY

Culturally competent skill development is the core of a discussion of culturally competent practice because it affects the worker–client helping relationship. This chapter defined three types of skills—process, conceptualization, and personalization—and related them to the social work practice stages of contact, problem identification, assessment, intervention, and evaluation. Culturally diverse service delivery was discussed and related to agency linkage, design, and implementation. Finally, research on culturally competent skill development was examined.

CULTURALLY DIVERSE GROUPS   PART | 3

The focus of Part Three is on a wide continuum of culturally diverse groups who are part of building cultural competence with individuals, families, and small groups. There are chapters on First Nations Peoples, European Americans, African Americans, Latino Americans, Muslim Americans, Women, Gay, Lesbian, Bisexual and Transgender Persons, Persons with Disabilities, and the Older Adult written by guest contributors who have expert knowledge and practice with these groups. We have asked them to present demographics, group diversity, cultural competence, historical oppression and current social issues, values and ethical dilemmas, cultural awareness, knowledge acquisition, skill development, social and economic justice resolution, and case studies. The majority of contributors have covered these areas. However, we have allowed some contributors who have insights and convictions to move toward their own interpretation of their population groups. We hope that you will find these chapters helpful in your quest for valuable information and practice principles to work with a variety of culturally diverse groups as you strive for cultural competence and proficiency.

Cultural Competence with First Nations Peoples

CHAPTER 8

Hilary N. Weaver

Many First Nations Peoples have an image of a social worker as someone from a government bureaucracy who takes children away, not only from parents but also from the indigenous community. The child is then raised by a White family with no knowledge of culture, traditions, or an indigenous identity. In this sense, social workers threaten more than a particular family. If we forget our cultures, we will no longer exist as distinct people. Thus, social workers are perceived as a threat to the very existence of First Nations Peoples. Although it is common for clients from many cultural groups to hold negative perceptions of social workers, the social worker who serves Native American clients is likely to face distinct challenges.

Before moving further into a discussion of cultural competence with First Nations Peoples, it is important to clarify the terminology used in this chapter. There are many different terms for the indigenous people of North America including *American Indian*, *Native American*, and *First Nations Peoples*. There is no consensus about which term is best, yet some Native people have strong preferences for one term over the others. These terms all include many different groups of distinct people. Use of such broad terms tends to obscure diversity. Generally, when speaking of a particular Native person or nation (such as Comanche or Oneida), it is best to use the specific label used by those people rather than a more general term such as *Native American*. In the context of this chapter, which covers a variety of Native groups, the terms *Native American*, *Native*, *indigenous*, and *First Nations Peoples* are used interchangeably.

Social workers need to understand the vast diversity that exists among First Nations Peoples. As of July 1, 2008, the U.S. Census Bureau estimates that there were 4.9 million Native Americans in the United States (1.6% of the population). This includes individuals who identified themselves both as Native American and from another ethnic group (U.S. Census Bureau, 2009). Over 500 distinct Native American nations exist within the boundaries of the United States. These nations differ in terms of language, religion, social structure, political structure, and many other aspects of their cultures. Some of these nations are quite small and have fewer than 100 members, whereas five nations (Cherokee, Navajo/Dine, Choctaw, Lakota/Dakota/Nakota, and Chippewa/Ojibway) have populations of over 100,000. Additionally, many immigrants from Latin America identify themselves primarily as First Nations Peoples. The census identified more than 100,000 Latin American indigenous people living in the United States in 2000. These six different groups accounted for 42% of all Native Americans in the United States (Ogunwole, 2002).

Substantial variation among Native Americans exists in other areas such as land holdings. Some nations such as the Navajo/Dine of the southwestern United States have a large reservation, and inhabitants may live in very isolated areas. Other Native nations such as the Cayuga of New York State have no reservation land base at all. Indeed, the perception that most Native people live on reservations has not been true for some time. More than two-third of Native Americans live in urban areas (Ogunwole, 2002).

First Nations Peoples vary substantially in their income. Some Native people, most notably Native people in the northeastern United States and southeastern Canada such as the Mohawks, have entered the well-paid profession of iron working and are largely responsible for building many major structures such as the bridges around New York City (Mitchell, 1991). Some Native people also receive per capita payments from casino revenues. On the whole, however, Native Americans are some of the poorest populations in the United States. In 2008, 24.2% of Native Americans lived below the poverty level (U.S. Census Bureau, 2009). This was higher for those who identified solely as Native American than those having heritage from another ethnic group as well. Poverty rates are also higher for reservation dwellers. Although there has been some improvement over time, the poverty rate has fluctuated instead of following a steady trend. For example, the poverty rate of Native Americans in 1987 was 28.8%, dropped to 23.9% in 1989, rose to 31.3% in 1991, dropped to 23.6% in 1993, and rose to 31% in 1995 (U.S. Bureau of the Census, 2005).

Extensive diversity also exists among people within Native nations in terms of their cultural identity. Some people are very knowledgeable about and grounded in their indigenous culture, whereas others are not. Sometimes this is based on choices an individual has made; however, it is more often the result of decades of damaging U.S. policies designed to assimilate Native people. These policies were deliberate in their attempts to eradicate indigenous cultures. Many First Nations Peoples lost their ability to speak their language and lost touch with their cultural traditions when they were forcibly taken away from their communities and sent to government or church-run boarding schools. This sort of cultural loss impaired their ability to pass on cultural traditions to their children and left many Native people with limited knowledge of their indigenous heritage. As of 2008, 29% of First Nations Peoples spoke a language other than English in their homes (U.S. Census Bureau, 2009).

Individuals may also be more or less grounded in their indigenous culture at different stages of their lives. Waters (1990) found that it is common for people to report their ethnicity differently at different points in their life. This may be particularly true for people of mixed heritage. Many indigenous people who have grown up with limited knowledge of their culture take steps to learn more and claim their heritage as they get older.

Because Native Americans are a relatively small population, researchers rarely have adequate samples to examine intertribal differences. Overlooking diversity among Native Americans results in distorted data regarding strengths and challenges faced by indigenous people. One example of this can be found in the research on First Nations Peoples and the use of alcohol. Substantial variation exists in the drinking patterns of people from different Native nations. Men and women also tend to have very different drinking patterns. Likewise, drinking tends to be prominent in some age groups and not in others. Unfortunately, when researchers report only findings about drinking and Native Americans as a general category, it obscures the fact that alcohol abuse is more of a problem in some nations than others and that it tends to be most problematic for young men. Although clearly methodological challenges exist in getting an adequate sample of Native people to examine these differences, if researchers continue to treat indigenous people as a monolithic group, they will contribute to stereotypical images—in this case, the perception that alcohol presents a widespread problem for all Native people. This stereotype of the drunken Indian perpetuates the belief that indigenous people are biologically predetermined to alcoholism and that they are helpless, hopeless, passive victims.

The diversity among Native American groups and among people within these groups cannot be overemphasized. Significant differences continue to exist among the people who fall into the general category "Native American." Just as it would be inappropriate to assume that all Europeans are the same, it is often inappropriate to generalize one First Nations group to another. A Miccosuki person is likely to be quite different from a Klamath person, just as a Greek person is different from a Belgian. These differences must be considered in all aspects of social work practice, from clinical work to policy development to research.

This chapter presents information that social workers need to know in order to provide culturally competent services to First Nations Peoples. The chapter begins with a discussion of operationalizing cultural competence with First Nations Peoples and an overview of historical oppression and current social issues. The chapter presents information on values and ethical dilemmas in working with Native people and reviews the areas of cultural awareness, knowledge acquisition, and skill development. This information will help readers not only to provide culturally competent clinical services but also to use social work skills to advocate for social and economic justice. The chapter concludes with a discussion of social and economic justice resolution and a case study that illustrates key points.

CULTURAL COMPETENCE WITH FIRST NATIONS PEOPLES

The need for cultural competence has been identified as an ethical imperative by the National Association of Social Workers (1999) in its Code of Ethics. In fact, some scholars have determined that competent practice and culturally competent practice are so intertwined that it is impossible to be competent without being culturally competent (Coleman, 1998). The Council on Social Work Education (2000) has also recognized the importance of cultural competence and requires that content on diverse populations be included in all accredited social work programs. Clearly, there is a belief within the social work profession that cultural competence is important, yet operationalizing this concept can be challenging.

In current social work literature, knowledge, skills, and values/attitudes are consistently identified as important components of cultural competence. Until recently, these components had not been clearly operationalized or empirically tested. At this time, the profession is taking an important step in moving beyond practice wisdom as researchers begin to identify specific knowledge, skills, and values/attitudes associated with cultural competence or proficiency with particular populations.

Cultural competence with First Nations Peoples involves blending knowledge about specific First Nations cultures, history, and contemporary realities with social work skills and knowledge. Additionally, social workers must be self-reflective, non-judgmental, and willing to learn from clients. This will enable social workers to assess clients within their cultural context and to choose culturally appropriate interventions.

Cultural competence, a necessity in direct practice with First Nations Peoples, is also critical in other levels of practice. Administrators and policy makers must apply the principles of cultural competence in order to ensure social justice throughout all aspects of social services. Cultural competence includes an understanding of how organizational or institutional forces can enhance or impede services to diverse populations (Sue et al., 1998). For example, cost containment strategies such as managed care may undermine the work of culturally competent helping professionals by limiting the type and amount of service provided (Abe-Kim & Takeuchi, 1996).

Green (1999) asserts the following:

> The service provider who is culturally competent can deliver professional services in a way that is congruent with behavior and expectations normative for a given community and that are adapted to suit the specific needs of individuals and families from that community. (p. 87)

In order to strive for cultural competence with First Nations clients, social workers must develop a basic understanding of these culturally based behaviors and expectations. Cultural competence also involves a recognition of macro-level problems and ongoing social injustice. Activism and advocacy are key skills that culturally competent social workers can use to confront problems such as violation of treaty rights, threats to sovereignty, contamination of the environment, and lack of adequate housing. Social workers also have a role to play in educating the large government bureaucracies that serve First Nations Peoples and in educating social work agencies in order to make their programs more culturally appropriate and effective with this population.

This chapter frequently cites the findings of a study of Native Americans in the field of social work (educators, social workers, and students) and their beliefs about culturally competent practice. This study sought to identify what specific knowledge, skills, and values/attitudes are needed for culturally competent social work practice with First Nations Peoples. (See Weaver, 1999b, for a detailed description of this study.) As both Native people and social work professionals, the respondents were in a unique position to begin to identify the specific components of culturally competent practice with First Nations Peoples. The respondents emphasized that social workers need to be knowledgeable in four broad areas: 1) diversity; 2) history; 3) culture; and 4) contemporary realities of Native people. Likewise, they identified the importance of having strong skills in general and containment skills such as having patience and allowing silence in particular.

Culturally competent social workers also need to bring certain values and attitudes to their work with indigenous people. These values and attitudes include 1) helper wellness and self-awareness; 2) humility and willingness to learn; 3) respect, open-mindedness, and a nonjudgmental attitude; and 4) social justice.

HISTORICAL OPPRESSION AND CURRENT SOCIAL ISSUES

In order to effectively work with First Nations Peoples, it is important to have an understanding of the historical events that have led to the circumstances of today. Within many Native American cultures, there is a sense of existing within a time continuum. The people of today maintain strong connections with ancestors, and contemporary actions are undertaken with future generations in mind. The concept of Seven Generations is present in many First Nations cultures, although it is defined somewhat differently by different people. For some, the ancestors seven generations ago were planning for the people of today, and these plans are the reason there is still land, language, and culture left for indigenous people. The people of today have the responsibility to ensure that the needs of future generations will be met in the same way. Some Native people interpret the Seven Generations concept as looking back to the ancestors three generations ago, looking forward to the children of the next three generations, with the current generation in the middle. Either way, indigenous people typically have a sense of being related to other generations through a time continuum. This sense of responsibility for future generations is a frequent message in prevention programs such as those that encourage abstinence from alcohol during pregnancy.

The ancestral connection felt by many First Nations Peoples is important to be aware of in understanding the importance of history. Some scholars have suggested that Native Americans have never been able to adequately mourn the events that happened to ancestors, and this unresolved grief is the root of many contemporary social problems (Brave Heart-Jordan & DeBruyn, 1995). Historical events that may be relevant to a particular client's case situation will vary by individual and by tribal affiliation; however, the following key events are likely to be relevant to many First Nations clients.

After Europeans came to the Americas, disease epidemics devastated many Native nations. Many of these epidemics were not the result of unfortunate circumstances but the result of deliberate acts of germ warfare perpetrated on indigenous people. The fact that such devastating diseases were deliberately spread by both the British and the Americans has been clearly documented (Stiffarm & Lane, 1992). The decimation of Native populations, by some estimations the loss of 95% to 99% of all indigenous people in what is now the United States (Stiffarm & Lane, 1992), occurred largely because of diseases such as smallpox, measles, and cholera (Claymore & Taylor, 1989; Native American Leadership Commission on Health and AIDS, 1994). The intergenerational memory of the effect of disease on Native people helps support a climate of suspicion around contemporary issues such as HIV/AIDS. Some First Nations Peoples fear that HIV/AIDS will have an even more devastating effect on their communities than previous epidemics. Additionally, some Native people feel that HIV/AIDS has been deliberately spread or promising treatments have been purposefully withheld in First Nations communities.

Much has been written about the use of alcohol as a tool of oppression and a way to cheat indigenous people of their land and other natural resources. Although not all Native communities have been equally affected, alcohol has had a devastating effect on some Native communities and is often linked to other social problems such as violence, suicide, and sexual abuse (Bachman, 1992).

One of the most devastating parts of the history of colonization and oppression of indigenous people in the United States and Canada has only recently begun to receive significant attention. Beginning in the late 19th century and extending into the late 20th century, it was federal policy to separate Native children from their families and to educate them in boarding schools that were often hundreds or thousands of miles from their home communities. The slogan of these schools, "Kill the Indian: Save the Man," reflected the belief of the times that all cultural, linguistic, and spiritual practices of First Nations Peoples must be eradicated in order for them to be civilized and have a place within White society. The mission of the schools was essentially cultural genocide. Often, children were taken to these schools for years at a time, where they were beaten for speaking their languages or for following their spiritual practices. During this time, they had limited contact with their home communities. When they eventually left school, they no longer were able to speak to their relatives or fit into their home communities. Growing up in institutions with no models of parenting other than the severe discipline of the military or religious personnel who ran the schools led to generations of Native people with no parenting skills (Morrisette, 1994). The physical and sexual abuse that was pervasive in some boarding schools is now replicated with succeeding generations in many First Nations communities. Likewise, the devastating effects of the schools have left many Native people with a severe mistrust of education and other dominant-society institutions.

National policies of relocation and termination have also had negative effects on indigenous communities. Ever since first contact with Europeans, Native people have been forced by warfare and federal policies to leave their traditional lands. The most famous removal was that of the Cherokee people of the Southeast and their forced march on the "Trail of Tears" in the 1830s to what is now Oklahoma. Likewise, the Navajo people of the Southwest were subject to removal on a forced march called the Longest Walk. Since the inception of the reservation system, the federal government has forced First Nations Peoples onto land a fraction of the size of their traditional territories, only to have some reservations reduced in size or eliminated altogether at a later date.

Beginning in the 1950s, the United States entered what is known as the *termination era*, a time when the federal government took steps to legally end the existence of many Native nations such as the Klamath and the Menominee. Through legal maneuvers, the United States revoked its promises made in treaties and took land previously set aside as reservations. Thus, members of terminated nations lost all access to social and health benefits that had been previously guaranteed to First Nations Peoples under treaties and other laws.

It is important to remember that Native nations are recognized as sovereign by the U.S. government, as acknowledged in all treaty agreements. According to the U.S. Constitution, treaties are the supreme law of the land and are not subject to modification by subsequent legislation. Sovereignty means that indigenous people retain their own governments with the ability to make laws and policies to govern themselves. Although existing within the physical boundaries of the United States, Native nations often have their own courts, schools, and social welfare systems. Thus, Native Americans are not simply an ethnic group. In addition to cultural distinctiveness, they have legal distinction from other groups in the United States. Although some federal laws infringe upon and limit sovereignty, in most cases, Native nations retain as many or more rights to self-governance as states and localities retain.

Oppression and violation of the rights of First Nations Peoples is not a thing of the past. In the 1970s, the Alaska Native Claims Settlement Act (ANCSA) combined some of the most devastating parts of earlier federal policies and applied them to Native Alaskans. The status and sovereignty of these First Nations Peoples were severely eroded by legally deeming nations to be corporations with stockholders. Native people born after 1971 were not even entitled to be stockholders, thus effectively ending the future (legally speaking) of indigenous people in Alaska (Churchill & Morris, 1992). By establishing a cutoff date for new stockholders, the federal government was able to limit future claims for land and other resources. As a result of ANCSA, First Nations Peoples in Alaska have less legal recourse than other Native Americans. Some questions have even been raised about whether major pieces of federal legislation such as the Indian Child Welfare Act (ICWA) apply to Native people covered by ANCSA, because legally they are no longer defined as Native nations. Fortunately, most social policies continue to treat Native people in Alaska as having the same rights as First Nations Peoples in the rest of the country; however, ANCSA opened the door to the possibility of legally sanctioned loss of access for Native Alaskans to all Native-specific social programs.

The challenges to indigenous people continue as conservative, reactionary Americans try to deny indigenous people their inherent rights to traditional means of subsistence such as fishing, whaling, and gathering medicines. In some regions of the United States such as Washington state, Michigan, and Wisconsin where the battles over traditional subsistence have been heated, it is common to see signs and bumper stickers advocating violence such as "Spear an Indian, save a fish."

First Nations Peoples also face challenges when they try to make a living in more modern ways but within a context of sovereignty. In the late 1990s, the state of New York attempted to tax the First Nations within its borders for the sale of cigarettes and gasoline (Weaver, 2000). Such a tax, if collected, would have a devastating effect on the economies of these First Nations. Although many indigenous people and their advocates viewed the imposition of the tax as a violation of treaties and a devastation of their sovereignty, the Supreme Court of the United States found otherwise. The state of New York took steps to collect the tax, which included imposing an embargo on reservations that prevented the delivery of any fuel including home-heating oil. State troopers were frequently shown on the news beating indigenous people as part of the standoff.

Another example of the continued oppression of First Nations Peoples is the ongoing paternalism and mismanagement of resources overseen by the federal government. Native Americans are still often seen as not fully competent to manage their own lives; thus, the federal government continues to consider them its wards. Moreover, the federal government holds 11 million acres in trust and collects money from timber sales, oil and mineral exploitation, and agricultural leases, which is obligated to be distributed to Native people. This is called Individual Indian Monies (IIM). Although some money is distributed to Native people (about $450 million annually), there has been a growing scandal that the federal government has not been allocating all the money collected. Some Native people are not receiving payment for use of their lands at all, whereas others do not receive payments regularly. There have been accusations that billions of dollars owed to First Nations Peoples are unaccounted for. A pending class action lawsuit alleges the federal government has grossly mismanaged IIM accounts (Unclaimed Assets.com, 2005). A federal investigation has been ordered into historical accounting practices (U.S. Department of the Interior, 2005).

The large number of Native children in substitute care continues to be a pressing social issue. Social workers working with First Nations Peoples must be familiar with the ICWA of 1978, one of the most significant policies affecting First Nations Peoples. Although the act has existed for almost a quarter of a century and is a federal law that social workers must follow regardless of where they practice, many social workers are ignorant of the law's requirements or may not have heard of the law at all. The law was passed in response to the large numbers of First Nations children who were removed from their families and communities and were raised outside of an indigenous context, through either foster care or adoption. Under ICWA, a social worker who works for an entity other than a Native nation may not have jurisdiction to work with a Native child who is being taken into foster care or placed for adoption. Although the "best interest of the child" is a concept common throughout many child welfare policies, it is rarely defined. Under ICWA, the best interest of the child is clearly defined as cultural continuity. Indigenous children who must be removed from their parents should be placed with the extended family when possible or with someone from their own tribe/nation, with a First Nations family, or with any family, in that order of preference. (For more information on ICWA, see Barsh, 1996; MacEachron, Gustavsson, Cross, & Lewis, 1996; Mannes, 1995; Wares, Wedel, Rosenthal, & Dobrec, 1994; Weaver & White, 1999.)

Health disparities plague indigenous populations. First Nations Peoples experience some of the poorest health statistics of any people in the United States (Bird, 2002; Droste, 2005; Swan et al., 2006). These disparities can be linked to a complex combination of high risk behaviors (i.e., high rates of smoking, poor dietary practices), environmental racism that has degraded the land, air, and water where many Native people live, and inadequate access to quality health care. Indeed, the health status of Native Americans appears to be deteriorating as major problems such as obesity and diabetes increase.

Economic development is an issue that presents challenges as well as hope in First Nations communities. First Nations Peoples, particularly those living on reservations, experience some of the highest unemployment rates in the country. Many reservations offer few job opportunities other than working directly for the tribe. Casinos and other gaming enterprises have offered some First Nations reservation communities a major source of employment and revenue. Although some Native people view these as positive developments, others see them as violations of cultural traditions, as addictive influences, and as something that opens the door to organized crime.

Because Native nations still retain vestiges of sovereignty, they are able to operate casinos, even when this is prohibited by state law. Beginning in the mid-1980s, some First Nations began to look to casino revenue as a form of economic development. For some nations, this has proved to be quite lucrative. Tribal gaming has grown from earning revenues of $5.4 billion in 1995 to $19.4 billion in 2004 (National Indian Gaming Association, 2005). Some casinos with a prime location to bring in large numbers of tourists have been particularly successful. For example, in 2003, 43 tribal gaming enterprises (out of a total of 330) brought in over $100 million each. However, the largest number, 73 (out of 330), brought in under $3 million. Some casinos are not financially viable, particularly for tribes in remote locations. The 330 tribal gaming enterprises operating at the end of 2003 is a decline from the 348 operating at the end of 2002 (National Indian Gaming Association, 2005).

Those casinos that have become profitable have been able to invest profits in tribal infrastructure (i.e., supporting governance and social service programs) as well as supporting their members (i.e., scholarships and per capita payments). This may even be seen as a way to reclaim independence and reduce dependence on the federal government (Napoli, 2002). Gaming revenue has also been used for disaster aid to meet the needs of those affected by Hurricanes Katrina and Rita that devastated Gulf Coast regions in September 2005 (National Indian Gaming Association, 2005). On the other hand, gaming is still highly controversial in many Native communities as well as the larger communities that surround them. Some people (Native and non-Native) view gaming as bringing additional problems rather than being a solution. In particular, the compact that must be signed with states in order to operate casinos may be viewed as irreparably damaging tribal sovereignty and largely benefiting states and non-Native communities.

Casino revenues add another dimension to the sometimes contentious issue of who qualifies for tribal membership. As sovereign nations, all tribes set their own criteria for tribal membership often based on some minimum standard of blood quantum (i.e., one-fourth, one-eighth) and sometimes recognizing descent exclusively through matrilineal lines or exclusively through patrilineal lines. Some Native nations who allocate casino profits to members have become more strict about their membership criteria thus reducing the need to further "divide the pie."

Some First Nations communities have been approached by the federal government to act as storage sites for nuclear waste and other toxic materials. This presents a dilemma, particularly for impoverished communities. Federal contracts of this type are likely to bring in a substantial amount of money to struggling reservation economies, but what will be the cost in the long run? The value placed on planning for seven generations echoes in the minds of indigenous people confronted with such options. Although accepting toxic waste would give First Nations communities the money needed to feed hungry children and elders, fund social programs, and invest in college educations for young adults, the environmental destruction and health consequences are likely to compromise the future of generations to come. As it is, First Nations communities, like many other communities of color and poor communities, are disproportionately exposed to environmental hazards that present numerous health risks.

First Nations communities will continue to be faced with the challenge of seeking economic development opportunities that help the nations and their members to be self-sustaining without compromising their own well-being. The relatively small, sometimes isolated nature of most reservations, and the lack of technologically skilled labor make it difficult to attract many employers. Indigenous people are confronted with difficult decisions about developing sustainable and culturally appropriate types of jobs in their communities.

Just as Native Americans are not a thing of the past, neither are oppression and social injustice. Social workers can play an important role in fighting continued oppression by publicly opposing social policies and laws that seek to further undermine indigenous sovereignty. Policies such as ICWA that encourage First Nations control over Native children being placed in foster care or adoptive homes should be supported. Other important ways of combating oppression include fighting to remove stereotypical images of First Nations Peoples used as mascots for sports teams and challenging environmental racism that has led to a variety of health problems and birth defects in First Nations communities.

VALUES AND ETHICAL DILEMMAS

Rarely acknowledged or critically examined, ethical dimensions are embedded in many aspects of social work practice with First Nations people. It is important for social workers to reflect on their practice and examine any ways in which they might be replicating the colonizing practices implemented by the federal government and its representatives. This includes conscious reflection and acknowledgment of the power dynamics inherent in social work practice. These reflections must be expanded to include all aspects of social work practice. Areas to consider include 1) What are the ethical implications of not being culturally competent in service provision? 2) What are the ethical implications of not advocating for social justice? 3) What are the ethical implications of agency policies and administrative practices as they relate to First Nations Peoples? 4) What are the ethical implications of social policies as they apply to First Nations Peoples? and 5) What are the ethical issues to consider in conducting research with First Nations Peoples? In particular, ethical concerns arise for social workers engaged in work in Native communities around issues of sovereignty and the primacy of the group versus the rights of individuals.

Sovereignty, the inherent right to self-governance, is a reflection of the unique legal status of Native Americans. This makes them different from any other cultural group in the United States and is the foundation of separate policies, services, and funding steams that apply only to Native Americans. Although laws based on race are unacceptable in the United States, indigenous status is not a race-based category. This is a distinction that many people in the United States have difficulty grasping. To further muddy the water, the federal government has impinged on indigenous sovereignty and treats indigenous nations as "domestic dependent nations." Social workers are left to wrestle with shifting value stances as to whether tribes do indeed constitute separate nations and the implications that this has for jurisdiction of services. A child welfare example will be used to briefly illustrate this ethical quandary.

A county-based child protective services social worker receives a call to investigate child abuse on a reservation. If the reservation is a sovereign nation, does she have the right to conduct an investigation there? Is she legally "wrong" if she refuses to investigate in the name of sovereignty? What harm does she risk (to the child or to a Native nation's sovereign status) if she does or does not investigate? Although there may be ethical questions related to the authority to conduct an investigation on sovereign territory, the law is clear in this regard; county-based child protective services social workers do have a legal right to investigate allegations of child abuse on a reservation. On the other hand, if a child is to be removed from the home (as in foster care or adoption), the federal ICWA clearly states that should a tribe choose to exercise its jurisdiction it has a right to do so and an outside social service entity must relinquish the case. This example illustrates that the law is mixed on the circumstances under which tribal reservations can exercise sovereignty (i.e., their right to be independent from outside intervention). Indeed, laws are subject to change. Even when current laws are explicit, social workers may find themselves in ethical gray areas when it comes to issues of sovereignty. Collaboration and partnership models can provide good resolutions. In some instances, county social service departments have proactively partnered with their tribal counterparts to develop agreements about how each partner will proceed when the interests of tribal children are at stake.

Another ethical dilemma is also easily illustrated in the context of child welfare. Many indigenous groups place a high value on the primacy of the group as opposed to the high value placed on the individual in general American society. In many First Nations societies, a child is considered to belong to the tribe and not just to the parents or nuclear family. On the other hand, in U.S. society parents typically have substantial rights and responsibilities when it comes to a minor child. These different value stances become painfully apparent in the case of a pending adoption. Does a Native parent have a right to give a child up for adoption to a non-Native family? Does the tribe have a say in this decision? Who has the final decision-making authority if there is a disagreement between the wishes of the parent and the wishes of the tribe? As per tradition and as affirmed by the ICWA, the tribe has a vested interest in the future of its members and does have the authority to prevent or interrupt adoptions involving Native children adopted outside of the tribe. This may seem anathema to social workers steeped in dominant society culture who value parental rights. Although the law is clear in this case, as discussed earlier, laws are always subject to change and ethical dilemmas often persist.

CULTURAL AWARENESS

Cultural awareness involves both becoming knowledgeable about basic facts about a particular cultural group and the social worker's ability to reflect on his or her own feelings and beliefs and how these impact work with clients. Both these aspects are necessary components of cultural awareness. In order to be culturally competent, social workers must understand the extraordinary diversity that exists among Native people, be knowledgeable about the culture of specific clients or groups they are working with, and be knowledgeable about the history as well as contemporary realities of First Nations clients (Weaver, 1999b). Clearly, the diversity theme underlies the other three areas of knowledge, because culture, history, and contemporary realities will vary depending on the particular Native client or nation.

In particular, social workers need to learn about indigenous values such as the emphasis placed on family and community. Extended family networks and strong community ties are common in First Nations cultures. These connections are likely to exist among urban Native people as well as those living on reservations (Red Horse, 1978; Weaver & White, 1997). Respect, responsibility, and generosity are also key values commonly found among First Nations Peoples. Respect determines how people interact with each other and the environment. Native people are often reluctant to impose on each other or to interfere with each other. A classic article on noninterference by Native social worker Jimm Good Tracks outlines how these values may conflict with social work interventions (Good Tracks, 1973). Responsibility and generosity also influence interactions between people. The sense of responsibility to other members of the community often results in support and mutual aid in caring for the elderly or teaching children. The generosity that permeates Native value systems is clearly illustrated by contemporary "giveaways," particularly common among First Nations Peoples from the Northwest, in which someone who is celebrating an event such as a graduation, birth, or anniversary gives away possessions.

Elders are particularly valued members of Native American societies. Not only do they have important roles to fill but also there is a strong belief that they are entitled to be cared for in their later years. Native elders are often cared for by their children or younger relatives who view this as a natural part of their responsibilities. In fact, about half of Native elders aged 75 or older live with their families. It is important to note, however, that these families are more than three times as likely as White families to be living in poverty and thus could benefit from increased use of social programs (Kramer, 1992a).

Understanding the history of First Nations Peoples can help in comprehending contemporary realities. As discussed earlier in this chapter, some First Nations social workers attribute contemporary social problems, such as the substance abuse and violence that trouble some Native communities, to historical unresolved trauma and grief (Brave Heart-Jordan & DeBruyn, 1995). Thus, it is important to identify the root cause and to validate historical trauma when addressing contemporary problems.

First Nations Peoples as a whole appear to suffer disproportionately from substance abuse due to a variety of factors such as cultural loss, prejudice, and poverty. In part, these problems have persisted because of helping professionals' lack of cultural competence when working with indigenous peoples (Mitka, 2002). It is important to recognize, however, that substantial variation exists in the extent of substance abuse problems among the various First Nations. This variation typically has not been recognized by researchers and practitioners, and inappropriate generalizations have been made that substance abuse is a significant problem across First Nations groups. Reliable data on trends or patterns of alcohol and drug use are scarce due to significant problems in the research (Weaver, 2001). Although social workers may well recognize substance abuse as being a significant issue for some of their Native clients, the extent and nature of this problem for First Nations Peoples has not been adequately documented.

In order to understand the current realities of First Nations Peoples, social workers need to understand the urban Native community as well as the reservation experience (Weaver, 1999b). Urban First Nations Peoples deal with issues that are both similar to and different from their reservation-based peers. Social workers need to develop culturally appropriate programs tailored to meet the needs of urban youth (Moran, 1999) and elders (Kramer, 1992a & b). Social workers should recognize that urban Native people may be strongly grounded in their cultures. Walters (1999) found that urban First Nations Peoples "have survived by taking the best of both worlds, integrating them, maintaining and transforming native cultures, and, ultimately buffering against negative colonizing processes through the internalization of positive identity attitudes and the externalization of negative dominant group attitudes" (pp. 163–164). Some urban Native people experience homelessness; however, this phenomenon differs significantly from homelessness experienced by White urban dwellers. Even though First Nations homeless people experience higher poverty, less consistent employment, higher misuse of alcohol, and lower use of mental health services than their White peers, they receive a higher level of support from family and friends (Westerfelt & Yellow Bird, 1999). This illustrates the strong value that First Nations Peoples place on interpersonal connections, even under dire circumstances.

Many Native communities are taking positive steps to prevent further erosion of culture and language and are indeed working to reclaim these vital aspects of their heritage. As an example of this, one Native American social agency has recently been awarded a federal grant to assess the state of the six languages indigenous to New York State. This program, called Haudenosaunee Empowerment through Language Preservation (HELP), examined how prevalent these languages still are and identified steps to preserve them and keep them as vital parts of Haudenosaunee culture. It is particularly noteworthy that this effort is being made by an urban social agency, given that most Native people live in urban areas, but the majority of Native people who speak their language fluently are likely to remain on reservations.

Cultural competence with First Nations Peoples requires a basic understanding of sovereignty issues and policies that apply to indigenous people, such as the ICWA and the Indian Health Service (Weaver, 1999b). When Europeans first came to what is now the United States, they dealt with First Nations Peoples on a government-to-government basis as an acknowledgment that the people who were already here existed as members of sovereign nations, just like other countries with complete rights to self-governance. Sovereignty is not something that one nation can give to another. It is an inherent characteristic. Over the centuries, the U.S. government has passed laws that have infringed upon the sovereignty of First Nations Peoples. Because the United States has grown stronger and has become able to enforce its will upon the First Nations, it has been able to put limits on indigenous sovereignty, yet it still recognizes Native people as members of domestic dependent nations, with many rights of self-governance still in place. An edited collection, *The State of Native America: Genocide, Colonization, and Resistance* (Jaimes, 1992), provides important background information that can help readers develop a basic understanding of historical and contemporary issues of indigenous sovereignty. With an understanding of the sovereignty of indigenous people, it becomes clear why many laws and policies exist that apply exclusively to First Nations Peoples.

Many stereotypes exist about Native Americans, so it is important for social workers to make sure they are choosing interventions and designing programs that accurately target needs rather than fulfill assumptions that are not based on reality. The social service needs of each Native community are likely to vary, so it is important to do an accurate assessment. As with assessing an individual, the needs of Native communities must be assessed in a thoughtful, culturally competent manner.

Damaging Hollywood images have objectified indigenous people and have promoted stereotypes. Thus, social workers may have developed certain ideas about what indigenous people look like or what their values are. Rather than being guided by stereotypes, social workers must be open to understanding how their clients identify as Native people and what is meaningful to them. Additionally, social workers should be prepared to actively challenge damaging stereotypical images like that of the "drunken Indian" that are used to label Native people and deny their basic humanity and strengths.

KNOWLEDGE ACQUISITION

In becoming knowledgeable about indigenous cultures, social workers can seek information from reservation and urban social service agencies, from indigenous journals such as *American Indian/Alaska Native Mental Health Research*, *Indigenous Voices in Social Work*, and *American Indian Quarterly*, and from individual Native people who give public speeches or workshops and may be willing to serve as key informants or cultural guides in First Nations communities. It is important that knowledge be culturally and community specific. For example, information about the culture of one tribal group may not be generalizable to another tribal group. Even within tribal groups, information may not be generalizable. For example, knowledge about the Mohawk community at Akwesasne may not be applicable at the Mohawk community of Tyendinaga. Social workers must be tentative in applying what they know about indigenous people until they can confirm whether the information that they have is applicable to a particular client.

Although readings, classes, and workshops on social work with Native Americans can be helpful, it is also important to participate in experiential learning activities. Sometimes internships are available at urban or reservation-based Native American agencies. These can give valuable opportunities for social work students to have supervised practice experience with First Nations Peoples. Briefer experiential learning activities can supplement such internships or provide important contact with Native communities when internships are not a practical option.

Spending time in First Nations communities, even for short periods, can present valuable learning experiences. Some schools of social work have developed immersion projects that send students to reservation communities for several days or weeks to learn about indigenous cultures. For example, students at Arizona State University School of Social Work can participate in a five-day cultural immersion exercise on the Navajo reservation in a class entitled "The Ecological Context of Social Work Practice." This class gives students an opportunity to learn through participation, not simply by observation (DeGraw, 1989). This type of project can be a valuable source of learning, but students must be prepared to enter indigenous communities with respect and an open mind and to not treat community residents as subjects to be studied.

Attending Native American activities can be a good source of learning. One social work student who attended a powwow in the western United States was startled to hear so many people speaking an indigenous language rather than English.

Even though the reservation was just a few miles from his home, he had no idea that indigenous language and culture were still a vital part of the lives of many First Nations Peoples. Other social work students have become exposed to First Nations cultures through attending indigenous festivals that are open to the public. This is a good way of learning about cultures, values, and traditions. Sometimes cultural activities are sponsored by social service agencies. For example, a human service agency may sponsor an honoring event that includes social dancing to honor foster parents or graduates of a drug rehabilitation program. Such events give insight not only into indigenous cultures themselves but also into how cultural elements can be integrated into social services.

It is difficult to enter experiential learning activities with a truly open mind. One way to begin to consciously be aware of assumptions and preconceived notions is to write them down before entering the experience. The cross-cultural learner can ask himself or herself: What is it that I think I know about the people I plan to interact with? How do I think they will act? What do I think they will look like? How do I think they will react to me? By reflecting on questions like these, the learner becomes more aware of assumptions and thus more able to put them aside and enter the experience prepared to learn and to have assumptions challenged.

SKILL DEVELOPMENT

Many of the skills needed for work with First Nations clients are the same as those used with clients from other backgrounds. Good communication skills and problem-solving skills are important with this population (Weaver, 1999b). Social workers must be able to communicate clearly with their indigenous clients. Cross-cultural social work can often be hampered when clients and social workers do not share a mutual understanding of the work to be done. The problem-solving approach with clear and practical steps for addressing concerns has been identified by First Nations social workers as being culturally congruent for most Native American clients (Weaver, 1999b). It is also important for social workers to approach their work with indigenous clients from a strengths perspective, given the deficit perspective that permeates the stereotypes of Native Americans. Although it is true that as a whole Native Americans are among the poorest groups in the country, have many health problems, and have a comparatively short life span, they also have many strengths as a population that has survived more than 500 years of colonization and policies designed for assimilation and both physical and cultural destruction. Some of the strengths that have enabled indigenous people to survive include a strong sense of community, values placed on tradition and cultural continuity, and respect for all people and parts of creation. These strengths must not be overlooked.

In addition to possessing strong general social work skills, it is particularly important that social workers who work with First Nations Peoples have good containment skills (Weaver, 1999b). Containment skills are those that require less activity on the part of the social worker (Shulman, 1999). In particular, social workers need to display a lot of patience in working with clients. It is important to spend a lot of time listening rather than talking. Although many social workers, particularly those new to the profession, may be uncomfortable with silence in the social work interview, it is important that silence be allowed to happen. Many

Native Americans have a different pace to their communication than do people from the dominant society. Silence is common in communication and often reflects the Native person's thoughtfully considering things previously said or taking time to choose just the right words. A social worker who rushes to fill silence prematurely is likely to cut off the client and discourage further communication.

Once a social worker recognizes the importance of containment skills when working with First Nations clients, he or she can begin to reflect on this aspect of his or her work. The social worker can review past interviews to pinpoint times when the use of containment skills might have been important. When beginning new interviews, the social worker can consciously monitor the pace of the interview and allow the client additional time to respond to questions or statements. Showing patience in this way is likely to result in additional material being disclosed or a client discussing current material more fully.

Engagement

The process of engagement often must begin with outreach. Given the historical relationship between Native Americans and social workers, there is often significant mistrust and an understandable reluctance to seek services. Social workers in program planning roles can seek input from key people in Native communities who can assist in making programs meaningful to indigenous community members. They can also assist in marketing services and spreading the word about the type of help that is available. Indeed, key members of the Native community often serve in gatekeeping roles that either encourage or discourage Native people from accessing services. By engaging these gatekeepers, social workers can gain entry to a much larger base of potential clients.

An appropriate intervention is one that is culturally congruent for the client. Social workers who serve First Nations clients must learn to take time to form a relationship during the engaging phase prior to probing for sensitive information. The pace of the interaction is likely to be fairly slow, allowing time for trust to build. Respecting silence is important in the interview.

Social workers must give thoughtful consideration to the best ways to reach culturally diverse clients. Techniques that have proved effective with some Native people will not necessarily work with others. For example, Schafer and McIlwaine (1992) found techniques that worked well for engaging Seminole children who may have experienced sexual abuse were inappropriate and ineffective when applied to sexually abused Navajo children. Interviewers successfully engaged Seminole children and encouraged them to talk about what happened to them by stating that elders had already been notified of the allegations and urged the children to cooperate fully in the investigation. This approach backfired with Navajo children who were shocked that investigators would have talked with elders and refused to cooperate for fear that information would quickly spread throughout their community and damage their reputations.

As part of the engaging process, it is important for social workers to be aware of culturally based nonverbal communication norms. For instance, a light, gentle handshake is often expected at each meeting by many traditional Native Americans. The stronger, less frequently given handshake typical of many interactions in American society would be considerably less engaging. Likewise, many traditional Native Americans do not maintain continuous eye contact as a sign of respect. Social workers should be aware that lack of eye contact does not necessarily mean that an indigenous client is not actively listening. When interviewing Navajo and Hopi youth, it is helpful to respect personal space by sitting slightly off to the side and avoiding eye contact. It is also helpful to know the timing of ceremonies to decide when best to conduct an interview and to use these as markers to identify when an event happened (Schafer and McIlwaine, 1992).

ASSESSMENT

Given the vast diversity that exists among Native people, it is important that social workers examine cultural affiliation as part of a basic assessment. Only an individual client knows what his or her cultural identity means to him or her, and the social worker must take steps to seek out this information. An important first step is to identify whether a client is a First Nations person and, if so, his or her nation. It is not always possible to identify a Native person by physical appearance or name. There are many Native people who appear phenotypically White, Latino, African American, or Asian. Social workers often may not even be aware that they are working with a Native client unless they ask or the client volunteers this information. Likewise, the social worker who expects all Native people to have colorful names like in the movies is likely to overlook the fact that some clients are Native American. Indeed, many Native people have names such as Smith and Johnson, and the names White and Hill are particularly common in some First Nations communities.

A number of assessment tools have been applied with Native clients, but social workers should be cautious in using such tools. Some of these standardized instruments were initially developed for use with other populations. For many reasons, people may or may not speak a language associated with their cultural group. It is important to challenge the assumption that people have given up speaking their language as part of a free choice to assimilate. Indigenous people have been subjected to large-scale federal policies designed to eradicate language and culture. Although there is certainly a link between language and culture, it is a complex one. It would be inappropriate to assume that a Native person who does not speak an indigenous language does not value or have a strong connection to his or her culture. Indeed, social workers should be sensitive to the fact that many indigenous people feel awkward when they cannot speak their indigenous languages, and this may have an impact on their sense of self.

Another concern with standardized cultural assessment tools is that many still place culture on a continuum; for example, if you are more grounded in one culture, you must be less so in another. Scholars who focus on cultural identity have begun to move beyond linear models to orthogonal models. Although *orthogonal* is a term used commonly in geometry to identify a right angle, social scientists increasingly use it to identify factors that exist independently. In other words, a strong connection to one culture does not limit an individual's ability to be strongly grounded in other cultures. Studies of First Nations youth have found that it is common for them to identify with more than one culture, thus supporting theories of orthogonal cultural identification (Oetting & Beauvais, 1991; Weaver, 1996).

Given the limitations of the standardized tools available for assessing culture in First Nations clients, social workers may wish to avoid using these instruments or at least to use them with caution. Culture can be assessed in a less structured manner. The following are some possible areas of inquiry for exploring culture. Information about culture may be obtained, in part, by inquiring about family history. For example, it may be revealing to know about family members who were placed in boarding schools (a common policy through the 1970s) and what this has meant for the client's ability to continue cultural traditions. Additionally, it can be helpful to know whether the client follows traditional spiritual practices, follows pan-Indian practices such as the Native American church, or is affiliated with a Christian denomination. Choices about how children are raised and the client's relationships with extended family and other members of the Native American community can also reveal information about how a client experiences his or her culture. As the social worker continues to work with the client, issues of values, behavior, and priorities that emerge during sessions will also reflect aspects of the client's culture.

It is important to incorporate diversity in planning both for individual clients and for programs. All planning must be done based on the assessment in order for it to be relevant. Well-meaning service providers are likely to miss the mark if they attempt to incorporate diversity without considering the particular needs of the client or client population. For example, one Midwestern social service agency with many clients from the First Nations of the Great Plains region decided to incorporate traditional practices in their interventions. The staff were astonished when in spite of their efforts, the vast majority of clients left the agency before completing the program. In hindsight, the staff realized that although the interventions contained material that was culturally appropriate for the people of that region, the clients in this particular program were all alienated from their cultural heritage and, in fact, felt even more inadequate when presented with the culturally infused interventions (Gurnee, Vigil, Krill-Smith, & Crowley, 1990). In planning for interventions and programs, it is critical to assess the level of cultural connection of clients and to find an intervention that is a good match.

Weaver (1999a) presents a model of how one urban First Nations community conducted a needs assessment to determine the effectiveness of its current social service programs and to identify gaps in agency-based services. Focus groups were used as a culturally congruent method of gathering information on social service needs. Although outside observers might expect such a needs assessment to identify the need for services in areas such as substance abuse, this particular community identified its most critical challenge as integrating culture in all facets of service delivery from direct work with clients to agency administration. In addition to incorporating cultural factors in the helping process, the needs assessment revealed a need to change the physical layout of the agency so that members of the First Nations community would feel comfortable dropping in and spending time in the setting, something not supported by a typical agency setup with a receptionist and waiting room. Culture also needed to be integrated in service delivery through methods such as honoring foster parents at traditional dancing events known as socials and by making use of traditional knowledge and the teachings of the elders as well as the professional knowledge of social workers (Weaver, 1999a).

Empowerment and Advocacy

As part of striving for cultural competence, social workers must recognize how many social work practices and social policies have been antithetical to empowering indigenous peoples. Although the social work value system promotes empowerment and advocacy, the continued framing of Native nations as "domestic dependent nations" and treatment of indigenous peoples as wards of the federal government perpetuates dependency and a variety of social problems. Indeed, empowerment of indigenous peoples necessitates a significant change in attitudes and policies on a large scale.

In choosing an intervention or designing a program, social workers should keep in mind the following principles:

1. The intervention should fit with the particular culture of the clients being served. In other words, a program based on Hopi culture is not likely to be a good fit for an Abenaki client.
2. The intervention should be based on the needs and level of cultural connection of the specific client. For example, offering an intervention grounded in Choctaw culture to a Choctaw client who knows nothing about his or her traditions is not likely to be productive. The exception to this would be an intervention designed specifically to reconnect a client to his or her culture.
3. The best information on whether an intervention or program is a good cultural fit will come from clients. Social workers should acknowledge that clients are experts on their own lives and needs. This acknowledgment can be very empowering for clients.
4. Some culturally based interventions, particularly those of a spiritual nature, are likely to be outside the purview of social work. Social workers should support clients who choose to seek help from traditional healers in addition to or instead of social work services.

Social work interventions that are most likely to be helpful for First Nations clients are ones that acknowledge, validate, and respect indigenous cultures. Empirical validation has been found for a variety of culturally grounded prevention programs that use a cognitive behavioral approach. Programs that target substance abuse prevention for First Nations youth have been effective at reducing the use of alcohol and drugs in many instances (Parker, Jamous, Marek, & Camacho, 1991; Schinke, Tepavac, & Cole, 2000). Although research has yet to test the effectiveness of most types of interventions with First Nations Peoples, those that incorporate culture clearly have face validity, are aligned with the principles of empowerment, and have the support of many experienced clinicians (Thomason, 2000).

In order to empower indigenous clients, social workers must thoughtfully critique the theories and models for cultural appropriateness before applying them in their work. Although extensive diversity exists among First Nations clients, some theoretical models may be more appropriate than others for guiding interventions. Models that tend to focus heavily on the individual may not be a good fit given the importance placed on extended family and community connections in many Native cultures. Interventions that are based on systems theories that emphasize the importance of the social environment are likely to be most effective.

It is helpful not only to acknowledge the importance of family and community members but also to incorporate them in the work. Connecting youth with elders can reinforce both their cultural identity and their positive behaviors that serve as protective factors against substance abuse and other social problems. Elders are typically perceived to be strong and vibrant members of their communities who are able to pass on the core elements of culture to others. Angell, Kurz, and Gottfried (1997) give a poignant example of how a social worker assisted a troubled adolescent who had attempted suicide by connecting him with a respected elder who helped him become more grounded in his culture. Additionally, helping elders to reestablish or strengthen meaningful roles in their communities can be therapeutic and empowering. One urban First Nations social agency had elders make beaded red ribbons that were later sold to promote awareness and raise funds for HIV prevention. This task gave the elders a way to make a difference in their community while using traditional skills.

The social service needs of urban Native American elders are extensive and often go unmet. Native people residing in urban areas often do not have access to health and social services offered under tribal auspices. A study of urban elders found that they suffer from many health problems. They often do not seek help from agencies and helping professionals because of significant mistrust of dominant-society organizations (Kramer, 1992a & b). Helping professionals need to do culturally appropriate outreach in order to successfully engage this population. Additionally, social workers must be prepared to advocate for needed funding and services for indigenous populations.

The importance of self-awareness is mentioned repeatedly in the social work literature. It is critical that social workers be able to reflect on their own feelings and biases and how these may influence their work with clients (Mason, Benjamin, & Lewis, 1996; Ronnau, 1994; Sowers-Hoag & Sandau-Beckler, 1996). Supervision can be an important venue for developing self-awareness and examining biases. It is important that a social worker feel safe enough to openly discuss these feelings in a confidential setting with a trusted senior colleague. One tool that can be helpful in this task is the process recording. Process recordings are an important learning tool in which social workers are encouraged to write down their feelings and reactions next to a description of the content of an interview with a client. The process recording is used as a learning tool that encourages self-reflection and is not something that becomes part of a client record; thus, it is a safe place for a social worker to begin to disclose feelings honestly.

Closely related to self-awareness is the value of helper wellness. Social workers must be able to take care of their own well-being and make sure they are not trying to inappropriately meet their own needs through interaction with clients. In recent years, Native values and spirituality have often been exploited through the New Age movement. This cultural and spiritual misappropriation has a devastating impact on First Nations Peoples. People with a spiritual hunger and need for balance in their lives have sought these out through attempting to replicate (often in inappropriate ways and with gross distortions) indigenous practices. Social workers need to make sure they are not trying to meet their own needs through asking Native clients questions about their culture, values, and traditions. Social workers need to find other ways to maintain their own well-being in this often stressful profession and to not do it at the expense of their clients.

Humility and willingness to learn are important values for social workers to have, regardless of the type of clients they serve, but these attitudes/values are particularly important in doing cross-cultural work. Social workers must realize that there are many different ways of helping and that they do not know everything; they should always display a willingness to learn. Sometimes learning comes through formal channels such as workshops, but some of the most important learning comes through less formal channels such as listening to and learning from clients. This is particularly important when working with Native American clients. Social workers must be willing to learn from clients the role that culture plays in their lives. Through active listening, the social worker will learn whether clients have strong cultural connections and the nature of those connections. Some clients who do not have a strong cultural connection may feel a sense of pain and loss that can be traced back to federal policies that promoted assimilation and cultural loss, such as boarding schools. It is important to learn how clients experience such losses. Are they filled with self-blame because they do not know their traditions? Are they angry at the dominant society (and those they perceive to be its representatives, such as social workers) over what has been taken from them? Only by careful listening and learning from clients will social workers be able to choose and implement appropriate interventions.

Respect, open-mindedness, and a nonjudgmental attitude are also important values for working with First Nations Peoples. In doing cross-cultural work, social workers are faced with clients whose values and lifestyles may be quite different from those of the social worker. It can be challenging to be open-minded enough to respect differing practices when they seem to be diametrically opposed to the social worker's own values. Voss, Douville, Little Soldier, and Twiss (1999) emphasize that social workers must be knowledgeable about and respectful of the traditional, non-Christian value systems held by many indigenous people. A social worker who comes from a strong Judeo-Christian orientation may have difficulty working with a client who follows traditional indigenous spiritual practices. For many years, ceremonies such as the Sun Dance were outlawed and perceived as barbaric because they differed from spiritual practices more commonly found in the dominant society. Indigenous spirituality was often seen as pagan and un-Christian rather than simply as a different and equally valid spirituality. Although it may be challenging for social workers to respect practices that differ significantly from their own, displaying a nonjudgmental attitude is an important part of cultural competence with First Nations Peoples.

Striving for social justice is inherent in culturally competent practice. Social workers can begin the struggle for social justice by examining the policies and procedures in their own agencies. This level of self-reflection must go hand in hand with a growing awareness of individual biases that influence practice. For example, a social worker in a foster care setting might reflect on the agency's policies and examine whether criteria for foster parents may contain a bias against Native families who may have limited income, space limitations, and several children already in the household. Likewise, social workers need to reflect on national policies and bureaucracies. For instance, a culturally competent social worker can reflect on legislation such as the Adoption and Safe Families Act and question how its implementation may interact with and possibly undermine legislation such as the ICWA. Social workers can use advocacy skills to work to implement culturally appropriate policies and to confront policies that have a differential or negative impact on First Nations Peoples. It is impossible to do culturally competent practice in an environment filled with social injustice; therefore, social workers must focus efforts on the macro level as well as the micro level.

SOCIAL AND ECONOMIC JUSTICE RESOLUTION

Social justice is a crucial element of cultural competence with First Nations Peoples (Weaver, 1999b). Social workers must be prepared to use their advocacy skills to confront the social and economic injustices that continue to be perpetrated upon First Nations Peoples. Native children are still removed from their families and communities in numbers large enough to threaten the future of indigenous nations. Knowledgeable social workers can play an important role in educating other social workers, people in the legal system, and the general public about the ICWA. This act has always been under attack by people who misunderstand or feel threatened by it. Thus far it has withstood all legal challenges, and it has not been affected by later legislation such as the Multiethnic Placement Act and the Adoption and Safe Families Act. It is likely that attacks on ICWA will continue. Social workers can assume an important role in helping others to understand the importance of this law and in making sure that the law is not overturned or watered down.

Currently, Native nations still retain some sovereignty that includes the right to govern themselves, set laws, and develop social policies. Reservations often have their own tribal social service offices, health clinics, and legal systems. Through the years, sovereignty has been infringed upon by the passage of various federal laws and by Supreme Court decisions (Robbins, 1992). Given the current political climate in the United States, challenges to sovereignty are likely to continue, and long-established treaty rights may be lost. The current configuration of the Supreme Court has consistently ruled against the rights of First Nations Peoples. Likewise, former President George W. Bush made public statements that there is no such thing as sovereignty for Native American nations. On the other hand, President Barack Obama has made particular efforts to reach out to Native people and get Native input on social issues. This provides a much-needed opportunity to shape social and health services in ways that take into account the needs of Native Americans. Social workers can play an important role in advocating for just and fair social and economic policies.

Social workers can play a number of activist roles on behalf of First Nations Peoples while still respecting a context of indigenous sovereignty. A much-needed role for social work activists is that of putting political pressure on federal and state entities that make policies and laws affecting First Nations Peoples. Social justice in a First Nations context means challenging the colonial structures and mindset that undermine sovereignty and self-governance. This can be done through traditional advocacy efforts such as letter writing, voting, and community organization, as well as through more radical methods that challenge U.S. and state governmental structures (Weaver, 1999a).

Case Study

You have been meeting with Ho Chunk client Dean Marshall for three months. The Ho Chunk (formerly known as the Winnebago) is a nation of people who traditionally farmed in Wisconsin near Green Bay before being relocated several times. Some remain in Wisconsin and have repurchased 2,000 acres of their traditional homelands. You have been trying to assist Dean in his goals of completing his GED and obtaining employment that would enable him to support his family of five. During your time working with him, he has disclosed how his grandparents were forced to go to boarding school where they were punished for speaking their language and were not allowed to practice their religion. His mother spent most of her childhood in various non-Native foster homes and was eventually adopted by a non-Native family where she suffered sexual abuse. There are few jobs in the area where Dean lives, and he struggles with having to leave the area and his extended family in order to find employment. He has expressed hopelessness in his ability to remain in his community and support his children at the same time. He feels overwhelmed and powerless.

1. Describe how you could empower Dean to look at his family's endurance and survival using tools such as a genogram to identify resilience across generations.

2. Describe how you could empower Dean to find employment opportunities and perhaps facilitate economic development that would bring opportunities to his community. It may be helpful to begin with an assessment of Dean's skills and interests as well as reviewing what the economic base of the Ho Chunk people has been in the past.

3. Describe how societal oppression and institutionalized racism have impacted Dean's life.

4. What clinical skills will be most useful in exploring Dean's feelings about himself and his environment?

5. Identify how social work skills might be used to work toward societal change and social justice to reduce oppression and racism. Are there oppressive factors in the contemporary social environment of First Nations Peoples that may be relevant to Dean's situation?

6. How can community organizing and advocacy skills be used to enhance employment?

7. How can you, as a social worker, address your own feelings of being overwhelmed by the situations of clients such as Dean who face many difficult obstacles?

This case, like many others, contains micro, meso, and macro dimensions. Interventions can be appropriate at various levels. The case begins on a direct practice level with a combination of counseling around issues of employment and may include concrete referrals to a GED class and temporary food and clothing resources.

It is often easiest to engage First Nations clients around issues of resolving basic needs before exploring more emotionally charged areas. Indeed, it appears that the engagement phase has been successful since Dean felt safe enough to disclose that boarding school trauma and sexual abuse have been issues in his family. At this point, the case is likely to require more use of clinical skills in exploring the history of trauma in Dean's family and its contemporary implications. Dean's statements about being overwhelmed and hopeless are also important areas to explore including whether he may have thoughts of suicide. Some Native communities have very high rates of suicide, so you will need to gather more information on whether various self-harming behaviors are present in Dean's social environment. Dean has also disclosed some ambivalence about education given his family's history with forced education as a tool of assimilation. You may want to do some additional reading or consult with someone more knowledgeable about the impact of Native American boarding schools.

Clearly, the social environment, both historically and at the time of this case, has a shaping influence on Dean and his feelings. It may be appropriate for interventions to target larger scale change. If Dean is one of several clients in similar situations, you may seek to create appropriate change at an agency level such as initiating a job seekers or GED support group. The social stressors felt by clients with limited education and job skills during a bad economy can indeed feel overwhelming to both clients and social workers counseling about these issues, but social work advocacy skills can be instrumental in pursuing large-scale change. Indeed, you may be able to use grant application skills to leverage funding to create new agency-based job readiness programs to assist Dean and similar clients.

Clients with multiple needs such as Dean may raise ethical dilemmas for social workers who are unsure how to prioritize areas for work. Dean presents with both concrete needs and the need for clinical counseling. Both are likely to absorb considerable resources. Decisions must be made about how best to meet Dean's needs. Using supervision is an important way to reflect on appropriate strategies as well as manage your feelings about the case.

CONCLUSION

Social workers must continue to strive for cultural competence. This involves the ability to interact with clients in a way that is knowledgeable and respectful of the clients' cultural context. Although it is not possible to know everything about every indigenous group, culturally competent social workers will take steps to be knowledgeable about the culture, history, and contemporary realities of the indigenous people they work with, keeping in mind the extraordinary diversity that exists among Native people. Culturally competent social workers will possess strong skills in general and will make sure they use containment skills that emphasize patience and listening and that allow for silence. Social workers must show respect, have an open mind, and be nonjudgmental with First Nations clients. Self-awareness and helper wellness are critical attributes, as are humility and a willingness to learn. Cultural competence is not just relevant to direct practice but also must permeate the way programs and policies are developed and administered.

Without social and economic justice, cultural competence on a micro level is severely limited.

Social workers who work with First Nations Peoples face the challenge of overcoming stereotypes to be effective in their work. In addition to gaining realistic, strengths-based perspectives of their Native clients, social workers must help clients see social workers in a new way. Many First Nations clients see social workers as culturally incompetent representatives of government bureaucracies that pose a threat to Native families, communities, and nations. Through culturally competent work, social workers can demonstrate respect for indigenous values and traditions. Once both clients and social workers are able to get past the stereotypes they hold of each other, it will be possible for them to work together in healthy, productive ways within a climate that respects indigenous cultures.

CHAPTER 9

CULTURAL COMPETENCE WITH EUROPEAN AMERICANS

Nocona L. Pewewardy, Rhea V. Almeida, Lisa Dressner, and Caroline Hann

INTRODUCTION

Lum suggested in the first chapter of this book that reading critiques on issues confronting the cultural competence discourse may prompt social work students to explore this area in more depth. Such an inquiry could result in a research paper or thesis emphasizing a cultural competence practice theme, deliberating on a dilemma within this discourse, or offering a revision to the paradigmatic scaffolding that undergirds culturally competent practice. This chapter provides a model for the third type of endeavor.

In the previous edition of this book Lum used a quote from Giordano and McGoldrick to reveal a pattern of thought that establishes whiteness as a cultural norm that does not require a racial or ethnic modifier in the United States, "Come on, White ethnics today don't have ethnic issues; they're totally American" (2007, p. 128). This statement reflected thinking that confounds notions of whiteness and European ethnicity and excuses both from interrogation as features of social location[1] that translates specific cultural values. It is a type of thinking that emanates from socialization that promotes White European ancestry as a value-neutral American cultural norm and reflects a conception of diversity grounded in what Jakobsen (1998) termed *binary oppositions*.

> Binary oppositions define social positions as oppositional pairs, one of which is defined in terms of the other.... So, for example, gender relations work to produce opposing types of persons where woman is defined in terms of man and where only these two positions are available as "genders." (p. 7)

Binary oppositions establish two possibilities for lived experience, and in the case of gender, "man" is advanced as a position of identity and that which is different is "woman" (Jakobsen, 1998). This way of conceptualizing diversity reinforces hierarchical binary relationships and negates the lives of people who are transgender and gender nonconforming. It also denies that the meaning of gender is itself differentiated by other axes such as race and class (Jakobsen, 1998).

One of the key aspects of cultural competence discourse is strengthening knowledge acquisition in order to promote social work practice that furthers the purpose of the profession (Lum, 2007). All people experience social group memberships and social roles that influence how power, privilege, and oppression manifest in their lives. The rationale for social workers to understand these dynamics emanates from the purpose of the profession, which is defined by the Council on Social Work Education (CSWE, 2008) as:

> The purpose of the social work profession is to promote human and community well-being. Guided by a person and environment construct, a global perspective, respect for human diversity, and knowledge based on scientific inquiry, social work's purpose is actualized through its quest for social and economic justice, the prevention of conditions that limit human rights, the elimination of poverty, and the enhancement of the quality of life for all persons. (p. 1)

A critical element of the paradigm shift in the cultural competence discourse is the emphasis on established hierarchies of power, privilege, and oppression with a focus on the "shifting kaleidoscope" of identity comprised from intersections between identity characteristics (Almeida, Dolan-Del Vecchio, & Parker, 2008; Hernandez, Almeida, & Dolan-Del Vecchio, 2005; Jakobsen, 1998).

> The singular politics of "difference" produces a version of diversity which is made up of multiple "units" of differences, but which ignores complexity. These coherent "units" of difference are placed in horizontal lists, producing a liberal pluralist version of diversity which assumes coherent separations and clear boundaries. The horizontal placement of various "differences" fails to articulate either power relations or historical conflicts among "different" groups. (Jakobsen, 1998, p. 9)

CULTURAL COMPETENCE WITH EUROPEAN AMERICANS: A RED HERRING CONCEPT

When it comes to conceptualizing social work with European Americans, it is crucial to understand that whiteness, rather than ancestry, determines a privileged social location that warrants critical interrogation in cultural competency discourse (Nylund, 2006; Pinderhughes, 1989; Sue, 2004). Pinderhughes's (1989) work revealed that race is a bigger barrier to self-awareness among White people than European ethnicity. A recurrent theme in the study of whiteness is that White people do not consider their "whiteness" an identity trait or cultural marker for group membership because it is not problematic and, therefore, salient to most respondents (Hurtado & Stewart, 1997). Helms (1992) maintained that White people comprise the only group in the United States "that spends more time and effort wondering about the implications of race for other groups than it does for itself" (p. i).

Confounding race and ethnicity and proposing that White European identity is a benign social location reflects a manifestation of White supremacy culture. Two premises guide this chapter: 1) the conceptualization of working with European Americans is flawed in the absence of a power analysis of whiteness in all of its permutations and 2) models of practice that uncritically focus on how to work with "cultural others" emanate from foundations of White supremacy and White privilege.

Oppression cannot be erased and healed until the equivocating connections of power and privilege are simultaneously deconstructed and dismantled. The National Association of Social Workers (NASW, 2006) Code of Ethics compels this work:

> Social workers should promote the general welfare of society, from local to global levels, and the development of people, their communities, and their environments. Social workers should advocate for living conditions conducive to the fulfillment of basic human needs and should promote social, economic, political, and cultural values and institutions that are compatible with the realization of social justice. (p. 414)

Social work has failed to challenge the beleaguering influence of White supremacy culture effectively (Herrick, 1978; McMahon & Allen-Meares, 1992; Pewewardy & Severson, 2003; Prichard, 1998; Weeks, 1988). For this reason, features of White supremacy culture replicate daily in social work practice without being proactively named or chosen because what are really cultural beliefs and values are articulated as unquestionable standards of behavior (Okun, 2008). Perfectionism, a sense of urgency, quantity over quality, worship of the written word, only one right way, paternalism, either/or thinking, and the right to comfort are features of White supremacy culture illuminated by Okun.

White supremacy culture replicates false consciousness, that is, internalized beliefs based on myths and lies translated by socialization to create perceptions of difference that safeguard the power and privilege of people in dominant positions (Fritze, n.d.). Interrogation of the multiple narratives that perpetuate false consciousness through social work practices and discourses reveals the need for a perpetual focus on the global destruction precipitated by colonization, imperialism, genocide, capitalism, neocolonialism, and globalization. False consciousness results from social work conceptions of diversity management that disarticulate diversity from complexity (Jakobsen, 1998).

CONSEQUENCES OF DIVERSITY DISARTICULATED FROM COMPLEXITY AND REALITY

Diversity disarticulated from complexity perpetuates competing personal and political struggles that insulate, conceal, and protect hierarchies of domination (Hobgood, 2000; Jakobsen, 1998). It is no coincidence that what are currently perceived of and discussed as "natural disasters" have the most deleterious impacts in the geographic regions most disrupted and shaped by global capitalism. The research and scholarship that dominates the current social work discourse lack the types of critical analyses that can prepare social workers in the 21st century to understand how the severity of devastation precipitated by the earthquake in Haiti on January 12, 2010, emanated from neocolonialism perpetuated by the United States and France.

Haiti is an impoverished nation that lacks the resources and infrastructure to moderate the destruction of natural disasters and deal with the aftermath because the United States and France colluded in stealing Haiti's resources (Matthewson, 2003). A few key features of the U.S. and French complicity in plundering Haiti are presented here in the hope that readers are troubled enough to think more critically about the cultural narratives that inform their practices.

When Haiti sought and gained independence in the 18th-century rebellion, their sovereignty came with a huge debt. Haiti was forced by France, with coercion from the United States, to pay 90 million gold francs in order to be recognized as a sovereign nation. France (the country that colonized Haiti) demanded remuneration for the loss of economic capital in slave ownership and labor. Haiti emerged as the hemisphere's first independent Black nation 200 years ago with a debt that placed their homes underwater permanently. Haiti never defaulted on its payments to France, which depleted the country of its resources (HaitiAction.net, n.d.).

Haiti's impoverishment was the direct result of foreign (United States and French) oppression, and both nations are, therefore, culpable for the level of destruction exacted by the January 12 earthquake. Increasing social work discourses about cultural equity interrupts narratives that couch the U.S. support of Haiti as a transfer of foreign aid. Any support the United States and France provide Haiti in recovering from the earthquake is a small down payment for reparations required to restore what was stolen from that nation. Social workers informed by this type of knowledge are positioned more powerfully to participate in efforts to redistribute how U.S. tax dollars are used. Resources now earmarked for war and the destabilization of nations (Sharlet, 2008) can be used otherwise for investments in a future that redresses 600 years of Eurocentric diffusionism.[2]

Mainstream models of social work practice are based on human behavior and developmental theory steeped in Eurocentric processes. Discussions of cultural competence that do not address these biases perpetuate hierarchical binary oppositions and circumvent the proliferation of practice strategies that support healing the wounds of oppression and dismantling its causes.

"Race is inscribed in every issue of the day" (Ignatiev & Garvey, 1996, p. 2). In early January 2010, some of Senator Harry Reid of Nevada's racist comments received media attention in a political tit for tat that perpetuated White supremacy culture by exploiting race as a wedge issue.[3] Reid's comments reflected the pervasive type of White supremacist beliefs passed around among White people when they think people of color will not hear, that is, Whites do not see themselves as people of color.

RACE: A FALSE NOTION WITH CONSEQUENCES TOO REAL TO IGNORE

A lack of White racial identity awareness is a feature and propagator of White supremacy culture. Thandeka (1999) invented the Race Game for a White colleague that asked what it felt like to be Black.

> The Race Game, as my luncheon partner very quickly discovered, had only one rule. For the next seven days, she must use the ascriptive term white whenever she mentioned the name of one of her Euro-American cohorts. She must say, for instance, "my white husband Phil," or "my white friend Julie," or "my lovely white child Jackie." … I guaranteed her that if she did this for a week and then we met for lunch, I could answer her question using terms she would understand. We never met for lunch again. Apparently my suggestion made her uncomfortable. (p. 3)

Helms (1992) maintained that "White people have difficulty accepting they have a race and therefore are threatened by groups who have no such difficulties" (p. i).

The "socially constructed concept of race" was the foundation for a society "in which superficial physical differences would be used to determine an individual's worth" (Graves, 2004, p. xxvi). In *The Race Myth: Why We Pretend Race Exists in America*, biologist Joseph Graves explained how the notion of race was socially constructed. Graves also discussed the historical and contemporary costs of operating from a false construction: "In popular discourse, racial groups are viewed as physically distinguishable populations that share a common geographically based ancestry" (American Sociological Association [ASA], 2003, p. 4).

When biological research evidenced that the DNA of human beings is 99% alike—regardless of race—it undermined the notion that race is a meaningful determinant in terms of a physiological explanation for differences (Graves, 2004, 2006). However, when White people dismiss the power and privileges that correspond with their racial identity, they are ignoring social science research that documents "the role and consequence of race in primary social institutions and environments, including the criminal justice, education and health systems, job markets, and where people live" (ASA, 2003, Executive Summary). White supremacy culture must be named and dismantled without being reified. This is a paradox that contemporary social workers are compelled by their professional mission to resolve.

CULTURAL COMPETENCE DISCOURSE: COMPETING PERSPECTIVES AND PARADOXICAL DILEMMAS

Developing increased knowledge of histories of oppression based on identity characteristics is a starting place for analyses that surface lies and inaccuracies perpetuated through dominant narratives (Lum, 2007). Discourse that promotes liberation, however, deliberately focuses on oppressive narratives and oppressor actions. Only learning about the contexts of oppression and circulating discourses of resistance with the idea of helping the oppressed fails to manifest social justice because people who are active and passive beneficiaries of "socio-cultural and political systems of domination" (Giulfoyle, 2005, p. 101) are not required to interrogate their privileged positions.

Throughout the 20th century social workers challenged White supremacy, promoted anti-racist alternatives, and contributed to positive social transformations (Aptheker, 1981; Berman-Rossi & Miller, 1994; Fibush & Turnquest, 1970; Johnson, 1991; McMahon & Allen-Meares, 1992; Peebles-Wilkins, 1989; Platt & Chandler, 1988; Ross, 1978; Shannon, 1970). These social workers' contributions have, however, been largely ignored and marginalized in the White-dominated discourses of the profession, which is an assertion that can be validated by the following exercise. Take out a sheet of paper and write down everything you can remember from your social work education about Jane Addams and Mary Richmond. Now, set that paper aside and write down everything you can remember from your social work education about Mary Church Terrell, Ida B. Wells Barnett, E. Franklin Frazier, and Fredricka Douglass Sprague Perry. Consider whose names are more readily recognized and whose biographical narratives are easiest to recall from your social work education. Now ask yourself why this is the case.

Social workers have options for developing liberation-based healing strategies that are informed by power analyses and interrogating why and how structural inequalities morph and persist. Instead of, for example, solely working within the conditions of economic recession and focusing on how to generate funding to serve clients in times of economic crises, social workers are compelled by their professional mission to investigate what precipitates funding scarcity, work with clients to hold more perpetrators of unscrupulous business practices accountable, and actively incorporate social action into their practice. As this chapter reveals in subsequent sections, the work to redress and abolish oppressive norms and hold actors accountable is not a matter of micro, mezzo, or macro practice. It is a matter of focus within all social work practice contexts.

Resistance to liberatory social work practice is intense, and there can be a correlation between the capital of unearned social privileges and the ferocity of opposition. There is an established precedent of blocking, erasing, suppressing, and underutilizing the work of activist and scholars that do not perform their liberation activity within the White proffered boundary. How the past influences the present is, however, primarily undetected because people who uncritically operate from the features of White supremacy culture are unable or unwilling to check their internalized ethnocentrism. Internalized White ethnocentrism is protected with denial and pride fueled by historical translations that distort perceptions (Loewen, 2007).

The choices historians make about which facts to emphasize in telling U.S. history are ideological in nature (Zinn, 1999). The "historian has been trained in a society in which education and knowledge are put forward as technical problems of excellence and not as tools for contending social classes, races, and nations" (p. 8). The ideological biases that emanated from European colonialism determined the discourse that dominates accounts of U.S. history (Loewen, 2007) and perpetuates what King (1991) termed *dysconsciousness*. "Dysconsciousness is an uncritical habit of mind (including perceptions, attitudes, assumptions, and beliefs) that justifies inequity and exploitation by accepting the existing order of things as given" (King, 1991, p. 135).

Social work scholars' perpetual focus on the importance of Jane Addams and Mary Richmond (Franklin, 1986; Harold, 2003; Kendall, 1989; Pottick, 1989) in the origins of the social work profession, for example, reflects what Loewen (1999) exposed as a White American predilection to remember and only publicize positive things. Loewen (1999) contended that America has ended up with a landscape of denial that keeps "us ignorant as a people, less able to understand what really happened in the past, and less able to apply our understanding to issues facing the United States today" (p. 19).

Contemporary social work would be a different profession had the work of Mary Church Terrell, Ida B. Wells Barnett, E. Franklin Frazier, and Fredricka Douglass Sprague Perry been heralded to the same extent as that of Jane Addams and Mary Richmond (Aptheker, 1981; Jones, 1990; Peebles-Wilkins, 1989; Platt & Chandler, 1988). Widely honoring the legacies of these social workers would, however, require exposing the influence of White supremacy on social work practice, research, and education. It would reveal why social work discourse has largely cooperated with the philosophy that racism can be redressed by focusing "on the effects on those who are oppressed as if there are no oppressors or beneficiaries" (Transnational Racial Justice Initiative, 2001, p. 5).

Graves (2004) established five pillars of racist thought:

- Biological races exist in the human species.
- Races have genetic differences that determine their intelligence.
- Races have genetically determined differences that produce unique diseases and cause them to die at different rates.
- Races have genetically determined sexual appetites and reproductive capacities.
- Races have genetically determined differences in athletic and musical ability. (p. xxx)

Graves contended that many people in the United States hold most or parts of these views, and "not everyone that believes these ideas is an evil person" (p. xxx). Failing to recognize these beliefs when they are implicitly and explicitly perpetuated is, however, a manifestation of the ongoing translation of White supremacy culture in social work discourses.

What would happen if the social work discourse was opened to the possibilities that our most heralded White leaders were racist? In an occasional paper that analyzed a public dialogue between Jane Addams and Ida B. Wells Barnett about the relationship (i.e., the lack of relationship, which was empirically documented by Wells Barnett) between the rape of White women and the lynching of Black men, Aptheker (1981) surfaced that Addams perpetuated racist stereotypes that undermined intersectional analyses of oppression. Addams articulated, through her own words, beliefs that reflected Graves's (2004) pillars of racism when she described Blacks and Whites as "alien races" and proffered an assumption that lynching emanated from a White southern belief that it was "the only successful method of dealing with a certain class of crimes" (Addams's essay "Respect for Law" is reprinted in total as is Wells Barnett's response, "Lynching and the Excuse for It," in Aptheker's *Occasional Paper, Lynching and Rape: An Exchange of Views* [1981]).

Wells Barnett rebutted Addams's contentions by providing empirical evidence that Addams's views about lynching being a response to rape were incorrect and baseless assumptions. Aptheker's analysis of Wells Barnett's response to Addams exposed three elements of racism in the United Stated that are as relevant today as they were when the exchange occurred 109 years ago:

1. People who don't have the shield of White privilege can face lethal repercussions for advocacy and resistance.
2. Only strategies generated from the interstices of oppression and that abolish the root causes, that is, dismantle privilege and oppose coercive power, result in sustaining changes.
3. The social work profession has acquiesced to and perpetuated oppression as a result of failing to hear the voices of leaders and visionaries that contested White supremacy culture throughout the 20th century.

It may be seductive to dismiss an assertion that Addams's essay revealed racist beliefs. It could be argued that selected statements from a single article are not enough to warrant such an interpretation and that Addams was among the most progressive White women of her time. To dismiss the racism in Addams's essay is, however, the articulation of defensive tactics that derail an honest interrogation of hegemony in the United States (N. Pewewardy, 2003).

Deconstructing and dismantling White supremacy culture in the 21st century require honesty about the racist beliefs Jane Addams articulated. Jane Addams "was a social activist, an accomplished organizer, suffragist and civil rights advocate, a courageous opponent of the First World War, and founding president of the Women's International League for Peace and Freedom" (Aptheker, 1981, p. 1). She also actively acquiesced to preserve her White privilege and participated in White supremacist culture, which she defended with utilitarianism (Aptheker, 1981).

Reviewing Addams's work from this perspective provides the opportunity to interrogate the influence of utilitarianism in White supremacy culture and to expose the manipulation inherent in a dangerous philosophy that justifies and perpetuates oppression. It also potentiates liberation by revealing that Jane Addams manifested internalized dominance in her social work practice and how contemporary social workers do the same.

A qualitative study[4] that explored how the contemporary discourse regarding White privilege can be used in social work education to promote individual and collective social and economic justice generated the following insights:

> Interrogating Jane Addams social location and beliefs about race is perceived as blasphemy because it is viewed in terms of denigrating her image. People are afraid that you're going to throw the baby out with the bath water. Social workers do not have to discount all the good things Jane Addams did in order to acknowledge she held and perpetuated racist beliefs. Suppressing this information is a way to keep white privilege in place and to make icons of the people who've made a difference so that you can't ever hope to have that many who really can make a difference. If we can critically analyze Jane Addams's legacy in total, which is not the same as denigrating, we can see how we can make a contribution by going further.

People have argued that "judging people of the past by the standards of our time" is anachronistic (Loewen, 1999, p. 40), but ignoring Jane Addams's racism gives it credibility in our time.

White supremacy emerges from critical analyses of the work of many leaders who are heralded as uncompromising advocates for human rights in White social work discourses. When Eleanor Roosevelt's life and work are discussed in *Affilia* (Brandwein, 2002; Coss, 2006) in a manner that conceals her complicity with racial terrorists,[5] it obliterates possibilities for White social workers to interrogate the duplicity that results in compromising human rights for group rights (Anderson, 2003, 2006, 2009). Explicating the features of White supremacy culture is a precursor to abolishing its influences. When the narratives of transformational leaders and activists such as Jane Addams and Eleanor Roosevelt detail the translation of White supremacy in their work, they provide opportunities to transcend White individual and cultural denial and repression.

What Addams's and Roosevelt's legacies provide is evidence that human beings, even the most distinguished, valued, and successful, commit treasons to human rights that have deleterious effects. Features of White supremacy culture, however, perpetuate separate and unequal consequences for these transgressions. Interrogating the failings of venerated historical figures provides opportunities to improve their efforts and further their work. All social workers will inevitably fail to articulate justice through their practice. Literacy about White cultural supremacy initiates opportunities for accountability and reparations that illiteracy precludes.

White social workers can learn a great deal about their cultural identity by studying how White suffragists used racism to promote their cause (Vernon Johns Society, 1994) and why feminism in the United States has been criticized for replicating White supremacy (hooks, 1994; Hurtado, 1996). Ignatiev and Garvey (1996) acknowledged "how devilishly difficult it is for individuals to escape whiteness" (p. 37).

> The white race does not voluntarily surrender a single member, so that even those who step outside of it in one situation find it virtually impossible not to step back in later, if for no other reason than the assumptions of others. But we also know that when there comes into being a critical mass of people who, though they look white, have ceased to act white, the white race will undergo fission, and former whites will be able to take part in building a new human community. (p. 37)

The following discussion elucidates features of White supremacy culture that regularly influence social work.

EXAMPLES OF WHITE SUPREMACY CULTURE: TRANSLATION, SEDUCTION, AND MAINTENANCE

How Can I, as a White Person Who Cares and "Gets It," Help a Person of Color?

A White teacher who attended a racial justice conference asked a multiracial group for advice about how to help a youth (age 14) avoid racial bullying by a White youth of approximately the same age, that is, the teacher reported the youth were all in the same grade. In describing the situation the teacher asserted that the administration turned a blind eye to the problem and that she was the only one at her school who cared about racial justice. The people the teacher entreated for help began brainstorming about how to interrupt racial bullying. Their responses reflected a multipronged approach that contextualized the situation within a predominantly White community and focused on individual and community accountability. Recommended strategies focused on immediate safety concerns and community change, that is, what social workers refer to as a multisystemic approach that incorporates micro, mezzo, and macro interventions.

1. Expose the problem and leverage school administrators' responsibilities and resources for safety. If the school administrators don't attend to the problem, initiate a letter-writing campaign—people in the group were eager to write letters to promote administrative accountability.
2. Utilize community organizing techniques to decrease the bullied student's isolation by promoting

critical thinking about the specificity of racial bullying and bullying in general.
3. Sponsor youth from the school to attend the Youth Leadership Conference at the 11th Annual White Privilege Conference (WPC11, n.d.), which provides "youth-friendly and youth-specific workshops, caucuses and space that engage issues of white privilege, white supremacy, and oppression" (p. 1).

One by one these recommendations were discounted and rebutted by the White teacher who entreated the group for help. She explained that she had tried many of the recommended strategies already. She expressed concern that a letter-writing campaign would alarm the administration, and there was not enough money to implement other recommendations. She communicated that she felt her situation was hopeless. After all, she explained, she had to be careful. If she lost her job by rocking the boat, the bullied youth would have no support at school. Her responses revealed that she was more aligned with the school administration and their comfort than with the student's safety.

Discussion

White supremacy culture was translated and maintained in this example by how the problem was presented and how support was rebutted. In this example the teacher was focused on how to help someone she perceived as a "racially other" victim. She wanted to situate her helping with the youth being bullied, which leaves the White supremacy and White racial violence uncontested. She confounded her perceived risks and sense of powerlessness with that of the youth being bullied and abdicated her capacity and responsibility to intervene. Ultimately, she defended the school's administration and refused the help of concerned people who were willing to provide her with support beyond a conversation at a conference.

In the book, *Why Are All the Black Kids Sitting Together in the Cafeteria? And Other Conversations about Race*, Tatum (1999) encouraged readers to break their silence about racism. She also revealed that racism may make White people uncomfortable, but it can have lethal implications for people of color.

Racism Is NOT the Problem Here

The hierarchical service model that most social workers follow supports a professionalism in which "experts" believe they should divorce their personal experiences, and certainly their lives, from the service users with whom they work (Weeks, 1988). These are the types of ideas that institutionalized fragmentation in social work practices (e.g., social workers quest for expertise about a specific community, efficacy with a therapeutic approach, or focus on a discreet problem) and perpetuate personal and political power dynamics that subjugate challenges to White supremacy culture.

Often social workers fail to consider the intersections between peoples' experiences and acquiesce to funding sources that dictate parameters of their practice without critically examining opportunities to undermine fragmentation and promote community and social healing rather than individual approaches. When White privilege is explicated as a pervasive destructive influence in peoples' lives in the United States, and identified as a root cause of inestimable oppression, White social workers often counter that White privilege is not an issue for White people or there are no benefits for being White. The liberatory potential of discussions with White people about White supremacy culture has heretofore been excluded from broad-based social work discourses. Explicating the influence of White privilege in White lives reveals interlocking power dynamics and can be the catalyst for development of liberatory critical consciousness.

Funding sources most typically target problems and populations, and this reinforces contexts of "otherness." Segregating services based on diagnostic criteria and identity characteristics replicates social control functions through social work practices that reinforce dominant positions in society.

Discussion

It is a challenge for those who seek social justice to keep in mind not only the ways that their own identities make them vulnerable to oppression (as middle-class, White women face oppression by middle-class, White men) but also the ways that their identities grant privilege (the White women's movement forgets the plight of women of color, women in poverty, and lesbians). To be effective, professional helpers working to foster social justice must keep the entire matrix of power, privilege, and oppression at the center of their thinking and at the center of therapeutic conversations and interventions (Almeida et al., 2008, p. 56).

White supremacy culture promotes individualized and personalized relationships and reinforces social work interventions that fragment problems. Dialogue about intersecting features of identity and the power and privilege that perpetuate and sustain oppression promotes relational healing. Falk (2007) suggested that social workers must purge the mechanisms of social control from within the profession and "speak freely to expose the ways that they believe social and economic policies are eroding human rights and creating oppressive and destructive social conditions for a significant portion of the world's population" (p. 6).

White social workers can feel trapped in systemic processes of racism that benefit them and oppress people of color (Pinderhughes, 1989). Awareness of White privilege and attempts to distance from White identity leave the social, material, and political manifestations of White supremacy culture embedded in society and do nothing to further the purpose of the social work profession.

To name White privilege as an outcome of White supremacy culture identifies people who are perceived as White and afforded that status in social interactions as constituents. White people often resist being implicated in the transactions of White privilege and deny the existence of White supremacy culture. The current era of global capitalism depends on and exacerbates racist, patriarchal, and heterosexist relations of rule (Mohanty, 2003). Colonization, imperialism, capitalism, neocolonialism, and globalization began with Eurocentric diffusionism in the 16th century. These processes have destroyed in

continued

some cases and jeopardized in others traditions of harmony and justice in "micropolitics in everyday life" and "macropolitics of global and political processes" (p. 230). Developing critical consciousness about a world order influenced by White supremacist culture is an important focus for the social work discourses on cultural competence. It potentiates practice strategies that disrupt social and political processes that perpetuate social stratification and structural inequalities.

DISMANTLING WHITE PRIVILEGE: DEFLATING WHITE SUPREMACY CULTURE

The salience of whiteness as a cultural identity characteristic is well established (Dalton, 1995; Helms, 1992; Ignatiev, 1995; Kivel, 2002; Tatum, 1999; Thandeka, 1999). White supremacy emerged in the British colonies of North America in the 17th century as Europeans arrived from Germany, England, France, and the Netherlands (Kivel, 2002). The term, *White*, was a political construct developed "as an organizing tool to unite Europeans in order to consolidate strength, increasing their ability to maintain control and dominance over the Native Americans and African slaves, which in many places outnumbered Europeans" (Rogers & Bowman, 2003, p. 12).

Rogers and Bowman (2003) detailed how religion, science, medicine, philosophy, and government participated in the construction of White supremacy and noted that White identity has a constantly shifting boundary. Powerful incentives of profit for the slave trader and planter, the temptation of superior status for poor Whites, and the legal and social punishments for challenging racism institutionalized White supremacy as the American colonies grew.

> The material benefits of racial exclusion and subjugation functioned, in the labor context, to stifle class tensions among whites. White workers perceived that they had more in common with the bourgeoisie than with fellow workers who were Black. Thus, W. E. B. Du Bois's classic historical study of race and class, Black Reconstruction, noted that for the evolving white working class, race identification became crucial to the ways that it thought of itself and conceived its interests. (Harris, 1993, p. 1741)

This resulted in structural advantages that perpetuated a possessive investment in whiteness and seduced groups that were initially excluded to assimilate into whiteness (Ignatiev, 1995; Lipsitz, 1998).[6] Irish assimilation occurred during the 19th century and the 20th century for ethnic Italians, Poles, Russians, and Greeks (Kivel, 2002).

A number of people who have participated in the contemporary discourse about White privilege in the United States credit Peggy McIntosh with being a pioneer in the effort to expose a particular type of unchallenged advantage, which she identified as White privilege (Dalton, 1995; Garcia & Melendez, 1997; Hobgood, 2000; Hurtado, 1996; Shipler, 1997; Wildman, 1996). McIntosh (1988) stated that she was thinking through unacknowledged male privilege as a phenomenon with a life of its own when she realized that since hierarchies in our society are interlocking, there was most likely a phenomenon of White privilege, which was similarly denied and protected. McIntosh operationalized the daily effects of White privilege in her life and provided anti-racist advocates with a language for identifying the ways White people benefit from the structural and institutional racism in the United States. The discourse about White privilege initiated by McIntosh's ideas has, however, too often stopped short of social action.

bell hooks (1995) illuminated how White people perpetuate racism by operating as if it were only embodied through individual prejudice. The work of McIntosh and hooks suggested that, in addition to continuing to oppose blatant forms of racism, people who are committed to racial justice must also engage in efforts to dismantle White supremacy culture. Wise (2004, 2008a & b) demonstrated that White privilege is a dividend of advantages accrued through slavery, segregation, exploitation, and genocide that continues to benefit generations that were not present during the initiation of these oppressions.

What follows are examples of contemporary benefits derived through sustained generations of White supremacy culture:

Stereotypes	19 men that were Arab and Muslim flew planes into buildings and otherwise rational human beings insist everyone perceived to be like them must be stopped and searched at the airports. Nothing remotely like this happened when Timothy Mcveigh and Terry Nichols bombed the Alfred P. Murrah Federal Building in Oklahoma City—even though Mcveigh's and Nichols's bombing was just as lethal as flying planes into the World Trade Center and Pentagon. (Wise, 2008a)
Profiling	Black and Latino males are three times more likely than white men to have their cars stopped and searched for drugs—even though white males are four and a half times more likely to have drugs [when they are stopped]. (Wise, 2008a, p. 3)
Income	A full-time black male worker in 2003 makes less in real dollar terms than similar white men were earning in 1967. Such realities are not merely indicative of the disadvantages faced by blacks, but indeed are evidence of the preferences afforded whites—a demarcation of privilege that is the necessary flipside of discrimination. (Wise, 2003, p. 4)
Wealth	White baby boomers will inherit $7–10 trillion in property assets that were obtained by their white families during US formal apartheid (i.e., Slavery, GI Bill, redlining). (Wise, 2003)
Presidential Politics	White privilege is when you can get pregnant at seventeen like Bristol Palin and everyone is quick to insist that your life and that of your family is a personal matter, and that no one has a right to judge you or your parents, because "every family has challenges," even as black and Latino families with similar "challenges" are regularly typified as irresponsible, pathological and arbiters of social decay.... White privilege is when you can attend four different colleges in six years like Sarah Palin did (one of which you basically failed out of, then returned to after making up some coursework at a community college), and no one questions your intelligence or commitment to achievement, whereas a person of color who did this would be viewed as unfit for college, and probably someone who only got in because of affirmative action. (Wise, 2008b, p. 1)

Privilege and oppression permute to accommodate the social and economic conditions of every era. For example, the oppression of slavery during the antebellum South was channeled through the convict lease system during the post-Reconstruction era (Ayers, 1984; Myers, 1998). This legacy of racial bias persists today through White privilege, which undergirds the disproportionate incarceration of people of color (Pewewardy & Severson, 2003).

> [T]he fault lines of race, gender, culture, class, and age help shape our history and experiences as surely as the fault lines of sexual and gender identity. Candid discussions about the interrelationships of these factors in the creation and administration of crime policy is often discouraged, if not outright suppressed, or characterized by the dynamics of accusation and defensiveness. (American Friends Service Committee, n.d., p. 1)

Throughout the U.S. history human and civil rights have been appraised, assigned values based on identity characteristics, and bartered for privilege. A focus on cultural equity can bankrupt White supremacy culture by diminishing the value of White privilege.

Almeida, Hernandez-Wolfe, and Tubbs (2010) described how focusing on cultural equity can empower social workers to move beyond thinking of cultural competency as a professional achievement so they can disrupt manifestations of privilege and power through their practices. Social work that is informed by critical thinking and focused on cultural equity can redress power imbalances by infusing healing processes with means for accountability and reparations (Almeida et al., 2008; Hernandez et al., 2005; Waldegrave, Tamasese, Tuhaka, & Campbell, 2003).

CULTURAL CONTEXT MODEL: A CULTURAL EQUITY APPROACH

Cultural equity (Almeida et al., 2010) approaches are organized around relational healing and circumvent several dimensions of White cultural supremacy that are imbedded in social work practices that advance compartmentalization. The Cultural Context Model (CCM) was originated by Rhea Almeida as an approach that promotes thinking about "ways to connect past, present, and future legacies within the matrix of critical consciousness, empowerment, and accountability" (Almeida et al., 2008, p. 6).

A guiding principle of the CCM is that liberation is a healing endeavor informed by critical consciousness. Freire (1970/1997) maintained that only discourse that requires critical thinking is capable of generating critical thinking. Freire's concept of *conscientizacao*, which "refers to learning to perceive social, political, and economic contradictions, and to take action against the oppressive elements of reality," (p. 17) is a basis for understanding the significance of critical awareness in liberation. Critical consciousness is a standpoint that emanates from structural analyses of the interactions between privilege and oppression and results in behavioral changes that challenge structural inequities.

"Healthy families, whose members demonstrate love, mutual respect, caring, support for differences, reciprocity, and equal distribution of power among adults, thrive with the support of communities that embody these values" (Almeida et al., 2008, p. 1). Models of social work practice that transcend the beliefs, behaviors, and structural arrangements that dehumanize people and compartmentalize and fragment communities promote and reflect challenges to White supremacist culture. The CCM is organized around the interrogation of how power, privilege, and oppression intersect to perpetuate abusive and coercive power. People are provided opportunities to draw comparisons between processes that feed from compartmentalization and social norms that perpetuate segregation.

The CCM links social justice to interventions (Almeida et al., 2008). A liberation-based model of healing built on social justice and cultural equity, it foregrounds intersectionality (Cesaire, 1972; Crenshaw, 1994; Freire, 1978; Said, 1993; Spivak, 1989, 1990) and, therefore, circumvents the fragmentation that occurs through therapeutic processes that attempt to understand people through compartmentalized features of their identity and diagnostic categories. A perpetual focus on interlocking systems of oppression, privilege, and power supports the development of healing alliances among diverse people. Connections between individual problems and broader social contexts are exposed, which helps people recognize that they are part of a network of domination (Almeida et al., 2008). From this standpoint they can "envision being part of a framework for liberation. With more options, [people] are freed from the burden of individual pathology and empowered toward change through social action" (p. 6).

This approach incorporates conversations that expose how features of White supremacy culture result from and protect dominating power structures, which helps people reflect on their situation so that they can understand oppressive systems and work for change. McMahon and Allen-Meares (1992) revealed that social workers have no neutral position in their practice. Social workers must acknowledge and understand their social locations, roles, and sanctioned power and incorporate responsibility and accountability into their practices.

Challenging the trajectories of power and privilege is as crucial in this work as voicing the subjugation of oppression.

> Imagine consulting with a white husband and wife, both top executives at Fortune 500 firms, whose 13-year-old son has been caught stealing from classmates. Many therapists would help the family seek the origin of the boy's stealing by exploring intergenerational legacies of loss and displacement. Most therapists would not, however, initiate a conversation about the wave of corporate crime grabbing headlines these past several years, nor would they ask the parents to describe their own business practices. While the individual sense of responsibility must be balanced within the collective, these legacies are at least as likely as multigenerational patterns to contribute to the presenting problem, and they need to be examined. (Almeida et al., 2008, p. 5)

Processes in White culture that depend on the subjugation and oppression of others have not been questioned through social work practice because they are perceived rights instead of choices. The CCM is the type of approach that McMahon and Allen-Meares (1992) promoted in response to findings of racism in the social work knowledge base.

Gems of wisdom in the social work knowledge base have exposed White supremacy culture in social work and provided guidance for liberatory practice alternatives for decades (Fibush & Turnquest, 1970; Pinderhuges, 1989; Shannon, 1970). The focus of this scholarship has not, however, rallied widespread professional interest and investment because it is not perceived as economically viable or socially valued. Most social workers are educated and invested in providing treatments and interventions "that stand in the way of the implementation of better solutions" (Sarnoff, 2001, p. 27).

Service providers routinely define the "needs" of others as the services they provide. This makes a mockery of the needs-assessment process considered the first step in any type of program development, and it comes as no surprise that counseling is often defined as a need, because government agencies and private funders traditionally ask social workers and other counselors to conduct needs assessments. So, for example, although crime victims consistently report that emergency funds and security items (such as locks) are the things they most need after crimes [Davis & Henley as cited in Sarnoff], they instead tend to be provided with more and more counseling [Sarnoff as cited in Sarnoff].... Another problem is that service providers often draw conclusions based on preconceived beliefs rather than seeking the truth. (p. 108)

The CCM promotes an inductive approach to relational healing by situating what are traditionally defined as "clients' problems" in social contexts of peoples' lives. Social justice, rather than pathology, is the focus of interventions that promote liberation beyond resolution of individualized problems and emotional duress.

Almeida et al. (2008) detailed how the following features of the CCM can be the catalysts for "effective resistances against culturally dominant discourses and practices" (Guilfoyle, 2005):

- Promoting critical awareness of diversity and power,
- Emphasizing how "normal" hierarchies of power, privilege, and oppression perpetuate suffering,
- Demonstrating the link between fairness and relational healing,
- Expanding the therapeutic encounter to include a community with critical consciousness rather than promoting consciousness one family at a time,
- Defining empowerment in collective rather than individual terms,
- Linking social activism to therapy as a means for empowering communities, families, and self,
- Inviting and embracing systems of accountability for all participants, including therapists,
- Creating a basis for developing authentic relationships across diverse communities, and
- Helping people think about ways to connect past, present, and future legacies within the matrix of critical consciousness, empowerment, and accountability. (p. 101)

Contextualizing problems within "larger crucibles of historical and contemporary public abuse toward marginalized groups" (Almeida et al., 2008, p. 5) invites White clients to begin a process of dismantling their White privilege. Understanding the translation of White privilege through intergenerational behaviors that promote privacy, ownership, and hierarchical statuses can help White clients restore their ability to engage in equitable relationships instead of confounding well-being with perceptions of status.

The goal of raising White privilege to consciousness in social work practice with White clients is to promote empowerment and accountability. Interactions between internalized dominance and repression and externalized dominance and oppression can be exposed through the development of critical consciousness. This process requires looking at self in relation to others (Hernandez et al., 2005).

Helping Whites to name injustices that they participate in and benefit from is an early step in moving toward liberation (Waldegrave et al., 2003). This is very different than starting at a personal point where most Whites will say that they are not racist or they have moved beyond the overt racism of their parents' generation. Examining White supremacy culture through public discourse takes the focus off the personal moral motive of the individual and situates White people within a systemic context for change.

Social workers want to foster the ability for their clients to think systemically, and this is a way to provide that guidance. However, resistance to this process can happen, and it is important for social workers, particularly White social workers, to understand how to assess resistance in their White clients, as well as themselves. The New Zealand Just Therapy team has defined three forms of resistance in working with White clients (Waldegrave et al., 2003):

Paralysis:	When Whites are challenged with their own racism and gender oppression, they have a guilt response that focuses only on their shame. Most White people become stuck in this position.
Individualizing:	When White people are challenged with their own racism and gender oppression, they separate from their cultural history and claim they can only be responsible for their "personal behavior." Examples: "I wasn't a part of slavery, so therefore I am not responsible for it." "I didn't deny women the right to vote, so therefore I am not responsible for it."
Patronizing:	When White people are challenged with their own racism and gender oppression, they become "self-appointed spokespersons" for the group their culture oppresses. In this definition, White people will "put words into the mouths" of people of color. These statements are usually inaccurate and create resentment.

In response to this, the Just Therapy team developed a system of caucusing, where discussions can occur between same race groups on concepts of equality and all caucuses will eventually meet to present their ideas in a collective community (Waldegrave et al., 2003). This is done so that the White people do not burden people of color with a process of discovery denied through their own socialization process (Tatum, 1994). Likewise, people of color have time and space to caucus about experiences of racism without having to explain it to White people (Waldegrave et al., 2003). When the caucuses come back together to discuss equity issues, there is increased potential for authentic collaboration.

INSTITUTE FOR FAMILY SERVICES: ORIGINS AND FEATURES OF THE CCM

The structure of the CCM departs from traditional Eurocentric models where there is one therapist in the room and individual or group sessions are the modality through which service is provided. The CCM incorporates a team of diverse therapists and clients. Concepts and processes that are specific to the CCM are socio-education, gender-specific circles, community culture circles, and critical consciousness.

Engagement begins when clients have an intake at the Institute for Family Services (IFS) and a genogram is completed (Hernandez et al., 2005). The genogram is revisited in subsequent sessions and shared with other members of gender-specific and community culture circles. Sharing the genogram enables therapists and community members to hold/remember the family story and patterns of interaction.

In addition to questions and content gathered for a traditional genograms, the CCM poses questions regarding race, class, gender, and sexual orientation. For White clients, therapists want to understand the history of White privilege over several generations of the family and link it to the public context of power and oppression. White clients may be asked, for example:

- How did your ancestors acquire their land? How has that benefited you and your family today?
- What organizations did your family belong to, or what public status did your family hold in their community?

Clients can respond about prior generations and their present situation.

After the initial intake is completed, family members participate in an eight-week gender-specific socio-education phase of therapeutic treatment. Socio-education is where film clips, books, articles, and sponsor narratives are used to create dialogue and inquiry among clients, therapists, and sponsors regarding the ways relationships are constructed in society around race, class, gender, and sexual orientation (Hernandez et al., 2005). This process helps to raise critical consciousness around the intersections of power, privilege, and oppression in society and how families are impacted. This eight-week socio-education process enables clients and therapists to discuss empowerment and accountability.

Although gender specific, the socio-education culture circles are not formed around presenting problems. Rather, members in the circle are seeking treatment for different reasons. The CCM joins clients around witnessing stories of liberation that are different from their own experiences, which circumvents focusing on the pathology of a problem (Hernandez et al., 2005).

One therapist works in the room with clients, and the remainder of the therapists work from behind a mirror giving input into the room via a device in the therapist's ear. This ensures a team of therapists, rather than an individual, hears all the information and serves to balance the process of accountability and empowerment in the room (Hernandez et al., 2005). For White clients, this begins the process of dismantling their White privilege as privacy and ownership maintain hierarchal statuses (Wise, 2004).

Once the eight-week socio-education process is complete, clients are placed into larger community culture circles where men and women meet together and have their own gender-specific circles in alternating weeks. Sponsors are adult members of the community who are farther along in their therapeutic process and have completed a 12-week training (Hernandez et al., 2005). Sponsors are assigned to same gender clients and help build compassion, relatedness, and critical consciousness in clients by expanding conversations about family life and sharing their own family stories. Whether in session or at community events, sponsors model equity in relationships.

Critical conscious raising is a way to challenge unexamined beliefs and initiate transformation within families and between families that become part of healing communities. This process is built upon looking at self in relation to others (Hernandez et al., 2005). For White families this is very important to their therapeutic process as most White families have never discussed White privilege or their relationships to communities, that is, White families typically view themselves as discrete units with loose and variable community relationships.

Therapists use film clips, and other socio-education materials, to provide a public context in which to discuss White privilege as it intersects with other oppressions. This helps White families take the focus off their personal story and begin to think systemically. In addition to this, it helps White families move through their White guilt or shame and not remain paralyzed in a victim role (Waldegrave et al., 2003). Empowerment and accountability evolve from critical consciousness as perpetual polyrhythmic processes instead of as treatment goals. The following case examples evidence the effectiveness of CCM in clinical practice.

Case Example: Sandra

Sandra was a 45-year-old White woman who presented to treatment after being turned away from several public and private systems of care. Sandra's ex-husband threatened to sue providers that became involved in supporting her. He used the court system to deplete her energy and resources in a five-year period following their divorce. He had a documented history of domestic violence that included severe physical abuse that required Sandra to be hospitalized. Additionally, he had a substantiated history of physical and emotional child abuse to two of the four children Sandra and he had together.

Despite Sandra having been given custody of her four children (two boys and two girls), teenagers at the time of treatment, the court continued to entertain her ex-husband's motions and conducted continuous hearings questioning her abilities to parent the children. The court system seemingly ignored the impact of the abuse the children witnessed and experienced by their father. Using a claim of parental alienation syndrome, a tactic often employed by men who have used domestic violence and then attempt to turn the responsibility of their children's responses on to the mothers who have custody of the children, Sandra's ex-husband continued to exploit Sandra and the children using the power of the court as a mechanism of control.

Sandra joined treatment with an agency that used the CCM, which is a social justice approach to mental health. The team of therapists included a White woman and African American man, the co-directors of the agency, a White female therapist, and several men and women of color who served as sponsors. The sponsors were individuals who had made a commitment to social justice and nonviolence; they supported others in their treatment as they continued working on their own personal goals.

Sandra and her children had an intake session with two of the therapists from the team and were introduced to sponsors immediately. They then became part of gender-specific circles for socio-education. Subsequently, they met every other week in a mixed-gender community and continued meeting in gender-specific circles on alternating weeks. All treatment was done in the context of the culture circles, a healing community that worked on developing a critical consciousness of race, class, gender, and sexual orientation. This consciousness then informed Sandra's efforts to address individual treatment goals and community goals of social justice.

The culture circle was made up of a diverse group of people who came in for various presenting issues. There were several men, mainly Black and Latino, who had recently returned home from incarceration and were required to receive mental health treatment as part of probation. There were many women, mainly African American, who were attending to support their children who had been involved in the juvenile justice system. There were also a few men and women, White and Black, who were coming in voluntarily for family issues, that is, marital conflict or problems with their children's behavior. Two of the sponsors had joined the group after losing their children to community violence and needed support to grieve and heal from this traumatic loss.

Sandra came into a culture circle that offered an alternative community for healing. As a White woman struggling with overcoming the impact of domestic violence and continued exploitation by her husband through the court system, she had been seeking a safe place for her and her family to heal. Through the process of socio-education, she developed a critical consciousness of the patriarchal system that upheld and perpetuated physical and emotional violence toward women and children. At the same time, this oppressive force was made explicit and validated as a debilitating influence on her and her family, and she was also supported and challenged to address the privilege she owned as a White member of the community and society.

Although Sandra had serious financial constraints, and at times had relied on public assistance to support her family, she came to understand that her experience as a White person afforded her benefits even in the midst of her struggle. Listening to the experiences of women of color who struggled with domestic violence and the court system, Sandra was able to become more present to both her experience of oppression as a working-class woman and her privilege as a heterosexual White person.

As clients undergo this process of reflection and dialogue, there are opportunities for growth as the pull to retreat to the safety of privilege rears its head. Sandra experienced this when she came to the culture circle one night and had been feeling especially frustrated and distraught about her oldest daughter's behavior. Her daughter had been breaking curfew, smoking marijuana, and engaging in promiscuous behavior. In the midst of court proceedings initiated by her husband to prove her an incapable parent, her daughter's behavior posed a threat to Sandra maintaining custody of her children.

By this time, Sandra had been part of this therapeutic community for three years. She had worked on her own treatment goals and participated in social justice activities that the culture circle had designed—the most recent being a basketball tournament that raised money for the victims of Hurricane Katrina and a gay rights organization that was representing victims of a local bias crime. On this night, Sandra came into the group and felt the urgency of her personal circumstances. Despite her tenure with the community and her understanding of the treatment process, Sandra wanted her needs addressed immediately.

A new woman came into the circle that night. The group subsequently began with a socio-education process of viewing a movie clip and having a dialogue about power, privilege, and oppression in order to create a framework for the new group member's understanding of the social and political dynamics of her situation. Sandra became frustrated with having to hold her personal story through this process and repeatedly interrupted the circle and the dialogue in attempts to get her needs met. After becoming visibly frustrated that her attempts were not working, she left the circle but not before disrupting the group.

She later called sponsors to discuss what happened and to again try to get some support about her immediate situation. She called two male sponsors and did not call any of the female sponsors whom she had known for three years and who had undergone similar experiences with their own children. Sandra received support from the team and community around her use of White privilege in this scenario and after several weeks of dialogue and analysis among the culture circle members, Sandra wrote a letter of accountability to the community for her misuse of power and privilege. It read,

> Initially, when my behavior at group a number of weeks ago was brought to my attention and feedback was given to me about it, I felt defensive and did not grasp what you were all trying to tell me. I was so caught up in my own feelings of distress. I was focused on feeling like you didn't understand me and how I felt. However, as time went on and I was supported to listen to the feedback I have come to the following understanding.
>
> I know that on that night, I was being rude and selfish—more concerned about how I was feeling than anyone else. Specifically, I know that I should have waited and participated in the socio-ed piece—especially since it was Debra's first night with us. Instead I was demanding and immature—wanting the session to revolve around me so that I could get immediate relief from my discomfort and distress.
>
> In thinking about the hierarchy of power, privilege, and oppression, I understand that as a white woman I have privilege in society that gives me this sense of entitlement and excuses my selfish behavior at the expense of others. I kept focusing on my motives, which were not bad or meaning to hurt anyone else, but my behavior did have an impact on others regardless of my conscious intent. The reality is I have privilege and I used it selfishly, which diminished, disrespected, and hurt the other women in the room, especially the women of color. I have a long relationship with the female sponsors in this circle and when I called the men rather than you, I understand how disrespectful and disempowering that was considering how you have so much to offer from your experience and how much you have supported me these past three years.
>
> I have been and will continue to work on sorting this out and monitoring my behavior in this area, and I welcome your feedback to me as you see me fall back into these patterns. I also used my privilege when I disrupted the group. This is typical of how whites operate in society, circumventing the standards laid out for everyone when it doesn't meet our needs and expecting special treatment. While I am in distress, I recognize that everyone comes in here with a struggle. My sense of entitlement that my pain was greater than everyone else's and that the process should have stopped and been altered to meet my needs came out of the abuse of my white privilege.
>
> I am so sorry for my behavior. I want you to know that this is the first place I have received support and even more than that a sense of hope for the future of my family and for the world. I am committed to receiving your feedback in the spirit of wanting to grow in maturity and awareness of privilege and social injustice. Please let me know if there are any issues that I missed or did not address sufficiently in this letter.
>
> *Sandra*

The community processed this letter and much of the dialogue focused on how the people of color in the circle had never heard or experienced a White person assuming responsibility for the misuse of White privilege and explicitly detailing what White privilege looks like in interpersonal and social interactions. They discussed slavery and the distortion of history that obscures White supremacy and White privilege, focusing on oppression alone, which results in people of color feeling the brunt of the responsibility with this one-sided account of "truth."

In hearing the account of privilege, the community expressed a sense of relief for having the connection made between the unspoken process of privilege and its multiple effects on people of color, their value to others, and the possibility for a community redefined.

Case Example: Ben

Ben was a 23-year-old White man who was charged with federal offenses for trafficking drugs across national borders. He was caught with large amounts of cocaine and over $35,000 cash and arrested in a large drug ring that included others being charged with extortion and murder. Ben grew up in a White, middle-class neighborhood and his family was devastated by his arrest. His father was involved in textile manufacturing and traveled to China often and his mother was a registered nurse. Ben's older sister was about to be married and the family had been focused on planning for this joyful occasion. Ben's father had hired a prominent attorney and they had presented for treatment about six months before Ben was to be sentenced.

Ben's father called the office and said that he was seeking treatment at this site because of the program's reputation for supporting families impacted by incarceration. He then went on to say that he was concerned about privacy and wanted to ensure that his family's situation would be kept confidential. He struggled with the idea of working with a team of therapists and was adamantly opposed to entering the culture circle. He wanted a private consultation with one of the co-directors to discuss the specific nature of what was happening with his son and the impact it was having on his family, especially his wife who he said had been very depressed and fearful for her son's well-being in a federal prison.

Ben, his mother, and his father came in for their first session and met the team and several sponsors during their intake in spite of their initial struggle with the community model of treatment. As they joined the gender-specific culture circles, Ben and his dad in the men's circle and his mom in the female circle, they participated in socio-education and deconstructed their own family story within the larger context of patriarchy, capitalism, power, privilege, and oppression. In a therapeutic community that included several men of color who had been charged with lesser offenses than Ben and had received harsher sentences due to oppressive laws such as mandatory minimum sentences and longer terms for selling drugs in school zones, Ben and his family began to have a different perspective of their family situation.

As Ben's mom became involved with the female sponsors, she began to discuss her role as the emotional caretaker of the family. While Ben's father was distraught about losing his son for years to a jail term, he focused on the practical issues and left the emotional work to his wife. The men supported Ben's father to be more responsible for the emotional caretaking of the family and helped him through the use of rituals in the community to express his feelings, hopes, disappointments, and dreams for the future with his wife and children. They also challenged him around understanding the connection between his son's involvement with the drug scene and his white-collar exploitation of laws in textile manufacturing.

Ben's father explored systemic patterns of White supremacy in disparities in legislation and sentencing for the poor and communities of color as compared to white-collar crime and the protection of White, upper-class criminals from harsh sentencing. In a process of dialogue and reflection Ben's father struggled with appreciating how this benefited his family while hearing how other young men, and their families, received no such protection. The families of color in the community supported Ben's parents around their process of accepting the consequences of Ben's behavior and its impact on their family and holding onto the vision of their family healing from this loss and the grief it brought them. This mutual support, along with the challenges of addressing simultaneous privileges and oppressions, opened up a space for White clients and clients of color to join around social injustice and develop personal and political plans for social action.

Ben's father shared resources from his business connections with other men in the community to assist in employment searches, resume building, and interview training. Ben's mother and father became involved in events that supported communities that were being destroyed by alarmingly high rates of incarceration. Ben received support from the men who had experienced incarceration around preparing for prison practically, mentally, and spiritually. Ben's father, in a session shortly before Ben was to be sentenced for his three-year incarceration, summarized his understanding of their situation as follows:

> I know we are losing our son for three years and the pain that this disruption will cause to our family cannot be lessened. But you all [the therapeutic community] have helped me to understand how fortunate we are even in the midst of this devastating situation. I feel torn—understanding how white privilege is benefiting us and appreciating that—and understanding that many of you and your families do not have the benefits of that privilege. When I came into this process, I had no idea that this would be the direction of therapy—I only wanted and thought I needed support for my family and our personal situation. I felt guilty about the situation my son was in and personally responsible for the course his life was on. I was not conscious at all of the bigger picture that we are a part of.

This family's experience is an example of the benefits that a model promoting cultural equity and social justice offers to White clients as well as clients of color. Training and practice that demands an examination of both privilege and oppression opens up the space for Whites and people of color to work collaboratively within a system of accountability and true empowerment. This type of healing community and the social action that comes from it is the answer to the question of why we need to incorporate an analysis of White privilege in the training and practice of social work. Critical consciousness reminds us of our humanity and moves us that much closer to making liberation a possibility.

REFLECTIONS ON DESCRIPTION OF CCM AND CASE EXAMPLES

The NASW Standards for Cultural Competence clearly outline the ethics of and principles for promoting social justice, which is a core mandate of the profession. The discourse regarding cultural competence often focuses on embracing diversity and difference with respect and sensitivity. Some of the critique of cultural competence presented in the first chapter indeed arises from the inability of cultural competence to effect individual or collective social change.

Notions of cultural competence that promote a focus on "the other" and social workers' internalized feelings and beliefs about "the other" reinforce reductive pluralism, hierarchies of domination, and centers of power (Almeida et al., 2008; Jakobsen, 1998). Social work practice that generates critical consciousness, however, links social justice to individual and collective healing. Revealing the interactions between power, privilege, and oppression creates a basis for developing authentic relationships across diverse communities and opens spaces for White people to participate in efforts to redefine humanity in a culture marked by violence, greed, and dogged competition (Almeida et al., 2008).

Agents of oppression and strategies to promote equity warrant deeper consideration in the social work discourse about cultural competence. White social workers resist accountability when they retreat to socialization processes that insulate White supremacy culture. If they are honest with themselves, for example, White social workers likely view the need to become culturally competent as related to working with people of color particularly in the early stages of their racial identity development. Some White social workers, even in the 21st century, explicate the position that cultural competence is of peripheral concern because they work primarily with White clients. The authors of this chapter experienced both of those sentiments during recent attempts to redress White supremacy culture in a professional social work organization.

Cultural equity approaches focus on reducing the effects of historical and current oppression by challenging power, privilege, and discrimination. Social work practices that focus on cultural equity are undergirded by critical consciousness, empowerment, and accountability and promote connections across differences that humanize all involved. Exploring typical questions that are rooted in White supremacy, such as "Why should I question my social location?" and "How will this benefit me?" while considering who has the privilege not to know, can begin a process of discovery that initiates critical consciousness. Consciously analyzing power systems in the United States in order to understand the interlocking relationships between power, privilege, and oppression bring the mission of social work into sharper focus.

As a profession with an explicit commitment to promoting individual and collective social justice, social work should be informed by a political framework and structural analyses.

Entitlement and privilege are rarely the focus of practice, and the field of social work has not made good on its commitment to social justice. Social work education that fails to prepare emerging practitioners to recognize and challenge White supremacy is incomplete.

Often, in trainings and classrooms that address White privilege, White students will talk about "not feeling safe." This false notion of danger is, as Okun

(2008) maintained, a feature of White supremacy culture that interrupts attempts to expose dysconscious racism. Without focused study of how White supremacy culture influences social work practice, efforts to promote cultural equity are muted.

When White social workers practice from a place of consciousness about the social construction of whiteness and the social and political influences that shape White identity, they have increased potential for understanding how White supremacy transforms interpersonal and collective social relationships. This place of consciousness is also the starting point for developing an understanding of personal agency and liberatory possibilities for manifesting power.

Personal and professional power is often difficult for White social workers to acknowledge. Learning to be responsible and accountable in using power to challenge White supremacy requires focused study of the misuse of power, participation in collective efforts to redefine how power is translated, and the humility to be accountable. Webb (2009) advocated that social work should not be distracted from inequality and injustice through a focus on difference. This chapter calls for social work that promotes critical consciousness about White supremacy culture in order to participate in contemporary efforts to promote individual and collective healing and dismantle White supremacy culture.

NOTES

1. Social location determines how identity characteristics and socially defined categorizations confer *privilege* (e.g., being a middle-class, able-bodied man) or elicit *oppression* (e.g., being a Muslim of Middle Eastern descent) (Pitner & Sakamoto, 2005).

2. Eurocentric diffusionism emanated from the belief that European civilization—'The West'—had "some special quality of race or culture or environment or mind or spirit, which gives this human community a permanent superiority over all other communities, at all other times in history down to the present" (Blaut, 1993, p. 1). Blaut depicted Eurocentric diffusionism as a product of European colonialism and as the colonizer's model of the world. According to Smith (1999), colonialism is an expression of imperialism, and over the past five hundred years, European imperialism has resulted in unprecedented economic expansion through a series of events related to discovery, conquest, exploitation, appropriation, and redistribution. Colonialism created a contemporary world economy that is dependent on resource exploitation and individual competition (Alfred, 1999). Through colonization, economic and social injustice have

become part of a framework of morality in the United States that tolerates exploitation and oppression based on a rationale that people get what they deserve based on their own merit or lack of merit (Pharr, 1996).

3. Any issue can become a wedge issue, that is "a divisive topic to sow discord in your opponents' ranks and peel support away from them" (Good, 2010, p. 1). Issues that can be confounded with elements of race and ethnicity are, however, among the most divisive. Race has been a wedge issue in the United States from the beginning (Dionne, 1991). Indeed, Ignatiev (1995) contended that democratic development in the United States "cannot be understood without reference to white supremacy" (p. 68). Harry Reid's comments (as were reported by the New York Times and CNN) reflected white supremacist biases and stereotypes. Perhaps the most authentic thing Senator Reid can do is to publicly acknowledge that he operates from stereotypes, which he can think critically about and outgrow. More typically when a person's white supremacist beliefs surface, responses focus on justification, denial, and rationalization.

4. The qualitative study from which this excerpt was derived was undertaken between 2001 and 2003 as dissertation research (Pewewardy, 2003). The purpose of the research was to explore how discourse regarding white privilege can be used in social work education to promote individual and collective social and economic justice. The excerpt referenced in this chapter addressed a theme that was beyond the scope of the dissertation research and has heretofore never been published.

5. Anderson (2003, 2006, 2009) detailed Eleanor Roosevelt's deliberate participation in efforts to deceive the United Nations about the severity of human rights abuses in the United States, specifically with regard to white lynching of African Americans. She deterred the National Association for the Advancement of Colored People (NAACP) from pursuing a human rights agenda with the United Nations and placated southern Democrats who buttressed white supremacy by protecting lynching from federal prosecution. Following the Civil War, lynching was a form of terrorism whites exacted with extreme brutality to exert control and perpetuate segregation.

6. White supremacy is reinforced in almost every aspect of socialization in the United States. Graves (2004) contended, "We cannot expect people to willingly reject the ideology of *whiteness* and the practice of social domination, so long as being defined as white in America means you receive so many social benefits" (p. 206). Social workers that fail to think critically about their own socialization are unprepared to interrupt the translation of white supremacy culture.

Cultural Competence with African Americans

CHAPTER 10

Ruth G. McRoy and Margaret Lombe

DEFINING CULTURAL COMPETENCE WITH AFRICAN AMERICANS

Numerous definitions of cultural competence exist. For example, Lum (1999) defines cultural competence as "the ability to understand the dimensions of culture and cultural practice and apply them to the client and the cultural/social environment" (p. 29). Other scholars have looked at cultural competence as practice guided by the acquisition of skills, knowledge, attitudes, and values equipping the practitioner to effectively and adequately work with clients of diverse cultural backgrounds (Williams, 2009). Similarly, scholars have also used the lens of cultural humility to underscore the need for a practitioner to have a long-term commitment to ongoing self-evaluation and flexibility, to be sufficiently humble when seeking knowledge about cultural differences, and to be able to redress the power imbalances in a cross-cultural encounter (Tervalon & Murray-Garcia, 1998). In a social work practice context, cultural competence involves the mutual consent of the worker and the client to become culturally proficient by participating together in the exploration and learning of cultural and ethnic history, values, and behavioral issues that are relevant to understanding particular problems in the helping relationship as part of the micro practice process and to work toward the development of meso and macro policies and programs that benefit clients who are culturally and ethnically diverse (Ridley, Baker, & Hall, 2001). Cultural competence is achieved through the development of personal and professional cultural awareness, knowledge acquisition, skills, and inductive learning about a specific population. This chapter examines these dimensions in relation to African Americans.

In 1989, Cross, Bazron, Dennis, and Isaacs proposed a continuum of competence that ranges from cultural destructiveness to cultural incapacity, cultural blindness, cultural precompetence, cultural competence, and finally, cultural proficiency. According to their continuum, cultural destructiveness refers to situations in which individuals exhibit attitudes and behaviors designed to crush or destroy a culture. In practice, this includes harmful acts such as denying people who are often disempowered access to resources. Historical practices that have denied African Americans employment or educational opportunities due to race are examples of cultural destructiveness (*Oppression*, 1998). Practitioners who are culturally incapacitated are not actively culturally destructive, yet they may adhere to values and beliefs that perpetuate racist stereotypes of African Americans. For example, those who fall in this domain of the cultural competence continuum might believe that African American families are pathological or all African American children perform poorly in school and might expect that they will be overrepresented in special education classes. They are likely to "blame the victim" (Ryan, 1976). The consideration of systemic factors as potential causes is unlikely among these individuals.

Cultural blindness refers to situations in which practitioners deny any differences between groups and assume that practices used with the majority population, generally Whites, may work equally as well with African Americans. For example, an adoption worker who finds that the majority of families who attend an adoption information meeting are White might assume that Whites are the only families who want to adopt, without considering factors that may be serving as barriers to African American families coming forward to adopt. Moreover, culturally blind practitioners may assume that no special efforts or changes in services are needed to recruit and retain African American prospective adoptive families.

Individuals who have cultural precompetence recognize their strengths as well as weaknesses in providing services to African Americans and seek to become more culturally sensitive and aware. Social workers at the precompetence level might suggest the need for staff diversity training, might enroll in prejudice awareness training, or might express the need for greater diversity among the staff or board. They are less likely to "blame the victim," and sometimes they begin to recognize their own personal biases. These practitioners are often comfortable attending diversity trainings that increase awareness of difference but are not yet comfortable acknowledging the existence of oppression or "White privilege" (McIntosh, 1992).

Culturally competent practitioners openly express a commitment to diversity and obviously value diversity. For example, they recognize the impact of societal institutions and systemic factors that may lead to an increase in African American single-parent families rather than blaming the families or culture. These practitioners tend to understand the need to consider the social context and diversity among African Americans. They may seek guidance from experts in diversity and may commit to training for their staff. Culturally competent practitioners often recognize the need to hire more than one African American staff member and insist that African Americans are included in the pool of all potential staff hires or board members.

Finally, those practitioners who are culturally proficient hold African American culture and diversity in high esteem. They recognize the need to go beyond tokenism in hiring and are likely to include on a regular basis mandatory diversity or anti-racism training for all staff, may hire a director of diversity, and may include and continually assess the effectiveness of diversity and/or social justice mission statements and goals in their policies and procedures. They believe in holding the agency accountable for diversity and may evaluate collaborators in terms of their willingness to require diversity training and to demonstrate their valuing of diversity. To these practitioners, diversity training means more than awareness; it means a commitment to hire African American staff and to train all staff in prejudice reduction or undoing racism, as well as a commitment to social and economic justice. It also means a commitment to gaining knowledge about effective strategies for serving African American clients including Afrocentric practice approaches based on African principles and values.

The following sections are designed to highlight the multidimensionality of cultural competency with African Americans. They focus on knowledge, skills, and inductive learning. More specifically we review the diversity that exists among African Americans in terms of sociodemographic characteristics and interpersonal styles. Besides providing an overview of "Black" immigrant populations, the chapter offers insight into the experiences of African Americans including past and current oppression. In addition, social services needs of African Americans are addressed. Strategies for knowledge development and skill acquisition for culturally competent practice are included. Also highlighted are Afrocentric practice approaches and strategies for social and economic justice advocacy.

UNDERSTANDING DIVERSITY AMONG AFRICAN AMERICANS FOR ASSESSMENT, PLANNING, PRACTICE, AND RESEARCH

There is much diversity among the African American population in terms of origin, appearance, experiences with oppression, identity, demographic characteristics, residential patterns, social class, interpersonal styles, and patterns of functioning and lifestyles. It is essential to understand each of these aspects of diversity in order to effectively assess, intervene, and become involved in research and practice involving African Americans.

PHYSICAL CHARACTERISTICS, ETHNIC LABELS AND IDENTIFICATION, AND RESPECTFUL LANGUAGE

African Americans range from those having much African genetic ancestry to those with primarily European ancestry. Phenotypic characteristics vary in terms of body size, skin color, and physical characteristics (Diller, 1999). Skin tones may range from very fair (almost white) to very dark. These variations reflect the racial mixing that has occurred over many generations. It is important to understand that oppression stemming from slavery is linked to "skin color." During slavery, the offspring of interracial unions, *mulattoes*, were often given more favored status on the plantation (e.g., as house servants) and may have been sold for higher prices at slave auctions (Comer & Poussaint, 1975; Drake & Cayton, 1962; McRoy, 1999; Myrdal, 1962; Neal & Wilson, 1989). In addition, higher social status was often accorded to those Africans who had more "Whitelike" characteristics. Just as there is diversity in skin tones, there is diversity in other physical attributes. For example, lips may be pencil thin to large and full (McRoy & Grape, 1999). Hair texture may vary from very straight to very curly or kinky. Although some believe the stereotype that "all Blacks look alike," the tremendous variation in physical attributes as well as skin shade demonstrates that there is great diversity within this population.

The diversity in appearance among African Americans mirrors the diverse opinions about how they refer to their ethnic background. It is important for practitioners to know what racial category to use in referring to the population in general as well as how to refer to the racial identity of an individual client. *African Americans* and *Blacks* are the terms generally used in the 21st century to refer to this racial group.

Some scholars differentiate between African Americans and Blacks by using *African Americans* to refer to Blacks who are descendents of African slaves brought to the United States and *Blacks* to refer to all people and cultures of African descent, including but not limited to Black people from the West Indies, Africa, and the Americas (Grace, 1992). Some believe that the term *African American* is the most appropriate of all as it gives respect to the African heritage. Historically, however, African Americans have been referred to as *colored*, *Negroes*, and later *Blacks* and *Afro Americans* (Diller, 1999). Some individuals, however, may resent being called African American and may express a preference for being called Black. Others use the terms interchangeably, as will be done in this chapter primarily for readability purposes. As practitioners develop rapport with clients or in the community, it is best to listen closely to see how individuals refer to one another or to ask specifically how they prefer to be identified. Some persons of mixed racial descent do not want to be referred to by one racial label at all and define themselves as bicultural, mixed, or biracial.

Similarly, in interactions with African American youth, practitioners must feel comfortable asking them to explain terminology with which the practitioner may not be familiar. Terms and phrases such as *That's legit*, *It's ill*, or *That's fresh* (fun, a happening place, good) are often used by African American youth today. It is better to ask questions about these cultural idioms and thus empower the client rather than make assumptions about their meaning or fail to clarify and therefore reduce the chances of developing rapport and forming an effective, therapeutic relationship (Lum, 2000).

Use of titles such as Mr., Mrs., Ms., or Dr. followed by their last names represents a sign of respect for African Americans. This is necessary until the client gives the practitioner permission to use first names. This not only empowers the client but also demonstrates a rejection of historically dehumanizing precedents when Whites called African American adults by their first names (e.g., Susie) while expecting African Americans to refer to White adults and often children by title and name (e.g., Mr. Bob or Miss Jones) (*African Americans*, 1998; Robinson, 1989).

RESIDENTIAL PATTERNS

Data on African American residential patterns suggest that in 2002/2003 the majority, 56% of the 36.2 million African Americans in the United States, resided in the South. This is compared with 18.1% in the Northeast, 18.1% in the Midwest, and 8.6% in the West (McKinnon, 2003). The 2008 population statistics suggest similar patterns. Specifically, 55% of the 39.1 million African Americans in the United States reside in the South. This is compared with 17.6% in the Northeast, 18.1% in the Midwest, and 9.4% in the West (U.S. Bureau of the Census, 2008).

Moreover, most (52%) African American families live in central cities of metropolitan areas. In contrast, only 21% of Whites[1] live in central cities. Those who live in inner cities have greater susceptibility to the negative consequences of downturns in the economy (Burbridge, 1995; Curry, Latkin, & Davey-Rothwell, 2008).

MARITAL STATUS

Many believe that African American families have always been predominantly female-headed. However, up until 1925, just before the Great Depression, the following was true:

> [With] the modernization of southern agriculture afterward—the typical African American family was lower class in status and headed by two parents. This was so in the urban and rural south from 1880 to 1900 and in New York City from 1905 to 1925. Such families were just as common among farm laborers, sharecroppers, tenants, and northern and southern urban unskilled laborers and service workers. This family style accompanied the southern Blacks in the great migration to the North that has so reshaped the United States in the twentieth century. (Harrison, 2000, p. 189)

In fact, from the mid-1700s to the mid-1920s, less than one-fourth of Black families were female-headed. In 1960, only 22% of Black families were female-headed (Billingsley, 1992, p. 36). However, this number began to significantly increase, and by 1970, 33% were female-headed. In 2002, 48% of African American families were headed by married couples, 43% were headed by women with no spouse present, and 9% were headed by men with no spouse present. This is compared with 82% of non-Hispanic White married-couple families, 13% of White families headed by women, and 5% of White families headed by men with no spouse present (McKinnon, 2003). The 2008 census data indicate similar trends. Specifically, 46.7% of all African American households were headed by married couples, 44.7% had a female head, and 8.6% had a male head with no spouse. This is compared with 79% of non-Hispanic White married-couple families, 14.8% of female-headed White families, and 6% of male-headed White families with no spouse present (U.S. Bureau of the Census, 2008).

In looking at the profile of African American children, during the first half of the 21st century, only 35% of African American children lived in married-couple families compared with 75% of non-Hispanic White children. Forty-six percent of African American children lived in single-parent families, 12% lived with neither parent, and 13.1% lived in grandparent-headed households (Annie E. Casey Foundation, 2003). The profile of African American children remained unchanged in 2008: only 35% of Black children were living with two parents compared with 75% of non-Hispanic White children and 64% of Hispanic children. Nine percent of all Black children did not live with either parent compared with 5% of Hispanic children, 3% of non-Hispanic White children, and 3% of Asian children (Forum on Child and Family Statistics, 2009; U.S. Bureau of the Census, 2008). The figures reviewed suggest African American children are much more likely than children of other racial backgrounds to live in single-parent homes; often characterized by limited income and other resources.

Sexual Orientation

Another important issue that must be considered in developing cultural competence in working with African American families is understanding the unique challenges faced by African Americans who are lesbian, gay, bisexual, or transgender (LGBT). The challenges of being a member of a racial and ethnic minority group are compounded when one is also a member of a sexual minority group. The limited research on African American gays and lesbians suggests that many men and women are reluctant to disclose their sexual orientation due to fear of rejection by family members and the church (Mays, Chatters, Cochran, & Mackness, 1998; Meyer & Ouellette, 2008). These institutions have historically provided support to African Americans, yet often have very negative attitudes toward homosexuality. Such attitudes have led some LGBT African Americans to engage in self-denial and sometimes bisexuality "out of cultural guilt or to salvage a bruised sense of masculinity" (Banerjee, 2006; Icard & Nurius, 1996, p. 39). Perceptions of racism within the predominantly White LGBT community also play a significant role in the formation of identity among African American LGBT individuals (Rosario, Schrimshaw, & Hunter, 2004). In any considerations of identity formation, family and community relationships, and help-seeking behaviors, practitioners must be aware of the impact of sexual orientation, racial identity, and socialization experiences on African American LGBT. An appreciation of the limited resources and support that may be available to African Americans as they negotiate their sexual identity is also important to acknowledge.

Age, Education, Social Class, Employment, and Gender

To better understand and assess African American families, it is important to understand their diversity in terms of age, education, social class, employment, and gender. African Americans are generally younger than Whites, with 33% under the age of 18 compared with 23% of Whites. Similarly, African Americans are less likely to be over the age of 65. In 2003, only 8% of African Americans were aged 65 or older compared with 14% of Whites. Although the population over the age of 65 is smaller in comparison with Whites, the poverty rate of African Americans aged 65 or older is 23.9%, which is more than twice the rate of the elderly in general. African American women over the age of 65 are especially vulnerable, as almost 28% live below the poverty line. A primary reason for the high poverty rate among older African Americans is that most (80%) rely on Social Security as their primary and often only source of income. Only 5.3% of older African Americans receive income from dividends, and only about 24% receive income from interest (Beedon & Wu, 2004). The limited income of African American elders has a direct bearing on their lifestyles and options available to them. In African American families, many elderly parents who are no longer able to live on their own live with an adult child, rather than in a nursing home. Historically, these shared housing arrangements have allowed the elderly family member to remain active in the community and often in the church, as adult children often provide transportation and ongoing connections to extended family and friends (Chatters, Taylor, & Neighbors, 1989).

African American families historically and still today tend to view education as the vehicle most likely to ensure economic security (Logan, 1990). In 2007, between 80 and 89% of all Blacks aged 25 and over had at least a high school degree. Black women were more likely to have a college degree compared with Black men. In 2002, 18% of Black females and 16% of Black males aged 25 and above had completed at least a bachelor's degree. This trajectory has continued unchanged into the second half of the 21st century (*The Journal of Blacks in Higher Education*, 2009).

A look at leading economic indicators suggests that although Blacks represent only about 13% of the population, they continue to be disproportionately poor. In 2001, 23% (8.1 million) of African Americans were poor compared with 8% (15.3 million) of Whites. Thirty percent of Black children under the age of 18 were poor, and 22% of Blacks aged 65 and over were poor. Black women are more likely to be poor than Black men. In 2001, 20% of Black men and 25% of Black women were poor. These percentages are two and a half to nearly three times higher than the rate of Whites in the same age and gender categories: 7% of White men and 9% of White women. The highest poverty rates are among families headed by women. Thirty-five percent of Black families and 19% of White families headed by women with no spouse present are in poverty (McKinnon, 2003). The poverty rate of African Americans is the lowest ever measured by the Census Bureau; however, it is still much higher than of non-Hispanic Whites.

Further, for over 50 years, the African American male unemployment rate has been over twice that of White males (Jaynes & Williams, 1989, p. 308). In 2001, 9.3% of Black men and 8.1% of Black women were unemployed compared with 4.2% of White men and 4.1% of White women. In 2005, Black unemployment rates were 10.8% compared with national unemployment rate of 6.2% (U.S. Bureau of Labor Statistics, 2009). Although a notable decline in unemployment figures indicated by 2007, unemployment rates stood at 8% for Blacks and 4% for Whites (9% for Black males vs. 4% for White males and 8% for Black females vs. 4% for White females); Black unemployment rates were still twice that of non-Hispanic Whites (U.S. Bureau of Labor Statistics, 2009). Among workers between the ages of 20 and 24, 16.8% of Blacks are unemployed, whereas only 6.5% of Whites are unemployed. For Black males between the ages of 16 and 19, 60% are not in the labor force compared with 43% of Whites in that age range (Cose, 1999). These figures may even be higher for older workers, a group in which only less than 5% are employed or actively looking for work (U.S. Bureau of Labor Statistics, 2009). This review suggests that some African Americans are doing better than in prior times, but in comparison with Whites, significant differences remain.

The median annual income for African Americans in 2001 was $29,470 compared with $53,635 for Asian and Pacific Islanders, $46,305 for Whites, and $33,565 for Hispanics (U.S. Bureau of the Census, 2002). In 2009, the U.S. Bureau of the Census reports a median income of $33,916 for African American households in comparison with $54,920 for non-Hispanic White households. Although 8% of African American married couples and 3% of White married couples are poor, married couples in general are likely to have more income; 52% of African American married couples, 13.7% of African American female heads of households, and 25.5% of African American male heads of households earn $50,000 or above. About 19% of African American married couples, 58.1% of African American female householders with no spouse present, and 37.6% of African American male householders with no spouse present make less than $25,000 a year. Moreover, current data from the U.S. Bureau of the Census (see Austin, 2008) suggest that 24.5% of African American households compared with 8.2% of non-Hispanic Whites live at the poverty level.

Despite income gains, the racial-wealth gap has widened considerably during the last 20 years (Oliver & Shapiro, 2008). The average net worth for Blacks is $6,166 compared with $67,000 for Whites (Fairie & Robb, 2007; U.S. Bureau of the Census, 2005). The root of the wealth inequality lies in a past in which African Americans were denied opportunities to accumulate assets. The discrepancies in wealth mean that many African Americans do not benefit from the cushion that assets provide in poverty reduction and social mobility across generations.

Much diversity exists within African American communities, and culturally competent practitioners need to recognize that poverty is not synonymous with African American culture. Nineteen percent of Black men and 27% of Black women are employed in service occupations, and 28% of Black men and 9% of Black women are likely to be employed as operators, fabricators, and laborers (McKinnon, 2003). Twenty-six percent of Black women are in managerial and professional specialty positions, and 18% of Black men are in such jobs. Many of these African Americans are classified as being in the middle or upper classes.

Generally, African American families/households have more difficulty moving into the middle class, and households that do enter the middle class are less secure and at higher risk than the middle class as a whole. Overall, more African American middle-class households are at risk of falling out of the middle class (Wheary, Shapiro, Draut, & Meschede, 2008). This is in sharp contrast to the middle class as a whole, where 31% are secure and 21% are at risk. Evidence suggests that only 26% of African American middle-class families have the combination of assets, education, sufficient income, and health insurance to ensure middle-class financial security.

The upper middle class, sometimes referred to as the *Black bourgeoisie* (Diller, 1999) after the Great Depression, historically meant a privileged class of persons who aspired to send their children to elite schools. Currently, many members of the African American upper middle class live in predominantly White communities; hold professional positions such as doctors, lawyers, professors, engineers, and computer scientists; and often define themselves as bicultural or acculturated. Some participate in traditionally upper-middle-class Black organizations such as The Links, Jack and Jill of America, and the Sigma Pi Phi Boule. However, it is important to note that indicators of social class used by Blacks (e.g., income, education, and occupation) are sometimes different from those used in the White community (Billingsley, 1968; Hill, 1978). For example, Logan (1990) notes, "[U]pper class Blacks comprise families of judges, businessmen, and physicians who would be middle class on the basis of criteria used by Whites" (p. 26). In 1987, Hill described African American households with incomes of $50,000 or more as upper class, and those with incomes between $20,000 and $49,999 were designated as middle class. Upper-class status, by White standards, is often based on much greater wealth (e.g., millions) that is either inherited or acquired through a successful independent business and less often from a salaried position.

Finally, there is a very rich group, in a class by themselves (multimillionaires), among African Americans who often serve as prominent role models for children. This group, mostly composed of wealthy athletes and entertainers such as Oprah Winfrey, Michael Jordan, Tiger Woods, and Janet Jackson, is considered among the Black elite.

LEADERSHIP IN THE AFRICAN AMERICAN COMMUNITY: THE OBAMA PHENOMENON

In each generation, leaders have risen and have responded successfully to challenges faced by the African American community. During the period of the civil rights movement, public figures such as Jesse Jackson and Al Sharpton demanded the elimination of Jim Crow practices. This signified the entry of Black politics into the mainstream in a fashion similar to the Irish and Italians (Ware, 2009). On January 20, 2009, millions of people witnessed the inauguration of Barack Obama[2] as the first African American president of the United States. The election of the Senator from Illinois was seen as a turning point in America's history. For many, Obama's entry into the Oval Office is seen as symbolic representation of the belief that systemic racism and inequality have been eliminated (Bobo & Charlse, 2009; Harlow, 2009; Ware, 2009). The election was marked by unprecedented fervor, especially in the Black community. For Black people all over the world, Obama generates pride, hope, and full inclusion and suggested that they are finally "worthy," a recognition of their humanity deserving respect (Harlow, 2009). Within the African American community, Obama is seen as the fulfillment of the American Dream. To many, he is an unprecedented role model for youth, the fulfillment of the promise of freedom and equality. Many Whites and Blacks view his election as a symbolic healing of the pain and shame of hundreds of years of denigration and humiliation of racism. This, however, does not mean problems for Blacks in the United States have been solved. As noted earlier, Blacks still disproportionately reside in poor, segregated neighborhoods and lack economic opportunities and resources for upward mobility. The effects of intergenerational transfers of disadvantage cannot be undone in a year—"the playing field is not level" (Better, 2008; Gilliam, 2006). Having a Black president may not necessarily affect the structures of inequality that have been in place for hundreds of years. However, there is no denying that significant barriers to inclusion—symbolic or otherwise—have been broken.

"BLACK" IMMIGRANT POPULATIONS

In recent years, increasing numbers of "Black" immigrants from the Caribbean and from sub-Saharan Africa have come to the United States. The 2000 U.S. Census reported 881,300 Africans, representing almost 3% of the total "foreign-born" population, entered the United States. Today, estimates have risen to 6% (Osirim, 2008). More than half of these African immigrants entered the United States between 1990 and 2000. Most enter under categories such as refugee, diversity programs, and family unification programs (Osirim, 2008). Thirty-six percent are from West Africa including countries such as Ghana, Nigeria, and Sierra Leone

(Wilson, 2003). The group consists of a wide range of educational and occupational backgrounds. This may range from unskilled laborers to professionals.

Caribbean immigrants comprise a significant number of Black immigrants in the United States. There are approximately 420,000 Haitians in the United States, and the majority live in Miami and New York. However, growing numbers are relocating to Massachusetts and New Jersey. Many were refugees from the political crisis in Haiti. Some Haitian immigrants seeking asylum in the United States had been diplomats or professionals in their home countries. They continue to fight for their identity and recognition in the United States, and they advocate for their homeland (Newland & Grieco, 2004; Stepick, 1998). They are accustomed to referring to themselves based upon their country of origin and may be called *Africans*, *Haitians*, *Nigerians*, or *Somalis*, among others. Although the group shares a pan-African identity, and are often referred to in the United States as *Black*, and viewed as "Black" based upon their phenotypic characteristics, they have a completely different history and cultural background. Also, their experiences vary by social characteristics such as country of origin, reason for migrating, and the capital they bring (Portes & Rumbaut, 2001). Many recent immigrants resent being "grouped" despite the fact that they share a history that is rooted in exploitation, domination, and subjugation through colonization by western countries. Understanding their history and the transnational identity that define people in this category and how this influences the way they navigate social institutions is essential in becoming culturally competent.[3]

It is also essential to understand the impact of globalization on "Black" immigrants. Globalization is characterized by substantial movement of capital, services, ideas, and people across countries and regions (Johnson, Burthey, & Ghorm, 2008). The situation, however, is paradoxical in that while trade and financial flows have been liberalized, mobility of humans, especially from countries of the global south, is severely restricted (Johnson et al., 2008). As a result, a substantial number of immigrants are undocumented, lacking official papers. Within this group may be found victims of one of the most outrageous crimes against humanity—persons who have been tracked across frontiers. Women and children, due to their vulnerable position, are overly represented in this group. This overview suggests globalization presents both challenges and opportunities to social work practitioners. It is very important for practitioners working with immigrants to understand their past experiences and history as well as their present goals. New paradigms may be needed to understand the experiences of people in this group. The cultural humility[4] approach may be one such approach.

INTERPERSONAL STYLES

Patterns of interaction exhibited by African Americans are shaped by culture, racial identity, and the social environment. These factors interact to influence attitudes, behaviors, belief, values, and patterns of communication that are passed on from one generation to the next (Parillo, 2003; Rovai, Gallien, & Wighting, 2005). They also determine one's degree of acculturation. Bell and Evans (1981) suggested that African Americans demonstrate four interpersonal styles that are associated with one's degree of acculturation. Those persons who have assimilated into the

White mainstream culture and whose actions suggest that they wish to deny or reject their Blackness in favor of White mainstream culture are often identified as having an acculturated interpersonal style. Many are more comfortable relating to Whites and limit their social and business contacts with other Blacks.

Those who choose to adopt a Black frame of reference and reject White mainstream culture, norms, and values are defined as culturally immersed. Their orientation is very Africentric, and they are less likely to have many White close friends. They may view many Whites with suspicion and distrust.

There are others who are considered to be bicultural as they are comfortable in both Black and White society. They may have both Black and White friends, and they usually work in settings in which they have to exhibit "double consciousness" (Du Bois, 1903). They function well in both the African American and the Anglo-American culture. They typically adjust their behavior to the identity of the persons with whom they interact and demonstrate bicultural competence (*African Americans*, 1998; LaFromboise, Coleman, & Gerton, 1993).

Finally, those who adopt a traditional interpersonal style tend to value their Blackness and typically have limited contact with persons outside the Black community. Many are elderly or from impoverished backgrounds and adhere to traditional Black family norms. Some may show deference to Whites as was expected many years ago. They may be reluctant to call themselves Black and instead still feel comfortable with the term *Negro*.

Some theorists exploring the development of interpersonal styles, such as Sanders-Thompson (1994), suggest the need to go beyond racial identification as the key component of interpersonal styles for African Americans. Sanders-Thompson proposes a multidimensional model that includes four parameters: the physical parameter involves an acceptance of African American physical features, the cultural parameter indicates an awareness of African American culture and values, the sociopolitical parameter includes attitudes toward economic and social issues, and the psychological parameter includes one's sense of belonging to the group.

Other theorists have begun to examine factors that may influence differences in cultural orientation among African Americans. Noting that racial identity (one's beliefs or feelings about the racial group to which one belongs) is possibly independent of level of acculturation, Landrine and Klonoff (1994) suggest,

> [H]ighly acculturated African Americans (e.g., who have adopted some aspects of White culture in order to succeed in some specific predominantly White context) may accept and take pride in their race or may reject and deny their racial group membership. (p. 125)

These authors have developed a new acculturation scale to further empirically examine ethnic differences in acculturation (Klonoff & Landrine, 2000). Whichever approach is taken, it is essential for practitioners to be cognizant of the within-group diversity among African Americans. As mentioned earlier, some persons of African American descent do not value a particular racial identity at all and may suggest that they are multiracial due to mixed racial genetic origins. In fact, according to anthropologist Munro Edmonson, the average American Black person has 25% traceable White genes ("What Makes You Black?" 1993).

In exploring an individual's racial and cultural identity to determine appropriate treatment approaches, as well as to assess whether the client is experiencing any conflict regarding his or her identity or racial background, a number of factors can be considered, including 1) racial self-identification, 2) physical appearance, 3) race of mother and father, 4) economic status and occupation or profession, 5) education, 6) church membership and other social affiliations, 7) relationship with extended family, 8) language (i.e., use of Ebonics), 9) lifestyle factors (i.e., living environment—predominantly White, African American, or racially mixed), and 10) experiences with racism. Data collection on all of these factors can provide useful information in better understanding the client's interpersonal style and the significance of race and culture in the client's life (McRoy, 1990).

It is essential to understand the diversity among African Americans in order to provide effective services as well as to conduct research with this population and interpret findings appropriately. Questions that must always be asked of researchers studying African American populations include the following: Who was in the study? What was their socioeconomic class? What was the attrition? How was the sample selected? What attempts were made to get greater participation? What was the race of the interviewer? Who was involved in conducting the evaluation? What types of instruments were used? Have the instruments or measures been normed on African American populations? A lack of knowledge about the myriad of systemic factors that affect this population and the extreme diversity of economic conditions, lifestyles, and interpersonal styles can lead researchers to make false generalizations or erroneous assumptions about the population or program (Grace, 1992). Culturally proficient researchers recognize this and use a variety of data-gathering methods, including case studies and ethnographic techniques, to examine cultural uniqueness.

To better understand the cultural uniqueness of African Americans, the following section examines the impact of their African origins on the history of race relations in the United States.

RECOLLECTING THE AFRICAN AMERICAN HISTORICAL AND CURRENT OPPRESSION EXPERIENCES

African Americans have a unique historical background characterized by involuntary migration, slavery and segregation, and continued oppression (Billingsley, 1968, 1992). From the 16th to the mid-19th century, coastal West Africans were forcibly removed from their homes and transported to America. They came from various ethnically distinct tribes (e.g., Mandingos, Yorubas, Ibos, Fantins, Ashantis, and Hausas) who spoke different languages and ascribed to different cultural traditions. They were taken from their homelands in which the family, children, and elders were highly valued. Their rich culture was characterized by "communal aid, religious rituals and celebrations, music and art" (McRoy, 1990, p. 4). Historians have noted that Africans were a very proud people who did not consider themselves inferior to Europeans (Bennett, 1982, p. 33).

Despite this rich history, European slave traders who supplied the labor to the huge American plantations enslaved Africans to provide cheap labor to work in tobacco, sugar, and cotton fields to support the southern agricultural economy.

Originally, unsuccessful attempts were made to use European immigrants as indentured servants and then to enslave Native Americans, but many died from diseases or were able to escape because they knew the land. Africans were more visible and could not blend in, did not know the land, and seemed to be in great supply. They were captured in large numbers, separated from their families, shackled, and forced to march hundreds of miles to the African coast, where they were examined like cattle and packed tightly like parcels into the hull of ships for the dreaded Middle Passage to the Americas. Many were tortured and murdered at sea, others were thrown overboard due to sickness, and some committed suicide. Ten to fifteen percent of slaves who left Africa died along the Middle Passage (Alter, 1997). It is estimated that over two and a half centuries, more than 100 million Africans in all were involved in the African Diaspora, the forcible dispersion of peoples from Africa. Many who survived the journey were taken to Brazil, Cuba, Jamaica, and Haiti, and some were later sold to America from there.

Most African slaves in America arrived on slave ships landing in the southern ports of Virginia and the Carolinas (Winkelman, 1999). They were auctioned and sold to the highest bidder. Considered bondsmen, or slaves for life, these Blacks were treated as "objects" or "things" that were owned by the master and could be bought and sold like any property. In many cases, families were separated to increase profitability. Children of slave mothers also became slaves. Slaves had no civil status and could not enter into legal contracts, so they could not legally marry, own property, sue, or be sued. They were not allowed to be educated, and they were forbidden from assembling, voting, and holding political office (McRoy, 1990, pp. 4–5).

The majority of slaves lived on southern plantations located in seven states, but an estimated 500,000 Blacks worked in cities as domestics, factory workers, or skilled artisans (Bennett, 1982). Women worked either in the fields or as house servants. Typically viewed as sexual objects or property, they were often exploited sexually by plantation owners. To further dehumanize slaves for the purpose of determining the number of congressional representatives, the 1787 U.S. Constitution stipulated that each slave would be counted as three-fifths of a person (Alter, 1997).

Some Blacks were free because they were born in a nonslave state, had been set free by a master, had run away, or had bought their freedom. However, they were only free from physical bondage, but not free from oppression. In the late 1780s, there were about 59,000 free Blacks and about 697,000 Black slaves. By 1860, the number of free Blacks had increased to about 500,000, and most lived in the Southeast. The rights of free Blacks varied from state to state. However, most had low-status and low-paying jobs. Most sought education as a means of self-improvement and advancement, and many were engaged in antislavery organizations and developed natural helping networks to combat poverty and provide services to Blacks (McRoy, 1990, p. 8).

The church played a major role in protecting slave families. According to McRoy (1990), church gatherings gave slaves a brief respite from the toils of their day, gave them a place to release their pent-up feelings of despair and to express their desires for freedom, and gave them an opportunity to develop group solidarity and promote mutual aid.

Drawing upon the helping tradition characteristic of African society, slave families helped one another, whether biologically related or not. Individual slaves looked out for one another and felt a sense of obligation to support family and nonfamily. Fictive kin (nonkin adults close to the family) were often referred to as *Aunt* or *Uncle*.

Slave rebellions, the abolitionist movements, the secession of the southern states from the Union, and the Civil War were among the factors that eventually led to the end of slavery. On January 1, 1863, the Emancipation Proclamation freed slaves living in the rebel states of the South during the Civil War. At that time, an estimated 5 to 20 million Africans were enslaved in the United States (Bennett, 1986). Slavery was officially abolished for all slaves with the signing of the Thirteenth Amendment in 1865.

However, the abolition of slavery did little to alter the historically oppressive relationship between Blacks and Whites in the United States. The dehumanization and "thingification" of Blacks, justified by theories of inferiority and subhuman status, laid the groundwork for the economic, political, and social discrimination and oppression that characterized the postslavery era. During this period, Black codes of conduct restricted the movement of freedmen, and "Jim Crow" laws legalized segregated facilities for Blacks. The systematic separation of Blacks and Whites in places such as schools, restaurants, theaters, buses, cemeteries, funeral homes, water fountains, and restrooms had legal sanction for over 58 years. These segregated facilities for Blacks were not only separate but also inadequate or inferior to comparable White facilities. In 1954, the Supreme Court began to dismantle the policy of "separate but equal" in the *Brown v. Board of Education, Topeka, Kansas* decision, making school segregation unconstitutional.

Beginning in the 1950s and 1960s, the civil rights movement, led by African American religious leaders such as the Reverend Dr. Martin Luther King, Jr., eventually led to the passage of the Civil Rights Act of 1964 and the Voting Rights Act of 1965. Over the years, the struggle has continued for African Americans to be given equal access to housing, jobs, and educational opportunities. In recent years, efforts to redress past wrongs, such as affirmative action policies in higher education, have come under siege.

Another form of oppression that stemmed from slavery is "skin color" oppression. During slavery, the offspring of interracial unions, *mulattoes*, were often given more favored status on the plantation (e.g., as house servants) and may have been sold for higher prices at slave auctions (Comer & Poussaint, 1975; Drake & Cayton, 1962; McRoy, 1999; Myrdal, 1962; Neal & Wilson, 1989). Higher social status was often accorded to those Africans who had more "White characteristics." However, according to laws in the upper south and in the north, any person with "one drop" of Black blood had the legal status of a pure African (Russell, Wilson, & Hall, 1992, p. 14).

Some African Americans have internalized this racist belief that characteristics associated with Whites (straight hair, thin lips, small pointed nose, and light eyes) are considered to be "good" or preferable, as they are more "Whitelike" and thus may be more acceptable to Whites. Those physical characteristics associated with Blacks (kinky hair, large lips, wide, flat nose, and dark eyes) are considered by some to be less desirable because they are less like the appearance of Whites (McRoy & Grape, 1999). Historically, persons with lighter skin tones were more likely to obtain higher status positions and earn more money than those with darker skin tones (Keith & Herring, 1991). As a result of the Black pride movements of the late 1960s and 1970s and changing perspectives on beauty over the years, many began to reject White standards of beauty. Despite this change in attitude, however, "the consequences of having a particular skin shade have not disappeared" (p. 777).

Still today, those with more "Whitelike" characteristics are defined by many Blacks and Whites as more acceptable to Whites and, therefore, may be given more opportunities. Bond and Cash (1992) found that although the majority of African American college women in their study were satisfied with their skin tone, those who desired a different skin color preferred a lighter tone. Keith and Herring (1991), using data from the National Survey of Black Americans (1979–1980), reported that skin tone is a more consequential predictor of occupation and income than parental socioeconomic status. They found that darker-skinned respondents were twice as likely to report being victims of discrimination within the last month than lighter-skinned respondents (p. 775). They concluded that despite progress in race relations, skin tone variations, both historically and now, have an influence on stratification outcomes.

Similarly, Blacks were not only systematically oppressed during slavery, but they continue to suffer discrimination. Equal rights for Blacks in the United States have always had to be fought for, and despite greater access and opportunities, Blacks still experience a great deal of discriminatory and oppressive attitudes and behaviors from the dominant White society. Legislative gains have been made, but it is not possible to legislate White attitudes (Billingsley, 1968).

Even the term *minority*, often used to refer to African Americans and other groups of color, is based on underlying racist assumptions. As Logan (1990) states, the term *minority* actually refers to "power and privilege, not to numbers" (p. 19). The emphasis on power differentials can become an obstacle to helping, as it exacerbates the already unequal power relationship between the client and clinician.

VALUES AND ETHICAL DILEMMAS IN WORKING WITH AFRICAN AMERICANS

In the Council on Social Work Education (CSWE) Code of Ethics, which defines values and moral principles that guide social work practice, emphasis is given to culturally competent practice with diverse client groups including African Americans. These ethics and values are also reflected in the CSWE (2008) Educational Policy and Accreditation Standards (EPAS; EP1.1) (see also National Association of Social Workers, 2007, "Standard 1. Ethics and Values"). When dealing with ethical dilemmas, which may arise in working with clients of African descent, social work practitioners are mandated to seek guidance from the profession's code of ethics.[5] Moreover, according to the standards, social workers should have knowledge about their client's culture and should seek knowledge and an understanding to the client's culture as well as the nature of diversity and oppression experienced by the client.

IDENTIFYING CULTURAL AWARENESS AND SOCIAL SERVICE NEEDS OF AFRICAN AMERICANS

Historically, many African Americans have been reluctant to seek help from social service agencies for a variety of reasons stemming from a distrust of society due to the history of institutional racism and discrimination. *Institutional racism* refers to the recurring ways in which injustice is perpetuated on Blacks in the United States. According to the National Council of Churches: "Both consciously and unconsciously, racism is enforced and maintained by the legal, cultural, religious, educational, economic, political, environmental and military institutions of societies. Racism is more than just a personal attitude; it is the institutionalized form of that attitude" (as cited in Feagan & Sikes, 1994, p. 3). Institutional racism is a form of oppression maintained through a reliance on White norms, stereotyping, assimilation, and tokenism in which people with power mismanage cultural differences (*Oppression*, 1998; Pinderhughes, 1989). One of the most blatant forms of oppression was the enslavement of African Americans in the United States, which was followed by legalized segregation. These racist practices have negatively impacted the economic and social lives of African Americans and therefore must be acknowledged in considering the social service needs of this population.

Neighbors and Taylor (1985) reported that the majority of Blacks still did not use social services. Those who did (14.4%) tended to be poor and sought services from public assistance programs (McRoy, 1990, p. 13). After slavery, however, as segregation and discrimination limited social services to African Americans, self-help efforts including daycare centers, orphanages, private services, and other forms of mutual aid developed within Black communities for families in need. Although never referred to as *volunteerism*, Blacks have always cared for each other in their homes, in their neighborhoods, and throughout their communities (Harper, 1990, p. 240). The Black church in particular has always been very much involved in serving Black families and is one of the few institutions that is Black-owned and controlled. It remains a source of material, emotional, and spiritual assistance (McRoy, 1990). Agencies must find ways to collaborate with families and communities to build on these natural helping tendencies and to enhance service provision.

Understanding spiritual belief systems also offers some guidance in the provision of services to African Americans. Spirituality for African Americans may include church attendance but actually includes more of a belief in a superior power who can provide solutions for problems. Some view problems as punishments from God, and others see the church as one's personal salvation. Because of these beliefs, many African Americans are very involved in missionary societies, Bible study groups, and prayer meetings and have a great deal of faith in preachers (Dana, 1993). For this reason, social service agencies need to recognize the influence of the church and use this as a resource to build relationships within the African American community. Some Blacks maintain a belief in voodoo, witchcraft, and folk medicine. These are beliefs that remain from African belief systems; they also must be explored (Dana, 1993).

According to data from the National Survey of Black Americans (Neighbors & Jackson, 1984), gender, age, and type of problem may influence help seeking among Black families. African American women are more likely than men to seek help as well as to use informal networks. Men are less likely than women to talk with informal helpers about their concerns and problems. This study also found that older Blacks are less likely than younger Blacks to use professional and informal networks. Crawley and Freeman (1992) reported similar findings. Logan (1996) noted other factors that may influence African American help-seeking behaviors, including "lack of diversity among service staff, location of service delivery system, negative perception of the service system, manner in which Black families conceptualize problems and needs and the manner in which Blacks conceptualize strategies for resolving problems" (p. 196).

Assumptions that race is nothing more than a physical attribute can lead to misunderstandings in client–worker relationships. Robinson (1989) notes that "by choosing not to acknowledge the clients' perspective regarding race, the therapist risks disrupting the formation of an alliance that the client experiences as sympathetic" (p. 323). This can lead to early withdrawal from therapy by the African American client. Practitioners must understand racial dynamics as well as racism and oppression and be willing to address these issues in treatment.

As agencies strive to become culturally competent and proficient, their staff must first become acutely aware of how personal stereotypical assumptions about African Americans can affect interactions. It is important for social workers to become self-aware of their own biases and recognize how these can act as an impediment not only to the use of services but also to the accurate assessment of problems (Gary, 1985). Moreover, practitioners must acknowledge that racist behavior can occur within social service agencies. A commitment to "undoing" racism, through trainings, ongoing self-assessments of practitioners, and agency policies and procedures, is needed to better meet the needs of African American clients.

Therefore, it is critical for social workers to adopt a multicultural perspective that "recognizes the multifaceted configurations of ethnicity and race in social work practice" (Dungee-Anderson & Beckett, 1995, p. 459) and accounts for the impact of environmental stresses such as racism and discrimination (*African Americans*, 1998). It is also important to utilize the ecological perspective in developing social service programs for African Americans, in order to focus on the dynamic interaction between the person and environment over the course of the life span.

Dana (1993) suggests that African American clients may go through some of the following stages as they consider becoming involved in the helping process. In the first stage, "appraisal," the African American client may appear very guarded, reserved, or aloof. In the second stage, "investigative," the client may begin to try to equalize the power differential between the client and practitioner by challenging the practitioner and raising questions about the practitioner's background and approach. For example, an African American client may ask a clinical supervisor why he or she was assigned an African American worker instead of a White worker. This "challenging" or "investigative" approach begins to alter the status disparity. In the third stage, "partial identification with the practitioner," the African American client attempts to establish a more personal relationship. The final stage, "loyalty and personal regard for practitioner," occurs when the African American client begins to feel comfortable with the practitioner and becomes less defensive. These stages are considered fluid, and clients may alternate between these responses at various times in the therapeutic relationship (Dana, 1993).

To further establish trust, the culturally sensitive practitioner must acknowledge any racial concerns of the client. If the client and practitioner differ in their ethnic background, African American clients often may assume that the practitioner has less familiarity with their situation and may not be likely to recognize or acknowledge the impact of racism and oppression on the presenting problem. Some may exhibit "healthy cultural paranoia" (Grier & Cobbs, 1968) in their interactions with the practitioner by demonstrating uneasiness and lack of trust in the initial encounters. This may manifest in more "hostile" reactions or reluctance to confide in non–African American practitioners. Instead of assuming this is resistance, practitioners should recognize that it is adaptive coping.

Because of the hesitancy of many African Americans to utilize a social service agency, the practitioner needs to demonstrate sensitivity by acknowledging that the client may have experienced lengthy waits for service in the past or may not have received adequate services in the past. Devore and Schlesinger (1996) suggest adjusting agency hours and service delivery patterns to facilitate the involvement of African American men in the helping process.

In assessing African American clients, workers should use a "strengths perspective" rather than defining all behaviors and problems as pathological. Finding positive coping strategies and looking for family strengths are essential in working with African American families. The pathological deficit approach is a sure way of losing a potential opportunity to help an African American client.

Some practitioners overlook the concrete needs of a family and want to immediately begin to address psychosocial problems. However, many families cannot begin to address issues such as parenting behaviors until the immediate stressors are eliminated through the provision of concrete services. Lum (2000) noted that many problems may be triggered by environmental deficits, and coping is often enhanced when these deficits are reduced.

Because African Americans are more likely to use informal helping networks, Logan (1996) suggests ways to empower African American communities by developing community directories of resources and making them available to families, creating community support groups for single parents or others with special needs, and creating linkages with churches and fraternal groups to aid in planning and implementing programs.

Finally, in working with African American clients, it is essential to consider the practitioner's level of acculturation and experiences with racism. It should not be assumed that African American workers are automatically able to accept and communicate with African American clients. Many African American social workers are products of traditional educational experiences and may not have had much experience with the realities of African Americans in other social classes. Similarly, White workers who believe that race is not an important factor to an African American client or who believe traditional stereotypes of African American clients will have difficulty in establishing positive working relationships with African Americans. Those who overemphasize the significance of race, blame racism and discrimination for everything, and fail to help the client see his or her part in an issue are also not going to be effective practitioners with African Americans (McRoy, 1990).

SOCIAL SERVICE NEEDS OF BLACKS

1. List questions or comments you have heard social workers, educators, or other service providers raise or state about reaching the African American community.
2. Identify five factors that may influence help seeking among African Americans and African immigrant populations.
3. Discuss pitfalls or problems agencies may encounter in appropriately serving African American clients.
4. List ways to address these problems or pitfalls.

EXPLORING KNOWLEDGE ACQUISITION AREAS ABOUT AFRICAN AMERICANS

In order to prepare to meet the needs of African American clients, social work practitioners need to have knowledge of the unique history experienced by African Americans in the United States and to understand the impact of contemporary racism and oppression. These factors must be integrated into assessment, intervention, and evaluation of service delivery to this population. Moreover, the impact of social and economic issues that have affected African Americans in the United States is essential knowledge in preparing to serve this population.

In developing cultural competence with African Americans, social workers need to have general knowledge in the following areas:

- The diverse demographic profiles of African Americans
- African American history, culture, values, and traditions
- The impact of racism, discrimination, oppression, and poverty on behavior, attitudes, and values
- Relationships between African Americans and immigrant populations
- Challenges faced by African American gays and lesbians
- Help-seeking behaviors of African Americans
- Language, speech patterns, and communication styles
- The impact of social service policies and practices on African Americans
- Resources (informal helping networks)
- Power relationships with Whites and other ethnic groups and their impact on African Americans
- Levels of acculturation and their impact on the helping relationship
- Possibility of conflict between professional values and values and needs of clients (Saldana, 2001)
- Theoretical approaches that work well with diverse African American populations, including a range of social classes and levels of education and acculturation (Pinderhughes, 1989)
- Ways to apply ecological theory and psychosocial theory to African American families
- Theories of ethnicity, culture, African American identity, and social class
- Africentric helping approaches

- Stereotypes African American clients may hold toward service providers
- The impact of gender, class, age, sexual orientation, and race on African Americans
- Strengths of African American men, women, and children, as well as of the community
- Critical analysis of contemporary issues and problems faced by African Americans
- Ways to operationalize the strengths perspective
- African American family functioning and family forms
- Disproportionate representation of African American children in special education and in foster care
- The differential impact of social policies on African American families

Social workers also need to have specific knowledge about these areas for each client or client system. For example, the worker needs knowledge about the following:

- Specific issue or problem facing the client
- Client's culture (history, traditions, values, family systems, etc.)
- Prior experiences of client or client's population with service providers
- Client's strengths, family resources, informal helping, network, and help-seeking behaviors
- Client's family functioning and family forms
- Potential stereotypes toward service providers
- History of help seeking
- Impact of gender, class, and ethnicity on client
- Experiences with racism, discrimination, and oppression
- Power and privilege and their impact on the family
- Client's interpersonal style and perceptions of racial identity and relationships

Diller (1999) suggests,

To the extent that White providers can acknowledge the centrality of race to a non-White client and at the same time grasp the nature of their own attitude toward racial differences, the cultural distance between them can dramatically be reduced. (p. 23)

To accomplish this, social workers working with African American populations should possess self-knowledge about the following:

- Level of cultural competence in relation to African Americans
- Ways in which racism, oppression, and discrimination have affected the worker both personally and professionally
- Worker's own racial and cultural heritage as well as how the worker's interpersonal style can affect his or her personal and professional relationships with African American clients (Diller, 1999)
- Ways in which power and privilege have differentially affected African Americans and Whites in the United States

EXPERIENCE AND KNOWLEDGE SELF-ASSESSMENT

Please complete the following self-assessment of your experiences with and knowledge about African Americans. Answer true or false, unless otherwise specified.

1. When I was growing up, my parents had many friends who were African American. ____ True ____ False
2. When I was growing up, African Americans were among my closest friends. ____ True ____ False
3. I have taken a course on African American families or social work practice with African Americans. ____ True ____ False
4. I feel that I have a very open communication style. ____ True ____ False
5. I believe I can learn a great deal from African Americans. ____ True ____ False
6. I see myself as being a. acculturated b. bicultural c. culturally immersed (within own culture) d. other (please explain)
7. When I hear others make pejorative comments about African Americans, I challenge them. ____ True ____ False
8. I am uncomfortable when I hear others make pejorative comments about African Americans. ____ True ____ False
9. I believe knowledge about African Americans will assist me in my practice. ____ True ____ False
10. I have had mostly positive experiences with African Americans. ____ True ____ False
11. I grew up believing the following stereotypes about African Americans:

12. I have the following questions about providing services to African Americans:

FOSTERING PRACTICE SKILL DEVELOPMENT ABOUT AFRICAN AMERICANS

Be aware of client perspectives

According to Saldana (2001), there is much potential for failure in cross-cultural therapeutic work. In each phase of the process, from engagement through case closure, it is important to recognize and acknowledge the potential for miscommunication. For example, African American clients who are seeking help, exhibiting the healthy cultural paranoia discussed earlier, may begin the encounter as follows: 1) assuming the therapist will not understand the situation due to the racial or cultural difference; 2) perceiving social distance between the therapist and client; 3) expressing fear of being judged by the professional; and 4) exhibiting anxiety due to these concerns. Therapists who are unaware of these potential client perceptions may sense the social distance, feel anxious, fall back on stereotypes to explain the client's behavior, and fail to recognize, acknowledge, and address their own or the client's anxiety.

As the therapeutic relationship continues, a client may maintain feelings of being misunderstood, fail to develop rapport, have greater feelings of distrust, and become less communicative in the encounter. The therapist may respond to the lack of disclosure by assuming the client is resistant and may view the client as unmotivated. A client may then cancel appointments or drop out of treatment without any further interaction with the therapist. In such a case, the therapist may exhibit frustration and could potentially misdiagnose, attributing failure to the client rather than to the worker for failing to appropriately develop rapport and overcome the initial social distance with the client.

Freeman (1990) and Saldana (2001) identified specific professional skills needed to work with culturally diverse populations. Many of these skills can be considered "good practices" with all populations. However, the following is an adaptation of these skills for specific use with African American families:

- Ability to communicate accurate information: being comfortable in assuming a "one-down" position and asking sensitive, nonjudgmental questions to obtain information from the client's perspective
- Ability to openly discuss racial and ethnic differences: acknowledging obvious differences between the worker and client and exploring how they may affect the interaction
- Ability to assess the meaning that ethnicity has for individual clients: identifying and understanding the worldview of African American families as being distinct from that of larger society
- Ability to discern between the symptoms of intrapsychic stress and stress arising from the social structure
- Interviewing techniques that enable the client to feel comfortable sharing personal information
- Ability to apply strengths perspective in evaluating strengths within the client, family, and community: assuming the existence of strengths such as strong kinship bonds; spiritual orientation; work orientation; adaptability or fluidity of family roles; high tolerance for environmental stress, ambiguity, and ambivalence; and high achievement orientations (Hill, 1972; Jones, 1983)
- Ability to utilize the concepts of empowerment on behalf of African American clients and communities: assessing strengths within the family and community, including the role and impact of significant others on the client
- Ability to recognize self-help structures in the community: recognizing the traditional family self-help approaches such as the fluidity of family roles, taking in kin, and the role of community agencies and churches in the family's life
- Ability to use resources on behalf of African American clients and their communities: giving appropriate referrals for concrete services if needed before more psychosocial services are provided
- Ability to recognize and combat racism, stereotypes, and myths about African American families: challenging self and others in an attempt to begin to undo the impact of racism and stereotypes in society
- Ability to evaluate the validity of using new therapeutic approaches, research findings, and knowledge with African American populations (Saldana, 2001, pp. 4–5)
- Ability to overcome client resistance and reduce communication barriers
- Ability to self-disclose lack of experience or information and to ask questions in a respectful manner
- Ability to modify services to make them accessible and culturally sensitive
- Ability to recognize the need for having African American professional staff as part of the agency

Social workers may need specific interpersonal skills in working with African Americans. Suggested interpersonal skills include (Madden, Faulkner & McRoy, 2010):

- Ability to use open communication style
- Ability to refrain from seeking permission to call a client by his or her first name until they volunteer their permission
- Ability to appropriately use both verbal and nonverbal cues in communication
- Ability to communicate professionally in a sincere, respectful, and warm manner
- Ability to appreciate the role of humor in dealing with difficult situations
- Ability to recognize and respect the centrality of religion and spirituality to the client
- Ability to demonstrate attentiveness and responsiveness through "active listening"
- Ability to maintain a balance between humility, openness, and expertise

Practitioners working with people of African descent may also need to have an appreciation of the indigenous approaches to helping and the great emphasis these may place on cooperation, collaboration, and community (Obasi & Leong, 2009).

SKILL ASSESSMENT

Please complete the following self-assessment of your skills in working with African Americans. Answer true or false, unless otherwise specified.[6]

1. I have an understanding/appreciation of the value system of African Americans. _____ True _____ False
2. Relationship building skills are essential to authentic partnership with clients of African origins. _____ True _____ False
3. Appropriate use of both verbal and nonverbal cues is important in communicating with African American clients. _____ True _____ False
4. Ability to use input from the client to develop assessments/interventions that are culturally meaningful is valuable in working with African American clients. _____ True _____ False
5. I am able to take stock of my own weaknesses and strengths when working with African American clients. _____ True _____ False
6. I possess the necessary skills to work with African Americans. _____ True _____ False
7. Knowledge of indigenous approaches to helping will assist me in my practice with African American clients. _____ True _____ False
8. I have respect and appreciation for differences. _____ True _____ False
9. Factors that may influence the worldview of many African Americans are:

10. I have the following questions about skills I need to work effectively with African Americans:

AFROCENTRIC PRACTICE APPROACHES

It is important to understand the diversity as well as the commonalities within African American communities. As someone once said, Black families are like all other families, some other families, and no other families. Nevertheless, an understanding of the ethos of African Americans allows one to appreciate the special characteristics that identify them as a group and that set the group apart from other groups. Ethos refers to the common beliefs and emotional responses that stem from a common historical heritage and worldview based upon contemporary experiences that include discrimination, oppression, biased media portrayals, and struggles for equality (Crawley, 1996).

Many believe that the prevailing Western/Eurocentric perspectives are not suited for remedying the conditions faced by most African Americans. Instead, an Afrocentric paradigm has been proposed. The term *Afrocentricity* (sometimes used interchangeably with *Africentricity*) has been used to describe "the cultural values of people of African descent" (Akbar, 1984; Daly, Jennings, Beckett, & Leashore, 1995; Everett, Chipungu, & Leashore, 1991; Schiele, 1996, p. 284, 2000). According to Oyebade (1990), "Afrocentricity is a search for those values that will make man relate to man in a humanistic way and not in an imperialistic or exploitative way" (p. 237). Most social service programs are not designed using African-centered principles for service delivery, rather they are based upon Eurocentric behavioral theories. Although these approaches have merit, they do not adequately account for the worldview of African Americans (Schiele, 2000).

The Afrocentric paradigm presents an innovative approach for understanding behavior and social problems affecting people of African descent. The paradigm acknowledges the collective identity of humans and individual as well as collective responsibility for the welfare of others. This is articulated in the African adage "I am because we are" (Mbiti, 1975; Schiele, 2000, p. 27). Coupled with this is the centrality of spirituality to the welfare of the individual and community. Another idea that is emphasized in this paradigm is the dependence of thought and rationality on feelings. It also underscores oppression and spiritual alienation as sources of human/social problems.

This paradigm has great promise in working with African American clients including youth. It emphasizes the utilization of factors that humanize clients, validate their experiences, and personalize the provider–client relationship. The paradigm accentuates caring for the individual and acknowledges the positive potential inherent in all people—a factor important for African Americans given their history of oppression and discrimination. Another point of emphasis is mutuality and reciprocity between the client and provider, underscoring potential to learn from each other in a relationship guided by respect and validation of knowledge the client possesses on the issue(s) affecting him or her.

Another transformative paradigm is the approach utilizing cultural humility. As stated earlier, cultural humility is a process outlining a lifelong commitment to learning and self-reflection. It involves reexamination of power imbalances that exist between the client and practitioner and uses client-focused interventions. The approach demands humility in development and maintenance of mutually respectful partnerships (Tervalon & Murray-Garcia, 1998). The process of cultural humility begins with the practitioner getting in touch with his or her own cultural identity and background. It also calls for acknowledgment of the practitioner's biases including unintentional and intentional racism, classism, and homophobia (Pew Health Profession Commission, 1995; Tresolini & Pew-Fetzer Task Force,

1994). In working with African American and other minority groups, this approach does not discount the value of knowing about clients' needs, rather it underscores the importance of honest and ongoing self-appraisal and commitment to long-term learning of the cultural dimensions of the experiences of diverse client groups. The paradigm places value on the client's agenda and validates the perspective the client brings to the encounter. The client is seen as uniquely qualified to assist the practitioner in understanding the intersections of race and other identities in shaping the client's experiences. This role reversal—the client as expert and the practitioner as learner—is essential for the development of strategies that truly reflect priorities, beliefs, as well as life stressors from the client's perspective.

The following principles, based on the Nguzo Saba value system, have also been known to be effective in working with people of African descent (Oliver, 1989, pp. 27–32):

- *Umoja* (unity)—to strive for and maintain unity in the family, community, nation, and race
- *Kujichagulia* (self-determination)—to define ourselves, name ourselves, create for ourselves, and speak for ourselves instead of being defined, named, created for, and spoken for by others
- *Ujima* (collective work and responsibility)—to build and maintain our community together, to make our sisters' and brothers' problems our problems, and to solve our problems together
- *Ujamma* (cooperative economics)—to build and maintain our own stores, shops, and other businesses and to profit from them together
- *Nia* (purpose)—to make our collective vocation the building and developing of our community in order to restore our people to their traditional greatness
- *Kuumba* (creativity)—to do always as much as we can, in the way we can, in order to leave our community more beautiful and beneficial than when we inherited it
- *Imani* (faith)—to believe with all our hearts in our people, our parents, our teachers, our leaders, and the righteousness and victory of our struggle (Crawley, 1996, p. 119)

By using such a collective approach, workers may be able to design practice strategies emphasizing group and family strengths that may work more positively with African American populations.

A collective Afrocentric practice approach recognizes that African American families reflect African traditions, Christian beliefs, and adjustments made to slavery ("The American Black Family," 1987, p. 26). According to Schiele (1996), this approach calls for the personalization of the professional relationship by downplaying "aloofness between social worker and client" (p. 291). Similarly, this perspective calls for reciprocity in the helping relationship as social workers recognize the potential for learning from the knowledge and experiences of the client. Social workers who acquire the aforementioned practice skills are likely to be very successful in providing culturally competent services to a variety of African American clients.

GENERATING NEW INDUCTIVE LEARNING ABOUT SOCIAL WORK WITH AFRICAN AMERICANS

According to Lum (1999), inductive learning "is a lifelong process of continuous discovery about the changing nature of multicultural individual, family, and community dynamics" (p. 146). It is based upon the premise that we must move beyond cultural stereotypes through listening to the meanings clients give to their lives and experiences and through observing clients within their ecological systems. Workers' assessments are based upon learning and discovering with clients, asking questions, using a strengths perspective, and embracing clients' behavioral styles, belief systems, and coping patterns (p. 152). Moreover, this approach draws upon qualitative research strategies that include inductive data gathering to seek an understanding of clients' perspectives on their problems. This approach empowers clients, as they assume the role of teacher, and the social worker is in the role of learner.

The inductive process leads the practitioner to approach the client with questions such as "What does X (an experience, belief, person, family, etc.) mean to you?" As the client describes the meaning, the practitioner engages in a data-gathering process through the client's narrative as well as the practitioner's observations. Using such narrative-generating questions and observations, the worker is able to develop an understanding of the client's reality. This data is then used to look for common themes that can be discussed with the client, who can then "confirm them, build upon them, or reject them" (p. 158). This approach leads to a more client- and culture-specific understanding of issues.

In practice with African American clients, the inductive approach suggests moving away from generalized, often stereotypically negative beliefs about African Americans to more of a practitioner–researcher approach. It means that the worker will utilize a strengths perspective by looking for positives rather than pathologizing clients. This is particularly important with African American clients, as so much has been written on this population from a pathological perspective. Using a strengths approach, the worker is able to form a client–worker partnership, and jointly the client and worker examine the client's knowledge and experience. This allows the worker to understand and embrace the client's behavioral styles, belief systems, and coping patterns (Lum, 1999). In this perspective, the worker clearly values the client's knowledge, beliefs, strengths, talents, and coping strategies. This approach is empowering to the client and serves to move the client from a position of learned helplessness to one of learned hopefulness. Instead of workers being in the role of informants to clients, the clients inform the workers and offer their own perspectives on how they think, feel, and behave in specific situations. This tends to broaden the knowledge of practitioners and to increase the likelihood of a successful intervention based on client reality rather than only the worker's evaluative perspective, which is often more narrow.

THE CASE OF MARIAH

Review the following case and respond to the questions listed after it.

Mariah is an 18-year-old African American female who is currently single and pregnant with her first child. She dropped out of high school during her senior year but hopes to get her GED and eventually to become a special education teacher. Currently, she is living in a transitional living program for pregnant and parenting teens because she has just aged out of foster care and has no permanent home. Her baby is due in three months. Her current boyfriend is not the father of her baby. She met the African American boyfriend at a shelter for drug-dependent youth that is located not far from the transitional living program. Her boyfriend hopes to "get clean" and get a job and support Mariah and her child. Mariah is having difficulty getting employment right now because she is six months pregnant, so she is very hopeful that her boyfriend will be able to support her. She has no contact with the Anglo father of her child but believes he is in jail for burglary. Her White foster parents moved to another town right after Mariah turned 18. She planned to be on her own but discovered she was pregnant, and she had no job or place to live. Mariah was physically abused in the home of her birth parents by her stepfather and was removed at the age of 4. She has been living in foster homes since her removal. She has two older brothers who were also removed; she has had no further contact with either of them. The social worker, Martin, first met Mariah when she was assigned her case at the transitional living program.

1. Using an inductive approach, what questions would Martin want to ask to better understand the meaning of this situation for Mariah?
2. What other forms of data collection should Martin use to better understand Mariah's situation?
3. How would Martin utilize a strengths perspective in working on this case?
4. How would Martin develop a positive client–worker partnership with Mariah?

UNDERSTANDING AND ADVOCATING SOCIAL AND ECONOMIC JUSTICE FOR AFRICAN AMERICANS

Gaining knowledge and understanding of the historical as well as contemporary inequities that many African Americans have experienced leads social workers to become more involved in advocating for social and economic justice. Social justice "refers to the manner in which society provides resources for its members" (Miley, O'Melia, & DuBois, 1995, p. 17). Historically and currently in the United States, the dominant White society has differentially held power, privilege, and resources and has treated persons of color inequitably. To maintain this sense of power, some members of dominant groups try to obscure or rationalize the unequal distribution of resources through the process of moral exclusion by assuming that some groups do not merit fair treatment (Staub, 1987). This allows those who have power and privilege to justify maintaining this system. For example, the lower educational attainment of African Americans, as compared with Whites, is often attributed to their lack of ability rather than to the fact that they have had limited access to well-funded public schools and, therefore, have not had access to equal educational opportunities.

Slavery, segregation, and "Jim Crow" laws are all examples of oppressive uses of power (Billingsley, 1992; *Oppression*, 1998). Society's unwillingness to challenge everyday practices of discrimination that result in oppression is defined as structural–cultural violence (Van Soest & Bryant, 1995). A related aspect of oppression is the internalization of oppression in which disempowered people carry out stereotypes and sometimes behave in ways that conform to the negative images society has of them. This internalization process further limits the opportunities for members of oppressed groups. Moreover, some disempowered people find that not only are they isolated from dominant society but also they are made to feel that the problems they experience are self-imposed rather than being imposed by society. For example, in 1965, the Moynihan report characterized African American families as primarily "female-headed," deviant, and pathological. However, in reality, a number of social and political factors were responsible for the undermining of the Black family, including social welfare policies beginning in the 1950s (e.g., Aid for Dependent Children [AFDC], which required male absence from the house for a woman to receive assistance). Such policies began to force men out of the family while "systematically entitling women, and not their husbands, to benefits" (Jewell, 1988, p. 25).

Culturally competent and proficient practitioners can acknowledge and explore the effects of power and privilege, look beyond cultural stereotypes and explanations, and recognize the impact of social policies on families. They seek to become effective advocates for African Americans and to develop strategies for shifting power to and sharing power with African American clients (*Oppression*, 1998). The use of the inductive method of data gathering (discussed earlier) is an example of one of these empowering strategies. Moreover, social workers must commit to the development of strategies for moral inclusion, operate from a strengths perspective, build coalitions with oppressed groups, call attention to inequities, and commit to advocating for social and economic justice in their professional lives.

SUMMARY

This chapter has focused on the unique attributes of African Americans in the United States. Beginning with their forced transplantation from Africa that started four centuries ago and continuing with the ongoing racial oppression and discrimination that they experience in U.S. society today, African Americans are the most racially stigmatized and stereotyped ethnic group in the United States. Due to the history of exclusion, segregation, and separation, much distrust, paranoia, and hostility still exists between Whites and Blacks. Although Blacks have made substantial economic gains in the recent past, major economic disparities still exist in terms of employment opportunities and earnings. African Americans continue to be underserved in many service areas, including the health care delivery system, and to be overrepresented in the population of persons who are poor, in prison, and in out-of-home care.

Vast diversity exists among African Americans, including physical characteristics, socioeconomic status, perceptions of racial identity, and interpersonal styles. Most African Americans have experienced racism, oppression, and discrimination, and those experiences influence their interactions and worldviews.

Many social service agencies continue to find it difficult to reach this population, and social workers are challenged to become more culturally competent to facilitate communication, interaction, and intervention. The utilization of a strengths-based, inductive, practitioner–researcher approach tends to increase the likelihood of effective interventions with African Americans. Afrocentric approaches also need to be implemented and evaluated to determine whether they may be more effective than traditional Eurocentric approaches with some African American clients. Finally, social workers must become cognizant of and be willing to challenge the effects of ongoing inequities and oppression and to advocate for social and economic justice for African Americans.

NOTES

1. In this chapter, White or Whites refer to persons of non-Hispanic origin.
2. Although Obama has a White mother and a Black father, making him biracial, the rule of hypodescent that applies to U.S. racial classification identifies him as Black (Harlow, 2009; Russell, Wilson, & Hall, 1992).
3. Identities extending across national borders involve exhibiting strong connections to home and host.
4. Cultural humility is a long-term commitment to self-evaluation and critique and aims at redressing the power imbalances in a cross-cultural encounter (Tervalon & Murray-Garcia, 1998).
5. The opening chapter of this book gives an extensive review of this (see "NASW Code of Ethics" section).
6. Davis (2001) and Grant (2001) serve as the basis for the assessment questions.

CULTURAL COMPETENCE WITH LATINO AMERICANS

Betty Garcia

INTRODUCTION

DEMOGRAPHICS AND GROUP DIVERSITY

The growth of the Latino population in the United States in the second decade of the 21st century continues to increase at exceedingly fast rates. Latinos represent 15.1% of the U.S. population (U.S. Census Bureau, 2008a). Moreover, Latinos are projected to represent 24% of the U.S. population by 2050 (Bergman, 2004). Mexicans represent the largest group at 64.3% (29.2 million) followed by Puerto Ricans at 9.1% (4.1 million) (Pew Hispanic Center, 2009a,b), Cubans at 1.6 million (Pew Hispanic Center, 2009c), Salvadorans at 1.5 million (Pew Hispanic Center, 2009d), and Dominicans at 1.2 million (Pew Hispanic Center, 2009e). As the largest ethnic group in the United States, the Latino population is projected to triple in size from 46.7 million in 2008 to 132.8 million by 2050 (U.S. Census Bureau, 2008a,b).

The median age of all Latinos is younger than other populations at 27, compared to 31 for African Americans, 36 for Asians, and 41 for Euro-Americans; approximately 1 out of 4 newborns in the United States are Hispanic (Pew Hispanic Center, 2009j). Educationally, Gandara and Contreras (2009) point out that Latinos are "now stalled" at the high school level with only about half of Latino students who enter high school having completed their degree in 2005 (U.S. Department of Education, 2007). Moreover, only 13% of Latinos have completed college, compared to 33% of Whites and 20% of Blacks (Edwards, 2009). Educational levels will be addressed further in relation to national origin and social justice issues. The effects of educational marginalization are manifested in the high poverty level of 23.2% compared to that of the Whites, which is 8.6% (U.S. Census Bureau, 2009). Future census reporting will indicate how devastating the national economic downturn that began in 2007 was for the entire Latino community in the United States.

Immigrant populations are projected to increase from one in eight (12%) in 2005 to one in five (19%) in 2050 (Pew Hispanic Center, 2008a,b). The shift toward the spreading out of Latino immigrants into areas other than the southwest, such as in the midwest, northeast, and the south, has led to increased interest in understanding incentive for the new destinations (Guarnaccia et al., 2007; Light & Johnston, 2009) and unique population profiles. Factors such as political, economic, social network, and language dominance are viewed as instrumental in selection of region for settlement.

Latino elders represent 5% of the total population aged 65 and over, whereas Euro-Americans represent 15% (Bernstein, 2005). Delgado's (2007) review of findings on the status of Latino elders illuminates that Latino elders 65 years and older are more likely to be employed at lower wages when compared with elders of other communities and only 28% of retired Latinos have an income other than social security. The following discussion suggests that it may be valuable to consider the Latino communities in their unique historical and experiential contexts in order to appreciate and grasp the Latino American identity.

While Latinos of Mexican origin represent the majority of Latinos in the United States, the Latino population is a highly heterogeneous group in relation to national origins, historical political context, motives for immigration, and settlement experiences. The differences and similarities between Latinos in the United States are borne of origins arising from nationalities that span the Caribbean, Central, and South America with distinct historical and political contexts that framed migration to the United States. These origins influenced unique qualities of Latinos expressed in, among other things, phenotype (i.e., appearance), language, and religion. Spain's dominance in Latin America often leads to the misperception of Latinos in monolithic terms at the expense of making invisible the richness and variation of Latino heritage. It is also notable, for example, that some immigrants from rural areas such as Oaxaca, Mexico, speak an indigenous language, and not Spanish.

There are some shared traditional, cultural values related to family, interpersonal interaction, and community among most Latinos. However, it is wise to keep the caveat in mind that the role of immigration, national origin, phenotype, and sociopolitical and economic (e.g., privilege, discrimination) factors are highly significant in shaping the experience and identity of individuals. The following points on historical, social, and political distinctions among Latino national origins, while too brief, are presented with the intention of stimulating curiosity on the heterogeneity among Latinos, rather than as reductionist information that obscure the complexity of individuals and their communities. It is hoped that the reader will pursue further knowledge building about Latin American origins and more importantly apply this knowledge as a hypothesis to what Sue (1998) calls "dynamic sizing" where one matches one's preconceptions about someone with the uniqueness of that person.

LATINOS OF MEXICAN AND CENTRAL AMERICAN NATIONAL ORIGIN

MEXICAN NATIONAL ORIGIN The Treaty of Guadalupe Hidalgo at the end of the U.S.–Mexican war led to the sale of the Southwestern states to the United States in 1848. This was followed by tensions between the native Mexican residents and new U.S. settlers that resulted in violence against Mexicans (Acuna, 1972). Early activism in the 20th century focused on land appropriation in New Mexico by Euro-American interests to divest residents of their property and the role of the U.S. government in supporting these interests (Acuna, 1972) . The combination of Spanish land grants in New Mexico and its geographical isolation led to Latinos' strong identification as Hispanics, that is, identification with Hispania, the European Iberian Peninsula. The history of Mexico as a country primarily of mestizos (i.e., combination of Spaniard and indigenous backgrounds) is reflected in the phenotypes of many Latinos in the United States. The heritage of Spanish and French colonizers has resulted in Latino appearance that includes various degress of mestizo and white.

In the early part of the 20th century, during and after the Mexican Revolution, the southwest witnessed one of several waves of immigration from Mexico. The budding presence of Mexican Americans in southern California and growing ethnic tensions erupted in several remarkable historical episodes. The national context of anti-immigrant sentiment and legislation on the national level at the turn of the century and 1920s was felt by many immigrant groups in the United States, including Latinos. The 1931 Lemon Grove Incident in San Diego (Alvarez, 1986) represents one of the earliest successful desegregation cases where the Mexican American community rallied to protect their children's rights to attend desegregated schools. The Los Angeles Zoot Suit Riot of 1943 represents an episode where discrimination exploded into violence in a week-long clash between White, off-duty U.S. sailors and Mexican American youths who dressed in what were called "zoot suits." The incident began when several Mexican American youths were assaulted on the same evening that 11 White sailors on leave were attacked. Claiming that their assailants were Latinos, and perceiving lack of police response, several hundred sailors caravanned in taxicabs into a Latino neighborhood the following night, randomly assaulting all Latinos, with no interference by local police (Parrillo, 2009).

The 1960s led to the inception of the Chicano movement in response to social injustice against the Latino, particularly Mexican American community. The term, "Chicano," previously used pejoratively in reference to Mexican Americans, was brandished in the 1960s as a symbol of self-determination, self-definition, political awareness, and recognition of the importance of strengthening community. The loss of the social movement context of that period leaves that term for many Mexican Americans today with some degree of ambivalence due to its earlier negative significance. Movements such as farmworker rights and international struggles for political self-determination, as in Chile and Puerto Rico, contributed immeasurably to critical thinking on social justice issues in relation to Latinos and to other disempowered populations (i.e., people belonging to low-income group, African Americans, women).

In 2007, an estimated 29.2 million Latinos of Mexican origin resided in the United States, 4 out of 10 were first generation immigrants compared to 39% of other Latinos, and the median age was 25 compared to the U.S. population that was 36 (Pew Hispanic Center, 2009a). A significant proportion of Mexicans (62%) arrived in the United States after 1990 (Pew Hispanic Center, 2009a), and although the majority of Mexicans live in California (37.6%) and Texas (25%), as reported previously, recent analyses indicate that Mexicans are dispersing throughout other parts of the United States. Latinos of Mexican heritage have the lowest level of education, with 9% of those 25 and older having a college degree compared to 12.5% of all U.S. Latinos (Pew Hispanic Center, 2009a).

SALVADORAN NATIONAL ORIGIN As a colony of Spain, El Salvador, like several other Central American countries, was granted independence in 1821 following the independence of Mexico from Spain. In recent history, the rise of revolutionary movements in El Salvador in the 1980s in response to repression, led to paramilitary death squads that terrorized peasant leaders, union militants, and political activists (Parrillo, 2009, p. 415). Escalation of conflict led to massive assaults on communities including obliteration of villages (Hamilton & Chincilla, 1991). Political tensions, marked by civil wars, oftentimes split families along political lines, led to the deaths of thousands, and left others seeking refuge in the United States. Many immigrants arrived in the United States with histories of witnessing beheadings and shootings as well as fear of death should they return to their homeland.

Parrillo (2009) points out there was little support from the Reagan administration for the refugees and that to some degree these events had a role in the beginning of the sanctuary movement in the United States as a way to assist these refugees seeking political amnesty. The civil war that ravaged El Salvador in the 1980s ended in 1989; however, the vestiges of that war have been felt internationally. For example, the growth of gang activity by the "Mara Salvatrucha" in the United States began with the deportation of a small group of Salvadoran youths from Los Angeles to El Salvador in the early 1980s. The combination of gang activity in Southern California and civil war experiences resulted in violence between gangs in as many as 33 states spanning the west and east coast of the United States, and El Salvador, Honduras, and Guatemala. It is estimated between 40,000 and 100,000 gang members exist in Central America alone (Salinas, 2005).

In 2007, a significant proportion of the Salvadoran population was estimated to be first generation immigrants (66.1%); most (56%) had arrived since 1990 and almost a third were U.S. citizens. Also, the median age of Salvadorans was older than most Latinos (29); 38.5% of them were estimated to live in California and have a lower educational level than other Latinos, with 53% who were 25 or older holding a high school degree compared to 39.4% of all Latinos (Pew Hispanic Center, 2009d). The poverty rate was also found to be high at 14.6% compared to the U.S. population poverty rate of 10.3%.

NICARAGUAN NATIONAL ORIGIN Nicaraguans experienced political oppression first with the Somoza government, which ended in 1979, and later with the subsequent Sandinista regime. "Nicaraguans have entered the country as undocumented immigrants" (Parrillo, 2009, p. 415). U.S. immigration policies regarding securing asylee or refugee status have presented an oppressive challenge that could overwhelm immigrants who had already suffered so much in their former country (Potocky-Tripodi, 1999). By the 1990s, the political situation was not as volatile and the scale of immigration to the United States slowed down to approximately 3,000 in the 21st century (U.S. Office of Immigration Statistics, 2006).

GUATEMALAN NATIONAL ORIGIN Historically, Guatemala was populated by the Mayans, was colonized by Spaniards, and achieved independence, following Mexico, in 1821. With a legacy of government-sponsored genocide against the indigenous population, today the Guatemalan government is a democratic republic. The resistance to oppressive governments was recognized with the awarding of the Nobel Peace Prize to Rigoberta Menchu in 1992. In 2007 approximately 40% lived in the West (42.3%), 19% were estimated to live in poverty, and 54.1% over the age of 25 had not obtained a high school degree (Pew Research Center, 2009f). The Pew Research Center (2009f) analyses report that there were a total of 860,000 Latinos of Guatemalan origin who were either first generation immigrants or had Guatemalan ancestry. A greater proportion are native born (69%) compared to 39% of Latinos in general, and similar to Mexican-Americans, Guatemalans are younger than the Americans with a median age of 27.

HONDURAN NATIONAL ORIGIN Honduras was formerly known as Spanish Honduras, is different from its neighbor Belize, formerly British Honduras, and was part of the Central American Mayan empire. European settlers arrived as early as the 15th century and immediately developed the silver mining industry. Honduras and several other Central American countries were granted independence immediately following Mexican Independence from Spain in 1821; by 1880 Tegucigalpa was chosen as the national capital. With a long-standing intense political history, recent history shows Honduras in the process of managing strife regarding a politically agreed-upon presidential administrative structure and status.

The political, economic, and social demographics of Central American immigrants in the United States are yet to be fully understood. The above information, provided by the U.S. Census Bureau, is yet to be expanded to inform us of immigrants from other Central American countries. Appreciation for the social identity of Central American immigrants needs to be understood in relation to political and colonizing elements of a particular country's history. Factors such as patterns of immigration into those countries, colonial dominance, and experience of indigenous groups led to tremendous variation in contemporary demographics. Diversity in phenotype varies across Central America in relation to high profile and/or dominance of Euro-American, indigenous, mestizo, or African Latino phenotypes. For example, in countries such as Belize or Panama, colonizers left a legacy of English and Spanish bilingual cultures. Also, the influx of immigrants from Jamaica and other Caribbean islands for the building of the canal in Panama in the early 1900s resulted in a multiracial society. Learning about political conditions, such as the late 20th-century dictatorship by Panamanian President Noriega, is essential as we learn about individuals from that region.

LATINOS OF CARIBBEAN NATIONAL ORIGINS

PUERTO RICAN NATIONAL ORIGIN Puerto Rico, first populated by the Taino indigenous population, was first annexed in 1898 and later declared an unincorporated territory by the United States in 1900 by the Foraker Act (Montijo, 1985). The Jones Act of 1917 mandated U.S. citizenship on its residents; moreover, during this period, the English language was imposed in schools (Parrillo, 2009). However, it was not until 1948 that a formal policy to reinstate instruction in the Spanish language was instituted. Although, Puerto Ricans are oftentimes referred to as immigrants, their status as American citizens, service in the American military, and governance by many American federal laws often go unacknowledged.

The historical relationship with the United States has produced several tensions. Not the least is the ongoing question over commonwealth versus statehood status. This issue remains a flashpoint for heated debate among Puerto Ricans on the island and in the United States. The 1950s witnessed extensive testing of birth control methods in remote mountainous parts of southeast Puerto Rico that left a significant portion of women in that generation infertile. There has been heightened attention since the 1980s to the presence of the U.S. military and bombing maneuvers on the island of Vieques off the east coast of Puerto Rico. Attention in the United States to the opposition of U.S. presence on Vieques assists in recognizing issues that may be significant for Puerto Rican communities (Orlando Sentinel, 2001).

In 2007 it was estimated that there were almost as many Puerto Ricans in Puerto Rico (3.9 million) compared to those in the United States (4.1 million). Data show that Puerto Ricans have low levels of education and underemployment compared to the general U.S. population (Pew Hispanic Center, 2009b).

DOMINICAN REPUBLIC NATIONAL ORIGIN   The Dominican Republic's history is similar to that of Haiti, its neighbor on the island formerly known as Hispaniola, which was initially populated by the Taino indigenous population. Population characteristics reflect the introduction of slave commerce by French and Spanish colonizers, who were fought off by the laborers. Its history is rife with political conflict that includes U.S. occupation between 1916 and 1922, dealing with heavy debt until the late 1940s, and a repressive regime by Trujillo until 1961. The period of resistance to the regime is in part memorialized through the International Day of the Elimination of Violence Against Women, observed in memoriam of the execution of three sisters from the privileged class, known as the Mariposas (Butterflies), who opposed the regime.

Approximately 60% of Dominicans are first generation immigrants with 56% having arrived in the United States since 1990. It is an older population than other Latinos with a median age of 29, has a higher level of education with 15%, 25 years and older, having a college degree, and 24% are in poverty, which is twice the rate of the U.S. population. Significantly 80% live in the northeast with 52.4% living in New York alone and home ownership is lower at 27.9% compared to other Latinos at almost 50%, and the U.S. population at 67.2% (Pew Hispanic Center, 2009e).

LATINOS OF CUBAN NATIONAL ORIGIN   Cuba's history with the corrupt regime of the Cuban dictator Fulgencio Batista began with a coup in 1933 that supported a regime that benefited from collusion with U.S. corporations and endured until the Marxist revolution led by Fidel Castro in 1959. As an economy based on gambling and international commerce, there was much support for the revolution that pushed for a government that was more responsive to the needs of the Cuban community, particularly the disenfranchised and low income. The revolution initially resulted in thousands of Cubans, primarily from privileged classes, fleeing their homeland to the United States and settling in Florida. Cuban immigrants have settled in the United States since the mid-19th century, in areas such as New Jersey; however, since the 1960s, "more than 910,000 Cubans – far more than came from the entire West Indues [during the preceding] 130 years have entered the U.S." (Parrillo, 2009, p. 408).

The high profile of Cubans in cities such as Miami transformed into anti-Cuban reactions manifested in English-only initiatives. In 1980 the arrival of refugees from Mariel, Cuba (i.e., Marielitos) was received with criticism and ambivalence in that this refugee group allegedly was comprised of individuals with histories of court involvement. However, research confirmed that only about 10% of this population had, in fact, been jailed in Cuba (Clark, Lasaga, & Reque, 1981, as quoted by Puig, 2001). Moreover, one of the reasons often cited for the critical reception was that 35% of the Mariel refugees were Black males with low education levels and employment skills (Clark, Lasaga, & Reque, 1981).

Most waves of immigration from Cuba to the United States represented privileged classes of European phenotype. One consequence of this phenomenon is that the demographic profile of Cuba has become increasingly African Latino with Cubans of European phenotype becoming the minority. The growth in the United States of Cuban professional refugees and the subsequent growth of the Cuban business owners have resulted in increased visibility of anti-Castro, conservative attitudes among Cubans. Cuban immigrants have uniquely developed a large presence in the media industry, and to some degree in federal appointments and political office, particularly in the east and southeast. The intersection between socioeconomic class privilege, European phenotype, and conservative political leanings within the Cuban Latino community is important to understand in relation to the experiences of Cuban American individuals, families, and communities.

Over 60% of Cubans are first generation immigrants, their median age at 40 is older than Latinos in general, and the majority (68.7%) live in Florida. Their educational attainment is higher with 25% of those over 25 having a college degree. Cuban poverty levels are equal to American poverty levels at 12.3% and thus lower compared to other Latinos, at 19.5%; however, home ownership is higher than for other Latinos (61.1%) yet lower for the U.S. population as a whole (67.2%) (Pew Hispanic Center, 2009c).

SOUTH AMERICAN ORIGIN   The following national statistics identifies limited information on additional Latino groups from South America who have immigrated to the United States. Columbians in the United States are primarily first generation immigrant (69.4%), tend to be older at 35, and have higher levels of education with 30.3% of Columbians over 25 years of age have obtained a college degree (Pew Hispanic Center, 2009g). Analyses show that 67.9% of Ecuadorians in the United States are immigrants, are older (30) and tend to live in the northeast (66.4%) with 42.4% in New York alone, and have higher levels of education with 18.2% of those 25 and over having a college degree (Pew Hispanic Center, 2009h). The profile of Peruvians in the United States indicates that 73.8% are first generation immigrants, tend to be older (35 years or more), are very dispersed throughout the United States (e.g., Florida, California, New Jersey), and have higher levels of education with 31% of those 25 and older having a college degree (Pew Hispanic Center, 2009i).

This discussion is all too brief due to limitations related to the purpose of this chapter; however, it suggests an inkling of the vast differences in histories and social identities within the Latino communities. Hopefully, this brief information will promote curiosity and learning.

ELDERLY LATINOS

Research on Latinos includes a broad range of issues including family roles, health, caregiving, end of life issues, protective factors, and effective interventions. Fuller-Thomson's (2007) findings with Central American grandparents showed that they were younger (age 45 and older), had not completed high school, and were not employed. This profile suggests the importance of learning about family role adaptation to changing socioeconomic conditions. Similar to other ethnic groups, there is evidence that most often, females are the caregivers for their parents or parents-in-law who have Alzheimer's disease and who tend to underutilize social services (Ayalon & Huyck, 2002). Interestingly, Latino Alzheimer's caregivers report lower levels of stress, greater perceived benefits of caregiving, and greater use of religious coping compared to Euro-American caregivers (Coon et al., 2004). Other studies show caregivers reporting a higher rate of satisfaction in caregiving along with lower depression levels and a sense of personal gain (Morano, 2003). This is meaningful in light of the toll on aging caregivers related to health problems and depleted finances (Kim & Lee, 2005).

Limited knowledge of hospice programs, fear of discrimination, possible costs, low-income status, lack of health insurance, low levels of education, and language concerns have been associated with Latino elders' lower rates of utilization of hospice services compared to Euro-Americans (Colon & Lyke, 2003; Gelfand, Balcazar, Parzuchowski, & Lenox, 2004; Randall & Csikai, 2003). Likewise, there is some indication of lack of awareness of high glucose levels (Bertera, 2003).

While grandchildren's problem behavior appears to contribute to negative affect of elders, the parents' presence in the home during grandparenting was found to contribute to a greater sense of well-being (Goodman & Silverstein, 2005). Somewhat in line with traditional values, Zunker, Rutt, and Meza (2005) report that Mexican elders value knowledge of life experience and raising a family, and view quality of health as being related to socioeconomic status, family support, chronic disease, and earlier life circumstances. Puerto Rican elders with low incomes who recently arrived in the northeast and perceive themselves as having poor health, limited interaction with relatives, and a need for emotional support were found to be more likely to be depressed compared to other Puerto Rican elders (Robison et al., 2003).

In relation to health, attending church once a week is associated with longevity among Mexican Americans (Hill, Angel, Ellison, & Angel, 2005). Also, Weitzman, Chang, and Reynoso (2004) report that middle-aged Latino women prefer female doctors, compared to older Latino women who prefer male doctors. Trustworthiness in physicians, Spanish-speaking physicians, and physicians of a different ethnicity were preferred by both groups.

Angel, Angel, and Hill's (2008) research on elder Latinos cautions about the importance of the time-consuming research methods that get at meaning and that "statistical techniques [cannot] serve as a substitute for … understanding the economic, political and organizational environment in which individuals … make choices about health care" (p. 21). Understanding the relationship between level of acculturation in Latino elders and expressions of mental health issues (Chiriboga, Jang, Banks, & Kim, 2007) is one example of research areas that benefit by mixed method approaches.

Delgado's (2007) summary on the socioeconomic condition of Latino elders highlights how low-income jobs during years of productivity often lead to social security as the sole source of income. Most often the immense lack of support to Latino elders from additional sources such as a pension, savings, and investments is known to affect their mental health (Aranda, 2006). The projected increase in life expectancy for Latino men, to 83 years of age, and women, to 83 years of age (U.S. Census Bureau, 2000), suggests that Latino elder quality of life issues loom even larger.

Latino Gay and Lesbian Sexual Orientation

A major theme in the literature on Latino gay and lesbian sexual orientation is the role of Latino culture in creating an experience that is different from the experience of White gays or lesbians. Ethnic identity and the connection with the Latino community place greater significance on the coming out process regarding fears of rejection and loss of a "refuge from … racism" (Marsiglia & Kulis, 2009, p. 168), and for adolescents a delayed coming out process can slow down the integration of identity (Rosario, Schrimshaw, & Hunter, 2004). For males, cultural expectations of control and dominance create conflict; likewise the coming out process for gays and lesbians is perceived as particularly threatening in that rejection would mean loss of "refuge from … racism or ethnocentrism" (p. 168). Findings indicate that gay males experience verbal and physical abuse, mistreatment, and increased psychological distress (Diaz, Ayala, & Bein, 2004) as well as sexual abuse among those who are HIV seropositive (Williams et al., 2004). Other researchers have dealt with ethnographic exploration of gay and bisexual Latino males in relation to immigration, acculturation, cultural values, health, and mental health beliefs (Colon, 2001); prejudice from one's ethnic group; and issues related to identity management in the workplace (Adams, Cahill, & Ackerlind, 2005). The findings of Parks, Hughes, and Matthews (2004) indicated that lesbian women reported having to confront norms and expectations of both majority and ethnic cultures.

CULTURAL COMPETENCE WITH CLIENT GROUP(S)

Cultural competence in social work practice is guided by several works that set a context for practice premised on person–environment interaction, social justice perspectives, and micro, meso, and macro (Cross, et al., 1989; National Association of Social Workers [NASW], 2007) frameworks. The work of Cross, Bazron, Dennis, and Issacs (1989) outlines the significance of organizational proficiency as a requisite factor in culturally relevant practice and defines cultural competence as a set of congruent behaviors, attitudes, and policies that become integrated in a system, agency, or among professionals and, in turn, enable that system, agency, or those professionals to work effectively in cross-cultural situations. Five elements are identified as part of the process of developing effectiveness in diverse settings: 1) valuing diversity; 2) having the capacity for cultural self-assessment; 3) being conscious of the dynamics inherent when cultures interact; 4) having institutionalized cultural knowledge; and 5) having developed adaptations to diversity, basing practice on accurate perceptions of behavior, constructing impartial policies, and demonstrating unbiased attitudes (p. v).

The NASW (2007) cultural competence indicators clarify the operationalization of ethics, self-awareness, knowledge, service delivery, empowerment and advocacy, workforce issues, professional education, linguistic competence, and leadership in culturally relevant practice. Social work values and ethics underscore the importance of framing culturally relevant practice in the context of social justice (Garcia & Van Soest, 2006) from the perspective that effective practice in diverse settings requires awareness of and working with social power and social location factors imbued in the interaction. Anti-oppression concepts (Curry-Stevens, 2009; Dominelli, 2002) identify relevant practice interventions such as client advocacy within the organizational setting and coalitional work that expand understanding about macro- and meso-level interventions that promote practice effectiveness. Advocacy can take place in supervision, staff meetings, and networking with staff to promote a constituency to raise issues to examine and potentially improve agency policy, and change-oriented activities (e.g., coalitions) can include attending community-based boards and committees that address diversity service delivery and disparities concerns. Mere firsthand observation or participation in such activities is expected to have an impact on practitioner awareness that will translate into enhanced interactional skills with diverse others.

Within a context that culturally relevant practice is a process and not a status to be achieved and clients are to be viewed in their historical context and in their wholeness as a unique individual, several key guidelines stand out. First, while it is essential to have some knowledge of the client's ethnic and cultural background (content skill) as the basis of a hypothesis until the real person reveals himself or herself to you (Sue, 1998), the process skills needed to engage, connect, explore, and convey safety may be more important. Second, having self-awareness premised on one's social identity (e.g., ethnicity, class, biases) is essential as the basis of attunement to biases related to privilege that are dealt with. Such practice is informed by an "informed, not knowing" perspective (Anderson & Goolishian, 1992; Laird, 1998) and compassionate posture. Third, sustainable culturally relevant practice requires a culturally proficient organization that values diversity and recognizes the role of organizational leadership and policy in promoting effective micro-level practice.

Culturally relevant practice with Latinos foremost recognizes the heterogeneity within the population, meaning the differences related to migration, reception in the United States, how and why they came, and that for some, the acculturation processes began in their countries of origin due to effects of neocolonialism and globalization (Guarnaccia et al., 2007, p. 528). Most often the reasons for migration shape the reception and settlement in the United States (Guarnaccia et al., 2007).

Culturally relevant practice requires bicultural and bilingual effectiveness. There is evidence that the matching hypothesis (Latino professional with Latino client) is not consistently effective. Attention to bicultural identification and language preference are basic competencies that social workers of all backgrounds can develop, particularly because as Guarnaccia et al. (2007) point out, language is often an indicator of acculturation and is associated with health outcomes.

The unique background that each social worker brings to practice with Latinos relates to potential biases that can get triggered. For Latinos with privileged backgrounds working with low-income clients, the expectations arising from class and culture can manifest in differences in meaning-making or value preferences of clients. Nativity, phenotype, acculturation, generation level, and native-born and foreign-born differences can influence how the worker will relate to a client and the kinds of interventions that are deemed relevant with individuals and families. The immigrant status of clients is a factor that social workers of all ethnicities may find challenging particularly if the client has undocumented status. The terminology that we use can convey strength-based, social justice perspective as demonstrated in the use of nondocumented versus illegal alien and promotes the dehumanization of immigrants by seeing them as less moral. These perspectives are the foundation of viewing others as with little to no compassion. These are but a few examples of challenges in practice that require recognition for the purpose of suspending one's assumptions and modifying one's perceptions in the process of engagement, assessment, and practice.

HISTORICAL OPPRESSION AND CURRENT SOCIAL ISSUES

Human rights issues are at the center of the discussion on historical oppression in relation to premigration and migration factors as well as experiences in the United States. Historically, all Latin American countries have dealt with colonial and imperialist interference with national development that introduced foreign settlements, appropriation of national resources, and influenced decision making. These political dealings have taken their toll in political and economic ways that motivate immigration based on factors such as seeking refugee status or a life where one can work and create a life of one's choice for self and family. Recent history has witnessed the growth of empire as the new form of global domination that supercedes imperialism and is characterized by collaborating powers (e.g., nation states, financial entities, major corporations) predicted to promote even more harsh structures leading to poverty and exploitation on an international scale (Hardt & Negri, 2004). These forces suggest that immigrants' hopes of a break from oppressive economic and political structures face confronting marginalization and devaluation in the new setting.

Oppression is defined as limitations placed on where one can go, how one spends their time, what activities consume their energy, and access to information and mobility (Bulhan, 1987). Like racism, oppression is a relational phenomenon that is characterized by institutional exclusion, its ability to define an individual, for example in relation to one's worth and status, and the view of the oppressed in terms of generalizations thus rendering the oppressed invisible (Memmi, 2000).

Several social justice issues surface as one examines the context of oppression in the lives of most Latino Americans. Several of these current social issues arising from social justice inequities are identified as follows.

1. *Access to education:*
   Research shows, as discussed earlier, Latino adolescents continue to drop out of high school at twice the rate in comparison to other groups and Latino males who enter higher education are less likely than Latino females to complete college. Factors related to oppression and social justice such as segregation, quality of K-12 education, and experiences with teachers and school administrators take their toll in undermining securing a professional education that will support quality-of-life factors such as home ownership and a career of one's choice. The lack of significant improvement on this front has direct consequences for long-term social justice concerns.

2. *Mental health disparities:*
   Research on disparities between identified need for mental health services and access to provision of quality services for Mexicans and Latinos in general documents the challenges to mental health professionals in providing effective services. There is evidence that Mexican immigrants arrive with healthier mental health and nutritional status; however, within several years of working in the United States they develop mental health disorders, worsened nutrition, and, in addition, substance abuse problems (Vega et al., 1998). Mexican immigrants with family members in the United States have been found to be more at risk for suicide (Borges et al., 2009) and more likely to have a substance abuse disorder compared to other Mexicans (Borges, et al., 2007). Also, greater attention is needed to stressors associated with acculturation with third generation Latino males in relation to substance abuse concerns (Alegria et al., 2007) as well as exercising carefulness in generalizing about the immigrant paradox in that there is variability in at-risk status to various mental disorders among different Latino nationalities (Alegria et al., 2008).

3. *Immigration reform initiatives:*
   Effective immigration reform legislation remains elusive, at times because of its controversy (flashpoint); at other times it is overshadowed by other national priorities. Discussion of new legislation includes the provision of citizenship for nondocumented residents who have been in the United States for several years; still several components endure through the various manifestations of the legislation. These include 1) border security, detention, and enforcement; 2) detention centers; 3) employment verification; and 4) legalization of undocumented residents. One long-standing issue that occasionally garners support for change is to restrict the authority to implement immigration policy to the federal government, rather than local authorities. This change would resolve the decades-long problems of unlawful arrests by deputized police and contracting with private sector entities (e.g., mercenaries) to implement border immigration practices.
   Lack of a legislative directive has allowed the anti-immigrant climate in the United States to worsen as witnessed by increasing deaths in detention centers (Bernstein, 2010), violent and sometimes fatal attacks on immigrants,

detention of nondocumented residents resulting from contact with police for minor incidents such as traffic violations, detention without notification of whereabouts to family, and workplace raids that include incarceration of legal residents and citizens based on racial profiling. The interface between detention and increasing intergenerational differences between minors born in the United States (citizens) and nondocumented parents has led to families being separated. The anti-immigrant sentiment fuels several initiatives that range from prohibiting nondocumented residents from receiving public health services, social services, and education and welfare benefits (Cowan, Martinez, & Mendiola, 1997). Workplace raids directed at detaining nondocumented individuals, particularly those with histories of court involvement, have resulted in the criminalization of immigrants and apprehension of legal residents, which creates fear and promotes a breakdown of community life.

An increasingly difficult issue is the escalation of border deaths that in part is due to the border fence shifting migrant passage through desert terrain as well as exploitation by "coyotes" who arrange transit between countries. The oppression of Mexican-heritage persons is buttressed by the abuse of academic scholarship, for example, by Harvard political scientist Samuel Huntington, who warns that Mexican immigration to the United States "looms as a ... disturbing challenge to our cultural integrity...." (Lindsay & Michaelidis, 2001, p. B7).

Immigration rights are connected to abusive practices described earlier and also to international policies. Globalization represents a paradigm shift that requires migration, creates displaced "illegal" populations, and connects to refugee policy, trafficking, and smuggling conditions (Bacon, 2008; Dauvergne, 2008). Legal arrangements that allow Latino immigrants into the United States for legal residence, however, promote conditions that lead to living in the shadows for society. The Temporary Bracero worker program of 1942–1964 and the current federal H-2 worker policy (Romo, 2009) are examples of programs that hoped for legislation that will create routes for citizenship for immigrant workers. Moreover, effective immigration policy has to improve on the management of logistics of immigration (e.g., who can immigrate, review motivation for employment as well as human rights issues; Castaneda, 2007). It is significant that the intensification of anti-immigrant initiatives led to rallies by Latinos in 2006 to show community support and solidarity with immigrants (Barreto, Manzano, Ramirez, & Rim, 2009; Martinez, 2008; Pantoja, Menjivar, & Magana, 2008).

4. *Human trafficking:*
   The vulnerability of nondocumented immigrants seeking passage into the United States creates conditions that leave some, particularly women and children, susceptible to predatory smugglers or even "friends" whose interests are exploitation. The advantages of modern transport and global communications make deception, abduction, violence, and coercion into sexual or slave labor possible (NASW, 2009b; U.S. Department of State, 2007). Recent history demonstrates a growing number of states that have strengthened their human trafficking penalties; for example, in 2010 California implemented a new law that raised fines to $20,000 and provides for apprehension of the trafficker's assets. Although U.S. citizens and legal residents are subject to human

trafficking, U.S. Department of State statistics indicate the immigrants from Mexico and Central America are highly represented among this population in the United States. A wide range of policy issues address the importance of public awareness, advocacy, services to survivors, professional education, legal and political action (NASW, 2009a). There is also discussion on the values that underlie policy assumptions regarding women's sexual labor and the need for more attention to women's labor, economic and human rights, and vulnerability in relation to globalization (Desyllas, 2007; Limoncelli, 2009).

VALUES AND ETHICAL DILEMMAS

The NASW Code of Ethics (1999) identifies professional responsibilities for ethical practice on micro, meso, and macro levels based on dignity and worth of the individual, importance of human relationships, integrity, competence, social justice, and human rights. Ethical practice within this framework is explicitly based on a commitment to social change that addresses the systemic aspects of barriers to client self-determination. Ethical practice with Latinos demonstrates knowledge, values, and skills premised on the NASW Achievement of the Standards for Cultural Competence (2007), developed by the National Committee on Racial and Ethnic Diversity (NCORED) that identifies criteria related to self-awareness, cross-cultural knowledge, cross-cultural skills, service delivery, empowerment and advocacy, diverse workforce, professional education, language diversity, and cross-cultural leadership.

Several macro-level ethical issues related to research practice arise in practice with Latinos. Cooper et al. (2004) point out that research with migrant farm workers take into account their vulnerability based on low socioeconomic status. Researchers who study this population should be rigorous in their human subjects protocol, inhibit potential harm by providing clear information on informed consent, and not assume participants will indicate if they do not understand (Adams, 2004). Potential ethical dilemmas and policy issues can arise in relation research on caregiving practices with undocumented children (Young, Flores, & Berman, 2004) and overlooking community-based participatory designs with this population (Martin & Lantos, 2005). An example of the need for ethics in interpreting research data is the finding that stressors related to immigration (e.g., poverty, discrimination) can lead to greater parental involvement in their adolescent children that can compete with education aims and peer engagement, and lead to a greater sense of personal and interpersonal competence (Jurkovic et al., 2004).

Additional macro-level ethical issues arise in relation to service delivery in human services and health settings. Historically, there have been regional initiatives that blur the boundaries of agency responsibility to nondocumented individuals leading in some cases to service delivery cutbacks and withholding of life-threatening medical services (e.g., dialysis). Agency policy can promote negative stereotyping of legal and nondocumented Latinos. Social workers risk practicing in ways that criminalizes Latinos rather than viewing them as individuals who have a right to resources.

The NASW Code of Ethics directs social workers to facilitate access to resources for those clients who come to them in need. They must respond to the client's plight in an unbiased fashion and suspend any negative sentiments toward those who are nondocumented; anything less is unethical (Zuniga, 2001). Socioeconomic or immigrant status differences between worker and client can evoke discomfort that benefits by framing within ethical standards that provide a context for effective practice.

CULTURAL AWARENESS

Cultural awareness is based on awareness of the multiculturality of individuals (i.e., identification with several cultures), recognition of stressors, socioeconomic marginalization, recognition of shared (etic) cultural factors, as well as unique qualities of individuals (emic) and how these translate into practice. The complexity of Latino experience based on national origin, immigrant status, generation in the United States, level of acculturation, and regional differences related to where they live in the United States are a few of the factors that reflect the heterogeneity with the population. Stressors may be related to preimmigration trauma, trauma in transit to the United States, and/or the experience of discrimination in the U.S. economic marginalization suggests particular vulnerability to economic stressors on a national level.

Awareness of historical and sociopolitical factors in the lives of Latinos also illuminates the need to be knowledgeable about the consequences of low social power and institutional racism in relation to social identity and perceptions of access to options. Rather than make assumptions about an individual based on class and/or phenotype (i.e., appearance), mindfulness about exploring the meaning and experiences of these elements in their lives is essential. All too often assumptions are made about Latinos based on their appearance, which leads to loss of the opportunity to learn about the subjective perspective arising from a diverse ethnic and "racial" heritage.

Learning how to be culturally attuned without contributing to negative stereotypes about Latino clients involves workers being willing to examine their own cultural backgrounds. They must examine their socioeconomic status and discern the degree and extent of their own cultural programming. If workers come from recent immigrant backgrounds, what is their level of acculturation, and what insights do they have about the complexities of this process? Are countertransference issues that might evolve from having similar backgrounds to clients present? If immigration experiences are not part of workers' backgrounds, they can learn by reading novels or films that deal with experiences. These activities serve to assist the social worker in becoming more familiar with difference.

Each Latino client system also teaches us about how Latinos utilize their culture—that is, in what ways they are unique and in what ways they share similar Latino values, attitudes, and behaviors. The one commonality we can agree on, however, is that all Latino clients are unique; therefore, we cannot make cultural assumptions about them.

KNOWLEDGE ACQUISITION

Effective practice is also premised on knowledge acquisition relevant to the populations one works with in relation to points identified previously regarding cultural awareness, and incorporating that knowledge through the utilization of critical thinking (Gambrill, 2005) and conceptual frameworks that guide in putting that awareness into practice. Critical thinking assists in identifying underlying assumptions of perspectives. Awareness of cultural values, gender issues within cultures, and the influence of these differences on the working relationship is aided by theories such as social construction and social identity development and those that address class issues (e.g., conflict theory) and oppression.

Professional accountability requires combining professional knowledge of relevant research, concepts, and theories with the realities of the individuals that we work with. This perspective minimizes the professional as expert, and more in line with the ethnographic approach, promotes the professional participating in the client–worker interaction within an "informed not knowing" stance (Laird, 1998) that promotes learning about one's own cultural biases as one learns about the client's cultural world.

Knowledge acquisition for practice with Latinos suggests being knowledgeable about the heterogeneity of the Latino population as well as findings that assist in engaging with and providing relevant services. The growing population of immigrants and evidence of the association of trauma with the immigration process and nondocumented status suggest knowledge of the effects of trauma, loss, and separation. Also, research on help-seeking pathways in mental health service delivery examines the "sequence of contacts with individuals and organizations" arising from the client's efforts to secure assistance (Rogler & Cortes, 2008, p. 32) and has found that Latinos most often first seek help through health professionals. Also, variations in substance abuse patterns between immigrants and U.S.-born Latinos indicate that immigrants may not drink regularly and drink more heavily when they do drink compared to U.S.-born Latinos (Worby & Organista, 2007).

Issues identified in the literature that bear attention are discussed as follows:

The re-sorting of gender roles and power has major implications for immigrants (Comas-Diaz & Greene, 1994) in that women may take low-paying jobs in instances where the male is unable to secure employment. The reshuffling of marital and familial roles can result in despondent men who have difficulty sustaining such power shifts. Immigrants often find themselves without the moral support and networks that enabled them to function in the past due to separation from family who remained in the country of origin. In his investigation of the social integration of Salvadoran refugees in Canada, Jacob (1994) found that social relationships were critical to satisfying the refugee's need for communication and to mitigate isolation. Such places as the workplace provided the most significant nonfamily support networks. These major adaptations suggest that workers need to develop knowledge of the varied kinds of social support that can be developed in immigrant communities (Valle & Bensussen, 1980; Vega & Kolody, 1980).

Research on Latino youth has examined how exposure to violence can result in suicidal behaviors, serious antisocial acts, insomnia, separation anxiety, defiance, somatic complaints, and school problems (Arroyo & Eth, 1985). Moreover, issues such as differences between teachers' pedagogical style and cultural factors (Brown, 2008), Latina college students' commitment to assisting family needs (Sy & Romero, 2008), and the need to engage parents in school activities to assure their children's academic success (Jarsky, McDonough, & Nunez, 2009) all have relevance for the practitioner knowledge based on what is known of challenges faced by Latinos.

Knowledge can be enhanced by seeking consultation from culturally competent workers with extensive experience serving this population. Volunteering one's case for formal case review provides another avenue for exploring the variety of perspectives that can be applied to understanding and enabling the worker to develop his or her own perspective. In addition, comparing how one social worker who is culturally aware assesses a case with workers with less awareness will elucidate the cultural perspectives that are crucial for effective service delivery.

Regardless of ethnic, racial, or class background, social workers must learn how to develop the appropriate knowledge, value, and skill repertoire to work with this diverse population in a culturally relevant and proficient way. Evidence show that the "matching hypothesis" has no base in reality. Latino professionals cannot be assumed to be the most effective. Allowing the term Hispanic to obscure differences based on class, occupation, and national origin can (Guarnaccia, 2007; Worby & Organista, 2007) result in a disconnect between you and your client. Recognition and working within the limits of one's personal attitude strengthen one's professional effectiveness. The earlier discussion in this chapter on oppression and social justice issues identifies areas for ongoing professional development (e.g., social power, cultural context, effects of devaluation, and invisibility).

SKILL DEVELOPMENT

Skill development with Latinos is premised on cultural attunement with attention to language, cultural values, and contextual stressors (Falicov, 2009), recognition that culturally relevant practice is a lifelong process not a status, and is grounded in a framework that integrates content and process skills that enable effective engagement, and problem solving on micro, meso, and macro levels. Lum (2010) identifies several skills necessary in engagement and rapport building, which include process, conceptualization, and personalization skills. Application of these three skills to each stage of problem solving (e.g., assessment, intervention, termination) highlights worker self-awareness, interpersonal skill in engagement with clients, and assessment that identifies problems, goals, and interventions within the context of a client's individual and cultural strength.

Ethical and culturally relevant practice requires both content and process skills. Knowledge about the history and context of your client provides a foundation for the development of hypotheses to guide the worker's learning about the reality and social identity of the client. Process skills promote effective engagement, rapport building, and transparency by the worker that facilitate expressing curiosity and appreciation of diversity.

Exploration of problem-solving methods, for example, with a low-income person may evoke devaluation in comparison to a worker's middle-class expectations. A middle-class practitioner who is accustomed to using a budget and anticipating long-term goals may view a Latino client's decisions on how to spend a lump sum of money as a source of conflict based on value preferences and differences. This gap might reflect a client's worldview assumptions of functioning in a survival mode compared to a worker's more privileged life that presumes a flourishing mode of functioning. The challenge is to refrain from devaluation of the client's spending choices and enable the client to learn to problem solve in future-oriented ways. Enabling a client to view a problem in a new way with new options is a tool; devaluing the way a client uses his or her money is unethical; the negative criticism can only diminish the client's self-esteem.

The Council on Social Work Education's (CSWE) Educational Policy and Accreditation Standards (EPAS) (2008) and the Indicators for the Achievement of the NASW Standards for Cultural Competence in Social Work Practice (2007) further contribute to identifying criteria for skilled professional practice with Latinos. CSWE mandates that the curriculum contains skill building in engagement, assessing, intervention, and evaluation with individuals and families. Emphasis on the dynamic and interactive aspects of these skills via reflective practice and utilization of approaches that promote learning from the client, such as with ethnographic interviewing, fit well with the challenges of learning about the uniqueness of Latinos with whom one is working. CSWE's mandate for biopsychosocial assessment facilitates exploration of Latinos' distinction in relation to national origin heritage, level of acculturation (e.g., biculturality), generation in the United States, socioeconomic status, and experiences in the United States. The EPAS reinforce interventions based on mutuality in formulating goals and intervention planning, building on strengths and evidence informed practice. NASW's indicators for cultural competence provide a framework for workers' ongoing professional development and interventions at all levels. The standards reflect social work's heritage of social justice and person–environment interaction perspective by addressing the value of empowerment-based practice and advocacy efforts.

Application of the principles and standards identified previously in practice with Latinos suggests several considerations in relation to engagement problem identification, assessment, and interventions. The following addresses some points to be mindful of as one works with Latinos.

RELATIONSHIP PROTOCOLS

Effective practice skills required to match the general cultural mode of Latinos require and ability to convey that one is personable and respectful (Tsui & Schultz, 1985; Zuniga, 1992). The capacity to build trust is particularly important when working with those who fear deportation. Worker self-disclosure can be valuable in establishing connection, for example sharing perceptions of family responsibilities; however, there must always be clarity about how the disclosure will assist the client. Workers might display concern about the special stressors immigrants face, and demonstrate optimism by noting how, with little help, most Latino individuals and families or individuals adapt very well.

Style of communication must be personable, patient, and formal, yet with warmth and consideration. If Spanish is not the worker's first language, but he or she speaks it well enough to work with the family, the worker can share their feelings about their limited proficiency in the language (e.g., discomfort), which displays humility and a respect for the client's culture. This transparency can act to even the playing field. A worker also can use a dicho (i.e., folk saying) to create a cultural ambiance clients will be comforted with, for example to express humor and allow the family to relax (Zuniga, 1991).

Workers who are delving into sensitive areas with clients, especially if a mental status exam is being undertaken, must recognize the importance of clients responding to questions in their first language to ensure a more accurate assessment. In mental health scenarios, the assessment of Spanish-speaking clients using their second language has shown greater degree of inaccurate mental status assessment (Marcos, 1994).

If the social worker is also Latino, he or she could disclose some history about his or her family's immigration experience (e.g., where they immigrated from, when they immigrated) and thus convey that they have some familiarity with the experience. Sharing reflections of how difficult it was for one's family (or parents) initially but how with time things worked out can signify the worker's insight on the client's issues and a sense of optimism.

Problem Identification

When clients present, noting a problem or a need, underlying issues and needs may exist that are difficult to disclose out of fear, shame, or distrust. From a strengths perspective, the worker can express regard for seeking help, and acknowledge the difficulty of this process. During problem identification, the worker can explore legal documentation, with clarification that the reason for asking is not to report the clients but to seek services that will not endanger them. When the worker highlights client concerns about deportation, this offers a respite from their anxiety about this matter. In acknowledging legal documentation, the worker can more easily evaluate what level of problem exists.

Assessment

Acculturation is critical to assess because of its influence on meaning-making, values, beliefs, and behavior. In the past the perspective that Latinos identified on to a larger degree on an either/or basis with traditional Latino cultural values or American culture. However, it has become clear that Latinos fall along a continuum of identification with both traditional culture and mainstream American cultures that is better described of "more or less of" both cultures, rather than "either/or." Guarnaccia et al. (2007) and Alegria et al. (2004) assert that the importance of taking a contextual and processual approach requires acculturation indicators that consider enculturation that deals with the "process of preserving the norms of the native group, whereby individuals retain identification with their ethnic cultures of origin" (Guarnaccia, 2007, p. 513). These researchers also point out that we need to keep perspective on the exposure of many immigrants to neocolonial and globalization forces prior to migration that impact acculturation. Directly related to accurate assessment of acculturation is the potential for cultural bias in instruments that have been standardized with non-Hispanic populations or English-only protocols.

Assessment of where individuals fall along the cultural identification continuum informs what intervention formats respect their value and behavior preferences, which can be particularly sensitive regarding sex roles that often change in the acculturation process (Comas-Diaz & Greene, 1994). Heterogeneity among

Latinos (e.g., socioeconomic status) and increasing dispersal of Latinos throughout regions of the United States as a function of best fit between needs and access to resources (McConnell, 2008; Umana-Taylor, 2009) has obvious consequences for acculturation processes.

Working with a traditional family requires knowledge about and sensitivity to the father's dominant role in relation to interventions. For example, if a member of the family must undergo surgery, the father must be consulted so that he comprehends what is needed and supports the procedure. Families encounter stressors when women obtain employment more easily than the men; this can result in an unbalanced family system, often leading to violence and substance abuse (Comas-Diaz & Greene, 1994). Respectfulness toward traditional family roles can become particularly sensitive when it relates to the wife's health needs. In relation to contraception decision making, social workers with strong empowerment, advocacy, and feminist beliefs may have to deal with resolving a conflict regarding the woman's right to free choice within a context of a traditional marital scenario. The worker is caught in a bind of not wanting to further contribute to a woman's oppression, yet intervention goals need to be formulated in the context of client needs in a culturally relevant way. How do social workers support a woman who wants to change traditional family roles? It is critical that they help her anticipate the consequences of this power change so her choices are informed and are truly choices, and not those of the worker. By mutually working with women to examine closely the costs of their choices or gender-based preferences, workers can assist them to determine change goals and weigh the pros and cons of different options. Change may initially appear so formidable (i.e., costly) that the client will not be willing to act on it. However, this need not necessarily exclude a long-term perspective of a more measured exploration of desired change.

Acculturation can become problematic when it is related to intergenerational dynamics such as varying levels of traditional and mainstream values within family systems (Szapocznick et al., 1997). Traditional parents may feel threatened by the new culture's values and behaviors manifested by their children. Parents often react to the threat of what they perceive as sexualized music, dress, and values by becoming more rigid and inflexible with their teenagers. The teens then react, sometimes with drugs, poor school performance, or other acting-out behaviors as they attempt to break from what they consider "old ways." Ascertaining what cultural conflicts exist between traditional, especially immigrant, parents and their teenagers helps to lay the foundation for competent planning and intervention formats. An acculturation instrument developed by Szapocznick et al. (1997) helps to identify generational differences that provide workers with insight when working with families.

RELIGION

The Spanish colonization of the New World with a goal of conversion of native peoples to Catholicism has led to a "the common thread of Catholicism at the core of national and cultural identities" (Maldonado, 2000, p. 99). Yet, over the years, religious diversity has increased among Latinos and includes Protestant denominations such as Methodists, Baptists, Presbyterians, Lutherans, Mormons, Seventh-Day Adventists, Jehovah's Witnesses, and Buddhists. The fastest-growing

Latino religious groups are the Pentecostal and evangelical denominations (Diaz-Stevens & Stevens-Arroyo, 1998).

Why is knowing about the religion of a Latino client important? The increase in religious diversity has prompted an increase by Catholic and Protestant denominations to engage in outreach activities. Also, Catholic, Lutheran, and Episcopalian churches have earmarked social service resources for this population via Spanish-speaking workers and programs structured to address their unique needs, such as special immigration and advocacy services. Puig (2001) describes the partnership the Cuban community developed with the Archdiocese of Miami to address the need to teach English to the "balseros" or Cuban refugees who left Cuba in 1994.

In different regions across the country, many denominations provide special support to Latinos in need and thus are a resource for social workers for referral making. It is helpful to know if a Latino client belongs to a certain denomination, or if needed to ascertain if services are offered in the Spanish language or if programs address specialized issues such as immigration. This information is particularly helpful if clients are not eligible for public sector services.

Another reason why determining the religious preference of Latino clients or families is crucial is that clients' or families' specific religion may be a profound asset in their ability to find meaning in their struggles and to find emotional resources (Hutchinson, 1999). In working with an elderly, acculturated Mexican American woman, for example, asking about her belief system may allow the worker to incorporate her daily prayer ritual as a clinical prescription for enabling her to address a situational crisis she is experiencing (Zuniga, 1991). Moreover, in enabling families like recent immigrants to develop social ties and a sense of relatedness, referral to a place of worship may be an important adjunctive intervention for enabling them to initiate their cultural networking. Also, if one is helping a family learn to become more cohesive, asking them to attend church service as a family may provide a family systems intervention that will help them function in a more collaborative and connected manner (Minuchin, 1974).

FAMILY

The value of family is a core dimension in the Latino culture. Despite acculturation, even third generation Latinos still have strong family-centered values. Roland (1988) points out the importance of a family orientation in most traditional cultures, a value stance that supports a collective sense of oneself in relation to the world. In a society like the United States that has such an ingrained sense of individual rights and the value of independence, it is difficult for a worker who is unaware of his or her own individualistic stance to be objective or unbiased about the more collective approach that Latinos utilize both in their problem solving and in their sense of interpersonal responsibility.

Latinos can be easily misassessed as being enmeshed with their family when they choose to live at home and/or not move out as other young adults in the majority culture often do. For example, one social work student felt that two teenagers she was working with, a 14- and 16-year-old sister and brother, were enmeshed with their grandmother. When asked to identify the behaviors on which she based her assessment, the student noted that each time the teens left their house, especially for recreational activities, they went to their grandmother, knelt before her, and asked for her blessing. The student was viewing a ritual as a weakness when, in fact, it was a family strength. It honored the role of the grandmother as the wise "protector" of the family and also depicted a strong intergenerational tie that is a strength for a Latino family, especially when acculturation processes often work to place young and old at odds with one another (Szapocznick et al., 1997).

The "connections" and sense of responsibility that Latino family members experience must be evaluated to assure that enmeshment is not occurring. However, workers must be cautious not to misconstrue interactions that are unfamiliar, like the example of the grandmother's blessing, as dysfunctional. They must seek consultation to learn what the rituals can mean and reevaluate whether they are viable in their own right or in fact may be contributing to enmeshed or dysfunctional behaviors.

LANGUAGE

Exploration of language dominance and preference opens many doors in understanding Latinos, making it essential to determine the client's language preference. Individuals who are bilingual may have preferences to communicate in Spanish if the agency offers that resource. Others can be served effectively only in Spanish, in which case the agency needs to ensure this resource is available—at a minimum, through the services of a translator who is bicultural and bilingual. Ideally, the worker is proficient in the language of the client.

The process of acculturation frequently leads to loss of Spanish language skills, especially by the third generation. Although this is an important marker of acculturation and integration of the American culture, this is not to be confused prematurely with internalization of American value on individualism. Values of family centeredness that characterize traditional values within this population may still be operating in acculturated individuals and families and need to be woven into the planning and intervention processes.

Each Latino national origin group speaks Spanish with a cultural style that highlights group differences as reflected in idioms and accent. Workers who are bilingual in Spanish and English must look for differences in expressions and idioms and need not inhibit themselves from asking clients to clarify the terms they use. Workers can also ask clients whether they comprehend the workers' idioms.

IMMIGRATION

The social justice issues related to immigration that were identified earlier in this chapter set a framework for the following considerations in relation to assessment with immigrants. Intergenerational considerations also encourage social workers to understand relevant immigration factors and subsequent functioning that may have transgeneration implications. While there are many dimensions of immigration to explore, the following are particularly significant:

- Motivations for immigration (e.g., political repression, economics, join family)
- Who was left behind and why (e.g., siblings, parents)
- How the immigration transit was arranged and managed (e.g., "agents" for a fee? Cost? Friends? Any "surprises" by those who offered to help?)

- What were the experiences during the transit? How eventful was it (e.g., robbery, rape, injury)?
- Legal status
- Reception in the United States

Exploring these areas focuses the social worker on exploration of premigration trauma, trauma encountered in transit, possible trauma related to settlement difficulties (e.g., asylum-seeking), and dealing with poverty-level living conditions, isolation, and/or discrimination in the United States. There is some evidence that women traveling alone from Central America or Mexico are at risk for months-long sexual assaults and forced labor as payments to coyotes or illegal travel brokers (Perez Foster, 2001). The heightened border security and creation of fencing has led many undocumented Mexicans to cross the U.S. border under treacherous conditions that risk death and can lead to development of post-traumatic stress disorder (PTSD) and/or related disorders such as anxiety and depression (Desjarlais et al., 1995).

Attachment theory suggests that age at the time of immigration is a significant psychosocial factor (Rodriguez, 2004) due to the various developmental tasks during childhood, adolescence, adulthood, and older adulthood. The intersection between developmental tasks and behavioral coping can be very challenging. Several stages of coping with migration have been proposed, which include 1) predominant feelings of sorrow, fear of the unfamiliar, loneliness, and isolation. Prior feelings of unresolved loss can get activated through this process. An ability to move into a role (i.e., work, career) and create connections in the new location that are similar to those in the homeland can assist the transition. Other variables that can exacerbate or assist the transition are the extent to which the new culture is different from that of the national origin, the quality of responsiveness of the host culture, the success or failure in the new environment, and the acquisition of legal status. The language adjustments are critical because of the role of language in identity; 2) feelings and thoughts that the immigrant had denied in order to manage the potentially overwhelming task of moving and adjusting can begin to surface and/or break through his or her awareness; and 3) the immigrant has worked through feelings of loss and mourning for what was left behind and is well underway integrating into life the elements of the new host environment and culture. He or she feels like a member of the new society and maintains a positive relation to his or her national origin, language, and culture. It is possible that for some, the process of mourning remains a lifelong process (Rodriguez, 2004).

When working with immigrants, workers' knowledge base should include some preliminary information on the populations they serve. Workers must be sensitive to the needs of traumatized immigrants and not avoid delving into important experiences thus colluding in denial (Perez Foster, 1998, 2001) or move into such content more quickly than the person's emotional readiness to do so. It is important to assess immigration history in a way that does not exacerbate negative emotions, such as fearfulness and anxiety, associated with the immigration process. Because the immigrant may be at a point where he or she has not begun to process the experiences and may be dissociating from the painful aspects of the experience (Perez Foster,

2001; Rodriguez, 2004), workers need to learn how to probe these experiences with sensitivity by beginning with asking "safe" questions about the experience and slowly, once rapport is established, moving into more sensitive areas. Workers must know what services undocumented immigrants are eligible for rather than jeopardize any opportunity for future legal immigration (Zuniga, 2001).

NEW GEOGRAPHIC SETTLEMENTS

The latter part of 20th century and early part of the 21st century have seen more Latino settlement in the midwest, northeast, Atlantic states, and the south in part related to employment but also in relation to small but present enclaves (McConnell, 2008). An essential area to explore, particularly with Spanish-dominant immigrants and in relation to experiences with discrimination, is the presence of networks and cultural supports. Are there resources by churches or community organizations that will support the immigrants' adaptation?

INTERVENTIONS

Although intervention will depend on the presenting problem, social workers should always consider the following questions about practice:

- Does the intervention help solve the problem without putting the client in harm's way regarding detection by immigration authorities?
- Does the intervention respond to the cultural orientation and preferences of this client rather than imposing societal or worker's cultural values and priorities?
- Does the intervention include natural support networks that would make the intervention more culturally relevant?
- Does the intervention acknowledge the stressors that immigration presents by offering resources or solutions that mitigate adaptation risks?
- Does the intervention give priority to survival issues before imposing talk therapy?
- Is the intervention offered in such a manner that facilitates adaptation, especially in such areas as development of competence, autonomy, relatedness, and esteem?
- Does the intervention utilize such resources as the client's religion, spirituality, or belief system?
- Does the intervention incorporate known culturally viable techniques such as narrative therapy (Falicov, 1998), use of metaphor or dichos (Zuniga, 1991), or family systems work (Szapocznick et al., 1997)?
- Does the intervention address different-sized system elements that may demand advocacy types of work?

SOCIAL AND ECONOMIC JUSTICE RESOLUTION

In U.S. society, each person has a right to benefit from societal resources, especially the right to a fair wage and decent working conditions as mandated by legislation. Moreover, society's resources such as health care, education, and housing should be accessible to all segments of the population. Demographic data on the labor force participation rate of Latinos indicate it is high; Latinos represent approximately 15% of the population and make up approximately 14% of the labor force (Pew Research Center, 2008b). Latinos who live in the United States or who come to the country as immigrants have a strong work ethic underpinned by their value on providing for their families' sustenance. Yet, the experience of Latinos continues to be one of labor-related exploitation. Exploitation in wages and/or lack of benefits, employment and housing, as well as lack of access to education present major barriers to adaptation to the culture. Moreover, institutional and individual discrimination have denied Latinos equal access to societal resources like health and mental health services.

Lack of documentation can leave families vulnerable to landlords charging excessive prices, or not responding to requests to correct housing problems (e.g., infestation, plumbing). Landlords realize these families may not make formal complaints out of fear of apprehension. Social workers can identify organizations that support advocacy efforts (e.g., community-run or sponsored by religious organizations), and work with such entities when undertaking advocacy efforts. Working with organizations that support advocacy efforts can provide the expertise and momentum that will make system entities more responsive. For example, in one instance parents worked with a community agency in seeking the removal of a local school principal who was insensitive to their children's needs (Zuniga, 2003). Parents who form groups become empowered and feel less threatened by their undocumented status because they know they will be supported in their efforts to ask for system change (Suarez-Orozco & Suarez-Orozco 1995).

Although advocacy efforts may expand clinical social workers' roles, culturally relevant practice with Latinos demands that social workers take on multiple roles at all levels (i.e., micro, meso, macro) and, from a social justice perspective, work with all systems that the clients live in. Workers must learn to be flexible in their roles so that they can facilitate empowering experiences for clients (Zuniga, 2003). This demands a role repertoire that includes not only the role of clinician but also that of educator, organizer, collaborator, counselor, broker, and advocate.

Social justice clinical models integrate marginality issues with insight-oriented therapy (Van Soest, 1994). This approach is practiced in office based 50-minute hour, as well as the clients' communities for the purpose of establishing collaborative efforts to develop resources that did not exist or were previously not accessible. By participating in community work, therapists become schooled in the clients' culture and their contextual or ecological realities. Such an experience offers therapists the opportunity to see the problems from the client's perspective; it gives them a real sense of the "stressors" their clients experience when they leave the therapist's office.

Making home calls to provide service when possible helps to lessen the threat of the situation for the family and offers the parents and family more control. This is also a viable manner by which to ensure that the worker's assessment truly incorporates an ecological perspective because the worker sees firsthand what kinds of streets, stores, bus transportation, and resources surround the family's home.

A worker who encounters gang graffiti close to where a family lives, for example, can ask the family about their experiences with gang phenomena. This may provide insights that otherwise might not be provided and uncover important areas to examine, such as the safety of children.

In short, many Latinos need social services that are offered in Spanish and with the cultural frameworks that respect and utilize a family and its cultural strengths. Information and referral services to enable the client and family to address survival issues should always be given priority. The need for knowledge of culturally relevant community services and agencies demands that the worker become familiar with the Latino community and its resources (Zuniga, 2003).

THE VALUE OF THE COLLECTIVE: GROUP SERVICES

The family-centeredness that characterizes Latino culture is interwoven with a concern for and emphasis on the collective. This emphasis can be used by workers to provide educational, informational, and problem-focused services by using group formats. In particular, the use of parent groups to inform parents about school policy or to address special topics, if driven by a culturally sensitive format, can be especially effective. Because so many Latino families immigrate to this country to ensure good educational resources for their children, developing services in collaboration with schools to strengthen the relationship between parents and the school systems is a critical need area.

Cultures like those of Latinos are viewed as "high-context" cultures wherein communication not only involves the words offered to convey a message but also relies heavily on personal delivery that resonates the affective as well as the factual (Hall, 1976). The meaning includes personal perceptions and is dependent on personal interaction. In contrast, low-context cultures use written communication such as letters or memos to parents, a device often used in U.S. public school systems. Utilizing a group process in which parents feel the support of other parents as they interact with representatives, professionals, and social workers from the sending institution or agency is a method that lessens the threat of dealing with a foreign institution, allows parents to provide support to one another, and incorporates the ideas and recommendations of these parents to ensure more culturally appropriate outcomes. It offers the parents the opportunity to assess the affective dimensions presented by the professional; if this affective component is genuine and shows the worker has *"un corazon buena,"* or a good heart, that helps to support culturally sensitive communication avenues. Although this speaks more to the style and format that social workers must incorporate if they are to provide culturally competent services to Latinos, there are also arenas of knowledge acquisition that must be recognized.

The Lopez vignette in this chapter illustrates how workers can use a process-stage approach in working with Latinos (i.e., contact, problem identification, assessment, intervention, and termination) (Lum, 2011). We will highlight some of the worker–system practice issues, noting the workers' tasks as they proceed through this stage approach.

CASE STUDY | THE LOPEZ FAMILY

The Lopez family came to the social service agency very concerned about their oldest son, Mando, who was in a gang, had been involved in various gang activities, and had been in the emergency room twice in the past year for a stabbing and a gunshot wound that was the result of a rival gang attack. The family had not been to a social service agency before, although they had asked for help from the school Mando attended. The worker, Andrea, was a young Euro-American woman who did not speak Spanish. The worker spent a few minutes greeting them, talking to them about the resources the agency provided, and explained the kind of questions she would need to ask and why they were important for her to be able to assist them. She also acknowledged her lack of familiarity with the Spanish language and the importance of their comfort in proceeding in English. Later in supervision, she raised questions about her work with the family that touched on relevance of interventions, assessment, and the personal meaning of working with this diverse family.

Although Mando, 18, wanted out of gang life, he was fearful that he would be gravely hurt if he left his gang. He expressed to his mother that he felt his life was worthless and that he knew he would be dead within a year. He was fearful of accompanying his family in asking the agency for help and did not participate in the meeting because of his concern that gang members would discover this and retaliate.

Mrs. Lopez and her two oldest daughters—Irene, age 27, and Maribel, age 20—came to the agency to seek help. They did not know what to do. They were fearful for Mando's welfare. They also felt embarrassed about this problem and were afraid the worker would look down on them because Mando was in a gang. The worker listened, nodding at times, indicated how their taking initiative to seek help was an example of a family strength.

The daughters were also fearful for their mother's health because she suffered from chronic insomnia that was triggered by her fear for her son's welfare. In later sessions, they hesitantly disclosed another family secret: all members of the family were legal residents except for Mrs. Lopez. Because of this immigration problem, the daughters feared for the safety of their mother in seeking health care.

Mrs. Lopez had not been examined by a doctor in years, and the daughters were anxious that she might have more medical problems that she was willing to disclose to them. The worker listened, attuned to their concerns, and said "with so much going on, you must feel very worried about your mother."

The family was reeling from the recent separation of the parents. The father had returned to Tijuana, Baja California, Mexico, leading to increased difficulties in sustaining themselves economically; they were struggling to maintain their economic stability. The mother and daughters felt helpless and incompetent in their ability to ensure the safety of their son/brother; they also had apprehension about issues related to Mrs. Lopez's undocumented status. The neighborhood and school systems that would normally provide resources for a teenager were viewed as alienating aspects of this family's environment. The school system had claimed that its hands were tied and that it did not have resources to offer the family when they asked for help with getting Mando out of his gang. Mando's fellow gang members were enrolled in the same high school, yet gang intervention efforts were not available. One of the reasons Mando dropped out of the school was to remove himself from gang influences while at school.

Moreover, Mando's neighborhood, which offered affordable housing for his family, was on the border of rival gang turf. Weekly gang struggles occurred in that area to such an extent that children were not allowed to play outside their homes. The neighborhood, which normally provides social, recreational, and support networks, was instead a system that was dangerous and resulted in families being cut off from each other, fearful of gang activity and disempowered. There was little interaction in their neighborhood between the school and the community with many families feeling isolated from the school and perceived it negatively as a challenge rather than as a resource.

During several planning sessions with the family that attempted to identify options that would enable Mando to exit his gang without reprisal, the 20-year-old daughter suggested that they move to San Diego where they had relatives, and would still be in proximity to their father. She raised the question whether it would be possible to move the family to San Diego as a way to remove Mando from his gang turf, freeing him in a legitimate way from gang membership. This would offer a new beginning for this teenager and his family members, albeit at some costs. Perhaps establishing a new environment would change the quality of family interactions. Andrea, the social worker, responded by engaging the family in exploring their feelings about this move and affirmed their brainstorming.

Mrs. Lopez worked cleaning hotel rooms, but she felt that the move would not be a problem related to work because a niece in the area would be able to obtain similar employment for her despite her undocumented status. The worker's sensitive inquiries about whether support systems existed for this family led to the family agreement that they would in fact have more support by moving to San Diego. Assessment of the father's relation to the family indicated that the mother felt having Mando's father in close proximity would provide the male input she could not provide for her son's socialization.

The worker and family listed all the positive reasons for moving and then identified all the difficulties and resources that would be needed for this change. A critical area that was assessed was whether the move and resettlement in a new city might be more risky for the mother's undocumented status. Although the worker felt uncomfortable in asking this sensitive question, the discussion helped the family assess this important area and consider this theme as a critical element in their planning. She also inquired if the family would like information on immigrant services in the area; Mrs. Lopez expressed interest in learning more about those services. The family examined the issues over several sessions and formulated an agreed-upon plan and commitment to move.

Between sessions, the worker found human service agencies in San Diego that would support Mando's need for a gang prevention resource once he returns to school and also located a community-based clinic that could attend to Mrs. Lopez's health needs without concern for her legal status. Although Mando had dropped out of school, he was motivated to start again if they moved to San Diego.

Planning with this family took several sessions where they examined budget issues, how to obtain rent deposit resources, how the move would take place, and how Mrs. Lopez would obtain employment before the move to ensure a source of income. Also, Maribel, the 20-year-old daughter, initiated a job search to find herself employment in San Diego. The move to San Diego meant the family would not have to pass through the U.S. Homeland Security Customs and Border Protection station; thus, the move would not place the mother at risk for detection. Even though the oldest daughter, Irene, was married and had her own family, she participated in all the planning activities because her mother did not speak English well. Irene also helped to make telephone calls regarding employment, human service contacts, and housing contacts before the move actually occurred. The social worker stayed in communication with Irene as she assisted with these tasks.

Assessment by the worker after the move indicated that Mando and his younger brother were enrolled in new schools. With the assistance of a contact made by the social worker in the new city, Mando was enrolled in an alternative high school that would allow him to take extra credits to make up for the time he had lost. This school had a collaborative gang prevention program that 1) provided Mando with pre-employment training; 2) offered counseling and support services; and 3) provided a tutor so that he would be eligible for graduation within the year. Mando graduated from high school, obtained a job through the gang prevention program, and began contributing to his family's welfare as they continued to struggle economically. He developed his ability to speak to teenagers on the dangers of gangs, and used his experiences to illustrate the dangers that he and his family survived.

Although the family also needed to address their grief related to the parents' separation, the worker focused first on the survival issues they faced. The life-or-death issue related to gang membership constitutes a major threat to teens who live in inner cities (Morales, 1995). Workers must be flexible and offer creative problem solving in their work with families that have scarce resources and limited options. A major underpinning in this family's solution strategy was consideration of what extended family and social supports would be most available. Coupling the family's natural networks with the worker's understanding of formal networks provided a solution, though difficult, that was acceptable to this family. Together, the worker and the family figured out a way to provide the family with a different environment, with the worker's mindfulness about

continued

CASE STUDY | THE LOPEZ FAMILY *continued*

identification of resources that would not jeopardize the mother's undocumented situation.

In the assessment process, planning endeavors, and implementation of strategies, the worker always asked for the family's evaluation of the worthiness of the plan and their affirmation. The fact that the 20-year-old daughter identified a most viable option that became real illustrates the importance of working with as many family members as possible. Although the mother's legal status was not part of the core problem, it was potentially related to the types of resolutions that were needed to help her son, Mando, and had to be acknowledged and addressed.

Case Vignette Reflections
The Lopez family vignette highlights many challenges faced by similar Latino families and demonstrates skill standards related to CSWE standards, NASW,

and Lum (2011). Social worker interventions illustrate identification of practice issues and interventions at micro, meso, and macro levels, framing service delivery goals in relation to social issues, and demonstrate worker awareness of possible ethical considerations by her awareness of the kinds of issues to raise in supervision. Cultural issues were factored in regarding family roles and family worldview. Macro-level social and economic justice issues regarding immigration documentation, employment, and education comprised part of the intervention strategy for the purpose of promoting empowerment on individual and family levels. Examples of specific interventions are manifested in the worker's engagement with all family members, empathy, and the ability to create a safe, holding environment for the family to use the agency services.

MICRO-LEVEL PRACTICE

On a micro level of practice, the vignette addresses how the family managed their anxiety and stress when all but one of the family members have documentation, coping with gang issues, problem solving on survival themes, and also referral making to counseling services focused on growth (flourishing). Growth issues focused on processing their grief and anger regarding the parental separation. Crisis intervention facilitated building rapport and relationship with the family and provided a foundation for the trust that needed to be in place for referral to counseling. The worker's affirming interventions normalized the family's difficulties in asking for help and promoted development of a safe, holding environment needed for change to occur.

MESO-LEVEL PRACTICE

The family work based on the Lopez's definition of "family" (i.e., including Irene, the married daughter) benefited by including many members of the family that it desired to participate assisted in utilizing family resources, for example with the 20-year-old's creative suggestion to move to another city.

"Platicas," or educative forums of group work with parents, is another format that is preventive and offers Latinos experiences with professionals that promote legitimizing professional credibility and the value of professional input. Support groups to address stressful issues and groups to promote advocacy efforts play into the cultural ethos of collective effort that is valued among Latinos. The group context enables parents or youth in groups to feel less threatened or embarrassed about participating. Creating a "social" atmosphere to group work, by asking parents to bring refreshments also plays into the Latino cultural format that values quality interpersonal activities. Both individual and group formats must be based on a humanistic stance that conveys to Latino clients that their culture is respected and that racist elements are not present (e.g., institutional practices that result in marginalization by "experts," stereotyping, patronizing, imposition of others values).

MACRO-LEVEL PRACTICE

In this vignette, knowledge acquisition included information on types of programs that are effective with Latino high-risk youth and identification of a Spanish-speaking counseling center (e.g., culturally appropriate referral). An ecological perspective (Germain, 1981) with a focus on improving the fit between a client's needs focused the worker on finding needed formal resources, that is, services offered in Spanish, services that would not jeopardize the mother, and a location where they could access natural support systems, which is crucial for the adaptation of Latino families (Valle & Vega, 1980). The Lopez family case points to provision of services many Latino client situations demand, and although there was attention to bolstering parenting to protect the children, autonomy in identifying options, and connection to social supports, there was little attention to issues of identity. Rather, the referral to counseling services was made with the intention of emotional aspects the family was contending with getting addressed with more depth. Because the worker understood the effects of acculturation (i.e., knowledge acquisition, relevant theory) within Latino families and how it can exacerbate identity issues for children and parents, she realized this also needed attention; however, this was not within the realm of her role.

Student Learning Exercise

Purpose: This exercise promotes critical thinking that support your practice skills.

1. How would you feel about working with Mando, knowing his history of gang involvement and assaults?

2. Mando claimed that he did not come to see the worker because he feared retaliation from his gang members. Do you think this was his real reason for not attending the meetings with his family or just an excuse for not facing his responsibilities?

3. Irene, the 27-year-old daughter, attended each session, even though she had her own family. Do you think there were any boundary issues here, and if so, which ones? If not, why not?

4. What was your comfort level when you read about Mrs. Lopez's undocumented status, what did it evoke for you, and what insights do you have into how you feel about her status?

5. How would you identify resources in another city for a family if you were not familiar with that city and its resources?

6. What value differences might you have with the family? How would you discuss these in supervision and in the feedback you might seek?

7. What approach or interventions would you use to learn more about the family and its culture? What wasn't explored that you would like to learn about (e.g., parenting, possible substance abuse, religion/spirituality)?

Student Learning

Purpose: This exercise enables you to reflect on the anxiety and vigilance that non-documented immigrants often experience when they live in the United States.

Go to a shopping mall and undertake several routine shopping experiences such as buying groceries for your family, buying stamps at the post office, and picking up medication at the pharmacy. Pretend you are an immigrant without documents, although you can speak some English. First, think about how lack of documents might affect each transaction. What things, people, or circumstances might raise concern or create anxiety for an immigrant? When you return home, think about the emotional costs an immigrant parent, in particular, experiences in undertaking even during normal tasks of a few hours of shopping.

- What incidents could have been especially sensitive?
- What transactions might have made an immigrant particularly concerned (e.g., asked to show identification to pick up a prescription)?
- Which officials, such as security guards monitoring stores, who might make an immigrant feel self-conscious did you encounter?
- How tired did you feel at the end of this exercise?

Implications: Workers need to be sensitive and have insights into the kinds of experiences that, although others may consider normal, add to the pressures and anxieties of an undocumented person. Such insights allow workers to consider how to ask clients about their experiences and enable workers to debrief clients and alleviate their anxieties. It also teaches workers how to prepare immigrants for referrals and help them to address normal tasks with less emotional distress.

CULTURAL COMPETENCE WITH ASIAN AMERICANS

CHAPTER 12

Rowena Fong

INTRODUCTION

Diversification among the ethnic groups has been evident with the growing census population numbers. The 2000 U.S. Census reflects how Asian and Pacific Islander Americans and other ethnic groups have evolved. Historically, Asian Americans were clumped together to include all groups of Asians, and Pacific Islanders were included in that group. However, during the 10-year period between 1980 and 1990, the total Asian American population increased 107% (Sandhu, 1997, cited in Ross-Sheriff & Husain, 2001).

But the 2000 U.S. Census subdivides the peoples of Asian countries into the major groupings of Asian, Southeast Asian, Asian Indian, and other Asian. These groups include people who are Chinese, Filipino, Japanese, Korean, Vietnamese, Cambodian, Hmong, Laotian, Indian, Pakistani, Thai, and other Asians; whereas the peoples of the 25 islands in the Pacific are categorized as Native Hawaiian, Guamanian or Chamorro, Samoan, or other Pacific Islander. Leung and Cheung (2001) report that prior to the 2000 U.S. Census, "[even though] Asians and Pacific Islanders represent at least twenty-three ethnic groups with thirty-two linguistic groups and more than one hundred dialects, these culturally diverse populations have been conveniently grouped for statistical purposes" (p. 426). Historically, Pacific Islanders were grossly omitted from considerations of reporting mechanisms. But with growing Pacific Islander populations throughout the United States, particularly on the West Coast, it is very important not only to acknowledge them but also to understand and respect their distinct cultural values and history.

DEMOGRAPHICS

According to the 2000 U.S. Census, Asian, Native Hawaiian, and other Pacific Islander are each considered to be separate race categories. The total U.S.

population in 2000 was 281,421,906 with 3.6% (2,475,956) reported to be Asian and 0.1% (398,835) to be Native Hawaiian and other Pacific Islander. The population of two or more races was 6,626,228. Of the Asians and Pacific Islanders (API) population, the subgroupings according to the 2000 U.S. Census are as follows:

Asian Americans	Chinese, Japanese, Filipino, Korean
Southeast Asians	Cambodian, Hmong, Vietnamese, Laotian, Thai, Malaysian, Singaporean
Asian Indian	Bengalese, Bharat, Dravidian, East Indian, Goanese
Other Asian	Bangladeshi, Burmese, Indonesian, Pakistani, Sri Lankan

Among the Pacific Islanders, the largest groups are Hawaiians, Samoans, and Guamanians (Chamorros). Other groups are Tongan, Fijian, Palauan, Tahitian, North Mariana Islanders, and other Pacific Islanders.

In a 2000 U.S. Census special report entitled "We the People: Asians in the United States," current demographics report Asians to be 11.9 million or 4.2% of the total population (Reeves & Bennett, 2004). Within the 11.9 million, 10.2 million are Asian only (3.6%) and 1.7 million or 0.6% are Asian and at least one other race. This report offers a breakdown of the 10.2 million Asian-only population: Chinese 2,422,970; Filipino 1,864,120; Asian Indian 1,645,510; Vietnamese 1,110,207; Korean 1,072,682; Japanese 795,051; Cambodian 178,043; Hmong 170,049; Laotian 167,792; Pakistani 155,909; Thai 110,851; and Other Asian 3, 478,636.

Another U.S. Census Special Report entitled, "We the People: Pacific Islanders in the United States" reports Native Hawaiian and other Pacific Islander Groups alone to be 378,782 or 0.13% of the total population (Harris & Jones, 2005). Within the 378,782 count, 139,495 are Native Hawaiian (0.05%); 85,243 are Samoan (0.03%); 55,130 are Guamanian (0.02%); 27,686 are Tongan (0.01%); 10,265 are Fijian; 5,843 are Marshallese; and 55,120 (0.02%) are other Pacific Islanders.

GROUP DIVERSITY

Diversity has made its impact on racial categorizing. Lott (1998) criticizes the racial groupings of Asian Americans and claims that "Asian Americans in the United States were first defined not as a racial category or ethnic group but as a legal status. For almost a century they were defined as aliens ineligible for citizenship" (p. 87). Thus, it was only in the 1970s that the Asian American category was expanded to include Pacific Americans. Only 30 years later, however, the 2000 U.S. Census was recategorized to include six race-alone categories (White, Black or African American, American Indian and Alaska Native, Asian, Native Hawaiian and other Pacific Islander, and some other race such as one of Hispanic origin including Spanish, Hispanic, or Latino) and one category for two or more races (U.S. Bureau of the Census, 2001).

Diversity in multiple races and ethnic identities challenges social workers in the 21st century to reexamine culturally competent practices in serving ethnic minority populations. The 2000 U.S. Census (U.S. Bureau of the Census, 2001) now reports seven possible categories of race and origin rather than the "one-drop" rule (Daniel, 1992). Thus, individuals can now self-identify with various race mixings. Spickard, Fong, and Ewalt (1995) forewarned that no one ethnic grouping would be sufficient and that the "multiplication of racial categories suggests a deconstruction of the very notion of race" (p. 581).

Because of the growing diversity among and within ethnic groups, social workers are to be evermore aware of subtle differences (Almeida, 2005; Kim & Ryu, 2005; Nath, 2005; Percy, Soekandar, Limansubroto, & Davis, 2005; Pillari, 2005; Root, 2005; Shibusawa, 2005). In delivering culturally competent social work services, cultural awareness, knowledge acquisition, and skill development need to be reexamined for each ethnic grouping. Asian Americans and Pacific Islanders are no exception. Within the last two decades, the Vietnamese, a Southeast Asian group, had a growth rate of 134.8% (Hing, 1993). With growth comes challenges and problems. Fong and Mokuau (1994), in their literature review on API, reported that researchers, educators, and practitioners would need to distinguish between Asians (South Asians and Southeast Asians) and Pacific Islanders, separate Asian Americans into different ethnic groups, and discern the differences between immigrants and refugees.

Social problems within the API groups have expanded (Vakalahi & Fong, 2009). Substance abuse and family violence are growing concerns with Native Hawaiians and other API populations (Mokuau, 1999, 2001; Straussner, 2001); stress, coping, and depression among the Korean and Chinese elderly (Mui, 1996, 2001); cultural conflict and pressure for scholastic achievement among Hmong and other Southeast Asian children (Caplan, Choy, & Whitmore, 1991; Chan, 1994; Trueba, Jacobs, & Kirton, 1990). Asian American mental health researcher Dr. Stanley Sue (2008) reported that in family suicide risk among Asian Americans, family conflict affects Asian American families more adversely than other risk factors such as poverty or depression. Social work professionals are reminded that Asian Americans are very hesitant to disclose their mental health problems. Harmony and family integration are highly valued and expected in Asian American families, which contribute to creating severe tensions and conflicts, especially between parents and college students whose attempts at suicide are becoming more noticeable and alarming. Sue warns that although prevention interventions are needed, mental health practitioners working with Asian American families still need to precisely determine the kinds of family conflicts that are associated with suicide risks with Asian Americans.

Risk factors in areas of health, mental health, and substance abuse are fueled by macro issues of bigotry, racism, discrimination, and oppression. Unfair employment, hate crimes, and insufficient funding for immigrants services were expected to be problematic for Asian Americans in the 1990s and 2000s (U.S. Commission on Civil Rights, 1992). Victims of human trafficking from Southeast Asia and South Asia suffer health and mental health problems (Fong & Berger, 2009; Fong & Urban, 2009 and somatic and social suffering exist among survivors of the Cambodian killing fields (Morelli, 2001; Uehara, Morelli, & Abe-Kim, 2001).

Thus, theories, practices, and social services should be modified and delivered in a manner that addresses the diverse, complex, and multifaceted needs of these clients. Social workers ought to examine new paradigm shifts and integrate the intersection of ethnicity, gender, age, social class, physical and mental abilities, and religion into present and future culturally competent practices (Fong & Furuto, 2001; Fong, 2004; Guadalupe & Lum, 2005). Rather than using the traditional paradigm of approaching API with ethnicity as the primary variable, social workers need to create new paradigms that also embrace sexual orientation and religion and physical and mental abilities as equally important factors in the clients' lives.

Within each ethnic group, distinctions may exist among individuals based on immigrant, refugee, and transnational status (Lott, 1998, p. 99). Immigrant status would distinguish between those people who are native and those who are foreign. Transnational status would distinguish those people who, like the Chinese, emigrate from one country to two or more countries, such as Hong Kong to Canada and then to the United States. Within the transnational identity, some immigrants have left living environments because of political policies affecting family size, structure, and functioning.

Besides the immigrants, two other growing populations within the Asian and Pacific Island American (APIA) population who are encountering stressors and are in need of attention are biracial and mixed-race children, adults, and families. This category encompasses the children born from intermarriages who will become biracial or multiracial adults. Dhooper and Moore (2001) report the major needs and problems of biracial/mixed-race American groups to be related to mixed-race status, mixed-race families, biracial homosexuals, and biracial children and adolescents. Identity formation, divided loyalties, and conflicted choices between cultural heritages are some of the common dilemmas for this population.

Another growing population within the Asian group that will need attention in the future is the rising number of Chinese female (mostly) babies from the People's Republic of China who are being adopted by families. This trend eventually will cause social workers to examine their practice and deal with diversity issues. Fong and Wang (2001) write about the differing political and social environments between the United States and the People's Republic of China and the potential identity conflicts these infants may face as young adults with the absence of birth family knowledge. Chinese infants in both Chinese and non-Chinese families will struggle with the same issues of identity that American-born Asian children and adolescents face, but they also will have to struggle with national identity because the values and traditions of the People's Republic of China differ greatly from those of Hong Kong and other non-Communist environments. National identity issues may arise when the Chinese girls ask their adoptive parents about their birthplace, and parents might have to grapple with their personal and political thoughts about the People's Republic of China's stance on human rights. As Ross-Sheriff and Husain (2001) remind social workers, "[O]verall the common concern regarding work with Asian Americans is that the practitioner must recognize and plan to address the complex and multifaceted nature of their diversity" (p. 87). Certainly, the Chinese infants, many of them with physical disabilities, born in a Communist country but raised in a democratic political environment, some with parents of a different race, might someday need very skilled social workers who can explain when these teenagers ask why their Chinese parents abandoned them. Culturally competent skills are needed in working with all these facets of diversity.

CULTURAL COMPETENCE WITH CLIENT GROUPS

Cultural competence, defined in Chapter One, is a relational, dialogical process between the worker and the client. The emphasis is on the conversation exchange, mutual understanding, and egalitarian relationship. It involves the participatory relationship between the worker and the client. The paradigm shift is from building the cultural competence of the worker to having the worker and the client work together in learning to be competent and proficient in cultural ways of coping with the problems of the living.

To address competency and proficiency in cultural ways, one needs to have a discussion about what is culture. The definition of culture is often presented as the starting point (Lum, 1999, p. 2) to the discussion on cultural competence. Gordon (as cited in Lum, 1999) defines culture as "the way of life of multiple groups in a society and consists of prescribed ways of behaving or norms of conduct, beliefs, values, and skills" (p. 2). However, in social work practice, the term cultural competence has evolved in the last couple of decades with a range of conceptualizations including culturally competent system of care (Cross, Bazron, Dennis, & Issacs, 1989), ethnic sensitive practice and ethnic realities (Devore & Schlesinger, 1999), social work practice and people of color (Lum, 2000), culturally competent social work practice (Lum, 1999), and biculturalization of interventions (Fong, Boyd, & Browne, 1999).

Lum (1999) has defined cultural competence as "the set of knowledge and skills that a social worker must develop in order to be effective with multicultural clients" (p. 3). He advocates for cultural awareness, knowledge acquisition, skill development, and inductive learning. Operating from a strengths-based, solution-focused, culture-valued framework, this was modified by Fong (2001), and the terms were redefined as follows:

- Cultural awareness: The social workers' understanding and identification of the critical cultural values important to the client system and to themselves.
- Knowledge acquisition: The social workers' understanding of how these cultural values function as strengths in the client's functioning and treatment planning.
- Skill development: The social workers' ability to match services that support the identified cultural values and then to incorporate them in the appropriate interventions.
- Inductive learning: The social workers' continued quest to seek solutions, which includes finding other indigenous interventions and matching cultural values to choose appropriate western interventions. (p. 6)

Fong's framework presupposed that social workers are fully familiar with the cultural values important to the client system. The traditional values of ethnic groups represent strengths in the assessment process of social work and provide resources in treatment planning and implementation. For example, in traditional Asian cultures values of patriarchy, family loyalty, cohesion, and harmony are highly revered. Thus, it is important to include these variables in the planning of how to treat these clients. Galan (2001) states that the "culturally competent relationship is helping each family member achieve internal consistency among values, beliefs, behaviors, and identity within a social context" (p. 264). He describes the "processing of cultural beliefs" and defines it to be "helping the client [to] know how to weigh cultural information and how to prioritize with respect to choosing appropriate behavior in order to maintain integrity in one's belief and behavior nexus" (p. 263).

The definition of cultural competence as it applies to APIA groups includes knowledge of cultural values, indigenous interventions, and Western interventions to support and not contradict or detract from the traditional cultural values. With many ethnic groups, macro-level societal values dominate the meso and micro levels of functioning of family and individual. Fong (1997) warned that in working with immigrants from the People's Republic of China and assessing problems and issues, social workers must study the macro-level societal values that shape the behaviors and performance of family members and individuals. This approach serves to address cultural competence at the macro, meso, and micro levels of practice. However, to build upon Cross, Bazron, Dennis, and Issacs's work (1989), cultural competence also needs to be addressed at the macro level in working with communities that support the ethnic families. In most Asian groups, the community family associations may play a big role in offering support and services to people within their own ethnic group.

This framework of starting with macro-level societal values supports and builds upon the previous literature of cultural competence. Devore and Schlesinger's (1999) ethnic sensitive practice framework examined the layers of understanding in ethnic-sensitive social work practice. These seven layers covered social work values, knowledge of human behavior, knowledge and skill in agency policy and services, self-awareness into ethnicity, impact of the ethnic reality, and the relationship between social worker and the delivery of social services. Cross, Bazron, Dennis, and Issacs (1989) examine cultural competence from a macro system of care framework that includes attitudes, behaviors, and policies as they apply to individuals, agencies, and organizations. For Hawaiian, Samoan, and Chamorro communities, cultural competence is "having staff, with a deep understanding of the people and place, an understanding reflected in program content, policies, procedures, and the living character of the program" (Furuto, San Nicolas, Kim, & Fiaui, 2001, p. 329). Each ethnic community program is a representation of a distinct part of the culture reflected in different languages and customs. The "living character of the program" is reflected when bilingual and bicultural social workers are hired to bring cultural meaning in words and behaviors into the agency and services for clients.

In defining cultural competence, this chapter will emphasize Lum's new paradigm shift in Chapter One of emphasizing the participatory relationship between the worker and the client: 1) it is expected that both the social worker and client will be learning the way of their respective lives that consists of values and beliefs; 2) it involves cultural awareness, knowledge, skills, and inductive learning (Lum, 1999); 3) it includes cultural values as strengths, which should be included in assessments and biculturalization of interventions (Fong, 2001); 4) it is the "processing of cultural beliefs" (Galan, 2001); and 5) it starts at the macrosocietal level and interacts with meso and micro levels (Fong, 1997).

With this new paradigm, cultural competence with Asian Americans will force social workers to understand the traditional values and beliefs of Asian Americans, who when seeking social services will be expected to learn about and adapt to the professional values and ethics of social work. In the same vein, cultural competence with Pacific Islanders will now demand that social workers not ignore the possibility that a worker–client participatory relationship may include extended family members and indigenous interventions because of the cultural values and practices of Native

Hawaiians and other Pacific Islander groups. Pacific Islanders, in a participatory relationship with their social worker, will learn more about the different levels of resources that social work offers and may become more familiar with the multilevels of receiving and getting help in a social work social systems approach. Thus, cultural competence shifts from an exclusive focus of the cultural competence of the worker to an inclusive relationship between the worker and the client based on the development of cultural competency and proficiency of both parties in the helping process.

HISTORICAL OPPRESSION AND CURRENT SOCIAL ISSUES

The history of the oppression of API is best told by recounting the discriminatory experiences of Asian immigrants, the racist attitudes and behaviors toward American-born Asians, and the colonialist practices toward Pacific Islanders, particularly Native Hawaiians. Although it is acknowledged that probably all Asian, Southeast Asian, South Asian, and Pacific Islander groups have endured unfair discriminatory, racist, and colonialist attitudes and behaviors, space limitations allow for only a brief discussion of some Asian and Pacific Islander groups' experiences.

DISCRIMINATORY EXPERIENCES OF ASIAN IMMIGRANTS

Discriminatory experiences of Asian immigrants have been many and are ongoing. The first Asian immigrant group to enter the United States was the Chinese in the 1840s. Mostly single men, these sojourners were looking for their "mountain of gold" (Sung, 1967) in order to make good money, buy a business or land, and return to China as prosperous successes. This was their dream. Their reality in California in the 1800s and 1900s was hostile confrontations, exclusions, and even fatalities because of riots against them. In 1882, legislation was passed (the Chinese Exclusion law) that halted immigration and exacerbated the already discriminatory practice of not allowing Chinese immigrants to become citizens. Although in 1943 the Exclusion Act was finally repealed, much pressure, such as being driven out of their work and communities, was put upon the Chinese laborers to return to China. Some succumbed, but despite the racist and discriminatory practices against them because they worked for wages lower than their Euro-American counterparts, many remained in the United States and formed Chinatown communities (Fong, 1992; Takaki, 1993).

The next Asian groups of Japanese, Korean, and Filipino immigrants fared no better than the Chinese in adjusting to the United States except that they could learn from experiences of the Chinese. Japanese immigrants, mostly laborers and indigent students who started coming to America in the 1890s, were carefully screened before being allowed to leave Japan. They were "predominantly males who worked at difficult low paying jobs; they faced racism and were relegated to the bottom of society" (Kitano & Nakaoka, 2001, p. 9). Although in 1907 the Gentleman's Agreement passed between the U.S. and Japanese governments restricted the emigration of male laborer immigrants, it did not apply to female immigrants. Between 1910 and 1920, the Japanese government allowed farmers and laborers to summon their wives in order to avoid the bachelor society the Chinese men had had to endure (Fong, 1992; Ichioka, 1988). Japanese women were able to join their husbands and form a "family society" in the United States, but many women also came as "picture brides" or prostitutes (Ichioka, 1988). Whether male or female, single or married, the Japanese immigrants, like the Chinese, experienced hostility and discrimination. The anti-Japanese movement was as virulent in the 1900s as was the anti-Chinese movement in the 1800s.

When the next immigrant groups of Koreans, Asian Indians, and Filipinos entered the United States in the 1900s, they too experienced exclusion, harassment, and violence. Filipinos confronted difficulties and hardships created by the U.S. government despite their U.S. national status. Anti-Filipino sentiment was rampant on the West Coast because of competition for jobs with white laborers. Asian Indians and Koreans also experienced prejudice, discrimination, and racism in jobs, workplace, housing, and educational opportunities.

In 1900, Asian immigrants consisting mostly of Chinese and Japanese occupied 1.5% of the total foreign-born U.S. population (Kitano & Nakaoka, 2001, p. 12). But Hing (1993) reports that demographic predictions are that by the year 2020, Asian Pacific Americans will be 54% of the foreign-born population (p. 127). Foreign-born Asians will dominate social work services, and culturally competent services will need to be changed to reflect that change in status.

RACIST ATTITUDES AND BEHAVIORS TOWARD AMERICAN-BORN ASIANS

First- and second-generation Asians, Southeast Asians, and Asian Indians born in the United States experience many discriminatory practices, as did their forefathers from overseas. Employment discrimination with unfair labor laws and below-normal wages continues to be practiced. In the 1940s, the Japanese interned during World War II experienced what the American Civil Liberties Union described as the "greatest deprivation of civil liberties by government in this country since slavery." Evacuation, incarceration, and resettlement were imposed on Japanese American citizens who felt that "their government did not trust them and that the Constitution did not protect them from forced removal and incarceration without charges or trial" (Nishi, 1995, p. 103).

Almost 30 years later in the 1970s, at the end of the Vietnam War, the Amerasian children, offspring of American GIs and Southeast Asian women, were also treated with racial bias and hostile attitudes, despite negotiations between the South Vietnamese and American governments. These refugees, although given U.S. citizenship by birth, were not well received in America. Nor were their other Southeast Asian counterparts. Poverty and poor housing and living conditions are some of the many problems these Southeast Asians have faced living in America.

COLONIZATION AND IMPERIALISM TOWARD PACIFIC ISLANDERS

The history of Pacific Islanders and the story of their oppressive encounters with people who forcibly try to dominate the land and the peoples document colonization and imperialist practices. In the history of the kanaka maoli or indigenous Hawaiians, it is written that James Cooke arrived in Hawaii in 1778 and "unleashed five devastating interrelated forces of depopulation; foreign exploitation; cultural conflict; adoption of harmful foreign ways; and neglect, insensitivity, and malice from the ruling establishment" (Blaisdell & Mokuau, 1991, p. 132). Native Hawaiians and other Pacific Islanders have experienced imperialism and colonization, which diminish their attempts and ability to self-govern (Trask, 1984–1985). Foreigners have come to the islands and exploited native lands for private ownership. They have supplanted ruling chiefs by indebtedness to avarice merchants and suspended native language, dances, and healing methods for Westernized religious practices (Mokuau, 1991). The sovereignty nation movement of Hawaiians in the 1990s was an attempt to empower the entire nation (Ewalt & Mokuau, 1995), but opposition remains to Native Hawaiian self-determination from internal (factions among the Hawaiian people) and external (practices of colonization) sources. Ethical questions arise when the practices of colonization go unquestioned, and social and economic injustices continue to plague the Native Hawaiian population.

IMPACT OF OPPRESSION

Native Hawaiians have struggled to own their land and receive the federal rights and entitlements bestowed upon Native peoples. Federal legislation was proposed to give Native Hawaiians the same federal recognition as Native Americans by Senator Daniel Akaka, who has been spearheading this effort since 1999. In January 2005, he introduced S147, the Native Hawaiian Government Reorganization Act of 2005, which would 1) establish the Office of Native Hawaiian Relations in the Department of Interior to focus on Native Hawaiian affairs; 2) establish the Native Hawaiian Interagency Coordinating Group; and 3) provide a process of reorganizing the Native Hawaiian governing entity. Akaka's bill was proposed and passed through the House in 2000 but was not immediately approved by the Senate. The delay perpetuates the denial of Native Hawaiians' rights and entitlements.

The United States Commission on Civil Rights (1992) reported that in the 1990s Asian Americans faced discrimination and barriers to equal opportunities because of the "model minority" stereotype that wrongly labels some Asian groups with high average family incomes, educational achievement, and occupational status as representing all or most Asian American family situations (p. 19). The poverty of recent immigrants and "glass ceilings" in employment and academic admissions in higher learning institutions for second-, third-, or fourth-generation individual members are ignored. Negative perceptions of being "foreigners," of lacking communication skills, of having limited English proficiency, and of adhering to non-Western religious beliefs and practices tend to still plague many American-born Asians (pp. 20–21).

IMPACT OF GLOBALIZATION AND TRAUMA OF IMMIGRATION

The issues for immigrants and refugees overlap concerns for American-born Asians, but a host of complex issues plague these growing populations (Lee & Mock, 2005; Leung & Boehnleim, 2005; Kim & Ryu, 2005). They have problems with undocumented-alien status and discriminatory Immigration and Naturalization Service (INS) experiences. Lee, Lei, and Sue (2001) report anxiety stressors associated with the process of leaving family members behind and encountering poor living conditions upon arrival in America.

Besides differences in political status, language, foods, beliefs, and traditions, the Asian and Pacific Islander immigrant and refugee populations can be further distinguished by religions, marriage patterns, and occupations. Although no one ethnic group is the same and there are many within-group differences, historically and even in current practices, Buddhism, Hinduism, and Catholicism have been major religions for several Asian groups. Interracial marriage tended to be more dominant in some Asian groups than others, and depending on the time cohort of the immigrant and refugee arrivals, occupational choices also tended to differ by Asian ethnic group. For example, Ross-Sheriff and Husain (2004) write:

> As a group, South Asians who came after 1980, as a result of the family reunification laws and green card lottery, are different from their previous counterparts. There is a much greater chance that neither parent of these immigrant families speak English or have a college degree. Unlike their predecessors who arrived after 1965, these immigrants have not settled in suburbs but rather in neighborhoods with low-cost or public housing. (p. 166)

Some of the Asian immigrant groups have settled into communities such as Chinatowns, Japantowns, or Koreatowns. These communities historically have been located in large cities such as San Francisco, Los Angeles, New York City, and Seattle. However, Asian communities have grown in Monterey, California (Chinatown); Portland, Oregon, and San Jose, California (Japantowns); and Atlanta, Georgia (Koreatown). In April 2005, *The Korea Times* newspaper printed an article entitled "Grocery Giants Battle in Atlanta Koreatown," reporting competition among five big grocery stores for the Asian and Latino customers (Chang, 2005). The Asian immigrant population continues to grow, sometimes with overlapping and tension-filled issues related to their own ethnic community or other minority groups.

VALUES AND ETHICAL DILEMMAS

In the CSWE 2008 EPAS the values of social work are grounded in areas related to service, social justice, the dignity and worth of the person, the importance of human relationships, integrity, competence, and human rights. Social workers are to uphold these values, as stated in the National Association of Social Workers (NASW) Code of Ethics. However, ethical dilemmas may occur when there are value conflicts or the special needs of diverse clients involving ethical-decision making related to the above mentioned areas become problematic.

Asian and Pacific Islander clients have traditional cultural values, which include working with extended family members, respecting the elders, honoring the male gender more than the female gender, putting family needs before oneself and making self-sacrifices. To behave appropriately is very important so that the Asian or Pacific Islander family would not be shamed or "lose face."

In working with Asian and Pacific Islander families in which domestic violence is a problem for the family, the social worker may find himself or herself in an ethical dilemma, especially if the social worker is of the same ethnicity and was called upon to help the family because of the assumption that if the social worker came from the same ethnic background there would more understanding of cultural values and norms. The social worker needs to be respectful of cultural norms but may have an ethical dilemma in being forced to choose to uphold the NASW Code of Ethics and to advocate for the rights of the abused woman although traditional Asian cultural values support the respect and honoring of the man in the family. Domestic violence that involves abuse done to the woman forces the social worker to choose safety and protection for the woman at the risk of not upholding the cultural norm of obeying the elders and honoring the male person in the family. Value conflicts may occur and social workers need to be able to discern how to be culturally appropriate yet still be respectful while processing cultural differences.

CULTURAL AWARENESS

Cultural awareness is defined as "the learning of the cultural background, issues, and relationships in a contextual sense" (Hardy & Laszloffy, 1995, as cited in Lum, 1999). Understanding the cultural background and the contextual sense is important because the context will dictate the services needed. Sanders (as cited in Mokuau, 1991) predicted a decade ago that the services for API would include the following considerations:

1. More changes and intergenerational problems impacting parents, children, and the elderly
2. A need for a more holistic perspective in services addressing "life, relationships, and services" and less of a "dichotomy between the body and mind, psyche and soma"
3. An emphasis on change that comes from a "preventive and developmental perspective" committed to "maximizing the strengths and capacities of individuals, families, and communities"
4. A cross-cultural, pluralistic perspective in working with clients and services
5. Greater emphasis on "total family and family support systems" (pp. 236–239)

Sanders identifies some needs, but developing the services to meet those needs is challenging. Even if the services are developed, they need to be made culturally competent and appropriate if APIA needs are truly to be met.

The social needs for services are great for Asian and Pacific Islanders. Among Japanese Americans, the impact of internment on families may still require services dealing with PTSD issues. Asian and Pacific Islander elderly suffer from depression and Alzheimer's disease, and caregivers' stress due to filial piety and obligation cultural values is also problematic (Mui, 2001). Chinese immigrants deal with language discrimination, employment, and naturalization problems. Intergenerational conflicts arise in parent–child relationships, and acculturation difficulties exist because of value conflicts, communication misunderstandings, and psychological isolation (Lee, 1997).

Filipinos struggle with employment discrimination and often end up in service-oriented jobs because of their immigrant status. Asian and Southeast Asian immigrants need bilingual services. Vietnamese and other Southeast Asians struggle with mental health problems because of acculturation stress and drastic changes in environmental disruptions (Ngo, Tran, Gibbons, & Oliver, 2001). Families have been separated, and Amerasian children have been forced to relocate to an American environment that initially did not welcome or support them. In Vietnamese and Korean immigrant family systems, there are role reversals and abuse of the women (Scheinfeld, Wallach, & Langendorf, 1997; Tran & Des Jardins, 2000; Zhou & Bankston, 1998).

Morelli (2001) writes that, in working with Cambodian refugees, social workers need to pay attention to five areas in assessment:

1. The need for trained competent language translators who have a sound understanding of differences in cultural beliefs and values regarding family, social customs, and health care between the host and immigrating cultures
2. The need for understanding of sociocultural traditions and health care
3. The need to be in consultation with community leaders and family elders regarding health care issues
4. The need for social workers to understand the disorders from both a Western and a culturally specific perspective
5. The role that policies and geopolitical histories have played and the consequent importance of macro perspectives when assessing needs for service provision (p. 208)

Among the Pacific Islander populations, abuse of Hawaiians continues because their cultural traditions have been stolen and their land is largely owned by trusts and oligopolies, forcing Native Hawaiian families to live in poverty. Native Hawaiian families experience disproportionate levels of substance abuse and family violence, and their children may consequently experience or witness domestic violence more than others will (Mokuau, 1999). Samoan children suffer high rates of child abuse, and their parents have financial difficulties, environmental and mental health concerns, and domestic violence problems. Chamorros suffer from high suicide rates among youth, drug abuse, alcoholism, family violence, and high crime rates.

Among the Asian and Pacific Islander gay, lesbian, bisexual, and transgender (GLBT) population, Kanuha (2001) makes the point that the gay or lesbian person from an ethnic group has sexual orientation needs in addition to ethnicity. Poon (2000) reports interracial same-sex abuse between Asian and Caucasian gay men and concludes that same-sex violence in Asian communities produces a need for 24-hour hotlines, shelters and safe houses, public awareness, and advocacy in the criminal justice system. Poon offers six risk factors contributing to intimate violence in Asian–Caucasian relationships:

1. Homophobia in Asian cultures
2. Issues of professional assistance and support
3. The dominant idea of beauty and Asian images in western countries
4. Age differences
5. Income disparity and its implications in relationships
6. Cultural values of family (p. 40)

Although the cultural value of family is usually a positive attribute, the shame and "loss of face" as well as privately keeping affairs within the family may discourage or prohibit help-seeking efforts.

In addressing these many needs for services within the API population, social workers need to be ready to provide social services that are based on cultural values and include indigenous strategies and interventions. They must also grapple with the interactions of ethnicity, sexual orientation, gender, and national origins that may result in cultural tensions.

KNOWLEDGE ACQUISITION

For social work practitioners, knowledge acquisition is the process of acquiring information that will enhance their understanding and effectiveness in providing culturally competent services to Asian and Pacific Islander clients. The question to be asked is this: What kind of knowledge is needed to enhance culturally competent practice with API? One proposal would be to explore how knowledge acquisition relates to the interaction of theory development, cultural values, and practice methods to affect Asian and Pacific Islander clients.

Although the theoretical framework of person-in-environment, the ecological model, and the oppression or colonization theories are germane to APIA knowledge development, theory development still needs to be compatible with the cultural values of the ethnic group. In the culture of First Nations Peoples, colonization theory guides the understanding of oppression (Brave Heart, 2001; Yellow Bird, 2001). Traditional Native culture also advocates historical trauma theory (Yellow Bird, 2001) to help explain the Lakota tribe's response to "massive cumulative group trauma across generations and within the current lifespan" (Brave Heart, 2001). This is an example of how cultural values guide theory development in Native people's culture.

In the Chinese culture, Chung (1992) offers the Confucian model of social transformation. It is a model for social change used in Asian countries that has been adapted for use in the universal generalist social work practice (p. 131). This theory is based on the values of Confucianism. There are seven steps in the model to change individuals and society:

1. The investigation of things or variables
2. The completion of knowledge
3. The sincerity of thought
4. The rectifying of the heart
5. The cultivation of the person
6. The regulation of the family
7. The governance of the state (p. 131)

This model demonstrates taking cultural values from Confucianism and creating a theory that supports those cultural values.

Another example is Morelli's (2001) statement:

[C]ritical to deeper understanding of Cambodian constructions of trauma and healing is the knowledge that the Khmer concept of pain and its expression in suffering is significantly different from western beliefs and forms. In the Khmer culture, the concept of pain extends beyond pain as an indication of illness. It is part of a larger process of suffering, which continually contributes to their kinship and familial solidarity and reciprocity, and ethnic identity maintenance. (pp. 202–203)

Morelli's point is that the Cambodian cultural value of suffering shapes the building of family and extended family relationships and connects them to the cultural value of suffering.

Thus, in working with Asians, Southeast Asians, Asian Indians, or Pacific Islanders, social workers must have a planned way to explore areas of knowledge acquisition that will allow them to better know the ethnic culture of their API clients and to use the cultural values to develop theories to explain their ways of thinking and behaving. This is closely tied into skill development and generating new inductive learning. Social workers need to know that if a Khmer client is expressing suffering and pain (a biological and psychological adjustment), the client may be using the strength of the Khmer cultural norm as a reciprocal endeavor to solidify kinship and ethnic identity. In other words, the suffering and pain should be taken as a strength for family solidarity rather than family dysfunction.

New theory development and practices need to be formulated for API families affected by policies and societal change. For example, Lee (1997) describes five types of constructs by which to understand Asian American families: traditional, "cultural conflict," bicultural, "Americanized," and interracial (pp. 11–13). Lee's five constructs assume that the Asian American families are intact families and that the differences stem from generational gaps (traditional) in differing environments with labels such as "cultural conflict" or "Americanized." Missing from Lee's constructs are Asian American families that are not intact, where the husband and wife are divorced; families where the partners are of the same sex or not married; and families with adopted children from other countries. Chinese infants from the People's Republic of China are now creating Asian American families that are more complex, with multifaceted factors. In working with Asian families, particularly Chinese families who have come from the People's Republic of China since the passing of the 1979 single-child policy, it would be erroneous for a social worker to assess the family's problem without understanding the cultural value of having only one child, particularly a male child to continue the traditionalist custom of name and family preservation.

Another area for knowledge acquisition is the interaction of the various diversity variables. Cultural values need to inform theory development and be interwoven with ethnicity, sexual orientation, gender, age, social class, religion, and physical or mental ability. This leads to some questions: How do social workers develop a framework that integrates these variables rather than treating them as separate entities? How does a social worker, for example, use knowledge about a lesbian Japanese woman to discern whether she is most concerned about her gender, sexual orientation, or ethnic cultural values? Probably all of these are important to her. To compound matters, how does a social worker take culture-specific problems and sift them though the lenses of a multicultural client? How do we help clients with the "processing of cultural beliefs" (Galan, 2001) in the midst of dealing with severe problems such as chronic depression, sexual abuse, or domestic violence? These are the questions and areas that social workers need to continue to explore in knowledge acquisition to improve their abilities as culturally competent social workers.

SKILL DEVELOPMENT

The Council on Social Work Education 2008 EPAS requires social workers to do "professional practice involving the dynamic and interactive processes of engagement, assessment, intervention, and evaluation at multiple levels. Social workers are to have the knowledge and skills to practice with individuals, families, groups, communities, and organizations" (2008, p.7).

Skill development, according to Lum (1999), is "the creation of a repertoire of behaviors for the social worker to use in the helping situation. Skills represent the practical application of cultural awareness and knowledge" (p. 112). In working with Asian Americans, it is important for social workers to learn how to foster the development of relevant and culturally sensitive and competent skills.

Because of the diversity within an ethnic group and the growing numbers of mixed groupings, skills development in culturally competent practice needs to continually be examined in several ways to accommodate changes. Questions to ask include the following: 1) Does the diversity within the single ethnic group warrant practice modifications? 2) Do practice methods account for the interactions of ethnicity, gender, sexual orientation, age, religion, social class, and physical or mental ability? 3) Do practices include indigenous strategies? 4) Are new practice models being developed to reflect cultural values? When social workers discuss practice methods and diversity, there should be a recognition that indigenous strategies, which are usually grounded in cultural values, ought to be an integral part of practice methods.

Examples would be o'hana conferencing or deep cultural therapy in the Hawaiian culture in which cultural values of family and land are reflected in the interventions. Fong, Boyd, and Browne (1999) look at combining Western interventions and indigenous interventions in the process of biculturalization of interventions. Lee (1997, p. 15) recommends structural family therapy because of the hierarchal and structural orientation to most Asian families, the generalist practice problem-solving approach, and the Bowenian approach to explore family dynamics. Structural family therapy reinforces the emphasis of many Asian cultures on family structure, roles, and authority domination. Jung (1998) advocates working with Chinese families from a Chinese American family therapy (CAFT) perspective, which also examines Chinese traditional values and Western-oriented therapies for families.

Because API are mostly family oriented, various family theoretical models have been used in social work practice. Family group conferencing (FGC) is another model being used in Asian and Pacific Islander family work. Having originated with the Pacific Islander Maori group in Australia, FGC has been used in child welfare and mental health fields. Pennell and Buford (2000) report how family group conferencing and decision making tap into the strengths of the families and communities and bring families who may be struggling with domestic violence and child welfare issues together. With the rising incidence of family violence and substance abuse among Native Hawaiian families, Mokuau (2001) proposes "culturally-based solutions" such as ho'oponopono, a Native Hawaiian family-focused approach to problem prevention and resolution.

Social workers need to develop skills in assessment from alternative paradigm perspectives. Rather than following the traditional paradigm of using Western treatment models, social workers need to start skill development of treatment planning with Asian and Pacific Islander traditional ways of healing and then match them with Western interventions. They need to evaluate whether the Western interventions foster the cultural values and ask whether programs that they are designing are accessible, available, and accountable to the ethnic community. For example, Chow (2001) advocates that a "multiservice, one-stop neighborhood center is considered a culturally appropriate approach for Chinese immigrant communities in the United States" (p. 217).

Another area in which to foster skill development is selecting the assessment and intervention skills that meet the complexities of problem situations involving the intersection of multiple variables such as physical disability, national origin, ethnicity, and multiple race. For example, in the area of international adoptions, Fong and Wang (2001) researched how parents prepared for and shaped the identity development of their adopted daughters from the People's Republic of China. Findings included the following: 1) creating a birth heritage; 2) instilling pride in the child's Chinese identity; 3) integrating the adoptive parents' background; 4) explaining the abandonment; and 5) coping with physical and medical special needs. The authors concluded:

> [T]he adoptees in the study have a composite identity of having special needs, being orphans, and becoming Chinese Americans born in Communist China but who are raised by non-Chinese parents in democratic America. The findings in the study strongly suggest the monitoring of the development of the ethnic identity of the adoptees.... Because the Chinese adoptees are born in the People's Republic of China and because Chinese culture is different from America, Hong Kong, or Taiwan, this heralds a new Chinese-American experience completely different from the "Chinatown" or "model minority" Chinese Americanness.... Multiple identities will intersect, such as adoptee, orphan, daughter, female, Chinese, American, and Chinese-American. The added intricacies of adoption, abandonment, foreign birthplace, and a second set of invisible parents [unidentifiable birth parents] call for new research endeavors. (p. 29)

New practice skills will also have to be developed to handle the complexities of these adoptive situations. Although the Korean, Romanian, and Russian international adoptive situations offer some comparative experiences and insights, the fact that accessibility to Chinese birth parents does not exist will create the need for social work skills to be developed to accommodate complex situations with adoptive parents, teachers, doctors, social workers, and therapists. Social workers working in international adoptions may have to develop closer ties with the medical community to understand the Chinese medical system and normative childhood medical conditions in China and compare them to American childhood diseases.

Newly developed practice skills would include understanding international social work; crossing disciplines between child welfare and health; and understanding Chinese language efficiency, health, mental health, and education. Research skills would be developed in alternative paradigms, and policy advocacy skills would be important in promoting human rights and social justice for the female special needs infant.

ENGAGEMENT

Engagement skills include making contact, identifying the problem, showing inductive learning, and engaging the person and problem through ethnographic interviewing.

Lee (1997) asserts that making contact and connecting to the client is very important to help identify the problem from the client's point of view. Helpful information needed in the contact and identifying the problem stage, which will later help with the assessment and data collection stages in working with APIAs, would be:

1. Family's ethnocultural heritage, migration stress, postmigration experience and cultural shock, impact of migration on individual and family life cycle, acculturation level of each family member

2. Work and financial stresses
3. Family's place of residence and community influence
4. Family stresses caused by role reversal
5. Stress caused by legal problems and sponsor relationships
6. Family's experiences with racism, prejudice, and discrimination
7. General skills plus specialized skills in substance abuse and family violence (pp. 16–24)

Leung and Cheung (2001) recommend that social workers use three principles when participating in the engagement stage in working with Asian and Pacific Islander clients and families in clinical practice:

1. To positively convey the concept of mental health and to address the purpose of counseling services according to cultural expectations
2. To evaluate the client's decision to seek, or not seek, family support
3. To recognize clients' strengths as well as evaluate their limitations that may block the optimal use of their potential in the environment (p. 426)

Inductive learning involves several steps and processes: 1) discerning the backgrounds and problems of the client; 2) improving the practitioner's skills; 3) collecting new information on problem formation; and 4) continuing to do informal and formal research to contribute to the enhancement of multicultural knowledge and skills. To generate new inductive learning, social workers will have to assess what they currently know about their minority client populations, discern what new information has been accrued recently, update their knowledge base and practices, and decipher where the gaps are and how to fill them.

Inductive learning about API will have to focus on the following areas: 1) new diverse groupings and identities; 2) clashes of cultural values when clients transition between differing social environments; 3) indigenous strategies; 4) commonalities between the APIA groups; 5) differences between the groups; and 6) differences within the same group. Another area where new inductive learning needs to occur is to develop a means to automatically intersect race and ethnicity with age, gender, sexual orientation, social class, religion, and disability with each ethnic grouping within the Asian American population. For example, Asian Americans and Pacific Islanders need to be addressed by life-span development from infancy to older adulthood with attention to male and female as well as gay and lesbian issues and needs. Disabilities need to be addressed during each developmental period, the differences between males and females need to be addressed; and attention must be paid to homo-, bi-, and heterosexuals and the impact social class and religion has on them. The perpetual argument given is that the populations of the various Asian subgroups are too small to warrant a separate discussion. This reasoning is no longer justifiable, given the increasing diversity among the Asian and Pacific Islander American minority groups as well as many other ethnic populations.

Engagement of people and problems can occur through ethnographic interviewing, a qualitative research method used to understand the participant's point of view. Research is an integral part of practice in that it evaluates the effectiveness of interventions, services, and programs. Historically, the traditional research paradigm had positivistic, scientific, objective, and quantitative characteristics (Schriver,

2001). However, an alternative paradigm for understanding human behavior and doing research is one with characteristics of interpretive, intuitive, subjective, and qualitative dimensions (Schriver, 2001). In doing research with API, several alternative paradigms have been used. Some of these alternative methods are participatory action research, oral histories and traditions, and ethnographies.

Matsuoka (2001) describes the need to do participatory action research (PAR) whose purpose is "documenting particular social realities in order to enable constituencies/communities to advocate for communities and the resources needed to sustain them" (p. 444). Matsuoka asserts that the traditional role of the researcher where participants play a passive role and are not actively engaged "in the technical and interpretative stages of research is antithetic to the goal of documenting indigenous realities" (p. 444). As described by Matsuoka,

> [PAR] is a process that involves establishing networks between representatives of a locale or community, research consultants, and bureaucrats. The goal of this process is to discover and document aspects of a community in order to preserve or ameliorate such aspects in an effort to sustain or improve the quality of life. (p. 444)

People's lives and indigenous realities are reflected in people's stories. In working with API, using oral histories is important. Mokuau, Lukela, Obra, and Voeller (1997), in their work about Native Hawaiian spirituality, capture oral histories and traditions from their focus group research. Oral histories and traditions are recorded through interviews using key informants in qualitative research methods. The histories and traditions are rich with descriptions of key events and their cultural meanings as well as human behavior affiliated with these activities. It is important for social workers to work on cultural competence skills in communication. Leigh (1998) advocates that social workers "must strive for the degree of understanding that can derive only from information provided by a member of the contrasting cultural group. Failure to achieve this means the social worker cannot enter the senses of the other. The social worker must comprehend the cultural context and meaning of these sensibilities. Only then will the social worker comprehend what is it that the person knows and how it is used in everyday life" (p. 15).

Ethnographies and ethnographic interviewing are other methods used in research. Ethnographic methods are "suggested for the culturally competent social worker because [they foster] a fellowship with the minority person of color" (Leigh, 1998, p. 12). Morton's (1996) ethnography on Pacific Islander children describes her research method as an ethnopsychological approach where she examined the "interaction of socialization, language socialization research, and accounts of tradition and cultural identity" (p. 10). She explains, "[T]he emphasis on interaction, agency, and context as a feature of recent psychological and sociological approaches to socialization is a feature of the ethnopsychological approach in anthropology" (p. 10). Interdisciplinary work often enhances the explanation of the contexts of the culture and the environments.

Leigh's (1998) work on communicating for cultural competence stresses the importance of ethnographic interviewing. He writes:

> Ethnographic interviewing holds much promise for social workers who wish to attain cultural competence. Ethnographic interviewing can be very helpful when working with

ethnic minority persons of color. Essentially, ethnographic interviewing is highly cognitive and word-oriented. It assumes that language and words, in particular, are windows to the world of the ethnic minority person. By ethnographic methods of inquiry, the social worker elicits the story. The story of a person can be seen as narrative through which the storyteller's perspective is revealed. Narrative is the universal metacode from which cultural messages and the nature of a shared reality are transmitted. For effective helping, it is essential that the social worker hear the content of the narratives, as the content provides valuable information about how other people experience others as well as themselves in interaction with others. (p. 13)

Although quantitative and positivistic research does occur with APIAs, Leung and Cheung (2001) write about the involvement of API in satisfaction surveys. They warn that in the Asian context,

> ... such an approach can be misinterpreted as either a dissatisfaction assessment or a means for pleasing others. Some API may think they should only report something that is undesirable and disregard the survey even if satisfaction is found. Others may solely focus on positives even if dissatisfaction is evident. (pp. 427–428)

Because many API tend not to express negative information or not to express their true thoughts and feelings, discernment is needed to discover what the clients truly feel and think about situations.

Furthermore, Leung and Cheung (2001) state: "No literature has addressed these phenomena because cultural factors [of APIs not expressing real feelings and emotions] are mixed with situational factors [of complying and responding to authority-associated activities] in Asian clients' responses to surveys" (p. 428). As social workers grapple with the complex issues that come with the diversity of the APIA population, it is hoped that innovative research endeavors will be created to meet new challenges encountered in evaluating traditional cultural responses in order to discern the real answers to ethnic clients' problems.

ASSESSMENT

Assessment and planning is the process of determining the problem and its roots from the biopsychosocial cultural perspectives of the client. It usually mandates an investigation of the impact of the social environment upon the client system. In working with people of color, when assessing and planning for problem identification, it is important to clarify and understand the role that cultural values play in the psychological, social, and biological functioning of the client. Cultural values acknowledge and reflect the diversity of social environments. Thus, in performing biopsychosocial cultural assessments with ethnic minority groups, a social worker would start with understanding of the culture of the client and determine how cultural values impact biological, psychological, and social functioning. For example, in Asian and Pacific Islander families, the unit of analysis or functioning is the family. Thus, the family unit has an impact on the individual's biological, psychological, and social functioning in API populations.

Usually in working with Asian and Pacific Islander populations, a biopsychosocial cultural assessment would have different emphases because of life-span development. When working with API youth, there may be a developmental life-span emphasis on the social rather than the psychological. However, in working with the aged population, the literature has documented that in working with the API elderly, assessment needs to be done in understanding the cultural component because psychosomatic symptoms frequently are indicators of mental health dysfunction as well as biological impairments (Browne & Broderick, 1994; Mui, 2001; Takamura, 1991). This is reflective of the traditional API cultural value of keeping problems in the family or denying that a psychological problem exists. It is a more common occurrence among the elderly who keep to traditional practices of not acknowledging mental health that they would acknowledge a biological rather than psychological problem.

Chinese American family therapist Marshall Jung (1998) describes his elderly mother's somatization of her psychological discomforts:

> As my mother grew older, she appeared to be plagued with an increasing number of physical ailments: headaches, backaches and stomach pains, and an inability to move joints. One day, my brothers Chester, Douglas, and I watched her coming out of the kitchen in the back area of our grocery store. She was dragging one leg and had her right hand on her forehead as she complained of having a severe headache. It looked [so] contrived that it seemed comical, instead of eliciting feelings of sympathy. We looked at each other thinking that she was a hypochondriac. Later, I learned that to the Chinese, somatization is a valid way of expressing inner conflicts and that physical, rather than psychological, complaints are an acceptable way to obtain attention. (p. 46–47)

Although some elderly do somatize feelings, others struggle with mental health issues. Studies have been done on Asian American elders and stress, coping, and depression (Mui, 1996, 2001; Mui & Burnette, 1996). But researchers and practitioners have found that "despite substantial prevalent rates, symptoms of depression can go unrecognized, undiagnosed, and untreated due to patient- and health-care-related barriers and problems in the organization and financing of mental health services for older adults, especially minority elders" (Mui, 2001, p. 283).

Whether the client is elderly or youthful, in Asian and Pacific Island cultures, there are many cultural values, with the most dominant ones to be love for and loyalty to family, respect of elders and authority, love of land and education, harmony and unity, and avoidance of loss of face and shame. These cultural values may be used as strengths in assessments in that they will explain much of the meaning behind behavior and thinking. In the area of Asian mental health, this is particularly important because the psychological and physical functioning of the individual are intricately related. The cultural components affect the psychological thinking, which may indeed affect the biological functioning.

Many cultural values dominate throughout the various Asian, Southeast Asian, and Pacific Islander cultures. A strong appreciation for family and extended family members is probably the most common. For some API groups, the cultural value of spirituality in various manifestations is very important. In working with Southeast Asians, Morelli (2001) writes about Cambodian meaning systems and the cultural value of spirituality and how it is intertwined with animism, sorcery, and magic. Asians hold strong Buddhist and Taoist beliefs as well as traditional Protestant and Catholic beliefs. Pacific Islanders honor their gods and strongly connect spirituality to their love of the land.

Although cultural values are related to religion and ethnicity, another diversity variable of sexual orientation adds complexities when these foci intersect. Kanuha (2001) warns that for gays and lesbians, another layer of complexity exists:

> ... due to the importance of family loyalty, "saving face," and other cultural values that are integral parts of many Asian and Pacific Island communities, social workers who work with individual or family levels with Asian/Pacific Island American (A/PIA) gay men and lesbians must be sensitive to the myriad ways this population balances cultural aspects of A/PIA family life while also learning to know themselves as gay and lesbian persons. (p. 315)

She suggests that social workers "assume that every A/PIA client who is dealing with his or her sexuality, whether or not they are gay, may also be conflicted in part by their racial/ethnic beliefs and traditions" (p. 320)

EMPOWERMENT AND ADVOCACY

In the NASW Standards for Cultural Competence in Social Work Practice, under Standard 6, is the section on Empowerment and Advocacy. Under this practice area social workers are to "be aware of the effect of social policies and programs on diverse client populations, advocating for and with clients whenever possible" (2001, p. 5).

Empowerment and advocacy should be applied to all Asian and Pacific Islander clients but it is particularly important for those clients who are victims of racism, discrimination, and oppression.

Those Asian immigrant and refugee clients who have language difficulty are particularly vulnerable and need resources which will empower them to seek and receive social services. Social workers may have to be insistent that non-English–speaking persons not be perceived or treated as if they are totally lacking in abilities. Many non-English–speaking Asian immigrants and refugees have skills and talents they used in their home countries. But as these people come to the United States and settle in, they usually find themselves unemployed or underemployed (Fong, 2004). Social workers need to be strong advocates for language and skill-building classes for this vulnerable population.

Another group of clients who need empowerment and advocacy are women and children who have been victims of human trafficking. There is still a lot of public misperceptions about human trafficking. Women who are forced into sex slavery are not understood to be victims but are wrongly labelled prostitutes. While trafficking can be a problem for both men and women, the majority of the victims are women who have been forced into sex slavery. Fong and Berger (2009) found that insufficient services were available for both women and children victims of trafficking. Much of the time the services that are available are time-limited and do not offer sufficient support to help the victims really resume their ways of living before they were forced into trafficking. Policies at the federal, state, and local levels need to be reexamined so that these women and children who are victims can receive adequate and culturally appropriate kinds of assistance.

SOCIAL AND ECONOMIC JUSTICE RESOLUTION

Social and economic justice is promoted by the Council on Social Work Education and the NASW. As early as the 1980s, the NASW standards for practice in social justice and economic justice were viable tenets for practice. Social workers were expected to understand the dynamics and consequences of social and economic injustice.

For API, social and economic issues revolve around land rights and welfare reform for immigrants. For Pacific Islanders, specifically Native Hawaiians, land rights are crucial. Fong and Furuto (2001) reiterate that "indigenous communities need to organize themselves around issues of sovereignty as a means by which to develop themselves and their communities" (p. 457). Furuto, San Nicholas, Kim, and Fiaui (2001) advocate that for Chamorros and Hawaiians, social justice would be the return of their land or the payment of fair compensation for it. For the Japanese internment people, social justice was achieved when they were compensated for their imprisonment.

For Asians, welfare reforms continue to economically oppress and intimidate immigrants. In writing about Public Law 104-193, the Personal Responsibility and Work Opportunity Reconciliation Act (known as the welfare reform law), Swingle (2000) states, "[T]he passage of the welfare reform rendered immigrants an 'undeserving group' and an 'economic drain' " (p. 605). He maintains that immigrants "are living in fear that if they utilize any public health services they will be considered a public charge resulting in possible deportation" (p. 605). This increasing fear is

> ... resulting in immigrant women not getting appropriate pre-natal care, and parents not getting their kids immunized or participating in nutrition programs. Health professionals are concerned that this problem will result in serious public health consequences affecting not only immigrants but also the larger population. (pp. 606–607).

Proposed is a public charge rule where legal immigrants are subject to public charge consideration if they receive "cash assistance for income maintenance." The protection offered under the proposed public charge rule is another form of labelling and does not really address the immigrants' economic dilemma. The fear of being rejected is not diminished by substituting one label for another. Social workers can assist immigrants to better cope with economic, social, and political pressures by understanding their situations and having as much background information as possible about their cultures in order to be competent cultural translators. Misunderstandings cause a lot of trauma for immigrants, who are often victims of racist and discriminatory practices.

Sanchez-Hucles (1998) asserts that racism is a form of emotional abuse and creates psychological trauma for ethnic minorities. She exhorts the mental health field to better understand racism to mitigate emotional abusiveness and trauma. She asserts that racism persists because of "inaction, passivity, tolerance, and denial" (p. 71). These discriminatory and racist practices will stop when API, and other ethnic minority groups, are treated equally, fairly, and justly. Despite the increasing census numbers, attitudes still need to be changed.

CASE STUDY	THE HAWAIIAN WAY

The presenting problem is a Hawaiian Chinese family with a 15-year-old son, who was suspended from school because of marijuana use. The Chinese mother phoned the family service agency wanting help, despite her hesitation to reveal family problems. The Hawaiian father did not want his son to be permanently hooked on drugs or kicked out of school, so he agreed to have the social workers come to his home. At the micro level the son has the drug problem. But at the meso level the mother is hesitant to reveal family problems and the father does not want the son hooked on drugs or kicked out of school.

The family had three children, ages 15, 12, and 9, but were part of a larger extended family system that generally could deal with all the problems presented by family members. Both parents admitted regular use of marijuana when younger. However, they were worried that their son was using "too much." They were worried that he might become incarcerated like the other cousins who used "too much." This may create social ethical problems for the parents in deciding how much they should tell the social worker about the parents' and family members' history of using drugs.

To show her cultural awareness and the knowledge that she acquired while working with Native Hawaiian families, the social worker works on developing goals for the family but is aware that the Hawaiian Chinese family may want to participate in a family problem solving method done in the Hawaiian culture. The social worker knows she first has to have the family work together on the problem. But extended family members may also be resources to this family in trouble. The mother wanted the father more involved and active in the parenting because she was tired of dealing with the son's problems on her own. The father wanted the mother to be less angry and demanding and more attentive to his (the husband's) needs. The other two kids wanted the parents to stop fighting all the time.

The social worker had to discern what values were important to the family that would help them direct the problem-solving process and select the appropriate culturally competent interventions for this family.

The following questions help to determine what values are important to the family as a system:

1. What cultural values are important to Chinese families?
2. What cultural values are important to Hawaiian families?
3. What cultural values are important to this Chinese-Hawaiian family?
4. How can social workers use these cultural values as strengths in treatment planning?

The Hawaiian Chinese parents agreed to work with the social worker but were uncomfortable with the proposed western intervention plan of having their son attend a group for substance users while they sought a marriage counselor to discuss their communication difficulties. Instead, FGC was proposed where this family and their extended members could gather to discuss how to go about treating the substance use and the parents' difficulties. The four phases of FGC (Merkel-Holguin & Ribich, 2001) were explained by the social workers as follows:

1. Phase One: Referral phase
2. Phase Two: Preparation and planning
3. Phase Three: The family group conference
4. Phase Four: Follow-up

The social worker worked with the parents in phases two and three, in preparing, planning, and actually holding the conference.

In the preparing and planning phases, the social worker had the parents define what they meant by family in order to determine which "family" members were necessary to invite. Relationship building among the extended family networks is important in order to protect emotional and physical safety during and after the family conference. Unresolved family issues are

continued

CASE STUDY | THE HAWAIIAN WAY *continued*

addressed as much as possible before the family conference begins. During the actual family group conference for this Hawaiian Chinese family, the co-ordinator made introductions of everyone present (family and relatives, professionals, school officials, community members). Professionals delineated the facts of the case during the time of information sharing. People present identified the strengths of the family and discussed available resources. Private family time was given after the concerns, strengths, and pertinent information on the case were laid out. All the professionals left it to the family, friends, and relatives to come up with a treatment plan to help the 15-year-old boy and his parents with his substance abuse problem.

Once a decision was made and a plan was developed, the professionals were invited into the room again to discuss the plan and make sure it was reasonable and could be implemented. When everyone present agreed upon the plan, it was signed and a copy was offered to all participants. The follow-up phase was very important because resourcing and monitoring needed to be carefully implemented.

Despite the proposed changes in practices, social workers need to be culturally sensitive as to why ethnic clients may refuse social work practice services. Leung and Cheung (2001) report that API may refuse to seek help for mental health problems either to avoid shame or because they assume natural healing will occur. Clients may not seek help for the following reasons:

1. They do not recognize or acknowledge there is a mental health problem.
2. They are afraid of being stigmatized if they seek help.
3. They do not want to address negative comments about their traditional healing practices.
4. They do not have access to bilingual, bicultural services.
5. They assume the social service provider will not be culturally competent.

Thus, the social worker is not thought to understand the client's culture even if the provider is the same ethnicity as the client (Leung and Cheung, 2001, pp. 428–429). Social workers need to try to work with the refusals and hesitations of clients by creating culturally competent practices. This would include helping the clients feel safe in knowing that a psychosomatic problem can be treated without shame-based activities or negative stigmas. Bilingual and bicultural workers who are of the same level of acculturation and who speak the same dialect can assure API clients that they will receive help in a manner that is sensitive to and respectful of their culture. Using indigenous treatments in place of or in addition to Western interventions assures API clients through familiar experiences that they are receiving help in a culturally competent manner. To ignore these preferred culturally competent practices can lead to social injustices because culturally insensitive and culturally inappropriate interventions may be imposed upon this or other Native Hawaiian, Pacific Islander, or Asian families.

Morelli (2001) asserts that "in cross-cultural practice we fail to fully assess, advocate for, and facilitate culturally appropriate interventions and services that have a greater potential for meeting the clients' needs" (p. 427). Ross-Sheriff and Husain (2001) warn:

> [P]ractitioners must realize that, regardless of their efforts to customize current assessment and interventions techniques to suit Asian-Americans, there will remain biases from the dominant Euro-American worldview and its values. Guided by their zeal to assist the client, the practitioners may involuntarily impart notions of what is healthy and normal based on Euro-American standards. (p. 87)

Practitioners need to examine their worldviews and be sure to have enough knowledge about their clients' ethnic culture in order to plan and implement treatment based upon values, beliefs, and ethnic practices of the clients. This will work to counteract culturally biased definitions of normal and abnormal attitudes and behaviors.

Student Learning Exercise

In discussing this case, answer the following questions which are important to consider in conducting a family group conference:

1. How is "family" defined in the clients' culture, and who are the important participants to invite?
2. Are all the strengths of the family system identified and used as resources?
3. Did every participant "buy into" the plan?
4. What assurance is there for the resourcing and monitoring of the plan?

CONCLUSION

Culturally competent practice with Asian and Pacific Islander Americans is diversifying so that social workers in the 21st century have the task of clarifying that the Asian American category as a single category is obsolete. The 2000 U.S. Census offered 17 categories for Asians, Pacific Islanders, and mixed groups of interracial identities in which API are included. Thus, the single ethnic categories need to be broken down into the multiple racial combinations and variations within single ethnic groups. Culturally competent practice also involves the challenge of including the intersection of ethnicity and race with gender, sexual orientation, religion, social class, and physical and mental abilities.

In defining cultural competence, many aspects must be considered, but the main focus is on the participatory relationship between the social worker and the client. The paradigm shift is focused on the mutual inclusiveness of the both parties rather than the exclusive focus on the cultural competence of the social worker. Cultural awareness, the exploration of knowledge acquisition, the fostering of skill development are necessary practices with engagement, assessment, and empowerment and advocacy as important emphases in skill development. The definition of cultural competence primarily follows a strengths perspective, and cultural values are identified as key components to understanding diversity in engaging the client through contact, problem identification, inductive learning, and ethnographic interviewing. Cultural values are reflective of the culture, norms, and behaviors preserved by each ethnic group. Galan (2001) discusses the "processing of cultural beliefs whereby the client weighs cultural information, prioritizes to choose appropriate behavior, and maintains integrity in belief and behavior" (p. 456).

Social and economic justice needs to be achieved for the Asian and Pacific Islander groups because so many discriminatory, racist, and oppressive experiences have been imposed upon these people and other ethnic minorities in the United States. Macro-level shifts in attitudes and policies need to be made in order to achieve culturally competent practice with Asian and Pacific Islander clients.

CHAPTER **13** | CULTURAL COMPETENCE WITH
MUSLIM AMERICANS

Altaf Husain and Fariyal Ross-Sheriff

We know that our patchwork heritage is a strength, not a weakness.
We are a nation of Christians and Muslims, Jews and Hindus—and non-believers.
President **Barack Hussein Obama**[1]

INTRODUCTION

Muslim Americans represent the fastest growing religious community in the United
States due to natural births, immigration, and conversion (Hodge, 2005; Pew
Research Center, 2007). While the social work literature has of late increasingly included content on Islam and Muslims in the United States (Al-Krenawi & Graham,
2000; Hodge, 2005; Hodge & Nadir, 2008; Nadir, 2002; Ross-Sheriff & Husain,
2000, 2004), the sociopolitical climate and professional standards and ethics together
warrant an increase in the awareness of and familiarity with the teachings of Islam
and especially issues related to culturally competent practice with members of this
emerging and diverse community. The term *Muslim Americans* will be used throughout this chapter to refer to those individuals residing within the United States and
who, within the counseling and therapeutic setting, self-identify as Muslims, and/or
raise issues arising from their religious beliefs.

This chapter is divided into ten sections, beginning with this introductory statement, which includes a presentation of the demographics and group diversity
within the Muslim community, followed by a discussion of cultural competence
with this client group in section two. In section three, we present a historical overview of oppression of Muslim Americans, along with the major current social issues facing them. The values of this client group are presented in section four with
a special emphasis on the potential ethical dilemmas which might be encountered
by practitioners working with Muslim Americans. Sections five through seven provide information on the three functions of cultural competence namely, cultural

awareness, knowledge acquisition, and skill development, as they relate to Muslim Americans. In section eight the focus is on social and economic justice resolution, followed in section nine by a case study before the concluding section.

DEMOGRAPHICS AND GROUP DIVERSITY

Perhaps two of the most complex aspects of the exercise to learn more about the Muslim American community are its rapidly changing demographics and its tremendous intra-group diversity. The Muslim population in the United States is increasing; but, more directly relevant to the current focus on cultural competence is that there is tremendous intra-group diversity due to differing schools of religious thought and the fact that Muslims trace their roots to over 80 different countries (Ali, Liu, & Humedian, 2004; Smith, 1999).

DEMOGRAPHICS

There are over 1.57 billion Muslims worldwide (Pew Research Center, 2007), and the estimates of the total number of Muslims in America range from 2.5 million (Pew Research Center, 2007) to 6 million to 10 million (Ali, Liu, & Humedian, 2004). An exact count of the Muslim American population has not yet been realized owing largely due to the prohibition in the census data collection procedures to inquire about religious affiliation (Hodge, 2005; Nyang, 1999; Pew Research Center, 2007). According to a 2007 study by the Pew Research Center, an estimated two-thirds of the Muslim American population is foreign-born, arrived mostly after 1990, and is comprised mostly of people from Arab countries, followed by South Asians, Africans, and Europeans. Findings from the same study indicate that overall the Muslim American population is split almost evenly by gender with slightly more males (54%) than females, and is "youthful, racially diverse, generally well-educated, and financially about as well-off as the rest of the U.S. public" (Mogahed, 2009, p. 15).

Natural births account for a substantial portion of the increase since the grandchildren of the first generation of the post-1965 wave of Muslim immigrants are now getting married and starting families of their own. The Muslim American community is not comprised solely of recent immigrants but also of African, Caucasian, and Hispanic Americans who have converted to Islam. The *second generation* refers commonly to children born in the United States to foreign-born parents. The United States is presently experiencing a demographic surge in the *third generation* of Muslim Americans, that is an increase in marriages and natural birth rates of the grandchildren of the post-1960s immigrants. There is anecdotal evidence to show that generational differences account for variations in the understanding and practice of Islam and in the affinity to traditions and customs of one's ethnic origin. Haddad and Lummis (1987) note that for some adult Muslims who were not fully practicing Islam in their countries of origin, the process of adjusting to life in America was accompanied by a marked increase in their voluntary adherence to Islamic teachings. Additional research on these generation differences is needed to examine whether the Muslim community will follow a similar trajectory of assimilation as that of other minority groups in the United States.

The Muslim population in America is also increasing due to continued and different types of immigration from various parts of the world such as family-sponsored and sponsored immigration, lottery-based visa program, and refugees and asylum seekers. Muslim American immigrants continue to cherish the value of caring for their immediate and extended family members, which, among other things, is the motivation for them to sponsor the immigration of relatives from their homelands to the United States. Two characteristics to note about the sponsored families are potentially large family size and potentially lower education levels. Muslim Americans are reflecting dominant societal norms in having smaller families but the family sizes of the new arrivals are often larger (Pew Research Center, 2007). Similarly, although Muslim immigrants of the last quarter of the 20th century were often highly educated and even possessed specialized training in certain fields just to be eligible for the strict visa requirements (Nyang, 1999), it is quite likely that the family members they are sponsoring from developing countries have low levels of education and in some cases might be unskilled laborers. These two characteristics of large families and low levels of education are bound to pose challenges to successful social and economic adaptation of these new arrivals to the United States.

In addition to family reunification, Muslims are also arriving from those countries for which the United States has decided to allocate a certain number of immigration visas strictly via a lottery system as a part of the Congressional mandated Diversity Immigrant Visa Program (DIVP). Under the DIVP, the government extends opportunities for immigration annually to 50,000 individuals from countries which have historically low rates of immigration to the United States but the education and work skills criteria to be eligible are very low, that is high school education or equivalent or two years work experience in an occupation which requires two years of training (U.S. Department of State, 2009b). The 2010 results for the DIVP[2] indicate that countries with majority or at least substantial Muslim populations in Africa (Algeria, Cameroon, Ghana, Nigeria, and Sierra Leone), Asia (Bangladesh and Iran), and Europe (Albania, Turkey, and Uzbekistan) received visas as a part of the random visa allocation (U.S. Department of State, 2009a). In addition to sponsored immigration and lottery-based immigration, refugees and asylum-seekers also contribute to growth of the Muslim population in the United States. Maloof and Ross-Sheriff (2003), in their analysis of the Muslim refugees resettled in the United States between 1988 and 2003, concluded that they were from 77 different countries and accounted for 15% of the total number of refugees. With no end in sight to the wars and civil strife in several Muslim majority countries such as Afghanistan, Chechnya, Iran, Iraq, and Somalia among others, it is likely that the resettlement of Muslim refugees in the United States will continue.

A third factor impacting the rapidly changing demographics of Muslim Americans is converts to the religion. In the decades which followed the mass conversions of African Americans in the 1970s, more Americans of First Nation, European, and Hispanic ancestry have converted to Islam through self-study, befriending Muslim neighbors and co-workers, or marriage (Smith, 1999). Just how many converts to Islam there are in the United States is difficult to estimate as noted in the study of Muslim Americans by the Pew Research Center, "American-born converts to Islam also increase the U.S. Muslim population, and researchers say getting accurate estimates of this group may be the most difficult challenge of all" (Pew Research Center, 2007, p. 14). The same study estimates that native-born converts account for almost 35% of the total U.S. Muslim population. Although counting how many native-born

Americans have converted to Islam is challenging at best, there is sufficient evidence in the literature and in popular media accounts that most of the native-born converts to Islam tend to be African American and women (Anway, 2002; Byng, 1998; Dirks & Parlove, 2003; Maslim & Bjorck, 2009). As with the acculturation and adaptation challenges associated with a physical migration, of interest to the social work profession should be the psychosocial and mental health challenges native-born converts are likely to face due to their spiritual migration.

MUSLIM AMERICANS: STRENGTH IN DIVERSITY

The Muslim American community is diverse along demographic, cultural, and theological lines. The ethnic, cultural, and linguistic diversity of its members is discussed below, followed by a fuller presentation of the diversity in the beliefs and schools of thought. Briefly, Muslim Americans belong to a number of *tariqat* (sects) which have differing beliefs and customs. The main bifurcation is of *Sunni* and *Shia*, and within both there is further segmentation. The student and practitioner have few resources to draw upon regarding this diversity because the social work literature has not kept pace with the growth of the Muslim community in the United States. There is hope, however, because over the last 5 years, the social work profession has made a special effort to learn about Muslims through presentations of the Islam and Muslims symposium at the Annual Program Meeting of the Council on Social Work Education.

ETHNIC, CULTURAL, AND LINGUISTIC DIVERSITY

Muslim Americans are a diverse group, distinguished by their national origins, languages, ethnic and cultural backgrounds, and intra-group religious differences. Countering the misconception that most Arabs are Muslims, Barrett (2007) states that "most American Muslims are not Arab, and most Americans of Arab descent are Christian, not Muslim" (p. 6). Among Muslim Americans, one can likely come across Africans (mostly East, North, Sub-Saharan, and West), African Americans, Arabs (all regions of the Middle East and North-Africa), Asians (Central, East, South, and Southeast), and Europeans. The foreign-born Muslim Americans trace their roots to over 80 countries spanning Africa, Asia (including the Middle East), and Europe (Ross-Sheriff & Husain, 2004; Smith, 1999). According to the U.S. Census Bureau figures on the foreign-born population, the African nations represented in sizeable numbers are Algeria, Egypt, Morocco, Nigeria, Senegal, Somalia, and Sudan; the European nations represented are Albania, Bosnia, Kosovo, and Turkey; and the Asian nations represented in sizeable numbers are Afghanistan, Bangladesh, India, Iran, Iraq, Lebanon, Pakistan, Syria, and Yemen (2003). A majority of Muslim Americans live in states with high immigrant populations such as California, Florida, Illinois, Michigan, New York, and Texas, with the largest concentrations found in the respective cities of Los Angeles, Orlando, Chicago, Detroit, New York, and Houston (Mogahed, 2009; Nyang, 1999; Ross-Sheriff & Husain, 2004). The cultural diversity of the Muslim American community is most visible and pronounced at the local *masjid* (mosque).

Muslim Americans have a unique culture emerging primarily due to their adherence to a common set of religious beliefs and to their common experience in acculturating to the majority American society (Abd-Allah, 2004). The *masjid* in America is less a cultural center for a particular ethnic group and more a place of gathering for all Muslims, regardless of their racial or ethnic background. During the process of becoming integrated into American norms and cultural practices, Muslims are guided by a basic prescript, that is everything in a culture is permissible except that which is explicitly prohibited by Islamic teachings. Great emphasis is placed on the preservation of indigenous cultures and traditions as long as those cultural and traditional practices are in line with Islamic teachings (Abd-Allah, 2004; Hamid, 1996). As a result, the typical *masjid* in America is reflective of a blend of cultures from all around the world especially around religious celebrations and life-cycle events such as births, weddings, and funerals.

Variations in the style of dress are most apparent as some South Asians appear in their *shalwar khameez*, a tunic and loose-fitting pant combination, or a *saree*; some Arabs adorn themselves in *thawbs* (for men) and *jalabeyyas* (for women)—ankle-length, loose-fitting gowns; some Africans, such as the Somalis, arrive in brightly colored and intricately embroidered full-body wraps known as a *guntiino* for women or a sarong-type wrap known as a *macaawiis* for men; and second- and third-generation Muslims are likely to wear Western-style suits (for men), pantsuits (for women), and even combinations of ethnic and Western-style clothing. The religiously mandated guidelines common to all of their choice and style of clothing are the outfit must be loose-fitting, modest, not translucent (see-through), and cover the *awrah* or that part of the body which has been designated as private (Hamid, 1996). Creative adherence to the guidelines for modest clothing have given rise to a whole fashion industry which seeks to incorporate both traditional Islamic garb, such as the religiously mandated headscarf for women or *hijab*, used in some countries of origin, along with typical Western clothing that conforms with modesty (Abd-Allah, 2004).

Variations in cuisine are also reflective of the cultural diversity among the Muslim Americans ranging from a preference of certain types of meat (with the exception of pork, which is forbidden) and vegetables to a preference of certain spices and cooking techniques. The impact of indigenous, geographic, and climate-based differences on the cuisine is mitigated by requirement that the ingredients and the final meal are *halal*, that is, both permissible and prepared in accordance with Islamic dietary laws. Adherence to *halal* guidelines at the individual level has been documented from the earliest known sources about Muslims in America (Diouf, 1998; Takaki, 1998). During the last quarter of the 20th century and onwards there have been organized community-wide efforts to facilitate the availability of *zabiha* meat, which is essentially meat of animals that have been slaughtered upon the utterance of a brief prayer and according to humane and sanitary guidelines designed to cause the least suffering to the animals at the moment they are slaughtered and to ensure the meat is cleansed thoroughly of the blood of the animals (Zolbern & Woon, 1999). The *zabiha* meat is not unlike the meat prepared according to the *kosher* dietary laws in Judaism. Lastly, along with their ethnic and cultural diversity, there is also considerable linguistic diversity among the Muslims of America.

The language of the *Qur'an* is Arabic and although Muslims must without exception memorize and recite portions of the *Qur'an* in Arabic during their obligatory daily prayers, there is tremendous appreciation for the preservation of indigenous and ethnic languages. While there are geographic variations in dialect among Arabic-speaking Muslims, foreign-born Muslims of Asian and African origin often speak an ethnic language, along with the language of the respective colonizer, that is Dutch, English, French, Italian, Portuguese, and Spanish, among others. Attempting to recreate the spiritual experiences of their countries of origin, foreign-born Muslim Americans sometimes prefer to hear weekly sermons in their native languages, although the majority of the *masajid* (plural of *masjid*) utilize a combination of Arabic and English during the sermons (Nyang, 1999; Sonn, 1994). The challenge for most immigrant families is the preservation of their native language in the face of a dominant English-speaking society while for both immigrant and native-born families, the challenge is to encourage simultaneously themselves and their children to acquire basic proficiency in Arabic.

DIVERSITY IN BELIEFS AND SCHOOLS OF THOUGHTS

Another major factor contributing to the diversity among Muslim Americans is the diversity in their beliefs and schools of thoughts. Universally accepted among all Muslims is the belief in the oneness of *Allah* (God) and the status of Muhammad[3] (peace be upon him) as the last and final prophet from *Allah*, in a series of prophets beginning with Adam through Abraham, Noah, Moses, and Jesus (peace be upon them) (Ibrahim, 1997). Profound differences in belief exist between the *Sunnis* and the *Shiites*, although both groups have coexisted in peace around the world until only within the last few decades when their differences were exploited to the point of violent confrontations most notably in Lebanon, Iran-Iraq, and Pakistan.[4] Within the United States the *Sunni* and *Shiite* leadership have emphasized mutually respectful relationships, reaffirmed at the height of the recent sectarian bloodshed in Iraq by the public signing of an intrafaith code of honor (Grossman, 2007). Theological tensions are to be expected not so much between communities of these two groups rather at the individual and family level due to a choice to shift from being a *Sunni* to a *Shiite* or vice versa or perhaps due to intermarriage between members of the two groups. Barrett (2007) states that "the two major subgroups of Muslims, Sunni and Shiite, are found in the United States in roughly their global proportions: 85 percent Sunni, 15 percent Shiite" (p. 7).

Among Muslim Americans there are also differences with regard to the understanding and interpretation of certain Islamic teachings and practices resulting in what are known commonly as *madhahib* or schools of thought (Hamid, 1996; Ibrahim, 1997). The five well-known schools of thought are *Hanafi*, *Hanbali*, *Jaafari* (*Shiite*), *Maliki*, and *Shafi'i*. Each of the founders of these schools of thought sought very much to use the *Qur'an* and the teachings of the Prophet Muhammad (peace be upon him) to facilitate all aspects of a Muslim's life in accordance with Islamic teachings. While there are differences in the conclusions which each of these founders reached, two points are noteworthy: 1) their conclusions were sound, aligned with, and derived from the most authentic sources available to each of them during their life time; and 2) their own admonition for followers of their school of thought was to give deference to the other schools of thought, especially in instances where those schools of thought had irrefutable evidence to support a particular juristic position on the basis of the two sacred texts. Whereas among Muslim Americans discussions can and do occur about the differences between *madhahib*, this chapter intentionally only introduces the concept of the *madhahib* briefly because it is not likely that a Muslim American client would expect a social work practitioner to be aware of such juristic differences among the schools of thought. It is important to reiterate that practitioners may encounter Muslim clients with differing levels of religious and cultural practice and understanding.

CULTURAL COMPETENCE WITH CLIENT GROUP(S)

Developing cultural competence with Muslim Americans has become a professional imperative in light of the national and international sociopolitical climate of the first decade of the 21st century. This climate has thrust Islam and Muslims unwittingly into the public sphere with untold consequences to well-being at the individual, group, and community levels. There is increasing evidence that Muslim Americans are utilizing therapeutic and counseling interventions as well as social services in general. Al-Krenawi and Graham (2000) have cautioned that when the practitioner–client fit is not optimal or hindered, Muslims "may under-utilize or prematurely terminate services" (p. 300). Culturally competent social workers must therefore be familiar with the help-seeking behaviors of Muslim Americans, along with their belief and value systems since such familiarity will inform the practitioners' choice of a therapeutic modality or intervention. Social workers should also explore challenges arising from ethnic and tribal rather than religious differences.

HELP-SEEKING BEHAVIORS

Muslim Americans are increasingly seeking intervention from providers of mental health and human services due to at least three major factors, all of which combine to make a strong case for culturally competent social work practitioners and scholars with this client group: 1) the pace at which the population of Muslims in America is growing (Hodge, 2005; Hunter & Malik, 2002); 2) education and awareness efforts to reduce the stigma associated with seeking assistance outside existing informal support networks (Khan, 2006); and 3) mental health and psychosocial challenges associated with real or perceived feelings of discrimination, prejudice, and anti-Muslim rhetoric in post-9/11 America (Abu-Ras & Abu-Bader, 2009; Ali, Liu, & Humedian, 2004). It is critically important that social work educators, researchers, and practitioners become more aware, acquire knowledge, and develop skills to ensure culturally competent teaching, research, and practice with Muslim Americans.

Even as the social work profession is coming to the realization that Muslim Americans are not a homogenous group and that they are represented among the help-seeking population, the goal of developing cultural competence with Muslim Americans is challenging at best due to the fact that the increase in Muslim Americans' help-seeking from outside one's family and relatives and close friends is a relatively recent phenomenon. The good news for the profession is that there is increasing evidence that they are seeking professional intervention both within Muslim community–based formal counseling and support services as well as from mainstream mental health and human service providers. As a result of various individual- and group-level factors, Muslim Americans might be more or less in-clined toward help-seeking behaviors. Khan (2006) has addressed "counselors" in particular, but her admonition is broadly applicable, when she emphasizes the "need to recognize not only the diversity of Muslims in America, but what this di-versity means with regard to inclinations to help-seeking among the predominant Muslim subgroups" (p. 22).

Characterizing the national response of Americans to the steady growth in the population of Muslims as prejudicial and discriminatory belies the fact that for dec-ades in the 20th century the most striking aspect about the existence of Muslims in America was that theirs was an untold story or at least a story told in quiet, hushed tones. When Muslim Americans were presenting as clients prior to that pe-riod it was because of issues of daily living such as parent–child conflicts, marital therapy, family violence, and poverty for example, not unlike issues facing any other minority group in America. Most noteworthy for the social work profession therefore is the marked rise in the mental health and social services utilization rates of members of this client group due in large part to the complex and intense nature of the scrutiny, vilification, and outright hostility they began to face after 9/11 (Abu-Ras & Abu-Bader, 2009). In both the public and private sectors, and in both town and gown settings, there has been in the last decade and continues now to be an unrelenting attack on all things Islam and Muslim. As a profession whose founding mission at the turn of the 20th century, realized through the Settlement House Movement, was to provide refuge and assistance to the newly arrived, it is imperative that sufficient education and training be provided to students and cur-rent and future practitioners so that they are able to serve Muslim American clients effectively. The sub-sections which follow provide knowledge about the Islamic worldview, the tenets of Islam, and core values of the faith.

ISLAMIC WORLDVIEW

Understanding the Islamic worldview is central to culturally competent practice with Muslim Americans. Unlike the dominant secular worldview in which most practitioners are being trained, Islam promotes a harmonious co-existence between the private and the public, the sacred and the secular, and the present life and the afterlife. Central to the Muslim worldview is the relationship between *Allah* and man, which is that of the Creator and the creation. *Allah* created all of creation to worship Him. Human beings, unlike other creatures on earth, are endowed with the faculties of intellect and reason. The ability to think and to reason allows hu-man beings to choose of their own free will whether to worship *Allah* or not to worship *Allah*. In this sense, human beings enjoy a tremendous amount of freedom. The best among the human beings are those who are conscious of their duty to *Allah*, who submit to *Allah's* commandments and to struggle in life to uphold righ-teous speech and conduct. *Taqwa* denotes the highest levels of consciousness of one's obligations and duties to *Allah*. A person who has *iman* (faith) and *taqwa* lives his or her life blessed by *Allah* such that neither loss, nor fear, nor anxiety, nor grief causes them to waver in their conviction that *Allah* is in charge and wants only what is best for them. Practitioners should be aware of the possibility of intra-Muslim variations in both the strength of *iman* and the levels of *taqwa*, and worse, the potential for a life challenge such as the death of a loved one to have shaken up the *iman* of a particular client. A part of worshipping *Allah* is to exist on earth as the stewards or ambassadors of *Allah* since all of a person's existence is characterized in relationship to *Allah*. Even if a person does not speak Arabic, the practitioner is likely to notice an effort to retain Arabic words and phrases which often invoke the name of *Allah*. Before undertaking any action, the start of a meal for example, a Muslim remembers *Allah,* saying *Bismillah*—in the name of *Allah*. After endeavoring on a project of any kind, it is commonplace for a Muslim to say *Insha'allah* or *Allah*-willing the project will be successful and by saying *Alhamdulillah*—all praise is due to *Allah* that the project is complete. A person with firm *iman* attributes success and failure and the onset of trials and tribulations in life to *Allah* by glorifying *Allah* (saying *Subhan'allah*), by praising *Allah* (saying *Alhamdulillah*), and by giving thanks to *Allah* (saying *Shukr lillah*). After receiving assistance from another person, a Muslim is likely to refer back to *Allah* by saying "may *Allah* reward you with good" (saying *Jazak Allahu khairan*), or at least a variation of that sentiment if the practitioner belongs to another faith, that is God bless you. References to God are generally absent within current social work practice settings so the practitioner must not be put off upon hearing such references nor should such utterances be associated with fundamentalism, rather as language reflecting consciousness to do good deeds and to be socially just.

Integral to the overall Islamic worldview are the interrelated concepts of accountability, sin, forgiveness, and repentance. Part of the attributes of *Allah* is that He is oft-forgiving, most beneficent, and most merciful. Every male and female becomes accountable at the age of puberty to uphold the obligatory duties outlined in the Islamic teachings. In Arabic, the term *mukallaf* refers less to a particular chronological age when puberty might occur and more to the notion of individual responsibility and accountability as an adult. A young boy or girl who is *mukallaf* is considered an adult. Practitioners whose client population consists mostly of children and families will find it beneficial to understand potential conflicts between behaviors considered age-appropriate (dating and drinking alcohol, for example) in the Western tradition and those behaviors which are congruent with Islamic teachings (Ross-Sheriff & Husain, 2004). In the case of an act of transgression against others, any reconciliation of the differences between two individuals, two spouses, two families, or two communities is pinned first to the remorseful acknowledgement of the harmful speech or conduct and then to seeking forgiveness from the aggrieved; then and only then can one repent and seek forgiveness. Children who disobey their parents are also disobeying *Allah* because of a clear Islamic injunction to obey the parents. To restore a parent–child relationship gone awry due to either a perceived or real act of disobedience on the part of a child, the practitioner must be aware that in addition to the therapeutic intervention, achieving closure will not be complete until the child seeks forgiveness formally from his or her parents.

TENETS OF ISLAM

Islamic teachings are universal, comprehensive, and timeless in their applicability, so much so that Al-Krenawi and Graham (2000) note that "Islam is a total, all-embracing way of life for Muslims" (p. 300). Practitioners working with Muslim Americans should familiarize themselves with the notion that Islam is a "way of life," offering guidance in all aspects of life, both public and private and relevant for all times. Doing so is a challenging proposition given the dominance of the secular narrative throughout the profession. However, within Islam, there is a harmonious blend between the secular, the sacred, and the spiritual (Hamid, 1996; Ramadan, 2004). For Muslim Americans, knowledge of and adherence to the two authentic sources of religious knowledge, the five pillars of Islam, and the six articles of faith culminates in the resultant Islamic ontological foundation which sustains and perpetuates their belief in *Allah*.

Qur'an and Sunna: Two Authentic Sources

The religion of Islam in its present form is a product of the 7th century, but Muslims believe that Islamic teachings did not begin in the 7th century, but rather with the beginning of creation itself. The *Qur'an* chronicles in detail the creation of Adam and Eve (peace be upon them) and their momentary lapse in judgment, their repentance to *Allah*, and their subsequent dispatch by *Allah* to be His viceregents on earth. As the progeny of Adam and Eve (peace be upon them) multiplied on earth, *Allah* sent prophets and messengers with guidance so that each new generation would be reminded that the ultimate reason why *Allah* created mankind was to worship Him. The *Qur'an* together with the *Sunna*—what the Prophet Muhammad (peace be upon him) "said, did and agreed to" (Hamid, 1996, p. 32)—comprise the two authentic sources of Islamic teachings (Al-Krenawi and Graham, 2000). The teachings are universal and timeless because they are viewed as being applicable, relevant, and adaptable all over the earth, for all of time. A Muslim woman in Canada or China can rely on the *Qur'an* and the *Sunna* to practice Islam with the same ease as a Muslim woman in Uruguay or the United States of America. The teachings are as relevant in the 21st century as they were at the time of revelation some 14 centuries ago. As well, the teachings are comprehensive because they cover all levels (individual, group, community, and society) and all aspects (cultural, economic, legal, political, and social) of human life. The Islamic moral and legal system, derived from both revealed and canonical laws, is known comprehensively as the *shari'ah*.

The Pillars of Islam and the Articles of Faith

The foundation of Islam is built upon what are commonly known as the pillars of Islam, and the articles of faith. The five pillars are: 1) *shahada* (testimony), 2) *salat* (prayer), 3) *siyam* (fasting), 4) *zakat* (tax on wealth), and 5) *hajj* (pilgrimage to Mecca). Upon accepting the Islamic worldview described above, an individual makes a conscious declaration of faith or the *shahada*, testifying that there is no god but God and Muhammad (peace be upon him) is His messenger. *Salat* refers to the five daily prayers at fixed times. Some *Shiite* Muslims combine their prayers into morning and evening times. During the process of arranging for appointment times with a Muslim American client, the practitioner might be told by the client that the appointment time conflicts with a prayer time or especially the Friday congregational prayer. If the client expresses anxiety about missing a prayer to maintain an appointment with the practitioner, one option for the latter is to offer a private, quiet, clean room for the client to perform his or her prayers. If it is possible to delay or advance the appointment time in order not to conflict with the prayer time, that is most advisable. *Siyam* (fasting) occurs during Ramadan from dawn to dusk, therefore the practitioner should be sensitive to the start of the month of Ramadan[5] and inquire if the client is fasting before offering him or her a snack or drink. *Zakat* is an annual payment of 2.5% of accrued wealth and is obligatory on the head of the household. From a psychosocial perspective, *zakat* has a two-fold function: 1) the individual seeks to purify his or her wealth by giving a portion of that wealth in charity; and 2) vulnerable and at-risk members of society are guaranteed financial and social service assistance from their brothers and sisters in faith. Finally, the fifth pillar of Islam, the *hajj*, is the obligation on every man and woman to perform a pilgrimage to Mecca, health and finances permitting, at least once in his or her lifetime. Modern-day estimates place the total at over 3 million Muslims gathering annually at Mecca for the *hajj* to perform rituals taught by the Prophet Muhammad (peace be upon him), rituals which commemorate events from the life of the Prophet Ibrahim (Abraham, peace be upon him) and his family.

In addition to the five pillars, *Sunni* and *Shiite* Muslims believe in six articles of faith, with belief in devotion to the family of the Prophet Muhammad (peace be upon him) being a seventh article referred to as *wilayat/imamat* which is central to the *Shiite* creed. In *Shia* tradition the authority to interpret faith is reserved for *Ahlul Bayt*, the progeny of the prophet. The six articles of faith are: 1) One God, 2) Angels of God, 3) Books of God, 4) Prophets of God, 5) Day of Judgment; and 6) Predestination. Belief in the oneness of *Allah* is paramount. Among the creation of *Allah* are the angels, and belief in the existence of these angels is an article of faith. The names of some noteworthy angels are *Mikaeel* (Michael) and *Jibreel* (Gabriel), the archangel who brought revelation from *Allah* to the prophets. Islamic teachings acknowledge as chronological iterations of divine guidance or books such as the *Zabur* (Psalms) revealed to the Prophet David (peace be upon him), the *Taurat* (Torah) revealed to Moses (peace be upon him), and the *Injil* (Gospel) revealed to Jesus (peace be upon him). The final iteration of the divine guidance is the *Qur'an* revealed to Muhammad (peace be upon him). Muslims also believe in the prophets of God among whom are *Nuh* (Noah), *Ibrahim* (Abraham), *Ishaq* (Isaac), *Ismail* (Ishmael), *Musa* (Moses), *Esa* (Jesus), and Muhammad (peace be upon him). Another article of faith emphasizes a belief in the *akhira* or an afterlife which is to be preceded by a Day of Judgment to separate one's reward-worthy deeds from those worthy of punishment. Finally, Muslims believe in predestination or *qadr* as a divinely ordained narrative accounting for every incident from the creation of mankind until the Day of Judgment. According to this belief, clients are likely to attribute a life event as being the will of *Allah*. Similarly, the client is highly unlikely to question the occurrence of that event since doing so would be tantamount to questioning the will of *Allah* who is benevolent and omniscient.

ISLAMIC ONTOLOGICAL FOUNDATION

Islamic teachings cast human beings in a positive light starting from birth. A baby, according to the Prophetic teachings, is born in a state of *al-fitra* or a pure state, a state free of sin, inclined to the worship of *Allah* (Abd al Ati, 1975). Even according to Islamic teachings, the ancestors of every human being are Adam and Eve; however, every newborn child does not inherit the sin of Adam and Eve because they both repented and were forgiven by *Allah*. The *Qur'an* chronicles this incident as such:

> We [Allah] said: "O Adam! dwell thou and thy wife in the Garden; and eat of the bountiful things therein as (where and when) ye will; but approach not this tree, or ye run into harm and transgression." Then did Satan make them slip from the (garden), and get them out of the state (of felicity) in which they had been. We [Allah] said: "Get ye down, all (ye people), with enmity between yourselves. On earth will be your dwelling-place and your means of livelihood—for a time." Then learnt Adam from his Lord words of inspiration, and his Lord Turned towards him; for He is Oft-Returning, Most Merciful. We [Allah] said: "Get ye down all from here; and if, as is sure, there comes to you Guidance from me, whosoever follows My guidance, on them shall be no fear, nor shall they grieve. But those who reject Faith and belie Our Signs, they shall be companions of the Fire; they shall abide therein" (*Qur'an*, 1993, 2:35–39).[6]

As these verses make clear, the Islamic outlook on the origins of humankind is that although a man or woman might be inclined to sin, the best of humankind are those who adhere to the guidance sent by *Allah* (Al-Krenawi & Graham, 2000).

It is important to note that Islamic teachings do not cast Eve as the originator of the sin in paradise. The sin of Adam and Eve is attributed to both Adam and Eve. Consistently in the *Qur'an*, the reference to the lapse of judgment in paradise appears in the plural form, that is *they* sinned; He [*Allah*] accepted *their* repentance. Therefore, women and men are treated as equitable partners, each racing and vying with the other to seek the pleasure of *Allah* through having faith, enjoining the good, forbidding the evil, and advising one another to patience and truth. Gender equity is addressed in the *Qur'an* in very strong terms,

> For Muslim men and women and for believing men and women, for devout men and women, for true men and women, for men and women who are patient and constant, for men and women who humble themselves, for men and women who give in charity, for men and women who fast (and deny themselves), for men and women who guard their chastity, and for men and women who engage much in Allah's praise, for them has Allah prepared forgiveness and great reward (*Qur'an*, 1993, 33:35).

The subjugation and oppression of women in some parts of the Muslim world stand in contrast to the Islamic teachings. Examining the dignified and respectable position of women within Islamic teachings, it becomes clear that the subjugation and oppression are rooted in local culture and deep-rooted misconceptions of women as inferior beings and not in the Islamic teachings themselves.

CORE VALUES OF THE FAITH

Muslim Americans cherish certain core values of the Islamic faith, values which are not entirely unique to Muslims but which provide social work practitioners a starting point to achieving cultural competence with this group. In the Western social work practice context, harmonious and healthy human functioning is an end in itself and is very much an individual-level project. In contrast, within the Islamic value system, healthy human functioning is a goal achievable in direct proportion

Table 13.1 | Contrast between Western and Islamic Values

Western Values	Islamic Values
Individualism	Community
Self-determination	Consensus
Independence	Interdependence
Self-expression	Self-control
Egalitarian gender roles	Complementary gender roles
Explicit communication that clearly expresses individual opinion	Implicit communication that safeguards others' opinions
Identity rooted in work and love	Identity rooted in religion, culture, and family

Source: SOCIAL WORK by Hodge and Nadir. Copyright 2008 by NATIONAL ASSOCIATION OF SOCIAL WORKERS. Reproduced with permission of NATIONAL ASSOCIATION OF SOCIAL WORKERS in the format Textbook and in the format extranet posting via Copyright Clearance Center.

to the strength of one's relationship with *Allah*. In their seminal work on cultural competence with Muslims, Hodge and Nadir (2008) contrast the Western values and those of the Islamic faith (see Table 13.1).

The Islamic values discussed in Table 13.1 are universally accepted but the degree to which an individual client adheres to these values is predicated on the role of religion in that client's life. Hodge (2002) asserts that "Indigenous cultural, social, and class factors associated with the family's country of origin affect how Islam is interpreted and practiced ... the cultural dimension may be more salient in determining beliefs and practices than Islam itself" (p. 7). Similarly, in the case of Muslim children whose identity is evolving and who are negotiating the values of various spheres of their lives, it is important for the practitioner to assess just what those spheres are in the case of an adolescent client and which of the spheres if any is dominant in guiding their daily lives. In addition to the teachings of Islam, Muslim children draw from their family's culture, which increasingly must include an appreciation of whether the parents were born in America or arrived as children of immigrants themselves; their peers and mass media, which arguably could have a significant impact; and the larger American culture, which notably could be transmitted via the public education system. As discussed further in the section on skills development, it behooves the social work practitioner to gauge inductively from interactions with the client the extent to which these core values and in general, the practice of Islam forms the lens through which the client views the world.

Overall, developing cultural competence with Muslim Americans is a professional imperative. Acquiring familiarity with the help-seeking behaviors of Muslim Americans, along with their belief and value systems, will facilitate greatly the goal of achieving cultural competence with this group.

HISTORICAL OPPRESSION AND CURRENT SOCIAL ISSUES

Muslim Americans have experienced historical oppression although the root causes of the oppression differ for Muslims of immigrant origins and for African American Muslims. The factor common to all Muslims is the widespread though mistaken connection between Islam and terrorism. The African American Muslims have experienced racism because they are black and bigotry because they are Muslim (Byng, 1998). Arab and South Asian Muslims have experienced bigotry because they are Muslim but also because of their perceived connection with whichever country the United States has been either at war or has had less than amicable relations. This section provides a brief review of Muslim American experiences with historical oppression in three phases: 1) from the founding until World War II; 2) post–World War II; and 3) post–September 11, 2001.

FROM THE FOUNDING TO THE WORLD WAR II PERIOD

The Muslim presence in North America predates even the founding of the United States but an institutional presence of Muslims is a mostly post–World War II phenomenon (Diouf, 1998; Nyang, 1999). There is indisputable evidence that among the hundreds of thousands of Africans who were enslaved and brought to America via an involuntary migration, there were substantial numbers of Muslims, mostly from present-day West African nations (Diouf, 1998). However, even after the Civil War and the abolition of slavery, there is little evidence of a pronounced institutional Muslim presence or established communities and organizations in the United States. Muslim merchants from the Middle East (present-day Syria and Lebanon) and seasonal farm workers from northern India represented voluntary and temporary migratory pathways to the United States during the late 1800s and early 1900s (Dannin, 2002; Takaki, 1998). In both cases, however, there is little evidence to indicate that any injustice or oppression faced by the Muslim merchants or the farm workers was due to their religious beliefs, especially since the former blended in owing to their fair skin, among the White population (Haddad, 1991) and the farm workers were most often mistaken as either being Hindus or even more ironically as distant cousins of the "Whites" owing to their "Aryan" roots (Takaki, 1998).

POST–WORLD WAR II

The major shift in immigration policies following World War II, along with an unprecedented demand for skilled labor combined to spawn the exponential increase in the migration of Muslims to the United States. Their physical migration plus the spiritual migration of tens of thousands of African Americans to Islam meant that the United States experienced an increase in the Muslim population starting around 1965 (Nyang, 1999). As the Muslim population increased, they sought to increase their civic engagement along with participation in the national political scene and were therefore thrust into the spotlight from a heretofore quiet existence, characterized more by instances of racial and ethnic prejudice and discrimination and less a discrimination based on their religious beliefs (Al-Issa, 1997b). The attitudes of mainstream society toward Islam and Muslims seem not to have been based on daily interactions with Muslims at work, in school, or in the neighborhood, rather on American government policies toward majority

Muslim nations. If the dominant discourse in America inclined positively toward Muslims, so did societal attitudes. Whenever American interests or just Americans abroad were threatened or targeted by Muslim political groups or state actors, similarly American attitudes toward Muslims were less favorable (Zolberg & Woon, 1999). During the Cold War, Muslims in America on the most part found themselves supporting broader American foreign policy interests, with all out full support from Muslims to support American efforts to end the occupation of Afghanistan by the Soviet Union. Following the defeat of Communism and the end of the Cold War, American foreign policy interests centered increasingly on Islam as a threat (Esposito, 2002).

POST–SEPTEMBER 11, 2001

By the end of the 20th century, there was considerable evidence of an increase in anti-Islamic rhetoric and cases of religion-based prejudice and discrimination and the situation for Muslim Americans soon turned from bad to worse (Akram, 2002; Shaheen, 2001). Three critical and interrelated events during the first decade of the 21st century have resulted in outright acts of violence, bigotry, prejudice, and discrimination toward Muslim Americans: 1) the September 11, 2001 terrorist attacks on the United States; 2) the U.S.-led war against Afghanistan; and 3) the ongoing U.S.-led invasion of Iraq. The negative sociopolitical context is further exacerbated with the ongoing conflation of Arabs and Muslims despite the reality that many Arabs are not Muslims and most Muslims are not Arabs (Barrett, 2007). The Council on American Islamic Relations (CAIR) monitors the status of Muslim civil rights in America and has reported worrisome increases in anti-Islamic behavior (verbal and physical assaults against innocent Muslim Americans) and harassment (workplace) and discrimination against Muslims (CAIR, 2006). The numbers tell a bleak story of anti-Muslim hate crime complaints not withstanding those incidents which go unreported due to fear of retaliation by neighbors or employers: 93 complaints, to 141, to 153 in the years 2003, 2004, and 2005, respectively (p. 7).

A comprehensive presentation of the experiences of historical oppression of Muslim Americans is beyond the scope of this chapter. Practitioners whose client population includes members of this group should make an effort to monitor local and national reports about emerging patterns of prejudice, discrimination, bigotry, and acts of violence against Muslim Americans. There is emerging evidence of the mental health and psychosocial consequences on the lives of Muslim Americans due to their experiences with oppression (Abu-Ras & Abu-Bader, 2009; Akram, 2002).

CURRENT SOCIAL ISSUES

Along with coping with and thriving in a sociopolitical climate which increasingly casts Muslims as the "other," Muslim Americans are contending with social issues whose resolution or lack thereof could result in psychosocial stress and other mental health challenges. Among these social issues are: 1) Muslim Americans and *patriotism*; 2) the role and status of Muslim women; 3) family issues; and 4) addictions.

MUSLIM AMERICANS AND *PATRIOTISM*

Given the historical context within which the Muslim American community developed, along with the present sociopolitical and cultural reality of an increasingly ethnically and religiously diverse American landscape, Muslim Americans are likely to face similar scrutiny about the extent to which they can successfully establish and maintain dual identities as Muslims and Americans. There is precedent within American history for such scrutiny because the Irish Catholics, who arrived en masse in the 1840s, and in whose lives Catholicism and the supremacy of the Pope were intertwined, had to endure intense hostility because they were deemed unable to become "Americans" or to be *patriotic* (Higham, 1963). Even before the September 11, 2001 terrorist attacks, Muslims experienced various mental health and psychosocial challenges due to experiences with prejudice and discrimination (Davies & Webb, 2000), but especially so in the decade following the attacks (Abu-Ras & Abu-Bader, 2009). Unresolved and festering identity issues have the potential to impact daily functioning on the one hand to psychosocial well-being on the other hand. Without adequate family and social support systems and available and open channels of communication through which to express their frustrations, adolescents, especially Muslim American youth, are likely to experience low self-esteem, poor academic performance, and related psychosocial challenges such as a breakdown in parent–child relationships and even confusion about their faith (Ali, Liu, & Humedian, 2004; Portes & Rumbaut, 2001; Ross-Sheriff & Husain, 2004; Suarez-Orozco & Suarez-Orozco, 2001). Practitioners should attempt to explore during the engagement and assessment phase to what degree if any the presenting problem of a Muslim American client relates back to his or her efforts at reconciling a dual identity as a Muslim and an American.

ROLE AND STATUS OF MUSLIM AMERICAN WOMEN

Most recent data on the Muslim American community indicate that women comprise almost half of the community (Pew Research Study, 2007). Due mostly to disproportionate attention in the media to honor killings and female genital mutilation, misconceptions within American society persist about the role and status of Muslim women, with the most common concern among Americans being the perceived oppression of Muslim women (Esposito and Mogahed, 2007). In the case of Muslim American women, the data indicate that they are increasingly better educated and pursuing careers (Mogahed, 2009). Notwithstanding the stresses and strains a Muslim woman experiences in the process of negotiating her identity as a woman, a Muslim, an American, and most likely a woman of color, it behooves the practitioner to explore complex issues that arise from their multiple identities. Islamic teachings liberate women to achieve their highest potential but either personal, familiar, or cultural forces could oppress them. It is important to understand the role and status of Muslim women in America from the perspective of 1) Islamic teachings; 2) a woman's personal understanding and interpretation; 3) the family's understanding and interpretation; and 4) culturally mandated expectations.

According to Islamic teachings, Muslim American women are encouraged to be educated, and to pursue careers. They are also encouraged to marry and along with their husbands, to share the responsibility of raising righteous children. This understanding emerges from Islamic teachings which emphasize the equitable contributions of Muslim women to the family, community, and society at large (Abd al Ati, 1977; Hamid, 1996). There is significant diversity around the world in terms of how the role and status of Muslim women is interpreted. Esposito and Mogahed (2007) summarize this diversity among Muslim women as follows:

> Women in some Muslim societies cannot drive cars and are sexually segregated, but women in many other parts of the Muslim world drive cars, ride motorcycles, and even fly planes. Some Muslim women are required by law to fully cover themselves in public, while others are prohibited from displaying the Muslim headscarf. A growing number of Muslim women are choosing to cover their heads, while others do not. In the United Arab Emirates and in Iran, women make up the majority of university students. In other parts of the world, women lag behind men in even basic literacy.

> Women serve in government in parliaments and cabinets and have headed governments in Turkey, Pakistan, Bangladesh, and Indonesia, while in other Muslim countries, women are struggling for the right to vote and run for office. Muslim women may wear a sari, pantsuit, blue jeans, dress, or skirt, just as Muslim men may wear long flowing robes, blue jeans, pullover sweaters, or three-piece business suits and may be bearded or clean-shaven (pp. 3–4).

Based on their own reading of the *Qur'an* and the *Sunnah* and within theological boundaries defined by those two sources, Muslim women are increasingly choosing to define their role and status. Esposito and Mogahed (2007)[7] indicate that around the world there is tremendous variance in how Muslim women approach their position in family and society. Within the American context, education has been a critical factor in ensuring upward mobility and women of color especially, and Muslim women are no exception, have encouraged their daughters to be educated (Portes & Rumbaut, 2001). With regard to the personal interpretation of Islamic teachings, Shakeri (2000) indicates that "Muslims, particularly women, want to keep their religious identity, while adopting other aspects of the host culture such as language, educational system, employment patterns, and civic life" (p. 129).

The situation of Muslim American women in families in which the parents are educated and are informed about the Islamic outlook on the role and status of women is different than one in which the parents, either due to being uninformed about Islamic teachings or due to the personal preferences of the father and mother, seek to deny their daughter rights such as seeking education, a career, and marriage, which emanate directly from Islamic teachings. The latter situation is likely to create profound stresses for a Muslim woman.

While personal and familiar interpretations of the role and status can either liberate or oppress Muslim women, perhaps the most dominant factor impacting individual clients is culture. Islamic teachings focus on instilling in both men and women a sense of decency, modesty, and respect. However, there are significant cultural differences in how modesty is interpreted. Muslim American women must contend with these cultural differences in the process of adapting to mainstream society and upholding Islamic teachings. Defying cultural interpretations of modesty for example by working outside the home, or wearing Western clothing, could result in community members distancing themselves from such a woman, depriving her of a social support system and potentially evoking feelings of alienation and loneliness.

The process of navigating the theological terrain, along with familial and societal expectations and pressures can be daunting for Muslim women, especially adolescent girls. The practitioner can best assist a Muslim woman client who presents with such stresses by validating her feelings of resentment and anger and by eliciting from female Muslim American clients their personal narratives. A strengths-based approach will be most empowering for the Muslim women to achieve the goals they have set for themselves. The practitioner can also connect clients with community-based Muslim organizations and support groups in order to fill the void created by feelings of alienation and loneliness.

FAMILY ISSUES

A healthy marital relationship and harmonious family relations are valued in Islamic teachings. Unconditional respect for elders is a value ingrained in children since birth. Obedience and deference to parents and elders are also valued. Mutual consultation, respect, a collectivistic outlook, and cohesiveness characterize the relations between husbands and wives and parents and children (Ali, Liu, & Humedian, 2004). Issues for Muslims American families arise broadly in the realm of 1) husband–wife relations and 2) parent–child relations.

A marriage in Islam represents not only the union of a man and a woman, but also of their respective families, in further support of the importance given to collectivism and community. The union is solemnized through an actual written contract which is considered sacred. Ross-Sheriff and Husain (2004) indicate that "Marriage is not only a formal contractual commitment between a husband and wife but also an informal commitment between the family members of each partner to help maintain and sustain the union" (p. 168). Contemporary issues confronting Muslim American couples include tensions arising from varying levels of practice of Islam; challenges facing dual-income households especially when the burden of chores falls disproportionately on the wives; and decisions involving having children, their schooling, their choices of peers and entertainment, and their college and career choices. Complicating the situation are cultural forces discouraging the disclosure of marital problems to "outsiders," leading some couples to suffer in silence or file for a divorce without seeking counseling or other interventions. The Muslim community is recognizing these issues and addressing them through increased attention to training Muslim counselors as well as through the provision of seminars and continuing education opportunities for practitioners of other faiths working with Muslim clients. An entire recent issue of a magazine published by the Islamic Circle of North America was dedicated to the topic of marriage counseling.[8]

Parent–child relations are another area of family issues requiring the timely and effective intervention of culturally competent practitioners. Ross-Sheriff and Husain (2004) note that "Muslim children, and even young adults, wishing to explore the dominant culture are caught between the old and the new, the tradition and the nontraditional, and the parents' wish to perpetuate Islamic norms" (p. 169). Issues likely to cause parent–child conflicts include the child's choice of dress, friends, hobbies, and entertainment; the pressure to excel in academics; and tensions arising from an inclination generally to experiment with a lifestyle considered age-appropriate by Western norms but potentially at odds with Islamic teachings. Faced with navigating Islamic teachings, the family culture, and the dominant culture, children experience various levels of conflicts and mental health consequences.

ADDICTIONS

Muslim Americans face similar life challenges as members of other minority and religious groups, including managing and overcoming addictions to alcohol, drugs, pornography, and gambling. For self-identifying Muslims, feelings of intense shame and guilt can arise as a result of knowingly violating Islamic teachings which forbid or consider *haraam* the consumption of alcohol and drugs and also forbid entertaining oneself with pornography and gambling. The focus within Islam is on the harmful effects on the mind and body of such activities concurrent with the potential loss of income spent on such activities. Hamid (1996) notes that some contemporary Muslim scholars "also regard smoking tobacco as *haraam* because of its harmful effects on the lungs and on health generally and because it involves a waste of wealth or *israaf* which is condemned in the Qur'an" (p. 43). Exacerbating the torment of addictions is the fear among Muslim Americans to admit to having such problems out of feelings of personal shame, loss of family honor, and possibly being alienated from the community. Practitioners dealing with Muslim clients with addictions should be aware of potential discomfort the clients might feel with the use of psychoanalytic techniques and especially group therapy, in addressing their addiction.

VALUES AND ETHICAL DILEMMAS

Ethics are rooted in values. Ethics are defined as actions that convey values which are society's normative standards and ethical dilemma are choices "between two actions that are based on conflicting values" (Linzer, 1999, p. 35). Both values may be "morally correct and professionally grounded but cannot be acted on together in a situation" (Linzer, 1999, p. 38). Based on their personal values and code of ethics of the social work profession, and understanding about the values of their Muslim clients, social workers may be caught up in a dilemma between the two sets of values. As we have pointed out in previous publications (Ross-Sheriff & Husain, 2000, 2004), social workers must examine whether they have knowledge and understanding about the complexity of values held by their culturally different clients or whether the challenges facing them in their decision making are really ethical dilemmas or practice problems arising from misinformation or misconstrued situations. Especially in the case of Muslim clients with whose beliefs and values the practitioner might not be familiar, it is critical for the latter to revisit and reaffirm the interpretation of the first standard in the *Standards for Cultural Competence in Social Work Practice*: "Cultural competence builds on the profession's valued stance on self-determination and individual dignity and worth, adding inclusion, tolerance, and respect for diversity in all its forms" (National Association of Social Workers, 2001, p. 8). We caution social work practitioners to distinguish between genuine ethical dilemma and practice problems and use guidelines provided in this chapter to serve their Muslim clients. The case study provided at the end of this chapter includes examples of possible value conflicts and ethical dilemmas in practice with Muslim clients. In this case study an astute social worker uses her clinical skills to evaluate and support a young Somali teenage boy who was presumed to pose an imminent threat to himself and his peers.

CULTURAL AWARENESS

One of the three functions of cultural competence identified in this book is *cultural awareness*, more specifically, a social worker's conscious and deliberate exploration of among other things, his or her own ethnic identity, cultural background, and contact with individuals of other cultural backgrounds. Such an exploration serves a priming effect insofar as the social worker is expected to acquire an awareness of and comfort with his or her own ethnic identity and cultural background and in doing so to come to terms with certain beliefs and values which are central to his or her background (Lum, 2004). A pertinent task for social workers is an exploration of their own ethnic identity and cultural background which must include a candid assessment of the place of spirituality and religion (Ross-Sheriff & Husain, 2004), a task for which most social workers are not well prepared (Canda & Furman, 1999; Hodge, 2007). In addition to the aforementioned discussion on intra-group diversity among Muslims and some of the major social issues they are facing, it is important for the practitioner to learn about the emerging Muslim American culture.

EMERGING MUSLIM AMERICAN CULTURE

As the population of Muslims in the United States increases, there is evidence of an emerging Muslim American culture, which is a blend of mainstream American culture and unique elements of each ethnic group represented within the broader Muslim American community. As noted earlier, Islam's preservative outlook ensures that the language, cuisine, dress, and other customs from the culture of origin are retained if only with slight modifications to align them completely with Islamic teachings. Therefore, even for an American of another faith who converts to Islam, the following cultural modifications might be required by way of example depending on their pre-Islam customs: 1) cuisine: Islam forbids the consumption of alcohol and pork, for example; 2) dress: Islam enjoins dress that is modest, loose-fitting, and not translucent; and 3) other customs: since only *Allah* is worthy of worship, any form of idolatry and ancestor worship become forbidden.

Islam's generative outlook in turn promotes the modification of existing cultural practices to include or emphasize particular values which are of great importance in Islamic teachings. Abd-Allah (2004) elicits a powerful image in his explanation of the on culture-friendly nature of Islam, stating that, "In China, Islam looked Chinese; in Mali, it looked African" (p. 1).

As noted earlier, the universalistic and timeless nature of Islamic teachings liberates the migrant Muslim, according her considerable freedom to adjust to the host culture. In the case of refugee migration to the United States, a Somali refugee mother of four is therefore as much at home practicing Islam in Virginia as is a Bosnian refugee father of two practicing Islam in Kentucky. Both find that the

Islamic teachings offer them a sense of familiarity, a sense of being rooted when confronted with a strange land as a result of their uprooting. Even as they go about settling in the United States and raising their children here, both of these refugees will feel relieved because Islam is "culturally friendly" on the one hand and will feel distressed on the other hand because the sociopolitical climate in America is presently culturally unfriendly toward Islam and Muslims.

During the last few decades, a distinct Muslim American culture has emerged as reflected, among other aspects, in their intra-group dynamics, their dress, and their entertainment. First, among Muslim minority populations around the world, the Muslim American community stands apart for its acceptance and respect of intra-group diversity and harmonious relations, especially among *Sunni* and *Shiite* congregations (Hunter & Malik, 2002). Despite varying levels of religious practice, diverse cultural norms, and understanding of gender roles and responsibilities, Muslim Americans are making great strides in promoting community development and civic engagement, education for girls and career development and advancement for women, as well as improved interfaith relationships and partnerships (Bukhari, 2003). Second, with regard to dress, second- and third-generation Muslims are designing creative new fashion lines, incorporating Islamic guidelines of modesty, American occasion-appropriate, seasonal, and regional fashion trends, and elements from ethnic and national outfits. Third, Islamic teachings regarding modesty and decency also guide the choices of Muslim Americans with regard to entertainment. Some consume American entertainment wholesale, while others reject American entertainment entirely, and others are applying a moderate and balanced approach to adapt existing forms of entertainment to develop Islamic acceptable, wholesome alternatives. It is common these days to see Muslim hip-hop artists, spoken word and other performing artists, Muslim comedians, and Muslim movie and documentary producers. Finally, the practitioner might have to expand his or her understanding of cultural awareness to include spiritual awareness, striving even to achieve spiritual competence. David R. Hodge, whose pioneering work is on spirituality and religiosity in social work, has written about spiritual competence (2002) and more recently has developed a scale to measure it. Canda and Furman (1999), writing about the practitioner's self-examination in the context of working with clients having a spiritual or religious worldview, entreat the practitioner to include reflecting upon personal biases, negative attitudes, stereotypes, and personal prejudices. Hodge (2007) asserts that "Independent of any particular faith tradition, the Spiritual Competence Scale taps values that are essential for culturally competent practice with spiritual and religious believers: openness, acceptance, respect, and sensitivity, along with a desire to understand and assign value to different spiritually based cultures, perspectives, worldviews, beliefs, and narratives" (p. 293). In the case of Muslim American clients, the practitioner's acquiring cultural awareness is interconnected with his or her acquiring spiritual competence as well.

KNOWLEDGE ACQUISITION

Another function of cultural competence is *knowledge acquisition*, more specifically, acquiring a skill set which facilitates practice with multicultural clients and an effort to learn more about and appreciate the principles guiding practice with those clients. Whereas knowledge acquisition is a critical step in practice with ethnic others, it is especially indispensable in the context of cultural competence with Muslim Americans for two reasons: 1) since clients from this community are only recently showing an increase in help-seeking behaviors, the social worker might have been exposed to little or no information about practice with this community; and 2) given the current scrutiny of Islam and Muslims in both the public and private spheres, the social worker is likely to have heard much about the religion and its adherents from popular literature, news media, and professional conference presentations. Absent an intentional effort to learn more about Islam, Muslims in general, and social work practice with Muslim Americans, the social worker is likely unaware of the beliefs and values which constitute a set of boundary guidelines for practice with this client group. Social workers whose client population includes Muslim Americans should be familiar with some over-arching aspects of the role of faith as it relates to: 1) divine help-seeking; 2) concept of Divine forgiveness for sins; and 3) life challenges and problems, as tests from *Allah*.

DIVINE HELP-SEEKING: RELIANCE ON *ALLAH* AND PRAYER

A Muslim American client is likely to rely on *Allah* for strength and guidance to supplement the professional help he or she is seeking. This inclination is noteworthy because one of the main reasons why another Muslim American client might not seek help is precisely because he or she might have concluded that divine help-seeking through prayer suffices and that seeking help from human beings is not becoming of a Muslim. While there is support in Islamic teachings for reliance on *Allah* and prayer to overcome any trial or tribulation, there is unequivocal support as well for agency and the expectation that one must first exert effort to resolve the presenting issue while concurrently relying on *Allah* for spiritual guidance and assistance (Al-Krenawi & Graham, 2000). An oft-cited verse from the *Qur'an* and a saying of the Prophet Muhammad (peace be upon him) illustrate the point well. In the *Qur'an*, Muslims read that "Verily never will Allah change the condition of a people until they change it themselves (with their own souls)" (*Qur'an*, 1993, Chapter 10, Verse 11). Similarly, the Prophet Muhammad (peace be upon him) corrected a man who understood trusting and relying on *Allah* to mean leaving his camel untied and unattended without consequence. The Prophet (peace be upon him) is reported to have responded to the man saying, "Trust in Allah but tie your camel first" (Hamid, 1996). Without this understanding some scholars of other faiths writing about Islam have misinterpreted the position of sole reliance on *Allah* as being a teaching of Islam itself, leading wrongly to the conclusion that Muslims are therefore fatalistic in their worldview. Endowed with the faculties of reason and logic, human beings are therefore expected to assess all types of risk in their immediate environment and to be proactive in mitigating the risk and even extricating themselves from the situation entirely.

CONCEPT OF DIVINE FORGIVENESS FOR SINS

The Islamic worldview places great emphasis on *Allah* as a benevolent and merciful deity, overall, but especially with regard to the human inclination to seek forgiveness after committing sins (Abd al Ati, 1975; Hamid, 1996; Ibrahim, 1997).

Whereas the Code of Ethics of the social work profession places tremendous emphasis on the worth and dignity of each individual, the presenting problems of clients are never categorized as sinful behavior. Rather, the profession views presenting problems as issues and challenges which are in need of professional intervention to restore a client to a state of well-being or functioning. A Muslim American client who believes that her every activity of daily living must be aligned with Islamic teachings is likely to focus on her presenting problem as a *sin*. The client is likely to be suffering emotional and psychological turmoil along with spiritual discomfort knowing that her actions have displeased *Allah*. It is important therefore for the social worker to know the relationship in Islam between the commission of a sin and the act of repenting followed by the act of seeking forgiveness from the aggrieved party—if an individual was wronged in the process—and certainly from *Allah*.

The burden of determining whether a presenting problem is also perceived by the Muslim American client as a sin does not fall on the social worker. The social worker does not need to acquire knowledge about Islam which would allow him or her to determine a priori whether the presenting problem is also a sin in the eyes of the client. In the process of developing a rapport with the client during intake, the social worker should make a genuine inquiry whether the presenting problem itself or some aspect related to the presenting problem poses a religious challenge for the client. If the client confirms the presence of spiritual discomfort, the social worker should attempt to understand 1) whether the client perceives the presenting problem to be sinful according to his or her faith, and 2) what process the client knows within his or her faith tradition she must follow to rectify the situation.

LIFE CHALLENGES AND PROBLEMS, AS TESTS FROM *ALLAH*

A critically important aspect of knowledge acquisition to develop cultural competence with Muslim Americans is the need for the social worker to comprehend the categorization within Islamic teachings of life challenges and problems as being tests from *Allah* (Abd al Ati, 1975). The client who presents with marital difficulties, for example, might share with the social worker his or her perception that he or she is experiencing such difficulties as a test from *Allah* for disobeying his parents and marrying the woman he loved, against their wishes. Another client whose business is failing might share his or her perception that he or she is being tested by *Allah* for choosing to sell alcohol since Islam forbids the production, distribution, sale, or consumption of alcohol (Ibrahim, 1997). The *Qur'an* is explicit in reminding all of humanity that *Allah* the Creator tests the faith of individuals and even entire societies by examining their resolve and perseverance in the face of adversity. Similarly, presented or tested with several courses of action, a faithful person is expected to assess each course of action through the lens of Islamic teachings to ensure that the final choice of action comports most with what is pleasing to *Allah*. If intense feelings of guilt, shame, and even self-hating overcome the client, he or she is likely to experience spiritual discomfort strong enough to block the ability to process even the most basic constructive thought patterns. Some clients experiencing spiritual discomfort might incline to increase their prayers and remembrance of *Allah* while others might incline to disengage from prayers. Ultimately, the client's attribution of his or her dysfunction as being a test from *Allah* should not distract the practitioner from his or her responsibility to help the client to acknowledge and accept his role and responsibility in resolving the marital difficulties. Similarly, the practitioner should be astute enough to help the businessman assess his management and financial practices rather than attributing the failure to a third party (*Allah*).

SKILL DEVELOPMENT

Driven by a professional mandate codified by both the Council on Social Work Education and the National Association of Social Workers to become culturally aware and acquire knowledge, the social work practitioner working with Muslim American clients must complement those efforts with a concerted effort to develop skills to undergird a culturally competent perspective. Given the existing paucity of content on Islam and Muslims in the social work literature, a practitioner is likely to face a daunting task in grasping practice principles to guide his or her practice with Muslim Americans. As noted throughout, it is not expected that the practitioner will be proficient in Islamic teachings rather that he or she will is committed to inductively learning about the Islamic worldview, the Islamic values, and the role that Islam plays in the life of the self-identifying Muslim client. Having such a commitment will enrich the counseling and therapeutic experience for both practitioner and client during the phases of engagement and assessment. In addition, such a commitment will foster goodwill between the practitioner and client, allowing the former to empower the latter to take control of and resolve the presenting problem as well as to serve as an effective advocate for the client.

ENGAGEMENT

Principles of culturally competent engagement of the client and the presenting problem are derived from Islamic teachings and values. Preparing to establish contact in person with a Muslim American client is important because a competent practitioner will at once put the client at ease by demonstrating knowledge and awareness of and respect for the client's value-informed worldview. The overarching guideline for effective engagement is to take cues from the client with regard to greeting the client, sitting down with the client, and establishing eye contact with the client during problem identification. A common Western greeting style involves saying hello while extending one's hand to shake hands. In the case of a female client, upon greeting the client, one suggestion is to pause to see if the client extends her hand for a handshake especially with a male practitioner. Due to a religiously mandated emphasis on respect and modesty for interaction with the opposite gender, the client might either choose not to shake hands or shake hands but it is preferable for the practitioner to err on the side of caution and wait for the client to take the initiative. Similarly, it is advisable for the practitioner to sit down first and allow the client's own comfort level to determine how far he or she chooses to sit. The problem identification will be a priority for the practitioner, but the client might engage in niceties and prolong the introductions to establish rapport before sharing personal information and the presenting problem. Direct eye contact between practitioner and client is considered a critical component of the therapeutic relationship in the Western context; however, partly due to concerns for modesty and partly due to deference to authority figures, the Muslim client may lower or avert his or her gaze. The client's indirect eye contact should not be stigmatized as a sign of low confidence, weakness, low integrity, or dishonesty rather it should be viewed in the context of his or her worldview. Especially relevant to the cultural norms and values of Muslim Americans is the utilization of ethnographic interviewing skills to assist the client to identify the presenting problem as well as to explore the interplay between various systems such as the family, extended family, friends, the community, school and work.

ASSESSMENT

Due to the diversity and varying levels of adherence to Islamic teachings and values among Muslim American clients, moving from knowledge acquisition to culturally competent practice with this group calls for the practitioner to engage the client at a level which promotes inductive learning from the client and which guides the practitioner's efforts to choose a practice modality and generally a service delivery structure most suitable for the client. Critically important to the discussion at hand is the choice of Western practice modalities "with which a certain degree of congruence or incongruence with Islamic values exists" (Hodge & Nadir, 2008, p. 33). The authors examined four modalities: 1) psychoanalytic approaches, 2) group therapy, 3) strengths-based approach, and 4) cognitive therapy. Least congruent among these four practice modalities are the psychoanalytic approaches because "the exploration of intrapsychic conflicts and the elucidation of psychodynamic insights" (p. 33) stand in stark contrast with the Islamic emphasis on looking not inward but outward and preferring community actualization over self-actualization. Even so, with the increasing familiarity and utilization rates of counseling and therapeutic interventions among Muslim Americans, the practitioner could gauge from the client just how comfortable he or she is looking inward. The second and third generation Muslims whose birth and upbringing have been entirely in the Western context, might not feel as conflicted discussing openly some of the intrapsychic conflicts they have or are experiencing. Similarly, while community and interdependence are prominent Islamic values, the dominant Western approach to group therapy, whereby members are expected to lower their guard and share personal indiscretions, is frowned upon and likely to put off Muslim clients. Owing to their "belief that if people conceal the weaknesses of others in this world, God will conceal their weakness in the hereafter," (p. 33), Muslim clients are likely to feel uncomfortable at best and avoid group therapy all together at worst. Further complicating the matter could be the outright fear of clients, especially those who have immigrated from despotic and dictatorial regimes, to share their thoughts in a group setting because of well-founded fears of their thoughts being reported back to the authorities. Both the strengths-based approach and cognitive therapy are more congruent with Islamic values than the psychoanalytic approaches or group therapy. The strengths-based approach is a good fit because it incorporates "environmental resources drawn from one's spirituality, family, culture, and community" (p. 33). The self-identifying Muslim values the spiritual strength he or she acquires through prayer and perseverance, and also the psychosocial support derived from healthy family relations, from cultural assets such as certain traditions and customs, and from a sense of protection and cohesion gained from the community. Finally, despite the focus on the individual in cognitive therapy, Hodge and Nadir (2008) proffer that this modality is congruent with Islamic teachings because key constructs of cognitive therapy such as "reason, logical discussion, education and consultation are widely affirmed in Islamic discourse" (p. 33). Therefore, the culturally competent practitioner will be able to engage the Muslim client, predicated of course on the level of education of the client, more effectively by tapping into the following: 1) the faculties of reason and logic; 2) the client's appreciation for being taught new mechanisms and strategies for coping with and resolving life challenges; and 3) *shura*, or mutual consultation, which is enjoined upon in the *Qur'an* as a means of conducting one's affairs.

EMPOWERMENT AND ADVOCACY

While empowering the client and serving as an effective advocate for him or her are foremost concerns for the practitioner, such an outlook is especially critical in the post-September 11, 2001 sociopolitical climate in which Muslims are experiencing considerable scrutiny, prejudice, and discrimination (Abu-Ras & Abu-Bader, 2009; Akram, 2002). The challenge for the practitioner is to reach a high level of self-awareness in order to deal effectively with any personal biases in either working with self-identified religious clients or specifically Muslims, toward whom the practitioner might have an ambivalence at best and prejudicial or discriminatory attitudes at worst. Reassuring statements can be quite empowering for the client such as "I understand that it is not easy to constantly be under scrutiny as a community, but please know that I am committed to work with you to resolve the problem we have identified together." Similarly, for those clients expressing anxiety about their faith, "I find comfort in turning to God as well during difficult times."

The client might appreciate as well knowing that the practitioner demonstrates readiness for advocacy on his or her behalf. The complexity of the problems facing the Muslim American client are likely to require a multi-agency response, a process which could prove daunting for the client to have to navigate by himself or herself. Equally problematic could be the client's own perceived or real experiences with prejudicial or discriminatory behavior with both society and the social service delivery system. The practitioner could serve as an effective advocate by helping to make explicit through active listening and prompting the implicit concerns of the client.

SOCIAL AND ECONOMIC JUSTICE RESOLUTION

The maintenance of justice is a cornerstone of the Islamic worldview. According to the *Qur'an*, order on earth is maintained through a dual focus among human beings to meet their obligations to God and to respect the mutual rights and responsibilities of other human beings and indeed all of creation. The Arabic term *adl* denotes justice and means to divide two things equally or to keep the balance. *Adl* is used in the *Qur' an* to refer to the imperative to establish justice in all matters, including in the social and economic realms. The model of just relations for

Muslims is Prophet Muhammad (peace be upon him) who was known for being fair and just not only to his followers, other tribes, and religious groups, but also to his enemies. The *Qur'an* requires Muslims to let nothing prevent them from being impartial in discharging justice. The verse below addresses the establishment of justice in the various systems impacting the life of a Muslim:

> O you who believe! Be established in justice, as witnesses for Allah, even if it be against yourselves, or your parents, or your relatives, whether they be rich or poor: for Allah is the protector of both. Therefore follow not the desires (of your hearts), lest you swerve from being impartial, and if you deviate or turn away, surely Allah is well-acquainted with whatever you do (*Qur'an*, 1993, 4:135).[9]

Islam not only ordains Muslims to do justice among themselves but also exhorts them to carry out justice even in the case of their enemies, "And let not the hatred of others to you make you swerve to wrong and depart from justice" (*Qur'an*, 1993, 5:8).

The resolution of social and economic justice issues is predicated on the above-mentioned foundation of justice. Islamic teachings are replete with admonishments for the believers to safeguard the well-being of the vulnerable, at-risk, and marginalized populations in society. Business dealings are to be conducted in an honest manner, with integrity and zero tolerance for corruption and greed. A description of righteousness in the *Qur'an*, which is illustrative of the social and economic justice imperative, juxtaposes belief in *Allah* and the articles of faith with an encouragement to be charitable and to have integrity in dealings, as stated below:

> It is not righteousness that ye turn your faces Towards east or West; but it is righteousness—to believe in Allah and the Last Day, and the Angels, and the Book, and the Messengers; to spend of your substance, out of love for Him, for your kin, for orphans, for the needy, for the wayfarer, for those who ask, and for the ransom of slaves; to be steadfast in prayer, and practice regular charity; to fulfill the contracts which ye have made; and to be firm and patient, in pain (or suffering) and adversity, and throughout all periods of panic. Such are the people of truth, and conscious of Allah (*Qur'an*, 1993, 2:177).

While the overwhelming majority of Muslims aspire to uphold teachings related to social and economic justice, there are very real challenges confronting Muslim communities around the world. Corrupt business practices, child labor, the subjugation and oppression of women, extremist ideologies and a cult of terror, among other challenges, are contrary to Islamic teachings and are more a function of local tribal customs. The resolution of these social and economic justice issues is linked directly to the restoration of the mutual respect for rights and responsibilities, which is of increasing concern to Muslim scholars and lay members alike (Ramadan, 2004).

CASE STUDY | A SOMALI AMERICAN TEENAGER: MODEL STUDENT OR SUSPECT?

Abdi, a young Somali American boy, is a ninth grader in high school, who has been referred for counseling to a local social services agency contracted by his high school. Abdi's father was killed during the years following the fall of the Siad Barre government in 1991 and the ensuing civil war in Somalia. Millions of Somalis fled from the capital city of Mogadishu and ended up in rural areas within the country while others reached refugee camps in Kenya and Ethiopia. In August, 2001, when Abdi was 6-years old, his mother received news of being accepted for resettlement in the United States in Portland, Maine.

Coming to America

A local church group met Abdi and his family at the airport. Since no one in Abdi's family spoke English, the welcome and greetings at the airport were conducted via a Somali language interpreter. Abdi's family moved in to a furnished apartment in Portland, sponsored in full by the generosity of the local church members. It was for Abdi's mother the end of an arduous journey which had started back in 1997 when the family fled Mogadishu.

Settling Down

Following the Labor day holiday in 2001, Abdi and his siblings began school, with Abdi having to start in first grade despite having had no formal schooling, unlike his older brothers and sisters. Abdi adapted well to the school and grasped some English words. He showed tremendous interest in learning and his mother was proud of him and his siblings, who were also adjusting well to school. For a 7-year old in kindergarten with almost no comprehension of the English language, the impact on his immediate life of the September 11, 2001 terrorist attacks was minimal. Portland, like other cities in America, was reeling from the shock of 9/11. Abdi's mother understood that life would become very difficult and that she and her children would be better off in a city with more Somalis. The family packed up their belongings and moved to St. Paul, Minnesota to join other Somali families, at least one of whom were distant relatives of Abdi's father's side of the family.

Life in St. Paul

Just as soon as they had landed in Portland and settled down, Abdi and his siblings were repeating the routine once again, this time in St. Paul, Minnesota.[10] They began to attend public school in St. Paul and took comfort in the fact that among their classmates were other Somali youth, most of whom were born in St. Paul. As the years went by, Abdi had a typical Muslim American upbringing, with his weekdays spent at school, and his weekends spent in the masjid learning about Islam and socializing with Muslim children from all racial and ethnic backgrounds. What was atypical, however, was that by the time he entered middle school, Abdi had developed an intense interest in American foreign policy, and particularly American military involvement in Somalia. He had watched the movie "Black Hawk Down,"[11] released after the 9/11 attacks, and was having mixed feelings about being a Somali American—Somali by birth and American as a result of the generosity of the American government. Within the family, Abdi was considered snobbish and even disrespectful because he was always referring to books and authors to back up even a most trivial argument with his siblings. They increasingly left him alone, taunting him for losing his Somali values and referring to him in a derogatory manner as *al Amriki*, or literally, the American. Abdi's mother had high hopes for her youngest son and helped him to understand more about the culture and history of the birthplace he never knew. She also sought out a Somali American woman who was teaching civics and social studies in the local elementary school and arranged for private tutoring for Abdi. As he prepared to enter high school, Abdi was a model student, excelling in his studies, respectful of his teachers and other students, proud to be a Muslim, proud of his Somali heritage, and emerging as a basketball player with promise.

Onset of Challenges

By 2009, as he made his way through the ninth grade, Abdi kept to himself, occupying his time with reading both in and out of the classroom. His classmates would see him in the library reading, getting up only to take a break to pray facing Mecca. Knowing that Somalia was without a government now for almost two decades, he wanted to learn more about how the United States itself was founded and how democratic ideals took such firm rooting in American soil. Courses like American history became his favorite subjects. The election of Barack Hussein Obama in 2008, the first African American president, with an Arabic middle name, and East African Muslim ancestry, had instilled in Abdi tremendous hope that in America, indeed, if you dreamed it, it was yours. With experiments in democracy all over the Muslim world underway such as in Afghanistan, Iraq, and Palestine among others, Abdi dreamed of one day writing a book on how Islam is totally compatible with democracy. Among his major influences in

continued

Islamic thought was the work of Professor Tariq Ramadan, a Swiss-born Muslim of Egyptian descent, who has written extensively about being both Muslim and European and being proud of both identities. Then news broke that a Somali American teenager named Osman from St. Paul, someone Abdi had known in passing, was reported missing. The authorities were alleging that Osman was on his way to Somalia to join the Shabaab—a group with ties to Al-Qaeda, and which the United States designated as a terrorist organization.[12] Abdi was clearly shaken up and retreated further into his books. As news about Osman's disappearance spread, Abdi was ridiculed at school, and taunted with disparaging statements like "Somalis are terrorists" and "Muslims don't belong in America." Abdi did not retort but he was visibly shaken up. The real trouble started when Abdi wrote an essay in class in which he exclaimed, reflecting upon the state of Muslims all over the world, that given the choice between living a life filled with oppression and tyranny, he would choose to "live free or die." These words sent chills down Abdi's teacher's back and she went straight to the school principal. Without so much as a second glance, the school principal referred Abdi immediately to a local social work agency specializing in services for children and family. The principal alleged that Abdi posed an imminent threat to himself and to his classmates for espousing *Jihad*[13] by expressing thoughts about extremism and violence. Abdi, who had never been written up before for anything, never been marked tardy, never had an unexcused absence, and by all accounts was a gentleman and an athlete, was now being referred for counseling for having extremist and violent thoughts. The principal indicated that Abdi could continue to come to school only if the latter agreed to see a counselor and the counselor signed off that Abdi was not a threat to himself or anyone else.

Assessment Almost Gone Awry

Even before Tracy Starks met Abdi, she was preparing herself for the worst. She felt in her phone conversations with him that he was standoffish and potentially even being raised in a household which subjugated women. When she called Abdi's home to set-up the appointment, Abdi's mother seemed uncomfortable speaking to Ms. Starks and said something to the effect of, *it is better you talk to the man.* When Abdi himself came on the line, he was not very talkative. He offended Ms. Starks by treating her as if she was a secretary attempting to set-up the appointment and not actually the counselor, who, as he exclaimed over the phone, *I thought when the principal said I would have to see a counselor, he meant I was going to talk to a man.* Ms. Starks' organization happened to be located within walking distance from Abdi's home so the appointment was set for him to see her at 3:00PM after school. Abdi agreed to come, saying only, *Insha'Allah* I will come after prayers. On the day of the appointment, Ms. Starks waited until 3:30PM and was about to start writing a note in Abdi's record when he appeared at her door and said only, *My name is Abdi and my mother is sitting out there in the lobby if you need to see her.* Leaning from her chair, Ms. Starks saw a woman wearing what she thought was a nun's outfit, smiling and waving back at her. Before Ms. Starks could rise from her chair, hand extended to greet Abdi, he was already sitting down across from her, his head hung low, seemingly put off by having to go through this exercise. Ms. Starks had experience working with other immigrant youth but never with a Somali boy, and especially not someone of a Muslim background. Too many conflicting thoughts raced through her mind about her own inexperience with serving the Muslim American population. *Shouldn't he have apologized for being late? Why had he ignored her attempt to shake his hand to greet him? Was this another example of how he was taught to treat women?* To her credit, she composed herself and decided to let Abdi guide her through the introduction and in-take, choosing not to even remind him why he had been referred to her in the first place.

Ms. Starks made an instant connection with Abdi by asking him if he liked to read, and sharing with him that her own favorite pastime was reading. Seemingly interested in the topic of conversation but not looking up as he spoke, Abdi remarked that he wished the school principal and his teacher had taken time to read about Islam instead of jumping to conclusions. Ms. Starks leaned forward in her chair to listen, but looked up and asked, *do you know what it's like to be called names at school? To be sent for counseling because of an essay I wrote? Why do people keep hating my religion? My culture?* Ms. Starks indicated politely, half-reflecting her own state of mind, *well, it always helps me to talk things through and to ask questions when I am unsure about something.* For example, she said, choosing to delay an immediate discussion of the presenting problem, *perhaps you can help me with some questions of my own because from our phone conversation I did not feel we got off to a good start.* No one had ever asked Abdi to help them, to clarify things, to share his views. He warmed to the idea and smiled, saying, *I realize you are trying to help and I am sorry if I have offended you in anyway.* As he spoke, Ms. Starks forgot for a moment that a ninth-grade client sat before her and became immersed in what could have easily been a presentation on Islam and Somali culture by a very learned adult. Abdi apologized for being late but reminded her that on the phone he had said he would come after prayers. *Could you not pray before 3:00PM,* she asked. Abdi explained to her that Muslims pray five times a day during fixed time blocks and the afternoon prayer time began around 3:00PM so he prayed at home and walked to his appointment. Upon arrival he did not shake her hand because of rules of modesty which govern the interaction between members of the opposite gender.[14] But why did his mother not wish to speak to Ms. Starks on the phone? *Because of her limited English proficiency, my mother is uncomfortable speaking in English for such important matters and handed me the phone because she felt it was better that you speak directly to me.* No disrespect was intended nor was Abdi's mother relegating her authority as the head of household to him, rather she was referring to him as a man because in Islamic teachings children are held accountable for their actions when they have experienced puberty. *Why did you assume the principal was referring you to a male counselor?* Abdi explained that he again meant no offense but that he had been taken off guard at the thought of having to discuss the issues at school with a woman and had himself assumed that the counselor was going to be a man not because he thought women were incapable of serving as counselors, but rather based on his own comfort level in dealing with men more so than women. Ms. Starks was impressed with Abdi. She

realized that despite her inadequate knowledge base and limited experience in working with Muslim Americans, her social work skills base had allowed her to draw upon the Socratic method to explore her client's worldview through asking guiding questions. Having started the session over 30 minutes late however meant that further dialog with Abdi would have to wait until their next appointment. Abdi was equally relieved at how well the session had gone and pressed Ms. Starks to find time for another counseling session within that same week. She had had a cancellation for the day after and the second appointment was set.

Intervention: Cultural Awareness and Knowledge Acquisition

During the second and third sessions, Ms. Starks and Abdi were able to develop a strong rapport and she decided it was time to tackle the presenting problem at the micro, meso, and macro levels. To do so, she would have to deal with an ethical dilemma about reporting Abdi to the authorities if in fact her intervention led her to believe that he did espouse violence and extremism. *Could it be that such a charming, intelligent young man with so much potential would want to throw away his life motivated by slogans such as live free or die? What religion would teach such an outlook?* As she had done during the assessment phase, Ms. Starks chose to suppress her own preexisting views about Islam and to work through the presenting problem with Abdi directly. She inquired about his family background and was surprised to hear that Abdi was born in Somalia. She had assumed due to his American accent that he was born in the United States. He took great pride in sharing with her the sacrifices his mother had made to give him and his siblings a better life. Islam engenders tremendous respect and dignity especially to women he noted, and serving one's mother puts one on the pathway to paradise. Abdi spoke lovingly of his mother and siblings and admitted how his bookish and reclusive lifestyle caused fights between him and his siblings. *All very normal,* Ms. Starks thought to herself. As Abdi spoke about himself and his family, there seemed nothing at the micro level which was especially noteworthy—Ms. Starks herself had six siblings and was raised by her mother after her parents divorced early on in her life. *What about school, what could Abdi say about his school environment?* She expected him to carry a negative tone

continued

CASE STUDY | A SOMALI AMERICAN TEENAGER: MODEL STUDENT OR SUSPECT?
continued

but he expressed tremendous love for learning and shared proudly with her that he was an almost straight A student and kept mostly to himself because he simply did not care for the kinds of conversation topics his friends, even his Muslim friends at school, would take on such as girls, dating, drinking, etc. He found much more satisfaction in reading and learning and his teachers inspired him to achieve high performance in school. He wanted very much to grow up to help others, especially Muslim children around the world. *What went wrong then, how do you explain the essay you wrote in class?* Unexpectedly, instead of giving an answer, Abdi asked her a question which in her mind essentially bridged the meso and macro levels of addressing the problem. *You have read my essay, why do you think there was anything wrong with it; I was only reflecting an ideal which has been touted in history class and is a cornerstone of the American Revolution.* Ms. Starks was expecting a mention of Islam, of something about what she had heard on the news, about how young Muslim men were being seduced into committing terrorist acts with the promise of heaven for achieving martyrdom on earth. She could not grasp how Abdi was indicating essentially that his classroom environment and American society had shaped his thinking with no mention at all of Islamic teachings and especially not of *Jihad. You seem shocked Ms. Starks, as if you believe what the principal and my teacher were saying about my having extremist and violent tendencies because I am a Muslim!* Visibly shaken but resolved to help Abdi, she regained her composure and encouraged him to please say more but at each turn, he seemed to ask her questions which she was unprepared to answer. *Do you realize Ms. Starks that there is nothing in Islamic teachings which encourages extremism or violence? Islam is against terrorism and promotes instead the sanctity of life. What I know is that if you take one innocent life it is as if you have killed all of humanity. I am surprised that you do not know the origins of the statement, "live free or die."* Abdi went on to explain that in

fact he was quoting an American revolutionary era general named John Stark who had famously uttered the phrase "live free or die" at the height of the struggle for independence from the British. Abdi indicated that he categorically rejected as ill-conceived the choice of the few Somali boys to have traveled to Somalia to help liberate it. Looking around at the Muslim world, he was appalled at the conditions of the Muslim populations and inspired by his knowledge of American democratic ideals to help improve the quality of life for those Muslims. He was against the American occupation of Iraq and Afghanistan, and also of the Israeli occupation of Palestine, but there was nothing within his understanding of Islamic teachings which would push him to ever take matters into his own hands or even to engage in terrorism. Was it not possible, he wondered aloud half-jokingly, that Ms. Starks' own family name could somehow be traced back to this general John Stark?

Termination: Skill Development and Lessons Learned

Over a matter of 2 weeks, Ms. Starks came to know Abdi quite well and learned much about Islam and Somali culture in the process.[15] There was no evidence based on her interactions with Abdi and even her own readings about Islam outside of their counseling sessions that Abdi was in any way inclined to encourage or engage in extremism or violence. Writing up her report about the assessment, intervention, and imminent termination, Ms. Starks realized that there could be many Muslim children who might be experiencing similar internal conflicts about being Muslim and American. Who would these children turn to? What if other principals and teachers were being just as hysterical and misreading very real psychological and identity crises and sending off their Muslim American students for counseling or even worse, suspending them or expelling them?

CONCLUSION

Practitioners should aim to establish a participatory relationship with the Muslim American client, engaging the client fully and learning inductively about the client's worldview particularly as that worldview informs the client's beliefs, values, and decision-making system. Ten practice principles emerge for cultural competent practice with Muslim Americans:

1. Appreciate that Muslims are not a monolithic group. They represent intra-group diversity based on their beliefs, levels of practice, cultural and ethnic diversity arising from their origin from almost 90 countries including the United States, migration status (as refugees, asylees and immigrants, and so on), and generational differences.

2. Gain basic knowledge and understanding of the tenets of the faith of their clients, specifically the pillars of Islam and articles of faith, and the social practices of some clients such as reduced eye contact, not shaking hands, using head cover and so on; the goal should be to take cues regarding appropriate responses to social practices from the client.

3. Utilize the engagement phase to establish rapport, build trust, and free up both practitioner and client for in-depth therapeutic work.

4. Understand the Islamic worldview and respect the core values of their clients, specifically in terms of family relationships, gender roles, self control, and communal concerns. This understanding would be helpful in assessment as well as therapeutic intervention.

5. Keep the assessment phase as comprehensive as possible, eliciting the client's narrative about his or her religious beliefs and values, and maintaining respect for the client's religion, worldview and core values, which like those of most religious groups, are humanistic.

6. Examine their own biases and the biases and fears of the leadership of the referring institution (employers, teachers, principals, etc.) about Muslims so that they may demonstrate "respect for diversity in all its forms" (NASW, 2001, p. 8).

7. Differentiate between a practice problem and a genuine ethical dilemma, because a misclassification by the practitioner followed by a misstep could pose very real and potentially life-threatening consequences for Muslim clients ranging from loss of employment and expulsion from school to deportation in the case of immigrants.

8. For immigrant Muslim children and adolescents, explore intergenerational differences as a likely source of challenges that result in stress and mental health problems.

9. Appreciate that what might be considered paranoiac or extremely cautious behaviors of their clients may arise from prejudice, discrimination, or even fears of potential personal harm.

10. Lastly and most importantly, an understanding of the complex and comprehensive nature of diversity among Muslims will help in avoiding fear as well as ethical dilemma in practice with this population. Such understanding and sensitivity to the values of Muslim clients will help social work practitioners focus their energies on presenting problems and serving their Muslim clients.

NOTES

1. Inaugural address delivered on January 20, 2009. Available at: http://www.whitehouse.gov/blog/inaugural-address. Accessed on October 15, 2009.

2. There is a 2-year lag between application for the lottery and notification and eligibility for actual immigration so the latest data available are for the results from those individuals who applied in 2008.

3. As a sign of respect and appreciation of the prophets, Muslims add "peace be upon him" after mentioning their name(s).

4. See Rogerson (2007) for a detailed examination of the differences between *Sunnis* and *Shiites*.

5. Desk and wall calendars increasingly indicate the start and end of the month of Ramadan; when in doubt, it is advisable to confirm the occurrence of Ramadan with the client.

6. References to *Qur'anic* verses are cited in the form, chapter:verse(s).

7. For further reading, see Chapter 4, "What do women want?" in Esposito and Mogahed (2007).

8. See *The Message* magazine, November/December 2009 issue; contact Message Magazine Publishing Office 166-26 89th Avenue, Jamaica, NY 11432-4254, 718-658-1199 ext. 116.

9. For additional information on the Somalis in Minnesota, especially the youth, see Adan, S. (2006). *Report on Somali youth issues.* Minneapolis, MN: City of Minneapolis Department of Civil Rights. Available

at: http://www.ci.minneapolis.mn.us/council/2007-meetings/20070126/docs/Somali-Youth-Issues-Report.pdf. Retrieved on March 4, 2010.

10. For additional information on the Somalis in Minnesota, especially the youth, see Adan, S. (2006). Report on Somali youth issues. Minneapolis, MN: City of Minneapolis Department of Civil Rights. Available at: http://www.ci.minneapolis.mn.us/civil-rights/docs/somali-report.pdf. Accessed on August, 10, 2007.

11. The movie *Black Hawk Down*, released after the 9/11 attacks, is based on a true story in which American troops, on a peace-keeping mission in Somalia in 1993, were captured, killed, and dragged through the streets of Mogadishu by local warlords.

12. See Designation of al-Shabaab as a foreign terrorist organization. February 26, 2008, Available at: http://www.state.gov/s/ct/rls/other/des/102446.htm. Accessed on January 10, 2010.

13. See Esposito and Mogahed (2007), p. 75 for a definition of the term *Jihad*.

14. See Maloof and Ross-Sheriff (2003) for a discussion on hand shaking and other Islamic etiquette relevant to worker–client interactions.

15. For a primer on Somali culture, see also Heitritter, D. L. (1999). *Somali family strength: Working in the communities.* Minneapolis, MN: Family and Children's Services and the University of Minnesota Extension Service.

CULTURAL COMPETENCE WITH WOMEN

CHAPTER 14

Economics, Global Forces, Poverty and Social Work as if Poor People Mattered

Christine T. Lowery

Safety is a deep, basic wish of all people, no matter what race or nationality. Fear gives rise to violence. When we practice looking deeply, we will see that if the other people do not feel safe, then we will not have safety either. To secure safety for ourselves, we have to think about the safety of others. If we give others the impression that they are in danger, then we will be in danger, too. If we continue to create danger and instability for the other group, the danger will rebound on us. What we do to the other, we do at the same time to ourselves. Safety is not an individual matter; it is a matter that concerns all of us.

–Thich Nhat Hanh, 2003, p. 199

INTRODUCTION

The role of economics has always been central to social work, although myopically centered on social control of poor families and racially marginalized communities, including the gendered welfare state (Abramovitz, 1996). Feminists (liberal, cultural, socialist) have offered broader explanations (sexism and biology, patriarchy and power, gender division of labor and women's dependence, and social reproduction, including child bearing and socialization) of structured gendered inequality to build on research regarding class inequality.

The rise of communication technology and the effects of globalization and environmental concerns have spawned a growing body of shared knowledge that forces us to recognize the interlocking networks and structural systems that create wealth for some and violence, suffering, and disposability for others. Understanding how economics and race are structured and manipulated is paramount for social workers working with children, families, and women. This requires study and diligence. The phrase "the personal is the political" used by feminists since the 1960s and 1970s can be augmented with compassion and spirituality. Recognizing

391

how people who are poor can change the world *is* personal transformation *is* collective transformation *is* world transformation.

We all feel the effects of globalization and environmental change. The focus on the people who are poor and on sustainable agricultural or agroecology models (balancing ecology, economy, equity) in this chapter is purposeful. People who grow their own food worldwide work to solve problems of survival every day, and they work against structural forces, policies and bureaucracies. Recognizing strengths and potential is not enough; recognizing how the poor are kept in situations of poverty, such as structural adjustment, is required. And reframing our expectations and recognizing how people work together to address inequalities is critical. The Campesino a Campesino model, a culturally based model combining mutual aid, science, teaching/learning, and the creation and dissemination of knowledge, is described in this chapter and students are challenged to explore and test this model for "sustainable" social work.

AN ETHICAL DILEMMA: GLOBALIZATION, A HAITIAN NATIONAL EXAMPLE

Haiti was hit by a 7.0 with earthquake on January 12, 2010. Buildings collapsed, killing nearly two hundred thousand, and leaving over a million people homeless. World response was galvanized, and the future is uncertain. The earthquake is but one of the many upheavals Haiti has endured including a cruel history of slavery under the French, and a bitter 13-year fight for freedom as slaves fought for freedom. In the 1980s, globalization and increased poverty added to the Haitian burden, and four hurricanes in three weeks in 2008 pale in comparison with the earthquake of 2010. These events reflect a range of relationships found in the world, from humanitarian responses, the consequences of environmental disasters and global warming, to the long-term trauma of historical and economic oppression.

In his book, *Eyes of the Heart*, former Haitian president, Jean-Bertrand Aristide (2000) describes globalization and the dynamic impact on the poor. Globalization, with its "market before the person" machine, demonstrates the ethical crises he saw in Haiti (p. 6). Using the hand as an analogy for the world's population with $100 to share, the thumb represents the richest 20% with $86. The little finger represents the poorest 20%, the disposable people, with a $1 to share. The social, economic, and ethical distance between the thumb and the little finger creates an enormous chasm, makes refugees of children and pushes them into the streets to make a living (p. 35). Street life is harsh, Aristide acknowledges, and in a culture of sharing, their spirits are lifted and the children think with piercing clarity. Three 11-year-old girls saw democracy in realities: food, school, and health care for everyone. Democracy has no meaning, unless children can eat and feel safe. These are basic human rights, and require an investment in people, Aristide concludes. "It is the challenge of any real democracy to guarantee them" (p. 36).

The role of women in economic environments and countries around the world is central to this chapter and is critical in understanding how culture is shaped and changed in an environment of poverty and need. In many cultures, women bear a huge responsibility for feeding and ensuring the health of their families. Aristide (2000) notes that when household budgets are in the hands of women, the needs of the family are considered. And in the Haitian informal economy where 70–80% of the people make their living, women are the *poto mitan* (center pole) because of their skills in cooperation and leadership, when compared to men. Aristide predicts that when women are in leadership positions and the budgets of nations are in their hands, then food, education, and healthcare will be central to the health of a nation. (In 2004, Aristide was removed as president of Haiti with impetus from the U. S. State Department, and is currently in exile in South Africa. Many in Haiti still wait his return in spite of political and politically contrived controversy regarding his presidency. After the earthquake, Aristide voiced his desire to return to Haiti, but must be invited by the Haitian government.)

In the news analyses that have followed the earthquake, pundits have cited a history of poverty, instability of the government, and corruption as reasons why Haiti has been unable to address the overwhelming poverty. From a different perspective, Aristide (2000) traces a history of structured economic and social crippling based on oppression and exploitation. When Columbus claimed Hispaniola (now Haiti and the Dominican Republic) for Spain, it was the indigenous Arawak people who greeted him. In 1697, when France claimed Haiti as a colony, the Arawak had been decimated through slavery and disease. France relied on the African slave trade to develop the coffee and sugar plantations of Haiti that rivaled the wealth of the 13 North American colonies. By 1791, slaves outnumbered the French in Haiti 10 to 1 and revolted. Haiti's infrastructure and agricultural productivity were devastated by the 13-year war that followed. An example of early economic structural adjustment was forced on the free Haitians when France demanded reparations of 150 million francs in 1804 (1.1 trillion in today's dollars), reduced in 1830 to 60 million francs (*Haiti's Historic Debt Load*, 2008). By 1900, Haiti was paying 80% of its national income to debt; the debt was paid with interest in 1947 (Haiti's debt, 2008).

This is not the only economic vulnerability however. Aristide provides two recent examples of international and U. S. involvement that have burdened the poorest Haitians. In the late 1970s, the African swine-fever was found among some pig populations in Caribbean nations, including Haiti. (There is some controversy whether or not this was swine fever, depending on the source, but the eradication of the Haitian Creole pig population is not debated.) The Creole pig, a scrappy descendent of pigs from Spain and wild boars, was literally money in the bank for Haitian peasants in rural communities and used for everything from emergencies to school fees and books, and voodoo sacrifice (Angler & Dierderic, 1984). The pigs were stalwart, ate waste, fertilized the soil, could survive for three days without food, and never got sick (Aristide, 2000). In 1982 international agencies convinced the Haitians that the pigs were sick and the Haitian government spent $22 million to eradicate the pigs (Angler & Dierderic, 1984). The United States assisted to protect the $10 billion U. S. pig business (Angler & Dierderic, 1984). Within 13 months, they were gone, with devastating economic consequences for the most economically vulnerable (Aristide, 2000). Many claim they were not compensated for the pigs, school enrollments dropped, and protein consumption in rural areas declined. To repopulate the pig population, the United States sent pigs from Iowa. Dubbed four-footed princes, these pigs required clean water the Haitians did not have, and needed imported feed the Haitians could not afford (Aristide).

By 1980, globalization was propagandized as the way out of poverty by countries that would benefit most. Many poor countries opened their economies to world markets hoping for foreign investment and business development. In exchange, these countries allowed goods and services from the outside to flow in, with devastating results (Aristide, 2000). For example, in 1986, Haiti imported 7,000 tons of rice, a staple already grown in Haiti. When tariffs on rice from the United States—where the rice industry is subsidized—were lifted, the Haitian market was flooded with cheaper rice. Haiti's peasant farmers could not compete and the rice production dwindled; many farmers and agricultural workers were displaced. By 1996, 196,000 tons of foreign rice made its way into Haiti at a cost of $100 million a year; when dependence on foreign rice was assured, prices rose, and continue to rise, taxing the ability of mothers and fathers to feed their children.

Like many poor nations, Haiti struggles under staggering debts to the World Bank and International Monetary Fund (IMF), which continue to cancel out the nation's productivity in a cycle of "perpetual economic dependence" (Aristide, 2000, p. 33). In June 2009, Haiti was released from over half (63%) of a crippling $1.9 billion dollar debt; the monthly bill alone included $5 million in interest payments (Ives, 2009). The money from the loans, made during the corrupt and violent Duvalier period (which predates Aristide's presidency) never found its way to the Haitian people. Despite the debt forgiveness, the IMF and World Bank—through which American ideas flow—continue to impede Haiti's ability to chart its own economic growth.

In a breath of fresh air amid all reports on the devastation, Ruxandra Guidi, a Venezuelan freelance journalist featured in the *New York Times* editorial blog on January 14, 2010, commented on the difference between life in the capital of Port-au-Prince and life in the countryside before the earthquake.

> While people in the cities lacked basic services and relied on international aid for everything from a job to food, the quality of life in the countryside seemed much better, even as people faced a hard time finding employment and getting their kids to school. In communities like Papaye, in Haiti's Central Valley, people grow their own food, reforest their land, and have a sense of community. They could work outside the development aid system, and create solutions that addressed their needs and their way of life. (para. 25)

EXPANDING POSSIBILITIES: PEOPLE WHO ARE POOR ARE PRODUCERS AND CONSUMERS

Polak (2008) elaborates on "three great poverty eradication myths" (p. 30). 1) We can donate people out of poverty. 2) The great myth of globalization is that national economic growth will raise all boats (p. 40). 3) Big business will end poverty (p. 41).

Aid money from rich to poor countries rarely finds its way to the 800 million poor farmers living on small farms around the world (Polak, 2008). According to research from the International Food Policy Research Institute (IFPRI), 85% of 525 million farms in the world are smaller than five acres, and their contributions to food production should not be underestimated. "In Russia in 2001, farms less than five acres produced 51% of the milk, 57% of the meat, 80% of the vegetables, 93% of the potatoes, and 28% of the eggs" (Polak, p. 119). In many parts of the world, subsistence plots that feed families of five or more are less than one acre and growing smaller; these are the dollar-a-day farmers. There are "1.1 billion dollar-a-day people in the world" (p. 47) and the entrepreneurial capacity is strong (Polak).

UN MILLENNIUM DEVELOPMENT GOALS

1. Eradicate extreme poverty and hunger
2. Achieve universal primary education
3. Promote gender equality and empower women
4. Reduce child mortality
5. Improve maternal health
6. Combat HIV/AIDS, malaria and other diseases
7. Ensure environmental sustainability
8. Develop global partnership for development

Source: *http://www.un.org/millenniumgoals*

Although the [United Nations] Millennium Development Goals are admirable and impressive, the strategies to achieve them are fatally flawed—big infrastructure investments, big agricultural projects, big irrigation, and big budgets controlled by the government of developing countries—all efforts that bypass poor rural people living on one acre farms (Polak, 2008, p. 34).

Depending on big business to eradicate poverty is wishful thinking (Polak, 2008). Despite sustained economic growth, there is poverty in the United States, India, and China. According to the U.S. Census Bureau in 2005, 12.6% of the population or 37 million people still remained poor in the U.S. (Polak, 2008). In 1999, India reported 36% of the population or 360 million people survived on less than $1 a day (Polak, 2008). And in 2001, China—including the prosperous industrial China and the unrelenting poor rural China—reported 216 million people survived on less than $1 a day. This is 16.6% of 1.3 billion people in a country that has an overall "impressive sustained per capita GDP [Gross Domestic Product: a nation's income minus costs with data gathered from surveys of stable businesses and industry] growth rate of 8%" (p. 40). Most poverty is evident in rural areas, far from urban industrial centers, and it is industrial growth that contributes to per capita GDP growth. The immediate alternative to rural poverty is migration to urban areas for work, living in city slums, and working under poor conditions.

There are alternatives to poverty using business. If multinationals are to contribute to working on poverty, they must refocus (Polak, 2008). They must understand how to make a profit serving those who make less than a dollar a day, serving those who may be illiterate, and serving those who have no access to mass media (Polak). In this plan, priorities include the "design and marketplace delivery of income-generating tools and strategies" that can pay for themselves in a year; proof that poverty is decreased; and the capacity to refit business to reach millions of people who are poor, but who can afford to buy a product (p. 45). For example, 2 million treadle pumps have been sold to dollar-a-day farm families for $25 each. With technical assistance to invest in labor-intense, cash crops and the growth of private sector supply chains, 2.5 to 3 million dollar-a-day families increased their net annual income (Polak). Over 25 years, farmers have invested $139 million in income-generating tools for an increase in net annual income of

$288 million. The global impact on poor villages is estimated to be $500 million a year (Polak).

"People who survive on less than a dollar a day have the lowest labor rates in the world" (Polak, 2008, p. 45). This labor pool can contribute to financial growth without destroying the environment with mega-farms and corporate agri-businesses. In India, the Gujarat Cooperative Milk Marketing Federation (GCMMF), also known as Amul, found a way to take fresh milk—using 2.5 million small-farm milk producers with one to three buffalos—and process it for sale in markets for butter, cheese, and ice cream. Sales in 2005–2006 were $850 million. Worldwide there are 800 million dollar-a-day rural people who can produce labor-intensive, high-cost off-season fruits and vegetables and herbs. Big business can contribute in distribution and marketing, or finding methods of collection and getting this produce to high-end markets (Polak, 2008).

These ideas are not new. Using science and technology, Schumacher (1973) outlined a plan for sustainability and non-violence, acknowledging the human relationship to nature. "Methods and equipment must be cheap enough so that they are accessible to virtually everyone; suitable for small-scale application; and compatible with man's need for creativity".... If only one of these three is neglected, things are bound to go wrong" (p. 34). The work here is in progress, but on a relatively small scale. Innovators and social entrepreneurs, students and professors in architecture, design, and engineering have taken on projects that are accessible, functional, and contribute to the creativity and productivity of men and women. In the reality of the extremely poor, affordability is the rule (Polak, 2008).

What would consumers who make $1 to $6 a day be willing to buy as their incomes increase? Polak estimates that a billion people would buy $2 eyeglasses, "if an effective global distribution and marketing system for them were developed" (Revolutionary Designs, para. 12). More than a billion would buy a $10 solar lantern (LEDs) since an electric power grid is not in their near future; and more than a billion would buy a $4 "household-level filter" for safer drinking water (Revolutionary Designs, para. 12).

COMPLEXITY AND CHANGE: ECONOMICS THROUGH A CULTURAL LENS

The role of women to help create a sustainable and safer world is recognized. The education of young girls reduces fertility rates and helps balance an unequal world population to promote sustainable futures in food, water, energy (Krauss, 2009). Education alone is insufficient, since economic opportunities are critical (Krauss, 2009). And the impact of culture and economics cannot be underestimated. What cultural practices are reinforced or changed at the intersection of culture and economic development and gender (men and women)?

Cultural roles (religion, economics, care of parents in old age) may weigh heavier on males than females in economically sustaining the family unit in a patriarchal society (Rosenburg, 2009). What Westerners view as gender preference or valuing boys over girls, can be reinterpreted as the cultural necessity to maintain the family unit, including property rights passed down to males. In patriarchal societies, women leave their parents to contribute primarily to their husband's families, while sons are retained to support their parents in culturally determined roles

(Rosenburg, 2009). In these societies, expected dowries a daughter must bring to the husband's family may stress the family economic resources (Rosenburg, 2009).

The Western expectation is that women of India, for example, who are more educated would use their status to elevate the positions of their daughters (Rosenburg, 2009). However, when cultural expectations are over-laid, educated women still carry similar cultural expectations as less educated women (Rosenburg, 2009). Wealthier, more educated women in India have smaller families. In the cultural context of maintaining the family, anticipating two or three children, instead of seven, intensifies the hopes of having sons; likewise, the disappointment of having daughters may be intensified (Rosenburg, 2009).

Economic development often coincides with technology. In the reproductive arena, this includes ultra-sound technology to depict the sex of a fetus (Rosenburg, 2009). While infanticide is still practiced in China, technology can influence the decision to abort the fetus (Rosenburg). Sex-selective abortion is banned in India and China, and it is illegal to inform parents of the sex of the fetus (Rosenburg). As with many illegal or coerced practices, the reality is that sex-selective abortion is practiced and not punished (Rosenburg). Eventually, the consequences of fewer female births have a future economic impact—particularly for poor people—when there are not enough female partners with whom to create a viable economic and social unit and continue the family.

Poverty for males and females deprives both though not equally (Rosenburg, 2009). As the family grows economically, birth order and gender may determine who gets the economic resources (doctor's visits, educational opportunities). While the first-born daughter in a family may be treated like her brothers, each subsequent daughter faces the likelihood of discrimination, particularly when it comes to medical care (Rosenburg). Often these daughters are neglected and may die within the first five years of life (Rosenburg). Demographics in India and China predict 1.5 million more girls than are actually born each year; more girls die before they would be expected (Rosenburg, 2009). In China in 2007, there were 1.73 million births—and a million missing girls (Rosenburg, 2009). Millions more grow up stunted, physically and intellectually, because they are denied the health care and the education that their brothers receive (Rosenburg).

Policy makers, thinking from a Western perspective, operate on two assumptions. First, women will fight for all their children as development and economic change influence women and as they become more educated and wealthy (Rosenburg, 2009). However, in some cultures, having sons who marry raises a woman's status and culturally this may wield a heavier influence on how she uses her increased power (Rosenburg). Second, aid to women will increase women's decision-making power (Rosenburg). With strong cultural obligations for maintaining the male position in a patriarchal society, it could be likely that women will use their new-found economic power to help their sons, not necessarily their daughters (Rosenburg). These practices may take a generation or two to change, and the changes will be culturally shaped.

Social workers must understand the changing relational contexts of women's lives and be conscious of any classist, elitist or Westernized expectations of the women with whom they work. Social work becomes ethnography and one enters the world of the women, including the structural, cultural, and social demands on their roles and their understanding of the world and the ways in which they move through their daily lives to maintain their families within cultural contexts.

U.S. CULTURE: A CURRENT STATE OF ECONOMIC AFFAIRS (2000–2010)

We live in a world of paradox and seeming contradiction. Zakaria (2009) provides evidence that despite worldwide sociopolitical upheaval and two U.S. wars and a series of economic melt-downs, in a broader historical context, we are living in a period of relative calm. Minimalist media sound-bites and headlines create the perception that we are always in constant danger; however, violence worldwide actually grew more steadily throughout the Cold War period than now (Zakaria, 2009). (This is the period in which assassinations of three dynamic leaders shook the United States including President John F. Kennedy, Martin Luther King, and Robert Kennedy they were he was campaigning for the presidency.)

The world economy was robust between 2000 and 2007, and income per person rose faster at 3.2% than at any other time in history (Zakaria, 2009). While inflation was relatively low, the global economy doubled from 1999 ($31 trillion) to 2008 ($62 trillion) (Zakaria). "Everywhere, the prices of goods fell while wealth in the form of stocks, bonds, and real estate soared" and global growth promised global order (Zakaria, p. xii). And, while China's considerable economic growth lifted millions out of poverty and poverty in other countries is falling, the "50 countries where the earth's poorest people live are basket cases that need urgent attention" (Zakaria, p. 3).

What happened to these growing world economies in 2008 and 2009? Zakaria's (2009) analysis takes into account the positive contributions of world stability in politics; economics and the race toward prosperity promised by globalization; and the technological push toward a single global economy. With huge corporate profits and the perception of manageable risk, dangerous investments were rampant. Every one, from corporations to homeowners spent beyond their means, including the U.S. government and its citizens. Americans consumed more than they produced and made up the difference by borrowing (Zakaria, 2009). Household debt rose from $680 billion (the equivalent of the current U. S. military budget) in 1974 to $14 trillion in 2008. In 2007, the U. S. current-account deficit, reached $800 billion—a dangerous level—explained by a worldwide surplus of savings, U.S. stability, and its attractiveness to investors (Zakaria, p. 200).

It is troubling that U. S. consumers borrow 80% of the world's surplus savings for their own consumption—essentially "selling off our assets to foreigners to buy a couple more lattes a day"—contributing to the "strongest challenge in history" for the American economy (Zakaria, 2009, p. 202). Then again, numbers might not tell us everything we need to know, Zakaria (2009) contends. The economic statistics are an approximation based on late 19th century measures. In an interconnected global market, "with revolutions in financial instruments, technology and trade.... it is possible that we're not measuring things correctly" (p. 200). The growing inequality and the conflict that follows are "fueled by a triple force—the knowledge economy, information technology, and globalization" (p. 202).

THE AMERICAN DREAM HEADS NORTH   Inequality in the United States is demonstrated in one example, by the wealthiest 10% who now have 16 times more income than the poorest 10% of households (Lobe, 2008). Over the past 20 years, the "American Dream"—economic and social upward mobility as measured by earnings of fathers and sons—now has greater promise in the Nordic countries (Denmark,

Norway, Sweden) where wealth is more equitably distributed (Lobe, 2008). In the United States the income gap between rich and poor has grown rapidly since 2000, particularly under the administration of President George W. Bush. At 16 to 1, the United States has the third largest income gap, behind Turkey (17 to 1) and Mexico (25 to 1) among the 30 member states of the Organization for Economic Cooperation and Development (OECD) (Lobe, 2008). The United States is not alone; three of four OECD countries have seen the gap widen; the average is 9 to 1, and in the Nordic countries, under 5 to 1 (Lobe, 2009). The United States shares the second highest poverty rate among these countries, tied with Turkey at 17%; Mexico is highest at 20%. Denmark, Sweden, the Czech Republic, and Norway have the lowest poverty rates (Lobe, 2008).

The OECD report *Growing Unequal?* was released when criticism of the "free-market" economic model promoted by the United States, the World Bank, and the IMF was rising worldwide (Lobe, 2008). Since the administration of President Ronald Reagan, free market economics—sometimes called the "Washington Consensus"—relies on markets without government intervention to promote economic growth. One expected outcome is that incomes for the middle class and the poor will rise, but this is not happening. While poverty among the elderly in OECD countries has fallen, poverty has risen among young families with children, particularly single-parent families, and one in five children in the United States lives in poverty. Proportional taxes on the wealthy, serious *investments* in education, public services and job creation, and eradicating child poverty are among the most effective governmental changes in addressing both the poverty rate and the gap between the rich and poor cited in the OECD report (Lobe, 2008).

Wealth inequalities are generated in the labor market and such inequalities contribute to social resentment and unrest (Lobe, 2008). (Students should pay attention to socio-political activities in California, where voters and advocacy groups develop propositions that they bring to the ballot box.) Over the past 70 years, the U. S. economy has grown steadily, creating wealth for American households (Irwin, 2010). However, economic growth as measured by job creation is now stagnant. Since December 1999, there has been zero net job creation, a lost decade for American workers (Irwin, 2010). Not since the 1940s has job growth been less than 20% (Irwin, 2010). When adjusted for inflation, middle-income households made less in 2008 than in 1999, and home values and retirement funds have declined in value (Irwin, 2010). The expectation early in this decade is that new job creation is on the horizon, but how long this will take is not clear.

Historically, lessons learned indicate that economic downturns are systemic, not individual or community. The Great Depression of the 1930s underscored the far-reaching impacts of a financial system collapse; the Great Inflation of the 1970s reframed the credibility of the banking system and keeping inflation in check (Irwin, 2010). Lessons from the Bubble Decade, particularly the past two years, has again, emphasized the *systemic* risks that banks create for the whole economy and lessons in risk management (Irwin, 2010).

However the reality of business practice, quarter-to-quarter, rewards narrow, short-term, high-risk, high-profit behaviors (Wallace, 2010); for example, the bonuses paid to bankers. Yet, business and economic decisions cannot be made without understanding the changing socio-cultural contexts (a multicultural critical framework) within which global economics function. Education for U. S. business graduates and undergraduates has responded slowly and piecemeal to the demands of a global environment. Harvard Business School has reframed its leadership course as "authentic leadership development" (para. 39) including leadership at the skills level, teamwork, experiential exercises, and critical thinking—the flagship of a liberal arts education (Wallace, 2010). At Yale, a "problem-framing course" (para. 37) requires students to think broadly, question assumptions, view the problem from multiple perspectives, and learn from history (Wallace, 2010). The business school at the University of Virginia incorporates design-thinking, using one's understanding of the world as a point where creativity expands through field testing as one shapes solutions. Stanford and Rotman School of Management at the University of Toronto lead the way with revised curricula (Wallace, 2010). It is estimated that currently 25% of business schools are responding to global requirements for multicultural frameworks, multiple perspectives, critical thinking, innovation, sustainable leadership, and social responsibility. It may take the next decade for the other 75% to make headway (Wallace, 2010). Why this change in business cultures and practices will take time is explained in the next section.

CULTURAL DIFFERENCES: ECONOMICS OF CHARACTER, NOT CONSUMPTION

Schumacher (1973) reduces economics to buying and selling in a market that focuses on the current "monetary situation" (p. 44). The willing buyer-seller pair act "economically" to get the most for one's money. "In a sense, the market is the institutionalization of individualism and non-responsibility. Neither the buyer or seller is responsible for anything but himself "(p. 44).... with one exception—avoiding the purchase of stolen property—since private property is sacrosanct, or used to be.

Schumacher (1973) then compares these economics to what he calls Buddhist economics. Note the cultural differences and outcomes in two views of work. Work to an economist is necessary, but the goal is to streamline work to increase production for profit, and eliminate work to have more leisure (Schumacher, 1973). From a Buddhist perspective, the joy of work has three functions: to develop and increase one's faculties, to support one in a common task with others, to help forego ego-centeredness; and to produce goods and services that contribute to existence for all (Schumacher, 1973). In balance, work helps one appreciate leisure. *The essential difference is the purification of the human character, rather than the "multiplication of wants"* (p. 55). So, a higher standard of living and more consumption are culturally antithetical to the Buddhist perspective, which is more of a process (Schumacher). Essentially, *optimal* consumption or the best use of limited, physical resources, is antithetical to *maximum* consumption or having more.

Other Buddhist principles (simplicity, non-violence) are supported. Self-sufficient, local communities are less likely to engage in "large-scale violence" than communities dependent on worldwide systems of trade (Schumacher, 1973, p. 59). The care of local resources is conscious when one's existence depends on them.

Economically, the cheapest resources would be used; however, Buddhist economics emphasizes the use of renewable (wood, water) resources, as opposed to the use of non-renewable (coal, oil) resources that constitutes violence (Schumacher).

> What is the meaning of democracy, freedom, human dignity, standard of living, self-realization, fulfillment? Is it a matter of goods, or of people? If [economic thinking] cannot get beyond its vast abstractions, the national income, the rate of growth, capital/output ratio, input-output analysis, labour mobility, capital accumulation; if it cannot get beyond all this and make contact with the human realities of poverty, frustration, alienation, despair, breakdown, crime, escapism, stress, congestion, ugliness, and spiritual death, then let us scrap economics and start afresh. (Schumacher, 1973, p. 75)

CULTURAL CASE STUDY

WOMEN'S ROLES IN THE CAMPESINO MOVEMENT: ELVIA ALVARADO (HONDURAS)

The idea of reframing social issues, women's issues within larger socio-political frameworks is not new: for example, violence and women and human rights, and incarceration, capitalism, and the post-industrial complex. However, frameworks are often not comprehensive or deep enough, since the racial, cultural, and global economic spheres are not understood and/or omitted. Hence, we miss full understanding and visualizing informed strategies and interventions in our social work practice. We have been trained for amelioration and reaction, rather than social work for broad social change, peace, and non-violence. Often our social work with women omits men, which skews our expectations. And too often, time and inevitable change and indigenous knowledge and experience are not considered, whether this is historical, political, or at the group or community level.

The campesinos or farmers' movements in Latin America, demonstrate the viability of people working together and facing the daily tasks of growing food under chaotic circumstances: civil war, structural adjustment, and economic manipulation. These movements required the work of everyone in the community. Two case studies are included. The first is an historical account of one woman's role in the movement in Honduras in the 1970s and 1980s to lay groundwork for understanding the history of oppression. The second is a contemporary account of the movement and the model of sustained agriculture through relationships and knowledge of the environment.

Why is the work of sustainable agriculture important in social work? The model works and we could learn something from the campesinos who now have almost 40 years of experience in using their resources to enhance their creativity and their contributions to the world through agroecological methods that sustain their communities and enhance their social resilience. This is work of the heart, the mind, the body, and the land.

DON'T BE AFRAID, GRINGO!   As of 1987, when *Don't Be Afraid, Gringo* was published, Honduras had endured 126 changes in government and 16 different constitutions, mostly under military rule and power (Benjamin, 1987). Militarization of Honduras by the United States, the influx of dollars, and Honduras' geo-political space between Guatemala, El Salvador, and Nicaragua add historical and modern complexities that must be explored by the motivated student (Benjamin, 1987). In 1994, the campesinos (farmers) rejected an untenable, land reformation package. Not much has changed in this century: unemployment is high, the economy is dependent on U. S. aid, and wealth and poverty gaps are wider than ever.

In 1987, Elvia Alvarado was about 48. The well-known Honduran land activist, was the daughter of a campesino day-worker; her mother raised chickens and made bread to earn money to feed the children. Elvia was on her own at 13, when her mother left to live with another man. When Elvia settled with her campesino "husband" Alberto, she had three older children in her mother's care and bore him three more.

As an adult, she volunteered to work with the mothers' clubs in the Catholic Church. The women prayed together and talked about their problems, feeding their children and keeping their husbands sober. They helped one another, distributed food to pregnant women and children suffering from malnourishment, established gardens, and discussed food and nutrition (Benjamin, 1987). The mothers' clubs were successful and five women, Elvia included, were selected to continue the work with malnourished children and their mothers. Elvia was to work throughout the region of La Libertad, in villages she had never heard of. This meant a month away from her family, and fights with her husband who didn't like the way she was changing. (She would eventually take her children and go her own way.) Her $75 stipend had to pay for her expenses, so there was little left for her own children when she returned home.

Elvia flourished; she learned the importance of women and rights and organizing. The women in the mothers' groups flourished as well. The women organized and took up activities in their communities and even built portions of roads. But when the women began to question, the church pulled its resources. "The church forged the path for us, but they wanted us to follow behind. And when we started to work ahead of them, when we started to open new paths ourselves, they tried to stop us" (Benjamin, 1987, p. 16). The women questioned why there was malnourishment to begin with. The church encouraged the women to grow vegetables in the small plots near their houses to supplement the campesino diet of beans and tortillas. The women questioned why they didn't have enough land to feed themselves. They saw themselves at the bottom of the economic and social order, exploited by the upper and middle classes, and the men around them. And when they talked about change, the "church abandoned us" (p. 17). The disappointment was short-lived. The women decided that their work was too important to stop. They combined the savings from all the mothers' clubs and established the Federation of Campesina Women (FEHMUC). The year was 1977 and Elvia was primed.

Land is needed to grow the food that the campesinas and their families need to survive, and land is needed to change their economic and social situations. Poverty was not going to end and society was not going to change until they had land for food. Elvia eventually joined the National Campesino Union (UNC) and was one of thousands who helped create the National Congress of Rural Workers (CNTC). "We've built up a society that treats people like trash, a society that doesn't give people jobs, a society that doesn't give people a reason to stay sober, " Elvia observes. When campesinos organize and farm, their time is spent "plowing, planting, weeding, irrigating, cutting firewood for the house, carrying the produce to market"

(Benjamin, 1987, p. 55). When campesinos have a purpose, they drink less. They take care of their families and stop beating their wives. And when women organize, they pull their husbands in line. "Our struggle has to begin in our own homes" (p. 56).

Land conflict had a history in Honduras since the Spanish conquest began in 1524, and since 1962, land reform and recovery was serious, but legally weak (Benjamin, 1987). By the 1970s, campesinos armed only with machetes, bore most of the casualties. Six were killed in La Talanquera in 1972. The massacre at Los Horcones in 1975 is the most infamous. The unions were demonstrating for the passage of the Agrarian Reform Law when five demonstrators were killed by the military. Nine others—including two priests— were tortured and killed at the ranch of José Manuel Zelaya and their bodies were crammed into a well (Benjamin). Elvia recalls the death of four of her own compañeros who died in Talanguita. "We all had to look at the four of them in those boxes, with their heads blown to bits by the landowner's bullets. It pains me to remember those moments....[So] how can we stop now?" (p. 83).

Education is valued among the campesinos; what they know, may be all they have to leave to their children. Elvia finished the second grade and struggled with reading and writing. As an organizer through the Catholic church, she studied and improved her writing. Courses through the campesino organizations and at the Agrarian Reform Democratic Party on the Honduran reality—the relationship between the rich and the poor—shaped her education and experience. Before her organizing work, daily survival to feed her children absorbed her energy and diverted her attention from analyzing the root of her problems, and this was true for many campesinos. "They feel the pain of suffering. They feel the wounds in their bodies, but they don't know who holds the knife or why they're bleeding. They often don't even realize that the large landowners are the source of their misery," she concluded (Benjamin, 1987, p. 62).

The campesino education included protection of their rights by organizing. They learned from the 1954 banana workers strike—35,000 workers strong (Benjamin, 1987, p. 151)—against United Fruit "and other gringo companies" (p. 85). The strike spread to banana plantations throughout the country and marked the beginning of unions as a political force in Honduras. And they learned from the rich with the wealth of private enterprise organizations, and the government and military organized to protect them. "They're super organized; so if we ever want to change anything in this country, we have to be even more organized than they are" Elvia concluded (p. 85).

In 1975, Agrarian Reform Law was to be reinforced by National Agrarian Institute (INA). The law is clear; land must be used to fulfill a social function. If land is not used, it must be turned over to the campesinos. The INA process to reclaim the land was fraught with legalities, corruptible officials, and year-long bureaucratic delays. So, the Honduran campesinos "recovered" the stolen land themselves, parcel by parcel. The campesinos would plant corn and beans on unused land, and when the police or the military would kick them off; the campesinos returned to plant more. The landowners used cattle to trample the newly planted seeds; and the campesinos returned to plant more. Sometimes, a leader would be shot and killed; and they returned to plant some more. Marches were organized, sit-ins gained concessions, and hunger strikes required much patience, but there were strategies that worked. And there were allies: doctors who treated injuries without charge, lawyers who worked without fee, university professors who spoke in their behalf, and workers unions that bailed them out of jail. And as the leadership, with few personal resources, traveled from village to village organizing, there were other campesinos who shared what little food they had (Benjamin, 1987).

Land reform organizations were gradually co-opted by the military, the landowners, or the government. In 1985, thousands of men and women campesinos organized a union—with elected leadership at the local, regional, national levels—to actualize agrarian land reform with support credit, technical assistance and organized defense against landowners and the military. About half membership of the CNTC were women. Organizing women over the opposition of their husbands was difficult; it changed household priorities. For example, the long process of preparing a meal starts with grinding corn, a practical reality. However, when both men and women are involved, it is the women who work the fields, when the men are jailed. The women face the soldiers, they work to get the men out of jail, and they sleep in the fields to keep the land. The relationship between the men and women in the struggle must be one of respect and purpose, acknowledges Elvia (Benjamin, 1987).

Men and women working closely over long periods of time forge realities: "compañeras in the struggle, but not compañeras in bed" (Benjamin, 1987, p. 89). Gaining the confidence of homebound women while working with their husbands must be directly addressed; sleeping with men "on the job" destroys trust, a vital ingredient in the struggle. Elvia considers the male leadership and their behaviors. Some have their wives at home and another woman in the city and this violates the principles of the struggle. They talk loud about the vital role of women in the movement, but "I've never even seen the wives of some of the leaders, they're so well hidden" (p. 90).

CULTURAL CASE STUDY: CULTURAL RESISTANCE AND THE ECONOMICS OF SURVIVAL (GUATEMALA, MEXICO, AND NICARAGUA)

"To be well, we have to be well economically and spiritually " (Holt-Giménez, 2006, p. 45), comments a man called Celso. The indigenous Kaqchikel Mayan worldview recognizes this as "an era of reflection.... everything has a moment and a space and a reason.... many organizations are looking for justice" (p. 46). When justice comes, peace comes too; and the economic situation will change.

Holt-Giménez (2006) relates the compelling stories of cultural resistance and sustainable agriculture, starting in Guatemala and spreading through Mexico and Nicaragua over the past 50 years. The case study of sustainable agriculture in Latin America demonstrates the cultural realities and life potential. This comprehensive framework works at the micro and macro levels over time, and serves a strong example of the transformational personal as the transformational political. The applications to social work are woven into the fabric of these stories, which include a culturally based, community organizing model that transcends social work models that encourage client participation, participatory research, and empowerment.

Women's roles in the history of the movement are foundational to the movement. They not only bear and rear children needed for farm labor, but bear responsibility for feeding everyone. The work in the field during planting and harvesting adds to the heavy work in the home. "Over the last decade, globalization has increased the exploitation of campesina women, both directly—as underpaid workers in maquiladoras—and indirectly—for the cheap reproduction of the labor force (Holt-Giménez, 2006, p. 121).

Love of the land and farming are as foundational as survival, reinforced with the understanding that "agri-culture" is culture and includes men, women, and families. As a culture, one can see processes and knowledge through "farmer innovation, free association, mutual aid, food production, and environmental protection work through tools, organization, and language to fashion autonomous paths to equitable, sustainable futures" (Holt-Giménez, 2006, p. xii). The narrative or story of resistance is consistent with the campesino culture, for this is how culture is sustained: through stories, sharing knowledge, collective aid and helping in response to governmental abuses, and a grassroots understanding of the political in everyday life. Grounded in benevolent self-sufficiency, cultural values are dominant in the people's consciousness and "their will to feed themselves and others in fair, environmentally sustainable ways; to develop their own agriculture; and to provide for dignified livelihoods based on mutual respect and self-determination" (p. xiii). This is life, and development of the people and agriculture is part of this broad framework. Work that is relational is transformative. Rogelio Sánchez Ledezma, summarizes his experience.

> When one travels and sees the local context of other communities, of other producers, of other campesinos, and one starts to reflect and appreciate the things that surround us. That's when you say *"Hijole!"* How have these people, living in these conditions, accomplished so much? And I, who am in another context and in another situation, have not taken advantage of what I have. So I think this has been transformative because it has permitted us to reevaluate and acquire a great commitment and ideas of what to do. (Holt-Giménez, 2006, p. 59)

HISTORY: GUATEMALA

Historically, indigenous peoples and their cultures in Guatemala descended from Mayan ancestors. Since conquest by Spaniards and their descendants, they have lived as second-class citizens in their own lands. Guatemala's indigenous groups have seen few periods of respite and long periods of trauma and overwhelming grief—*la pena insoportable* (Holt-Giménez, 2006, p. 49). They have withstood overlapping waves of socialist, capitalistic, and neoliberal economic structures. A civil war lasting 36 years ended in 1994, with 200,000 fatalities, mostly indigenous innocents (Holt-Giménez, 2006).

In the 1970s, a period of relative respite, organizations such as World Neighbors and Oxfam came to San Martín, Guatemala and urged the campesinos to cultivate the land. "We started village by village.... with the themes of agricultural development, soil conservation, and water conservation" (Holt-Giménez, 2006, p. 45). A 7.5 magnitude earthquake in 1976 left 23,000 fatalities, destroyed homes and fields, exacerbated grinding poverty in rural areas, and forced emigration to the coasts where many were penniless, with no clothing, and little food. Between the 1980s and 1990s—the period known as *La Violencia*—organizing and development through agriculture was mired in fear and violence, when military occupation forced conscription, massacres, and disappearances (Holt-Giménez, 2006). When terraces and conservation ditches were found in the highlands, the military accused campesinos of digging the ditches for military purposes; these were filled with cornstalks and covered. The land improvements, social and cultural unity that had been built went underground for years, and sent people into exile in other countries including Mexico.

THE MEXICAN CONNECTION   Exile from Guatemala had unforeseen consequences for some of the campesinos. In Mexico, Campesino a Campesino started with rural development projects in Tlaxcala in 1977, funded by the Mexican Friends Service Committee. "North American volunteers for the project established a 'model farm' testing French intensive biodynamic gardens, rabbits, milk goats, and solar heating," using their own ideas of farming and agriculture (Holt-Giménez, 2006, p. 55). The reality in Tlaxcala was lack of water, drought, deforestation, soil erosion, poor health and poverty, and corrupt officials and only those who understood the sociopolitical environment could negotiate this gap. As campesino groups transitioned through political changes, forming and reforming, the exiled Guatemalans came in 1981 and the work of the campesinos continued—conserve soil and water, work on soil fertility, experiment with seeds, and learn from one another.

Felipe Tomas, a promoter with World Neighbors, recounts his exile to Mexico, a sad and lonely time, without family, friends, and culture. "The saddest thing about exile is to stop speaking our native tongue, Kaqchikel…This is very sad and hits me in the heart" (Holt-Giménez, 2006, p. 53). His work as a campesino continued, side-by-side with Mexican campesinos; he learned about their agricultural environment and culture. His family joined him at one point and eased his loneliness. After 17 years, when a relative peace came to Guatemala, he returned home at a time when the Guatemalan Campesino a Campesino groups had re-emerged (Holt-Giménez, 2006).

THE NICARAGUAN LAND REFORMS

Land reform during the Sandinista Revolution (1979–1990) was "both the central agrarian instrument for incorporating the campesinado into the Revolution and the main engine driving them toward the counterrevolution" (Holt-Giménez, 2006, p. 12). By 1988, a quarter of the peasant population had been given 2.3 million acres, medium-sized producers lost 1.73 million acres, and campesinos—in the tens of thousands—fought in the U.S.–financed counterrevolution (Holt-Giménez, 2006). The National Union of Farmers and Ranchers (UNAG) established in 1981 and controlled by large producers, was the only union that represented campesino interests through development projects. The Campesino a Campesino movement for sustainable agriculture emerged from these projects (Holt-Giménez, 2006).

THE MEXICAN CONNECTION   The visits by the Mexican farmers in 1987 had a profound cultural and ideological influence on the Nicaraguans (Holt-Giménez, 2006). The Mexicans had two generations of land reform experience and several years of farmer-to-farmer training experience. They carried themselves well, they spoke from experience with enthusiasm, they preached what they practiced, and they showed the Nicaraguans what they could become (Holt-Giménez, 2006).

In turn, when the Nicaraguans visited Mexico, they witnessed "the process by which the Mexicans had developed their own agriculture" (p. 16). Alicia Sarmientos at 18 was one of two young women who traveled to Nicaragua from Mexico to teach organic gardening. Children in Nicaragua were dying of hunger and she felt the fear of people living under the threat of attack by the counterrevolutionaries. "It marked a change for me, it matured me, and it especially made me value all of the things I have learned through the Grupo and everything I had in my life. Sharing my work with the people from [Nicaragua] made me more determined to learn" (Holt-Giménez, 2006, p. 17).

CAMPESINO A CAMPESINO: A MODEL FOR ENGAGED SOCIO-CULTURAL SOCIAL WORK?

The principles of Campesino a Campesino are outlined here and students are encouraged to think about how these principles can be used in cross-cultural situations from foster parent training to working in groups with people who are incarcerated or people in immigrant detention facilities; from single mothers working to raise, educate, and feed their children to men and women involved in domestic violence. At the macro level, educating for health changes or organizing communities to address environmental hazards are useful applications for this model. What is the history and context and timing of our work? What is our dominant philosophy? How is mutual aid and teaching/learning demonstrated? What do the people with whom we work teach us in our exchanges? How is this documented and tested? How is knowledge created in these exchanges disseminated?

To be able to teach, one must do, according to Chepe Chu, a Nicaraguan farmer (Holt-Giménez, 2006). At the center of doing and being, are the opportunities to learn, hand-in-hand with opportunities to serve. These experiences are encircled with opportunities to share; to adapt the learning within a cultural context; to experiment, test, and study the outcomes. The knowledge created must be shared within a mutual teacher–learner relationship. *Learning and sharing rejuvenates enthusiasm in the process of discovery, and cannot be ignored, for then the process dies* (Holt-Giménez, 2006).

> If there is anything that truly satisfies a person, it is helping others; to collaborate so others improve; collaborate so others overcome obstacles; collaborate so that others can live differently all those things one suffers from in the countryside. I have felt such beautiful things through these experiences even though I never had any schooling.... But with Campesino a Campesino, the Mexicans came to give us a workshop here in Santa Lucía, and everything changed. Before, when technicians came to give workshops, I never understood what they were talking about. But when the Mexicans came, I understood everything because I understood their experience. (José Jesús Mendoza in Holt-Giménez, 2006, p. 62)

TIMING AND THE CURRENT CULTURAL CONTEXT Ground work for the Campesino a Campesino movement already had an influential history of oppression and response to oppression. Social workers and intellectuals had incorporated Paulo Friere's work of problem-solving education through political consciousness raising in the Popular Education movement (Holt-Giménez, 2006). Liberation theology, with its "referential option for the poor" (p. 80) provided a spiritual and sociopolitical base in the response to severe oppression in the Latin American countryside in the 1970s. The two merged and supported thousands of "motivated, village-level advocates of social change" (p. 80). A second wave was already in the making as European governments tried to strengthen the culture of democracy struggling beneath oppressive military regimes, often supported by the United States to protect capitalistic ventures. Thousands of nongovernmental organizations or NGOs were funded to work with the poor, with a proliferation in the 1970s and 1980s across Latin America. The third wave—the growing interest in sustainable agriculture—was forming, to be followed by the growth of agroecology, the companion science. What are the movements and history (practice, political) of the work you are doing?

CAMPESINO PEDAGOGY   Campesino a Campesino transfers and broadly disseminates knowledge, a necessity in any community organization strategy. Not often acknowledged is the cultural production of knowledge (Holt-Giménez, 2006). The campesinos "access, adapt, create, use and defend agroecological knowledge on their own terms in an exercise in autonomy" (Holt-Giménez, 2006, p. 78). (What cultural knowledge and practices are created by the people with whom we work?) Campesino a Campesino has developed its own principles regarding farming and the environment. Through mutual aid—working side-by-side and talking—new insights and ways of doing are born, reflected on, tested, and refined.

Three basic phases of the Campesino pedagogy include the analytical, the experimental, and the socio-cultural transfer of knowledge. *Problematizing* explores the limits of production balanced by the ecological risks. The causes of common problems—water and soil conservation techniques, fertility, pest management—are analyzed and solutions are posed. (What are the parameters of the social work problem?) *Experiments* are designed to test alternatives (hypotheses formation); these are measured precisely and observed consistently without bias, and *recorded*. Experimental variables are controlled, comparisons made and results are shared. The final phase is *promotion*. Knowledge is shared through workshops and field days and visits to other groups, locally and with other farmers in other countries in cross-cultural experiences and introduction to new agricultural, social, and political environments (Holt-Giménez, 2006).

Significantly, the workshops are family affairs and locally, peer training and group communication skills can be included (Holt-Giménez, 2006). The cultural arena—field, patio, garden, household—for growing food integrates different family members into farming and tending tasks. Agroecological innovations and changes can influence roles, tasks, time, and even the relationships among the family members (Holt-Giménez, 2006). For example, the patio is the woman's domain, and she may experiment with medicinal plants. She also does the cooking and looks for cultivars that contribute to a good diet, taste good, and use little water and fuel to cook (Holt-Giménez, 2006). Family involvement in workshop opens space for education and health for the family. Children and teens take notes for their parents, who may not read or write. In this process, the cultural values and relationship to the environment nurtures the children and youth in common work with their parents. This work counters the urban educational values that pull young people from life on the farm (Holt-Giménez, 2006).

ONE STEP AT A TIME   The introduction of new technology is slow, one or two new technologies at a time. Experimentation, which encourages innovation and teaching others, reinforces learning and builds relationships. Key concepts are presented in different ways: spoken, demonstrated, and experienced, including creative drama, poetry, and song (Holt-Giménez, 2006).

One campesino in Cuba recognized that he had lost his "peace and quiet with experimentation" (Holt-Giménez, 2006, p. 36). Before new technologies, two varieties of beans and two varieties of corn were planted in season. Experimentation spurred food and economic security with greater diversity and an explosion of bean and corn varieties that resist pests and crop disease. "My mind has gone through even bigger changes than the farm! .... on our farm the boundaries are all fruit trees, plantains, coconut, and even royal palms. So where I used to produce nothing, now I have hundreds of plants that start producing in three years because we learned to graft them to speed up the flowering cycle" (p. 37).

SOCIAL SUPPORT AND REJUVENATION   Working in the fields is public work because people see your work. Criticism is part of change, particularly from one's own family and community, and especially in village life. Results are not recognized until they are proven useful and public mistakes can become lore. "This has been a stone in the shoe of the Movement, and we haven't been able to shake it out easily..." (Holt-Giménez, 2006, p. 94). In response, campesinos have learned that three or more farmers can provide moral support for one another. And when they need joy and rejuvenation, visits to other Campesino a Campesino groups with successful experiments disseminate knowledge from discoveries. (This is probably the most neglected step in social work. Learning from discovery and rejuvenation is usually not considered when we think of social support.)

KUCHUBAL: THE CULTURAL PHILOSOPHY OF RELATIONSHIP AND RECIPROCITY   The Mayan kuchubal is the "social and organizational root of Campesino a Campesino" (Holt-Giménez, 2006, p. 92). Farming the steep hillsides of the countryside requires constant digging to build the terraces and ditches to conserve soil and water, and one cannot do this alone. Teams work one day each week on the farm of one group member, and the next week, move to another. Labor is a product, certainly. More importantly, teams create, reinforce and sustain cultural values while supporting their families and communities with the work they love.

Through this process, group members develop their own sets of skills and expertise. Each has his own strengths that can be paired with skills and expertise of others, which broadens the work they will do next, makes training teams flexible, and the group life dynamic. This also strengthens the moral obligation or *compromiso morale* (Holt-Giménez, 2006, p. 95) to give back to the movement by teaching others. The new knowledge that is gained as one matures, is given in return. This serves as the cultural or common knowledge that comes out of an individual or group experience, and is shared and cultivated by all. This process "reawakens and quenches the thirst for learning" and creativity, brings in new experiences and people, and leads to "intellectual, social, and political experiences that were previously inaccessible" (Holt-Giménez, 2006, p. 96).

TRANSFORMATIVE LEARNING THROUGH RESEARCH   Understanding how and why agroecological knowledge—response to organic matter, weed reduction, zero tillage, maintaining biodiversity in the humid tropics—works is summarized in the story that follows. The Nicaraguan-Costa Rican border along the San Juan River is considered almost impenetrable. Clearing tropical forest for farming is hard work, and slash and burn methods have damaged the land on farms—accessible by boat or canoe—spread along the San Juan River. Experiments to test the nitrogen-rich, leafy biomass from the velvet bean, which could help fertilize damaged soil, had been set up by a Campesino a Campesino group with help from a local NGO. Weekly, the NGO technician took several days to visit each farm. He or she checked the test plots of velvet beans, reviewed farmers' journals recording their daily observations, and interviewed the farmers with a handheld recorder. The local radio station sound engineer helped him or her set up a weekly radio program so that farmers, up and down the river, could follow the step-by-step experimentation with the velvet bean, step-by-step. When the beans were harvested, hundreds of farmers showed up in San Carlos to buy beans to plant on their own land (Holt-Giménez, 2006).

IS THIS MODEL ADAPTABLE FOR SOCIAL WORK?   Social work requires a recommitment and action to address poverty and create sustained change, as the campesinos have done. They have found a workable model for sustaining their families and renewing their culture, by reaffirming their relationships with one another and with the environment. They have found a way to strengthen their creativity through the joy of learning and teaching. And they have contributed to sustained agriculture and the science of agroecology through serious study, experimentation, and dissemination of information. Significantly, this work supports peace, because it is based on love and considerate use of resources. It echoes the work of Schumacher and Buddhist principles of nonviolence discussed earlier in this chapter.

The moral obligation to give back is part of a social worker's creed and the NASW Code of Ethics contributes to our professional social work culture, but lacks the intimacy and immediacy of the Campesino a Campesino model. In social work, learning communities and shared power support parts of the model. Practice knowledge is akin to cultural knowledge in some aspects, but the experiential generation of knowledge in a community of learners/teachers is not usually a sustained practice in social work. Respect and self-determination are part of the Code of Ethics, but the kuchubal requires a deep commitment to sustain social change. Social workers trained in behavior analysis use the experimental process, but is this taught/learned with clients? In the model, work is done primarily with peers; what other variations are probable?

The potential for transformational learning through relationship and research is here. The challenge to students is to consider this model as they move through their education and the initial years of social work practice. Can it be useful for our work in social change? Is it useful for cross-cultural social work? Can it be useful in confronting the challenges of globalization?

STRUCTURAL ADJUSTMENT AND DISASTER ECONOMICS

In October, 1998, Hurricane Mitch waged a war of wind and rain for an unending week on Central America—including Honduras, Guatemala, and Nicaragua. Destruction, mudslides, and death followed. Foreign aid was needed and was generously given, and the deals brokered opened the floodgates for economic take-over by private corporations, usually at bargain prices (Klein, 2007). In Honduras, land reforms were sacrificed so that foreigners would benefit from buying and selling (Klein, 2007). The mining industry drafted a pro-business mining law, reducing environmental standards in their favor and included evictions from homes that blocked new mines (Klein, 2007). The privatization of four airports, seaports, and highways was passed through the Honduran Congress (Klein, 2007). The state telephone company, the national electric company, and parts of the water sector were put on the block for privatization (Klein, 2007). The telephone system in Guatemala went to a Mexico's Telmex, a privatized phone company. Nicaragua sold its electric company to Spain's Unión Fenosa and sectors of the petroleum industry were also sold. Klein (2007) calls this pattern "disaster capitalism". The pattern was repeated in countries—Sri Lanka, Thailand, the Maldives, and Indonesia—where the 2004 tsunami hit, as people around the world watched the disaster played and replayed on television. There was no grand fundraising for people who lived in slums, Klein contends. The United States directly sent $1 million for temporary shelters for the displaced fishing people, but this gesture may be misleading since privatization of beachfront property came next (Klein, 2007).

> But the World Bank and USAID understood something that most of us did not: that soon enough, the distinctiveness of the tsunami survivors would fade and they would melt into the billions of faceless poor worldwide, so many of whom already live in tin shacks without water. The proliferation of these shacks has become as much an accepted feature of the global economy, as the explosion of $800-a-night hotels. (Klein, 2007, p. 398)

Haiti presents the next disaster, played and replayed on television, and it is important to be aware of the structural adjustments that may follow. However, global and regional networks have already formed a response to any who are planning the exploitation of Haiti. The role of the Haitian people to help themselves is claimed.

> We call on governments and international organizations to immediately and unconditionally cancel the external debt claimed of Haiti, the servicing of which affects millions of lives. We also demand that the resources allocated for relief and reconstruction do not create new debt, or conditionalities that are imposed or any other form of external imposition which vitiates this goal, as is the practice of international financial institutions like the World Bank, the Interamerican Development Bank, the IMF, and the so-called donor countries. We also reject the intervention of private multinational companies who seek to take advantage of this tragedy to reap multibillion dollar profits in the reconstruction of Haiti, as happened in Iraq, or to exploit cheap labor and continue to plunder the country's natural resources. (Food First, 2010)

MEXICO: STRUCTURAL ADJUSTMENTS, CULTURAL CLASH, AND THE PROCESS OF DISAPPEARANCE

> We have to insist on the human space in development because neoliberalism and the politics of globalization are so violent, not just economically, but culturally. When they privatize, they don't just privatize the service, but the links that exist between the people and the environment. This is a strong danger of the loss of cultural identity. Our campesinos migrate and the drought drives them out. We are living a process of disappearance. I think that what we are seeing is the resistance of people who do not want to disappear!—Nelda Martínez, development worker, Managua, Nicaragua. (Holt-Giménez, 2006, p. 111)

How does globalization makes some countries rich and others poor? Globalization is trickle-down disaster for poor people around the world and the process of *structural adjustment* is mean and comprehensive. Mexicans felt globalization in the 1980s when oil prices fell, interest rates rose, and $57 billion in foreign debt could not be paid (Holt-Giménez, 2006). An appeal to the IMF resulted in structural adjustments to the Mexican economy, including the *privatization* of the telephone company, the state banks, the rail system and sectors of the transport industry (Holt-Giménez, 2006). Tariffs protecting national products were renegotiated and "allowed 100% of foreign ownership of national industries" in a process of *deregulation* (p. 126). Any progress in agriculture and social services was curtailed in a process *fiscal austerity*. And finally in a process of *devaluation*, the Mexican peso was devalued, subsequently devaluing Mexican products for the international market for dollars or capital investment and development. The next step was to push these austerity measures beyond the reach of the people to resist, by solidifying an international treaty—The North American Free Trade Agreement (NAFTA)—in 1994 (Holt-Giménez, 2006).

In this grand sweep to privatize state-owned enterprises, Article 27 or the Agrarian Law of the Mexican Constitution, the ejido—"the backbone of cultural, economic, and community life in the Mexican countryside" (p. 126)—was privatized in 1992 (Holt-Giménez, 2006). Article 27 protected the campesinos and ensured that ejido land could not be sold, but preserved and passed to the next generation (Holt-Giménez, 2006). Now ejido land can be sold. From 1994 to 2000, 13% of land sales involved the campesino sector and ejido land (Holt-Giménez, 2006). With this stake, some young people immigrate to the United States, compounding the disintegration of communities and gains in land reform (Holt-Giménez, 2006).

Historically, indigenous lands were taken during conquest and held by hacienda owners, until a revolution reclaimed the land. Now, both communal land and hacienda land are in danger of privatization in the hands of absentee, foreign owners and transnational corporations (Holt-Giménez, 2006). Loss of land *is* loss of solidarity, loss of culture, and leads to dependency and poverty.

In a more specific example of globalization, genetically modified organisms (GMOs), products of corporation giants such as Syngenta and Monsanto, contaminated Mexican maize varieties, even before they were legally sanctioned in 2003 (Holt-Giménez, 2006). Corporation-produced fertilizer, pesticides and herbicides have already damaged the land, and GMOs damage the food supply. For example, tortillas are the staple of the Mexican campesino diet. Tortillas made with GMO maize are cheap and people who work no longer have time to make their own tortillas, a practical reality. Continued use of GMO tortillas competes with locally grown maize varieties and with small tortilla-producing enterprises. Campesinos must change this landscape through organizing and relationship building with local tortilla factories (Holt-Giménez, 2006).

Campesinos recognize that the "last line of cultural defense is the seed" and this has taken campesinos in new directions (Holt-Giménez, 2006, p. 132). In Mexico, biodiversity has guided principles in the study and preservation of local seed varieties—120 varieties of maize and 230 varieties of beans have been identified—resistant to pests and environmental stress. Women's groups have processed different foods and assessed local, wild food varieties for propagation. Local seed varieties are vulnerable to giant seed companies across the globe, and this is also recognized (Holt-Giménez, 2006).

The work of the campesino and campesino culture is also vulnerable, and the challenges of globalization and climate change will push the movement in new directions. In the face of globalization, there has been little work to change the policies that discourage sustainable agriculture (Holt-Giménez, 2006). *Critically, land reform movements have partnered with NGOs whose major purpose is to support and implement projects (technical and social level), not to change policies or laws (political level).* "Farmers in the Movement can get the techniques in the field right, but the larger economic context still works against them" (Holt-Giménez, 2006, p. 134).

STRUCTURAL LITERACY: SAME MODEL, NEXT STEPS   While the farmers face challenges— "lopsided global markets, hostile agrarian policies, and the absence of any effective support from the state" (Holt-Giménez, 2006, p. 179)—they have studied and created a knowledge of agriculture that is specific to their environment, without violence and damage to the earth and without going broke. However, the success of the Campesino a Campesino programs has kept their eyes to the ground, literally. They are focused on agroecological practices rather the structural socio-political and economic conditions that work against sustainable agriculture (Holt-Giménez, 2006). However, based on the model that sustains them, there is every reason to expect that they could become "structurally literate" (p. 180).

"Structural issues like food sovereignty, agroecological agricultural versus genetically modified crops, intellectual property rights versus farmers' rights are themes that could be incorporated in the workshops, the cross visits, and regional gatherings" (Holt-Giménez, 2006, p. 181). The existing structures such as advocacy groups, farmers unions, and federations to sustainable agricultural development NGOs are in place (Holt-Giménez, 2006). It is expected that this new breed of campesinos would generate knowledge in a matter of time. Existing challenges now that require experimentation are formidable: "preserving agrobiodiversity in the face of transgenic contamination, resistance to colonization by the soy-beef industry, or the creation of local and regional markets for food sovereignty could all be easily shared alongside the agroecological innovations that constantly emerge and spread...." (p. 181).

CONCLUSION

Presenting a proven cultural model for social change, for analysis, and for experimentation in social work has emerged as product of this chapter. The consideration of the model and experimentation comes next as students enter the transcultural contexts with their clients. Becoming structurally literate—connecting the dots to deconstruct oppressive structures—is part of cultural proficiency and our work as social workers. This is concomitant with human rights discussed in another chapter in this book. Cultural proficiency is integrated in understanding oppression and the manipulated economic and contextual forces that exploit, manipulate, and destroy the spirits of women, men, and children, and the healthy future of nations and the natural environment. Structural literacy, cultural awareness and proficiency are also integrated in knowing when to listen deeply and when to speak; when to be taught and when to teach; when to exercise patience and when and how to act with compassion.

The economic health of Latin America is tied to the United States and the global economy. The fight for land is not over. An end to poverty and hunger requires that people in the United States take a stand with courage and character and spirit that defies our fear of loss of comfort. One must be convinced that the struggle is just and the objectives must be clear. One must educate as one finds more truth, and dialogue with others in groups is central. Making diverse allies to equitably divide the work of the large tasks is paramount.

In the closing sentences of the book edited by Benjamin (1987), Elvia Alvarado makes a plea for the readers to join the struggle. "We want you to denounce what your government is doing in Central America.... From those of you who feel the pain of the poor, who feel the pain of the murdered, the disappeared, the tortured, we need more than sympathy. We need you to join the struggle. Don't be afraid, gringos.... we're right there with you!" (p. 146).

Cultural Competence with Lesbian, Gay, Bisexual, and Transgender Persons

CHAPTER 15

Carol Tully

INTRODUCTION

Social work practitioners work with members of various population groups that may be viewed as being *outside* the majority and, as such, are often described as *disenfranchised*. Such groups include, but may not be limited to, the very young, the very old, women, racial minorities, ethnic minorities, those with physical or mental challenges, those in poverty, religious minorities, those who are not heterosexual, and so forth. While many people in these populations may be identified by physical characteristics or behavior (watching a hearing impaired person sign or looking at someone with a particularly fair complexion and blonde hair may give the worker some clues about another's culture), there are those who are members of numbers of various cultures who are virtually invisible and indistinguishable from the majority. Those who are lesbian, gay, bisexual, or transgender tend to fit into this category of invisibility, and, in many instances have no trouble hiding in plain sight in every race, ethnicity, age group, or other population descriptor.

To better understand these various populations it is important to realize how each construct is defined. Sexual orientation is commonly understood as how individuals define their primary, enduring sexual activities and emotionally intimate feelings (Kinsey, Pomeroy, & Martin, 1948; Tully, 1983). Sexual and emotional intimacies are conceptualized on a continuum where exclusive heterosexuality is at one end and exclusive homosexuality is at the other. Bisexuality lies between these two poles. While in the United States it is customary for exclusive heterosexuality to be considered the norm (Tully, 2000), this is not so worldwide (Kimmel, 2004) and sexuality perhaps is best perceived as being a fluid construct that may move back and forth across the sexual/psychological continuum during a lifespan.

415

Although same-sex practices have been present in all historical eras, the word *homosexuality* did not come into existence until 1869 when it appeared in a pamphlet authored by a German-Hungarian writer (Tully, 2000). As a term, today it has been replaced with others that include *gay persons, lesbians, gay men* and, in some sectors, *queer*. The generic term *gay* tends to include both men and women while *lesbian* refers only to women. Persons who identify their sexual orientation as exclusively or primarily *gay* find sexual and emotional intimacy with members of their own sex.

The construct *bisexuality*, or a sexual and emotional enduring attraction to both sexes, was first applied to human sexuality in translation of a work by Krafft-Ebing in 1892 but did not come into general usage until the 1950s (Online Etymology Dictionary, 2009). Those who identify as bisexual find sexual and emotional satisfaction with members of either sex. Bisexuality, like exclusive hetero- or homosexuality, should be viewed as a fluid entity that may ebb and flow across the lifespan.

As a construct the word *transgender* has the most recent lineage as it came into currency in the early 1990s. The term has a varied history: first used to describe those who appeared as a member of the opposite sex (cross-dresser) or a transsexual, the term has come to forge a distinction between sexual identity and gender identity (Dictionary.com Unabridged, 2009; Walters, Longres, Han, & Icard, 2007). Sexual identity is viewed as being biologically determined based on chromosomes while gender identity is based on one's personal ideology about being either female or male. Typically, a *transgender* person's gender roles and identity diverge from and do not match the gender roles normally associated with his or her biological sex. More simply, there is a disconnect between the person's biological sex and the individual's personal gender identification or that genitals alone do not determine identity. One who identifies as transgendered may fall anywhere along the sexual/emotional continuum and therefore can identify as exclusively hetero- or homosexual or anywhere in between.

The primary difference between lesbians, gays, bisexuals, and transgender persons is that lesbians, gays, and bisexuals are comfortable with their biological sex and tend to conform to fairly normative gender identity roles. Those who identify as transgender tend to reject their biological sex in favor of their perceived views of gender. Another distinction between bisexuals, gays, and lesbians and transgender persons is that gays, bisexuals, and lesbians identify and, in part, define themselves based on *sexual orientation* while those who are transgendered identify and, in part, define themselves based on *gender identity* (Walters, Longres, Han, & Icard, 2007).

There is no way to know precisely how many lesbian, gay, bisexual, and transgender persons live in the United States because of their ability to be chameleons. However, the U.S. Census first asked about same-sex households in the 1990 census and continued collecting those data in the 2000 census (U.S. Census Bureau, 2009). There are approximately 307,410,000 people currently living in the United States and, according to data from the 2000 census, 9.7% ($n = 29,818,770$) of the total number live in same-sex households (U.S. Census Bureau, 2009). Does this number accurately define the total number of gays and lesbians in our country? Of course it does not. Some have estimated that because of homophobia, lesbians and gays still do not self-identify as such and remain hidden in what may be called the culture of the heterosexual majority (Tully, 2000). While there are guesstimates that somewhere between 10 and 15% of the total population in the United States may be gay or lesbian, the reality is that no one knows the true number.

The numbers of bisexuals and transgender persons living in the United States are even more blurred. Given the lack of conclusive population figures for gay and lesbian persons, it is not surprising to learn that there are also no absolutely accurate population numbers for those who identify themselves as bisexual. In 1948, data on men noted that 48% of all men surveyed had engaged in sexual activities with both women and men (Kinsey, Pomeroy, and Martin, 1948) but the estimates of those who see themselves as bisexual today is between 1.0% ($n = 3,074,100$) and 2.0% ($n = 6,148,200$) of the total population (Centers for Disease Control, 2008). There are some data related to the number of transgender persons. The Human Rights Campaign (2009b) posits that between 0.25% ($n = 768,525$) and 1.0% ($n = 3,074,100$) of the total population may be transgender. However, as with lesbians and gays, there are no conclusive statistics related to how many transgender people actually reside within our borders.

As is evident from the data, there are far more individuals who identify themselves as gay or lesbian when compared to those who self-identify as either bisexual or transgender. Admittedly, the United States has had more time to acclimate itself to the reality of lesbians and gays than it has to bisexuals or transgender persons, but there still exists sufficient discrimination to force those of sexual orientation and gender identity minorities into hiding. This chapter will undoubtedly lead the reader to want to do more in-depth study about transgender persons, lesbians, gays, and bisexuals because the chapter's content will be able to provide only the most basic of information. The content will include information related to a historical overview; value and ethical dilemmas; cultural awareness and competency needed to interact with members of these groups; specific skills that will assist the social worker when confronted with a lesbian, gay, bisexual, or transgender person; and social and economic justice resolution. Finally, a case study will be provided that will allow the student practitioner an opportunity to apply theory to practice in a safe setting.

CULTURAL COMPETENCY

As noted, lesbian, gay, transgender, and bisexual people are ubiquitous and not easily discerned within society. Since many members of these groups adequately function within the mainstream of society, ferreting out a unique *culture* associated with some of these sexual minorities presents somewhat of a challenge. Before we can more clearly understand cultural differences, it is important to understand what is meant by the construct *cultural competency*.

Cultural competency as a defined entity must be explored from both words that have been united into one view. *Culture* is traditionally viewed as being related to various integrated patterns of human behavior, beliefs, and values that are handed down from one generation to another. These may include beliefs about religion, views on what is socially acceptable, values that are deemed congruent with everyday life, and specific beliefs about what activities are seen as deviant (Merriam-Webster Online Dictionary, 2009). *Competency* is related to one's ability to have the required knowledge, skills, and values to function in a capable and knowledgeable manner (Merriam-Webster Online Dictionary, 2009). When combined and when specifically related to social work practice, the construct has come to mean:

> a measurable professional standard that evaluates the incorporation of the differential historical, political, socioeconomic, psychosocial, spiritual, and ecological realities, their interaction, and its impact on individuals or groups. Here culture is used in its broadest sense to include race, ethnicity, gender, and sexual orientation and considers other dimensions of individual or group experiences that are salient to their understanding of the world and of themselves. This definition also suggests that factors that are prominent in contextualizing the identity and relational development of one racial/ethnocultural group may differ significantly from those of another. (Lum, 2007, p. 9)

Using this operational definition it will be a bit easier to tease out variances between the predominantly heterosexual culture and the subcultures comprised of lesbians, gays, bisexuals, and transgender persons.

The Gay/Lesbian Life and Culture

While it has been argued that there is no actual lesbian/gay culture apart from mainstream society (Tully, Craig, & Nugent, 1994), it is generally an accepted reality that the more than 29 million gay/lesbian persons in the United States do constitute a defined entity that can be viewed as having its own culture (Lum, 2007). Here we must remember that the definition of *culture* must be expanded to include the reality that lesbian and gay people are united only by a sexual orientation that deviates from the heterosexual norm. As such, it has no specific geographic, racial, or common characteristics thus making the gay/lesbian culture as diverse as its heterosexual counterpart. And, while lesbians and gays interact daily within mainstream America, there exists an identifiable gay/lesbian segment of the larger society that is unique in its structure and beliefs (Tully, 2000). Learning about the myths and realities of this lesbian/gay culture will hopefully enable the practitioner to work with gays and lesbians without prejudice and with the necessary requisite knowledge, skills, and values.

Transgender Life and Culture

Determining the existence of an actual transgender culture becomes a bit more complex mostly because the transgender population of the United States is quite small (0.25–1% of the total population or 700,000–3 million people) and while some transgendered individuals may opt to live in large metropolitan areas where mores tend to be more liberal, some simply disappear into the heartland (Transgender Blogs, 2009). Complicating the picture is the fact that the term transgender must be differentiated from transsexual and the definitions of these terms tends to be somewhat fluid.

While some use the term *transgender* only to refer to those persons whose view of self, behavior, or dress do not conform to normative gender roles it is probably more correct to see the term as an umbrella under which various groups fit. As such it includes not only those who do not conform to normative gender roles, but also *transsexuals* and *cross-dressers* too (APA, 2009). *Transsexuals* are defined as a segment of the transgendered population who wish to live their lives as members of the sex opposite to their original biological sex and who are at some stage of undergoing sexual reassignment (female-to-male [FTM] or male-to-female [MTF]) (APA, 2009). *Cross-dressers* or *transvestites* are yet another segment of the extremely diverse transgender population and are those individuals who choose to wear apparel of the opposite sex (either entirely or in part) (APA, 2009). (Of course in this age of androgyny it is no longer considered cross-dressing or gender-bending to see a woman in trousers or a man carrying a "man-purse.")

Whether or not there exists in the United States an actual transgender culture is difficult to say. There are organizations, websites, blogs, and dating services devoted to the transgender population but traditional communities comprised solely of transgendered persons, with uniquely inherent belief systems handed down from generation to generation, are not part of the transgender tradition. It seems safe to consider those who comprise the transgender population as a small, extremely diverse subculture within the dominant culture who, because of their traditionally disenfranchised status, have unique social service needs.

BISEXUAL LIFE AND CULTURE

Defining lesbian, gay, and transgender life and culture is complex but determining the reality of a bisexual culture becomes virtually impossible. Bisexuality itself is not a hard construct to define as it is generally perceived as individuals who have a physical sexual attraction or romantic/emotional connection to both sexes (Merriam-Webster Online Dictionary, 2009; PFLAG, 2009), but what is hard to distinguish is specifically who comprises the bisexual population. Data suggest that perhaps between 1 and 2% of the population in the United States may be bisexual (3–6 million persons) (Centers for Disease Control, 2008), but there is no real way to know for certain how many bisexuals exist. Coupled with that reality is the apparent invisibility of the bisexual within both the heterosexual culture and gay subculture. Probably the best way to conceptualize the bisexual population is to acknowledge that within the culture there exist a number of individuals who identify themselves as bisexual. As such they tend to remain virtually invisible unless they choose to identify themselves. So, to say that bisexuals comprise a unique culture or even subculture is not particularly accurate; but to say they are not unique in their social service needs is not accurate either. Bisexuals are prone to the sting of biphobia just as homosexuals are subjected to institutionalized homophobia and transgender persons experience transphobia.

In sum, lesbians, gays, bisexuals, and transgender persons all exist within the mainstream of the United States culture but each group does have unique "group experiences that are salient to their understanding of the world and of themselves" (Lum, 2007, p. 9). As such they have differing social service needs that require the professional social worker to put in the context of the *culture* of the particular minority being served. To help contextualize this, the remainder of the chapter will focus on the historical oppression faced by these minority groups; current social issues related to GLBT persons; possible value conflicts and ethical dilemmas workers may face when dealing with these groups; and knowledge, skills, and values needed to provide excellent social services to these populations.

HISTORICAL PERSPECTIVES AND CURRENT ISSUES

This section will attempt to put the constructs of homosexuality, bisexuality, and transgenderism into a brief historical perspective within the United States. While narrowing this discussion to one country across little more than 125 years may seem arbitrary, the topic is, for the scope of this chapter, too broad to include other cultures or eras. For those interested in a more broad based view of these terms, ample documentation exists and the reader is encouraged to explore them (Boswell, 1980; Faderman, 1981; Tully, 2000). Each of these three constructs has a distinct historical lineage; because homosexuality has the longest historical pedigree it will be examined first.

HOMOSEXUALITY IN HISTORICAL CONTEXT

It is generally accepted that same-sex sexual relationships and practices have existed in all historical eras and across all cultures since the beginning of recorded history, but the word *homosexuality* did not come into being until 1869 when a German-Hungarian writer, Karl Maria Kertbeny included it in a pamphlet he had written. At the time, same-sex liaisons were condemned by some, accepted by others, or simply ignored. By the beginning of the 20th century terms like *congenital inversion,* *homosexual,* and *perversion* were being used to define same-sex romantic alliances between either women or men.

The decades between 1900 and 1980 are seen as vitally important to the gay rights movement for it is within this time period that homosexuality moved from being viewed as a sin, criminal act, or mental illness to being perceived as simply an acceptable lifestyle different from heterosexuality (Altman, 1982; D'Emilio & Freedman, 1988; Faderman, 1981). This early idea that same-sex romantic friendships were a perversion or mental illness has its roots in the medical community's developing views of sexuality as a scientific component. These newer *scientific* ideas were supplanting the more traditional church views of same-sex liaisons as sinful. It was thought that science could define what was considered *normal* human behavior. Because the norm was heterosexual, homosexuality, by definition, became *abnormal* or *deviating* from the norm. With the growing development of psychiatry at the same historical time, it became easy, even if incorrect, to begin to define homosexuality as a mental illness because same-sex relationships did differ from the heterosexual norm. This stigma of mental illness persisted until the American Psychiatric Association (APA) removed homosexuality from the third edition of its diagnostic manual of mental disorders in the early 1970s.

Of course, if it was no longer thought to be a mental illness, lesbians and gays were still perceived to be sinners in the eyes of many mainstream religious organizations. But, with changing cultural norms toward homosexuality came softening views of same-sex relationships within the church. Gays and lesbians created their own churches (e.g., Metropolitan Community Church), created church-supported organizations (e.g., Dignity in the Catholic Church), and became more visible in traditional religious arenas.

The trend toward a more accepting view of lesbians and gays can be traced to New York's Stonewall Riots of 1969 when gays, lesbians, and transgendered persons stood up to the New York police who were raiding the Greenwich Village Stonewall Bar. This was the first time these minorities had fought back and their courage that June night marks the start of the current gay and lesbian movement in the United States. Since that event enormous changes have occurred in laws, policies, and procedures related to the gay community. In the public sector many states, cities, and jurisdictions have instituted legal protections for lesbians and gays to ensure them equal protection. Several states now allow same-sex couples to legally marry, enter into civil unions, or adopt children together. In the private sector numerous companies include same-sex domestic partnership benefits equal to those provided to heterosexually married couples and have dropped their previously existing policies discriminating against gays and lesbians in hiring (Human Rights Campaign, 2009a). In television, gay and lesbian characters now play a visible role in genres ranging from afternoon soap operas to prime-time dramas and situation comedies. In the film industry, lesbians and gays, while always present in some form, have moved from the ranks of supporting actors to being the main character. The Internet provides incredible resources for gays and lesbians. Web-based same-sex dating services, chat rooms, and social networking sites abound and at some level it seems lesbian and gay relationships are becoming more and more accepted. Data from the National Opinion Research Center (NORC) indicate that attitudes toward homosexuality and same-sex marriage have become more accepted during the past three decades (NORC, 2009) and yet even with all these positive steps toward equality there still exists enormous misunderstandings and prejudices related to same-sex relationships and families.

Homosexuals have endured an elaborate history of discrimination including torture, murder, stigmatization, and oppression that dates back centuries (Tully, 2000). It is therefore not surprising that discrimination still exists. Many fundamental religions continue to condemn same-sex relationships; hate crimes toward gays and lesbians happen routinely (U.S. Department of Justice, 2009); institutionalized homophobia (a generalized societal fear of homosexuality) abounds, and gay and lesbian persons are still denied many fundamental rights accorded routinely to heterosexuals. In sum, enormous cultural stigmas still exist for this disenfranchised minority.

THE TRANSGENDER EXPERIENCE IN HISTORICAL CONTEXT

Although there is historical evidence that demonstrates transgendered persons have existed across all recorded historical eras (TransgenderZone.com, 2009), the most current transgender movement emerged from 1910 when Magnus Hirschfeld, a German, coined the term *transvestite* and then went on to found the Institute for Sexology in Berlin (the first known clinic to treat transgendered people). The term *transsexual* came into existence in 1923 when Hirschfeld distinguished between those who were cross-dressers (transvestites) and those who perceived themselves to be physiologically the wrong sex and who wanted sexual reassignment surgery (Brown, 2009). The term *transgender* seems to have a more current genesis although its origins are uncertain. It may stem from Virginia Prince, who in the 1970s, described herself as a *transgenderist*. The term begins to appear with regularity in the early 1980s and has emerged as an umbrella term that includes transvestites (cross-dressers), transsexuals (those undergoing some phase of sexual reassignment), and intersexed (hermaphrodite) people (Brown, 2009; Tittsworth, 2005).

A significant amount of the history related to transgendered persons centers on transsexuality and gender reassignment surgery. The development of hormone therapy starting in the 1930s, allowed transsexuals an opportunity to receive treatment that created physiological changes. The 1940s, 50s and 60s saw the development of clinics for transsexual treatment, and the first surgeries performed on non-intersexed persons were performed in the late 1960s.

Mentioned earlier were the Stonewall Riots of 1969. What is often overlooked in this watershed event is the reality that it was transgendered people who began the riots by throwing coins and then bottles at the New York police who were harassing patrons at the Stonewall Inn (Feinberg, 1998). One such combatant was Sylvia Rivera, a self-proclaimed Puerto Rican drag queen who said after having been shoved and pushed by the police during the fracas, "You get tired of being just pushed around" (Rivera as quoted in Feinberg, 1998).

While the events at the Stonewall Inn became the cornerstone of the current lesbian and gay movement, it also signaled a new awareness of the needs of members of the transgender community. Following the riots transgendered individuals began organizing their own advocacy groups and joined with more established gay and lesbian organizations. The entry of transgendered persons into lesbian organizations was fraught with anger and hostility on the part of lesbians (especially lesbian separatists) who did not want MTF persons in their groups. The Michigan Womyn's Music Festival (MWMF) banned transsexuals in the early 1990s, then allowed post-operative MTF's entry in 1999, but lesbian separatists protested. What has emerged since then is an extremely uneasy association at the festival where *transphobia* (the irrational fear of transgendered persons) is still in evidence.

The decades since the 1970s provided more advances in medical treatment for transsexuals and also brought about some small legislative changes that ban discrimination on the basis of gender identity. Currently 13 states and the District of Columbia have laws that specifically prohibit discrimination against transgender people and 93 cities have legislation prohibiting gender identity discrimination (American Civil Liberties Union, 2009). Traditionally such legislation has been coupled with legislation dealing with discrimination related to lesbians, gays, and bisexuals and may or may not cover those who are transgender. Whether or not transgender persons are included depends on the locality.

As with gays and lesbians, the mainstream popular media of television and film have included transgender persons in prime-time television series and mainstream movies. Felicity Huffman was nominated for an Academy Award for her portrayal of a transgender person in *Transamerica*. But despite these positive steps, transgender members of our country continue to be ridiculed, persecuted, misunderstood, and marginalized by not only the heterosexual community but also by the gay and lesbian community.

The transgender population is beset by institutional transphobia just as the lesbian and gay community struggles because of institutional homophobia. Because the transgender population is significantly smaller than the gay community, organizing and advocacy is difficult. Because many members of the gay community fail to embrace the plight of the transgender person, those with gender identity differences face discrimination from both mainstream society and the marginalized gay community.

While numbers of transgender individuals go about their lives with little fanfare, it is the stories of people like Thomas Beatie who gain media attention and create controversy. Mr. Beatie, an FTM transgender person who, while being born female, legally became male although he maintained his original female reproductive organs and became pregnant twice. He and his infertile wife wanted children and Mr. Beatie retained female reproductive organs and a vagina during sexual reassignment surgery that removed his female breasts. The family now consists of two healthy children and their parents Thomas and Nancy. For many in our culture such a story is difficult to comprehend and embrace as either acceptable or normal. Yet, had Mr. Beatie opted not to become pregnant, he and his wife would have remained an invisible couple perceived as heterosexual living in a typical American small town.

In sum, stories such as that of Mr. Beatie challenge us to rethink what it means to be female or male and to become more aware of the ongoing struggles confronting transgender individuals. Those who are transgender face unimaginable discrimination from family, friends, coworkers, and society itself. Yet, the drive to be who they perceive themselves to be propels many on a courageous journey of discovery in a world that is often unrelenting in its lack of understanding.

BISEXUALITY IN HISTORICAL CONTEXT

Putting the construct of bisexuality into a historical context presents challenges. While bisexuality, as the construct is now commonly defined, has been part of the human experience across time, the term *bisexual* was coined in the 19th century when it was defined as an attraction to both sexes. Prior to that, a common term was *hermaphroditic* meaning that an individual physiologically possessed characteristics of both sexes. Bisexuality as we currently use the term came into general usage in the 1950s (Angelides, 2001; Harper, 2001).

The bisexual movement, as it has been called, began in the 1970s and was interwoven with the gay liberation movement of the same decade. However, as gays and lesbians faced confrontations between themselves related to sexism, the rise of the women's movement, and separatism, bisexuals (who were often perceived as heterosexuals) were excluded from the gay movement. Not only were bisexuals excluded from gay and lesbian organizations of the 1970s and 1980s, they were also alienated from organizations that were seen as heterosexual (in such organizations, bisexuals were often perceived as lesbian or gay).

With this exclusion from many emerging social rights groups bisexuals reacted with, in 1972, the formation of The National Bisexual Liberation Group in New York City. Other cities such as San Francisco and Chicago followed and created their own bisexual groups. In the late 1970s and 1980s bisexual women who were systematically excluded from lesbian separatist groups responded by forming bisexual networks in several major cities including Boston, Washington DC, San Francisco, Seattle, and New York City (Highleyman, 2001).

The 1980s brought HIV/AIDS to the gay male population and likewise the male bisexual population. In this context bisexual men were viewed as pariahs who were systematically spreading the virus to both homosexual and the larger mainstream heterosexual populations. As with gay men, many self-defined bisexual men died and along with many in the lesbian and gay community became politically active in the war against HIV/AIDS and equal rights for sexual minorities.

The North American Bisexual Network was created in 1987 and in the early 1990s became the North American Mulitcultural Bisexual Network. Renamed as BiNet: The Bisexual Network of the USA, it continues and identifies itself as an umbrella organization for bisexuals, lesbians, gays, transgender, and questioning allies and friends (BiNet, 2009). Along with the creation of more bisexual affirming organizations, websites, and social networking opportunities have come more overt discussions about bisexuality as a legitimate sexual orientation. The 1990s and 2000s have seen more students becoming involved in the bisexual movement and gay, lesbian, and transgender groups including bisexuals in their ranks. With this inclusion by other disenfranchised sexual minority groups, bisexuality is becoming more openly discussed and visible.

While bisexuality has not been the topic of as many books, research, or media attention as has homosexuality and transgenderism, more scholarship related to bisexuality has emerged since the 1990s. Amazon.com has more than 10,000 books related in some way to bisexuality and more and more research is being conducted with this population. One such publication that presents such is the *Journal of Bisexuality*, a peer-reviewed academic scholastic journal that publishes research data and conceptual articles related to bisexuality.

In sum, while the bisexual movement has been interwoven with gay and lesbian liberation, bisexuals have and continue to create a history that is unique to their experiences. Discriminated against by both the dominant heterosexual culture and the lesbian and gay subculture, bisexuals face multiple challenges. These challenges as well as other social issues confronting sexual minorities will now be discussed.

CURRENT SOCIETAL ISSUES CONFRONTING SEXUAL MINORITIES

Generally, the sexual minorities we are discussing face societal issues related to religious intolerance, societal discrimination, and denial of rights. Each of these will be discussed in the broadest of terms here. For a more detailed exploration of these issues, the reader is invited to consult the evolving literature.

RELIGIOUS INTOLERANCE   Historically organized religion has condemned any type of sexual activity that deviated from the so-called heterosexual norm. This remains the case in many Catholic and evangelical churches where homosexual behavior is not tolerated. Gays and lesbians are not able to join the church, take communion, become ordained, or enjoy the sacraments of marriage. Sexual deviation is traditionally viewed as a sin, the perpetrator headed for a life of eternal damnation both in his or her earthly experience and the afterlife. Religious communities may see those who are members of a lesbian, gay, transgender, or bisexual subculture as somehow psychologically in charge of their sexual orientation and as such, able to change in order to conform to the heterosexual norm. One such *cure* has included the practice of reparative therapy, a therapeutic intervention condemned by the National Association of Social Workers and proven to be largely ineffective.

Although Jesus never said anything about homosexuality, transgenderism, or bisexuality, religious intolerance toward these minorities has been part of the landscape for thousands of years and continues to be the basis for discrimination that endures today. Change is slow and religious traditions tend to be particularly resistant to change.

SOCIETAL DISCRIMINATION   Religious intolerance may be one reason for the continuing societal discrimination faced by bisexuals, transgendered persons, gays, and lesbians. There exists in the United States a continuing fear of these sexual minorities that has come to be known as *institutionalized homophobia, transphobia,* and *biphobia.* This irrational fear of these sexual minorities results in generalized anxiety and disenfranchisement of these populations. The most heinous reality of this discrimination is found in hate crimes perpetrated against gays, transgendered persons, bisexuals, and lesbians.

Hate crimes are those offenses that are motivated by a bias against the victim's perceived sexual orientation, religion, disability, race/ethnicity. The most current data from the Federal Bureau of Investigation (FBI) related to hate crimes indicate that in 2007, there were a total of 7,621 single-bias incidents that involved 9,527 victims (FBI, 2007). Of these, 1,460 (15.3%) were hate crimes associated with sexual orientation. Almost 60% ($n = 864$) of these crimes were against gay men while 12.6% ($n = 184$) were against lesbians and 1.6% ($n = 23$) were against bisexuals. No data are available for hate crimes against transgender persons, but of the 24.8% ($n = 362$) crimes classified generally as anti-homosexual, one could infer that transgender persons were included as victims in this (as well as other) anti-gay defined hate crimes (FBI, 2007).

Hate crimes are only one manifestation of the discrimination faced by these populations. Societal disenfranchisement and alienation that includes the irrational fear of transgender persons, bisexuals, lesbians, and gays also results in specific denials of rights accorded to the heterosexual majority.

DENIAL OF RIGHTS   Overt discrimination against any minority is often seen in the denial of rights afforded others who are perceived as being members of the mainstream culture. Certainly this is the case with lesbians, transgenders, bisexuals, and gays. Gay and lesbian couples, because they are generally recognized as not having any legal relationship, may be denied a host of benefits afforded to heterosexual couples. Such include the right to marry; the right to two-party adoption of children; the right to family medical health insurance; the right to visit one's partner in the intensive care unit (ICU); the right to inherit as a spouse; the right to a partner's social security benefits; the right to a protected status in the areas of housing, employment, and, all of the other rights and privileges granted to members of the heterosexual majority. Lesbians and gays may face discrimination in the area of employment where there may be homophobia that hinders hiring them as teachers, day care providers, or coaches. Organized religion may require that priests and other ordained clergy not be gay or lesbian and even in the film industry there may be stigma attached to gay and lesbian actors who are too overt in their appearance or actions.

Transgender persons can face similar discrimination, but in some instances institutional transphobia and the internalized transphobia that can emanate from it causes great suffering. As noted earlier, those who are transgender push those who are not to rethink and deal with gender stereotypes in new ways. Often, this is difficult and the result can be misunderstanding and disenfranchisement. For the married transgender man who can no longer deny his true identity the struggles are enormous and the discrimination potential huge. What happens to the legal marriage, the relationship with the teenage son, the employment that supports the family? Transgender persons not only face discrimination from the heterosexual majority but also from the gay and lesbian subculture. Lesbian separatists especially have been less than charitable to MTF persons who are viewed as "not real women," but rather imposters who have had the opportunity of male privilege and are now masquerading as female. Both FTMs and MTFs can face discrimination as they move through their physical transitions. Even simply using a public bathroom can be a minefield for transgender persons.

A most poignant story is that of Bethany, an MTF woman who lost everything that was dear to her because of her gender orientation. She lost a well-paying job as an engineer, her health benefits, her family, her house, her car, and her friends. Her employer told her she would be terminated if she ceased being male; with her termination went her health benefits; paying for her transition treatment and surgery cost her the home and car she owned; and the friends she had when male, deserted her. Despite these extraordinary losses, she persevered, had the surgery, found a new job, made new friends, and is a tireless advocate for the transgender community.

Transgender persons, like lesbian and gay persons, face discrimination in the United States mostly because of a lack of tolerance, understanding, and condemnation related to their lifestyle. As such, there are legal barriers and lack of a protected status in such things as employment and housing. They may be seen as freaks of nature unworthy of acceptance by the majority. The discrimination faced by this group is comparable to other kinds of discrimination faced by bisexuals.

Bisexual people in our country live on a continuum between heterosexuality (or normalcy as defined by society) and homosexuality (or deviancy). While many proclaim bisexuality as a valid sexual orientation, others do not agree. To many, bisexuality may be viewed as a phase in the gay/lesbian coming-out process and not a "real" sexual orientation. Others simply see bisexual behavior as an experimentation with sexuality that will ultimately be left behind for preferred heterosexual normalcy. Bisexuality is not recognized as a legally protected status and bisexuals are subjected to discrimination in housing and employment.

The reality is that gays, lesbians, transgenders, and bisexuals all face discrimination and disenfranchisement in our society. The legal system favors the majority and until social mores change, this long-standing institutionalized homophobia, transphobia, and biphobia will continue to create unimaginable strife for these groups. Additionally, none of these groups is immune from discrimination such as ageism, sexism, racism, etc., faced by other minority groups. This persistent historical discrimination and the values held by many in our society may pose ethical dilemmas for social workers struggling to empower bisexuals, transgenders, lesbians, and gays.

ETHICAL DILEMMAS

Both the Council on Social Work Education (CSWE) Educational Policy of Accreditation Standards (EPAS) (CSWE, 2008a) and the National Association of Social Workers' (NASW) Code of Ethics (NASW, 2008a) have policy statements related to ensuring that social workers provide services to clients that respect the worth and dignity of every individual and that honor human rights by demonstrating a respect for all persons and a commitment to social and economic justice. Professional services are to be given with integrity and competence. Competence not only means providing services for which the professional is trained and licensed but also has a broader implication. Specifically, the NASW ethical code demands that social workers need an understanding of oppression and social diversity with respect to gender identity and sexual orientation (NASW, 2008b). These policy standards related to the values and ethics expected of professional social workers.

It is not uncommon for social work practitioners to encounter ethical and value dilemmas in situations where personal and professional values may seem at odds with one another. An ethical dilemma may be defined as a situation that arises when two or more values found in something like the ethical code of NASW or the accreditation standards of CSWE are contradictory. In both NASW and CSWE the policy mandates are quite clear in noting that sexual orientation or gender expression should not be areas for disenfranchisement or discrimination. When working with these minorities, ethical dilemmas are more likely to arise when a social work professional's personal values collide with those espoused by the profession.

While social work educators train students to provide services from a bias-free, neutral stance, pragmatically this is impossible. One cannot simply check one's values at the office door and be value-free when working with clients. Rather, social workers must know themselves and know the values, beliefs, and attitudes they bring to the therapeutic process that will shape the services they provide to their clients. When ethical dilemmas do emerge (and they always do), it is incumbent upon the worker to identify the value conflicts, weigh each competing value, and make a decision based on the clinician and client's ethical philosophy. Many excellent ethical decision making tools are available and should be consulted if necessary (Dolgoff, Loewenberg, & Harrington, 2008; Linzer, 1999; Mattison, 2000), and if you are confused about the construct *ethical philosophy*, explore such authors as Elaine Congress, Black and Strom-Gottfried (2009), Stephen Freeman (2000), or Frederic Reamer (2006).

When dealing with lesbian, gay, bisexual or transgender clients, ethical dilemmas may arise when a conflict exists between the profession's professed value stance and the social worker's personal beliefs, values, and attitudes. Often these are related to church doctrine about these minorities; institutionalized or internalized homo-, trans-, or biphobia; or simply generalized misunderstandings about gays, bisexuals, lesbians, and transgender persons.

Social work practitioners are not the only ones who face ethical dilemmas related to sexual orientation or gender identity. Bisexuals, transgender persons, lesbians, and gays, too, may face enormous ethical dilemmas when recognizing and affirming their identities. The *coming-out* process for these minorities can be viewed in distinct phases all of which can pose ethical dilemmas for the individual or clinician. In the simplest model the four phases include: feeling different, questioning and experimentation, tolerance, and acceptance.

The first phase occurs when the individual first has feelings that he or she is somehow different from others. For transgender persons this may occur at very early ages; for lesbians and gays perhaps around puberty. However, some people do not experience this phase until they are adults. Data exist that demonstrate the process of coming-out occur at any age (Tully, 2000). This feeling of difference may present ethical dilemmas for not only the individual, but also for his or her family, or social work practitioner who may be working with the family. Assuming the feelings of difference persist, the second phase of coming-out involves questioning and sexual experimentation. Such may include bisexual activity or cross-dressing. The third phase centers on the individual's gradual tolerance for the lifestyle and the final phase includes the person's internalized acceptance of identity. At any point along this coming-out continuum, ethical dilemmas can arise and could include the individual going through the process, their family members, members of the community, or the social worker providing services to the individual. Such dilemmas might include facing difficult decisions regarding the acceptance (or denial) of what is occurring in various phases, based on prevailing societal values and the best interest of the individual.

In sum, ethical dilemmas are seemingly inevitable when working with highly volatile values, beliefs, and attitudes around sexuality. Sexual orientation and gender identity may be difficult for practitioners to struggle with because of persistent discrimination against these groups on the basis of fear and religious prejudice. In order to overcome such injustice and bigotry, it is imperative for social workers to become culturally sensitive and aware of these groups by gaining accurate knowledge about them.

CULTURAL AWARENESS AND KNOWLEDGE ACQUISITION

As a construct, the term *cultural awareness* has been described as the cornerstone of communication including the ability for us to step back and analyze ourselves in terms of our societal beliefs and values (Quappe & Cantatore, 2007). Lum (2007) adds that culture awareness also involves an understanding of traditions, customs, and practices that are transmitted from one generation to another. Further, Lum notes that cultural awareness includes both cognitive and sensory inputs. We *know* things both intellectually from being taught certain values, attitudes, and beliefs and we emotionally *feel* specific ways about them. Assuming everything we have been taught about any culture or minority is not 100% accurate, the feelings we have about these groups might also be suspected of being incorrect (remember, at one point the prevailing *truth* was that the world was flat). Gaining true cultural awareness of another's way of life requires us to be open to questioning, learning, and feeling differently than we may have been used to. It also requires that we put aside (as much as is possible) previously held values, attitudes, and beliefs until they are either confirmed or denied. Finally, with new knowledge must come new emotional feelings about the culture or group. When becoming culturally aware of the gay, lesbian, bisexual, and transgender lifestyles social workers will, no doubt, learn that their previous cognitive and sensory beliefs and feelings have failed to adequately prepare them for a culturally sensitive social work practice.

It is not enough for culturally competent social work practitioners merely to know that gays, lesbians, bisexuals, and transgender persons exist. In order to provide competent services to these minorities practitioners must also have knowledge about them. *Knowledge* means having an understanding and mastery of theories, facts, and information related to these populations (Lum, 2007). Knowledge is the cognitive piece of learning and what is most often thought of as those things we are taught and learn. Knowledge about any minority requires an understanding of the demographics of the group, critical thinking about it, how the minority has been historically oppressed, and various theories related to minority status and culture. Working with transgender persons, bisexuals, lesbians, and gays requires the same in-depth scrutiny and knowledge base. *Knowledge acquisition* is how the social work practitioner gains realistic information about whatever minority he or she wants to learn about.

With the advent of the Internet learning about any population different from one's own has been made much easier than it once was. Search engines enable us to simply enter keywords and instantly data related to the concept are made available. For the novice, an excellent way to begin is to simply Google keywords and see what pops up. The danger in this approach is that there are no filters to screen what may be prejudicial from what is true. So, since you are going to use the Internet, start by reading a well-accepted encyclopedia article about the topic (e.g., *Encyclopedia of Social Work* or *Encyclopedia Britannica*) and going to some reputable related websites such as that run by Parents, Families, and Friends of Lesbians and Gays (PFLAG) at http://www.pflag.org. PFLAG has accurate information about all the minorities discussed in this chapter and is an excellent resource for anyone working with gay, lesbian, bisexual, or transgender persons. Links to other reputable sources can be found at the PFLAG website. While articles about the populations and websites can provide a wealth of practical information, it is incumbent upon the social work clinician to also understand prevailing theoretical positions on these groups and be able to critically think about the content.

This chapter has already discussed the demographics and historical oppression related to transgender, bisexual, gay, and lesbian persons and will now explore a few relevant theories and how one can critically analyze content related to these minorities. The three current theories associated directly with lesbian, gay, transgender, and bisexual persons include feminist theory, queer theory, and gender theory. Of course, many theories have included thoughts on sexuality and theories that deal with the populations at hand are relatively recent. The oldest of the three, feminist theory, explores gender inequalities between women and men and seeks to discover whether there is a female way of knowing and women's knowledge. Modern feminism has had a significant impact on lesbian philosophy and how lesbians see themselves in contemporary society. Queer theory emerged in the 1990s and grew out of content related to feminist studies and the emerging field of lesbian and gay studies. Although not well developed, it embraces postmodern thought and social constructionism. It explores the intersections of gender and sexual orientation and posits that sexual identity is not fixed, but rather is fluid and that heterosexuality should not be perceived as the natural order. This theory embraces the naturalness of bisexuality and supports the empowerment of all individuals. The most recent theory to materialize is that of gender theory as a separate entity from feminist theory or queer theory. However, its ideology may not yet rise to the level of being described as a true theoretical system. Perhaps a better descriptor of it would be a conceptual framework or paradigm related to gender. This view holds that children born into whatever societal and cultural setting learn what gender norms are expected and follow them. Or, gender is not determined by biological sex, but rather by learned behaviors that mirror what has been considered the norm. Those who believe this think such behavior is nothing more than stereotyping, and that all individuals should not be labeled according to gender.

While it is helpful to understand current theoretical positions associated with minorities, a broad-based approach toward understanding cultural competence practice theory provides the practitioner with the basis of practice. Cultural competence theory holds that there are a number of competencies necessary for effective practice. According to Leung and Cheung (2001), these include competencies related to information, intellect, interpersonal, intrapersonal, and intervention. Perhaps the most important component of applying these competencies is for the practitioner to critically analyze each and then act.

When confronted with new information the practitioner must, in concert with the client, and using intellectual processes, analyze and assess the presenting problem or issue, sort fact from fiction, and think about possible points of view related to the issue. Interpersonal skills aid the worker in formulating approaches to the issue and developing relationships between the worker and client. Intrapersonal skills become important when the worker's values and gut reactions may differ from the values and beliefs of the client. Finally, from a host of interventive possibilities, the worker and client come to an agreement about what will provide the best course of action. All these steps require critical thinking skills that take into account social and economic justice issues, the empowerment perspective, and the needs of the client.

In sum, cultural awareness and knowledge acquisition when working with bisexual, transgender, gay, and lesbian persons is similar to working with any minority group. The process of becoming skilled clinicians when working with these groups may present challenges simply because of the invisibility of many members of these groups. As noted at the beginning of this chapter, passing as heterosexual presents an adaptive coping mechanism for many lesbian, gay, bisexual, and transgender persons. Developing clinical skills to effectively provide services to these minorities follows.

SKILL DEVELOPMENT

Interventive skills refer to those professional behaviors social workers use when providing services to clients. In social work the skills represent a pragmatic application of knowledge of prevailing theory and personal values. Skills are the tools by which the clinician provides culturally competent services to all clients and comprise the foundation of professional practice. This section will discuss specific skills necessary for working with lesbian, gay, transgender and bisexual clients.

PROFESSIONAL STANDARDS FOR CULTURAL COMPETENCY

Both NASW and CSWE have standards related to what skills and interventive techniques professionally trained social workers should be able to provide when dealing with clients (CSWE, 2008a; NASW, 2008a,b). Generally these policies require that social workers be aware of how culture influences behavior, gain education specific to various populations at risk, and be able to demonstrate competence in the provision of services sensitive to the needs of the population seeking services (CSWE, 2008a). Specifically the educational standards required by NASW state that "social workers should obtain education about and seek to understand the nature of social diversity and oppression with respect to race, ethnicity, national origin, color, sex, sexual orientation, gender identity or expression ..." (NASW, 2008a, 1.05c). The CSWE also has specific standards related to professional practice. CSWE notes that such practice "involves the dynamic and interactive processes of engagement, assessment, intervention, and evaluation at multiple levels ... where practice knowledge includes identifying, analyzing, and implementing evidence-based interventions designed to achieve client goals; ... and promoting social and economic justice" (CSWE, 2008a, 2.1.10, pp. 6–7).

Interventive skills related to working with bisexual, transgender, gay, or lesbian persons are not different from the skills used in working with any other client or group and require the same levels of competency. The generalist roles of conferee, broker, mediator, therapist, case manager, group worker, and community organizer (Wood & Tully, 2006) are still germane and should be applied. The most salient of these skills when related to lesbian, transgender, bisexual, or gay clients center on engagement, assessment, intervention, and empowerment.

ENGAGEMENT

Engaging the client (or client group) is the most important element in creating a client–worker connection and relationship. Engaging the client involves creating a safe space for the relationship to develop, attending, creating empathic connections, checking out inferences, reaching for information, and giving feedback (Wood & Tully, 2006). When working with clients who may not be open about their sexual or gender identification the first skill in engaging the client is to provide an office space that does not espouse a *heterosexual assumption*. Having intake forms that include options for "partner" (and not simply "spouse"), "in a long-term relationship" (not just "married, single, or divorced") is one way of showing cultural sensitivity. Including gay-friendly literature in the waiting room is also a sign that heterosexuality is not assumed by the social workers in the office. Similarly, when first engaging the client in conversation, do not assume his or her sexual or gender identity. Leave stereotypical thinking outside the client–worker relationship, attend to what the client is saying, and develop empathic connections with the client.

Attending is the interactional part of listening where the worker occasionally nods, leans forward, and maintains eye contact. This leads to a better understanding of what another is feeling thereby creating empathic connections. These connections are nonjudgmental and the worker often checks out inferences by stating what the client has noted and asking whether or not the inference is correct. New knowledge of the client's situation is gained by reaching for further information that further explore the values, facts, opinions, etc., that increase the awareness of the event. Finally, the worker provides feedback to the client that asks whether or not the worker truly understood what the client was sharing. If incorrect, the client has the opportunity to correct misinterpretations.

Client work with lesbian, gay, bisexual, and transgender persons follows the same path. This work does require, however, that the worker has adequate knowledge and skills required to work with these groups, that all biases about these minorities have been analyzed, and that the worker feels comfortable and competent to provide services in a professional manner that is in keeping with professional ethical demands.

ASSESSMENT

Assessment deals with the clinician appraising, with the client, the client's current strengths, needs, resources, and interests. It also encompasses an evaluation of potential strengths, supports, and resources available to the client as well as the client's level of functioning. During the assessment phase of interaction, the social worker and the client work together to first assess why the client is seeking services, what resources are available, and tentatively agree on how to best approach and deal with the presenting problem or issue. In this stage of treatment with transgender, lesbian, bisexual, or gay persons the approach and skills required are identical to those needed when working with any client. What may differ is that, as a social worker you may not know the sexual or gender orientation of the client with whom you are trying to form a relationship.

What a social worker can deduce from a first meeting with a client may include race, sex, and general age (if that). Merely looking at someone may not provide much realistic information about the person. For example, the client may actually be a 70-year-old, marathon running, biracial, lesbian but what the worker may *see* at first is an older, physically fit, white woman. Or, a client may be a 47-year-old, African American, FTM transgender person who *looks* like a middle-aged, bearded man. In sum, it is the development of the interpersonal relationship with a client that will provide the actual details of who the client really is. Developing this relationship with lesbian, gay, transgender, and bisexual people requires that the worker keep an open mind, not assume that all persons are heterosexual, and be willing to let the client determine the pace of how and when revelations about sexual and gender orientation are made. Members of these disenfranchised minorities face problems and issues similar to others in our society; and, what brings them to seek help may or may not be related to their sexual or gender identification. It will be in the assessment phase where the client and worker will determine the exact reason for the visit and proceed accordingly using appropriate interventive strategies.

INTERVENTION

Intervention is the phase in the client–worker relationship where, working with one another, the client and worker determine which actions will enhance client capacities and help resolve current issues. As with other minority groups or any client population, determining what intervention will be the best is totally dependent on the presenting problem.

If the presenting problem happens to be related to sexual or gender identification the worker must have the repertoire of interventive skills necessary for cultural competency in the needed area. This may mean having knowledge of a variety of resources that are germane to the gay, lesbian, transgender, and bisexual community and simply being culturally sensitive to the needs of these groups. Because sexual or gender orientation is only one defining characteristic, the worker also must be culturally competent to deal with other minority statuses in clients. Clients may face double or triple jeopardy in a culture where a 17-year-old, bisexual teenager or an 88-year-old, Hispanic, gay man may face threats other than their gender or sexual orientation. (Please see Walters, Longres, Han, & Icard [2007] for a more complete discussion of working with gay and lesbian persons of color.)

In sum, interventive skills must be unique to the situation at hand and must include knowledge of client strengths, weaknesses, social supports, and personal and community resources. Also, the clinician must understand the historical discrimination faced by these groups and the role homophobia, biphobia, and transphobia plays at the institutional, interpersonal, and intrapersonal levels.

EMPOWERMENT AND ADVOCACY

The NASW ethical code demands that social work professionals not only have an ethical responsibility to clients but also to the broader society (NASW, 2008a,b). This includes ensuring that clients have equal access to employment, resources, opportunities, and services necessary to meet basic needs and that special attention is paid to those groups vulnerable to discrimination because of their status (NASW, 2008b). Empowerment and advocacy are the two primary methods by which social work professionals help clients and communities gain power in situations where the disenfranchised may have little or no influence or power.

Empowerment and advocacy for lesbian, transgender, gay, and bisexual persons and groups utilizes the same techniques used for empowering any group. At the micro level it involves mobilizing client strengths and self-determination to foster positive coping mechanisms and behaviors that allow the client to become self-sufficient and control his or her life. At the meso level it includes mobilizing communities to develop group consciousness around particular issues of importance and to act in ways that will facilitate community change. At the macro level it embraces solutions related to institutional discriminations. For sexual- and gender-orientation–related issues the following could be considered. At the micro level empowerment could mean that a transgender client struggling with a new identity finds a supportive fellowship in a group run by a social worker. At the meso level it might mean that a political action committee is formed to support an openly lesbian candidate for mayor. And, at the macro level it could mean the collective efforts of supporters to rid a particular institution of policies and procedures that discriminate on the basis of sexual or gender identification.

In sum, empowerment and advocacy on the part of any minority involves personal and political action to ensure that the rights of all individuals are protected and that the most vulnerable populations in our society are not denied equal protection. Helping those who have been systematically disenfranchised and exploited serves as a basis for professional social workers and provides the foundation for social and economic justice.

When thinking about developing interventive skill related to working with lesbian, gay, bisexual, or transgender persons it is important to remember that the skills used in working with any population are appropriate. What you will need to remember is that members of these disenfranchised populations live in a society rife with misinformation, stereotypes, confusion, and fear about them. Being culturally sensitive to the realities of these groups and learning as much as possible about them will determine the best interventions. And, remember that just because one is transgender, bisexual, lesbian, or gay does not mean that that reality is the reason for seeking professional assistance.

SOCIAL AND ECONOMIC JUSTICE

The constructs *social justice* and *economic justice* relate to how members of society have access to equal rights and privileges. Specifically, *social justice* speaks to society's need to ensure that all people have access to basic human rights that espouse equal protection and opportunities related to rights and privileges, protections, and obligations while *economic justice* looks at how societal institutions guarantee all societal members' ability to earn a living, gain adequate education to be gainfully employed, and financially meet their needs (Van Soest, 2007). The NASW ethical code instructs social workers to "promote social justice" (NASW, 2008b, 6.04a) when speaking of a worker's ethical responsibility to society in general. This expectation then moves from the micro level of interaction with individuals, families, or groups, into a more meso- or macro-level approach. To explore all the ways social workers should seek to empower populations of lesbians, gays, bisexuals, and transgenders to ensure social and economic justice is beyond the scope of this chapter. The following two suggestions should help social workers better guarantee social and economic justice for these groups. First, social work professionals must educate themselves about the reality of each of these groups so as to realistically portray who they are and to dispel lingering and damaging stereotypes. Once well educated on these matters, the social worker should seek to educate others. How this occurs is as varied as the creativity of the worker. Panel discussions at public forums, testimony at public hearings, or personal testimonials in appropriate forums are some ways of public education, but let your own creativity guide the process.

Now that you have educated yourself as to all the nuances about bisexual, transgender, lesbian, and gay culture and have overcome whatever homophobia, transphobia, and biphobia that may have been lurking in your psyche, you may want to move into a more meso- or macro-level role of advocacy by confronting existing laws, policies, and procedures that continue to discriminate against these disenfranchised minorities. With the continuing influence of those who still believe that reparative therapy can "cure" homosexuality and lingering fears about each of these groups, the opportunities for social workers to engage in work that will ensure social and economic justice are enormous. The following case examples will provide an opportunity to apply what has been discussed in the previous pages and should engender spirited discussions.

FROM THEORY TO PRACTICE: APPLYING THE PRINCIPLES

The following case examples are designed to facilitate class discussion, role plays, debates, activism, or other creative solutions. Put yourself in the position of being the social worker who is assigned to each of these cases. When analyzing the scenarios please be certain to address the following questions:

1. Who is/are the client/s? What is the presenting problem/issue? Is it a micro-, meso-, or macro-level problem?

2. What do you already know about the person/group/organization? What resources are you aware of that could be beneficial to your client? What do you not know about your client? Where can you look to find out additional information that would be helpful?

3. What is your *gut* reaction to the client and the client's situation? What personal values, beliefs, attitudes, and biases do you have about the client and the client's situation? What role does institutionalized and internalized homophobia, transphobia, or biphobia play in your relationship with the client? What stereotypes do you have about the client? How does your personal situation (e.g., socioeconomic status, sex, age, race, sexual orientation, etc.) influence your interactions with the client? Beyond discrimination based on gender identity or sexual orientation, what other minority groups define the client?

4. How does the client view himself or herself and his or her situation? What role does institutionalized and internalized biphobia, transphobia, or homophobia play in the client's life? Where is the client in relation to his or her coming-out process?

5. What ethical dilemmas could be faced when dealing with the client? What culturally competent skills are necessary for the worker to have in order to provide the necessary services? Specifically, what micro-, meso-, or macro-level skills will be required to ensure appropriate intervention? What role does empowerment play and what are the factors related to social and economic justice?

CASE STUDY | CHRISTINE AND CECILIA

Christine is a 74-year-old African American lesbian who has been with Cecilia, a Caucasian, aged 69 years, for the past 25 years. The two of them retired to a one-story cottage in New Orleans 5 years ago and both are very physically fit, active, and have lots of friends in the lesbian/gay community where they are seen as "a prototype for successful lesbian living." On Thanksgiving Day, Christine fell at home and broke her hip. She was taken to the emergency room and ultimately wound up in the ICU of the hospital due to complications related to respiration and coronary problems. Christine's daughter, Mahala, age 37, lives close to the hospital but has never approved of her mother's lifestyle and does not get along with Cecilia or any of the couple's friends. For the past 25 years, Christine and Mahala have been estranged and not in communication unless absolutely necessary. The ICU policies state that only family members can visit. You are the hospital social worker assigned to Christine's case.

CASE STUDY | TOMAS

Tomas, who calls himself Tomi, is a 19-year-old, Hispanic man and the only child of his parents. Tomi has always believed he was trapped in a male body when in actuality he believed himself to be female. His strict Catholic upbringing and familial heritage caused him to question his feelings and his family dismissed his protestations at wearing masculine clothing as a "phase." He recently left home to attend a college hundreds of miles from home and discovered a GLBT organization on campus that he joined. The more he learned about the transgender community, the more he believed that he was transgendered, but he is having an internal clash trying to make peace between his religious beliefs, his family's expectation that he marry and carry on the family name, the Hispanic culture's beliefs about MTF persons, the overall societal views of transgender persons, and some of his friends who think he is nuts. He is becoming more and more confused and has stopped eating, is sleeping poorly, his grades have nose-dived, he is drinking more, and is questioning his existence. You are the social worker in the mental health clinic on campus and have been called in by Tomi's physician to work with Tomi.

CASE STUDY | ANGELICA

Angelica is a 34-year old who is biracial. Her father is African American, her mother, Vietnamese. She is married to an African American Army sergeant, Derek, who has been deployed to Afghanistan. She is pregnant with the couple's first child that is due in 7 months. Shortly after she discovered she was pregnant Derek had to return to Iraq and she joined a military wives support group. She has become extremely close to Juanita, another member of the group. This closeness reminds Angelica of a lesbian experience she had when she was in college and that she had told Derek about. Derek seemed fine with her college dalliance, so she pursues a sexual relationship with Juanita. Angelica and Juanita's relationship blossomed and both seem to think they are bisexual. Derek and Angelica have discussed this but Juanita and her husband have not. Derek is due home on leave in a week; Juanita has just found out that her husband was killed in battle. You are the social worker on base and both Angelica and Juanita have come to see you.

CASE STUDY | CHUCK AND GARY

Chuck is a 55-year-old Jewish store owner. He and his partner, Gary, age 58, have been in business together for the past 30 years. They are, in gay parlance, "proud and loud." Meaning that they are pleased to let everyone know their sexual orientation and do it in ways that might offend some. Their store, which is in a trendy up-scale, "straight" neighborhood, is festooned with rainbow banners and the windows adorned with pro-gay bumper-stickers. The store has been located in the same spot for two decades and is a well-known hangout in the gay community. The landlord, an 85-year-old woman who loved "her boys" recently died and left the property to her decidedly homophobic son who wants Chuck and Gary out of the building immediately. The gay community and Chuck and Gary are trying to determine what course of action would be appropriate. You are the social worker at the local community outreach center in Chuck and Gary's neighborhood and they have sought you out.

CULTURAL COMPETENCE WITH PERSONS WITH DISABILITIES

CHAPTER 16

Romel Mackelprang

INTRODUCTION: DISABILITY DEFINITIONS AND PREVALENCE

The inclusion of disability in this latest edition of the text represents a major leap in conceptualizing diversity. Historically and contemporarily, disability is generally treated in a negative light. Definitions of disability vary widely; therefore, coming up with a universally accepted concrete characterization of disability is impossible. For example, disability as defined by the Social Security Administration to qualify for social security benefits will always differ from census estimates, and disability definitions for college students requesting reasonable accommodation for extended test times will differ from both. Definitional differences arise when attempting to describe other diversities as well. For example, whether one qualifies as Native American is often determined by a blood percentage. Barak Obama is widely considered an African American, yet he was raised by his Caucasian mother's family.

Because disability definitions are so divergent, estimates of the incidence and prevalence are difficult to obtain. Mont (2007), writing for the World Bank, states that prevalence rates range from 1% in Kenya to 20% in New Zealand. He suggests, "that there is no single correct definition of disability, that the nature and severity of disabilities vary greatly, and that how one measures disability differs depending on the purpose for measuring it" (p. 1). Marshaw and Reno (1996) document nearly two dozen context specific U.S. definitions of disability. A commonly used framework for defining disability in the U.S. was developed by Nagi (1969) and consists of four elements: 1) *pathology* that interrupts physical or mental processes, 2) *impairment* that limits a person's ability to function and that may result in, 3) *functional limitation* relative to the ability to perform or engage in life tasks, and 4) *disability* or the inability to perform socially expected activities.

437

The 1990 Americans with Disabilities Act estimated that 43 million Americans had disabilities and defined disability as:

(1) Disability.—The term 'disability' means, with respect to an individual—

    (A) a physical or mental impairment that substantially limits one or more major life activities of such individual;

    (B) a record of such an impairment; or

    (C) being regarded as having such an impairment.

The U.S. Census Bureau, defining disability relative to difficulties in performing tasks of everyday living, estimates that about 52.6 million Americans live with disabilities and 33 million live with severe disabilities. It estimates the poverty rate of adults with disabilities is more than three times (27.9% vs. 8.3%) the poverty rate of nondisabled individuals (McNeil, 2001). The 2007 U.S. Disability Status Report uses Census data based on employment criteria to determine disability prevalence among noninstitutionalized people, estimating that approximately 14.9% of Americans, ages 5 years and above, live with disabilities (Erickson & Lee, 2007). Prevalence of disability types was estimated as follows.

- Sensory: 4.2%
- Physical: 9.4%
- Mental: 5.8%
- Self-care: 3.0%
- Go-outside home: 5.4%
- Employment: 7.1%

It is evident from this data that many people have multiple disabilities and that these categories are not mutually exclusive. The Status Report estimates the prevalence of disability for working-age people (ages 21 to 64) was:

- 12.6 percent among Whites
- 17.0 percent among Black/African Americans
- 6.3 percent among Asians
- 22.5 percent among Native Americans
- 11.7 percent among persons of some other race (p. 3).

Prevalence of disability increases with age.

- 14.9 percent for persons ages 5+
- 6.3 percent for persons ages 5 to 15
- 6.8 percent for persons ages 16 to 20
- 12.8 percent for persons ages 21 to 64
- 29.7 percent for persons ages 65 to 74
- 52.9 percent for persons ages 75+ (p. 3).

The estimates of disability prevalence cited above utilize a medical/pathology model for defining disability. Essentially, they focus on deficits or impairments that make it difficult or render people incapable of performing activities and tasks. However, in recent years, the emphasis on disability has begun shifting away from individual pathology that requires individualized treatment to fix or modify. Instead, the problems associated with disability are increasingly being recognized as arising from the intersection of the individual and the environment. As evidence of this shift, the first major United Nations human rights initiative of the 21st Century is the 2007 UN Convention on the Rights of Persons with Disabilities. The UN Convention marked a paradigm shift to a civil rights perspective on disability. For example, traditionally, people with paraplegia have been considered unemployable because of their mobility limitations. Yet, as Johnson (2006) observes:

> Disability and nondisability are also constructed through the language used to describe people...There is a world of difference between using a wheelchair and being treated as a normal human being (who happens to use a wheelchair to get around) and using a wheelchair and being treated as invisible, unintelligent, frightening, passive, dependent, and nothing more than your disability... We think the way our culture defines something like race or gender (or disability) is simply the way things are in some objective sense. (pp. 19–20)

This chapter recognizes the importance of utilizing demographic information to estimate disability prevalence as well as the prevalence of other characteristics such as race, ethnicity, age, and gender. However, rather than assuming that the problems arising from disability are internally based, this chapter assumes that disability is an element of diversity rather than pathology. In contrast to the conventional, medical model approach of disability, the *social model approach* to disability recognizes disability as a diverse attribute in society. This means that self identification of disability is as important in determining disability as some external categorization according to diagnostic criteria.

CULTURAL COMPETENCE IN PERSONS WITH DISABILITIES

Traditionally, cultural competence has been defined primarily from a racial and ethnic perspective. However, this conceptualization is being challenged as myopic and incomplete (Colligan, 2004; Mackelprang & Salsgiver, 2009; McRuer, 2006). Cultural competence, "must address more than race. It must address multiple social identities and their unique intersection for each individual, organization, and society... Multiple social identities must always be considered" (Ridley, Baker, & Hill, 2001, p. 830).

Disability culture has arisen from identity based communities (Longres, 2000). As Fine & Asch (1993) contend, minority group status resulting from shared experiences within larger society, provide Disabled persons common identity and shared interest. "Consequently, disabled persons—that is, people who identify as disabled and embrace disability—have recognized the importance of moving the agenda of independence and equality forward through the political process. Disabled persons and their allies have become active in developing political agendas and establishing policies that recognize Disability culture and educating both disabled and nondisabled persons about Disability culture" (Mackelprang & Salsgiver, 2008, p. 113). Political advocacy and resistance to mainstream disability views have directly contributed to developing Disability culture (Riddell & Watson, 2003). They suggest that advocacy and political activism have led to a system of "signs, symbols, tools and beliefs," a kind of "social order," communicates, reproduces, and explores the common experience of persons with disabilities (p. 5).

Surviving and resisting oppression and marginalization have created a foundation for disability culture as disabled persons have forged a group identity as Disabled people. The resilience of disabled persons is manifest in the art, music, literature, and other expressions of their lives and their culture, drawn from the experience of disability (Brown, 1996).

The burgeoning disability rights movement and Disability culture eschew traditional pathology based approaches to disability. Disability advocates contend that social policies, environmental barriers, and discrimination are the primary employment obstacles faced by disabled persons. Like other diversities, the social/diversity model of disability relies on social contexts and personal identities to determine disability and nondisability. Consider the following discriminatory practices based on majority accepted perceived limitations. Two hundred years ago, Blacks in the U.S. were considered 3/5 of a person. In the 1800s, Native Americans were forced from their lands onto reservations. Less than 100 years ago, women were denied the right to vote. As recently as 50 years ago, social work, psychology and psychiatry considered homosexuality a pathological trait—and many in society still carry this belief. Similarly, disabled people have been institutionalized, imprisoned, and forced into poverty because of discrimination and ableism—not because disabled people are inherently incompetent or *invalid*. As a result, the last 40–45 years have seen a burgeoning disability rights movement and an embracing of disability as an attribute, disability community for support and validation, and a disability culture that celebrates disability and the lives of disabled people.

Disability culture is emerging and continually evolving. Disabled persons have formed communities based on their common interests, experiences, and minority status in society (Fine & Asch, 1993). Disabled persons who embrace and identify with their disabilities are developing disability culture as they promote independence and equality (Riddell & Watson, 2003). Several authors have identified elements of disability culture and the mechanisms by which it is being developed and promulgated (Longmore, 2003; Mackelprang & Salsgiver, 2009; Snyder & Mitchell, 2006). Longmore avers that disability culture repudiates nondisabled values of "overcoming" disability and embraces self-definition. He states that in this process,

> Disabled people began to celebrate themselves. Coining self-affirming slogans such as "Disabled and Proud," "Deaf Pride," and "Disability Cool," they seized control of the definition of their identities. This has been not so much as a series of personal choices as a collective process of reinterpreting themselves and their issues. It is a political and cultural task... For example, some people with physical disabilities have been affirming the validity of their own experience. Those values are markedly different from, and even opposed to nondisabled majority values. They declare they prize not self-sufficiency but self-determination, not independence but interdependence, not functional separateness but personal connection, not physical autonomy but human community. (p. 222)

The common experiences of devaluation, oppression, and marginalization are providing a common bond and resilience within disability communities. This has led to Disability art, music, literature and other manifestations of Disability culture (Brown, 1996). John Callahan, a quadriplegic humorist mocked disability stereotypes with his first book, *Don't Worry, He Won't Get Far on Foot* (1989) a tome with which mobility disabled people readily identify. Lewis (2006) has compiled a compendium of contemporary plays by disabled playwrights and critiqued common portrayals of disabled people in the entertainment media. Comedian Josh Blue won the 2006 *Last Comic Standing* by joking about his cerebral palsy. The disability rights magazine, *Disability Rag* was first published in 1980, embraced disability, and advocated for "Disability Cool." The *Rag* included news stories, poetry, fiction, and thousands of disability related articles. Its successor, the *Ragged Edge* continues the mission of embracing disabled people and Disability culture. The Avocado Press has published multiple titles on disability issues and rights and that contribute to a burgeoning Disability culture. The 2005 award winning film, *Murderball* documents the exploits of a group of elite disabled athletes who play quad rugby. Centers for Independent Living, located in every state, are disability advocacy organizations that require that a minimum of 51% of administrative staff and boards of directors be disabled. They also provide a safe environment for disabled people who are peers. The slogan, "Nothing about us without us," implies the rejection of traditional practices in which nondisabled people develop policies and make decisions for the benefit of disabled individuals and groups. A strong manifestation of developing Disability culture is the rapid development of Disability Studies programs in universities throughout the North America and Europe. Disability studies programs approach diversity similarly to ethnic studies programs and women's studies programs. Scholarly journals such as the *Disability Studies Quarterly* and the *Review of Disability Studies* provide a forum for critical analysis of disability in contemporary society.

Language to describe disability is a powerful determinant of perception so we will consider how language creates and fosters views of disability. We will also explore how evolving language is indicative of Disability culture. Traditionally, pejorative descriptors such as cripple, *in*valid, spastic, retard, imbecile, and handicap were common disability descriptors. These terms were used, not only to describe but to define disabled individuals. In recent decades, "person first" language was adopted as a means to value the lives of people with disabilities by placing people before their disability (e.g., person with deafness, person with paraplegia, person with mental retardation). Person first language has been used to describe disability as a problem individuals possess while not defining them by their disabilities.

The language of Disability culture and Disability pride challenges traditional disability views. For example, in Deaf culture, person first language has long been rejected. Instead, Deaf culture uses Deaf-first language and uses "big D" deaf to describe Deaf culture vs. "little d" deaf to describe deafness as a hearing impairment. Most in the deaf community reject terms such as "person with deafness" in favor of "deaf person." Being culturally Deaf is a source of identity and pride. In the non-Deaf disability community, one can often see the use of a big A disAbility to signify disability as diversity and to connote disability pride by emphasizing ability rather than *dis*ability.

This chapter adopts two approaches from Deaf culture. First, it uses "big D" Disability to discuss Disability culture and "little d" disability to describe disability as a characteristic or attribute. Second, it uses Disability first language rather than person first language. While person first language was an important step forward in validating the lives of disabled persons, this chapter assumes that the development of a rich disability culture signals that it is time to move beyond person first language. Arguably, person first language implies disability as pathology in the same way that describing a Black man as a "man with Blackness," or a female as a "person with femaleness," or a gay man as "person with homosexuality" would imply deficiency.

Culturally competent practice can be viewed as embracing five dimensions of knowledge and skills. First, social workers need to understand the social contexts in which disabled persons live. Disabled individuals live in a nondisabled world, and usually in nondisabled families and communities. Social workers need to recognize that disabled people are susceptible to, a) adopting the ableist attitudes of a nondisabled society, and b) that their nondisabled families may not buffer these attitudes. Exposure to disabled people and others who are disability positive creates social contexts to challenge ableist beliefs.

Exposing disabled persons to other disabled persons and allies aids social workers in helping disabled people develop alternate attitudes. This second element of cultural competence, helping disabled persons develop a positive disability identity, entails challenging disability stereotypes and replacing those stereotypical attitudes with disability positive perspectives.

A third element of Disability cultural competence involves language. Language evolution creates conundrums for social workers who strive to use politically correct language relative to disability and other diversities. Mackelprang and Salsgiver (2009) acknowledge the lack of universality in disability language and suggest that human service workers begin by ascertaining and using the descriptors utilized by the people with whom they work. Some prefer person first language while others utilize Disability first language. Still others may use other descriptors. Some people with characteristics that qualify for externally prescribed disability status do not consider themselves disabled and do not identify with disability community.

Within medical and professional settings, person first language is commonly used by disabled and nondisabled persons. For example, John might use a descriptor such as, "I have T 12 paraplegia," to describe his disability to a social worker. However, in describing disability from a diversity perspective, some disabled people are now eschewing person first language and adopting disability first language.

The fourth element of disability competent practice entails ascertaining and demonstrating respect for the disability perceptions of disabled participants. A common social work maxim is to "start where the client is." A better maxim, especially is it applies to disability might be, "start by learning where the client is." In working with disabled social work clients and colleagues, this learning begins with four components: a) what is the meaning of the disability to the person, b) does the person self-identify with a disability and with disability culture, c) how would connection to disabled persons and organizations benefit the person, and d) to what extent would it benefit the person to challenge his or her disability views?

Finally, social workers need to respect the disability perspectives and identities of participants. For example, some disabled persons may benefit from eschewing ableist attitudes but never self-identify as Disabled or even disabled. This is especially true for people who become disabled later in life. For example, elderly persons who become hard of hearing do not identify with Deaf or Disability culture and may not even self-identify as disabled. Culturally competent practitioners ascertain and respect how well participants' perceptions and attitudes are working for them.

ETHNIC AND DISABILITY VALUES ORIENTATIONS AND CULTURE

Culturally competent practice entails multiple identities and the intersection of these identities within society (Ridley, Baker, & Hill, 2001). Race and ethnicity influence people's attitudes about life and personal identity for both disabled and non disabled people. Racial and ethnic culture is a strong determinant of individual and group values. These values provide commonality of understanding and perceiving the world. Research by Kluckholm and Stodtbeck (1961), on ethnic and cultural groups in the United States, provided a foundation for value orientation theory that has been used as lens for viewing ethnic families in therapy (McGoldrick, 1982; McGoldrick, Pearce, & Giordano, 1982). Fernandez and Marini (1995) and Fernandez and Freer (1996) further expanded the values orientation framework to posit choices across ethnic groups and disabled persons in U.S. society. McGoldrick posits this theory as an eco-logically based taxonomy by which people from one ethnic background can gain an understanding of the orientations of people from differing backgrounds based on the five life dimensions listed below.

I.   Time: the temporal focus of human life

1.   Past: importance of personal and family history and prior learning
2.   Present: importance of here and now (one need not worry about tomorrow)
3.   Future: sacrificing today for an enhanced tomorrow

II.   Activity: preferred pattern of action in interpersonal relations

1.   Doing: emphasis on working hard, achieving to attain goals and rewards
2.   Being: taking life as it comes (it is enough to exist)
3.   Being in becoming: develop one's inner self, achieving self-actualization

III.   Relational: the preferred way of relating in groups

1.   Individual: self-determination and independence in thought and action
2.   Collateral: connecting with significant others to deal with life's issues
3.   Lineal/hierarchical: vertical, relying on leaders and followers

IV.   Humanity/nature: the ways people relate to nature or supernatural environments

1.   Harmony with nature: coexistence of people and nature
2.   Mastery over nature: seeking challenges to overcome or conquer
3.   Subjugation to nature: influence of external forces such as karma or a deity on life

V.   Basic nature of humanity: attitudes about the innate good or evil of human behavior

1.   Neutral/mixed: One is not born good or bad but is influenced by environment and life choices.
2.   Good: People are born inherently good and have a good basic nature.
3.   Evil: People are basically born corrupt and need redemption to change.

Table 16.1 provides a cultural lens through which to view ethnic groups and disabled persons. On the time dimension, African Americans' present orientation likely originated from slavery and continued as a consequence of racism and lack of opportunity. Native Americans' orientation to the present is a manifestation to their rhythmic and cyclical views of nature and life. In contrast, ancestral worship and connections to tradition leads to Asian Americans' past orientation, while Latino Americans' past orientation is influenced by a strong attention to family tradition and honor. The present orientation in Disability culture is related to the need to survive in the present and the lack of self-determination as a result of public policies and practices. This taxonomy suggests that culture affects first-, second-, and third-order choices for groups (Fernandez & Marini, 1995; Fernandez & Freer, 1996; Mackelprang & Salsgiver, 2009; McGoldrick, 1982; McGoldrick, Pearce, & Giordano, 1982). The first-order choices of value orientations of these groups are illustrated in table 16.1.

To ascertain the applicability of this taxonomy to individual clients, social workers engage in inductive processes. In culturally competent work with disabled persons, social workers engage in a mutual relationship to ascertain the meaning of disability and life with disability to the individual. It is especially important for social workers to understand how disability affects every day, lived experiences. For disabled persons who have been isolated from other disabled persons and from disability community, this exploration may provide an opportunity to learn that their experiences are shared by a larger community and may even connect them to Disability culture. For example, groups for youth born with spina bifida can provide an excellent mechanism for understanding common experiences and develop community. Commonly, people will begin to see how they have shared experiences with objectification of their bodies by health providers and ableism that limits their life choices. The sense of shared identity on the micro level is key in developing meso and macro policies and practices that lead to empowerment. The independent living movement and federally funded centers for independent living (CILs) in every state are illustrative. These centers must be governed and managed by a majority of disabled persons and provide an environment in which disabled people can go for support and mentoring. They provide a

TABLE 16.1 | First-Order Choices Across Ethnicities and Cultures

	European American	African American	Asian American	Hispanic American	Native American	Disabled Individuals
Time	Future	Present	Past-Present	Past-Present	Present	Present
Activity	Doing	Doing	Doing	Being in becoming	Being in becoming	Being
Relational	Individual	Collateral	Collateral	Collateral	Collateral	Individual
Person/Nature	Mastery	Harmony	Harmony	Harmony	Harmony	Subjugated
Basic Nature	Neutral	Neutral	Good	Neutral	Good	Good

sense of community. Concomitantly, these organizations are leaders in the disability rights movement, affecting policy on local, state, and federal levels. CILs are filled with disabled peers and are active at the micro-, meso-, and macro-levels. Social workers who wish to develop Disability cultural competence can utilize CILs as a resource. Often social workers are employed as independent living workers in these CILs.

HISTORICAL OPPRESSION AND CURRENT SOCIAL ISSUES

To understand perceptions in the US and the world contemporarily, we will consider the history of disability through the ages. From the first recorded history, disability was dreaded. Neolithic tribes believed disabilities were caused by evil spirits and performed skull surgeries to release these supernatural entities. Ancient Greeks believed disabled people were inhuman and the Greeks and subsequently the Romans abandoned disabled babies to die (Albrecht, 1992; DePoy & Gilson, 2004; Plato, 1991). Similarly, Persian society as long as 2500 years ago, envisaged a perfect world without disabled people (Miles, 2002). Ancient Hebrews banned disabled people from entering their holy temples and Jesus' disciples believed blindness was a punishment from deity; assuming a blind man was born blind because of sin.

Within Christian contexts throughout the last two millennia, disabilities were explained as resulting from phenomena such as sin, demonic possession, a curse from deity, or as a way for nondisabled people to achieve salvation. Sometimes disabled people have been thought of as having special powers and attributes (Mackelprang & Salsgiver, 2009; Snyder & Mitchell, 2006). In the middle ages, disabilities were explained as out of harmony with god and nature, and disabled people were often removed from society. Some, like lepers lived in isolated communities, others were institutionalized in subhuman conditions, and still others were cast out of communities to live in the countryside (Foucault, 2006).

The Enlightenment brought new ways of viewing people in society as an emphasis on rational inquiry began competing with moral explanations of disability. The Elizabethan Poor Laws defined disabled persons as "worthy" poor, in contrast to slackers and lazy people who were unworthy. As early as 1600, Sir Frances Bacon refuted moral explanations of disability. However, as noncontributors to societal economic well-being they were considered *in*valid. Acquired disabilities with obvious causes were more acceptable than the monstrosity associated with disabilities from birth (DePoy & Gilson, 2004). Disabled war veterans were provided special consideration because their disabilities were acquired in societal service.

Quetelet, a Belgian social statistician (1796–1874) was instrumental in developing rational explanations of disability. He applied mathematical concepts such as the normal curve to the human condition wherein the average man was the ideal. This provided a unifying framework in which people with disparate physical and mental attributes and atypicalities could be combined together as an identifiable abnormal group (Mackelprang & Salsgiver, 2009).

In the late 1880s Charles Darwin began challenging long held beliefs about the natural world. He posited that "natural selection" was a key to evolution in the biological world. However, his ideas gave rise to a new movement of Social Darwinism that advocated for social engineering to segregate and to limit the reproduction of undesirables to purify society (Wiggam, 1924). Social Darwinists developed the practice of eugenics that promoted policies such as sterilization of undesirables including non-Whites and disabled people. Alexis Carrel, a 1912 French Nobel Prize winner in medicine advocated for the "humane disposal" or euthanasia of people he considered physically and mentally defective (Carrel, 1935; Szasz, 1977) and in 1924, the U.S. Supreme Court decision *Buck vs. Bell* legitimized the forced sterilization of disabled people. Lifton (1986) recounts how American and European medical professions defined disability primarily as pain and suffering and advocated euthanasia, voluntary or otherwise, as a relief for disabled persons and to benefit and cleanse society.

The ultimate manifestation of Social Darwinism and eugenics occurred in Nazi Germany. The extermination of 6 million Jews is well known. What is less known is the fact that Hitler's minions perfected their killing techniques by exterminating between 75,000 and 200,000 disabled Germans in their Tiergartenstrasse 4 (T4) program. Before Franz Stangl became commandant of the infamous Sobibor and Treblinka extermination camps, he perfected his genocide skills at Hartheim, a hospital that the T4 program converted into an extermination center for the disabled (Garscha & Kuretsidis-Haider, 1997). Yet, as Longmore recounts, the Nuremburg war crimes judges avoided dealing with the mass genocide of disabled persons because they were a substantial burden to society and life was, "probably of little comfort to them... In other words, while genocide of Jews was a war crime, extermination of disabled people was tough minded mercy" (p. 153).

It is only in recent decades that pervasively accepted pathology based views of disability have been challenged. Disabilty rights advocates have been influenced by other marginalized groups who have rejected racist, sexist, attitudes and fought for their rights. Disabled people have much in common with other groups that have been similarly devalued, marginalized, and discriminated against. Marginalization and discrimination based on characteristics such as race and ethnicity is somewhat fluid and dependent on society and cultural contexts. For example, Mexican Americans have been subjected to widespread racism in the United States; however, in Mexico they are a majority. Attitudes toward Japanese Americans have changed dramatically over the last seven decades when they were incarcerated in concentration camps during World War II. Contemporarily, Arab and Muslim Americans contend with racism and religious discrimination; however, they also have rich cultural heritages. In contrast, Groce (1999) contends that disability is considered pathological in almost all known societies.

Disabled people and allies are challenging ableist societal attitudes and embracing their diversity. They have recognized that their primary problems stem from discrimination rather than their internal problems. This alternate view is that disability contributes to people's strengths and life choices. Consider, for example, Stephen Hawking, universally considered one of the greatest physicists of our time. He has lived with ALS, a progressive neuromuscular condition that has resulted in quadriplegia. He is considered successful "in spite" of his disability. However, in reading his account of his life, it becomes clear that internal strengths and positive external factors were more important than his internal impairments. "I have had motor neurone disease for practically all my adult life. Yet it has not prevented me from having a very attractive family, and being successful in my work." (Hawking, n.d.). Rather than defining his disability only as a tragedy, one might ask how his condition may have guided his positive life decisions, events and actions relative to marriage, family, and career. Justin Dart (1930–2002), a champion of the Americans with Disabilities Act and a civil rights advocate, credits his polio, as a teenager, as the event that made his life worth living. For Dart and others, disability proved to be an important determinant in leading a productive and happy life. Just as being Black contributed to the life experiences and success of leaders such as Martin Luther King and Barack Obama, being disabled contributed to the leadership of disability rights leaders such as Justin Dart, Ed Roberts, and Judy Heumann. And, even though Franklin D. Roosevelt hid his disability, he was elected New York governor and President of the United States after acquiring his disability from polio.

The disability rights movement arose in the wake of the turbulent 1960s. In a few short decades it has spread worldwide. The 1990 Americans with Disabilities Act (ADA) was revolutionary in its framing of disability as a civil rights issue (Mackelprang and Salsgiver, 2009). While the Civil Rights Act of 1964 prohibited discrimination in employment, school, and housing based on race, sex, national origin, or religion, people with disabilities were excluded from these protections. Subsequent laws such as the Rehabilitation Act of 1973 prohibited disability discrimination in federal agencies and organizations and those with federal contracts; however, private enterprises such as movie theaters, retail establishments, and telecommunication companies were free to exclude disabled people—and many did exactly that. However, ADA acknowledged that 43 million disabled Americans were subject to discrimination and included provisions to protect their civil rights.

The U.S. is not alone in its pursuing disability rights categorically. As early as 1975, France enacted Law 75–534 that made disability integration a national obligation (IDEAnet, 2003a). Argentina (2007) passed a disability rights law in 1981; Australia in 1992; Jordan (DREDF, 2006) in 1993; Chile (IDEAnet, 2004a) in 1994; United Kingdom (IDEAnet, 2003b), Hong Kong (Peterson, 2005), India (IDEAnet, 2005), Russia (IDEAnet, 2003c), and Bolivia (IDEAnet, 2004c) in 1995. Other countries such as Canada, Ghana, and South Africa have included disability in general protections rather than categorically. Canada's 1982 Charter of Rights and Freedoms includes disability along with all other diverse groups. Similarly, the constitutions of Ghana (1992) and South Africa (1996) treat discrimination universally with disability as one of multiple groups that must be treated fairly and without discrimination in society.

In recent decades, efforts to end disability discrimination and devaluation have been emphasized in international communities. In 1981, the United Nations declared the International Year of Disabled Persons and followed this up with the International Decade of Disabled Persons (1983–92). Multiple regions such as Africa (2000–09), Asia and the Pacific (1993–2002 and 2003–12), and Arab countries (2003–12) have also declared Decades of Disabled persons.

VALUES AND ETHICAL DILEMMAS

As a profession, social work has a rather checkered history with people with disabilities. Social work, along with other health and human service professions have been agents of social control over people with disabilities in institutions and agencies. And, while social work pioneers such as Jane Addams embraced diverse racial and ethnic groups, disability has been excluded from this diversity framework. Consider, for example, the 1992 *Curriculum Policy Statement* of the Council of Social Work Education. In this document that guided social work curricula in the U.S., programs could organize curricula around population groups (e.g., race, ethnicity, women) or problem areas (e.g., sexism, racism, disability). Note that disability and not ableism was defined as a problem area along with problems such as racism and sexism while other "vulnerable groups" were included in populations. Social work education has evolved significantly over the last two decades. In the early 1990s an informal disability task force was created in 1996, was afforded sanction as the Commission on Disability and Persons with Disabilities joining CSWE's other three "diversity commissions" on women, race and ethnicity, and sexual orientation and identity. Later, CSWE bylaws changes eliminated these four diversity commissions in favor of an overall diversity commission; with the four former diversity commissions having distinct councils under the overarching diversity commission. The 2008 CSWE Educational Policy and Accreditation Standards also address disability as a component of diversity, stating.

> Social workers understand how diversity characterizes and shapes the human experience and is critical to the formation of identity. The dimensions of diversity are understood as the intersectionality of multiple factors including age, class, color, culture, disability, ethnicity, gender, gender identity and expression, immigration status, political ideology, race, religion, sex, and sexual orientation. Social workers appreciate that, as a consequence of difference, a person's life experiences may include oppression, poverty, marginalization, and alienation as well as privilege, power, and acclaim (pp. 4-5).

These new policies place disability within the context of diversity. Further, it recognizes the social and societal factors that can negatively impact disabled people's lives. The National Association of Social Workers' approach to disability has been more ambivalent. Its publications include disability but they often address disability from a medical model perspective rather than a diversity framework. For at least a decade, disabled social workers have advocated for the NASW Board of Directors to apply a diversity based approach to disability. Yet, the 2009 NASW Diversity and Equity website (http://www.socialworkers.org/diversity/default.asp) continues to addresses sex, race and ethnicity, and sexual orientation, and NASW supports commissions to address each. However, disability continues to be absent. The 2008 Code of Ethics includes disability stating, "social workers should not practice, condone, facilitate, or collaborate with any form of discrimination on the basis of race, ethnicity, national origin, color, sex, sexual orientation, age, marital status, political belief, religion, or *mental or physical disability*". This designation medicalizes disability into two diagnostic categories rather than as an identity or characteristic. Further, it excludes major segments of the disability community such as those with sensory (e.g., hearing, visual) and cognitive disabilities. It also adopts the extant allopathic medical paradigm that separates the mental from the physical. The NASW Cultural Competence Indicators (2006) also shows ambivalence toward disability. It repeatedly uses terms such as "physical or mental disability," and one section excludes disability from its definition of cultural competence; replacing disability with "physical and mental abilities" (p. 8). However, in another section, it states, "The term culture includes ways in which people with disabilities or people from various religious backgrounds or people who are gay, lesbian, or transgender experience the world around them" (p. 10). The extant policy manual *Social Work Speaks* (NASW, 2009) offers the most inclusive approach to disability to date in that it, "advocates a national policy that ensures the rights of people with disabilities to participate fully and equitably in society," (p. 249) and "the inclusion of social workers with disabilities in all areas of the professional organization" (p. 250).

CULTURAL AWARENESS

A major crux of this text is that self evaluation and an understanding of one's own culture or cultures is essential for social workers to develop cultural competence in work with others. It is especially important for social workers from backgrounds of majority and/or power to understand the experiences of minority and/or non-empowered groups. Racial and ethnic majority and minority cultures vary from locale to locale; however, disability and disabled people are universally a minority, nonpower group. Thus, three models of disability are omnipresent in countries and cultures worldwide. As you learn about the three disability models, consider how your culture has influenced your embedded beliefs. As you do so, think about how your culture assumes the validity of these disability explanations.

The *moral* model of disability is as old as recorded human history. This model assumes that disability is unnatural and is out of order with nature. Within religious contexts, disability may be seen as a curse, test, or blessing from deity. Other cultures view it as a karmic problem. Contemporarily, in the U.S. the moral model is manifest by perceptions that keep disabled people institutionalized to mitigate their threat to society. In some cultures within Tanzania, discrimination against albinos has resulted in multiple murders in recent years (United Nations Radio, 2009) in the effort to procure their body parts for special powers that can bring economic wealth and luck. Fear, disgust, and pity are common feelings associated with the medical model.

By the mid-1800s, the *medical model* of disability emerged as a competing model to the moral model. The medical model is based on reason and rational thought and eschews moral explanations in favor of scientific and empirical explanations that explain disability as deviance that can be treated by professionals. Initially, there was misdirected optimism that those who were considered *abnormal* could be fixed and made *normal*. In modern capitalist society, individual and group worth is determined by industrial and financial productivity, and disabled people are considered among the least productive in society. Ironically, social work, medicine and other helping professions rely on caring for, serving, and working with disabled people—who often live in poverty—to maintain our middle and upper middle class lives.

The medical and moral models of disability give rise to ableism, the belief that disability is inferior, which in turn, produces disability stereotypes. Mackelprang and Salsgiver (2009) discuss several disability stereotypes that are articulated below, along with examples of each. As you read these, consider which combination of moral and medical models are inherent with each stereotype.

Perpetual children: Jerry Lewis telethons seek money for "Jerry's kids" and Jerry's kids are "kids" regardless of age.

Pitiable objects: Consider the film *Million Dollar Baby* in which euthanizing a disabled person is glorified.

Heroes: One of the most common stereotypes, disabled people are portrayed as "overcoming" great odds or for accomplishments "in spite of" their disability.

Menaces or threats to society: Mass media is full of examples of the "retarded" and the "mentally ill" who commit violent crimes. In reality, disabled people are much more likely to be victimized by others.

Sick: Common language such as "confined to a wheelchair," "afflicted with cerebral palsy," and "mental illness" reflect this stereotype.

Burdens to society: Eugenics and the Nazi extermination program are based on this stereotype. U.S. laws provide subsistence support for disabled persons while making it difficult for them obtain gainful employment.

Ugly and sexless: Forced sterilization was widespread during much of the 20th Century.

Incompetent: Throughout much of the 20th century, physicians and social workers routinely encouraged parents to institutionalize their children with Down syndrome because they would never be able to function in society. (Contemporarily, deinstitutionization has demonstrated that these children function in schools and in mainstream society.)

Curse from God: AIDS has killed millions of people worldwide, yet HIV was largely ignored by the U.S. government for years because it affected gay men. This disability was perceived as a punishment for immoral acts. Not coincidentally, the first federal HIV/AIDS legislation was passed in 1996 bears the name of a hemophiliac "innocent victim" Ryan White who acquired it from the blood of the guilty.

Freak: Circus shows have routinely charged patrons to view their freaks; people with atypical characteristics.

The *social/minority model* of disability is a constructive alternative to traditional models of disability. To engage in Disability culturally competent practice, social workers need to understand the concept that disability is an element of diversity "Whereas, traditional moral and medical paradigms define the nature of disability in terms of individual deficiencies and the biology of the disability... the social/minority model focuses on society, its beliefs, and resulting discrimination" (Mackelprang & Salsgiver, 2009, p. 17). Meyerson (1990) contends that, as a minority group, disabled people have been denied civil rights. Fine and Asch (1993) contend that the problems facing disabled persons must be viewed in the context of disability as a minority group who are subjected to pervasive discrimination. In contrast to traditional models, the social/minority model suggests that, rather than fixing individuals, eliminating discrimination and removing societal barriers to equal access are the primary ways to improve lives. By reconsidering cultural assumptions and redefining life with a disability, social workers begin to understand the lives of disabled persons, thus increasing our ability to practice in a culturally competent manner.

KNOWLEDGE ACQUISITION

A review of several theories of human behavior in the social environment demonstrates the consistent place of disability in multiple societies. Developmental theorists such as Freud, Erickson, and Piaget approach disability as deficiency and pathology. Development is addressed from a nondisability perspective and atypical characteristics are explained as barriers to adequate development. Never are the potential benefits of disability considered.

Social Darwinists placed nondisabled, Caucasian males at the apex of the evolutionary chain with non-Whites and disabled people designated as inferior (Snyder & Mitchell, 2006; Wiggam, 1924). Marx contended that the presence of disabled people in industrial society was indicative of the inherent corruption of capitalism (Marx & Engels, 1848). Capitalist societies place value on people according to their economic output while making it difficult for disabled people to work. For example, in the U.S., disabled people are often forced to rely on Medicaid to pay for health care costs. To qualify for Medicaid, one must be impoverished, yet without universal health care, people who are disabled are unable to work because they would lose Medicaid, would have no access to health care through employment, and would have no ability to pay the exorbitant costs to obtain private insurance.

Feminists have also treated disability harshly. Early feminists such as Charlotte Perkins Gilman and Margaret Sanger treated disability as a scourge (Snyder & Mitchell, 2006). Disabled feminist scholars contend that feminists have largely ignored disabled women—and men (Lloyd, 1992; Morris, 1992). Waldschmidt (2006) points out that feminism has advocated for women's reproductive rights while ignoring problems such as genetic selection. These scholars suggest that disabled voices are needed to prevent reproductive rights becoming a modern form of eugenics. Garland-Thomson (2002) presents a civil rights based framework for integrating disability and feminist theories, articulating four parallel mechanisms for women and disabled individuals: a) both are non-normative and deficient; b) appearance and the medicalization of women's and disabled bodies; c) cultural stereotypes consigning both to dependent roles; and d) commonalties in activism for women and disabled people.

Disabled people and homosexuals share a common history of widespread "pathologization." Homosexuality has been celebrated in some societies such as ancient Greece; however, contemporarily homosexual acts are considered a capital offense in some Middle Eastern countries. Homosexuals were incarcerated and exterminated in Nazi Germany. Canada sanctions marriage between gay men and lesbians; however, in the U.S., gay/lesbian marriages have recently been rejected by voters in several states. In 2009, Uganda introduced legislation to make homosexual acts a capital offense. Major religions such as Christianity, Judaism, Islam, and Baha'i define disability and homosexuality using the moral model. Despite commonalties between the two groups, gay and disability communities have remained separate. For example, American Sign Language has heterosexist and pejorative signs for gays and lesbians. Simon LeVay's research on brain differences and sexual orientation was criticized by gay rights advocates who, "accused him of legitimizing the argument that homosexuality is a biologically based disability" (Mackelprang & Salsgiver, 2009, p. 58). In recent years, connections have been made between the two groups. McRuer (2006) articulates shared cultural connections between queerness and disability. Colligan (2004) describes intersections between disability and queer theory. Onken and Mackelprang (1997) discuss similarities in the process of "coming out" for disabled people and gays/lesbians. They note that, unlike people from other diverse backgrounds, disabled people and LGBTs are usually raised as minorities in their own homes and communities.

There are multiple, and often conflicting explanations of race and ethnicity. As discussed, eugenicist and ethnocentric explanations have defined the white, Caucasian race as superior and non-White as inferior (Snyder & Mitchell, 2006; Wiggam, 1924). Geneticists like Cavelli-Sforza (2000) explain that the world's five primary genetic groups—African, Ocenaic, Asian, European, and American—arose from the African diaspora over the last 50,000–100,000 years. However, most contemporary geneticists also contend that the genetic differences within populations are greater than they are between the five genetic groups (Foster & Sharp, 2005; Krieger, 2005). The American Anthropological Association (1988) approaches race and ethnicity from a social constructionist perspective stating,

> Historical research has shown that the idea of "race" has always carried more meanings that mere physical differences; indeed, physical variations in the human species have no meaning except the social ones that humans put on them... The ideology magnified the differences among Europeans, Africans, and Indians, established a rigid hierarchy of socially exclusive categories underscored and bolstered unequal rank and status differences, and provide the rationalization that the inequality was natural or God-given.

Parallel to racism, *ableism* is the belief that atypicalities from "normal" are inherently inferior. Concomitantly, eugenics and other racist ideologies define non-White as defective or disabled. Non-White and disabled stereotypes include sloth and laziness, hypersexuality, and impulsiveness. In other words, racial and ethnic minorities are considered de facto disabled. "Racist and ableist connections of 'inferior' races to disability have motivated a disconnection between ethnic identity and disability" (Mackelprang & Salsgiver, 2009, pp. 59–60). Lukin (2006) contends that racism and ableism are parallel phenomena and argues that the civil rights and the disability rights movements would both benefit from identifying commonalities and working together. A major benefit of this collaboration is that disabled people will be better able to claim their dual identities. It is also important to recognize and reject internalized ableism and racism that lead people to devaluing themselves.

SKILL DEVELOPMENT

As discussed in previous sections, social work as a profession has begun the process of evolving away from a pathology-based view of disability that is necessary for disability competent practice. "For the social work profession to operationalize cardinal social work values, such as respecting the inherent worth of all persons and the right to self-determination, social workers must strive to eliminate discrimination and to work with persons with disabilities (rather than on their behalf). This means allying ourselves with disability advocates as well as including persons with disabilities as equals and embracing them as members of the profession. As we do this, the profession will be strengthened, just as it has been strengthened by embracing other diverse groups" (Mackelprang, 2002). This challenge applies to individual practitioners as well as the profession as a whole. This section addresses intervention with disabled persons. First, the process of intervention is discussed. Then, attitudes toward disability and disabled persons is addressed.

SOCIAL WORK INTERVENTION PRACTICES

Social work practice with disabled persons begins with assessment and evaluation that can be parsed into three components: a) what, b) so what, and c) now what. Figure 16.1 provides an assessment and evaluation tool for this work as outlined by Mackelprang and Salsgiver (2009, p.395).

Social work assessment begins with *what*: learning about people, situations, and histories. *So what* assesses and provides meaning to this information, and *now what* involves the plans to intervene with the person on the person's behalf. Historic and contemporary information derived from the *what* section must inform the *so what* section of an evaluation. Practitioners develop assessments and plans based on historical and contemporary information. Consequently, the *now what* interventions arise directly from assessments. Intervention plans entail both outputs—activities to be engaged in, and outcomes—expected and hoped for results of work together.

Assessment can be divided into three domains. The *biosocial* domain joins human biology and biological function with social contexts. For example, the biological characteristic of being female is the same worldwide; however, the biosocial implications of being female vary widely between the U.S. and Afghanistan. In the U.S., fifty years ago, children with Down syndrome were routinely institutionalized whereas today they are raised in family environments. Social work's expertise is in the *psychosocial* domain of assessment which involves people's living conditions, family environment, and communities and their psychological and emotional characteristics and coping mechanisms. Finally, the *social-structural* domain involves societal values, laws, policies, and institutional structures and the interchange between these macro elements of society and the lives of individuals and groups. The social structural domain supports and is supported by dominant culture (Mackelprang & Salsgiver, 2009). The use of ethnographic interviewing provides social workers a bridge to understanding the lives of disabled people in nondisabled society.

Assessments give rise to engagement and interventions. There are several elements to culturally competent disability practice and we will discuss them in the context of four roles (Mackelprang & Salsgiver, 2009).

WHAT?

IDENTIFYING INFORMATION (age, gender, ethnicity, residence, etc.)
Reason for admission, clinic visit, or agency involvement
Reason for referral to social work

FAMILY BACKGROUND
Family of origin or childhood
Current relationships
Adult family and significant others
Living situation—past, present, and anticipated

SOCIAL HISTORY
Educational history
Work history (including military background)
Friends—relationships
Cultural influences
Places of residence
Substance use history
Legal involvement

FINANCIAL STATUS
Income, expenses, obligations
Insurance—medical coverage and needs

PSYCHOSOCIAL SITUATION
Cognitive status
Emotional/psychosocial status
Psychiatric—mental health history
Family reactions, relationships, support, and adjustments
Sexuality concerns (e.g., questions, orientation, problems)
Judgment/planning—behavioral situation
Other relevant issues

TOOLS
Genogram
Ecomap

SO WHAT?

IMPRESSIONS
Personal strengths and limitations
Social supports
Resources

NOW WHAT?

PLANS
Counseling and direct services—individual and significant others
Social interventions, planning, advocacy
Micro, meso, macro interventions
Anticipated outcomes

FIGURE 16.1 | ASSESSMENT AND EVALUATION TOOL

Competent social workers are capable of engaging as counselors: a role that might include, but is not to be confused with psychotherapist. In a manner similar to that described by Solomon (1976) with African Americans, social workers sensitize disabled persons to how oppression affects their lives and help them begin to see their characteristics in a positive light (Blotzer & Ruth, 1995). Counselors help people with both individual life problems and coping skills (Wright, 1983) as well as develop the personal strengths and social advocacy skills to overcome devaluation and marginalization. Counselors promote empowerment by helping people to reject ableist attitudes and to develop the skills to navigate their lives in ableist communities and society.

A second social work skill entails the role of teacher/consultant. This role involves strong emphasis on common social and community factors affecting disabled people's lives and teaching them to reject dependency and isolation that are forced on them by society. It includes teaching people about the guilt and shame that are commonly associated with disability. It involves consulting with participants on how to change their expectations and demanding their personal rights to fully participate in society. For example, deaf people have the same right to telecommunication afforded to nondisabled people. This access is not a privilege or something special for which they should be indebted to other's largesse. As another example, people with physical disabilities who require assistance with activities of daily living deserve to determine who provides their attendant care. However, this control is commonly given to home health agencies and medical providers and disabled people are required to accept care from people over which they have little control. Teachers/consultants help individuals and groups develop self-advocacy skills to assume control over who provides personal care and the care they provide. This role also involves skill development. It may involve teaching people how to manage personal care attendants, use public transportation, and assertively interview for employment. Social workers can use role models, peer mentors, educational and support groups, and other resources to facilitate this process.

A third element of culturally competent practice involves the role of social broker. Social workers can identify societal resources and engage participants in a collaborative process to gain access to those resources. This involves knowledge of community organizations and institutional policies. Brokering involves helping people acquire resources as well as helping them develop personal brokering skills. Meso- and macro-level practitioners can also broker by working with individuals and groups by connecting them with organizations and communities to promote access. Social brokers utilize a variety of skills including community organization, policy planning, and mediation.

A fourth element of competent practice involves social workers as policy advocates and political advocates; and sometimes activists. This role bridges the personal and the political. It moves activities from case to cause and back to case. For example, disability rights activists joined with social workers and others to influence Congress to enact the 1990 ADA. In recent years, physically disabled people who were forced to rely on medical agencies have obtained the right to hire and manage the employment of personal care attendants. Disability competent social work practitioners recognize the need to promote disability rights; not only on the personal level but at the institutional and policy levels. Policy and political advocacy also includes challenging agency and organizational policies and practices as well as local, state, and national policies that devalue disabled people and groups.

Self-Assessment

Racial and ethnic cultural competence are universal values within social work profession because culturally competent practice with disabled persons is only now emerging. Thus, it is important for social workers to evaluate our personal attitudes to assure our assessments and interventions are relevant and effective. It will also promote the use of reliable and valid evidence based practice evaluation. To assess one's ability to work with disabled people, both individually and as a group, it may be helpful to engage in personal assessment along the following knowledge and attitude dimensions.

LEARNING (NOT STARTING) WHERE THE PARTICIPANT (NOT THE CLIENT) IS

Practitioners should develop an understanding of their lives and the meaning of disability for their disabled participants. The term participant rather than client is used here to signify the assumption of a partnership rather than a hierarchical professional-client relationship.) Developmentally, the age at which one's disability is acquired is significant. People born with disabilities or who acquire them in early childhood have no recollection of a life without a disability. Yet, unlike children from racially and ethnically diverse backgrounds who are raised in concordant families and communities, disabled children and youth are usually raised in nondisabled environments in which loved ones have little previous disability experience and are ill equipped to provide disability mentoring. Often, families and loved ones carry the ableist attitudes of mainstream society. Disabled children and their families can benefit greatly from exposure to positive disability role models and mentors. They may also need guidance as they obtain disability related resources and supports.

Youth and adults who acquire disabilities may experience concomitant, significant changes in family roles, education and employment, and in community mobility. They have developed pre-disability self-concepts but their identities may need to change to adapt to their new realities. Naturally, they may experience loss and grief, especially if they have been raised to believe disability stereotypes and life with a disability. Media like *Million Dollar Baby* and *Whose Life is it Anyway* have perpetrated the attitude that disability is worse than death. Social workers may have to help people maximize their pre-disability coping skills while helping them reject stereotypes that portray disability as a catastrophe.

The older a person is at the onset of an acquired disability, the less likely the individual is to adopt a disability identity. For example, social workers who work in the field of aging routinely work with people with acquired disabilities but who do not see themselves as disabled. It is not our task to impose a disability positive identity on participants. Instead, we can learn the meaning of an attribute, impairment or disability to the person, assess with them how well their beliefs are working for them, and develop interventions to facilitate positive outcomes.

PERSONAL ATTITUDES

Effective practice entails an evaluation of one's professional and personal beliefs. While college campuses and social work education routinely emphasize the importance of valuing diversity, more often than not, disability is treated as an at-risk group but rarely as diverse. The perception that people with disability have been devalued and marginalized is common. However, the second dimension, that disabled people are important contributors to a diverse society, is less accepted.

DISABILITY COMPETENT PRACTICE IN PROFESSIONAL CONTEXT

Social workers are ethically obligated to consider employing organizations in professional practice. In most social work settings, disabled patients and clients are defined by their personal problems and social workers are employed to intervene, treat, and ameliorate these problems. In settings such as mental health centers and special education, people's disabilities qualify them for the individual treatment and services that justify their social workers' employment. Interventions are usually devoted to helping people find solutions to problems such as unemployment, adjustment reactions, mental health difficulties, poverty, and social isolation. However, in addition to individual interventions typically mandated by employers, social workers are also responsible to change the agency practices, social policies, and societal conditions that lead to these problems.

INDIVIDUAL DIGNITY AND WORTH, AND SELF-DETERMINATION

Social work is distinctive among helping professions in our emphasis on self-determination and individual worth whereas, in contrast, medicine and nursing emphasize the principle of "doing no harm" above all. Social workers consider our relationships with those with whom we work (e.g., clients, patients, participants) as our primary responsibility, whereas public health considers "the public" in general as its primary "client." In working with disabled people, social workers must work to keep the locus of control with individuals to the extent possible. Social workers start with the assumption that people are competent and assume control only when absolutely necessary rather than making decisions on clients' or patients' behalf or for their own good. Similarly, our responsibility to our disabled clients/participants is primary. When employers and sanctioning organizations enforce ableist policies, we have a responsibility to facilitate change.

INVEST IN DISABILITY

The agencies and organizations in which social workers are most often employed provide "services" to clients, patients, families, communities and other constituents. However, service has a variety of meanings that depend on social policies, contexts in which one works, and the attitudes and actions of social workers providing services. *Charity service* is the most common approach used to serve disabled people from ancient to contemporary times. From almsgiving to charitable organizations, charity is given to help those who are disadvantaged. Contemporarily, Medicaid and Supplemental Security Disability Income are the largest charity services for disabled people in the U.S. *Control service* is a form of service in which social control is exercised over clients along with services they receive. Psychiatric hospitals and institutions that house the "mentally retarded" are two examples of social control service. They provide services but also protect society. *Benefit service* is a third type of service in which recipients have earned the service. Medicare and Veterans' benefits are two examples. Recipients are seen as deserving service based on their actions such as serving in the military or working, contributing to the economy, and paying taxes. *Investment service* is a service that is provided for recipients with the expectation of receiving a future benefit for providing the service. For example, public universities operate with the support of state funding. Students receive educational service with the expectation that will become employed, use their expertise to benefit society, and their taxes to contribute to the economy.

As you read about the services below, consider the policies and societal attitudes that guide the services provided. Which of the four service areas do each traditionally fit.

1. Giving a donation to the muscular dystrophy telethon.
2. Donating to your alma mater.
3. Volunteering for a free dental clinic.
4. Providing dental care for a military man and his family.
5. Public education for children 5–18 years of age.
6. Early intervention from birth for a child with Down syndrome.
7. Working for a free health care clinic.
8. Working for an employee assistance program.
9. Providing a wheelchair for a child with cerebral palsy.
10. Providing prosthetic legs for a veteran who lost her legs from an IED.
11. Working in a sheltered workshop for people with intellectual disabilities.
12. Supervising medical students in clinical rotations.
13. Teaching in a school of social work.
14. Coaching Special Olympics.
15. Coaching high school soccer
16. Working in a state agency that helps parents of disabled children qualify for SSDI.
17. Working for the Social Security Administration helping retirees receive SSA benefits.
18. Working at a student housing complex.
19. Working in an institution housing intellectually disabled children and adults.
20. Advanced placement math and science courses for high school students.
21. Special education classroom for students with learning disabilities.

Each of the situations above may fit multiple categories of service. However, disabled people are much more likely than nondisabled people to receive *charity services* and *control services.* Nondisabled people are more likely to receive *invest-ment services* and *benefit services.* The former are far more likely to be stigmatized, professionally controlled, and minimally resourced than the latter. Disability rights advocates blame modern professions, including social work, for promulgating paternalistic welfare and social service systems based on the assumption that disabled people are abnormal and irresponsible (Longmore, 2003; TenBroek & Matson, 1959), thus requiring charity and control services.

Disability competent social work practice requires a change in attitude from charity service to investment service. For example, in recent years some progress has been made with the deinstitutionalization. Community-based services for infants with Down's and their families that have demonstrated that people with Down's do not need to live their lives controlled and institutionalized. The next step will need to encompass invest in children as future contributors. As society invests in children with intellectual disabilities and their families, they will have greater opportunities to grow and contribute to society. Whereas traditional social service agencies have maintained social control over disabled people, federal law mandates centers for independent living (CILs) that operate in every state be governed and administered by disabled people. CILs invest in disabled people and honor their self-determination. They operate with the assumption communities and society is enriched by integrating people with disabilities.

Social workers often work in organizations that provide charity and control services as elements of their missions or mandates. Even in these organizations, social workers can honor disabled people by utilizing an investment approach that recognizes their individual and collective worth, maximizes self determination, and facilitates their empowerment. On meso- and macro-levels, social workers can advocate for social policies and agency practices that recognize the value of disability and invest in disabled people. Social workers should generally eschew charity service. Though control service may be necessary in some situations social workers should work to maximize self-determination, using social control only when necessary. Societal investment in disability will result in a return on investment that reciprocally benefits society.

SOCIAL AND ECONOMIC JUSTICE RESOLUTION

As a profession, social work has readily treated disability as an at-risk population. In fact, through our employing organizations such as mental health agencies, medical and mental health hospitals, child welfare agencies, institutions housing disabled people, and other service agencies, social workers serve more disabled people than any other human service profession. However, the profession is routinely perceived in negative and controlling terms by disabled people and disability activists. As Longmore (2003) states,

> So pervasive are the deficiencies of disabled people, so omni-incompetent are we, that an array of professionals with many kinds of expertise must superintend our lives. These arrangements force many people with disabilities to remain as permanent clients of, not must one, but many programs and agencies (p. 242–43).

Social work's commitment to diversity has been manifest in the ways that the profession has embraced diverse, underrepresented groups. The profession started out primarily with middle class Caucasians serving economically disadvantaged and ethnically diverse groups. Very quickly, the profession brought people from these diverse groups into the professional fold to serve people from groups from which they come and to enhance the profession. Social work has embraced marginalized people and groups such as women, people from diverse racial and ethnic backgrounds, and gays, lesbians, bisexuals and transgendered persons as full participants in the profession. When disabled people are similarly embraced as students, colleagues, and even supervisors, social work will be enriched by our contributions and life perspectives.

The primary problems facing disabled people today are problems related to social justice and *not* to individual pathology. Socially just social work practice with individuals, groups and families entails the following dimensions.

1. Removing barriers to housing, employment, education, health care, recreation, etc. will reduce the societal burden of disability far more effectively than charity and institutionalization.

2. Disabled people should be assumed as competent and as experts over their own lives. Too often, society treats disabled people as though they are incapable. Self-determination is a cardinal social justice matter and should be wrested from disabled persons only in the most dire of circumstances.

3. Social and economic service systems should be based on investing in disabled people and not in providing them with charity service.

4. Disabled people have the same rights and societal worth as nondisabled people. Just like nondisabled people, disabled individuals are interdependent on others. And while some physically disabled people may not be physically independent, they do have the right of self-determination to direct their personal care. Similarly, individuals with intellectual disabilities may not be able to fully manage their finances but they can choose who helps them with their finances and they have the right to maximal self-determination.

5. Disabled people have the right to live in the community and not in institutions. Nursing facilities house many disabled persons because less expensive resources are unavailable in communities. In the U.S., prisons and jails are a primary mechanism of social control over up to 300,000 people with mental health disabilities. This, in large measure, is a result of inadequate community resources (Human Rights Watch, 2003).

6. Self-control and social justice will be promoted as organizations that follow the social model, such as centers for independent living, are supported and legitimized. Professional organizations such as NASW should partner with disability rights based organizations to promote rights based approaches.

7. Social policies and organizational policies should promote the roles of people with disabilities as experts, advocates, and role models.

CASE STUDY 1

Tom is a 27-year-old Native American male with T 10 paraplegia as a result of an automobile accident at age 19. He was born and raised on a rural reservation where he continues to live today. His residence is 10 miles from the nearest town. Tom's auto accident occurred when his car left the rural road on which he was driving and crashed into a tree. It was 5 hours before he was found by another passing motorist.

Tom was flown by helicopter to an urban trauma center where he underwent spinal stabilization surgery followed by 6 weeks of inpatient rehabilitation. While hospitalized, a psychiatric consult was ordered when he began relating tales of spiritual vision that occurred while trapped in his car as well as spiritual manifestations subsequent to the accident. He was diagnosed as having a schizoaffective disorder, with symptoms precipitated by the trauma of his injuries.

Tom worked in building construction prior to his accident. Since his accident, he has been unemployed and he has relied on Medicaid and Supplemental Security Income for his economic needs. He uses tribal housing, so his rent is minimal. He has no vehicle so he relies on family and friends for transportation who are also his primary social contacts. He spends much of his time around his home and watching television and using the Internet. Tribal public healthcare worker, including a social worker, periodically visit Tom.

Answer the following questions based on the beliefs and attitudes you have held relative to disability and diversity.

1. Which would you more likely use to describe Tom's mobility status: "Tom is confined to a wheelchair," or "Tom uses a wheelchair for mobility."? Which of these terms implies a medical model approach? Which implies a social model approach?
2. Within formal service systems, Tom's diagnosis of schizoaffective disorder has stuck with him since his hospitalization. However, his peers value him for his spiritual gifts.
   - What are the cultural implications of this diagnosis?
   - How might this diagnosis reflect embedded ethnocentrism in mainstream medical systems?

- How might assumptions about disability reflect ableist attitudes in mainstream medical systems?
- What are the implications of Tom's dual diagnosis of paraplegia and "mental illness" relative to employment and other societal resources that would promote independence?
- What are the implications of Tom's diagnoses relative to social justice and cardinal social work values such as individual worth and dignity and self-determination?

3. Below are several statements relative to employment. How would you be most likely and least likely explain Tom's employment status? How do you think society would explain this?
   - "Tom is unemployed because he is disabled."
   - "Tom is unemployed because unemployment on reservations is rampant."
   - "Tom is unemployed because social policies punish disabled people who work."
   - "Tom is unemployed because he has no independent transportation."
4. How reflective are the following statements of extant social disability policies? To what extent do each of these reflect a commitment to social justice?
   - Society has a responsibility to provide charity benefits for its disabled poor.
   - As a disabled person, Tom is one of the worthy poor that society has a responsibility to care for.
   - All people, including disabled persons should have an opportunity to contribute to society.
   - Society benefits from the full participation of all its members.
5. Assume a social work admissions committee was considering Tom's admission to a BSW program. On a scale of 1-10 and based on your experiences, estimate the weight you believe a committee at your social work program would provide these rationales for admitting Tom.
   - "As a Native American, Tom would be a desirable candidate for admission because of his life experiences and the ethnic diversity to our program."

continued

CASE STUDY 1 | *continued*

- "As a wheelchair user, Tom would be a desirable candidate because of the diversity of experiences he brings as disabled man."

6. What are Tom's primary sources of cultural identity? How might a social worker intervene to help Tom expand this identity to include a disability identity?

Observations relative to the issues above.

1. The term confined assumes pathology whereas the second statement does not.

2. Tom was diagnosed with mental illness only after being hospitalized, thus residing in a culturally foreign living situation. The combination of his ethnicity and disability may lead to negative assumptions by professionals.

3. Extant social policies provide for a subsistence level existence. However, resources are always maintained at a minimal level. Consider the implications if Tom tried to work. Jobs he would have access to have no health insurance and if Tom started working he would lose Medicaid. Therefore, with his health expenses, he literally cannot afford to work.

4. Extant social and health policies reflect societal values that devalue disabled persons.

5. Most social work programs place high value on ethnic diversity. It would be rare for a program to consider his disability as a valued characteristic

relative to admission. In fact, it would be much more common for the program to assess the negative implications of his ability to successfully complete his education.

6. Tom maintains strong Native American cultural identity. He gets much satisfaction from the respect he holds in his community and tribe. However, his isolated living conditions provide him with no regular contact with other disabled people. Thus, he had no access to address everyday issues such as relationships and dating, wheelchair maintenance, and bladder care strategies. In this situation, the social worker actually referred Tom to internet resources that introduced him with other disabled people. As a result, Tom was connected, electronically to people who helped him navigate live as a disabled man. He received great strength from these relationships.

While medical and health interventions on Tom's behalf have been necessary for him to survive, Tom is no longer sick or ill. He lives with a permanent disability. He has knowledge and skills for self care. Meso- and macro-level interventions, policies, and practices that promote individual dignity, self-determination and full participation are far more important to ensuring his quality of life than any combination of individual treatments or interventions.

CASE STUDY 2

An ultrasound in her 4th month of pregnancy revealed that the fetus Martha was carrying had spina bifida. Because she was uninsured, Martha was receiving care at a community health clinic. Because of her lack of insurance, fetal surgery to ameliorate the spina bifida was not possible. However, her physician informed her that she could choose an abortion. Martha chose to carry to term and she delivered a daughter, Becky. Shortly after, Becky underwent surgical repair, and she was left with sensory and motor impairment. Because of the Individuals

with Disabilities Education Act, Becky was eligible for services from birth. A social worker, Ashley, who also had a mobility disability and used a wheelchair for mobility, began working with the family shortly thereafter. Below are some of the interventions that demonstrated culturally competent social work practice.

1. Martha and her husband Tim received criticism from friends for carrying a disabled child to term rather than choosing abortion. However, because

of religious beliefs they never considered abortion. Ashley supported their religious cultural beliefs and actions. Further, Ashley was a disability role model. While Ashley believed in a woman's right to choose, she reinforced the fact that her life—and Becky's life as well—was as valuable as a nondisabled child.

2. Subsequently, Martha and Tim were approached by another couple who were members of their church. The couple had just found out that the child they were carrying had Down syndrome. They were strongly encouraged by health providers to abort but they also rejected this option because of religious and spiritual values. Though the disabilities were very different, this couple was supported and prepared to welcome a disabled child into their lives without viewing their situation as a tragedy. Tim and Martha helped them through their grieving and adjustment processes prior to and subsequent to the birth. Their child received services from birth and his parents became aware of People First, a self advocacy organization for intellectually disabled people.

3. Ashley connected Tim and Martha with the parents of other children with spina bifida. This proved to be a great resource. This group mentored new parents and were emotionally supportive of each other. Further, as their children grew

and developed, they developed friendships with other disabled children. Feelings of isolation were mitigated. Disability became a part of everyday life.

4. The local center for independent living (CIL) sponsored advocacy supports for disabled youth. Martha and Tim became involved with the center and were assisted in ensuring Becky received adequate educational plans and appropriate resources. Through the CIL, parents of children with various mobility, intellectual, sensory and other disabilities recognized the commonalities in interest and combined efforts.

5. The CIL provided recreational and support activities for Becky, her friends with spina bifida, and other disabled children. Disabled adults from the CIL mentored these children and the youth developed a sense of unity and identity.

Becky's situation is demonstrative of a burgeoning disability culture and identity. Early exposure to disability is critical to help parents develop attitudes and skills that are important for raising disabled children. Early exposure to other disabled children, as well as disabled mentors allow children to grow up understanding themselves positively and rejecting society's ableist views. These youth then become the leaders of tomorrow.

CONCLUSIONS

Culturally competent practice with disabled persons and groups will require most social workers to assess and modify their attitudes about disability, disabled people, and life with a disability. This process can begin with an individual evaluation of how they would react when faced with disability related situations. For example, one can consider how one would react, both personally and professionally, to the situations below.

1. How would I respond if I learned that a residence for people with intellectual disabilities or mental health disabilities was opening in my community?
2. If I (or my spouse or partner) found out that I/she was pregnant, how would I feel? How would I feel if I found out that the fetus had spina bifida?
3. If I were a social worker for my agency, would I be more or less likely to hire an applicant who had a history of an anxiety disability?
4. When I see someone who uses a wheelchair for mobility, what is my immediate reaction?

In self assessment you can determine, 1) what are the prevalent attitudes I carry about disability as a group and people with disabilities; 2) to what degree are my beliefs stereotypical and/or ableist; 3) what can I do to challenge ableist beliefs, educate myself, and change ableist attitudes; and 4) what is my responsibility to affirm the rights of disabled persons to fully participate in society.

As a profession, social work has a long history of working with diverse groups of people. It has been a leader in advocating for equal opportunity and the rights of devalued and marginalized populations. Values such as self-determination, dignity and worth of people, and social justice are at the profession's core. The social work profession must embrace disabled persons as valued members of society and as valued members of the profession in order for us to be a culturally competent profession. This begins with defining disability and the disabled community not only as an at-risk, marginalized, and oppressed group *but also* as a diverse population group in society.

By including a chapter on culturally competent practice with disabled people, this text represents a significant step in social work's commitment to embrace diversity in its broadest sense. The disability motto, "nothing about us without us," is extremely germane to the profession. As social workers redefine disability embrace disabled people as contributors to the diverse tapestry of society, the profession will be strengthened by diverse disability voices. Social workers will be better able to serve people with disabilities in a culturally competent manner and invest in their success. Disability competent social workers are equipped to help disabled individuals with problems and solutions. More important, disability competent social work recognizes that devaluation, discrimination, and marginalization and *not* individual pathology are the primary barriers disabled people face in their quest to live full and productive lives.

Our progress, individually and collectively can be measured by the extent to which we demonstrate attitudes and incorporate disability. The following are some measures by which we can evaluate ourselves.

- Our work begins with the assumption that disabled people are competent.
- Individually and collectively, we embrace disabled people in the profession.
- We learn about disability, disability community, and Disability culture in our educational programs and in the organizations in which we practice.
- Our practice approaches and methods demonstrate understanding of the biosocial implications of disability and life as a disabled person.
- Any social work assessments and interventions consider the implications of community and societal determinants of the challenges and experiences disabled persons face.
- The individual dignity and worth of disabled individuals is held sacrosanct and self-determination is honored. Social control is exercised only as a last resort.
- Solutions to the problems disabled persons and groups face are primarily located in changing social environments and societal policies—not in changing individuals.
- Disabled people deserve the same investment that nondisabled people deserve. Further, as society invests in disabled people, disabled people will enhance the diverse tapestry of society.

Finally, culturally competent social work practice involves attention to the individual and collective rights of disabled people to fully participate. In addition, society has a responsibility to provide opportunities for growth, self-determination, and self-fulfillment to all its citizens: majority and nonmajority, typical and atypical, male and female, gay and straight, white-black-brown-red-yellow, as well as disabled and nondisabled.

CHAPTER 17

CULTURAL COMPETENCE WITH THE OLDER ADULT

Linda A. Revilla and Donna L. Yee

Demographers tell us that in every century we seem to discover a new stage. In the last century it was adolescence. This period between 50 and 75 is probably the developmental stage of this century. We are living longer and living healthier much longer. I think that more and more we will accept that this is the time to spread our wings and take flight, to sing a new song.

—Sarah Lawrence-Lightfoot. (2009). Later-life lessons: An interview with Sarah Lawrence-Lightfoot, *The Boston Globe,* January 5.

Lum (2011) defines cultural competence as a relational, dialogical process (a dialogue rather than an emphasis on worker's competence) between the worker and the client, between cultures, and between people and context. Dialogue means conversation, interchange, discussion, and mutual understanding involving *an egalitarian relationship* of equal status and rights. Cultural competence with the older adult is an important topic of concern with the growing population of older persons, the elderly, and senior citizens in the United States. Senior status is usually granted to persons who arrive at their 65th birthday. It signals retirement from full-time active employment. While old age is measured in terms of years, persons who reach this stage of life are active, vibrant persons who have wisdom, experience, and skills yet to offer to society. Cultural competence with this age group signifies the mutual sharing of cultural wisdom and insight between the worker and the client in order to enrich the lives of the senior client and to assist with life problems with the social worker as a helper. In this chapter we will explore the demographics of the older adult; focus on cultural competence with four older persons of color groups; identify ageism as the major theme of historical oppression and the current social issue confronting this age group; address the issues of health and disparities as value and ethical dilemmas; and discuss cultural awareness, knowledge acquisition, and skill development principles. We will also touch on social and economic justice issues and offer two case studies regarding older adult issues.

DEMOGRAPHICS OF THE OLDER ADULT

Around the world, the older adult population, defined here as people aged 65 and older, is growing at a rapid rate. We will discuss what it means to be an older adult in some populations later. Advances in modern medicine and sanitation, which have positively impacted health and longevity, coupled with improved nutrition, declining fertility, and other factors have contributed to this unparalleled explosion in the global older adult population. A recent report by the U.S. Census highlights the statistics and impact of global aging (Kinsella & He, 2009). In 2008, the number of older adults was estimated at 506 million globally; that number will *double* in about 30 years to 1.3 billion by 2040. For the first time, within the next decade, older adults will outnumber children under age five. With the exception of some developing countries devastated by HIV/AIDS, most countries around the world show a trend for increasing life spans. Looking at numbers alone, the 2008 rank order of countries with the world's largest older populations (in millions) was China (106.1), India (59.6), United States (38.7), Japan (27.5), and Russia (19.9). European countries will continue to have the highest population proportions of older adults, with one in four persons aged 65 or older by 2040. With the exception of Japan, whose older adult population is 21.6%, and Georgia at 16.6%, the rest of the 25 countries with the largest percentage of older adults are all in eastern or western Europe. By 2040, however, developing countries will be home to 76% of the international older adult population. The Caribbean has the oldest population of developing regions (7.6%). Latin America has 6.4%, Asia (with the exception of Japan) has 6.2%, and Africa has 3.3%, respectively. Older adult population gains of more than 250% by 2040 are projected in developing countries such as Singapore, Colombia, India, Malaysia, Egypt, Costa Rica, Bangladesh, Kenya, and the Philippines. Another 20 countries will experience a 100% increase in older adult populations. None of those countries is in Europe except Turkey; the only developed countries on the list are the United States, Canada, New Zealand, and Australia.

Additionally, within the older adult population, the growth of the "oldest old," defined here as aged 80 and above, is the fastest growing segment of the population of many countries. Worldwide, the oldest old population will increase more than 200% between 2009 and 2040. In 2008 the oldest old was almost one-fifth of the older adult population. More than half of them lived in just five countries—China, the United States, India, Japan, and Russia. Individuals born today in countries such as Japan, Singapore, France, Sweden, Italy, Australia, and Canada can expect to live to reach their 80th birthday. People in developed countries such as the United States and those of western Europe can expect to live to their 78th birthday. Most people of Latin America, the Caribbean, and Asia can expect to live to their 70s. The exception is for people in India, Pakistan, and Bangladesh. There is considerable variation in the life spans of people in Africa: people in Tunisia, Egypt, and Morocco may live to be in their 70s; people in Kenya, Uganda, and Botswana may only live to their 50s; and South Africans and people from

Malawi may only live to their 40s. One of the lowest life expectancies can be found in Zimbabwe, where people live an average of only 39.7 years.

The impacts of the global older adult population surge are manifold. An increasing aging population coupled with declining fertility rates will force many countries to revise programs such as health and pension systems, as fewer workers support more retired older adults. As longevity increases, family households may change to accommodate living and care-giving requirements across four generations. Public policies will need to evolve to account for the growing older adult population's quality-of-life needs, including wellness and long-term care.

AGING IN THE UNITED STATES: AGE IS NOT ABOUT CHRONOLOGY

"Aging is an *Active* Verb" is a multi-media public education campaign by Aging Services of California, promoting a redefinition of "aging as a lifelong process everyone experiences rather than a label placed on the elderly" (Aging Services of California, 2010). *Aging Well* is a magazine reflecting a new model of positive aging. "You're only as old as you feel" and "sixty is the new forty" are catchphrases of a paradigm shift coming at a time when the older adult population in the United States, similar to the rest of the world, is rapidly increasing in number. Census data reveal that in 2007, the older adult population, aged 65 or older, numbered 37.9 million. This means that one in eight Americans, or 12.6%, is an older adult. Older adults are not evenly distributed across the United States (Figure 17.1). More than half live in only nine states: California, Florida, New York, Texas, and Pennsylvania had more than 2 million older adults in 2007, while Illinois, Ohio, Michigan, and New Jersey each had over 1 million (Administration on Aging, 2009). Older adults comprise more than 14% or more of the population of Florida, Pennsylvania, Rhode Island, West Virginia, Iowa, North Dakota, Connecticut, Arkansas, South Dakota, and Massachusetts. About 80% of older adults live in metropolitan areas. The highest poverty rates for elders are found in the south, including Washington D.C., the southwest states of Texas and New Mexico, and North Dakota.

Within the older adult population, there are differences in the rate of growth for some segments. For example, there has been growth in the older adult population from 2000 to 2005 with a 25% increase in the 55 to 64-year-old age group, a 20.2% increase in the 85+ group, but only a 1.4% increase for ages 65–74, a 5.6% increase for ages 75–84, and a 3.2% increase for those under age 55. Population projections have forecast that by 2020 there will be 55 million adults aged 65 and over and 6.6 million adults aged 85 and over. This "silver tsunami" indicates the aging of the boomer generation (those born between the years 1946 to 1964) and reflects advances in modern medicine and technology, and public health policies that have enabled the average life expectancy of American men and women to dramatically rise in the 20th century. In 2008, men reaching age 65 have an average life expectancy of 17.4 more years, while women reaching the same age have an average life expectancy of 20.3 years. Accordingly, gender ratios decrease as the population ages. Americans are living longer, enjoying better health, and are redefining what it means to grow older in America.

There is also increasing diversity among the older adult population. In 2008, there were 21.9 million older women and 16 million older men. This trend of

Numbers	Number of Persons 65 and Older	Percent 65+ of the Total Population	Percent Increase in Numbers from 1997 to 2007	Percent Below Poverty 2007
US Total (50 States + DC)	37,887,958	12.6	11.2	9.7
Alabama	625,756	13.5	11.5	11.9
Alaska	47,935	7.0	49.6	5.0
Arizona	820,391	12.9	36.2	8.6
Arkansas	397,108	14.0	10.3	11.9
California	4,003,593	11.0	12.1	8.1
Colorado	492,685	10.1	25.2	8.9
Connecticut	472,284	13.5	0.6	6.2
Delaware	117,678	13.6	24.7	8.6
District of Columbia	69,741	11.9	−5.0	14.6
Florida	3,098,364	17.0	14.4	9.5
Georgia	942,832	9.9	27.7	12.2
Hawaii	183,994	14.3	17.4	6.5
Idaho	174,946	11.7	27.8	8.6
Illinois	1,548,781	12.1	4.6	8.6
Indiana	795,441	12.5	8.4	7.8
Iowa	438,448	14.7	2.1	8.1
Kansas	360,216	13.0	2.5	8.7
Kentucky	549,504	13.0	12.4	13.1
Louisiana	522,334	12.2	5.1	13.1
Maine	194,986	14.8	12.5	8.2
Maryland	661,809	11.8	13.4	7.8
Massachusetts	858,939	13.3	−0.4	9.2
Michigan	1,280,152	12.7	5.4	8.1
Minnesota	636,216	12.2	10.1	8.1
Mississippi	364,614	12.5	9.5	14.5
Missouri	788,371	13.4	6.5	9.4
Montana	133,578	13.9	15.0	8.9
Nebraska	236,648	13.3	4.0	8.4
Nevada	285,654	11.1	48.3	6.6
New Hampshire	165,742	12.6	17.2	6.2

FIGURE 17.1   (CONTINUED)

Numbers	Number of Persons 65 and Older	Percent 65+ of the Total Population	Percent Increase in Numbers from 1997 to 2007	Percent Below Poverty 2007
New Jersey	1,134,636	13.1	2.6	8.5
New Mexico	250,235	12.7	29.7	13.0
New York	2,546,405	13.2	4.9	11.8
North Carolina	1,103,413	12.2	18.9	11.0
North Dakota	93,285	14.6	0.8	14.4
Ohio	1,545,085	13.5	3.4	8.1
Oklahoma	480,140	13.3	8.0	10.3
Oregon	488,936	13.0	13.6	8.6
Pennsylvania	1,889,660	15.2	–0.8	8.8
Rhode Island	146,847	13.9	–5.9	9.1
South Carolina	573,098	13.0	26.3	12.1
South Dakota	113,555	14.3	7.9	10.9
Tennessee	793,117	12.9	18.4	11.8
Texas	2,394,157	10.0	22.2	12.0
Utah	233,982	8.8	30.0	5.3
Vermont	84,425	13.6	16.9	7.3
Virginia	909,522	11.8	20.4	9.3
Washington	757,852	11.7	17.1	7.5
West Virginia	280,666	15.5	2.3	10.4
Wisconsin	736,301	13.1	7.7	8.3
Wyoming	63,901	12.2	17.7	4.6

FIGURE 17.1 | THE OLDER ADULT POPULATION BY STATE (2007)

Source: Administration on Aging aoa.gov website

women outnumbering men as they age is expected to continue. Older men are much more likely to be married (73%) than older women (42%). Thirty percent of all older adults live alone; half of older women aged 75+ live alone.

CULTURAL COMPETENCE WITH OLDER ADULTS

As indicated at the beginning of this chapter, cultural competence with older adults is a crucial topic with the growth of older people of color in the United States who are first generation immigrants or second and third generation American born seniors.

Often older persons have a great appreciation for their cultural history and practices and utilize these resources when confronted with problems of living. For example, they remember their cultural history (their culture of origin and family stories) and practices (family support and spiritual prayer) which strengthen their fortitude to cope with current issues facing them. In this section, we will focus on socio-economic demographics and specific characteristics of Latinos, African Americans, Asian Pacific Islanders, and American Indians and Native Alaskans who are older persons.

More older adults are enjoying a level of wealth than preceding generations. Increasing numbers of older adults have high incomes, while decreasing numbers live in poverty, and in low income groups. These changes may be attributed to many reasons, including more older people, especially older women, in the workforce (Federal Interagency Forum on Aging-Related Statistics, 2008). Despite these gains, median household income of older persons shows large differences between men and women, and between ethnic groups. The median incomes of individual men compared to that of individual women are greater than $10,000. Some of the variation in median income of households headed by an older adult may be attributed to the number of wage earners in each household. For example, Asian American households have the highest median income of all groups; however, Asian Americans tend to live in large households with multiple wage earners, which is not accounted for in the data. Additionally, while the median income of Asian American households is higher, actual buying power may not be reflected in the income, as Asian Americans predominantly live in California, Hawaii, and New York, geographic regions that have higher costs-of-living than most of the United States. It is also important to note that many households with an elderly member (1 of every 14) had incomes less than $15,000 (Administration on Aging, 2009). A recent study in California reports that half of the older adults aged 65 and above (495,000), living alone in the state, lacked the income to pay for basic needs of housing, food, health care, transportation, and other expenses. Latino elders had the highest rates of what the study defined as "economic insecurity" (i.e., incomes below the actual costs by county of basic expenses needed for the aged to live independently and with dignity in their own homes). These incomes are often just above the Federal Poverty Level. Almost 75% of Latino elders living alone and about 50% of Latinos residing with their spouse are unable to meet their basic needs. Older women, who are 72% of all older Californians living alone, are more likely than men to be unable to meet their basic needs financially. Age status, living alone, and being a female of color add up to the increased likelihood of being economically insecure. More than 90% of Latino or Asian women aged 75 years or older, 85% of African American women, and 66% of White women had incomes categorizing them as economically insecure (Wallace & Smith, 2009).

Elder people of color are projected to increase in population from 5.7 million in 2000 to 8 million in 2010 to 12.9 million in 2020, or account for 23.6% of the population (population projections by race and Hispanic Origin for persons aged 60 and over from 2000 to 2050). Variation in education, income, and living arrangements is also related to health, wellness, and quality-of-life issues among diverse groups. Ethnicity, age, gender, and socio-economic status are key factors. (Figure 17.2)

Ethnicity	Median income of households headed by older adult (in $)	Individual personal income: Males (in $)	Individual personal income: Females (in $)	Poverty rate (in %)
Latinos	31,544			17.1
African Americans	32,025	16,074	11,578	23
Asian Americans	47,135	18,460	11,226	12
American Indians				
Non-Hispanic Whites	43,654			7.4
All older adult households	41,851	24,323	14,021	9.7

FIGURE 17.2 | ETHNICITY, AGE, GENDER, AND SOCIO-ECONOMIC STATUS (2007)

Source: Compiled from data at Administration on Aging (www.aoa.gov).

LATINOS

The Latino older adult population numbered 2.5 million in 2007 and is projected to be over 17 million by 2050, or almost 20% of the total older adult population. The majority of older Latinos live in four states: California, Texas, Florida, and New York. In 2007, among Latinos aged 65+, 42% had high school diplomas, compared to 76% of the total older population, 70% of the Asian American population, and 57% of the African American population. Looking at living arrangements, Latino older men lived with spouses (65%), with other relatives (20%), with non-relatives (3%), or alone (15%). Latinas lived with spouses (39%), with other relatives (33%), with non-relatives (2%), or alone (26%).

AFRICAN AMERICANS

The African American older adult population numbered 3.1 million in 2007 and is projected to be over 9.9 million by 2050, or 11% of the older adult population. Half of older African Americans live in eight states: New York, Florida, California, Texas, Georgia, North Carolina, Illinois, and Virginia. Looking at living arrangements, older African American men lived with spouses (75%), with other relatives (10%), with non-relatives (4%), or alone (29%). Older African American women lived with spouses (25%), with other relatives (32%), with non-relatives (2%), or alone (40%).

ASIAN PACIFIC ISLANDERS

The Asian Pacific Islander (API) older adult population numbered 1.3 million in 2007 and is projected to be over 6.8 million by 2050, or 7.8% of the older adult population. More than half (60%) of older APIs live in three states: California, Hawaii, and New York. While 70% of older APIs have finished high school, almost 30% have at least a bachelor's degree. Looking at living arrangements, older Asian American men lived with spouses (84%), with other relatives (6%), with non-relatives (2%), or alone (8%). Older Asian American women lived with spouses (47%), with other relatives (30%), with non-relatives (3%), or alone (20%).

AMERICAN INDIANS AND NATIVE ALASKANS

The American Indian and Native Alaskan older adult population numbered 212,605 in 2007 and is projected to be about 918,000 by 2050, or 1% of the older adult population. Currently, there are an additional 369,399 older persons who report American Indian and Native Alaskan identities or heritage. Just over half (51%) of older American Indians and Native Alaskans live in six states: California, Oklahoma, Arizona, New Mexico, Texas, and North Carolina. The small size of this group, relative to others, results in a lack of reliable estimates about living arrangements.

HISTORICAL OPPRESSION AND CURRENT SOCIAL ISSUE

Outwardly, every society in the world offers care in various forms (e.g., pension, health care) for their older adults. Yet a case could be made for identifying and interpreting various social undercurrents confronting older persons which can be called historical oppression in terms of age discrimination. In addition to understanding the complexities of cultural and ethnic diversity as delineated in other chapters of this volume, for the professional social worker interacting with older clients of color, cultural competence includes recognizing diversity *across generations* in terms of lifespan experiences, values, and access to technology, among other issues. Part of recognizing diversity includes attitudes about older adults and aging. "Ageism" is one of the issues in an unabashedly youth-driven American culture.

Ageism is defined as a process of systematic stereotyping and discrimination against people because they are old, just as racism and sexism accomplish this for skin color and gender. Older people are categorized as senile, rigid in thought and manner, and old-fashioned in morality and skills. They may be seen as boring, stingy, cranky, demanding, and useless.... Ageism allows the younger generation to see older people as different from themselves; thus they suddenly cease to identify with their elders as human beings. This behavior serves to reduce their own sense of fear and dread of aging. Stereotyping and myths surrounding old age are explained in part by a lack of knowledge and insufficient contact with a variety of older people. (Butler, 2008, pp. 25–27)(25-26)

The 2008 presidential campaign provides macro-level examples and a lens to observe stereotypical views of aging in the United States. Senator John McCain, who was then 72 years old, was running against 47-year-old Senator Barack Obama. The difference alone provided plenty of material for the late-night comedians, who targeted McCain's age. Jokes were made about McCain being confused, non-technologically savvy, and needing help going to the bathroom. While there is swift negative public and institutional reaction against racist and sexist humor aired on network television, there is no such response against ageist humor. In a time when many Americans recognize racist and sexist humor as offensive, ageist humor is still accepted. Perhaps more significant was that in addition to providing fodder to provoke laughter, for some, McCain's age called into question his suitability for the job of President. McCain was forced to emphasize the soundness of his health, publicize his fitness routine, and put the spotlight on the healthiness of his 95-year-old mother (Associated Press, 2007).

According to the American Psychological Association (APA), ageism exists on many levels:

1. discriminatory attitudes toward older adults;
2. discriminatory behavior against older adults;
3. prejudicial comments and poor treatment by service providers; and
4. discrimination of older adults by institutional practices and policies (American Psychological Association Resolution on Ageism, 2010)

APA's strategy to combat ageism includes providing accurate information to reduce stereotypes and incorrect information about aging.

In addition to humor, discriminatory attitudes and behavior against adults is manifested on many meso levels, including mandatory retirement ages, restrictions or extra conditions on activities (i.e., some states have shorter renewal cycles for older adult drivers' licenses and other driving restrictions) (Insurance Institute for Highway Safety, 2010). Gerontologist Carol Austin (2005) says social workers must be mindful that the American culture glorifies youth, denies death, and transforms aging into a medical condition that can be cured and a cosmetic challenge that can be fixed. Ageism is not just profound and pervasive. Its ultimate power is that ageist attitudes are uncritically internalized and ageist behavior is too often viewed as acceptable.

The International Longevity Center (2007) posits age discrimination is deeply embedded and widespread in American society. Their report, "Ageism in America," documents numerous examples of ageism. They estimate the frequency of elder abuse ranging from 2% to 10%, with only one out of six incidents being brought to the attention of authorities. Likewise, an estimated 5 million older adults are financially exploited, but a fraction of the cases are reported. Age discrimination at the micro level in health care takes many forms, including faulty knowledge about the aging process by physicians, a lack of preventive services for older adults, under-treatment of certain cancers in older adults, and under-representation of older adults in clinical trials for pharmaceuticals. The report also documents age discrimination in nursing homes, emergency services, the workplace, the media, and marketing.

The following joke, recounted by aging services providers, illustrates the sometimes unthinking ageist attitudes of health-care providers: A man goes to his doctor because his right arm is stiff. The doctor brushes off his concerns, saying, "Your arm is stiff because you're getting older." The man replies, "But doctor, my left arm is just as old as my right arm, and it is not stiff." But, ageism in health care is no laughing matter, as lives are at stake.

International research shows under-treatment of older cancer patients. Pritchard's (2007) meta-analysis of cancer research discusses the paradigm, prevalent in the United Kingdom, in which women aged 70 and older with breast cancer are treated differently than younger women. Older women get chemotherapy alone, versus chemotherapy in conjunction with surgery for younger women. The rationale given was that older women are less fit for surgery because of age and co-morbidity. The life expectancies of older women are also underestimated. Ironically, older women have been specifically excluded from research on breast cancer therapy around the world, despite the fact that incidence of breast cancer increases with age.

Other researchers show under-treatment of older women with breast and gynecologic cancers can include lowered doses of chemotherapy to no chemotherapy. Under-treatment was also found for palliative care, pain management, and reconstructive surgery. The researchers conclude, "Undertreatment in older cancer patients is a well-documented phenomenon responsible for preventable cancer deaths" (Bouchardy et al., 2007).

Ageism in emergency services is also prevalent as emergency safety measures are often not adequate for older people. Stunning data from the Hurricane Katrina disaster show that of the 917 identified deceased (several more were unidentified) in Louisiana (among evacuees that passed away as a result of the disaster), 49% were older than 75 and fewer than 10% were younger than 45 (Brunkard, Namulanda, & Ratard, 2008). Poor, African American elderly were disproportionately victimized by the hurricane. Seventy-one of the deceased were nursing home residents who passed away in their facilities. Almost half of the nursing home residents were from one nursing home outside New Orleans (CNN, 2005). Another New Orleans nursing home accounted for 22 deaths (Associated Press, 2007). The fates of elderly in assisted living, board and care, and other private facilities is not known (Centers for Disease Control, year unknown). Among the 23,000 people who were evacuated from the hurricane zone to the Astrodome in Houston, Texas, were scores of older adults. Many did not arrive with family members or others who could assist and advocate for them and were unable to access the services provided at the Astrodome; some were too frail to walk to the restrooms, hear announcements over the loudspeakers, see announcements on electronic displays, or feed themselves. Some were very ill and needed immediate hospitalization. At the Astrodome a team of gerontological health professionals came together to address the needs of the elderly evacuees. They developed a rapid triage tool to assess cognitive function, medical status, financial and social service needs, and ability to perform activities of daily life. They were able to assist 228 vulnerable older adults (Dyer et al., 2008). Hurricane Katrina and other natural disasters are a wake-up call for increasing focus on disaster preparedness for vulnerable populations by emergency response experts and the aging services network (Centers for Disease Control, year unknown).

VALUES AND ETHICAL DILEMMAS

Ethical dilemmas are value conflicts or special needs of diverse older adult clients involving such ethical decision-making issues such as services, social justice, the dignity and worth of the older person, the importance of human relationships, integrity, competence, and human rights. While we admit that there are a host of other values and ethical issues that are connected to older adults, in this section we will concentrate on two areas: the health of older adults and the disparities among elders of color.

THE HEALTH OF OLDER ADULTS

As mentioned earlier, Americans are living longer than before. Among industrialized countries, however, longevity after age 65 in the United States lags behind Japan, Canada, and France. In Japan a woman at age 65 can expect to live an average of 3.2 years longer than her American counterpart. Japanese men at age 65 can expect to live 1.2 years longer than their American counterparts. The leading causes of death among all adults aged 65 and older in 2007 were heart disease and cancer, followed by cerebrovascular disease (stroke), respiratory diseases, Alzheimer's disease, diabetes mellitus, and influenza and pneumonia (Federal Interagency Forum on Aging-Related Statistics, 2008). Note that chronic conditions are the leading cause of death for older adults. In the United States, 85% of adults aged 65 or older have been diagnosed with at least one chronic condition and 62% of adults aged 65 or older have two or more chronic diseases (Anderson & Horvath, 2004). In 2008, 12.2 million seniors report having some form of cardiovascular disease (American Heart Association, 2009). Diabetes affects the daily lives of 12.2 million seniors, while arthritis afflicts half of Americans aged 65 or older (Centers for Disease Control website, www.cdc.gov). Seven of every ten Americans die of a chronic disease every year (Stanford University Chronic Disease Self-Management Program website, patienteducation.stanford.edu).

The prevalence of chronic disease such as diabetes, heart disease, and arthritis among seniors presents a serious problem to their continued well-being and the capability of hospitals to care for them. The effects of chronic disease in seniors can be severe. Chronic disease leads not only to physical deterioration but psychological deterioration and isolation which, when combined, result in neglect and frequent hospitalization. Chronic conditions negatively affect quality of life for elders and hamper their ability to remain active in the community.

DISPARITIES AMONG ELDERS OF COLOR

Race and ethnicity are correlated with persistent disparities in health. For example, fewer elders of color felt the same way, with 34.1% of Asian Americans, 28.9% of Latinos, 23.7% of African Americans, and 24.3% of American Indians/Alaska Natives, rating themselves similarly (Administration on Aging website, 2009). Diseases affect elder minority populations disproportionately in terms of incidence, prevalence, and severity (Centers for Disease Control National Center for Health Statistics, 2007). The Department of Health and Human Services identifies areas in which people of color experience serious health disparities among older adults:

1. *Cancer screening and management.* African American women are more likely than White women to die from cervical cancer and more likely than women of all ethnic and racial groups to die of breast cancer.
2. *Cardiovascular Disease.* Rates of death of African Americans from heart disease were 29% higher than White adults. Rates of death of African American from stroke were 40% higher.
3. *Diabetes.* American Indians, African Americans, and Latinos were more likely to have diagnosed diabetes than Caucasians.

4. *Immunizations.* Latinos and African American elderly were less likely to receive influenza and pneumococcal vaccines.

Other conditions demonstrating disparities are mental health, with American Indians and Alaska Natives having high prevalence of depression and substance abuse. People of color in general have less access to available mental health services; receive poor-quality mental health services; and are underrepresented in mental health research. Tuberculosis and hepatitis also have a high prevalence among API (Centers for Disease Control, 2010). Other disparities are apparent in access to health care and medications.

CULTURAL AWARENESS

Cultural awareness involves the self in a cultural context. Cultural context or knowledge of the cultural environment is a critical determinant of how one evolves as a cultural being. In terms of jeopardy befalling the older adult, illness is the enemy of the older person. In this section we discuss two disease entities which illustrate how a person afflicted with illness responds in terms of cultural environmental context, particularly with family and community concerns.

ALZHEIMER'S DISEASE AND DEMENTIA

Dementia is the loss of a person's cognitive functioning, including memory. Dementia negatively affects problem-solving ability, decision making, judgment, and spatial relationships. Personality changes may also occur. There are multiple causes of dementia (American Psychiatric Association, 1994). Alzheimer's Disease (AD) is the leading cause of dementia, accounting for 50–70% of dementia cases. AD is a progressive brain disorder, destroying brain cells and causing impairments in cognitive and behavioral functioning. Early symptoms of AD are difficulty remembering names and recent events, apathy, and depression. As the disease progresses, later symptoms may include impaired judgment, disorientation, confusion, and behavior changes and the inability to control one's body (i.e., difficulty swallowing), leading to death. Autopsies will reveal "plaques," deposits of the protein fragment beta-amyloid, and "tangles," twisted strands of the protein tau in the brain (Alzheimer's Association, 2009). One in eight persons aged 65 and older have AD. Vascular dementia is the second most common type of dementia, caused by decreased blood circulation to parts of the brain. Thus, it is also known as multi-infarct or post-stroke dementia or vascular cognitive impairment. The symptoms are often similar to AD; loss of intellectual abilities is the major feature (Alzheimer's Association, 2009).

The elderly are the population most affected by dementia and AD. As the disease progresses, persons affected are eventually unable to care for themselves (APA, 1994). Women are more likely than men to have Alzheimer's disease and other dementias, primarily because they live longer. The Alzheimer's Association reports that 14% of all people aged 71 and older have dementia; Women aged 71 and older had higher rates than men: 16% of women aged 71 and older and 11% for men in the same age range. Prevalence of dementia varies among ethnic groups.

Research finds that African Americans have a higher prevalence of dementia (Gurland et al., 1999) and increased risk for Alzheimer's Disease (Danner et al., 2008). Contributing factors include the high prevalence of risk factors such as hypertension and diabetes in African American communities (Danner et al., 2008). AD will significantly increase among all ethnic groups; APIs with AD are projected to increase by 67% from 2008 to 2030.

The results from the longitudinal Honolulu-Asia study (White et al., 1996) indicate that among older Japanese American men in Hawaii, prevalence of AD is similar to that of Caucasian Americans whereas the prevalence of vascular dementia appears to be higher than Caucasian men. A study of the clients at nine California Alzheimer's Disease and Diagnostic Centers found only 0.7% of the cases were Filipino Americans (Yeo & Lieberman, 1993), indicating a need for more dementia research on this population. Among Chinese Americans the prevalence of AD is unknown because the population has not been included in any population-based studies of AD (Wang et al., 2006). Even when dementia may be present in an individual, it is often unrecognized in primary care settings (Valcour et al., 2000) and by family members. Even when memory loss is noticed by family members, sometimes no physician is consulted (Masaki et al., 1997). In many Asian cultures, the value of "filial piety," traditionally conceptualized as "children expected to obey and respect their parents, bring honor to their parents by succeeding in work, and support and care for their parents in their old age" (Tanabe, year unknown) is manifested today by adult children assuming a duty to care for aging parents, no matter what the emotional, physical, or financial toll. Cultural explanations of AD and dementia may contribute to lack of help-seeking among APIs. A study of Hmong in Wisconsin found few cases of dementia among the population. Hmong see dementia as a natural part of the life cycle, thus no treatment is sought (Olson, 1999). There is evidence that dementia is seen as a form of normal aging also among Japanese and Chinese American families. Cultural notions of shame prevent many families from seeking help for mental health conditions. Mental illness may be perceived as stemming from a flawed genetic background, which can shame and stigmatize the family as a whole and perhaps even future generations. Additionally, the pressure to "keep family secrets" may prevent families from seeking information and assistance.

KNOWLEDGE ACQUISITION

Social workers should learn about the Older Americans Act, Area Agency on Aging, and Titles XVIII, XIX, and XX of the Social Security Act. They should familiarize themselves with the aging services network, with local, state, and federal resources, and their efficacy and accessibility for older adults and their caregivers.

In addition to understanding resources, understanding attitudes is just as important. One of the reasons for a fear of aging might be a lack of knowledge and lack of contact with older people. The solution is to get to know diverse groups of older people. Interacting with older people and volunteering at places where older adults frequent provides opportunities to interact with older adults, as this MSW student, interning at a nonprofit providing older adult services describes:

Learning from others has proven time and time again to be a very enriching experience. My volunteer work has taken me on journeys into the lives of many people—youth, the homeless and older adults. Being around the older generation has provided me with a personal connection to history. Conversations with my grandmother have given me a glimpse of what it was like to survive the Japanese invasion of China—the chaos, the lost of a loved one and the strength to move forward with life. No history book that I have encountered has ever provided me with such vibrant account of a historical event.

Modern senior centers, in particular, replete with hockey rinks, ceramics studios, and fitness offerings of yoga, pilates, and zumba appeal to elders of all ages. Mather Lifeways "cafes" in Chicago offer coffee, computer classes, and lectures (www.matherlifeways.com). Likewise, Osher Lifelong Learning Institutes, housed at colleges and universities around the country, have intellectually and socially stimulating classes for older adults. During Fall, 2009, UCLA's Osher Institute had an artist-in-residence program, as well as class offerings on the "History of Rock and Roll" and "Psychological Poetry" (www.uclaextension.edu).

Reading books is another way to learn more about older adults. Sawako Ariyoshi's *The Twilight Years* sensitively portrays end-of-life issues and care giving in Japan. Sarah Lightfoot-Lawrence's book, *The Third Chapter: Passion, Risk, and Adventure in the 25 Years After 50*, describes new opportunities for creativity and self-fulfillment for older adults. Gene Cohen's books, *The Mature Mind: The Positive Power of the Aging Brain* and *The Creative Age: Awakening Human Potential in the Second Half of Life* also reject myths about the abilities of older adults.

Some movies also provide insight into the diverse worlds of older adults. *Young@Heart* is a documentary about the "Young@Heart Chorus," formed in Northampton, Massachusetts, in 1982. Current performers, all over age 70, sing only rock and roll, have released a CD, and perform concerts nationally and internationally. Their website describes the chorus as follows:

Young @ Heart has become infamous for its defiant and moving performances. As its name suggests, age is integral to this company. Slaughtering any good-natured sympathy by using age as an ironic weapon, the Young @ Heart has crafted surprising and hilarious work that is not about old people performing, but rather a performance that happens to feature older people (www.youngatheartchorus.com).

A four-part documentary by HBO, National Institute on Aging, and Alzheimer's Association, *The Alzheimer's Project* not only presents leading-edge research on the disease, but also the disease from the perspective of grandchildren and the experience of caregivers (www.hbo.com/alzheimers/about-the-project.html). The Alzheimer's Association worked with Hallmark Hall of Fame to ensure actress Sissy Spacek's depiction of a woman living with AD was accurate in the television movie *Pictures of Hollis Woods*, based on the book of the same name by Patricia Reilly Giff. An animated film with an interesting portrayal of an older adult is Disney/Pixar's *Up*. While the film begins with an elderly widower (voiced by actor Edward Asner) stereotypically portrayed as a lonely, grouchy curmudgeon, the characterization evolves into one showing courage, strength, and warmth as a shared adventure deepens the elderly man's relationship with a little boy. This character is an alternative to Disney's portrayals of older women as mean (i.e., Cruella de Vil in *101 Dalmations*), wicked stepmothers (i.e., Cinderella's), evil queens who transform into old hags (i.e., Snow White's), and older men who are wicked (i.e., the "Vizier" in *Aladdin*), easily fooled, (i.e., the king in *Aladdin*), or infirm (i.e., Mulan's father).

SKILL DEVELOPMENT

Skill development (Lum, 2007) involves using practical tools for working with the older adult client. It is generally process-oriented in social work practice with a beginning, middle, and end, during which the worker exercises skills having to do with engagement (contact and problem identification), assessment, intervention, and evaluation. These skill areas serve as stepping stones to move the worker and the older adult client through the helping process to a successful conclusion.

ENGAGEMENT

The establishment of the relationship between the worker and the older adult client is basic to the engagement stage of the helping process. We term this phase "care giving." An estimated 10 million Americans needed long-term care in 2000 (Rogers & Komisar, 2003). Sharlach and colleagues (2003) estimate that 16% of all households have at least one caregiver for someone aged 50+, and estimate a minimum of 1.8 million caregivers in California. They found that 75% of caregivers are women and 5% are Asian American, but since the finding is based on a telephone survey conducted in English, it is likely an underestimate. APIs have a long and well-documented history of health, mental health, and social services underutilization (Braun & Brown, 1998). A 2001 community assessment in Sacramento, California, showed few APIs self-identify as family caregivers, although informal investigations revealed that over two-thirds were caregivers of an older family member (Asian Community Center, 2006). Compared to other ethnic groups, AARP (2001) found APIs to have the highest proportion of caregiving for an elder. The research on the stressful and health impacts of caregiving is abundant (Pinquart & Sorenson, 2003). In particular, caregivers of people with dementia are more likely to report more hours of caregiving per week (54 hours), financial hardship, physical strain, and emotional stress (Sharlach et al., 2003).

Family caregivers of color are difficult to identify and reach unless organizations with strong ties to community-based organizations facilitate access. The combination of historic patterns of service underutilization among older adults of color and persistent reliance on family members, cultural beliefs, lack of knowledge about dementia and other health conditions, limited English skills, and lack of language/culturally competent services combine as barriers to service, resulting in a need to better address caregivers' support service requirements (Asian Community Center, 2006).

As a part of the engagement phase, care giving (Lum, 2007) means asking ourselves as workers what older adult clients are saying about themselves, their problems, their families, and their friends who are concerned about their well-being. We must mentally record the words, thoughts, and feelings of our older clients and then translate them into teachable moments for us to learn and uncover new and different ways of understanding and relating to this client group.

ASSESSMENT

Assessment skills (Lum, 2007) involve a psychosocial perspective that analyzes person and environment. Some factors in the social environment may relate to maintaining basic survival needs, such as food and nutrition, housing, clothes, health care, and care giving. Other related environmental stressors may include intergenerational disputes, financial conflicts, illness (gradual or catastrophic), and other tragedies. The older adult client interacts with and responds to the environment. People generally use coping skills to process environmental stressors. Ego strength, support systems, and community resources play a part in coping with the environment. However, the older adult client may have inadequate resources due to physical and/or mental disparities.

The social worker's assessment includes assessing his or her own skills, his or her expectations of client and helper, and his or her "professional" role:

1. The social worker does not judge the client. The helping relationship does not require us to "like" the client, it requires us to understand his or her perspectives, values, and wants/needs and to make care plans that are helpful and that achieve care-plan objectives.
2. The social worker is challenged to respond to the oppressive relationship between the client and the situational environment.
3. The social worker is challenged to help the client understand multi-cultural aspects of the care relationship and reflect on the problem. Should nothing be said to challenge the client's thinking or understanding the meaning of the helping process?
4. How does the social worker "protect" or assure the helper gets a fair hearing? How does the social worker work toward a remedy—to repair the client–helper relationship and get it on track toward mutual respect and a broader understanding of each person's perspectives and life experience.

Interpreting these points to the older adult client helps the worker to keep the perspective on the interaction between the person and the environment. Older clients, particularly Asian Americans, may have psychosomatic reactions such as anxiety and depression with accompanying insomnia, weight loss, and lack of energy; headache, back pain, and shoulder pain; hypertension; and loneliness and isolation. It is important to find out medical and health information about older adult clients from their physicians and to work in conjunction with these health-care providers.

INTERVENTION

The purpose of intervention (Lum, 2007) is to come between the older adult client and the problems confronting him or her in order to affect a positive change. In this text the intervention approach is empowerment. For the older adult client this means the gaining of power by an individual, family, group of persons, and community to affect change of a previously powerless situation. On the individual level empowerment entails mobilizing the unique client to take charge and control his or her life, to learn new ways of thinking about the problem situation, and to adopt new behaviors that provide more satisfying outcomes. On the family level it means drawing on the collective good will and strengths of family members to assist the older adult who may no longer be able to help himself or herself. On the group level the social worker may connect the older adult client to resource centers that have senior programs, independent living facilities, and intermediate and long-term nursing care as well as community services for the blind, the disabled, and the terminally ill. On the community level empowerment means marshalling advocates for the older adult so that adequate legislation for senior services are funded and protected from budget cuts.

SOCIAL AND ECONOMIC JUSTICE FOR THE OLDER ADULT

Social justice and economic justice for the older adult involve two separate but related issues. On the one hand, social justice entails monitoring how social institutions deal fairly and justly with the social needs of the older adult in such a way that this age group has access to what is good for older adult individuals and groups. Goodness means that there is the securing of social rights and benefits for such social provision of well-being (e.g., nutrition, housing, clothing, pension and related benefits, health care). Social justice for the older adult also addresses historical and current forms of oppression (e.g., ageism and related discrimination and exploitation) and seeks legal safe guards and societal means to protect and correct elder abuse and establish an equal playing field for the older adult regardless of age, ethnicity, gender, economic status, social class, and sexual orientation. On the other hand, economic justice is an equal partner of social justice but it has a different mission. Economic justice for the older adult sets forth moral principles to govern how to design economic institutions so that an older adult can be provided economic dignity and an adequate income in retirement. Economic justice ensures that society establishes social and economic contracts on behalf of the older person (e.g., Social Security, Medicare) and that the older adult can have goods and services to produce an independent material foundation for economic sustenance. It also ensures a nurturing environment based on economic security and when an older adult is unable to provider for himself or herself, economic justice fosters supplementary assistance until a person can resume functioning again.

Egalitarian social and economic justice is reflected in the writings of John Rawls (1971). Rawls sets forth two basic principles which should govern how society ought to treat such groups as older adults. His first principle (the ideal) holds that basic liberties must be equal because citizens of a just society have the same basic rights to freedom, equality of opportunity, access to goods and services, and self-respect. The second principle (the real) observes that although the distribution of income and wealth need not be equal, any inequalities in power, wealth, and other resources must be taken into account that they benefit the worst-off (the least advantaged) members of society. Thus, one could argue that there should be a standard for how society treats and provides for the older retired adult and ensures a basic quality of living as well as ensures that the least advantaged of older adults should receive additional resources and assistance based on age and need.

Case Study 1: Asian American Care-Giving Family

You get a call from a client whose father is now living with him and his family after being widowed 5 years earlier. The father has dementia, is increasingly frail, and uses a walker to get around. The father, who had previously been very independent and, in his son's words, "stubborn," is having a difficult time adjusting to being dependent upon his son, daughter-in-law, grandchildren, and the paid caregiver. He refuses help bathing, but has fallen in the shower. Although he needs help, he does not want help while toileting and instead leaves a mess in the bathroom. He refuses assistance with his medications, but forgets to take them. He is also not eating well. The son and daughter-in-law are exhausted and unhappy trying to balance work, children, and care-giving responsibilities. They are arguing more often and are short-tempered with each other, the father, and their children. Both your client and his wife have started losing sleep. Their large, extended family is sympathetic to their situation, but family members are unable to offer help beyond emotional support. The son, who has no siblings, tells you, "No one in my family has ever put their parent in a nursing home, and I won't be the first one who breaks that tradition. If I do that, I'll feel guilty as heck and I won't be able to look any of my aunties in the eye. Besides, I wouldn't want my children doing that to me."

How would you work with this family, using principles from the cultural awareness, knowledge acquisition, and skill development sections of this chapter?

Case Study 2: Recognizing Diversity Across Race, Class, and Generations

A 77-year-old White client requests home visit by the social worker, to talk about the homecare helper, who is Chinese. The visit results in a complaint that the homecare helper is not good, particularly with her shopping and cooking. The client complains that the helper refuses to purchase Swiss cheese, can't tell the difference between Grape-Nut Flakes and Grape-Nuts, and cooks rice all the time. The client also complains about the helper's cleaning skills, saying, "She uses a cloth to dust lampshades, and the dust is flying in the air, how can I breathe with that going on?" "She sweeps the carpet and does not seem to know how to use the vacuum cleaner," and "She leaves the mop out on the deck. Why can't she use a rag to clean the floor like I used to do?"

The social worker, who is a person of color, must grapple with the following issues:

1. What is the helper's experience with client? Does she feel and think the client is oppressive? Does the helper pity the client, thereby excusing her? Does she expect that these underlying thoughts about people of color will always come out?

2. How does the social worker report and resolve the "complaint"? Can the social worker just tell the helper not to prepare rice, stating that client was unable to tell her directly of her dislike?

3. The social worker asks helper to reflect on the context of the caring relationship—is the helper required to accommodate a client's abusive attitude?

4. Does the homecare helper want something done about the complaint?

5. Client's white skin privilege (i.e., "how do you expect me to eat rice?").

6. Client–helper relationship assumes the client is "right" and the helper is "wrong."

7. Do we fail to expect older persons to change, to take on relationships outside of their life experiences (i.e., relating to uneducated women of color, immigrants, domestic workers, and people from different races and classes in general)?

8. Quality of care in this setting is about providing care and conducting daily living tasks in ways the client would do it, if she could. What are the limits of client preferences and prejudices? When client's life experience with theft or battery by an Asian American results in her refusing to accept Asian American workers? When the cooking of the helper, while nutritious, is not what the client prefers to eat? Or when the cooking of the helper is not "good" enough?

SUMMARY

In this chapter we have sought to provide an update on the current demographic changes that have recently occurred with the older adult in the United States and throughout the world.

The rapid growth of older persons based on good health and health care means that society must recognize the needs and contributions of this age group and must integrate them as a vibrant part of the population. It must guard against ageism and age discrimination in full-time and part-time employment, social benefits, health-care resource distribution, and other areas where older adults might be short changed. It must monitor the actual and potential physical and financial abuse of older persons often by greedy family members and persons who prey on this age group in the community.

For the social worker, becoming culturally competent with the older adult means that the social work student should be introduced to gerontological social work education. We have mentioned some of the multiple areas of study in various parts of this chapter: care giving, chronic disease, the literature of the field, and practice skills with the older adult. We have also identified the specific needs of culturally diverse groups of older adults. We trust that you will cultivate a major interest in working with this age population group.

PRESENT AND FUTURE DIRECTIONS

Part Four includes summary reflections on culturally competent practice that cover the major growth moments of cultural competence; the social context of realities related to social stratification and strategies to cope with these contentual realities; the strivings for human rights and social and economic justice; cultural and ethnic diverse groups and cultural competence; and reflections that we hope will make you a better person, a more perceptive student, and an effective social worker.

At the November 2005 Cultural Competence and Mental Health Summit XIII in Fresno, California, the theme of the conference was Building Bridges to Recovery and Wellness in our Communities. Since 1992, mental health professionals in California have gathered annually to discuss a wide array of topics ranging from Creating Culturally Blended Communities to Overcoming Health Disparities through Cultural Competency and to focus on such learning vehicles as Hmong Narratives: Narrative as Identity, Treatment, and Renewal. In a workshop that I led called Culturally Competent Intervention Strategies, I asked the question: Where is cultural competence going? Various answers were given but one woman observed: "It's not so much cultural competence that we are concerned about. Rather, it is about delivering culturally effective services to our clients." I did not answer this participant but I silently responded: "But cultural competence is a practice approach that can help to deliver culturally and ethnically effective services to clients."

SOME REFLECTIONS ON CULTURALLY COMPETENT PRACTICE

CHAPTER 18

Doman Lum

This book has taken you on a journey that started with an introduction to cultural competence. We began by giving you a thorough understanding of this concept, particularly how it is defined and implemented in competencies. We are pleased that the National Association of Social Workers (NASW) has Standards and Indicators for Cultural Competence in Social Work Practice and that the Council on Social Work Education (CSWE) has specific curriculum standards based on a set of core competencies. These criteria and content areas have been discussed and applied in this text.

Culturally competent practice is emerging as an integral part of social work practice and education. We have sought to present a culturally competent practice model that addresses a number of areas: definition, history, levels and dimensions, beliefs, and research issues; social context; human rights and social and economic justice; and diverse groups. Rather than reiterate the essence of these themes we need to press on to an urgent issue: *What are the new horizons and the unfinished agenda for cultural competence* particularly in light of the rich contributions which has been made by social work and counseling psychology during the last 20 years?

The purpose of this chapter is to think with you about a number of new challenges facing the culturally competent practice movement as we enter the second decade of the 21st century and to leave with you an agenda that you may be willing to assume and own in your own rights as social work students, educators, and practitioners.

NEW HORIZONS AND THE UNFINISHED AGENDA

Part of the challenge of participating in a relatively new practice approach called culturally competent practice is the fresh tasks of envisioning new horizons and defining the unfinished agenda of a practice movement. In part I have a selfish reason for discussing horizons and agendas. My own sense of mortality and finitude tells me that I might not live to be a witness to the future innovative contributions of my social work colleagues who labor in the harvest fields of cultural competence. As a retired professor of social work, I am in the process of disengagement. Teaching classes, reading and grading papers, participating in faculty meetings, and going on CSWE accreditation site visits are no longer a part of my daily professional routine. At best, reading the cultural competence literature and finding out the latest state-of-the-art research and publications have been my joys as I endeavor to piece together and write about the present practice state of this approach for this book. So let me leave with you *a legacy of what I hope will unfold in the next 10 years* of cultural competence development in social work education and to have you as students, educators, and practitioners buy into the parts and the whole of the new horizons and agenda.

OPERATIONALIZATION OF THE DEFINITION

As indicated in Chapter One, a major effort has been to assess current definitions, propose a formal definition, present a working definition, and find supportive evidence toward conceptualizing formal and working definitions of cultural competence and culturally competent social work practice. Previous definitional conceptualizations have missed the mark, concentrating on the functions of the culturally competent worker, the tasks of cultural competence, and other peripheral features. The definition of cultural competence in a social work practice context is the essential element in the epistemology (theory of knowledge) of cultural competence. One is required to build the definition from the etiology and the root meaning of the term and to apply the scientific research methodology (the construct, the operationalization of the construct, and the working definition and purpose). We have endeavored to do so in Chapter One. However, formulating current and future definitions of cultural competence are continuous tasks, particularly as new data emerges about the dynamic nature of culture and competence.

The formulation of a precise and accurate definition of cultural competence and the operationalization of the definition have implications for practice, behavior, research, policy, and field. Without an operationalized definition the worker might not know how to implement cultural competence in helping a client with a culturally related problem; understanding the dynamics of cultural behavior; formulating culturally based policies, legislation, and programs; constructing a culturally competent measurement instrument and conducting culturally competent research; and establishing culturally competent field placement experiences *in a culturally competence sense.*

We need to articulate an accurate working definition that has language syntax and addresses the essential meaning.

OUTCOME MEASUREMENT

The NASW 2007 *Indicators for the achievement of the NASW standards for cultural competence in social work practice* is a major milestone for the social work profession and culturally competent practice. It demonstrates a serious commitment of professional social work to cultural competence, but it underscores the need to determine how to measure these indicators in order to provide evidence that cultural competent practice was implemented properly with individuals, families, and groups in a social work agency setting.

A review of the indicators uncovers 106 competencies and sub-competencies identified in ten standards with supporting interpretation. The present task is to devise an instrument to measure these indicators and to provide agency data to determine the degree of the NASW member worker's cultural competence with clients. The instrument could be a part of a monograph entitled *Cultural competent research: Measuring NASW cultural competent indicators*. It is imperative to carry out this follow-up project, because one suspects that the standards for cultural competence in social work practice and the indicators might not be fully appreciated and used because of the lack of certainty about how to use and measure the indicators.

CLIENT COMPETENCE AND PROFICIENCY

We have discussed the importance of the client to become culturally competent and proficient in working through culturally based problems. This is part of the dialogical helping relationship between the client and the worker. Together, in a dialogical egalitarian relationship, the client and the worker name reality in order for it to be changed. Naming the reality applies to the goal of attaining interpersonal cultural competence between client and worker, as it applies to specific behaviors and situations of the client, problems facing particular cultural groups, and macro-level systemic injustice. What seems like a simple act-naming reality, calling things what they are, can be the impetus for the client or worker who may be the victim of oppression and historically dehumanized to reclaim his or her identity as a subject and become an active participant in history rather than simply the object of oppression.

It is also an occasion for the client and worker who may have knowingly or unknowingly, actively or passively participated in the dehumanization of others (and, as a result, the dehumanization of himself or herself in the Freirean sense) to acknowledge complicity and to begin working toward humanization. By doing this, it concretely situates the helping relationship in the broader context of a social justice struggle and it contains within it the possibility of changing the trajectory of the ways of being for both the client and the worker and the possibility of disrupting the dominant historical, political, and economic narratives.

No one is leading anyone anywhere, and no one is practicing the banking (I owe you) concept of helping, but rather, in the substitution of the oppressive teacher–student (I am competent—I am teaching you to be competent) binary (two by two) with an egalitarian relationship and with mutual client and worker competence and proficiency, the client and the worker are freed to see the world and their situation as it is, rather than as it has been prescribed. Thus, the nature and definition of cultural competence as mutual participation and exploration are an exercise in dialogue between concrete experience and theory, between action and reflection, and between the dialogical self of the client and the worker talking and listening to each other and themselves in the dialogical process that is cultural competence and proficiency. By beginning the dialogue between the client and the worker we work through problems that are not just culturally, but also historically, sociopolitically, and economically based. In this sense we are achieving breakthroughs in the dialogical process.

If we have turned the corner and shifted the cultural competence paradigm from worker competence to client and worker competence and proficiency, we must begin to write about client competence and proficiency. That is, what are the benchmarks that characterize a competent and proficient client who can draw upon his or her culture to assist with the problem-solving of his or her life's situation? Moreover, it is important to name the reality of the following cultural resources which can be a source of strength and solace. A number of areas (Lum, 2004) related to client competence and proficiency are:

- The use of cultural beliefs, customs, celebrations, and rituals as means to overcoming social problems
- Culture as a source of strength and renewal, particularly the rediscovery of past heritage to cope with present and future life problems
- Reframing the problem to include positive cultural strengths within a strategy of change
- A mix which consists of directive task-centered approaches, environmental approaches to changing the problematic condition, the interdependent extended family, and practical advice-giving
- Cultural explanations of the individual's problems which include disharmony and imbalance manifested in psychophysiological or somatic symptoms as well as shame and social withdrawal or isolation
- Dreams, visions, and cosmic messages which may be culturally accepted means of resolving problems
- Culturally significant resources and social supports such as self-help groups, extended family, and the church (perceived as a community of accepting people who are involved in practical helping programs)
- The development of identity pride which involves defining one's self in ways to affirm one's identity in order to promote self-love, to free one's self from internalized stereotypes, and to value one's ethnicity, gender, disability, sexual orientation, faith, and/or age
- Building on client's strengths and mobilizing resources to enhance the capacity to recover from, survive, and overcome oppression; deal with powerlessness and discrimination; and use personal and interpersonal power to obtain concrete resources and information
- Increasing client access to power by mobilizing resources to achieve control over their lives (self-empowerment) and to seek changes in external conditions
- Seeking changes in oppressive conditions by self-affirmation and love or identity pride which has a transforming effect and by advocacy activities to obtain necessary services

Advocates of client competence and proficiency are encouraged to develop these themes and related areas in order to balance the literature related to worker competence and client competence and proficiency.

CULTURAL COMPETENCE RESEARCH

An effort toward strengthening the research methodology of culturally competent practice is essential in the development of quantitative and qualitative studies in this field. While counseling psychology has developed individually focused cultural competent instruments, social work research is concerned about the development of cultural competent instruments which study the interaction between the worker and the client, client and agency effectiveness, and related micro-meso-macro dimensions of research. Along with instrument development is the need to evaluate existing cultural competence research as far as individual clients, organizational behavior, and program development are concerned. New categories of research analysis in these areas (e.g., revised version of Cross and associates Culturally Competent System of Care) reflecting current cultural competence organizational behavior is an example of social work meso research which would make a contribution to future studies.

CULTURAL COMPETENCE AND THE CORE COMPETENCIES

The 2008 CSWE Educational Policy and Accreditation Standards (EPAS) moved social work education to a competency-based curriculum model with a set of core competencies. As indicated in Chapter One, six of the ten core competencies are covered in various chapters of this book. Out of the ten competencies, there are cultural competence dimensions which could be identified for each competency.

For example, the competency on *diversity* in practice (CSWE, 2008, EPAS, Educational Policy 2.1.4) is: "Social workers understand how diversity characterizes and shapes the human experience and is critical to the formation of identity." Measuring this curriculum competency with cultural and ethnic diversity parameters is a task for culturally competent research and outcome measurements. It should be noted that diversity is operationalized based on the concept of *intersectionality*. Intersectionality theory holds that there are multidimensional client characteristics which intersect at various points. Educational Policy 2.1.4 continues: "The dimensions of diversity are understood as the intersectionality of multiple factors including age, class, color, culture, disability, ethnicity, gender, gender identity and expression, immigration status, political ideology, race, religion, sex, and sexual orientation." How would one operationalize "diversity" and "intersectionality" to create corresponding categories in order to devise outcome measurements for curriculum evaluation?

Moreover the competency on *difference* in practice (CSWE, 2008, EPAS, Educational Policy 2.1.4) is: "Social workers appreciate that, as a consequence of difference, a person's life experience may include oppression, poverty, marginalization, and alienation as well as privilege, power, and acclaim." The concept of difference is operationalized as "the importance of difference in shaping life experiences"(Educational Policy 2.1.4). Factors central to cultural competence in this standard include variables such as color, culture, ethnicity, gender, race, sex, and sexual orientation. What are the program guidelines on diversity and difference which result on determining outcome measurements and useful to ascertain curriculum competencies for a particular social work education program in the accreditation process (e.g., program self-study guidelines to determine and implement core competencies and accompanying significant variables)? Like the need for outcome measurements for the 2007 NASW cultural competence indicators is the need for similar efforts with the 2008 CSWE core competencies.

CULTURAL COMPETENCE AND EVIDENCE-BASED PRACTICE

The Whaley and Davis proposal to integrate cultural competence and evidence-based practice (a wedding of two popular movements in social work and counseling/clinical psychology) is an interesting agenda item on the table. As indicated in Chapter One, Whaley and Davis (2007) made the proposal based on two concerns: the need to introduce the concept of cultural adaptation to the evidence-based practice approach and the need to provide a scientific practice methodology to culturally competent practice. The question is whether both practice approaches would benefit from the exchange in the process. To this date there has been no significant review of the literature and conceptual proposal to integrate cultural competence and evident-based practice. Since Whaley and Davis proposed such a practice merger, it seems logical for them to pursue this matter and conduct a series of follow-up studies involving propositional principles of these two practice approaches. Interfacing two practice approaches with content and methodology from the other offers a new avenue of exploring and developing practice theory conceptualization.

CULTURAL COMPETENCE PUBLICATIONS

The cultural competence practice movement should evaluate the present state of cultural competence publications and determine the areas for future research and writing contributions. Among the social work education curriculum areas for cultural competence publications are cultural competent perspectives in diversity and difference; human rights and social and economic justice; research-informed practice and practice-informed research, human behavior and the social environment; policy practice, practice process, and field education. An examination of the 2008 CSWE EPAS curriculum design reveals alternative curriculum configurations beyond the categories of practice, human behavior, policy, diversity, policy, and field. The present EPAS core competencies reveal a flow of curriculum content which is joined together in various combinations and which intersects traditional boundaries. This curriculum design can be the source of publications which require innovative avenues of researching and writing because it brings new interpretations of social work education curriculum with a competencies perspective. Social work educators ought to research and write about these curriculum areas with curriculum competencies and cultural competence perspectives.

CULTURAL COMPETENCE BEST PRACTICES

With professional practice in cultural competence at a high point of interest, NASW should plan a national conference on Cultural Competence Best Practices. The purpose of the conference is to identify the existing models of cultural competence best practices and to invite outstanding cultural competence theorists and practitioners for presentation, dialogue, and action. Major components of the conference would be: 1) the presentation of a variety of cultural competence best practice models with panels of discussants; 2) the construction of research design and evaluation to validate cultural competence best practice models; and 3) the implementation of cultural competence best practices models in selected agency programs across the country which would promote practice-oriented research test centers for culturally competent practice. A series of short-term longitudinal studies of cultural competence best practices models would occur in these sites and findings would be published by NASW.

CULTURAL COMPETENCE AND INTERDISCIPLINARY STUDIES

Historically the cultural competence movement in the United States started with multicultural counseling and clinical psychology and spread to social work, medicine, nursing, and other health and human services disciplines. Cultural competence is an authentic interdisciplinary subject area. It is noteworthy that Dr. Derald Wing Sue, professor of counseling/clinical psychology, teaches at Columbia University Teachers College and has a part-time appointment at Columbia University School of Social Work. Dr. Sue has been the leading proponent and authority of the cultural competence movement and is an example of an interdisciplinary studies resource in cultural competence. Rather than propose that Columbia University establish a National Center on Cultural Competence and Interdisciplinary Studies, I suggest that university social work education programs identify existing social work faculty with interest and expertise in culturally competent practice and similar faculty in related disciplines such as psychology, ethnic studies, medicine, nursing, and other areas. A preliminary step toward establishing interdisciplinary studies in cultural competence would be to create a course on Interdisciplinary Cultural Competence and to involve a number of instructors from various departments with interest and perspectives on cultural competence. Professors of medicine, social work, and psychology teaching such a course would offer interesting insights and content emphases. They could collaborate on significant interdisciplinary research in cultural competence and work on common local social services programs with cultural competence components. The possibilities and potentials for creative interdisciplinary collaboration are endless.

CULTURAL COMPETENCE RESEARCH AND TRAINING CENTER

At the present time there is a National Center for Cultural Competence (NCCC) housed at Georgetown University in Washington, D.C., which is funded by the Health Resources and Services Administration (HRSA), Department of Health and Human Services (DHHS). The mission of NCCC is to increase the capacity of health-care programs to design, implement, and evaluate culturally competent service delivery systems. The Cultural Competence Research and Training Center (CCRTC) would complement the NCCC. The purpose of CCRTC is to serve as a clearinghouse for cultural competence practice research, to promote new innovative research in the field, and to serve as a training center for practitioners and educators who are seeking alternative ways of practicing and teaching cultural competence. A possible site is at a major research education university with a full-time director and a support staff. Facility and accompanying resources (e.g., library, computer technology) are important for the success of such a center. Practitioners and professors on leave and sabbaticals from various parts of the country with cultural competence interests comprise research and teaching fellows. Federal research and training grants and university matching funds are revenue sources for the center.

CULTURAL COMPETENCE CENTER FOR CHILDREN AND FAMILIES

A Cultural Competence Center for Children and Families (CCCCF) envisions a culturally competent practice site for the promotion of cultural competence and proficiency for parents, children, and families. The purpose of the center is to gather children and families from diverse backgrounds together and to examine culturally competent indigenous beliefs and practices, to evaluate diverse problem children and families in order to determine social contextual factors, and to identify and promote culturally competent ways of dealing with child and family problems. Since the child and the family comprise the basic group of households in the United States, it is crucial to have a number of regional centers located in major metropolitan and rural areas near university-based social work education programs for resources and support. Social work practitioners from local agencies and social work professors from surrounding universities as volunteers could staff a regional center and work with selected children and families. The primary purpose is examination, evaluation, and promotion of ways to effect culturally competent practice on these target systems (child, siblings, parent(s), and family). The secondary purpose is to provide social service assistance to a selected population on a limited basis.

We have presented 11 examples of new horizons and the unfinished agenda that offer possibilities and potentials for the culturally competent movement. There are a mix of academic and research concerns, curriculum design innovations, practice approach integrations, and program structures which will have an effect on the growth and development of cultural competence. As you consider each one, I want you to consider which ones interest you, which ones have the potential to reach fruition, and which ones could be realistically funded. Set your own horizon on cultural competence and put an agenda item on the table. You may be a catalyst and leader of culturally competent practice as you make a commitment to this movement.

DIVERSITY GROUPS

Sixteen social work educators contributed original, theme-related chapters on First Nations Peoples, European Americans, African Americans, Latino Americans, Asian Americans, Muslim Americans, women, gays, lesbians, bisexual, and transgender persons, persons with disabilities, and older adults. Although distinctive emphases have been made in the discussion of each group, a number of themes have emerged from the contributors' efforts of writing from a common outline chapter format.

The contributors have enlarged our understanding of defining cultural competence. Weaver emphasizes the need to develop knowledge competencies for working with First Nations clients in diversity, history, culture, and contemporary realities of Native people. The social worker's values and attitudes for cultural competence should include helper wellness and self-awareness, humility and willingness to learn, respect and open-mindedness, a nonjudgmental stance, and social justice. Pewewardy, Almeida, Dressner, and Hann point out that in order to be culturally competent, European Americans must recognize that whiteness determines a privileged social location and that deconstruction and dismantling of the connections of White power and privilege is needed. For African American clients, according to McRoy and Lombe, culturally competent workers should commit to diversity, recognize social factors leading to single-parent families, and seek out African American staff. McRoy and Lombe makes African American client applications to the Cross, Bazron, Dennis, and Isaacs (1989) continuum. Garcia reminds us that for Latino American clients, cultural competence means unbiased worker attitudes, particularly toward undocumented people (which is underscored in their chapter).

For Asian Americans and Pacific Islanders, Fong believes that cultural competence involves knowledge of cultural values, indigenous interventions, and Western interventions that support traditional cultural values. The starting point is macro-level societal values and issues and their implications for communities, families, and individuals. Husain and Ross-Sheriff underscore that in order to be culturally competent with Muslim Americans, one must understand their religious culture and integrate it into the helping process. They speak about the Islamic worldview which promotes a harmonious co-existence, and the tenets of Islam found in the *Qur'an* and *Sunna*, the Pillars of Islam and the Articles of Faith, the Islamic Ontological Foundation, and Core Values of the Faith. Husain and Ross-Sheriff explain these principles in depth and encourage social workers to grasp these concepts. For work with women, Lowery emphasizes culturally competent practice with regard to the multiple identities (ethnicity, gender, social class, and related areas) and interventions at the multiple levels of micro, meso, and macro systems. Tully points out the multiple dimensions for gay, lesbian, bisexual, and transgender clients in terms of understanding their history of oppression and exclusion, membership in many groups, racial and sexual identity processes, stress, and the functions of heterosexism, racism, and sexism. Understanding and balancing these issues on behalf of this client group calls for an extra portion of culturally competent wisdom, grace, and skill.

Our understanding of the multiple meanings of cultural competence is broadening to include client and community, worker and staff, values, and multiple identities and interventions beyond our present meanings. That is, a culturally competent worker must have respect for the client and knowledge and skills to deal culturally with the client and the community of which the client is a part; must focus on the worker as a part of a culturally competent and integrated staff; must have appropriate and coherent values that culturally fit the populations served; and must recognize that people have complex and multilayered identities that require micro, meso, and macro multiple interventions. In his advocacy for persons with disabilities, Mackelprang stresses the multiple social identities that must be part of our understanding of cultural competence. This includes the disability culture arising from identity-based communities. These insights should make us revisit our understanding of cultural competence.

For understanding diversity among and between the various groups, Weaver reminds us of the rich and widespread diversity within First Nations Peoples. One must ask to what extent a First Nations Peoples client is culturally affiliated as far as identification is concerned. Culture, spiritual practices, the social environment, and family and community are important areas to explore in building an understanding of diversity. McRoy's and Lombe's view of African American diversity involves explaining ten ethnic population demographic areas that must be understood by the social worker. For Latino Americans, Garcia portrays the richness of diversity as we conduct assessment on language, acculturation, and immigration; planning from an ecological, cultural, and practical perspective; and practice that is family based, involves crisis intervention, and is support-group oriented. In her portrayal of Asian American diversity, Fong is concerned for a number of emerging groups of Asian American immigrants and refugees, biracial and mixed racial children, adults, and families, including families adopting children from the People's Republic of China. Husain and Ross-Sheriff cover the ethnic, cultural, and linguistic diversity of Muslim Americans which span Africa, the Middle East, Asia, and Europe as well as the diversity in beliefs and schools of thought among Muslims.

The Lowery study of women is from the perspective of Central American women who have taken the leadership in grassroots movements. Given the international concern for earthquake victims in Haiti in 2010, Lowery gives us historical and economic background of Haiti where women have a major responsibility for feeding and ensuring the health of their families. When the 2010 earthquake struck in Haiti, relief workers discovered that it made sense to have the women of families receive the food in order to avert riots when food distribution encountered unruly mobs. Lowery also points out that in Haitian informal economy, women are central due to their skills in cooperation and leadership. She champions the Campesino Movement among farmers of Latin America and the role of women in leadership positions. Likewise, Tully gives us vital information about distinguishing the unique life and culture and histories of gays, lesbians, bisexual, and transgender persons rather than viewing these groups as similar. Revilla and Yee estimate that the diverse older adult population was 506 million in 2008 globally and will reach 1.3 billion by 2040. Moreover the "oldest old" aged 80 and above is the fastest-growing segment of the population of many countries according to them.

Inter- and intragroup diversity causes us to realize how similar and how different we are both as members of an ethnic and cultural group and as we relate to other ethnic and cultural peoples. Mackelprang has an interesting chart which identifies first-order choices across ethnicities and cultures. The chart includes the common themes of time, activity, relational, person/nature, and basic nature for five major ethnic groups and disabled individuals. It illustrates the similarities and differences of diversity. Individuality and uniqueness and difference and distinction are present in a single group, yet we are able to transcend these realities and come together with common concerns, bonding with each other.

Pertaining to conceptualizing oppression, all contributors reiterated the major events of historical oppression inflicted upon these groups. We gain an understanding of the particular history of clients who are a part of these groups. The theme of historical trauma helps us to understand the psychohistorical pain of people who still carry these events in their inner selves. That is, ethnic people and groups carry and pass on a sense of collective trauma and pain over what happened to them and their ancestors that affects their individual and group psyches. Colonization and other forms of oppression require people to revisit these events, re-experience them, and learn new ways through re-education to deal with the trauma and pain. Weaver's sharing of the concept of the Seven Generations provides a historical perspective—for First Nations Peoples' cultures, ancestors seven generations ago were planning for future generations to preserve land, language, and culture. The message is that people today have the same responsibility to ensure that the needs of future generations will be met. Peweardy, Almeida, Dressner, and Hann observe that historically the term *White* was a political construct to unite Europeans, particularly to consolidate strength and increase their ability to control and dominate Native Americans and African slaves. McRoy and Lombe remind us of the historical background of African Americans: involuntary migration, slavery, segregation, and continued oppression. In numerous ways, racism and oppression are still daily experiences for African Americans.

Garcia offers a multidimensional view of oppression affecting Mexicans, Puerto Ricans, Cubans, and Central Americans and its impact on new geographical settlements in parts of the country where there is limited Latino presence. Likewise, Fong traces the historical oppression of Asian immigrant groups in the United States during the last two centuries, and she traces racist attitudes and behaviors during World War II with Japanese Americans and during the Vietnam War with Amerasian children. She also highlights the past colonialist practices toward Pacific Islanders, particularly Hawaiians, and the current oppression experiences faced by native Hawaiians who are struggling with the issue of sovereignty and the return of their lands. Husain and Ross-Sheriff describe three periods of historical oppressions and current social issues for Muslim Americans: from the founding until World War II, post World War II, and post September 11, 2001. Understanding oppression from the Muslim American viewpoint helps us humanize this group rather than viewing all Muslim Americans as potential terrorists. Likewise addressing the role and status of Muslim American Women in terms of pursuing education and careers helps us to see the equitable contributions of Muslim women in their community. Tully points out that among gays, lesbians, bisexual, and transgender persons there is still religious intolerance, societal discrimination, and denial of rights. According to Revilla and Yee, ageism or age discrimination is a process of systematic stereotyping against people because they are old and has been a constant societal problem.

Our task is to realize that people carry their histories with them and are cautious of how they relate to others, particularly in the helping process. Learning how historical events of oppression affect the client and how these past happenings influence present thoughts, feelings, and behaviors is crucial to our development of cultural competence.

Addressing cultural awareness and social service needs, Weaver offers suggestions on how to structure needs assessment, intervention choice, and program design for First Nations Peoples to achieve a cultural fit and connection with a particular client in a particular cultural setting. McRoy and Lombe offer practical suggestions for working with African American clients in the establishment of relationship building and trust, the use of the strengths perspective in assessment, the use of helping networks and community intervention support, and awareness of spiritual belief systems and the role of the Black church. The strengths approach, in finding positive coping strategies and looking for family strengths, moves away from a pathological, deficit view. Garcia identifies a number of areas crucial to fostering Latino American cultural awareness and social service needs: an understanding of Latino American religious trends and family structure and composition, the importance of engaging and including fathers as heads of households, and the use of group services to reach Latino families. Fong surveys the wide array of cultural and service needs of Asian American groups: the elderly, the immigrant, the refugee, the victim of substance abuse and family violence, and gay, lesbian, bisexual, and transgender Asians and Pacific Islanders. Needs and services vary among these different but similar populations. Husain and Ross-Sheriff explain cultural awareness of Muslim Americans in terms of their cuisine, dress, and worship. Mackelprang walks us through three stages of cultural awareness in our evolution of how we have perceived persons with disabilities: the moral model, the medical model, and now hopefully the social/ minority model where disability is an element of diversity. Lowery points to the high poverty levels of women of color, the effect of poverty on health and mental health, and the availability of health care services and systems for such women to meet their needs.

Cultural awareness areas underscore the need for social services delivery planning to be based on a cultural orientation foundation of particular service intent according to the groups served and for the maintenance of cultural awareness throughout the beginning, middle, and end of the helping process. That is, cultural awareness should permeate how to begin the relationship, how to couch the problem, how to articulate a strengths-based assessment, and how to form an intervention that will encompass the many cultural and social needs of people.

Concerning knowledge acquisition, there are so many knowledge areas to become familiar with and master. Weaver underscores the worker's knowledge of Native people's diversity, extended family networks and community ties, historical trauma and grief, distinctiveness of urban and reservation communities, sovereignty issues and policies surrounding the Indian Child Welfare Act and the Indian Health Service, and attitudinal values of the worker toward the client (worker wellness and self-awareness, humility and the willingness to learn, respect and open-mindedness, nonjudgment, and a sense of social justice). McRoy and Lombe identify numerous general knowledge areas about African Americans and specific knowledge concerns about a particular African American client. The many knowledge areas include help-seeking behaviors of African Americans, the use of the strengths perspective, and the client's interpersonal style and perceptions of racial identity and relationships.

Garcia is concerned about the acquisition of knowledge about Latino immigrants in terms of their mental health and social/environmental needs. They trace the stages of migration and isolation issues, and their effects on families, particularly children and youth. Fong looks at knowledge theories that may be pertinent to Asians and Pacific Islanders: colonization theory, historical trauma theory, Confucian philosophy, and related areas. She also encourages us to construct new theories that address policy and social change, which will broaden our understanding of family subgroups such as Chinese children abandoned and then adopted from the People's Republic of China, and the various interacting diverse variables that force us to view and understand clients in multidimensional levels. Concerning knowledge acquisition for Muslim Americans, Husain and Ross-Sheriff help us to understand divine help-seeking (reliance on Allah and Prayer), the concept of divine forgiveness for sins, and life challenges and problems as tests from Allah. Revilla and Yee encourage social workers to acquire knowledge through studying older adult legislation (the Older Americans Act, Area Agency on Aging, titles XVIII, XIX, and XX of the Social Security Act), reading books (e.g., Gene Cohen's *The Mature Mind: The Positive Power of the Aging Brain* and *The Creative Age: Awakening Human Potential in the Second Half of Life*), and seeing movies on older adults (e.g., *Young@Heart*).

I encourage you to choose a few of the knowledge concepts that catch your interest and to begin to study and focus on them. Family-related knowledge areas, such as extended family support networks and family structure and dynamics, and immigrant and refugee transitions are areas with overlapping themes that bridge various cultural and ethnic groups.

Focusing on practice skill development, Weaver stresses good communication skills, problem solving with clear and practical steps, and good containment skills such as listening and patience as key to working with First Nations Peoples. Pewewardy, Almeida, Dressner, and Hann teach a Cultural Context Model (CCM) which offers a liberation model of relational healing based on cultural equity and social justice. McRoy and Lombe pinpoint the development of the therapeutic relationship, communication skills, worker abilities, and Afrocentric practice approaches. Garcia identifies relationship protocols (self-disclosure, style of communication), problem identification, and interventions that realize realistic cultural support network approaches. Fong teaches the need to develop indigenous and traditional ways of healing and to match them with Western interventions in a treatment plan that makes sense to the client, as well as with interventions that meet the multiple variable dimensions and needs of the client. Husain and Ross-Sheriff stress knowledge, awareness, and respect for the Muslim American client's value-informed worldview. Lowery encourages social work to adopt a socio-cultural approach to working with people, much like the Campesino Movement of Central America. She calls for social work to recommit itself to address poverty, to reaffirm relationships, to learn and to teach, to create learning communities and shared power, and to promote transformational learning. Tully summarizes intervention on three levels: the micro level of mobilizing client strengths and self-determination, the meso level of mobilizing communities to develop group consciousness, and the macro level of embracing solutions related to institutional discrimination.

One must combine traditional social work interventions such as problem solving and empowerment with indigenous approaches that come from the culture itself. The biculturalization and integration of the two offer an opportunity to create interventions that make sense in the cultural context and that are functional and practical for both the worker and the client. Weaver believes in experiential learning opportunities such as spending time in First Nations communities in a classroom context, attending cultural and ethnic activities that are open to the public, and becoming a cross-cultural learner. McRoy and Lombe suggest the use of gathering clients' life narratives and workers' observations through meaningful questions that generate understanding, and the use of the strengths perspective, which looks for positives. Garcia recommends seeking the consultation of culturally competent Latino workers who have worked with and understand Latino Americans, asking for assistance on a Latino case, and finding the literature and pertinent conferences that will foster inductive learning of this population. Fong is keen on such new inductive learning areas for Asians and Pacific Islanders as new diverse groupings and identities, transitional cultural value conflicts, indigenous strategies, and commonalities and differences within and between groups. Husain and Ross-Sheriff suggest that for Muslim Americans a strengths-based approach and cognitive therapy are most effective rather than a psychoanalytic or group therapy perspective. Revilla and Yee talk about the importance of care giving and being a caregiver in skill development with the older adult client.

Finally, with human rights and social and economic justice, Weaver identifies a number of concerns for First Nations Peoples: Indian child welfare removal, economic development that offers employment with a future; environmental and health concerns such as the use of Native lands for dumping toxic waste; and indigenous sovereignty. McRoy and Lombe are concerned about equal access to resources (education and the public schools in the African American community), everyday practices of oppression that become internalized, and strategies of empowerment. Garcia focuses on Latino employment exploitation, inequitable educational facility resources, and immigrant exploitation in employment and housing. She suggests the need for empowering clients through community participation in collaborative resource development in the local Latino communities. Fong zeroes in on land rights and welfare reform for Asian and Pacific Islander immigrants as the most important human rights and social and economic justice issue for this population. For Muslim Americans, social and economic justice are a part of their religious culture: obligations to God and respect for the mutual rights and responsibilities of other human beings. For women, Lowery presents Elvia Alvarado, a Honduran land activist, who worked in the Catholic Church helping others, distributing food to hungry women and children, establishing gardens, and discussing food and nutrition through mothers' clubs. Ms. Alvardo was an advocate for women's rights, spoke against economic classism and injustice, joined the National Campesino Union, and helped to create the National Congress of Rural Workers which was instrumental in agrarian land reform for Hondurus. Tully offers practical suggestions for social workers as far as social justice for gays, lesbians, bisexual, and transgender persons is concerned: educate yourself about the realities of sexual minorities and endeavor to dispel stereotypes and then seek to educate others. For women, Lowery discusses the following human rights and social and economic justice concerns: health coverage, employment, education and training, and safeguards against sexual harassment.

Human rights and social and economic justice reveals past and present incidents of injustice and fuels the need to practice and maintain equality for all. We constantly strive for the ideal but struggle with the real. The contributors point out the realities of our imperfections and the need to empower others for access to resources.

SOCIAL WORK AND CULTURAL COMPETENCIES

PRELIMINARY RESEARCH RESULTS ON SELF-ASSESSMENT TESTS

We have discussed the importance of measuring cultural competencies. You may find useful the following preliminary research results examining cultural competencies described in this text.

This author administered the Social Work Cultural Competencies Self-Assessment Pretest and Posttest to his Social Work 102 Multicultural Theory and Practice undergraduate classes from the Spring 1999 to the Fall 2004 semesters at California State University, Sacramento. A reliability analysis scale (alpha) of the pre- and posttests was established with the reliability coefficients of 388 cases and 44 items of the questionnaire. There was an alpha of .9437 reliability for the pretest and an alpha of .9245 for the posttest. Instrumentation reliability was very high.

The demographics of these 388 undergraduate students revealed the following characteristics:

- Age: ranged from 17-years old to 59-years old with a mean of 26 years
- Gender: 336 females and 52 males
- Ethnicity: 158 European Americans, 55 Asian Americans, 48 Latino Americans, 48 African Americans, 18 Native Americans, 16 Middle Easterners, 6 Jewish Americans, and 25 others (3 unanswered)
- Education: ranged between 12 years and 19 years of school with a mean of 15 years (undergraduate junior year)
- Number of years as a volunteer in social services: ranged from 1 to 5 years with a mean of 1.6 years
- Number of years in social work employment: ranged from 1 to 4 years with a mean of 1.2 years
- Previous diversity courses taken in college: ranged from 1 to 4 courses with a mean of 2.2 courses

Pretest and posttest mean scores for the following areas revealed increases in understanding: 1) cultural awareness pretest score (25.8080) and posttest score (28.6108); 2) knowledge acquisition pretest score (22.4575) and posttest score (31.2487); 3) skill development pretest score (51.2977) and posttest score (75.4472); and 4) inductive learning pretest score (10.2371) and posttest score (11.9588). The category of skill development experienced the most growth (+24.1494), followed by knowledge acquisition (+8.7912), cultural awareness (+2.8028), and inductive learning (+1.7216). The course content was devoted to the skill areas of contact, problem identification, assessment, intervention, and termination along with knowledge concepts. The total pretest cultural competencies mean score was 109.8003, whereas the total posttest cultural competencies score was 147.2655. There was a total increase of +37.4652, which was a high outcome measure for a social work diversity course teaching culturally competent practice.

Paired sample *t*-tests revealed two-tailed significance of .000 for all pairs of pre- and posttest categories (cultural awareness, knowledge acquisition, skill development, and inductive learning) and for the total pre- and posttest cultural competencies scores.

The companion Social Work Cultural Competencies with Diverse Groups of Color and Social and Economic Justice Pretest and Posttest was administered to the author's Social Work 102 Multicultural Theory and Practice undergraduate classes from Fall 2002 to Fall 2005 semesters at California State University, Sacramento. The demographics of 168 undergraduate students were as follows:

- Age: ranged from 18 years to 55 years with a mean age of 24
- Gender: 142 females, 24 males, 2 missing
- Ethnicity: 59 European Americans, 34 Asian Americans, 22 African Americans, 17 Latino Americans, 15 Middle Easterners, 5 Native Americans, 1 Jewish American, 8 others, and 7 missing
- Years of education: ranged from 12 to 19 years with a mean of 14.81 years

Pretest and posttest mean scores revealed the following increases for six groups and for social and economic justice: 1) First Nations Peoples pretest (18.4524) and posttest (24.3661) with a 5.9136 increase; 2) African Americans pretest (15.9196) and posttest (23.5446) with a 7.6250 increase; 3) Latino Americans pretest (17.7768) and posttest (24.6518) with a 6.8750 increase; 4) Asian Americans pretest (16.4970) and posttest (24.2589) with a 7.7619 increase; 5) Women of Color pretest (14.5000) and posttest (24.1786) with a 9.6785 increase; 6) Gay and Lesbian Persons of Color pretest (16.0000) and posttest (24.2560) with a 8.2559 increase; and 7) Social and Economic Justice pretest (17.2560) and posttest (27.3631) with a 10.1071 increase. The total pretest scores were 116.4018 and the total posttest scores were 172.6190.

Paired samples correlations were conducted on these six groups and subject area and revealed a two-tailed significant difference of .000 for all.

Further follow-up studies in various social work programs in the United States are important to compare results. However, these preliminary findings indicate that the Social Work Cultural Competencies Self-Assessment and the Social Work Cultural Competencies with Diverse Groups of Color and Social and Economic Justice instruments measure positive outcomes in a social work education diversity course.

SELF-ASSESSMENT INSTRUMENTS

In Chapter One, you were asked to complete the Social Work Cultural Competencies Self-Assessment instrument as a pretest that measured your level of cultural competence at the start of a course on culturally diverse social work practice. Now it is important for you to take a posttest to determine the extent of your cultural competence at the end of the course.

The cultural competence areas may have been foreign and unfamiliar to you at the beginning of this book. I hope that the lectures, discussions, exercises, and assignments have contributed to your understanding of cultural competence and cultural competencies and to an enthusiastic passion for culturally diverse social work practice.

As you complete the Social Work Cultural Competencies Self-Assessment instrument for the second time, compare your levels of competence as indicated by the pretest and the posttest scores. Write a two-page analysis comparing the results of your pretest and posttest. Indicate the particular items where your score shows a significant difference and those where there is no change.

A companion instrument measures your knowledge and understanding of the culturally diverse groups and of the social and economic justice issues you have read about and studied in your class. You took the pretest of this instrument in Chapter One of this text; now we would like you to take the posttest here. You and your instructor now have two research instruments to measure your learning outcomes based on this text. We hope that they also will be the source of further discussion, research, and inquiry into various aspects of culturally competent practice.

TOOLS FOR STUDENT LEARNING 18.1

Social Work Cultural Competencies Self-Assessment Posttest

Written by Doman Lum, PhD (all rights reserved)

Introduction

This instrument measures your level of cultural competence at the beginning and end of the semester. The results of this self-assessment will be evaluated by your social work instructor. Strict confidentiality is observed regarding the results of this self-assessment.

Rate yourself on your level of competency on a scale of 1–4: 1 = Unlikely; 2 = Not very likely; 3 = Likely; and 4 = Definitely. Circle the appropriate number.

Social Security # (last four digits):   Course: Instructor: Campus:

Background Information

1. Age: ____

2. Sex: Male ____ Female ____

3. Ethnicity: (please check all that apply)
   African American _____ Asian American _____ European American ____
   Jewish American _____ Latino American _____ Middle Eastern _____
   First Nations Peoples ____ Other (please specify) _____

4. Years of education (e.g., 12 = high school graduate) (circle correct number)
   12   13   14   15   16   17   18   19   20   21 or more

5. Highest degree earned/major:

6. Years of previous social service volunteer experience:
   None ____ 1–3 years ____ 4–6 years ____ 7–9 years ____ 10 years or more ____

7. Years of previous social work employment:
   None ____ 1–3 years ____ 4–6 years ____ 7–9 years ____ 10 years or more ____

8. Prior courses on cultural diversity:
   None ____ 1 course ____ 2 courses ____ 3 or more courses ____

Cultural Awareness

1. I am aware of my life experiences as a person related to a culture (e.g., family heritage, household and community events, beliefs, and practices).

   1–Unlikely   2–Not very likely   3–Likely   4–Definitely

2. I have contact with other cultural and ethnic individuals, families, and groups.

   1–Unlikely   2–Not very likely   3–Likely   4–Definitely

3. I am aware of positive and negative experiences with cultural and ethnic people and events.

   1–Unlikely   2–Not very likely   3–Likely   4–Definitely

4. I know how to evaluate my cognitive, affective, and behavioral experiences and reactions to racism, prejudice, and discrimination.

   1–Unlikely   2–Not very likely   3–Likely   4–Definitely

5. I have assessed my involvement with cultural and ethnic people of color in childhood, adolescence, young adulthood, and adulthood.

   1–Unlikely   2–Not very likely   3–Likely   4–Definitely

6. I understand such terms as positionality, intersectionality, and the dialogic self.

   1–Unlikely   2–Not very likely   3–Likely   4–Definitely

7. I have had or plan to have professional employment experiences with culturally diverse clients and programs.

   1–Unlikely   2–Not very likely   3–Likely   4–Definitely

8. I have assessed or plan to assess my academic and professional work experiences with cultural diversity and culturally diverse clients.

   1–Unlikely   2–Not very likely   3–Likely   4–Definitely

Knowledge Acquisition

9. I understand the following terms: critical thinking, identity development, social constructionism, and marginalization.

   1–Unlikely   2–Not very likely   3–Likely   4–Definitely

10. I have developed a critical thinking perspective on cultural diversity

    1–Unlikely   2–Not very likely   3–Likely   4–Definitely

11. I know information about knowledge theories related to cultural competence.

    1–Unlikely   2–Not very likely   3–Likely   4–Definitely

12. I understand the history of oppression and multicultural social group history.

    1–Unlikely   *2–Not very likely*   *3–Likely*   *4–Definitely*

13. I know about culturally diverse values.

    1–Unlikely   *2–Not very likely*   *3–Likely*   *4–Definitely*

Skill Development

14. I understand how to overcome the resistance and lower the communication barriers of a multicultural client.

    1–Unlikely   *2–Not very likely*   *3–Likely*   *4–Definitely*

15. I know how to obtain personal and family background information from a multicultural client and determine the client's ethnic/community sense of identity.

    1–Unlikely   *2–Not very likely*   *3–Likely*   *4–Definitely*

16. I understand the concepts of ethnic community and practice relationship protocols with a multicultural client.

    1–Unlikely   *2–Not very likely*   *3–Likely*   *4–Definitely*

17. I use professional self-disclosure with a multicultural client.

    1–Unlikely   *2–Not very likely*   *3–Likely*   *4–Definitely*

18. I have a positive and open communication style and use open-ended listening responses.

    1–Unlikely   *2–Not very likely*   *3–Likely*   *4–Definitely*

19. I know how to obtain problem information, facilitate problem area disclosure, and promote problem understanding.

    1–Unlikely   *2–Not very likely*   *3–Likely*   *4–Definitely*

20. I view a problem as an unsatisfied want or an unfulfilled need.

    1–Unlikely   *2–Not very likely*   *3–Likely*   *4–Definitely*

21. I know how to explain problems on micro, meso, and macro levels.

    1–Unlikely   *2–Not very likely*   *3–Likely*   *4–Definitely*

22. I know how to explain problem themes (racism, prejudice, and discrimination) and expressions (oppression, powerlessness, stereotyping, acculturation, and exploitation).

    1–Unlikely   *2–Not very likely*   *3–Likely*   *4–Definitely*

23. I know how to find out about problem details.

    1–Unlikely   *2–Not very likely*   *3–Likely*   *4–Definitely*

24. I know how to assess socioenvironmental impacts, psychoindividual reactions, and cultural strengths.

   1–Unlikely   *2–Not very likely*   *3–Likely*   *4–Definitely*

25. I know how to assess the biological, psychological, social, cultural, and spiritual dimensions of the multicultural client.

   1–Unlikely   *2–Not very likely*   *3–Likely*   *4–Definitely*

26. I know how to establish joint goals and agreements with the client that are culturally acceptable.

   1–Unlikely   *2–Not very likely*   *3–Likely*   *4–Definitely*

27. I know how to formulate micro, meso, and macro intervention strategies that address the cultural needs of the client and special needs populations such as immigrants and refugees.

   1–Unlikely   *2–Not very likely*   *3–Likely*   *4–Definitely*

28. I know how to begin the evaluation phase which links the client to an ethnic community resource, reviews significant progress and growth development, evaluates goal outcomes, and establishes a follow-up strategy.

   1–Unlikely   *2–Not very likely*   *3–Likely*   *4–Definitely*

29. I know how to design a service delivery and agency linkage and culturally effective social service programs in ethnic communities.

   1–Unlikely   *2–Not very likely*   *3–Likely*   *4–Definitely*

30. I have been involved in services that have been accessible to the ethnic community.

   1–Unlikely   *2–Not very likely*   *3–Likely*   *4–Definitely*

31. I have participated in delivering pragmatic and positive services that meet the tangible needs of the ethnic community.

   1–Unlikely   *2–Not very likely*   *3–Likely*   *4–Definitely*

32. I have observed the effectiveness of bilingual/bicultural workers who reflect the ethnic composition of the clientele.

   1–Unlikely   *2–Not very likely*   *3–Likely*   *4–Definitely*

33. I have participated in community outreach education and prevention that establish visible services, provide culturally sensitive programs, and employ credible staff.

   1–Unlikely   *2–Not very likely*   *3–Likely*   *4–Definitely*

34. I have been involved in a service linkage network to related social agencies that ensures rapid referral and program collaboration.

   1–Unlikely   *2–Not very likely*   *3–Likely*   *4–Definitely*

35. I have participated as a staff member in fostering a conducive agency setting with an atmosphere that is friendly and helpful to multicultural clients.

1–Unlikely   2–Not very likely   3–Likely   4–Definitely

36. I am involved or plan to be involved with cultural skill development research in areas related to cultural empathy, clinical alliance, goal-obtaining styles, achieving styles, practice skills, and outcome research.

1–Unlikely   2–Not very likely   3–Likely   4–Definitely

What are your questions and views on cultural competence and cultural competencies?

What are your reactions to this self-assessment instrument?

Please count your scores on the 36 self-assessment items and rate your level of cultural competence. Circle the appropriate level and write your raw score in one of the following levels:

Level 1: Unlikely (scores 36–69)

Level 2: Not very likely (scores 70–94)

Level 3: Likely (scores 95–128)

Level 4: Definitely (scores 129–144)

Thank you for your cooperation on this self-assessment instrument. You have made a significant contribution to our research on social work cultural competence.

TOOLS FOR STUDENT LEARNING 18.2

Social Work Cultural Competencies with Culturally Diverse Groups and Social and Economic Justice Posttest

Written by Doman Lum, PhD (all rights reserved)

Introduction

This instrument measures your level of cultural competence with culturally diverse groups and social and economic justice at the beginning and end of the semester. The results of this test will be evaluated by your social work instructor. Strict confidentiality is observed regarding the results of this instrument.

Rate yourself on your level of competence on a scale of 1–4; 1 = Unlikely; 2 = Not very likely; 3 = Likely; and 4 = Definitely. Circle the appropriate number.

Social Security # (last four digits):   Course: Instructor: Campus:

First Nations Peoples

1. I know about the diversity of Native nations, which differ in terms of language, religion, social structure, political structure, and many aspects of culture.

1–Unlikely   2–Not very likely   3–Likely   4–Definitely

2. I understand the concept of Seven Generations, which provides a historical and current perspective on oppression experiences.

   1–Unlikely   *2–Not very likely*   *3–Likely*   *4–Definitely*

3. It is important to choose interventions and design programs that accurately target the needs of First Nations Peoples, which may be different for each community.

   1–Unlikely   *2–Not very likely*   *3–Likely*   *4–Definitely*

4. Knowledge about First Nations Peoples requires an understanding of sovereignty issues and policies that apply to indigenous people.

   1–Unlikely   *2–Not very likely*   *3–Likely*   *4–Definitely*

5. Patience, listening, and silence are important skills to practice when working with First Nations Peoples clients.

   1–Unlikely   *2–Not very likely*   *3–Likely*   *4–Definitely*

6. I know about First Nations community immersion projects to increase inductive learning.

   1–Unlikely   *2–Not very likely*   *3–Likely*   *4–Definitely*

7. The Supreme Court has consistently ruled against the rights of First Nations Peoples.

   1–Unlikely   *2–Not very likely*   *3–Likely*   *4–Definitely*

European Americans

8. Whiteness determines a privileged social location in the United States.

   1–Unlikely   *2–Not very likely*   *3–Likely*   *4–Definitely*

9. American society is oriented around Eurocentric processes.

   1–Unlikely   *2–Not very likely*   *3–Likely*   *4–Definitely*

10. A lack of White racial identity awareness is a feature of White supremacy.

    1–Unlikely   *2–Not very likely*   *3–Likely*   *4–Definitely*

11. White supremacy culture must be named and dismantled.

    1–Unlikely   *2–Not very likely*   *3–Likely*   *4–Definitely*

12. Jane Addams, an early social worker who won the Nobel Prize for Peace in the early 20th century, was a racist who believed in White supremacy.

    1–Unlikely   *2–Not very likely*   *3–Likely*   *4–Definitely*

13. Peggy McIntosh coined the term, White privilege, and pointed out the ways that White people benefit from structural and institutional racism in the United States.

    1–Unlikely   *2–Not very likely*   *3–Likely*   *4–Definitely*

14. The cultural context model raises White privilege to consciousness and helps to name injustices that Whites participate in and benefit from.

    1–Unlikely   2–Not very likely   3–Likely   4–Definitely

African Americans

15. Diversity among African Americans involves such factors as physical characteristics, residential patterns, marital status, education, income, age, social class, and employment.

    1–Unlikely   2–Not very likely   3–Likely   4–Definitely

16. I understand the unique historical background of African Americans regarding involuntary migration, slavery, segregation, and continued oppression.

    1–Unlikely   2–Not very likely   3–Likely   4–Definitely

17. I am able to explain the four stages of the helping process that African American clients may go through with a practitioner.

    1–Unlikely   2–Not very likely   3–Likely   4–Definitely

18. I can identify several knowledge areas about the African American population and about the African American client.

    1–Unlikely   2–Not very likely   3–Likely   4–Definitely

19. I understand Afrocentric practice approaches, which are based on the Nguzo Saba value system.

    1–Unlikely   2–Not very likely   3–Likely   4–Definitely

20. I can explain the inductive learning strengths perspective approach for African American clients.

    1–Unlikely   2–Not very likely   3–Likely   4–Definitely

21. I comprehend the internalization of oppression that leads to disempowerment as a starting point for understanding how to achieve social and economic justice.

    1–Unlikely   2–Not very likely   3–Likely   4–Definitely

Latino Americans

22. I know the distinctions in Latino diversity pertaining to language differences, immigration history and patterns, and traditional and intergenerational acculturation.

    1–Unlikely   2–Not very likely   3–Likely   4–Definitely

23. I understand the historical and current oppression experiences of Mexican, Puerto Rican, Cuban, and Central American Latinos.

    1–Unlikely   2–Not very likely   3–Likely   4–Definitely

24. The religion of a Latino client is important because Catholic and Protestant denominations often establish social service outreach resources for the Latino community.

   1–Unlikely   2–Not very likely   3–Likely   4–Definitely

25. Knowledge of children and youth from war-torn countries such as El Salvador and Nicaragua indicates that exposure to violence may result in suicidal behaviors, serious antisocial acts, insomnia, and other physical, psychological, and social problems.

   1–Unlikely   2–Not very likely   3–Likely   4–Definitely

26. In social work practice with Latinos, it is important to use a "dicho" to create a cultural ambiance.

   1–Unlikely   2–Not very likely   3–Likely   4–Definitely

27. It is important to cover legal documentation with Latino clients in order to seek, in an inductive nonthreatening manner, services that will not endanger them.

   1–Unlikely   2–Not very likely   3–Likely   4–Definitely

28. I understand the dynamics of Latino immigrant exploitation in employment and housing as issues of social and economic justice.

   1–Unlikely   2–Not very likely   3–Likely   4–Definitely

Asian Americans

29. I know about the diversity between Asians and Pacific Islanders, among different ethnic groups of Asian Americans, and between Asian immigrants and refugees.

   1–Unlikely   2–Not very likely   3–Likely   4–Definitely

30. I am aware of the discriminatory experiences of Asian immigrants, the racist attitudes and behaviors toward American-born Asians, and the colonialist practices toward Pacific Islanders, particularly Native Hawaiians.

   1–Unlikely   2–Not very likely   3–Likely   4–Definitely

31. I understand the broad and varied social service needs of specific Asian American and Pacific Islander groups.

   1–Unlikely   2–Not very likely   3–Likely   4–Definitely

32. I know that Asian American and Pacific Islander knowledge acquisition consists of knowing the ethnic culture and using the cultural values to explain ways of thinking and behaving.

   1–Unlikely   2–Not very likely   3–Likely   4–Definitely

33. I understand that in developing treatment planning with Asians and Pacific Islanders, traditional ways of healing should be matched with Western interventions, and the Western interventions should be evaluated to determine whether they foster the cultural values of the ethnic community.

    1–Unlikely   *2–Not very likely*   *3–Likely*   *4–Definitely*

34. I am aware of the need to discuss Asian Americans and Pacific Islanders by life-span development, gender, and sexual orientation issues and needs in order to create an intersection of inductive learning themes.

    1–Unlikely   *2–Not very likely*   *3–Likely*   *4–Definitely*

35. I understand the social and economic issues of land rights and welfare reform for Asian and Pacific Islander immigrants.

    1–Unlikely   *2–Not very likely*   *3–Likely*   *4–Definitely*

Muslim Americans

36. I know about the increasing Muslim population in the United States due to natural births, immigration, and conversion and that the Muslim presence dates back to the arrival of slaves, many of whom were Muslims, from West Africa.

    1–Unlikely   *2–Not very likely*   *3–Likely*   *4–Definitely*

37. I know about the diversity among Muslim Americans, many of whom differ in terms of language, ethnicity, culture, and religious beliefs and schools of thought.

    1–Unlikely   *2–Not very likely*   *3–Likely*   *4–Definitely*

38. I understand the impact of the September 11, 2001 terrorist attacks on the mental health and psychosocial well-being of Muslim Americans, especially when examined through the lens of historical and current perspectives on oppression experiences.

    1–Unlikely   *2–Not very likely*   *3–Likely*   *4–Definitely*

39. I appreciate that developing cultural competence with Muslim Americans is challenging at best due to the fact that the increase in Muslim Americans' help-seeking from outside one's family and relatives and close friends is a relatively recent phenomenon.

    1–Unlikely   *2–Not very likely*   *3–Likely*   *4–Definitely*

40. I understand that unlike the dominant secular worldview in which most practitioners are being trained, Islam promotes a harmonious co-existence between the private and the public, the sacred and the secular, and the present life and the afterlife.

    1–Unlikely   *2–Not very likely*   *3–Likely*   *4–Definitely*

41. I know about the role of faith in the lives of Muslim Americans especially as it relates to divine help-seeking, the concept of Divine forgiveness for sins; and the concept of life challenges and problems, as tests from Allah.

    1–Unlikely   *2–Not very likely*   *3–Likely*   *4–Definitely*

42. I understand that as I prepare to establish contact in person with a Muslim American client, it is important that I put the client at ease by demonstrating knowledge and awareness of and respect for the client's value-informed worldview.

    1–Unlikely   *2–Not very likely*   *3–Likely*   *4–Definitely*

Women

43. In Haiti women have a major responsibility for feeding and ensuring the health of their families.

    1–Unlikely   *2–Not very likely*   *3–Likely*   *4–Definitely*

44. In Haitian informal economy women have skills in cooperation and leadership.

    1–Unlikely   *2–Not very likely*   *3–Likely*   *4–Definitely*

45. Aid to poor women will increase poor women's decision-making power.

    1–Unlikely   *2–Not very likely*   *3–Likely*   *4–Definitely*

46. Women in the National Congress of Rural Workers in Honduras played a major role in agrarian land reform.

    1–Unlikely   *2–Not very likely*   *3–Likely*   *4–Definitely*

47. The Campesino or Farmers' Movement in Latin American illustrates people, particularly women, working together and growing food under chaotic circumstances.

    1–Unlikely   *2–Not very likely*   *3–Likely*   *4–Definitely*

48. Women in the Campesino Movement used Paulo Friere's problem-solving education with political consciousness-raising.

    1–Unlikely   *2–Not very likely*   *3–Likely*   *4–Definitely*

49. The Campesino Movement is a model for socio-cultural social work.

    1–Unlikely   *2–Not very likely*   *3–Likely*   *4–Definitely*

Gay, Lesbian, Bisexual and Transgender Persons

50. I understand the different meanings of the terms gay, lesbian, bisexuality, and transgender.

    1–Unlikely   *2–Not very likely*   *3–Likely*   *4–Definitely*

51. I am aware of the distinctions between life and culture of gay/lesbian, transgender, and bisexual persons.

    1–Unlikely   2–Not very likely   3–Likely   4–Definitely

52. I am aware of the religious intolerance, societal discrimination, and denial of rights confronting sexual minorities in the United States.

    1–Unlikely   2–Not very likely   3–Likely   4–Definitely

53. I am aware of the ethical dilemmas facing sexual minorities and their families in the coming-out process

    1–Unlikely   2–Not very likely   3–Likely   4–Definitely

54. I am familiar with the organization Parents, Families, and Friends of Lesbians and Gays (PFLAG).

    1–Unlikely   2–Not very likely   3–Likely   4–Definitely

55. When working with lesbian, gay, transgender, and bisexual people in helping relationships, I endeavor to keep an open mind, not assume that all persons are heterosexual, and let the client determine the pace of revealing sexual and gender orientation.

    1–Unlikely   2–Not very likely   3–Likely   4–Definitely

56. I am in the process of educating myself about sexual minorities and am working through lingering and damaging stereotypes about this population group.

    1–Unlikely   2–Not very likely   3–Likely   4–Definitely

Persons with Disabilities

57. I understand that disability is an element of diversity rather than pathology.

    1–Unlikely   2–Not very likely   3–Likely   4–Definitely

58. I am aware that social policies, environmental barriers, and discrimination are the primary employment obstacles faced by disabled persons.

    1–Unlikely   2–Not very likely   3–Likely   4–Definitely

59. I can explain the moral model of disability, the medical model of disbility, and the social/minority model of disability.

    1–Unlikely   2–Not very likely   3–Likely   4–Definitely

60. I agree that the older a person is at the offset of an acquired disability, the less likely the individual is to adopt a disability identity.

    1–Unlikely   2–Not very likely   3–Likely   4–Definitely

61. I agree that disabled people are much more likely than nondisabled people to receive charity services and control services.

    1–Unlikely   *2–Not very likely*   *3–Likely*   *4–Definitely*

62. I agree that nondisabled people are more likely to receive investment services and benefit services.

    1–Unlikely   *2–Not very likely*   *3–Likely*   *4–Definitely*

63. I agree that solutions to the problems disabled persons and groups face are primarily located in changing social environments and societal policies, not in changing individuals.

    1–Unlikely   *2–Not very likely*   *3–Likely*   *4–Definitely*

The Older Adult

64. In 2008 the number of older adults was 506 million and by 2040 it will be 1.3 billion globally.

    1–Unlikely   *2–Not very likely*   *3–Likely*   *4–Definitely*

65. The leading country in the 2008 rank order of the world's largest older populations was China (106.1 million).

    1–Unlikely   *2–Not very likely*   *3–Likely*   *4–Definitely*

66. The growth of persons ages 80 and above is the fastest growing segment of the population of many countries.

    1–Unlikely   *2–Not very likely*   *3–Likely*   *4–Definitely*

67. Increasing numbers of older adults have higher incomes with decreasing numbers in poverty and in low income groups may be attributed to more older persons, especially older women, in the work force.

    1–Unlikely   *2–Not very likely*   *3–Likely*   *4–Definitely*

68. Almost 75 percent of Latino elderly living alone and about 50 percent of Latinos residing with their spouse are unable to meet basic needs.

    1–Unlikely   *2–Not very likely*   *3–Likely*   *4–Definitely*

69. Ageism is a process of systematic stereotyping and discrimination against people because they are old.

    1–Unlikely   *2–Not very likely*   *3–Likely*   *4–Definitely*

70. The two leading causes of death among adults aged 65 and older in 2007 were heart disease and cancer.

    1–Unlikely   *2–Not very likely*   *3–Likely*   *4–Definitely*

Social and Economic Justice

71. I understand the relationship between cultural diversity and social justice in terms of historical and ongoing oppression and privilege that different social identity groups experience in our society.

    1–Unlikely   *2–Not very likely*   *3–Likely*   *4–Definitely*

72. I understand the meaning of economic class as a prime indicator of oppression and the creation of a class system based on difference as a function of oppression.

    1–Unlikely   *2–Not very likely*   *3–Likely*   *4–Definitely*

73. I can explain the concept and perspectives of distributive justice and their implications for social and economic justice.

    1–Unlikely   *2–Not very likely*   *3–Likely*   *4–Definitely*

74. I can connect the concepts of moral exclusion and fairness.

    1–Unlikely   *2–Not very likely*   *3–Likely*   *4–Definitely*

75. I understand the human rights and oppression concepts of the United Nations Universal Declaration of Human Rights.

    1–Unlikely   *2–Not very likely*   *3–Likely*   *4–Definitely*

76. I am aware of the United Nations materials on human rights for social work.

    1–Unlikely   *2–Not very likely*   *3–Likely*   *4–Definitely*

77. I understand the meaning of and the connection between empowerment and social and economic justice.

    1–Unlikely   *2–Not very likely*   *3–Likely*   *4–Definitely*

78. I understand how the grieving cycle is related to how a person feels about oppression and injustice.

    1–Unlikely   *2–Not very likely*   *3–Likely*   *4–Definitely*

Please count your scores on the 78 items and rate your level of cultural competence.

Circle the appropriate level and write your raw score in one of the following levels.

Level 1: Unlikely (scores 78–155)

Level 2: Not very likely (scores 156–233)

Level 3: Likely (scores 234–254)

Level 4: Definitely (scores 255–272)

Thank you for your cooperation on this self-assessment instrument. You have made a significant contribution to our research on social work cultural competence.

CLOSING THOUGHTS

As social work education and culturally competent practice actively engage in a host of efforts during the 21st century, cultural competence has been an emerging topic that has catalyzed new growth and development. It is a topic taught in medical schools and undergraduate and graduate programs in psychology, social work, nursing, education, and related disciplines; mandated in the mental health and health-care programs of such states as California, New Jersey, New York, Washington, and South Carolina; and fostered on the federal level through the National Center for Cultural Competence. In many ways throughout the helping professions, cultural competence has been promoted as essential for working with client populations.

Cultural competence is clearly mandated in the NASW Code of Ethics and the Standards and Indicators for Cultural Competence in Social Work Practice. Cultural competence points toward the future of social work education and practice: outcome-based knowledge and skills, measurement accountability, and mastery of culturally competent practice with people.

It is now time to move ahead with cultural competence, which fits into the profession's emphasis on competency indicators and core competencies. As a retired social work educator, it has been my good fortune to teach and write about cultural competent practice. If you have any thoughts on culturally competent practice, please e-mail me: domanlum@gmail.com. I look forward to the future as I interact with social work education colleagues and students about this vital area of culturally competent practice.

REFERENCES

Chapter 1

Adams, D. (2005). Cultural competency now law in New Jersey. http://www.ama-assn.org/amednews/2005/04/25/prl20425.htm

Arredondo, P., et al. (1996). *Operationalization of the multicultural counseling competencies*. Washington, DC: Association for Multicultural Counseling and Development.

A rapid move to diversity. (2001, March 13). *Sacramento Bee*, p. A.

Blue Cross BlueShield of Florida. (2004, December 27). Diversity program. http://www.bcbsfl.com/index.cfm?secion=&fuseaction=Careers.diversityProgram

Boyle, D. P., & Springer, A. (2001). Toward a cultural competence measure for social work with specific populations. *Journal of Ethnic and Cultural Diversity in Social Work*, 9(3), 53–71.

California Social Work Education Center (CalSWEC) at the University of California at Berkeley. (2005, March). *CalSWEC II mental health initiative mental health competencies foundation year and advanced/specialization year: A competency-based curriculum in community mental health for graduate social work students*. Berkeley, CA: Author.

Casas, J. M., Ponterotto, J. G., & Gutierrez, J. M. (1986). An ethical indictment of counseling research and training: The cross-cultural perspective. *Journal of Counseling and Development, 64,* 467–349.

Center on an Aging Society, Georgetown University. (2004). *Cultural competence in health care: Is it important for people with chronic conditions?* Issue brief, No.5, February 2004, pp. 1–13. Retrieved May 7, 2010, from http://ihcrp.georgetown.edu/agingsociety/pubhtml/cultural/cultural.html

Constantine, M. G., & Sue, D. W. (2005). The American Psychological Association's guidelines on multicultural education, training, research, practice, and organizational psychology: Initial development and summary. In M. G. Constantine & D. W. Sue (Eds.), *Strategies for building multicultural competence in mental health and educational settings* (pp. 3–15). Hoboken, NJ: John Wiley & Sons.

Council on Social Work Education (CSWE). (2008). *Educational policy and accreditation standards*. Alexandria, VA: Author.

Cross, T. L., Bazron, B. J., Dennis, K. W., & Isaacs, M. R. (1989). *Toward a culturally competent system of care*. Washington, DC: Georgetown University Child Development Center.

Davis, T. S. (2007). Mapping patterns of perceptions: A community-based approach to cultural competence assessment. *Research on Social Work Practice, 17*(3), 358–379.

Dean, R. (2001). The myth of cross-cultural competence. *Families in Society, 82*(6), 623–630.

Devore, W., & Schlesinger, E. G. (1981). *Ethnic-sensitive social work practice.* St. Louis, MO: Mosby.

Fong, R., & Furuto, S. (Eds.). (2001). *Culturally competent practice: Skills, interventions, and evaluations.* Boston: Allyn & Bacon.

Green, J. W., & Associates. (1982). *Cultural awareness in the human services.* Englewood Cliffs, NJ: Prentice Hall.

Green, R. G., et al. (2005). The multicultural counseling inventory: A measure for evaluating social work student and practitioner self-perceptions of their multicultural competencies. *Journal of Social Work Education, 41,* 191–208.

Harper-Dorton, K. V., & Lantz, J. (2007). *Cross-cultural practice: Social work with diverse populations.* Chicago, ILL: Lyceum Books.

Harvard Medical School. (2005). Highlighting cultural competence education at the AAMC annual meeting. *Mentations News from the Office of Diversity and Community Partnership at Harvard Medical School News from Our Colleagues, 20,* Winter 2005.

Johnson, Y. M., & Munch, S. (2009). Fundamental contradictions in cultural competence. *Social Work, 54*(3), 220–231.

Kaiser Permanente. (December 2004). Diversity and inclusion. http://www.kaiser permanentejobs.org/ workinghere/diversity.asp

Kerlinger, F. K. (1973). *Foundations of behavioral research.* New York: Holt, Rinehart & Winston.

Kwong, M. H. (2009). Applying cultural competency in clinical practice: Findings from multicultural experts' experience. *Journal of Ethnic & Cultural Diversity in Social Work, 18* (1–2), 146–165.

Lonner, W. J. (1997). Three paths leading to culturally competent psychological practitioners. *International Journal of Intercultural Relevance, 21,* 195–212.

Lum, D. (1996). *Social work practice and people of color: A process-stage approach.* Pacific Grove, CA: Brooks/Cole.

Lum, D., & Lu, Y. E. (1997, March). *Developing cultural competency within a culturally sensitive environment.* Paper presented at the Council on Social Work Education annual program meeting, Chicago, Illinois.

Marsella, A. J., & Yamada, A. M. (2000). Culture and mental health: An introduction and overview of foundations, concepts, and issues. In I. Cuellar & F. A. Paniagua (Eds.), *Handbook of multicultural mental health: Assessment and treatment of diverse populations* (pp. 3–24). San Diego, CA: Academic Press.

Miley, K. K., O'Melia, M., & DuBois, B. I. (1998). *Generalist social work practice: An empowering approach.* Boston: Allyn & Bacon.

National Association of Social Workers (NASW). (1996). *NASW code of ethics.* Washington, DC: Author.

National Association of Social Workers (NASW). (2001). *NASW standards for cultural competence in social work practice.* http://www.naswdc. org/pubs/standards/cultural. htm

National Association of Social Workers (NASW). (2007). *Indicators for the achievement of the NASW standards for cultural competence in social work practice.* Washington, DC: Author.

Nybell, L. M., & Gray, S. S. (2004). Race, place, space: Meanings of cultural competence in three child welfare agencies. *Social Work, 49,* 17–26.

Office of Multicultural Services, South Carolina Department of Mental Health. (2005). *Cultural competence plan 2003–2005.* http://www.state. sc.us/dmh/cultural_ competence/cultural_plan.htm

Orlandi, M. A. (1992). The challenge of evaluating community-based prevention programs: A cross-cultural perspective. In M. A. Orlandi, R. Weston, & L. G. Epstein (Eds.), *Cultural competence for evaluators: A guide for alcohol and other drug abuse prevention practitioners working with ethnic/racial communities* (pp. 1–22). Rockville, MD: U.S. Department of Health and Human Services, Office for Substance Abuse Prevention.

Orlandi, M. A., Weston, R., & Epstein, L. G. (Eds.). (1992). *Cultural competence for evaluators: A guide for alcohol and other drug abuse prevention practitioners working with ethnic/racial communities.* Rockville, MD: U.S. Department of Health and Human Services, Office for Substance Abuse Prevention.

Paasche-Orlow, M. (2004). The ethics of cultural competence. *Academic Medicine, 79,* 347–350.

Pinderhughes, E. (1989). *Understanding race, ethnicity, and power: The key to efficacy in clinical practice.* New York: Free Press.

Ponterotto, J. G., Casas, J. M., Suzuki, L. A., & Alexander, C. M. (Eds.). (1995). *Handbook of multicultural counseling.* Thousand Oaks, CA: Sage.

Pope-Davis, D. B., & Coleman, H. L. K. (Eds.). (1997). *Multicultural counseling competencies: Assessment, education and training, and supervision.* Thousand Oaks, CA: Sage.

Ridley, C. R. (2005). *Overcoming unintentional racism in counseling and therapy: A practitioner's guide to intentional intervention.* Thousand Oaks, CA: Sage Publications.

Ridley, C. R., Baker, D. M., & Hill, C. L. (2001). Critical issues concerning cultural competence. *The Counseling Psychologist,* 29(6), 822–832.

Rothman, J. C. (2008). *Cultural competence in process and practice: Building bridges.* Boston: Pearson Education Allyn & Bacon.

Simmons, C. S., Diaz, L., Jackson, V., & Takahashi, R. (2008). NASW cultural competence indicators: A new tool for the social work profession. *Journal of Ethnic & Cultural Diversity in Social Work,* 17 (1), 4–20.

Smith, T. B., Richards, P. S., Granley, H. M., & Obiakor, F. (2004). Practicing multiculturalism: An introduction. In T. B. Smith (Ed.), *Practicing multiculturalism: Affirming diversity in counseling and psychology* (pp. 3–16). Boston: Allyn & Bacon/ Pearson Education.

Solomon, B. B. (1976). *Black empowerment: Social work in oppressed communities.* New York: Columbia Univerity Press.

Substance Abuse and Mental Health Services Administration. (1997a). *Cultural competence guidelines in managed care mental health services for Asian and Pacific Islander populations.* The Asian and Pacific Islander American Task Force: The Western Interstate Commission for Higher Education Mental Health Program.

Substance Abuse and Mental Health Services Administration. (1997b). *Cultural competence guidelines for Native American populations.* Native American Managed Care Panel: The Western Interstate Commission for Higher Education.

Sue, D. W., Arredondo, P., & McDavis, R. J. (1992). Multicultural counseling competencies and standards: A call to the profession. *Journal of Counseling and Development,* 70, 477–486.

Sue, D. W., & Sue, D. (2003). *Counseling the culturally diverse: Theory and practice.* New York: John Wiley & Sons.

Sue, D. W., & Sue, D. (2008). *Counseling the culturally diverse: Theory and practice.* New York: John Wiley & Sons.

Teasley, M. L. (2005). Perceived levels of cultural competence through social work education and professional development for urban school social workers. *Journal of Social Work Education,* 41, 85–98.

U.S. Census Bureau. (2004). Interim projection of the U. S. population by age, sex, race, and Hispanic origin: Summary methodology and assumptions. http://www.census.gov/ ipc/ www/usinterimproj/ idbsummeth.html

Whaley, A. L. (2008). Cultural sensitivity and cultural competence: Toward clarity of definitions in cross-cultural counselling and psychotherapy. *Counseling Psychology Quarterly,* 21(31), 215–222.

Whaley, A. L., & Davis, K. E. (2007). Cultural competence and evidence-based practice in mental health services: A complementary perspective. *American Psychologist,* 62(6), 563–574.

Williams, C. C. (2006). The epistemology of cultural competence. *Families in Society,* 87 (2), 209–220.

Zayas, L. H., Evans, M. E., Mejia, L., & Rodriguez, O. (1997). Cultural-competency training for staff serving Hispanic families with a child in psychiatric crisis. *Families in Society,* 78, 405–412.

Chapter 2

Aguilar, M. A., & Williams, L. P. (1993). Factors contributing to the success and achievements of minority women. *Affilia,* 8(4), 410–424.

Aguirre, A., Jr., & Baker, D. V. (2008). *Structured inequality in the United States: Critical discussions on the continuing significance of race, ethnicity, and gender.* Upper Saddle River, NJ: Pearson Education Prentice Hall.

Allport, G. W. (1954). *The nature of prejudice.* Reading, MA: Addison-Wesley.

Appleby, G. A. (2001). Dynamics of oppression and discrimination. In G. A. Appleby, E. Colon, & J. Hamilon (Eds.), *Diversity, oppression, and social functioning: Person-in-environment assessment and intervention* (pp. 36–52). Boston: Allyn & Bacon.

Appleby, G. A., & Anastas, J. W. (1998). *Not just a passing phase: Social work with gay, lesbian, and bisexual people.* New York: Columbia University Press.

Arredondo, P., & Perez, P. (2003). Expanding multicultural competence through social justice leadership. *The Counseling Psychologist, 31*(3), 282–289.

Bankston, C. L., & Zhou, M. (1995). Effects of minority-language literacy on academic achievement of Vietnamese youths in New Orleans. *Sociology of Education, 68,* 1–17.

Beeghley, L. (2008). *The structure of social stratification in the United States.* Boston: Pearson Education Allyn & Bacon.

Bonacich, E., & Goodman, R. F. (1972). *Deadlock in school desegregation: A case study of Inglewood, California.* New York: Praeger.

Brown, L. S. (1990). The meaning of a multicultural perspective for theory-building in feminist therapy. In L. S. Brown & M. P. P. Root (Eds.), *Diversity and complexity in feminist therapy* (pp. 1–21). New York: Haworth.

Butler, R. N. (1969). Ageism: Another form of bigotry. *The Gerontologist, 9,* 243–246.

Canales, G. (2000). Gender as subculture: The first division of multicultural diversity. In I. Cuellar & F. A. Paniagua (Eds.), *Handbook of multicultural mental health: Assessment and treatment of diverse populations* (pp. 63–77). San Diego, CA: Academic Press.

Carter, R. T., & Jones, J. M. (1996). Racism and white racial identity merging realities. In B. P. Bowser &

R. G. Hunt (Eds.), *Impacts of racism on white Americans.* Thousand Oaks, CA: Sage.

Collins, P. H. (1990). *Black feminist thought: Knowledge, consciousness, and the politics of empowerment.* Boston: Unwin Hyman.

Comas-Diaz, L. (1994). An integrative approach. In L. Comas-Diaz & B. Greene (Eds.), *Women of color: Integrating ethnic and gender identities in psychotherapy* (pp. 287–318). New York: Guilford.

Comas-Diaz, L., & Greene, B. (Eds.). *Women of color: Integrating ethnic and gender identities in psychotherapy.* New York: Guilford.

Congress, E. P., & Kung, W. W. (2005). Using the culturagram to assess and empower culturally diverse families. In E. P. Congress & M. J. Gonzalez (Eds.), *Multicultural perspectives in working with families* (pp. 3–21). New York: Springer Publishing Company.

Constantine, M. G. (2006). Racism in mental health and educatiuon settings: A brief overview. In M. G. Constantine & D. W. Sue (Eds.), *Addressing racism: Facilitating cultural competence in mental health and educational settings* (pp. 3–13). Hoboken, NJ: John Wiley & Sons.

Council on Social Work Education (CSWE). (2008). *Educational policy and accreditation standards.* Alexandria, VA: Author.

Davis, T. S. (2009). Diversity practice in social work: Examining theory in practice. *Journal of Ethnic & Cultural Diversity in Social Work, 18*(1 & 2), 40–69.

Devore, W., & Schlesinger, E. G. (1999). *Ethnic-sensitive social

work practice.* New York: Allyn & Bacon.

Fain, M. J. (2005). *Cultural competency for the older adult.* http://www.eddev. arizona.edu/courses/sbs/yl/ docs/Cultural Competency.pdf

Freire, P. (1970). *Pedagogy of the oppressed.* New York: Herder & Herder.

Friedman, M. B. (2004). Focus on geriatric mental health: Testimony regarding the New York State Office of Mental Health's 5-Year Plan, June 4, 2004. http://mhawestchester.org/ advocates/tfriedman60404.asp

Gil, D. G. (1998). *Confronting injustice and oppression: Concepts and strategies for social workers.* New York: Columbia University Press.

Greene, B. (1994). Diversity and difference: Race and feminist psychotherapy. In M. P. Mirkin (Ed.), *Women in context: Toward a feminist reconstruction of psyhcotherapy* (pp. 333–351). New York: Guilford.

Greene, R. R., Watkins, M., McNutt, J., & Lopez, L. (1998). Diversity defined. In R. R. Greene & M. Watkins (Eds.), *Serving diverse constituencies: Applying the ecological perspective.* New York: Aldine De Gruyter.

Gutierrez, L. M., & Lewis, E. A. (1999). *Empowering women of color.* New York: Columbia University Press.

Haberman, M. (1994). Gentle teaching in an intolerant society. *Educational Horizons, 72,* 2–29.

Holland, T. P., Gallant, J. P., & Colosetti, S. (1994). Assessment of teaching a constructivist approach to social work practice. *Arete, 18,* 45–60.

Iceland, J. (2009). *Where we live now: Immigration and race in *the United States.* Berkeley, CA: University of California Press.

Ivey, A. E., & Collins, N. M. (2003). Social justice: A long-term challenge for counseling psychology. *The Counseling Psychologist, 31*(3), 290–298.

Kemp, S. P., Whittaker, J. K., & Tracy, E. M. (2002). Contextual social work practice. In M. O'Melia & K. K. Miley (Eds.), *Pathways to power: Readings in contextual social work practice* (pp. 15–34). Boston: Allyn & Bacon.

Kliman, J. (1994). The interweaving of gender, class, and race in family therapy. In M. P. Mirkin (Ed.), *Women in context: Toward a feminist reconstruction of psychotherapy* (pp. 25–47). New York: Guilford.

Kopacsi, R., & Faulkner, A. O. (1988). The papers that might be: The unity of white and black feminist. *Affilia, 3*(3), 33–50.

Lee, M. Y. (2008). Violence among multicultural populations. *Journal of Ethnic and Cultural Diversity in Social Work, 17*(2), 102–107.

Lee, R. M., & Ramirez, M. (2000). The history, current status, and future of multicultural psychotherapy. In I. Cuellar & F. A. Paniagua (Eds.), *Handbook of multicultural mental health: Assessment and treatment of diverse populations* (pp. 279–309). San Diego, CA: Academic Press.

Liu, W. M., Soleck, G., Hopps, J., Dunston, K., & Pickett, T. (2004). A new framework to understand social class in counseling: The social class worldview and modern classism theory. *Journal of*

Multicultural Counseling and Development, 32, 95–122.

Longres, J. F. (1995). *Human behavior in the social environment.* Itasca, IL: F. E. Peacock.

Lott, B. (2002). Cognitive and behavioral distancing from the poor. *American Psychologist 57,* 100–110.

Lum, D. (2004). *Social work practice and people of color: A process-stage approach.* Belmont, CA: Brooks/Cole-Thomson Learning.

Mahoney, M. R. (1994). Victimization or oppression? Women's lives, violence, and agency. In M. A. Fineman & R. Mykitiuk (Eds.), *The public nature of private violence: The discovery of domestic abuse* (pp. 59–92). New York: Routledge.

Marsella, A. J., & Yamada, A. M. (2000). Culture and mental health: An introduction and overview of foundations, concepts, and issues. In I. Cuellar & F. A. Paniagua (Eds.), *Handbook of multicultural mental health: Assessment and treatment of diverse populations* (pp. 3–24). San Diego, CA: Academic Press.

McAleavy, T. M. (2002, January 21). Race colors views of job fairness. *Sacramento Bee,* pp. E1, E4.

McNamee, S., & Gergen, K. J. (Eds.). (1992). *Therapy as social construction.* London: Sage.

Messinger, L. (2004). Out in the field: Gay and lesbian social work students' experiences in field placement. *Journal of Social Work Education, 40,* 187–204.

Mirkin, M. P. (Ed.). (1994). *Women in context: Toward a feminist reconstruction of*

psychotherapy. New York: Guilford.

Miville, M. L., & Ferguson, A. D. (2006). Intersections of sexism and heterosexism with racism: Therapeutic implications. In M. G. Constantine & D. W. Sue (Eds.), *Addressing racism: Facilitating cultural competence in mental health and educational settings* (pp. 87–103). Hoboken, NJ: John Wiley & Sons.

Molina, L. E., & Wittig, M. A. (2006). Relative importance of contact conditions in explaining prejudice reduction in a classroom context: Separate and equal? *Journal of Social Issues, 62*(3), 489–509.

Murphy, B. C., & Dillon, C. (1998). *Interviewing in action: Process and practice.* Pacific Grove, CA: Brooks/Cole.

Nylund, D. (2006). Critical multiculturalism, whiteness, and social work: Toward a more radical view of cultural competence. *Journal of Progressive Human Services, 17*(2), 27–42.

Paniagua, F. A. (2005). *Assessing and treating culturally diverse clients: A practical guide.* Thousand Oaks, CA: Sage Publications.

Pederson, P. (2005). The importance of cultural psychology theory for multicultural counselors. In R. T. Carter (Ed.), *Handbook of racial-cultural psychology and counseling: Theory and research* (Vol. 1, pp. 3–16). Hoboken, NJ: John Wiley & Sons.

Pence, E. (n.d.). *Power and control wheel.* Duluth, MN: Domestic Abuse Intervention Project.

Ponterotto, J. G., Utsey, S. O., & Pedersen, P. B. (2006). *Preventing prejudice: A guide for counselors, educators, and parents.* Thousand Oaks, CA: Sage Publications.

Pope-Davis, D. B., Toporek, R. L., Ortega-Villalobos, L., Ligiero, D. P., Brittan-Powell, C. S., Liu, W. M., et al. (2002). Client perspectives of multicultural counseling competence: A qualitative examination. *The Counseling Psychologist, 30*(3), 355–393.

Portes, A., & Hao, L. (2002). The price of uniformity: Language, family and personal adjustment in the immigrant second generation. *Ethnic and Racial Studies, 25,* 889–912.

Portes, A., & Rumbaut, R. (2001). *Legacies: The story of the immigrant second generation.* Berkeley: University of California Press.

Radtke, H. L., & Stam, H. J. (Eds.). (1994). *Power/gender: Social relations in theory and practice.* Thousand Oaks, CA: Sage.

Ragg, D. M. (2001). *Building effective helping skills: The foundation of generalist practice.* Boston: Allyn & Bacon.

Renzetti, C. M., & Curran, D. J. (1995). *Women, men, and society.* Boston: Allyn & Bacon.

Ridley, C. R. (2005). *Overcoming unintentional racism in counseling and therapy: A practitioner's guide to intentional intervention.* Thousand Oaks, CA: Sage Publications.

Rose, S. M. (1990). Advocacy/empowerment: An approach to clinical practice for social work. *Journal of Sociology and Social Welfare, 17*(2), 41–52.

Schriver, J. M. (2001). *Human behavior and the social environment: Shifting paradigms in essential knowledge for social work practice.* Boston: Allyn & Bacon.

Stockard, J., & Johnson, M. M. (1992). *Sex and gender in society.* Englewood Cliffs, NJ: Prentice Hall.

Sue, D. W. (2006). The invisible whiteness of being: Whiteness, white supremacy, whie privilege, and racism. In M. G. Constantine & D. W. Sue (Eds.), *Addressing racism: Facilitating cultural competence in mental health and educational settings* (pp. 15–30). Hoboken, NJ: John Wiley & Sons.

Sue, S. (2003). In Facilitating defnse of cultural competency in psychotherapy and treatment. *American Psychologist, 58*(11), 964–970.

Takaki, R. (1990). *Iron cages: Race and culture in 19th century America.* New York: Oxford University Press.

Tully, C. T. (2000). *Lesbians, gays and the empowerment perspective.* New York: Columbia University Press.

Van Den Bergh, N., & Crisp, C. (2004). Defining culturally competent practice with sexual minorities: Implications for social work education and practice. *Journal of Social Work Education, 40,* 221–238.

Vera, E. M., & Speight, S. L. (2003). Multicultural competence, social justice and counseling. *The Counseling Psychologist, 31*(3), 253–272.

Weaver, H. N. (2005). *Explorations in cultural competence: Journeys to the four directions.* Belmont, CA: Brooks/Cole Cengage Learning.

Weaver, H., & Congress, E. (2009). Indigenous people in a landscape of risk: Teaching social work students about socially just social work responses. *Journal of Ethnic & Cultural Diversity in Social Work, 18*(1 & 2), 166–179.

Weinberg, G. (1972). *Society and the healthy homosexual.* New York: St. Martin's Press.

Worden, B. (2001). Women and sexist oppression. In G. A. Appleby, E. Colon, & J. Hamilton (Eds.), *Diversity, oppression, and social functioning: Person-in-environment assessment and intervention.* Boston: Allyn & Bacon.

Young, I. M. (1990). *Justice and the politics of difference.* Princeton, NJ: Princeton University Press.

Chapter 3

American Psychiatric Association. (1973). *Diagnostic and statistical manual of mental disorders* (3rd ed.). Washington, DC: Author.

Barker, R. L. (2003). *The social work dictionary* (5th ed.). Washington, DC: NASW Press.

Beverly, D. P., & McSweeney, E. A. (1987). *Social welfare and social justice.* Englewood Cliffs, NJ: Prentice Hall.

Bulhan, H. A. (1985). *Frantz Fanon and the psychology of oppression.* New York: Plenum.

Callahan, S. (1982, November 19). Peacemaking strategies for inertia. *National Catholic Reporter,* 1.

Conrad, A. P. (1988). The role of field instructors in the transmission of social justice values. *Journal of Teaching in Social Work, 2*(2), 63–82.

Council on Social Work Education (CSWE). (2008). *Educational policy and accreditation standards.* http://www.cswe.org/CSWE/accreditation

Cross, T. L., Bazron, B. J., Dennis, K. W., & Isaacs, M. R. (1989). *Towards a culturally competent system of care.* Washington, DC: Georgetown University Child Development Center.

Davis, K. E. (2004). Social work's commitment to social justice and social policy. In K. E. Davis & T. B. Bent-Goodley (Eds.), *The color of social policy* (pp. 229–241). Alexandria, VA: Council on Social Work Education Publications.

Derman-Sparks, L., & Brunson Phillips, C. (1997). *Teaching/ learning anti-racism: A developmental approach.* New York: Teachers College Press, Columbia University.

Ferguson, M. (1980). *The aquarian conspiracy.* Los Angeles: J. P. Tarcher.

Finn, J. L., & Jacobson, M. (2008). Social justice. In Terry Mizrahi & Larry E. Davis (Eds.), *Encyclopedia of social work.* New York City: National Association of Social Workers and Oxford University Press, Inc.

Flynn, J. P. (1995). Social justice in social agencies. In R. L. Edwards (Ed.-in-Chief), *Encyclopedia of social work* (19th ed.). (pp. 2173–2179). Washington, DC: NASW Press.

GATT and NAFTA: How trade agreements can change your life. (n.d.). San Francisco, CA: Global Exchange.

Gil, D. (1998). *Confronting injustice and oppression: Concepts and strategies for social workers.* New York: Columbia University.

Giroux, H. A. (2000). Racial politics, pedagogy, and the crisis of representation in academic multiculturalism. *Social Identities,* 6(4), 493–510.

Goldberg, D. T. (1993). *Racist culture.* Cambridge, MA: Basil Blackwell.

Ife, J. (1997). *Rethinking social work: Towards critical practice.* Melbourne: Longman.

Ife, J. (2001). *Human rights and social work: Towards rights-based practice.* Cambridge, UK: Cambridge University Press.

International Federation of Social Workers (IFSW). (2004). *Ethics in social work, statement of principles.* http:// www.ifsw.org/p38000324. html

Kubler-Ross, E. (1975). *Death: The final stage of growth.* Englewood Cliffs, NJ: Prentice Hall.

Lum, D. (1999). *Culturally competent practice: A framework for growth and action.* Belmont, CA: Wadsworth.

Macy, J. R. (1983). *Despair and personal power in the nuclear age.* Philadelphia: New Society.

Marris, P. (1974). *Loss and change.* London: Routledge & Kegan Paul.

Mill, J. S. (1863). On the connection between justice and utility. In *Utilitarianism,* Chapter V, as reprinted in J. P. Sterba (1992), *Justice: Alternative political perspectives* (pp. 171–184). Belmont, CA: Wadsworth.

Mills, K. W. (1997). *The racial contract.* Ithaca, NY: Cornell.

Morrow, A. (2008, September 9). *The four phases and tasks of grief.* http://dying.about.com/ od/thegrievingprocess/a/phases_04_tasks.htm

Mullaly, R. (2002). *Challenging oppression: A critical social work approach.* Don Mills, Ontario: Oxford University Press.

National Association of Social Workers (NASW). (2008). *Code of ethics.* Washington, DC: Author. http://www.

socialworkers.org/pubs/code/ code.asp

National Association of Social Workers (NASW). (1996b). *The violence and development project: Expanding capacities for community building and global learning* (preliminary funding proposal by the National Association of Social Workers in collaboration with the Council on Social Work Education and the Benton Foundation). Washington, DC: Author.

Nozick, R. (1974). *Anarchy, state, and utopia.* New York: Basic Books.

Opotow, S. (1990). Moral exclusion and injustice: An introduction. *Journal of Social Issues,* 46(1), 1–20.

Opotow, S., Gerson, J., & Woodside, S. (2005). From moral exclusion to moral inclusion: Theory for teaching peace. *Theory into Practice,* 55(4), 303–318.

Parsons, R. J. (2008). Empowerment Practice. In Terry Mizrahi & Larry E. Davis (Eds.), *Encyclopedia of Social Work.* New York City: National Association of Social Workers and Oxford University Press, Inc.

Pateman, C. (1988). *The sexual contract.* Stanford, CA: Stanford University Press.

Pinderhughes, E. (1989). *Understanding race, ethnicity, and power.* New York: Free Press.

Rawls, J. (1971). *A theory of justice.* Cambridge, MA: Harvard University Press.

Reed, B. G., Newman, P., Suarez, Z., & Lewis, E. (1997). Interpersonal practice beyond diversity and toward social justice: The importance of critical consciousness. In C. Garvin & B. Seabury (Eds.), *Interpersonal practice in social work: Promoting competence and social justice* (2nd ed.). (pp. 44–78). Boston: Allyn & Bacon.

Reichert, E. (2003). *Social work and human rights: A foundation for policy and practice.* New York: Columbia University Press.

Reisch, M. (2002, July/August). Defining social justice in a socially unjust world. *Families in Society, 83*(4), 343–354.

Reisch, M., & Taylor, C. T. (1983). Ethical guidelines for cutback management: A preliminary approach. *Administration in Social Work, 7*(3/4), 59–72.

Saleebey, D. (Ed.). (2006). *The strengths perspective in social work practice* (4th ed.). Boston: Pearson Education, Inc.

Schwartz, S. H. (2007). Universalism values and the inclusiveness of our moral universe. *Journal of Cross-Cultural Psychology, 38*(60), 711–728.

Slap-Shelton, L. (1998). *Go through the phases of grief work to overcome your loss.* http://www.selfhelp magazine.co/article/grief-work

Sterba, J. P. (Ed.). (1992). *Justice: Alternative political perspectives.* Belmont, CA: Wadsworth.

United Nations. (1987). *Human rights: Questions and answers.* New York: Author.

United Nations. (1992). *Teaching and learning about human rights: A manual for schools of social work and the social work profession.* New York: Author.

Van Voorhis, R. M. (1998). Culturally relevant practice: A framework for teaching the psychosocial dynamics of oppression. *Journal of Social Work Education, 34*(1), 121–133.

van Wormer, K. (2004). *Confronting oppression, restoring justice: From policy analysis to social action.* Alexandria, VA: Council on Social Work Education.

Wakefield, J. C. (1988, June). Psychotherapy, distributive justice, and social work. Part I: Distributive justice as a conceptual framework for social work. *Social Service Review, 62*(2), 187–210.

Witkin, S. (1998). Human rights and social work. *Social Work, 43*(3), 197–201.

Wronka, J. (1998). *Human rights and social policy in the 21st century.* Lanham, MD: University Press of America.

Wronka, J. (2007). *Human rights and social justice: Social action and service for the hleping and health professions.* Newbury Park, CA: Sage Publications, Inc.

Young, I. M. (1990). *Justice and the politics of difference.* Princeton, NJ: Princeton University Press.

Chapter 4

Alter, C., & Egan, M. (1997). Logic modeling: A tool for teaching practice evaluation. *Journal of Social Work Education, 33*(1), 75–84.

Arredondo, P., et al. (1996). *Operationalization of the multicultural counseling competencies.* Washington, DC: Association for Multicultural Counseling and Development.

Council on Social Work Education (CSWE), Commission on Accreditation. (2008). *Educational policy and accreditation standards.* Alexandria, VA: Author.

Flexner, A. (1961). Is social work a profession? In R. E. Pumphrey & M. W. Pumphrey

(Eds.), *The heritage of American social work: Readings in its philosophical and institutional development* (pp. 301–307). New York: Columbia University Press.

Kurfiss, J. G. (1989). Helping faculty foster students' critical thinking in the disciplines. In A. F. Lucas (Ed.), *New directions for teaching and learning* (No. 37). San Francisco: Jossey-Bass.

Lum, D. (1986). *Social work practice and people of color: A process-stage approach.* Monterey, CA: Brooks/Cole.

Pedersen, P. (1991). Multiculturalism as a fourth force in counseling. *Journal of Counseling and Development, 70*(1), 5–25.

Reid, W. J. (1978). *The task-centered system.* New York: Columbia University Press.

Smith, T. B., Richards, P. S., Granley, H. M., & Obiakor, F. (2004). Practicing multiculturalism: An introduction. In T. B. Smith (Ed.), *Practicing multiculturalism: Affirming diversity in counseling and psychology* (pp. 3–16). Boston: Allyn & Bacon/Pearson Education.

Sue, D. W., & Sue, D. (2008). *Counseling the culturally diverse: Theory and practice.* New York: John Wiley.

Van Den Bergh, N., & Crisp, C. (2004). Defining culturally competent practice with sexual minorities: Implications for social work education and practice. *Journal of Social Work Education, 40,* 221–238.

Chapter 5

Appleby, G. A., & Anastas, J. W. (1998). *Not just a passing phase: Social work with gay, lesbian, and bisexual people.*

New York: Columbia University Press.

Ashford, J. B., LeCroy, C. W., & Lortie, K. L. (2001). *Human behavior in the social environment: A multidimensional perspective.* Pacific Grove, CA: Brooks/Cole.

Collins, P. H. (1990). *Black feminist thought: Knowledge, consciousness, and the politics of empowerment.* Boston: Unwin Hyman.

Council on Social Work Education (CSWE), Commission on Accreditation. (2008). *Educational policy and accreditation standards.* Alexandria, VA: Author.

Delgado, M., Jones, K., & Rohani, M. (2005). *Social work practice with refugee and immigrant youth in the United States.* Boston: Allyn & Bacon/Pearson Education.

Freire, P. (1970). *Pedagogy of the oppressed.* New York: Herder & Herder.

Giordano, J., & McGoldrick, M. (1996). European families: An overview. In M. McGoldrick, J. Giordano, & J. K. Pearce (Eds.), *Ethnicity and family therapy* (pp. 427–441). New York: Guilford.

Green, J. W. (1995). *Cultural awareness in the human services: A multi-ethnic approach.* Boston: Allyn & Bacon.

Hardy, K. V., & Laszloffy, T. A. (1995). The cultural genogram: Key to training culturally competent family therapists. *Journal of Marital and Family Therapy, 21,* 227–237.

Keenan, E. K. (2004). From sociocultural categories to socially located relations: Using critical theory in social work practice. *Families in Society, 85,* 539–548.

National Association of Social Workers (NASW). (2007). *Indicators for the achievement of the NASW standards for cultural competence in social work practice.* Washington, DC: Author.

Perez, R. M., Fukuyama, M. A., & Coleman, N. C. (2005). Using the multicultural guidelines in college counseling centers. In M. G. Constantine & D. W. Sue (Eds.), *Strategies for building mullticultural competence in mental health and educational settings* (pp. 160–179). Hoboken, NJ: John Wiley & Sons.

Potocky-Tripodi, M. (2002). *Best practices for social work with refugees and immigrants.* New York: Columbia University Press.

Reed, B. G., Newman, P. A., Suarez, Z. E., & Lewis, E. A. (1997). Interpersonal practice beyond diversity and toward social justice: The importance of critical consciousness. In C. D. Garvin & B. A. Seabury (Eds.), *Interpersonal practice in social work: Promoting competence and social justice* (pp. 44–77). Boston: Allyn & Bacon.

Reynolds, A. L. (1995). Challenges and strategies for teaching multicultural counseling courses. In J. G. Ponterotto, J. M. Casas, L. A. Suzuki, & C. M. Alexander (Eds.), *Handbook of multicultural counseling* (pp. 312–330). Thousand Oaks, CA: Sage.

Ridley, C. R. (2005). *Overcoming unintentional racism in counseling and therapy: A practitioner's guide to intentional intervention.* Thousand Oaks, CA: Sage Publications.

Sanday, P. R. (1976). *Anthropology and the public interest.* New York: Academic Press.

Segal, U. A. (2002). *A framework for immigration: Asians in the United States.* New York: Columbia University Press.

Spencer, M., Lewis, E., & Gutierrez, L. (2000). Multicultural perspectives on direct practice in social work. In P. Allen-Meares & C. Garvin (Eds.), *The handbook of social work direct practice* (pp. 131–149). Thousand Oaks, CA: Sage Publications.

Suarez, Z. E., Newman, P. A., & Reed, B. G. (2008). Critical consciousness and cross-cultural/intersectional social work practice: A case analysis. *Journal of Ethnic & Cultural Diversity in Social Work, 89* (3), 407–417.

Weaver, H. N. (2005). *Explorations in cultural competence: Journeys to the four directions.* Belmont, CA: Brooks/Cole Cengage Learning.

Whaley, A. L., & Davis, K. E. (2007). Cultural competence and evidence-based practice in mental health services: A complementary perspective. *American Psychologist, 62*(6), 563–574.

Yan, M. C., & Wong, Y. L. R. (2005). Rethinking self-awareness in cultural competence: Toward a dialogic self in cross-cultural social work. *Families in Society, 86,* 181–188.

Chapter 6

Aguilar, M. A., & Williams, L. P. (1993). Factors contributing to the success and achievements of minority women. *Affilia, 8*(4), 410–424.

Anderson, H., & Goolishian, H. (1992). The client is the expert: A not-knowing approach to therapy. In S. McNamee & K. J. Gergen

(Eds.), *Therapy as social construction* (pp. 25–39). London: Sage.

Carter-Black, J. (2007). Teaching cultural competence: An innovative strategy grounded in the universality of story-telling as depicted in African and African American story-telling traditions. *Journal of Social Work Education, 43*(1), 31–50.

Council on Social Work Education (CSWE). (2008). *Educational policy and accreditation standards*. Alexandria, VA: Author.

Dean, R. (2001). The myth of cross-cultural competence. *Families in Society, 82,* 623–630.

Dhooper, S. S., & Moore, S. E. (2001). *Social work practice with culturally diverse people*. Thousand Oaks, CA: Sage Publications.

Epston, D., White, M., & Murray, K. (1992). A proposal for a re-authoring therapy: Rose's revisioning of her life and a commentary. In S. McNamee & K. J. Gergen (Eds.), *Therapy as social construction* (pp. 96–115). London: Sage.

Froggeri, L. (1992). Therapeutic process as the social construction of change. In S. McNamee & K. J. Gergen (Eds.), *Therapy as social construction* (pp. 40–53). London: Sage.

Geertz, C. (1973). *The interpretation of cultures*. New York: Basic Books.

Gelman, C. R. (2004). Empirically-based principles for culturally competent practice with Latinos. *Journal of Ethnic & Cultural Diversity in Social Work, 13,* 83–108.

Gergen, K. J. (1985). The social constructionist movement in modern psychology. *American Psychologist, 40,* 266–275.

Gergen, K. J., & Davis, K. E. (1985). *The social construction of the person*. New York: Springer-Verlag.

Guba, E. G., & Lincoln, Y. S. (1998). Competing paradigms in qualitative research. In N. K. Denzin & Y. S. Lincoln (Eds.), *The landscape of qualitative research* (pp. 195–220). Thousand Oaks, CA: Sage Publications.

Helms, J. E. (1990). An overview of black racial identity theory. In J. E. Helms (Ed.), *Black and white racial identity: Theory, research, and practice* (pp. 9–33). New York: Greenwood.

Holland, T. P., Gallant, J. P., & Colosetti, S. (1994). *Assessment of teaching a constructive approach to social work practice. Arete, 18,* 45–60.

Lee, R. M., & Ramirez, M. (2000). The history, current status, and future of multicultural psychotherapy. In I. Cuellar & F. A. Paniagua (Eds.), *Handbook of multicultural mental health: Assessment and treatment of diverse populations* (pp. 279–309). San Diego, CA: Academic Press.

Lum, D. (2004). *Social work practice & people of color: A process-stage approach*. Belmont, CA: Brooks/Cole Thompson Learning.

Manning, M. C., Cornelius, L. J., & Okundaye, J. N. (2004). Empowering African Americans through social work practice: Integrating an Afrocentric perspective, ego psychology, and spirituality. *Families in Society, 85,* 229–235.

Marsiglia, F. F., & Kulis, S. (2009). *Diversity, oppression, and change: Culturally grounded social work*. Chicago: Lyceum Books.

Morton, G., & Atkinson, D. R. (1983). Minority identity development and preference for counselor race. *Journal of Negro Education, 52*(2), 156–161.

Mumm, A. M., & Kerstling, R. C. (1997). Teaching critical thinking in social work practice courses. *Journal of Social Work Education, 33,* 75–84.

National Association of Social Workers (NASW). (2007). *Indicators for the achievement of the NASW standards for cultural competence in social work practice*. Washington, DC: Author.

Norton, D. G. (1993). Diversity, early socialization, and temporal development: The dual perspective revisited. *Social Work, 38*(1), 82–90.

Parker, I., & Shotter, J. (Eds.). (1990). *Reconstructing social psychology*. London: Routledge.

Passel, J. S., & Cohn, D. (2008). *U.S. population projections: 2005-2050*. Washington, DC: Pew Research Center.

Paul, R. (1992). Critical thinking: What, why, and how. *New Directions for Community Colleges, 77,* 3–24.

Pedersen, P. (2005). The importance of cultural psychology theory for multicultural counselors. In R. T. Carter (Ed.), *Handbook of racial-cultural psychology and counseling: Theory and research* (Vol. 1, pp. 3–16). Hoboken, NJ: John Wiley & Sons.

Pieper, M. H. (1994). Science, not scientism: The robustness of naturalistic clinical research. In E. Sherman & W. J. Reid (Eds.), *Qualitative research in social work* (pp. 71–88). New York: Columbia University Press.

Portes, A., & Rumbaut, R. G. (1990). *Immigrant America: A portait*. Berkeley: University of California Press.

Potocky-Tripodi, M. (2002). *Best practice for social work with refugees and immigrants*. New York: Columbia University Press.

Rosenblum, K. E., & Travis, T. C. (Eds.). (2000). *The meaning of difference: American constructions of race, sex and gender, social class, and sexual orientation*. Boston: McGraw-Hill.

Shriver, M., & The Center for American Progress. (2009). *The Shriver report: A woman's nation changes everything*. Washington, DC: The Center for American Progress.

Sim, S. (1999). Postmodernism and philosophy. In S. Sim (Ed.), *The Routledge critical dictionary of postmodern thought* (pp. 3–14). New York: Routledge.

Sivan, E. (1986). Motivation in social constructivist theory. *Educational Psychologist, 2*, 209–233.

Tanemura Morelli, P. T., & Spencer, M. S. (2000). Use and support of multicultural and antiracist education: Research-informed interdisciplinary social work practice. *Journal of Social Work, 45*(2), 166–175.

Weaver, H. N. (2004). The elements of cultural competence: Applications with Natve American clients. *Journal of Ethnic & Cultural Diversity in Social Work, 13*, 19–35.

Weaver, H. N. (2005). Re-examining what we think we know: A lesson learned from Tamil refugees. *Affilia, 20*, 238–245.

Westphal, D. (2001, March 13). Giant leap in U.S. diversity. *Sacramento Bee*, pp. A1, A18.

Williams, C. C. (2006). The epistemology of cultural competence. *Families in Society, 87* (2), 209–220.

Williams, F. (1996). Postmodernism and philosophy. In S. Sim (Ed.), *The Routledge critical dictionary of postmodern thought* (pp. 3–14). New York: Routledge.

Chapter 7

Acevedo, G., & Morales, J. (2001). Assessment with Latino/Hispanic communities and organizations. In R. Fong & S. B. C. L. Furuto (Eds.), *Culturally competent practice: Skills, interventions, and evaluations* (pp. 147–162). Boston: Allyn & Bacon.

Amato-von Hemert, K. (1994). Should social work education address religious issues? Yes! *Journal of Social Work Education, 30*(1), 7–11, 16, 17.

American Psychiatric Association (APA). (1994). *Diagnostic and statistical manual of mental disorders* (4th ed.). Washington, DC: Author.

Barnes, A., & Ephross, P. H. (1995). The impact of hate crimes on victims: Emotional and behavioral responses to attacks. *Social Work, 39*, 247–251.

Beach, M. C., et al. (2005, April). Cultural competence: A systematic review of health care provider educational interventions. *Medical Care, 43*(4), 356–373.

Bergin, A. E., & Garfield, S. L. (1996). *Handbook of psychotherapy and behavior change*. New York: John Wiley.

Bernard, J. M. (1979). Supervisor training: A discrimination model. *Counselor Education and Supervision, 19*, 60–68.

Bisman, C. (1999). Social work assessment: Case theory construction. *Families in Society, 8*(3), 240–247.

Boehm, A., & Staples, L. H. (2004). Empowerment: The point of view of consumers. *Families in Society, 85*, 270–280.

Bordin, E. S. (1979). The generalizability of the psychoanalytic concept of the working alliance. *Psychotherapy: Theory, Research, and Practice, 16*, 252–260.

Bricker-Jenkins, M. (1997). Hidden treasures: Unlocking strengths in the public social services. In D. Saleebey (Ed.), *The strengths perspective in social work practice* (pp. 133–150). New York: Longman.

Browne, C., & Mills, C. (2001). Theoretical frameworks: Ecological model, strengths perspective, and empowerment theory. In R. Fong & S. B. C. L. Furuto (Eds.), *Culturally competent practice: Skills, interventions and evaluations* (pp. 10–32). Boston: Allyn & Bacon.

Chen, S., Sullivan, N. Y., Lu, Y. E., & Shibusawa, T. (2003). Asian American and mental health services: A study of utlization patterns in the 1990s. *Journal of Ethnic & Cultural Diversity in Social Work, 12*, 19–42.

Clark, J. (1994). Should social work education address religious issues? No! *Journal of Social Work Education, 30*(1), 11–16.

Comas-Diaz, L. (1994). An integrative approach. In L. Comas-Diaz & B. Greene (Eds.), *Women of color: Integrating ethnic and gender identities in psychotherapy* (pp. 287–318). New York: Guilford.

Cowger, C. D. (1994). Assessing client strengths: Clinical assessment for client empowerment. *Social Work, 39,* 262–268.

Cox, C. B., & Ephross, P. H. (1998). *Ethnicity and social work practice.* New York: Oxford University Press.

Dana, R. H. (1993). *Multicultural assessment perspectives for professional psychology.* Boston: Allyn & Bacon.

Dore, M. M., & Alexander, L. B. (1996). Preserving families at risk of child abuse and neglect: The role of the helping alliance. *Child Abuse and Neglect, 20*(4), 349–361.

Dupree, D., Spencer, M. B., & Bell, S. (1997). African American children. In G. Johnson-Powell & J. Yamamoto (Eds.), *Transcultural child development: Psychological assessment and treatment* (pp. 237–268). New York: John Wiley.

Eaton, T. T., Abeles, N., & Gotfreund, M. J. (1988). Therapeutic alliance and outcome: Impact of treatment length and pretreatment symptomatology. *Psychotherapy, 25,* 536–542.

Eisenthal, S., Emery, R., Lazare, A., & Udin, H. (1979). Adherence and the negotiated approach. *Archives of General Psychiatry, 36,* 393–398.

Fassinger, R. E., & Richie, B. S. (1997). Sex matters: Gender and sexual orientation in training for multicultural counseling competency. In D. B. Pope-Davis & H. L. K. Coleman (Eds.), *Multicultural counseling competencies: Assessment, education and training, and supervision* (pp. 83–110). Thousand Oaks, CA: Sage.

Fong, R. (2004). Overview of immigrant and refugee children and families. In R. Fong (Ed.), *Culturally competent practice with immigrant and refugee children and families* (pp. 1–18). New York: Guilford Press.

Fong, R., & Furuto, S. B. C. L. (2001). *Culturally competent practice: Skills, interventions, and evaluations.* Boston: Allyn & Bacon.

Fortune, A. E. (1987). Grief only? Client and social worker reactions to termination. *Clinical Social Work Journal, 15,* 159–171.

Fortune, A. E., Pearlingi, B., & Rochelle, C. D. (1992). Reactions to termination of individual treatment. *Social Work, 37,* 171–178.

Frank, A. F., & Gunderson, J. G. (1990). The role of the therapeutic alliance in the treatment of schizophrenia. *Archives of General Psychiatry, 47,* 228–236.

Franklin, A. J. (1993, July/August). The invisibility syndrome. *Family Therapy Networker,* 33–39.

Gibson, C. M. (1993). Empowerment theory and practice: With adolescents of color in the child welfare system. *Families in Society, 74,* 387–396.

Giordano, J., & Giordano, M. A. (1995). Ethnic dimensions in family therapy. In R. Mikesell, D. Lusterman, & S. McDaniel (Eds.), *Integrating family therapy.* Washington, DC: American Psychological Association.

GLSEN (Gay, Lesbian, and Straight Education Network). (2001, January 2). *Building culturally competent organizations.* http://www.lgbthistorymonth.org/cgi-bin/iowa/all/news/record/339.html

Grant, D. (2001). Evaluation skills with African American organizations and communities. In R. Fong & S. B. C. L. Furuto (Eds.), *Culturally competent practice: Skills, interventions, and evaluations* (pp. 355–369). Boston: Allyn & Bacon.

Green, J. W. (1995). *Cultural awareness in the human services: A multi-ethnic approach* (2nd ed.). Boston: Allyn & Bacon.

Green, J. W. (1999). *Cultural awareness in the human services: A multi-ethnic approach* (3rd ed.). Boston: Allyn & Bacon.

Greene, G. J., Lee, M. Y., & Hoffpauir, S. (2005). The language of empowerment and strengths in clinical social work: A constructivist perspective. *Families in Society, 86,* 267–277.

Gutierrez, L. M. (1990). Working with women of color: An empowerment perspective. *Social Work, 35,* 149–153.

Helms, J. E., & Richardson, T. Q. (1997). How "multiculturalism" obscures race and culture as differential aspects of counseling competency. In D. B. Pope-Davis & H. L. K. Coleman (Eds.), *Multicultural counseling competencies: Assessment, education and training, and supervision* (pp. 60–79). Thousand Oaks, CA: Sage.

Henggeler, S. W., Schoenwald, S. K., Pickrel, S. G., Rowland, M. D., & Santos, A. B. (1994). The contribution of treatment outcome research to the reform of children's mental health services: Multisystem therapy as an example. *Journal of Mental Health Administration, 21,* 229–239.

Hepworth, D. H., Rooney, R. H., & Larsen, J. A. (2002). *Direct social work practice: Theory and skills* (5th ed.). Pacific Grove, CA: Brooks/Cole.

Hines, P. M., & Boyd-Franklin, N. (1996). African American families. In M. McGoldrick, J. Giordano, & J. K. Pearce (Eds.), *Ethnicity and family therapy* (pp. 66–84). New York: Guilford.

Horvath, A. O., & Greenberg, L. S. (Eds.). (1994). *The working alliance: Theory, research, and practice.* New York: John Wiley.

Iglehart, A. P., & Becerra, R. M. (2000). *Social services and the ethnic community.* Prospect Heights, IL: Waveland Press.

Kadushin, A., & Kadushin, G. (1997). *The social work interview: A guide for human service professionals.* New York: Columbia University Press.

Kochman, T. (1981). *Black and white styles in conflicts.* Chicago: University of Chicago Press.

Kumabe, K., Nishida, C., & Hepworth, D. (1985). *Bridging ethnocultural diversity in social work and health.* Honolulu: University of Hawaii Press.

Lefley, H. P., & Pedersen, P. B. (1986). *Cross-cultural training for mental health professionals.* Springfield, IL: Charles C. Thomas.

Leigh, J. W. (1984). *Empowerment strategies for work with multi-ethnic populations.* Paper presented at the Council on Social Work Education Annual Program Meeting, Detroit, Michigan.

Lipman-Blumen, J., Handley-Isaksen, A., & Leavitt, H. J. (1983). Achieving styles in men and women: A model, an instrument, and some findings. In J. Spence (Ed.), *Achievement and achievement motives.* San Francisco: Freeman & Company.

Longres, J. F. (1991). Toward a status model of ethnic sensitive practice. *Journal of Multicultural Social Work, 1,* 41–56.

Lu, Y. E., DuBray, W. H., Chen, S., & Ahn, J. H. (2000). *Culture and clinical social work: American Indian vs. European American achieving styles.* An unpublished paper.

Lu, Y. E., Lum, D., & Chen, S. (2001). Cultural competency and achieving styles in clinical social work: A conceptual and empirical exploration. *Journal of Ethnic and Cultural Diversity in Social Work, 9*(3–4), 1–32.

Lu, Y. E., Organista, K., Manzo, S., Jr., Wong, L., & Phung, J. (2002). Exploring dimensions of culturally sensitive clinical styles with Latinos. *Journal of Ethnic and Cultural Diversity in Social Work, 10*(2).

Luborsky, L. (1975). Helping alliance in psychotherapy. In J. L. Claghorn (Ed.), *Successful psychotherapy* (pp. 92–116). New York: Brunner/Mazel.

Lum, D. (1996). *Social work practice and people of color: A process-stage approach* (3rd ed.). Pacific Grove, CA: Brooks/Cole.

Lum, D. (2000). *Social work practice and people of color: A process-stage approach* (4th ed.). Pacific Grove, CA: Brooks/Cole.

Manning, M. (2001). Culturally competent assessment of African American communities and organizations. In R. Fong & S. B. C. L. Furuto (Eds.), *Culturally competent practice: Skills, interventions, and evaluations* (pp. 119–131). Boston: Allyn & Bacon.

Manning, M. C., Cornelius, L. J., & Okundaye, J. N. (2004). Empowering African Americans through social work practice: Integrating an Afrocentric perspective, ego psychology, and spirituality. *Families in Society, 85,* 229–235.

Mayer, J., & Timms, W. (1969). Clash in perspective between worker and client. *Social Casework, 50,* 32–40.

Muslim refugees in the United States (n.d.). *Muslim refugee populations and special concerns.* http://www.culturalorientation.net/muslims/mc4.html

Negroni-Rodriguez, L. K., & Morales, J. (2001). Individual and family assessment skills with Latinio/Hispanic Americans. In R. Fong & S. B. C. L. Furuto (Eds.), *Culturally competent practice: Skills, interventions, and evaluations* (pp. 132–146). Boston: Allyn & Bacon.

Paniagua, F. A. (2005). *Assessing and treating culturally diverse clients: A practical guide.* Thousand Oaks, CA: Sage Publications.

Pinderhughes, E. (1989). *Understanding race, ethnicity, and power: The key to efficacy in clinical practice.* New York: Free Press.

Potocky-Tripodi, M. (2002). *Best practices for social work with refugees and immigrants.* New York: Columbia University Press.

Proctor, E. K., & Davis, L. E. (1994). The challenge of racial difference: Skills for clinical practice. *Social Work, 39,* 314–323.

The question of race in America. (1997, June 15). *Sacramento Bee,* p. Forum 4.

Raue, P. J., & Goldfried, M. R. (1994). The therapeutic alliance in cognitive-behavior therapy. In A. O. Horvath & L. S. Greenberg (Eds.), *The working alliance: Theory, research and practice* (pp. 131–152). New York: John Wiley.

Reid, W. J. (1978). *The task-centered system*. New York: Columbia University Press.

Reynolds, A. L., & Pope, R. L. (1991). The complexities of diversity: Exploring multiple oppressions. *Journal of Counseling and Development, 70,* 174–180.

Ridley, C. R., Espelage, D. L., & Rubinstein, K. J. (1997). Course development in multicultural counseling. In D. B. Pope-Davis & H. L. K. Coleman (Eds.), *Multicultural counseling competencies: Assessment, education and training, and supervision* (pp. 131–158). Thousand Oaks, CA: Sage.

Saleebey, D. (Ed.). (2002). *The strengths perspective in social work practice*. Boston: Allyn & Bacon.

Schriver, J. M. (2001). *Human behavior and the social environment: Shifting paradigms in essential knowledge for social work practice*. Boston: Allyn & Bacon.

Sobeck, J. L., Chapleski, E. E., & Fisher, C. (2003). Conducting research with American Indians: A case study of motives, methods, and results. *Journal of Ethnic & Cultural Diversity in Social Work, 12,* 69–84.

Solomon, B. (1976). *Black empowerment: Social work in oppressed communities*. New York: Columbia University Press.

Spence, J. T. (1985). Achievement American style: The rewards and costs of individualism. *American Psychologist, 40* (12), 1285–1295.

Stanhope, V., Solomon, P., Pernell-Arnold, A., Sands, R. G., & Bourjolly, J. N. (2005, Winter). Evaluating cultural competence among behavioral health professionals. *Psychiatric Rehabilitation Journal, 28*(3), 225–233.

Tsui, P., & Schultz, G. L. (1985). Failure of rapport: Why psychotherapeutic engagement fails in the treatment of Asian clients. *American Journal of Orthopsychiatry, 55,* 561–569.

Vasquez, M. J. T. (2005). Independent practice settings and the multicultural guidelines. In M. G. Constantine & D. W. Sue (Eds.), *Strategies for building multicultural competence in mental health and educational settings* (pp. 91–108). Hoboken, NJ: John Wiley & Sons.

Waldinger, R. J., & Frank, A. F. (1989). Clinicians' experiences in combining medication and psychotherapy in the treatment of borderline patients. *Hospital and Community Psychiatry, 40,* 712–718.

Wallace, S. (1990). The no-care zone: Availability, accessibility, acceptability in community-based long-term care. *Gerontologist, 30,* 254–261.

Weaver, H. N. (2001). Organization and community assessment with First Nations People. In R. Fong & S. B. C. L. Furuto (Eds.), *Culturally competent practice: Skills, interventions, and evaluations* (pp. 178–195). Boston: Allyn & Bacon.

Yellow Horse Brave Heart, M. (2001). Culturally and historically congruent clinical social work assessment with Native clients. In R. Fong & S. B. C. L. Furuto (Eds.), *Culturally competent practice: Skills, interventions, and*

evaluations (pp. 163–177). Boston: Allyn & Bacon.

Yuen, F. (1999). Family health and cultural diversity. In J. Pardeck & F. Yuen (Eds.), *Family health: A holistic approach to social work practice* (pp. 101–114). Westport, CT: Auburn House.

Yuen, F. (2003). Critical concerns for family health practice. In F. Yuen, G. Skibinski, & J. Pardeck (Eds.), *Family health social work practice: A knowledge and skills casebook* (pp. 19–40). Binghamton, NY: Haworth Press.

Yuen, F. (2005). Family health social work practice and change. In F. Yuen (Ed.), *Social work practice with children and families: A family health approach* (pp. 1–11). Binghamton, NY: Haworth Press.

Yuen, F., Bein, A., & Lum, D. (2006). Inductive learning. In D. Lum (Ed.), *Culturally competent practice: A framework for understanding diverse groups and justice issues* (3rd ed.). Pacific Grove, CA: Brooks/Cole.

Yuen, F., & Lum, D. (2003). Family health practice with the spiritually diverse person. In F. Yuen, G. Skibinski, & J. Pardeck (Eds.), *Family health social work practice: A knowledge and skills casebook* (pp. 131–145). Binghamton, NY: Haworth Press.

Yuen, F., & Terao, K. (2003). *Practical grant writing and program evaluation for the human services*. Belmont, CA: Brooks/Cole Thomson Learning.

Yuen, F., Terao, K., & Schmidt, A. (2009). *Effective grant writing and program evaluation for human service professionals*. Hoboken, NJ: Wiley & Sons.

Chapter 8

Abe-Kim, J. S., & Takeuchi, D. T. (1996). Cultural competence and quality of care: Issues for mental health service delivery in managed care. *Clinical Psychology: Science and Practice, 3*(4), 273–295.

Angell, G. B., Kurz, B. J., & Gottfried, G. M. (1997). Suicide and North American Indians: A social constructavist perspective. *Journal of Multicultural Social Work, 6* (3/4), 1–25.

Bachman, R. (1992). *Death and violence on the reservation.* New York: Auburn House.

Barsh, R. L. (1996). The Indian Child Welfare Act of 1978: A critical analysis. In J. R. Wunder (Ed.), *Recent legal issues for American Indians, 1968 to the present* (pp. 219–268). New York: Garland.

Bird, M. E. (2002). Health and indigenous people: Recommendations for the next generation. *American Journal of Public Health, 92*(9), 1391–1392.

Brave Heart-Jordan, M., & DeBruyn, L. (1995). So she may walk in balance: Integrating the impact of historical trauma in the treatment of American Indian women. In J. Adelman & G. Enguidanos (Eds.), *Racism in the lives of women: Testimony, theory, and guides to antiracist practice* (pp. 345–368). New York: Haworth.

Churchill, W., & Morris, G. T. (1992). Key Indian laws and cases. In M. A. Jaimes (Ed.), *The state of Native America: Genocide, colonization, and resistance* (pp. 13–21). Boston: South End Press.

Claymore, B. J., & Taylor, M. A. (1989). AIDS—Tribal nations face the newest communicable disease: An Aberdeen area perspective. *American Indian Culture and Research Journal, 13*(3/4), 21–31.

Coleman, H. L. K. (1998). General and multicultural counseling competency: Apples and oranges? *Journal of Multicultural Counseling and Development, 26,* 147–156.

Council on Social Work Education (CSWE). (2000). *Educational policy and accreditation standards.* Alexandria, VA: Author. http://www.cswe.org/accreditation.htm

DeGraw, R. G. (1989). The Navajo cultural immersion project. In P. S. Denise & I. M. Harris (Eds.), *Experiential education for community development* (pp. 223–231). New York: Greenwood.

Droste, T. (2005). States and tribes: A healthy alliance. *State Legislatures, April,* 29–30.

Good Tracks, J. G. (1973, November). Native American non-interference. *Social Work,* 30–35.

Green, J. W. (1999). *Cultural awareness in the human services: A multi-ethnic approach.* Boston: Allyn & Bacon.

Gurnee, C. G., Vigil, D. E., Krill-Smith, S., & Crowley, T. J. (1990). Substance abuse among American Indians in an urban treatment program. *American Indian and Alaska Native Mental Health Research, 3*(3), 17–26.

Jaimes, M. A. (Ed.). (1992). *The state of Native America: Genocide, colonization, and resistance.* Boston: South End Press.

Kramer, B. J. (1992). Health and aging of urban American Indians. *The Western Journal of Medicine, 157*(3), 281–286.

Kramer, J. B. (1992). Serving American Indian elderly in cities: An invisible minority. *Aging, 363/364,* 48–52.

MacEachron, A. E., Gustavsson, N. S., Cross, S., & Lewis, A. (1996). The effectiveness of the Indian Child Welfare Act of 1978. *Social Service Review, 70*(3), 451–463.

Mannes, M. (1995). Factors and events leading to the passage of the Indian Child Welfare Act. *Child Welfare, 74*(1), 264–282.

Mason, J. L., Benjamin, M. P., & Lewis, S. (1996). The cultural competence model: Implications for child and family mental health services. In C. A. Heflinger & C. T. Nixon (Eds.), *Families and the mental health system for children and adolescents* (pp. 165–190). Thousand Oaks, CA: Sage.

Mitchell, J. (1991). The Mohawks in high steel. In E. Wilson (Ed.), *Apologies to the Iroquois* (pp. 1–36). Syracuse, NY: Syracuse University Press.

Mitka, M. (2002). Two new projects to help Native Americans end substance abuse and domestic violence. *Journal of the American Medical Association, 288*(15), 1834–1835.

Moran, J. R. (1999). Preventing alcohol use among urban American Indian youth: The Seventh Generation program. *Journal of Human Behavior in the Social Environment, 2*(1/2), 51–67.

Morrisette, P. J. (1994). The holocaust of First Nation people: Residual effects on parenting and treatment implications. *Contemporary Family Therapy, 16*(5), 381–392.

Napoli, M. (2002). Native wellness for the new millennium:

The impact of gaming. *Journal of Sociology and Social Welfare, 29*(1), 17–34.

National Association of Social Workers (NASW). (1999). *Code of ethics of the National Association of Social Workers.* Washington, DC: Author.

National Indian Gaming Association. (2005). http://www.indiangaming.

Native American Leadership Commission on Health and AIDS. (1994). *A Native American leadership response to HIV and AIDS.* New York: American Indian Community House.

Oetting, E. R., & Beauvais, F. (1991). Orthogonal cultural identification theory: The cultural identification of minority adolescents. *The International Journal of the Addictions 25* (5A & 6A), 655–685.

Ogunwole, S. (2002). *The American Indian and Alaska Native Population: 2000.* Washington DC: U.S. Census Bureau.

Parker, L., Jamous, M., Marek, R., & Camacho, C. (1991). Traditions and innovations: A community-based approach to substance abuse prevention. *Rhode Island Medical Journal, 74,* 281–286.

Red Horse, J. (1978). Family behavior of urban American Indians. *Social Casework, 59*(2), 67–72.

Robbins, R. L. (1992). Self-determination and subordination: The past, present, and future of American Indian governance. In M. A. Jaimes (Ed.), *The state of Native America: Genocide, colonization, and resistance* (pp. 87–121). Boston: South End Press.

Ronnau, J. P. (1994). Teaching cultural competence: Practical ideas for social work educators. *Journal of Multicultural Social Work, 3*(1), 29–42.

Schafer, J. R., & McIlwaine, B. D. (1992). Investigating child sexual abuse in the American Indian community. *American Indian Quarterly, 16*(2), 157–167.

Schinke, S. P., Tepavac, L., & Cole, K. (2000). Preventing substance use among Native American youth: Three-year results. *Addictive Behaviors, 25*(3), 387–397.

Shulman, L. (1999). *The skills of helping individuals, families, groups, and communities.* Itasca, IL: F. E. Peacock.

Sowers-Hoag, K. M., & Sandau-Beckler, P. (1996). Educating for cultural competence in the generalist curriculum. *Journal of Multicultural Social Work, 4*(3), 37–56.

Stiffarm, L. A., & Lane, P., Jr. (1992). The demography of Native North America: A question of American Indian survival. In M. A. Jaimes (Ed.), *The state of Native America: Genocide, colonization, and resistance* (pp. 23–25). Boston: South End Press.

Sue, D. W., et al. (1998). *Multicultural counseling competencies: Individual and organizational development.* Thousand Oaks, CA: Sage.

Swan, J., Breen, N., Burhansstipanov, L., Satter, D. E., Davis, W. W., McNeel, T., et al. (2006). Cancer screening and risk factors among American Indians. *American Journal of Public Health, 96*(2), 340–350.

Thomason, T. C. (2000). Issues in the treatment of Native Americans with alcohol problems. *Journal of Multicultural Counseling and Development, 28*(4), 243–252.

Unclaimed Assets.com. (2005). *Unclaimed individual Indian monies and tribal trust accounts.* http://www.unclaimedassets.com/US2.htm

U.S. Bureau of the Census (2005). http://www.census.gov.

U.S. Census Bureau. (2009). *U.S. Census Bureau News.* CB09-FF.20. Washington DC: U.S. Census Bureau. Accessed July 1, 2010, from www.census.gov/Press-Release/www/releases/pdf/cb09ff.20_americanind.pdf

U.S. Department of the Interior. (2005). *Historical accounting for individual Indian monies: A progress report.* http://www.doi.gov

Voss, R. W., Douville, V., Little Soldier, A., & Twiss, G. (1999). Tribal and shamanic-based social work practice: A Lakota perspective. *Social Work, 44*(3), 228–241.

Walters, K. L. (1999). Urban American Indian identity attitudes and acculturation styles. *Journal of Human Behavior in the Social Environment, 2*(1/2), 163–178.

Wares, D. M., Wedel, K. R., Rosenthal, J. A., & Dobrec, A. (1994). Indian child welfare: A multicultural challenge. *Journal of Multicultural Social Work, 3*(3), 1–15.

Waters, M. C. (1990). *Ethnic options: Choosing identities in America.* Berkeley: University of California Press.

Weaver, H. N. (1996). Social work with American Indian youth using the orthogonal model of cultural identification. *Families in Society: The Journal of Contemporary Human Services, 77*(2), 98–107.

Weaver, H. N. (1999a). Assessing the needs of Native American communities: A Northeastern example. *Evaluation and Program Planning: An*

International Journal, 22(2), 155–161.

Weaver, H. N. (1999b). Indigenous people and the social work profession: Defining culturally competent services. *Social Work, 44*(3), 217–225.

Weaver, H. N. (2000). Activism and American Indian issues: Opportunities and roles for social workers. *Journal of Progressive Human Services, 11*(1), 3–22.

Weaver, H. N. (2001). Native Americans and substance abuse. In S. L. A. Straussner (Ed.), *Ethnocultural factors in substance abuse treatment* (pp. 77–96). New York: Guilford Press.

Weaver, H. N. (2005). *Explorations in cultural competence: Journeys to the four directions.* Belmont, CA: Brooks/Cole Thomson Learning.

Weaver, H. N., & White, B. J. (1997). The Native American family circle: Roots of resiliency. *Journal of Family Social Work, 2*(1), 67–79.

Weaver, H. N., & White, B. J. (1999). Protecting the future of indigenous children and nations: An examination of the Indian Child Welfare Act. *Journal of Health and Social Policy, 10*(4), 35–50.

Westerfelt, A., & Yellow Bird, M. (1999). Homeless and indigenous in Minneapolis. *Journal of Human Behavior in the Social Environment, 2*(1/2), 145–162.

Chapter 9

Degruy Leary, J. (2005). *Post traumatic slave syndrome: America's legacy of enduring injury and healing.* Milwaukie, OR: UPTONE Press.

Graves, J. L. (2004). *The race myth: Why we pretend race exists in America.* New York: Penguin.

Ignatiev, N. (1995). *How the Irish became White.* New York: Routledge.

Lipsitz, G. (1998). *The possessive investment in Whiteness: How White people profit from identity politics.* Philadelphia: Temple University Press.

Loewen, J. W. (2007). *Lies my teacher told me: Everything your American history textbook got wrong* (Rev. ed.). New York: Simon & Schuster.

Shipler, D. K. (1997). *A country of strangers: Blacks and Whites in America.* New York: Alfred A. Knopf, Inc.

Takaki, R. T. (1993). *A different mirror: A history of multicultural America.* Boston: Little, Brown and Company.

Thandeka. (1999). *Learning to be White: Money, race, and God in America.* New York: The Continuum Publishing Company.

Washington, H. A. (2008). *Medical apartheid: The dark history of medical experimentation on black Americans from colonial times to the present.* New York: Anchor Books.

Zinn, H. (1999). *A people's history of the United States 1492-present: Twentieth anniversary edition.* New York: HarperCollins.

Chapter 10

African Americans: Cultural diversity curriculum for social workers and health practitioners. (1998). Center for Social Work Research, University of Texas at Austin.

Akbar, N. (1984). Africentric social sciences for human liberation. *Journal of Black Studies, 14,* 395–414.

Alter, J. (1997, December 8). The long shadow of slavery. *Newsweek,* pp. 58–63.

The American Black family: Looking back. (1987). *American Visions, 2*(6), 26–27.

Annie E Casey Foundation. (2003). *Kids count pocket guide: African-American children.*

Austin, A. (2008). *What a recession means for black America.* EPI Issue Brief #241. Retrieved December 14, 2009, from http://www.epi.org/publications/entry/ib241/

Banerjee, N. (2006, January 21). Black churches' attitudes toward gay parishioners spur debate at conference. *The New York Times.* Retrieved January 5, 2010, from http://www.nytimes.com/2006/01/21/national/21church.html?_r=1&scp=1&sq=black%20churches%20January%202006&st=cse

Beedon, L., & Wu, K. (2004, September). *African Americans age 65 and older: Their sources of income.* Washington, DC: AARP Public Policy Institute.

Bell, P., & Evans, J. (1981). *Counseling the Black client: Alcohol use and abuse in Black America.* Center City, MN: Hazelden.

Bennett, C. E., & Debanos, K. A. (1998). *The Black population.* In The official statistics. Washington, DC: U.S. Census Bureau.

Bennett, C. I. (1986). *Comprehensive multicultural education: Theory and practice.* Boston: Allyn & Bacon.

Bennett, L., Jr. (1982). *Before the Mayflower: A history of Black America* (5th ed.). Chicago: Johnson.

Better (2008). Institutional racism: A primer on theory

and strategies for social change. Lanham, MD: Rowman & Littlefield.

Billingsley, A. (1968). *Black families in White America*. Englewood Cliffs, NJ: Prentice Hall.

Billingsley, A. (1992). *Climbing Jacob's ladder: The enduring legacy of African American families*. New York: Simon & Schuster.

Bobo, L., & Charlse, C. (2009). Race in the American mind: From the Moynihan report to the Obama candidacy. *The ANNALS of the American Academy of Political and Social Science, 621*, 243–259.

Bond, S., & Cash, T. F. (1992). Black beauty: Skin color and body images among African-American college women. *Journal of Applied Social Psychology, 22*, 874–888.

Burbridge, L. C. (1995). *Policy implications of a decline in marriage among African Americans*. In M. B. Tucker & C. Mitchell-Kernan (Eds.), *The decline in marriage among African Americans: Causes, consequences, and policy implications* (pp. 323–344). New York: Russell Sage.

Chatters, L. M., Taylor, R. J., & Neighbors, H. (1989). Size of informal helper network mobilized during a serious personal problem among Black Americans. *Journal of Marriage and the Family, 51*, 667–676.

Comer, J. P., & Poussaint, A. F. (1975). *Black child care: How to bring up a healthy Black child in America: A guide to emotional and psychological development*. New York: Pocket Books.

Cose, E. (1999). The good news about Black America. *Newsweek*, pp. 28–40.

Council on Social Work Education (2008). *Educational Policy Accreditation Standards*. Retrieved January 19, 2010, from http://www.cswe.org/ Accreditation/Handbook.aspx

Crawley, B., & Freeman, E. (1992). Themes in the life views of older and younger African American males. *Journal of African American Male Studies, 1*(1), 15–29.

Crawley, B. H. (1996). Effective programs and services for African American families and children: An African centered perspective. In S. L. Logan (Ed.), *The Black family: Strengths, self-help, and positive change* (pp. 112–130). Boulder, CO: Westview Press.

Cross, T. L., Bazron, B. J., Dennis, K. W., & Isaacs, M. R. (1989). *Towards a culturally competent system of care*. Washington, DC: Georgetown University Child Development Center.

Curry, A., Latkin, C., & Davey-Rothwell, M. (2008). Pathways to depression: The impact of neighborhood violent crime on inner-city residents in Baltimore, Maryland, USA. *Social Science & Medicine, 67*(1), 23–30.

Daly, A., Jennings, J., Beckett, J., & Leashore, B. (1995). Effective coping strategies of African Americans. *Social Work, 40*, 240–248.

Dana, R. H. (1993). *Multicultural assessment perspectives for professional psychology*. Boston: Allyn & Bacon.

Davis, E. (2001). Evaluation skills with African American individuals and families: Three approaches. In R. Fong & S. Furuto (Eds.), *Culturally compentent practice: Skills, interventions, and evaluations* (pp. 343–354). Boston: Allyn & Bacon.

Devore, W., & Schlesinger, E. G. (1996). *Ethnic-sensitive social work practice*. New York: Allyn & Bacon.

Diller, J. V. (1999). Working with African American clients: An interview with Jimmie Turner. In *Cultural diversity: A primer for the human services* (pp. 174–188). Toronto: Wadsworth.

Drake, S., & Cayton, H. R. (1962). *Black metropolis: A study of Negro life in a northern city*. New York: Harper & Row.

Du Bois, W. E. B. (1903). *The souls of Black folk*. Chicago: McClurg.

Dungee-Anderson, D., & Beckett, J. O. (1995). A process model for multicultural social work practice. *Families in Society: The Journal of Contemporary Human Services, 76*(8), 459–468.

Everett, J. E., Chipungu, S. S., & Leashore, B. R. (Eds.). (1991). *Child welfare: An Africentric perspective*. New Brunswick, NJ: Rutgers University Press.

Fairie, R. W., & Robb, A. M. (2007). Why are Black-owned businesses less successful that White-owned businesses? The role of families, inheritance, and business human capital. *Journal of Labor Economics, 25*(2), 289–323.

Feagan, J., & Sikes, M. (1994). *Living with racism: The Black middle-class experience*. Boston: Beacon Press.

Forum on Child and Family Statistics (2009). *America's Children: Key National Indicators of Well-being 2009*. Retrieved May 5, 2010, from http:// childstats.gov/americaschildren/famsoc.asp

Freeman, E. M. (1990). Theoretical perspectives for practice with Black families. In S. Logan, E. Freeman, &

R. G. McRoy (Eds.), *Social work practice with Black families: A culturally specific perspective* (pp. 38–52). White Plains, NY: Longman.

Gary, L. E. (1985). Correlates of depressive symptoms among a select population of Black men. *American Journal of Public Health, 75,* 1220–1222.

Gilliam, F. (2006). *The architecture of a new racial discourse: A FrameWorks message memo.* Washington DC: FrameWorks Institute.

Grace, C. A. (1992). Practical considerations for program professionals and evaluators working with African-American communities. In M. A. Orlandi (Ed.), *Cultural competence for evaluators: A guide for alcohol and other drug abuse prevention practitioners working with ethnic/racial communities* (pp. 55–74). Rockville, MD: U.S. Department of Health and Human Services, Office for Substance Abuse Prevention.

Grant, D. (2001). Evaluation skills with African American organizations and communities. In R. Fong, & S. Furuto (Eds.), *Culturally compentent practice: Skills, interventions, and evaluations* (pp. 355–369). Boston: Allyn & Bacon.

Grier, W. H., & Cobbs, P. M. (1968). *Black rage.* New York: Basic Books.

Harlow, R. (2009). Barack Obama and the (in)significance of his presidential campaign. *Journal of African American St, 13,* 164–175.

Harper, B. C. O. (1990). Blacks and the health care delivery system: Challenges and prospects. In S. Logan, E. Freeman, & R. G. McRoy (Eds.), *Social work practice with Black*

families (pp. 239–256). White Plains, NY: Longman.

Harrison, D. D. (2000). "Wild women don't have the blues": Blues from the Black woman's perspective. In F. W. Hayes, III (Ed.), *A turbulent voyage: Readings in African American studies* (3rd ed.). San Diego: Collegiate Press.

Hill, R. (1972). *The strengths of Black families.* New York: National Urban League.

Hill, R. (1978). *The illusion of black progress.* Washington, DC: National Urban League, Research Department.

Hill, R. (1987). The black middle class defined. *Ebony, 42*(10), 30–32.

Icard, L. D. & Nurius, P. S. (1996). Loss of self in coming out: Special risks for African American gays and lesbians. *Journal of Loss and Trauma, 1, 1,* 29–47.

Jaynes, G. D., & Williams, R. M. (Eds.). (1989). *A common destiny: Blacks and American society.* Washington, DC: National Academy Press.

Jewell, K. S. (1988). *Survival of the Black family: The institutional impact of U.S. social policy.* New York: Praeger.

Johnson, J., Burthey, G., & Ghorm, K. (2008). Economic globalization and the future of Black America. *Journal of Black Studies, 38,* 883–899.

Jones, D. L. (1983). African-American clients: Clinical practice issues. In F. J. Turner (Ed.), *Differential diagnosis and treatment in social work* (pp. 565–578). New York: Free Press.

The Journal of Blacks in Higher Education. (2009). *Vital signs: Statistics that measure the state of racial inequality, 63.* Retrieved from http://www.jbhe.com/vital/index.html

Kantrowitz, B., & Wingert, P. (2001, May 28). Unmarried, with children. *Newsweek, 137* (2), 46–54.

Keith, V. M., & Herring, C. (1991). Skin tone and stratification in the Black community. *American Journal of Sociology, 97*(3), 760–778.

Klonoff, E., & Landrine, H. (2000). Revising and improving the African American acculturation scale. *Journal of Black Psychology, 26*(2), 235–261.

LaFromboise, T., Coleman, H. L. K., & Gerton, J. (1993). Psychological impact of biculturalism: Evidence and theory. *Psychological Bulletin, 114,* 395–412.

Landrine, H., & Klonoff, E. (1994). The African American acculturation scale: Development, reliability, and validity. *Journal of Black Psychology, 20*(2), 104–127.

Logan, S. (Ed.). (1996). Epilogue: Understanding help-seeking behavior and empowerment issues for Black families. In S. L. Logan (Ed.), *Black family strengths, self help and positive change* (pp. 193–206). Boulder, CO: Westview Press.

Logan, S. M. L. (1990). Black families: Race, ethnicity, culture, social class, and gender issues. In S. Logan, E. Freeman, & R. G. McRoy (Eds.), *Social work practice with Black families: A culturally specific perspective* (pp. 18–37). White Plains, NY: Longman.

Lum, D. (1999). *Culturally competent practice: A framework for growth and action.* Pacific Grove, CA: Brooks/Cole.

Lum, D. (2000). *Social work practice and people of color: A process-stage approach.* Pacific Grove, CA: Brooks/Cole.

Madden, E., Faulkner, M., & McRoy, R. (2010). *Cultural competency tip sheets*. Collaboration to AdoptUsKids Training and Technical Assistance Report.

Mays, V., Chatters, L., Cochran, S., & Mackness, J. (1998, Spring). African American families in diversity: Gay men and lesbians as participants in family networks. *Journal of Comparative Family Studies*, 29(1), 73–88.

Mbiti, S. J. (1975). *Introduction to Africa religion*. New York: Praeger.

McIntosh, P. (1992). White privilege and male privilege: A personal account of coming to see correspondences through work in women's studies. In M. L. Anderson & P. H. Collins (Eds.), *Race, class and gender: An anthology* (pp. 70–81). Belmont, CA: Wadsworth.

McKinnon, J. (2003). *The Black population in the United States: March 2002*. Washington, DC: U.S. Census Bureau, Current Population Reports, Series P20–541.

McRoy, R. (1999). *Preserving African American culture: Perspectives on transracial placements*. Los Angeles: Institute for Black Parenting.

McRoy, R., & Grape, H. (1999). Skin color in transracial and inracial adoptions. *Child Welfare*, 78(5), 673–692.

McRoy, R. G. (1990). A historical overview of Black families. In S. Logan, E. Freeman, & R. G. McRoy (Eds.), *Social work practice with Black families: A culturally specific perspective* (pp. 3–17). White Plains, NY: Longman.

McRoy, R. G. (Ed.). (1998). *Cultural diversity curriculum*. Final report to Texas Department of Health.

Meyer, I., & Ouellette, S. C. (2008). Unity and purpose at the intersections of racial/ethnic and sexual identities. In P. L. Hammack & B. J. Cohler (Eds.), *The Story of Sexual Identity: Narrative, Social Change, and the Development of Sexual Orientation*. New York: Oxford University Press.

Miley, K. K., O'Melia, M., & DuBois, B. I. (1995). *Generalist social work practice: An empowering approach*. Boston: Allyn & Bacon.

Moynihan, D. P. (1965). *The Negro family: The case for national action*. Washington, DC: Government Printing Office.

Myrdal, G. (1962). *An American dilemma: The Negro problem and modern democracy*. New York: Harper & Row.

National Association of Social Workers. (2007). *Code of ethics of the National Association of Social Workers*. Washington, DC: NASW Press.

Neal, A. M., & Wilson, M. L. (1989). The role of skin color and features in the Black community: Implications for Black women and therapy. *Clinical Psychology Review*, 9, 323–333.

Neighbors, H. W., & Jackson, J. S. (1984). The use of informed help: Four patterns of illness behavior in the Black community. *American Journal of Community Psychology*, 12 (5), 551–565.

Neighbors, H. W., & Taylor, R. J. (1985). The use of social service agencies by Black Americans. *Social Service Review*, 59, 259–268.

Newland, K., & Grieco, E. (2004). *Spotlight on Haitians in the United States*. Migration Information Source. Retrieved from http://www.migrationinformation.org/USFocus/display.cfm?ID=214

Obasi, E., & Leong, F. (2009). Psychological distress, acculturation, and mental health-seeking attitudes among people of African descent in the United States: A Preliminary Investigation. *Journal of Counseling Psychology*, 56(2), 227–238.

Oliver, W. (1989). Black males and social problems. *Journal of Black Studies*, 20(1), 15–39.

Oliver, M., & Shapiro, T. (2008). Sub-prime as a Black catastrophe. *The American Prospect*. Retrieved May 6, 2010, from http://www.prospect.org/cs/articles? article=sub_prime_as_a_black_ catastrophe

Oppression: *Cultural diversity curriculum for social workers and health practitioners*. (1998). Center for Social Work Research, University of Texas at Austin.

Osirim, M. J. (2008). African women in the new diaspora: Transnationalism and the (re) creation of home. *African and Asian Studies*, 7, 367–394.

Oyebade, B. (1990). African studies and the Afrocentric paradigm: A critique. *Journal of Black Studies*, 21(2), 233–238.

Parillo, V. N. (2003). *Strangers to these shores* (7th ed.). New York: MacMillan.

Pew Health Profession Commission. (1995). *Critical challenges: Revitalizing the health care professions for the twenty first century*. San Francisco: UCSF Center for the Health Professions.

Pinderhughes, E. (1989). *Understanding race, ethnicity, and power: The key to efficacy in clinical practice.* New York: Free Press.

Portes, A., & Rumbaut, R. (2001). Legacies: *The Story of the Immigrant Second Generation.* Berkeley: University of California Press.

Ridley, C. R., Baker, D. M., & Hall, C. L. (2001). Critical issues concerning cultural competence. *Counseling Psychologist, 29*(6), 822–832)

Robinson, J. T. (1989). Clinical treatment of Black families: Issues and strategies. *Social Work, 34,* 323–329.

Rosario, M., Schrimshaw, E. W., & Hunter, J. (2004). Ethnic/racial differences in the coming-out process of lesbian, gay, and bisexual youths: A comparison of sexual identity development over time. *Cultural Diversity and Ethnic Minority Psychology, 10*(3), 215–228.

Rovai, A., Gallien, L., & Wighting, M. (2005). Cultural and interpersonal factors affecting African American academic performance in higher education: A review and synthesis of the research literature. *The Journal of Negro Education, 74*(4), 359–370.

Russell, K., Wilson, M., & Hall, R. (1992). *The color complex: The politics of skin color among African Americans.* Garden City, NY: Anchor.

Ryan, W. (1976). *Blaming the victim* (Rev. ed.). New York: Vintage Books.

Saldana, D. (2001). *Cultural competency: A practical guide for mental health service providers.* Hogg Foundation for Mental Health, University of Texas at Austin.

Sanders-Thompson, V. L. (1994). Socialization to race and its relationship to racial identification among African Americans. *Journal of Black Psychology, 20*(2), 175–188.

Schiele, J. (1996). Afrocentricity: An emerging paradigm in social work practice. *Social Work, 41*(3), 284–295.

Schiele, J. (2000). *Human services and the Afrocentric paradigm.* New York: The Haworth Press.

Staub, E. (1987, August). *Moral exclusion and extreme destructiveness: Personal goal theory, differential evaluation, moral equilibration and steps along the continuum of destruction.* Paper presented at the American Psychological Association Meeting, New York.

Stepick, A. (1998). *Pride against prejudice: Haitians in the United States.* Boston: Allyn & Bacon.

Sudarkasa, N. (1993). Female-headed African American households: Some neglected dimensions. In H. P. McAdoo (Ed.), *Family ethnicity: Strength in diversity* (pp. 81–89). Newbury Park, CA: Sage.

Tervalon, M., & Murray-Garcia, J. (1998). Cultural humility vs. cultural competence: A critical distinction in defining physician training outcomes in multicultural education. Journal of Health Care for the Poor and Underserved, 9(2), 117–125.

Tresolini & Pew-Fetzer Task Force. (1994). *Health professions education and relationship-centered care.* San Francisco: Pew Health Professions Commission.

US Bureau of the Census. (1999). *Current population survey, racial statistics branch, population division.* Retrieved from http://www.census.gov/population/www/socdemo/race/Black99tabs.html

US Bureau of the Census. (2000a). *Current population survey, racial statistics branch, population division.* Retrieved from http://www.census.gov/population/www/socdemo/race/ppl-142.html

US Bureau of the Census. (2000b). *Poverty rate lowest in 20 years, household income at record high, Census Bureau reports.* Retrieved from http://www.census.gov/Press-Release/www.2000/cb00-158.html

US Bureau of the Census. (2002). *Poverty rate rises, household income declines, Census Bureau Reports.* Washington, D.C. US Department of Commerce News, p. 1.

US Bureau of the Census (2005). *Asset ownership of households, 2000.* Retrieved from http://www.census.gov/hhes/www/wealth/1998_2000/wlth00-1.html

US Bureau of the Census. (2008). *Population estimates.* Retrieved December 12, 2009, from http://factfinder.census.gov/ US Bureau of the Census. (2009). *Current Population Survey, 2008 Annual Social and Economic Supplement.* Retrieved November 30, 2009, from http://www.census.gov/cps/

US Bureau of labor statistics. (2009). *Current Popluation Survey.* Retrieved January 4, 2010, from http://data.bls.gov:8080/PDQ/outside.jsp?survey=ln

Van Soest, D., & Bryant, S. (1995). Violence reconceptualized for social work: The urban dilemma. *Social Work, 40*(4), 549–558.

Ware, L. (2009).What Obama means: For our culture, our politics, our Future. *Journal of African American St, 13,* 195–197.

What makes you Black? (1983). *Ebony, 38*(3), 115–118.

Wheary, J., Shapiro, T. M., Draut, T., & Meschede, T. (2008). *Economic Insecurity: The experienceo of the African-American and Latino middle classes.* By a Thread Report no. #2. The Institute on Assets and Social Policy and Demos.

Williams (2009). *Essay: Economic inequality and the African diaspora.* The Black Studies Center.

Wilson, J. (2003). *African-born residents of the United States.* Migration Information Source. Retrieved from http://www.migrationinformation.org/USfocus/display.cfm

Winkelman, M. (1999). *Ethnic sensitivity in social work.* Dubuque, IA: Eddie Bowers Publishing.

Chapter 11

Acuna, R. (1972). *Occupied American: The Chicano's struggle toward liberation.* San Francisco: Canfield Press.

Adams, C. (2004). Linguistic differences and culturally relevant interventions for involving monolingual Latino individuals in research efforts. *Journal of Hispanic Higher Education, 3*(4), 382–392.

Adams, E., Cahill, B., & Ackerlind, S. (2005). A qualitative study of Latino lesbian and gay youths' experiences with discrimination and the career development process. *Journal of Vocational Behavior, 66*(2), 199–218.

Alegria, M., Canino, G., Shrout, P., Woo, M., Duan, N., Vila, D., et al. (2008). Prevalence of mental illness in immigrant and non-immigrant U.S. Latino groups. *American Journal of Psychiatry, 165,* 359–369.

Alegria, M., Mulvaney-Day, N., Torres, M., Polo, A., Cao, Z., Canino, G. (2007). Prevalence of psychiatric disorders across Latino subgroups in the United States. *American Journal of Public Health, 97*(1), 68–75.

Alegria, M., Takeuchi, D., Canino, G., Duan, N., Shrout, P., Meng, X., et al. (2004). Considering context, place and culture: The National Latino and Asian American study. *International Journal of Methods in Psychiatric Research, 13,* 208–220.

Allen, M., Elliott, M. C., Fuligni, A. J., Morales, L. S., Hambarsoomian, K., & Schuster, M. J. (2008). The relationship between Spanish language use and substance use behaviors among Latino youth: A social network approach. *Journal of Adolescent Health, 43,* 372–379.

Almeida, J., Molnar, B. E., Kawachi, I., & Subramanian, S. V. (2009). Ethnicity and nativity status as determinants of perceived social support: Testing the concept of familism. *Social Science and Medicine, 68*(10), 1852–1858.

Alvarez, R. R., Jr. (1986, Spring). The Lemon Grove Incident: The nation's first successful desegregation court case. *Journal of San Diego History, 32,* 116–135.

Anderson, H., & Goolishian, H. A. (1992). The client is the expert: A not knowing approach to therapy. In S. McNamee & K. Gere (Eds.), *Therapy as social construction* (pp. 25–39). Newbury Park, CA: Sage Publications.

Angel, R. J., Angel, J. L., & Hill, T. D. (2008). A comparison of the health of older Hispanics in the United States and Mexico. *Journal of Aging and Health, 20*(1), 3–31.

Aranda, M. P. (2006). Older Latinos: A mental health perspective. In B. Berkman & S. D'Ambruoso (Ed.), *Handbook of social work in health and aging* (pp. 283–291). New York: Oxford University Press.

Arroyo, F., & Eth, S. (1985). Children traumatized by Central American warfare. In S. Eth & R. S. Pynoos (Eds.), *Post-traumatic stress disorders in children* (pp. 101–120). Washington, DC: American Psychiatric Press.

Ayalon, L., & Huyck, M. (2001). Latino caregivers of relatives with Alzheimer's disease. *Clinical Gerontologist, 24*(3–4), 93–106.

Bacon, D. (2008). *Illegal people: How globalization creates migration and criminalizes immigrants.* Boston: Beacon Press.

Barreto, M., Manzano, S., Ramirez, R., & Rim, K. (2009). Mobilization, participation, and solidaridad: Latino participation in the 2006 immigration protest rallies. *Urban Affairs Review, 44*(5), 736–764.

Bergman, M. (2004, March 18). U.S. Census Bureau projects tripling of Hispanic and Asian populations in 50 years: Non-Hispanic whites may drop to half of total population.

Bernstein, N. (2010, January 9). Officials hid truth about immigrant deaths in jail. *New York Times.*

Bernstein, R. (2005, June 9). *Hispanic population passes 40 million* (Census Bureau Report CB05-77). Washington, DC: U.S. Census Bureau.

Bertera, E. (2003). Psychosocial factors and ethnic disparities in diabetes diagnosis and treatment among older adults. *Health and Social Work, 28* (1), 33–42.

Borges, G., Breslau, J., Su, M., Miller, M., Medina-Mora, M., & Aguilar-Gaxiola, S. (2009). Immigration and suicidal behavior among Mexicans and Mexican Americans. *American Journal of Public Health, 99*(4), 728–733.

Borges, G., Medina-Mora, M., Breslau, J., & Aguilar-Gaxiola, S. (2007). The effect of migration to the United States on substance use disorders among returned Mexican migrants and families of migrants. *American Journal of Public Health, 97*(10), 1847–1851.

Brown, A. V. (2008). Effectively educating Latino/a students: A comparative study of participation patterns of Hispanic American and Anglo-American university students. *Journal of Hispanic Higher Education, 7*(2), 97–118.

Bulhan, H. (1987). The constrained-strained theory: A general theory of deviance. *BHM Review 1.* Boston, MA: Behavioral Health Management.

Cabassa, L. J. (2007). Latino immigrant men's perceptions of depression and attitudes towards help seeking. *Hispanic Journal of Behavioral Sciences, 29*(4), 492–509.

Campbell, M. E. (2009). Multiracial groups and educational inequality: A rainbow or a divide? *Society for the Study of Social Problems, 56*(3), 425–446.

Castaneda, J. (2007). *Ex-Mex: From migrants to immigrants.* New York: The New Press.

Chiriboga, D. A., Jang, Y., Banks, S., & Kim, G. (2007). Acculturation and its effect on depressive symptom structure in a sample of Mexican American elders. *Hispanic Journal of Behavioral Sciences, 29*(1), 83–100.

Clark, J. M., Lasaga, J. L., & Reque, R. S. (1981). The Mariel exodus: An assessment and prospects. *In Council for Inter-American Security: A special report.* Washington, DC.

Colon, E. (2001). An ethnographic study of six Latino gay and bisexual men. *Journal of Gay and Lesbian Social Services: Issues in Practice, Policy and Research, 12*(3–4), 77–92.

Colon, J., & Lyke, J. (2003). Comparison of hospice use and demographics among European Americans, African Americans, and Latinos. *American Journal of Hospice and Palliative Care, 20*(3), 182–190.

Comas-Diaz, L., & Greene, B. (1994). *Women of color.* New York: Guilford.

Coon, D., et al. (2004). Well being, appraisal, and coping in Latina and Caucasian female dementia caregivers: Findings from the REACH study. *Aging and Mental Health, 8*(4), 330–345.

Council on Social Work Education. (2008). *Policy and accreditation standards.* Alexandria, VA: Author.

Cross, T., Bazron, B., Dennis, K., & Isaacs, M. (1989). *Towards a culturally competent system of care.* Washington, DC: CASSP Technical Assistance Center, Georgetown University Child Development Center.

Cuellar, I. A. B., & Maldonado, R. (1995). The acculturation rating scale for Mexican Americans-II (ARSMA-II): A revision of the original ARSMA scale. *Hispanic Journal of Behavioral Sciences, 17,* 275–304.

Curry-Stevens, A. (2009). *Early considerations for defining Anti-oppression practice (AOP) outcomes for MSW students: A concept paper.* Unpublished Manuscript.

Dauvergne, C. (2008). *Making people illegal.* Cambridge, England: Cambridge University Press.

Delgado, M. (2007). *Social work with Latinos: A cultural assets paradigm.* New York: Oxford University Press.

Desjarlais, R., Eisenberg, L., Good, B., & Kleinman, A. (1995). *World mental health.* New York: Oxford University Press.

Desyllas, M. C. (2007). A critique of global trafficking discourse and U.S. Policy. *Journal of Sociology & Social Welfare, 34*(4), 57–79.

Diaz, R., Ayala, G., & Bein, E. (2004). Sexual risk as an outcome of social oppression: Data from a probability sample of Latino gay men in three U.S. cities. *Cultural Diversity and Ethnic Minority Psychology, 10*(3), 255–267.

Diaz-Stevens, A. M., & Stevens-Arroyo, A. (1998). *The Latino resurgence in U.S. religion.* Boulder, CO: Westview Press.

Dominelli, L. (2002). *Anti-oppressive social work theory and practice.* New York: Palgrave Macmillan.

Edwards, T. (2009). Current Population Survey. *U.S. Census Bureau.*

Falicove, C. J. (2009). Commentary: On the wisdom and challenges of culturally attuned treatments for

Latinos. *Family Process, 48* (2), 292–309.

Fortuna, L. R., Porche, M., & Alegria, M. (2008). Political violence, psychosocial trauma, and the context of mental health services use among immigrant Latinas in the United States. *Ethnicity and Health, 13*(5), 435–463.

Fritz, C. S. J. (2009). A post racial America: Myth or reality? [Review Article]. *Ethnic and Racial Studies, 32*(6 July), 1083–1088.

Fry, R. (2002). Latinos in higher education: Many enroll, too few graduate.

Fuller-Thomson, E. M. M. (2007). Central American grandparents raising grandchildren. *Hispanic Journal of Behavioral Sciences, 29*(1), 5–18.

Gambrill, E. (2005). *Critical thinking in clinical practice.* Hoboken, NJ: John Wiley & Sons, Inc.

Gandara, P., & Contreras, F. (2009). *The Latino education crisis.* Cambridge, MA: Harvard University Press.

Garcia, B., & Van Soest, D. (2006). *Social work practice for social justice: Cultural competence in action.* Alexandria, VA: Council on Social Work Education.

Gelfand, D., Balcazar, H., Parzuchowski, J., & Lenox, S. (2004). Issues in hospice utilization by Mexicans. *The Journal of Applied Gerontology, 23*(1), 3–19.

Germain, C. (1981). The ecological approach to people environment transactions. *Social Casework, 62,* 323–331.

Goodman, C., & Silverstein, M. (2005). Latina grandmothers raising grandchildren: Acculturation and psychological well-being. *International Journal of*

Aging and Human Development, 60(4), 305–316.

Guarnaccia, P., & Rodriguez, D. (1996). Concepts of culture: Their role in the development of culturally competent mental health services. *Hispanic Journal of Behavioral Sciences, 18,* 419–443.

Guarnaccia, P. P. I. M., Alegria, M., Shrout, P. E., Lewis-Fernandez, R., & Canino, G. (2007). Assessing diversity among Latinos: Results from the NLAAS. *Hispanic Journal of Behavioral Sciences, 29*(4), 510–534.

Hall, E. T. (1976). *Beyond culture.* New York: Anchor Books.

Hardt, M., & Negri, A. (2004). *Empire and multitude: War and democracy in the age of empire.* New York: The Penguin Press.

Hill, T., Angel, J., Ellison, D., & Angel, R. (2005). Religious attendance and mortality: An 8 year follow-up of older Mexican Americans. *Journals of Gerontology, 60B*(2), S102–S109.

Hutchinson, E. D. (1999). *Dimensions of human behavior.* Thousand Oaks, CA: Pine Forge.

Jacob, A. G. (1994). Social integration of Salvadoran refugees. *Social Work, 39,* 307–312.

Jarsky, K. M., McDonough, P. M., & Nunez, A. (2009). Establishing a college culture in secondary schools through P-20 collaboration: A case study. *Journal of Hispanic Higher Education, 8*(4), 357–373.

Kim, H., & Lee, J. (2005). Unequal effects of elders health problems on wealth depletion across race and ethnicity. *Journal of Consumer Affairs, 39*(1), 148–172.

Laird, J. (1998). Theorizing culture: Narrative ideas and practice principles. In M. McGoldrick (Ed.), *Re-Visioning family therapy.* New York: The Guilford Press.

Light, I., & Johnston, M. F. (2009). The metropolitan dispersion of Mexican immigrants in the United States, 1980 to 2000. *Journal of Ethnic and Migration Studies, 35*(1), 3–18.

Limoncelli, S. A. (2009). The trouble with trafficking: Conceptualizing women's sexual labor and economic rights. *Women's Studies International Forum, 32,* 261–269.

Lindsay, J. M., & Michaelidis, G. (2001, January 5). A timid silence on America's immigration challenge. *San Diego Union Tribune,* p. B7.

Lum, D. (2010). *Culturally competent practice* (4th ed.). Belmont, CA: Thomson Brooks/Cole.

Maldonado, D. (2000). The changing religious practice of Hispanics. In P. S. J. Cafferty & D. Engstrom (Eds.), *Hispanics in the United States: An agenda for the 21st century.* New Brunswick, NJ: Transaction.

Marcos, L. R. (1994). The psychiatric examination across the language barrier. In C. Telles & M. Karno (Eds.), *Latino mental health: Current research and policy perspectives.* Los Angeles: Neuropsychiatric Institute, University of California.

Marsiglia, F., & Kulis, S. (2009). *Diversity, oppression, and change.* Chicago, IL: Lyceum Books, Inc.

Martin, M., & Lantos, J. (2005). Bioethics meets the barrio: Community-based research involving children. In E. Kodish (Ed.), *Ethics and research with children: A case-based approach* (pp. 63–76). New York: Oxford University Press.

Martinez, L. (2008). Flowers from the same soil: Latino solidarity in the wake of the 2006 immigrant mobilizations. *American Behavioral Scientist, 52*(4), 557–579.

McConnell, E. D. (2008). The U.S. destinations of contemporary Mexican immigrants. *International Migration Review, 42*(4), 767–802.

Memmi, A. (2000). *Racism.* Minneapolis, MN: University of Minnesota Press.

Montijo, J. (1985). Therapeutic relationships with the poor: A Puerto Rican perspective. *Psychotherapy, 22,* 436–440.

Morales, A. (1995). Urban gang violence: A psychosocial crisis. In A. Morales & B. Sheafor (Ed.), *Social work: A profession of many faces* (pp. 433–463). Boston: Allyn & Bacon.

Morano, C. (2003). The role of appraisal and expressive support in mediating strain and gain in Hisapnic Alzheimer's disease caregivers. *Journal of Ethnic & Cultural Diversity in Social Work, 12*(2), 1–18.

NASW. (1999). *Code of ethics.* Washington, DC: Author.

National Association of Social Workers. (2007). *Indicators for the achievement of the NASW standards for cultural competence.* Washington, DC: Author.

National Association of Social Workers. (2009a). *Immigrants and refugees Social work speaks: National Association of Social Workers Policy Statements 2009–2012* (8th ed.). (pp. 196–201). Washington, DC: Author.

National Association of Social Workers. (2009b). *Slavery and human trafficking Social work speaks: National Association of Social Workers Policy Statements 2009–2012* (8th ed.). (pp. 317–321). Washington, DC: Author.

Organista, K. C. (2007). *Solving Latino psychosocial and health problems: Theory, practice and populations.* Hoboken, NJ: John Wiley & Sons, Inc.

Orlando Sentinel. (2001, June 15). Navy officials, GOP lawmakers fume at Bush Vieques decision. *Reprinted in San Diego Union Tribune,* p. A2.

Padilla, R. (2007). *Camino a la universidad: The road to college.* Indianapolis, IN: Lumina Foundation for Education.

Pantoja, A., Menjivar, C., & Magana, L. (2008). The spring marches of 2006: Latinos, immigration, and political mobilization in the 21st century. *American Behavioral Scientist, 52*(4), 499–506.

Parks, C., Hughes, T., & Matthews, A. (2004). Race/Ethnicity and sexual orientation: Intersecting identities. *Cultural Diversity and Ethnic Minority Psychology, 10*(3), 241–254.

Parrillo, V. N. (2009). *Strangers to these shores* (9th ed.). Boston, MA: Pearson Allyn & Bacon.

Perez Foster, R. M. (2001, April). When immigration is trauma: Guidelines for the individual and family clinician. *American Journal of Orthopsychiatry, 71*(1), 153–170.

Pew Hispanic Center. (2008a). U.S. Population Projections 2005–2050.

Pew Hispanic Center. (2008b). Latino labor report, 2008: Construction reverses job growth for Latinos.

Pew Hispanic Center. (2009a). Hispanics of Mexican origin in the United States, 2007.

Pew Hispanic Center. (2009b). Hispanics of Puerto Rican origin in the United States, 2007.

Pew Hispanic Center. (2009c). Hispanics of Cuban origin in the United States, 2007.

Pew Hispanic Center. (2009d). Hispanics of Salvadoran origin in the United States, 2007.

Pew Hispanic Center. (2009e). Hispanics of Dominican origin in the United States, 2007.

Pew Hispanic Center. (2009f). Hispanics of Guatemalan origin in the United States, 2007.

Pew Hispanic Center. (2009g). Hispanics of Columbian origin in the United States, 2007.

Pew Hispanic Center. (2009h). Hispanics of Ecuadorian origin in the United States in 2007.

Pew Hispanic Center. (2009i). Hispanics of Peruvian origin in the United States, 2007.

Pew Hispanic Center. (2009j). Between two worlds: How young Latinos come of age in America.

Potocky-Tripodi, M. (1999). Refugee children: How are they faring economically as adults? In P. Ewalt, E. Freeman, A. Fortune, D. Poole, & S. Witkin (Eds.), *Multicultural issues in social work: Practice and research* (pp. 622–633). Washington, DC: NASW.

Puig, M. (2001). Organizations and community intervention skills with Hispanic Americans. In R. Fong & S. Furuto (Eds.), *Culturally competent practice: Skills, interventions, and evaluations* (pp. 269–284). Boston: Allyn & Bacon.

Randall, H., & Csikai, E. (2003). Issues affecting utilization of hospice services by rural

Hispanics. *Journal of Ethnic & Cultural Diversity in Social Work*, 12(2), 79–94.

Robison, J., Curry, L., Gruman, C., Covington, T., Gaztambide, S., & Blank, S. (2003). Depression in later life Puerto Rican primary care patients: The role of illness, stress, social integration, and religiosity. *International Psychogeriatrics*, 15(3), 239–251.

Rodriguez, G. P. (2004). *Immigration: Its mourning and reformulation of identity implications for clinical practice*. Paper presented at the California Society for Clinical Social Work 33rd Annual Conference, October 29–31, Monterey, California.

Rogler, L. H. (1993). Help-seeking pathways: A unifying concept in mental health care. *The American Journal of Psychiatry*, 150(4), 554–561.

Rogler, L. H., & Cortes, D. E. (2008). Help-seeking pathways: A unifying concept in mental health care. In J. Mezzich & G. Caracci (Eds.), *Cultural formulation* (pp. 51–67).

Roland, A. (1988). *In search of self in India and Japan: Towards a cross-cultural psychology*. Princeton, NJ: Princeton University.

Romo, H. (2009, Spring). Immigrants, guest workers and policy issues: Perspectives on Mexican transnationalism. *Latin American Politics and Society*, 51(1), 149–163.

Rosario, M., Schrimshaw, E., & Hunter, J. (2004). Ethnic/Racial differences in the coming out process of lesbian, gay, and bisexual youths: A comparison of sexual identity development over time. *Cultural Diversity and Ethnic Minority Psychology*, 10(3), 215–228.

Salinas, M. E. (2005, August 30). Central American gangs toil in violence. *Fresno Bee*, p. B9.

Sue, S. (1998). In search of cultural competence in psychotherapy and counseling. *American Psychologist*, 53(4), 440–448.

Sy, S., & Romero, J. (2008). Family responsibilities among Latina college students from immigrant families. *Journal of Hispanic Higher Education*, 7 (3), 212–227.

Szapocznick, J., et al. (1997). The evolution of a structural ecosystemic theory for working with Latino families. In J. Garcia & M. Zea (Eds.), *Psychological interventions and research with Latino populations* (pp. 166–190). Boston: Allyn & Bacon.

Torres, L. (2009). Attributions to discrimination and depression among Latinos: The mediating role of competence. *American Journal of Orthopsychiatry*, 79, 118–124.

Umana-Taylor, A. J. (2009). Research with Latino early adolescents: Strengths, challenges, and directions for future research. *Journal of Early Adolescence*, 29(1), 5–15.

U.S. Census Bureau. (2000). Population projections of the U.S. population by age, sex, race, Hispanic origin, and nativity: 1999 to 2100.

U.S. Census Bureau. (2008a). An older and more diverse nation by midcentury (August 14).

U.S. Census Bureau. (2008b). U.S. Hispanic population surpasses 45 million: Now 15 percent of total.

U.S. Census Bureau. (2009). Income, poverty and health insurance coverage in the United States, 2008.

U.S. Department of Education. (2007). The *Nation's Report Card*, 2007. http://NCES.ed.gov/nationsreportcard/nies/nies_2007/n0029.asp

U.S. Department of State. (2007). Trafficking in persons report.

U.S. Office of Immigration Statistics. (2006). Yearbook of Immigration Statistics, 2006, Table 2.

Valle, R., & Bensussen, G. (1980). Hispanic social network, social support, and mental health. In R. Valle & W. Vega (Eds.), *Hispanic natural support systems* (No. 620047). Sacramento: State of California Department of Mental Health.

Valle, R., & Vega, W. (Eds.). (1980). *Hispanic natural support systems* (No. 620047). Sacramento: State of California Department of Mental Health.

Van Soest, D. (1994). Social work education for multicultural practice and social justice advocacy: A field study of how students experience the learning process. *Journal of Multicultural Social Work*, 3 (1), 17–24.

Vega, W. A., & Kolody, B. (1980). The meaning of social support and the mediation of stress across cultures. In R. Valle & W. Vega (Eds.), *Hispanic natural support systems* (No. 620047). Sacramento: State of California Department of Mental Health.

Vega, W., Kolody, B., Aguilar-Gaxiola, S., Alderete, E., Catalano, R., & Caraveo-Anduaga, J. (1998). Lifetime prevalence of DSM-III-R psychiatric disorders among urban and rural Mexican Americans in California. *Archives of General Psychiatry*, 55(9), 771–778.

Vega, W., Kolody, B., Aguilar-Gaxiola, S., & Catalano, R.

(1999). Gaps in service utilization by Mexican Americans with mental health problems. *American Journal of Psychiatry, 156*(6), 928–934.

Weitzman, P., Chang, G., & Reynoso, H. (2004). Middle-aged and older Latino American women in the patient–doctor interaction. *Journal of Cross Cultural Gerontology, 19*(3), 221–239.

Williams, J., Wyatt, G., Resell, J., Peterson, J., & Asuan-O'Brien, A. (2004). Psychosocial issues among gay and non-gay identifying HIV seropositive African American and Latino men who have sex with men. *Cultural Diversity and Ethnic Minority Psychology, 10*(3), 268–286.

Worby, P. A., & Organista, K. (2007). Alcohol use and problem drinking among male Mexican and Central American immigrant laborers: A review of the literature. *Hispanic Journal of Behavioral Sciences, 29*(4), 413–455.

Young, J., Flores, G., & Berman, S. (2004). Providing life-saving care to undocumented children: Controversies and ethical issues. *Pediatrics, 114* (5), 1316–1320.

Zuniga, M. E. (1991). "Dichos" as metaphorical tools for resistant Latino clients. *Psychotherapy, 28*(3), 480–483.

Zuniga, M. E. (1992). Families with Latino roots. In E. W. Lynch & M. J. Hanson (Eds.), *Developing cross-cultural competence: A guide for working with young children and their families* (pp. 151–179). Baltimore, MD: Brookes.

Zuniga, M. E. (2001). Latinos: Cultural competence and ethics. In R. Fong & S. Furuto (Eds.), *Culturally competent*

practice: Skills, interventions, and evaluations (pp. 47–60). Boston: Allyn & Bacon.

Zuniga, M. E. (2003). Latinos' needs: Flexible and empowering interventions. In L. Gutierrez, M. Zuniga, & D. Lum (Eds.), *Education for multicultural social work practice.* Alexandria, VA: CSWE.

Zunker, C., Rutt, C., & Meza, G. (2005). Perceived health needs of elderly Mexicans living on the U.S.-Mexico border. *Journal of Transcultural Nursing, 16*(1), 50–56.

Chapter 12

Almeida, R. (2005). Asian Indian families: An overview. In M. McGoldrick, J. Giordano, & N. Garcia-Preto (Eds.), *Ethnicity & family therapy* (3rd ed.). (pp. 377–394). New York: Guilford Press.

Blaisdell, K., & Mokuau, N. (1991). Kanaka Maoli: Indigenous Hawaiians. In N. Mokuau (Ed.), *Handbook of social services for Asian and Pacific Islanders* (pp. 131–154). New York: Greenwood.

Brave Heart, M. Y. H. (2001). Culturally and historically congruent clinical social work interventions with Native clients. In R. Fong & S. Furuto (Eds.), *Culturally competent social work practice: Skills, interventions, and evaluations* (pp. 285–298). Boston: Allyn & Bacon.

Browne, C., & Broderick, A. (1994). Asian and Pacific Island elders: Implications for research and mental health administration. *Social Work, 39*(3), 252–259.

Caplan, N., Choy, M., & Whitmore, J. (1991). *Children of the boat people: A study of*

educational success. Ann Arbor: University of Michigan Press.

Chan, S. (1994). The Hmong experience in Asia and the United States. In S. Chan (Ed.), *Hmong means free: Life in Laos and America* (pp. 1–60). Philadelphia: Temple University Press.

Chang, S. (2005, April 14). Grocery giants battle in Atlanta Koreatown. *The Korean Times.* http://times.hankooki. com/page/opinion/200504/ kt2005041414154054100. htm

Chow, J. (2001). Assessment of Asian American/Pacific Islander organizations and communities. In R. Fong & S. Furuto (Eds.), *Culturally competent social work practice: Skills, interventions, and evaluations.* (pp. 211–224). Boston: Allyn & Bacon.

Chung, D. (1992). The Confucian model of transformation. In S. Furuto, R. Biswas, D. Chung, K. Murase, & F. Ross-Sheriff (Eds.), *Social work with Asian Americans* (pp. 125–142). Beverly Hills, CA: Sage.

Council on Social Work Education. (2008). *Handbook of accreditation standards and procedures. Educational Policy and Accreditation Standards (EPAS).* Alexandria, VA: Author.

Cross, T., Bazron, B., Dennis, K., & Issacs, M. (1989). *Towards a culturally competent system of care.* Washington, DC: CASSP Technical Assistance Center, Georgetown University Child Development Center.

Daniel, R. (1992). Beyond black and white: The new multiracial consciousness. In M. Root (Ed.), *Racially mixed people in America* (pp. 333–341). Newbury Park, CA: Sage.

Devore, W., & Schlesinger, E. (1999). *Ethnic sensitive social work practice* (5th ed.). Boston: Allyn & Bacon.

Dhooper, S., & Moore, S. (2001). *Social work practice with culturally diverse people*. Thousand Oaks, CA: Sage.

Ewalt, P., & Mokuau, N. (1995). Self-determination from a Pacific perspective. *Social Work*, 40(2), 168–175.

Fong, R. (1992). History of Asian Americans. In S. Furuto, R. Biswas, D. Chung, K. Murase, & F. Ross-Sheriff (Eds.), *Social work with Asian Americans* (pp. 3–26). Beverly Hills, CA: Sage.

Fong, R. (1997). Child welfare practice with Chinese families: Assessment for immigrants from the People's Republic of China. *Journal of Family Social Work*, 2(1), 33–48.

Fong, R. (2001). Culturally competent social work practice: Past and present. In R. Fong & S. Furuto (Eds.), *Culturally competent practice: Skills, interventions, and evaluation* (pp. 1–9). Boston: Allyn & Bacon.

Fong, R. (Ed.). (2004). *Culturally competent practice with immigrant and refugee children and families*. New York: The Guilford Press.

Fong, R., & Berger, J. (2009). Child human trafficking victims: Challenges for the child welfare system. *Journal of Evaluation and Program Planning*.

Fong, R., Boyd, T., & Browne, C. (1999). The Gandhi technique: A biculturalization approach for empowering Asian and Pacific Island families. *Journal of Multicultural Social Work*, 7, 95–110.

Fong, R., & Furuto, S. (Eds.). (2001). *Culturally competent social work practice: Skills, interventions, and evaluations*. Boston: Allyn & Bacon.

Fong, R., & Mokuau, N. (1994). Social work periodical literature review of Asians and Pacific Islanders. *Social Work*, 39(3), 298–312.

Fong, R., & Urban, B. (2009). *Evaluation of coalition of South Texas*. Austin, TX: Center for Social Work Research. School of Social Work. The University of Texas at Austin.

Fong, R., & Wang, A. (2001). Adoptive parents and identity development for Chinese infants. In N. Choi (Ed.), *Psychosocial aspects of the Asian-American experience: Diversity within diversity* (pp. 19–33). New York: Haworth.

Furuto, S., San Nichols, R., Kim, G., & Fiaui, L. (2001). Interventions with Kanaka Maoli, Chamorro, and Samoan communities. In R. Fong & S. Furuto (Eds.), *Culturally competent social work practice: Skills, interventions, and evaluations* (pp. 327–342). Boston: Allyn & Bacon.

Galan, F. (2001). Intervention with Mexican American families. In R. Fong & S. Furuto (Eds.), *Culturally competent social work practice: Skills, interventions, and evaluations* (pp. 255–268). Boston: Allyn & Bacon.

Guadalupe, K., & Lum, D. (Eds.). (2005). *Multidimensional contextual practice: Diversity and transcendence*. Belmont, CA: Thomson/Brooks/Cole.

Harris, P., & Jones, N. (2005). We the people: Pacific Islanders in the United States. http://www.census.gov/prod/2005pubs/censr-17.pdf

Hing, B. (1993). Immigration policy: Making and remaking Asian and Pacific America. In *The state of Asian Pacific America* (pp. 127–140). Los Angeles: LEAP Asian Pacific American Public Policy Institute and UCLA Asian American Studies Center.

Ichioka, Y. (1988). *The Issei: The world of the first generation Japanese immigrants*. New York: Free Press.

Jung, M. (1998). *Chinese American family therapy: A new model for clinicians*. San Francisco, CA: Jossey Bass Publishers.

Kanuha, K. (2001). Individual and family intervention skills with Asian and Pacific Island American lesbian and gay men. In R. Fong & S. Furuto (Eds.), *Culturally competent social work practice: Skills, interventions, and evaluations* (pp. 313–326). Boston: Allyn & Bacon.

Kim, B., & Ryu, E. (2005). Korean families. In M. McGoldrick, J. Giordano, & N. Garcia-Preto (Eds.), *Ethnicity & family therapy* (3rd ed.). (pp. 349–362). New York: Guilford Press.

Kitano, H., & Nakaoka, S. (2001). Asian Americans in the twentieth century. In N. Choi (Ed.), *Psychosocial aspects of the Asian-American experience: Diversity within diversity* (pp. 7–17). New York: Haworth.

Lee, E. (Ed.). (1997). *Working with Asian Americans: A guide for clinicians*. New York: Guilford.

Lee, E., & Mock, M. (2005). Chinese families. In M. McGoldrick, J. Giordano, & N. Garcia-Preto (Eds.), *Ethnicity & family therapy* (3rd ed.). (pp. 302–318). New York: The Guilford Press.

Lee, J., Lei, A., & Sue, S. (2001). The current state of mental health research on Asian Americans. In N. Choi (Ed.), *Psychosocial aspects of the Asian-American experience: Diversity within diversity* (pp. 159–178). New York: Haworth.

Leigh, J. (1998). *Communicating for cultural competence.* Needham Heights, MA: Allyn & Bacon.

Leung, P., & Boehnlein, J. (2005). Vietnamese families. In M. McGoldrick, J. Giordano, & N. Garcia-Preto (Eds.), *Ethnicity & family therapy* (3rd ed.). (pp. 363–376). New York: Guilford Press.

Leung, P., & Cheung, M. (2001). Competencies in practice evaluations with Asian American individuals and families. In R. Fong & S. Furuto (Eds.), *Culturally competent social work practice: Skills, interventions, and evaluations* (pp. 426–437). Boston: Allyn & Bacon.

Lott, J. (1998). *Asian Americans: From racial category to multiple identities.* Walnut Creek, CA: Alta Mira Press.

Lum, D. (1999). *Culturally competent practice: A framework for growth and action.* Pacific Grove, CA: Brooks/Cole.

Lum, D. (2000). *Social work practice and people of color* (4th ed.). Pacific Grove, CA: Brooks/Cole.

Matsuoka, J. (2001). Evaluation and assessment in Hawaiian and Pacific communities. In R. Fong and S. Furuto (Eds.), *Culturally competent practice: Skills, interventions, and evaluations* (pp. 438–453). Boston: Allyn & Bacon.

Merkel-Holguin, L., & Ribich, K. (2001). Family group conferencing. In E. Walton, P. Sandau-Beckler, & M.

Mannes (Eds.), *Balancing family-centered services and well-being* (pp. 197–218). New York: Columbia University Press.

Mokau, N. (Ed.). (1991). *Handbook of social services for Asian and Pacific Islanders.* New York: Greenwood Press.

Mokau, N. (1999). Substance abuse among Pacific Islanders: Cultural contexts and implications for prevention programs. In B. Yee, N. Mokau, & S. Kim (Eds.), *Developing cultural competence in Asian-American and Pacific Islander communities: Opportunities in primary health care and substance abuse prevention* (pp. 221–248). Washington, DC: U.S. Department of Health and Human Services, Substance Abuse and Mental Health Services Administration, Center for Substance Abuse Prevention.

Mokau, N. (2001). *Substance use and family violence among Native Hawaiians: Problems and culturally-based solutions.* Paper presented at the National Institute on Drug Abuse, Differential Drug Use, HIV/AIDS, and Related Health Outcomes among Racial and Ethnic Populations.

Mokau, N., Lukela, D., Obra, A., & Voeller, M. (1997). *Native Hawaiian spirituality: A perspective on connections.* Honolulu, HI: University of Hawaii School of Social Work and Native Hawaiian Safe and Drug Free Schools and Communities Program at Kamehameha Schools Bishop Estate.

Morelli, P. (2001). Culturally competent assessment of Cambodian American survivors of

the killing fields: A tool for social justice. In R. Fong & S. Furuto (Eds.), *Culturally competent social work practice: Skills, interventions, and evaluations* (pp. 196–210). Boston: Allyn & Bacon.

Morton, H. (1996). *Becoming Tongan: An ethnography of childhood.* Honolulu: University of Hawaii Press.

Mui, A. (1996). Depression among elderly Chinese immigrants: An exploratory study. *Social Work, 41,* 633–645.

Mui, A. (2001). Stress, coping, and depression among elderly Korean immigrants. In N. Choi (Ed.), *Psychosocial aspects of the Asian-American experience: Diversity within diversity* (pp. 281–299). New York: Haworth.

Mui, A., & Burnette, D. (1996). Coping resources and self-reported depressive symptoms among frail, older ethnic women. *Journal of Social Service Research, 21*(3), 19–37.

Nath, S. (2005). Pakistani families. In M. McGoldrick, J. Giordano, & N. Garcia-Preto (Eds.), *Ethnicity & family therapy* (3rd ed.). (pp. 407–422). New York: Guilford Press.

Ngo, D., Tran, T., Gibbons, J., & Oliver, J. (2001). Acculturation, premigration, traumatic experiences, and depression among Vietnamese Americans. In N. Choi (Ed.), *Psychosocial aspects of the Asian-American experience: Diversity within diversity* (pp. 225–242). New York: Haworth.

Nishi, S. (1995). Japanese Americans. In P. Min (Ed.), *Asian Americans: Contemporary trends and issues* (pp. 95–133). Thousand Oaks, CA: Sage.

Pennell, J., & Buford, G. (2000). Family group decision-making: Protecting women and children. *Child Welfare, LXXIX*(2), 131–158.

Percy, F., Soekandar, A., Limansubroto, C. & Davis, S. (2005). Indonesian families. In M. McGoldrick, J. Giordano, & N. Garcia-Preto (Eds.), *Ethnicity & family therapy* (3rd ed.). (pp. 332–338). New York: The Guilford Press.

Pillari, V. (2005). Indian Hindu families. In M. McGoldrick, J. Giordano, & N. Garcia-Preto (Eds.), *Ethnicity & family therapy* (3rd ed.). (pp. 395–406). New York: The Guilford Press.

Poon, M. (2000). Inter-racial same sex abuse: The vulnerability of gay men of Asian descent in relationships with Caucasian men. *Journal of Gay and Lesbian Social Services, 11*(4), 39–68.

Reeves, T., & Bennett, C. (2004). *We the people: Asians in the United States.* http://www.census.gov/prod/2004pubs/censr-17.pdf

Root, M. (2005). Filipino families. In M. McGoldrick, J. Giordano, & N. Garcia-Preto (Eds.), *Ethnicity & family therapy* (3rd ed.). (pp. 319–331). New York: The Guilford Press.

Ross-Sheriff, F., & Husain, A. (2001). Values and ethics in social work practice with Asian Americans: A South Asian Muslim case example. In R. Fong & S. Furuto (Eds.), *Culturally competent social work practice: Skills, interventions, and evaluations* (pp. 75–88). Boston: Allyn & Bacon.

Ross-Sheriff, F., & Husain, A. (2004). South Asian Muslim children and families. In R. Fong (Ed.), *Culturally competent practice with immigrant and refugee children and families* (pp. 163–182). New York: Guilford Press.

Sanchez-Hucles, J. (1998). Racism: Emotional abusiveness and psychological trauma for ethnic minorities. *Journal of Emotional Abuse, 1*(2), 69–88.

Sanders, D. (1991). Future directions in social services: Asian and Pacific Islander perspectives. In N. Mokuau (Ed.), *Handbook of social services for Asian and Pacific Islanders* (pp. 233–242). New York: Greenwood Press.

Sandhu, D. (1997). Psychocultural profiles of Asian and Pacific Islander Americans: Implications for counseling and psychotherapy. *Journal of Multicultural Counseling and Development, 25*(1), 7–22.

Scheinfeld, D., Wallach, B., & Langendorf, T. (1997). *Strengthening refugee families: Designing programs for refugee and other families in need.* Chicago: Lyceum Books.

Schriver, J. (2001). *Human behavior in the social environment* (3rd ed.). Boston: Allyn & Bacon.

Shibusawa, T. (2005). Japanese families. In M. McGoldrick, J. Giordano, & N. Garcia-Preto (Eds.), *Ethnicity & family therapy* (3rd ed.). (pp. 339–348). New York: The Guilford Press.

Spickard, P., Fong, R., & Ewalt, P. (1995). Undermining the very basis of racism—Its categories. *Social Work, 40*(5), 581–584.

Straussner, S. (Ed.). (2001). *Ethnocultural factors in substance abuse treatment.* New York: Guilford.

Sue, S. (2008). A family suicide risk in U.S. Asians. *Time Magazine.*

Sung, B. (1967). *Mountain of gold.* New York: Macmillan.

Swingle, D. (2000). Immigrants and August 22, 1996: Will the public charge rule clarify program eligibility? *Families in Society, 81*(6), 605–610.

Takaki, R. (1993). *A different mirror.* Boston: Little Brown.

Takamura, J. (1991). Asian and Pacific Islander elderly. In N. Mokuau (Ed.), *Handbook of social services for Asian and Pacific Islanders* (pp. 185–202). New York: Greenwood Press.

Tran, C., & Des Jardins, K. (2000). Domestic violence in Vietnamese refugee and Korean immigrant communities. In J. Chin (Ed.), *Relationships among Asian American women* (pp. 71–100). Washington, DC: American Psychological Association.

Trask, H. (1984–1985). Hawaiians, American colonization, and the quest for independence. In G. Sullivan & G. Gawes (Eds.), *Social process in Hawaii, 31,* 101.

Trueba, H., Jacobs, L., & Kirton, E. (1990). *Cultural conflict and adaptation: The case of Hmong children in American society.* Bristol, PA: Falmer Press.

Uehara, E., Morelli, P., & Abe-Kim, J. (2001). Somatic complaint and social suffering among survivors of the Cambodian killing fields. In N. Choi (Ed.), *Psychosocial aspects of the Asian-American experience* (pp. 243–262). New York: Haworth.

U.S. Bureau of the Census. (2001). *Overview of race and Hispanic origin census of 2000 brief.* Washington, DC: U.S. Government Printing Office.

U.S. Commission on Civil Rights. (1992). *Civil rights facing*

Asian Americans in the 1990s. Washington, DC: U.S. Government Printing Office. http://www.census.gov/prod/2001/pubs/c2kbr01-1.pdf

Vakalahi, H., & Fong, R. (2009). Social work practice with Asian and Pacific Islander Americans. In A. Roberts (Ed.), *Social workers' desk reference* (pp. 954–958). New York: Oxford University Press.

Yellow Bird, M. (2001). Critical values and first nations peoples. In R. Fong & S. Furuto (Eds.), *Culturally competent practice: Skills, interventions, and evaluation* (pp. 61–74). Boston: Allyn & Bacon.

Zhou, M., & Bankston, C. (1998). *Growing up American: How Vietnamese children adapt to life in the United States.* New York: Russell Sage Foundation.

Chapter 13

Abd al Ati, H. (1975). *Islam in focus.* Indianapolis, IN: American Trust Publications.

Abd al Ati, H. (1977). *The family structure in Islam.* Indianapolis, IN: American Trust Publications.

Abd-Allah, O. F. (2004). *Islam and the cultural imperative.* Chicago: Nawawi Foundation. Retrieved January 24, 2007, from http://www.nawawi.org/downloads/article3.pdf.

Abu-Ras, W., & Abu-Bader, S. H. (2009). Risk factors for depression and posttraumatic stress disorder (PTSD): The case of Arab and Muslim Americans post-9/11. *Journal of Immigrant & Refugee Studies*, 7(4), 393–418.

Akram, S. M. (2002). The aftermath of September 11, 2001: The targeting of Arabs and Muslims in America. *Arab Studies Quarterly*, Spring-Summer, 58 pages. Retrieved February 4, 2005, from http://findarticles.com/p/articles/mi_m2501/is_2002_Spring-Summer/ai_95571887.

Al-Issa, I. (1997b). The psychology of prejudice and discrimination. In I. Al-Issa & M. Tousignant (Eds.),*Ethnicity, immigration and psychopathology* (pp. 17–32). New York: Plenum Press.

Al-Issa, I., & Tousignant, M. (Eds.) (1997). *Ethnicity, immigration and psychopathology.* New York: Plenum Press.

Al-Krenawi, A., & Graham, J. R. (2000). Islamic theology and prayer: Relevance for social work practice. *International Social Work*, 43(3), 289–304.

Alba, R. (2005). Bright vs. blurred boundaries: Second-generation assimilation and exclusion in France, Germany, and the United States. *Ethnic and Racial Studies*, 28(1), 20–49.

Ali, S. R., Liu, W. M., & Humedian, M. (2004). Islam 101: Understanding the religion and therapy implications. *Professional Psychology: Research and Practice*, 35(6), 635–642.

Anderson, P. (2004, July 22). Treasury department settles with grocers over losses. *The Associated Press State & Local Wire*. Available at: LexisNexis Academic database. Retrieved March 28, 2006.

Anway, C. (2002). Daughters of another path: Experiences of American women choosing Islam. Lee's Summit, MO: Yawna Publications.

Barrett, P. M. (2007). *American Islam: The struggle for the soul of a religion.* New York: Farrar, Straus and Giroux.

Bukhari, Z. H. (2003). Citizenship and its meaning for the U.S. Muslim community. In S. Hunter, & H. Malik (Eds.), *Integration of Muslim communities in Europe and the United States.* Washington, DC: Center for Strategic and International Studies.

Byng, M. D. (1998). Mediating discrimination: Resisting oppression among African American Muslim women. *Social Problems*, 45, 473–487.

Canda, E. R., & Furman, L. D. (1999). *Spiritual diversity in social work practice.* New York: Free Press.

Council on American-Islamic Relations (CAIR). (2006). *The status of Muslim civil rights in the United States, 2006: The struggle for equality.* Retrieved May 6, 2010, from http://www.cair.com/pdf/2006-CAIR-Civil-Rights-Report.pdf

Dannin, R. (2002). *Black pilgrimage to Islam.* New York: Oxford University Press.

Davies, M., & Webb, E. (2000). Promoting the psychological well-being of refugee children. *Clinical Child Psychology and Psychiatry*, 5(4), 541–554.

Diouf, S. A. (1998). *Servants of Allah: African Muslims enslaved in the Americas.* New York: New York University Press.

Dirks, D. L., & Parlove, S. (Eds.). (2003). *Islam our choice: Portraits of modern American Muslim women.* Beltsville, MD: Amana Publications.

Esposito, J. L. (2002). Islam as a Western phenomenon: Implications for Europe and the United States. In S. T. Hunter & H. Malik (Eds.), *Islam in Europe and the United States:*

A comparative perspective (pp. 3–10). Washington, DC: Center for Strategic and International Studies.

Esposito, J. L., & Mogahed, D. (2007). *Who speaks for Islam?: What a billion Muslims really think*. New York: Gallup Press.

Grossman, C. L. (2007). Tensions between Sunnis, Shiites emerging in USA. *USA Today*, September 24. Retrieved December 22, 2009, from http://www.usatoday.com/news/religion/2007-09-24-muslim-tension_N.htm

Haddad, Y. Y. (1991). Introduction: The Muslims of America. In Y. Y. Haddad (Ed.), *The Muslims of America* (pp. 3–10). New York, NY: Oxford University Press.

Haddad, Y. Y., & Esposito, J. L. (2000). (Eds.). *Muslims on the Americanization path?* New York, NY: Oxford University Press.

Haddad, Y. Y., & Lummis, A. T. (1987). *Islamic values in the United States*. New York, NY: Oxford University Press.

Hamid, A. (1996). *Islam the natural way*. London: Muslim Educational and Literary Services.

Handlin, O. (1951). *The uprooted*. New York: Grosset and Dunlap Publishers.

Hashim, A. (1997). Conflicting identities in Somalia. *Peace-Review*, 9(4), 527–531.

Haynes, A. W., Eweiss, M. M. I., Mageed, L. M. A., & Chung, D. K. (1997). Islamic social transformation: Considerations for the social worker. *International Social Worker*, 40, 265–275.

Higham, J. (1963). *Strangers in the land: Patterns of American nativism, 1860–1925*. New Brunswick, NJ: Rutgers University Press.

Hodge, D. R. (2002). Working with Muslim youth: Understanding the values and beliefs of Islamic discourse. *Children and Schools*, 24(1), 6–20.

Hodge, D. R. (2005). Social work and the house of Islam: Orienting practitioners to the beliefs and values of Muslims in the United States. *Social Work*, 50(2), 162–173.

Hodge, D. R. (2007). The Spiritual Competence Scale: A new instrument for assessing spiritual competence at the programmatic level. *Research on Social Work Practice*, 17(2), 287–295.

Hodge, D. R., & Nadir, A. (2008). Moving toward culturally competent practice with Muslims: Modifying cognitive therapy with Islamic tenets. *Social Work*, 53(1), 31–41.

Hunter, S. T., & Malik, H. (Eds.). (2002). *Islam in Europe and the United States: A comparative perspective*. Washington, DC: Center for Strategic and International Studies.

Ibrahim, I. A. (1997). *A brief illustrated guide to understanding Islam* (2nd ed.). Houston, TX: Darussalam, Publishers and Distributors.

Khan, Z. (2006). Attitudes toward counseling and alternative support among Muslims in Toledo, Ohio. *Journal of Muslim Mental Health*, 1(1), 21–42.

Linzer, N. (1999). *Resolving ethical dilemmas in social work practice*. Boston: Allyn & Bacon.

Lum, D. (Ed.). (2004). *Culturally competent practice: A framework for understanding diverse groups and justice issues* (2nd ed.). Pacific Grove, CA: Brooks/Cole.

Maloof, P. S., & Ross-Sheriff, F. (2003). *Muslim refugees in the United States: A guide for service providers*. Washington, DC: Center for Applied Linguistics.

Maslim, A. A., & Bjorck, J. P. (2009). Reasons for conversion to Islam among women in the United States. *Psychology of Religion and Spirituality*, 1(2), 97–111.

Mogahed, D. (2009). *Muslim Americans: A national portrait*. Washington, DC: Gallup Center for Muslim Studies. Also available at: http://www.muslimwestfacts.com/mwf/File/116074/AmericanMuslimReport.pdf. Accessed on November 3, 2009.

Nadir, A. (2002). Social welfare with Muslims in the U.S. In P. Popple, & L. Leighninger, (Eds.), *Instructor's Manual for Social Work, Social Welfare and American Society* (5th ed.). Boston: Allyn & Bacon.

National Association of Social Workers (NASW). (2001). *Standards for cultural competence in social work practice*. Washington, DC: Author. Available at: http://www.socialworkers.org/practice/standards/NASWCulturalStandards.pdf. Accessed on December 5, 2009.

Nyang, S. S. (1999). *Islam in the United States of America*. Chicago: ABC International.

Pew Research Center. (2007). *Muslim Americans: Middle class and mostly mainstream*. Retrieved May 6, 2010, from http://pewresearch.org/assets/pdf/muslim-americans.pdf.

Portes, A., & Rumbaut, R. G. (2001). *Legacies: The story of the immigrant second generation*. Berkeley, CA: University of California Press.

Qur'an. (1993). *The Meaning of the Holy Qur'an*. Brentwood, MD: Amana Corporation.

Ramadan, T. (2004). *Western Muslims and the future of Islam*. Oxford, New York: Oxford University Press.

Rogerson, B. (2007). *Heirs of the prophet Muhammad: Islam's first century and the origins of the Sunni-Shia schism*. Woodstock, NY: Overlook Press.

Ross-Sheriff, F., & Husain, A. (2000). Values and ethics in social work practice with Asian Americans: A South Asian Muslim case example. In R. Fong & S. Furuto (Eds.), *Culturally competent practice: Skills, interventions, and evaluations* (pp. 75–88). Needham Heights: Allyn & Bacon.

Ross-Sheriff, F., & Husain, A. (2004). South Asian Muslim children and families. In R. Fong (Ed.), *Culturally competent practice with immigrant and refugee children and families* (pp. 163–182). New York: Guilford Publications.

Shaheen, J. G. (2001). *Reel bad Arabs: How Hollywood vilifies a people*. Northampton, MA: Olive Branch Press.

Shakeri, E. (2000). Muslim women in Canada: Their role and status as revealed in the *Hijab* controversy. In Y. Y. Haddad & J. L. Esposito (Eds.), *Muslims on the Americanization path?* (pp. 129–144). New York, NY: Oxford University Press.

Smith, J. I. (1999). *Islam in America*. New York: Columbia University Press.

Sonn, T. (1994). Diversity in Rochester's Islamic community. In Y.Y. Haddad & J. I. Smith (Eds.), *Muslim communities in America* (pp. 279–292). New York: State University of New York Press.

Suarez-Orozco, C., & Suarez-Orozco, M. M. (2001). *Children of immigration*. Cambridge, MA: Harvard University Press.

Takaki, R. T. (1998). *Strangers from a different shore: A history of Asian Americans*. Boston: Little, Brown.

U.S. Department of State. (2009a). *Diversity Visa Lottery 2010 (DV-2010) Results*. Retrieved May 6, 2010, from http://travel.state.gov/visa/immigrants/types/types_4574.html

U.S. Department of State. (2009b). *Diversity Visa Program*. Retrieved May 6, 2010, from http://travel.state.gov/visa/immigrants/types/types_1322.html

Zolberg, A. R., & Woon, L. L. (1999). Why Islam is like Spanish: Cultural incorporation in Europe and the United States. *Politics and Society, 27* (1), 5–38.

Chapter 14

Abramovitz, M. (1996). *Under attack, fighting back: Women and welfare in the United States*. New York: Monthly Review Press.

Angler, N., & Dierderic, B. (1984, July 16). Environment: Eliminating the Haitian swine. *Time/CNN*. Retrieved May 6, 2010, from http://www.time.com/time/magazine/article/0,9171,951249-1,00.html

Aristide, J. B. (2000). *Eyes of the heart: Seeking a path for the poor in the age of globalization*. Monroe, ME: Common Courage Press.

Benjamin, M. (1987). *Don't be afraid, Gringo: A Honduran woman speaks from the heart*. San Francisco, CA: Food First.

Food First. (2010, January 26). *To the governments and organizations gathered in Montreal on the situation in Haiti*. Retrieved May 6, 2010, from http://www.foodfirst.org/en/node/2773

Haiti's Historic Debt Load. (2008, November 13). *Historical note*. Retrieved from http://historicalnote.com/2010/01/15/haitis-historic-debt-load/

Hanh, T. N. (2003). *Creating true peace: Ending violence in yourself, your family, your community, and the world*. New York: Free Press.

The Help That Haiti Needs. (2010, January 14). Opinion/Room for Debate: A running commentary on the news. *New York Times*. Retrieved from http://roomfordebate.blogs.nytimes.com/2010/01/14/the-help-that-haiti-needs/?ref=americas

Holt-Giménez, E. (2006). *Campesino a Campesino: Voices from Latin America's farmer to farmer movement for sustainable agriculture*. Oakland, CA: Food First Books.

Irwin, N. (2010, January 2). Aughts were a lost decade for U. S. economy, workers. *The Washington Post*. Retrieved January 9, 2010, from http://www.washingtonpost.com/wp-dyn/content/article/2010/01/01/AR2010010101196_2.html?hpid=topnews

Ives, K. (2009). *Haite liberte: Finally some debt relief for Haiti*. Retrieved October 25, 2009, from http://www.haitianalysis.com/2009/7/4/finally-some-debt-relief-for-haiti

Klein, N. (2007). *The shock doctrine: The rise of disaster capitalism*. New York: Metropolitan Books.

Krauss, L. M. (2009). How women can save the planet.

Scientific American, 301(5), 38.

Lobe, J. (2008, October 21). Economy: Rich-poor divide worst among rich countries. *Inter Press Service News Agency.* Retrieved January 9, 2010, from http://ipsnews.net/print.asp?idnews=44381

Polak, P. (2008). *Out of poverty: What works when traditional approaches fail.* San Francisco, CA: Berrett-Koehler Publishers, Inc.

Revolutionary Designs. *Paulpolak.com.* Retrieved November 23, 2009, from http://www.paulpolak.com/html/about.html

Rosenburg, T. (2009, August 19). The daughter deficit [Special issue: Saving the world's women]. *New York Times.* Retrieved from http://www.nytimes.com/2009/08/23/magazine/23FOB-idealab-t.html

Schumacher, E. F. (1973). *Small is beautiful: Economics as if people mattered.* New York: Harper and Row.

UN Millennium Development Goals. (2009). Retrieved May 6, 2010, from http://www.un.org/millenniumgoals

Wallace, L. (2010, January 10). Multicultural critical theory? At B-school? *New York Times.* Retrieved from http://www.nytimes.com/2010/01/10/business/10mba.html?em=&pagewanted=print

Zakaria, F. (2009). *The post-American world.* New York, NY: W. W. Norton & Company.

Chapter 15

Altman, D. (1982). *The homosexualization of America.* Boston: Beacon Press.

American Civil Liberties Union. (2009). Know your rights: Transgender people and the law. Retrieved October 20, 2009, from http://www.aclu.org/lgbt/transgender/kyr_-transgender.html

Angelides, S. (2001). *A history of bisexuality.* Chicago: University of Chicago Press.

APA. (2009). *Answers to your questions about transgender individuals and gender identity.* Retrieved September 25, 2009, from http://www.apa.org/topics/transgender.html#whatdoes

BiNet USA. (2009). *BiNet USA.* Retrieved November 12, 2009, from http://www.binetusa.org

bisexuality. (2009). In *Merriam-Webster Online Dictionary.* Retrieved October 7, 2009, from http://www.merriam-webster.com/dictionary/bisexuality

Boswell, J. (1980). *Christianity, social tolerance, and homosexuality: Gay people in Western Europe from the beginning of the Christian era to the fourteenth century.* Chicago: University of Chicago Press.

Brown, K. (2009). *20th Century transgender history and experience.* Retrieved October 20, 2009, from http://jenellerose.com/htmlpostings/20th_century_transgender.htm

Centers for Disease Control. (2008). *Lesbian, gay, bisexual and transgender health.* Retrieved September 9, 2009, from http://www.cdc.gov/lgbthealth/

competent (2009). In *Merriam-Webster Online Dictionary.* Retrieved September 22, 2009, from http://www.merriam-webster.com/dictionary/competency

Congress, E., Black, P., & Strom-Gottfried, K. (Eds.). (2009). *Teaching social work values and ethics: A curriculum resource.* Alexandria, VA: CSWE.

CSWE. (2008a). *Educational Policy and Accreditation Standards: Educational Policy 2.1.10 (a)—(d) —Engage, assess, intervene, and evaluate with individuals, families, groups, organizations, and communities* pp. 6-7. Alexandria, VA: CSWE Press.

culture. (2009). In *Merriam-Webster Online Dictionary.* Retrieved September 22, 2009, from http://www.merriam-webster.com/dictionary/competency

D'Emilio, J., & Freedman, E. B. (1988). *Intimate matters: A history of sexuality in America.* New York: Harper and Row.

Dictionary.com Unabridged (v 1.1). Retrieved September 10, 2009, from http://dictionary.reference.com/browse/transgender

Dolgoff, R., Loewenberg, F. M., & Harrington, D. (2008). *Ethical decisions for social work practice.* Itasca, IL: F.E. Peacock Publishers, Inc.

Faderman, L. (1981). *Surpassing the love of men: Romantic friendships and love between women from the Renaissance to the present.* New York: William Morrow.

FBI. (2007). *Incidents and offences.* Retrieved November 13, 2009, from http://www.fbi.gov/ucr/hc2007/incidents.htm

Feinberg, L. (1998). Leslie Feinberg interviews Sylvia Rivera: "I'm glad I was in the Stonewall riot." Retrieved October 20, 2009, from http://www.workers.org/ww/1998/sylvia0702.php

Freeman, S. J. (2000). *Ethics: An introduction to philosophy and practice.* Belmont, CA: Wadsworth.

Harper, D. (November 2001). Bisexuality. *Online Etymology Dictionary.* Retrieved November 12, 20009, from http://www.etymonline.com/index.php?term=bisexuality

Highleyman, L. A. (2001). *A brief history of the bisexual movement.* Boston: Bisexual Resource Center.

Human Rights Campaign. (2009a). *About workplace.* Retrieved December 20, 2009, from http://www.hrc.org/issues/coming_out/8055.htm

Human Rights Campaign. (2009b). *Transgender population and number of transgender employees.* Retrieved September 9, 2009, from http://www.hrc.org/issues/9598.htm

Kimmel, M. S. (2004). *The gendered society* (2nd ed.). New York: Oxford University Press.

Leung, P., & Cheung, M. (2001). Competencies in practice with Asian American individuals and families. In R. Fong & S. B. C. L. Futuro (Eds.), *Culturally competent practice: Skills interventions, and evaluations* (pp. 426–437). Boston: Allyn & Bacon.

Linzer, N. (1999). *Resolving ethical dilemmas in social work practice.* Boston: Allyn & Bacon.

Kinsey, A. C., Pomeroy, W. B., & Martin, C. E. (1948). *Sexual behavior in the human male.* Philadelphia: W.B. Saunders.

Lum, D. (2007). *Culturally competent practice: A framework for understanding diverse groups and justice issues.* Belmont, CA: Brooks-Cole.

Mattison, M. (2000). Ethical decision making: The person in the process. *Social Work, 45,* 201–212.

National Opinion Research Center. (2009). *General Social Survey.* Retrieved October 20, 2009, from http://www.norc.org/GSS

NASW. (2008a). *Code of ethics: Standard 1: Social Workers' Ethical Responsibilities to Clients.* Washington, DC: NASW Press.

NASW. (2008b). *Code of ethics: Standard 6: Social Workers' Ethical Responsibilities to the broader society.* Washington, DC: NASW Press.

Online Etymology Dictionary. Retrieved September 10, 2009, from http://dictionary.reference.com/browse/bisexuality

PFLAG. (2009). *Bisexuality 101.* Retrieved October 7, 2009, from http://pflag.org

Quappe, S., & Cantatore, G. (2007). What is cultural awareness, anyway? How do I build it? Retrieved November 18, 2009, from http://culturosity.com/articles/whatisculturalawareness.htm

Reamer, F. G. (2006). *Social work values and ethics.* New York: Columbia University Press.

Tittsworth, J. P. (2005). *Transgender umbrella chart.* Paper presented at the University of Houston-Clear Lake Student Leadership Conference.

Transgender Blogs. (2009). Retrieved September 25, 2009, from http://www.transgenderblogs.com

TransgenderZone.com. (2009). *Transgender history.* Retrieved October 20, 2009, from http://transgenderzone.com/features/timeline.htm

Tully, C. T. (1983). *Social support systems of a sample of older women.* Unpublished doctoral dissertation Virginia Commonwealth University, Richmond, VA.

Tully, C. T. (2000). *Lesbians, gays and the empowerment perspective.* New York: Columbia University Press.

Tully, C. T., Craig, T., & Nugent, G. (1994). Should only gay and lesbian community organizers work in gay and lesbian communities? In M. J. Austin & J. I. Lowe (Eds.), *Controversial issues in communities and organizations* (pp. 86–96). Boston: Allyn & Bacon.

U.S. Department of Justice. (2009). *Hate crime statistics: Victims.* Retrieved October 20, 2009, from http://www.fbi.gov/ucr/hc2007/victims.htm

Van Soest, D. (2007). Advancing social and economic justice. In D. Lum (Ed.), *Culturally competent practice: A framework for understanding diverse groups and justice issues* (2nd ed.). (pp. 73–107). Belmont, CA: Brooks/Cole.

Walters, K. L., Longres, J. F., Han, C., & Icard, L. D. (2007). Cultural competence with gay and lesbian persons of color. In D. Lum (Ed.), *Culturally competent practice: A framework for understanding diverse groups and justice issues* (2nd ed.). (pp. 389–426). Belmont, CA: Brooks/Cole.

Wood, G. G., & Tully, C. T. (2006). *The structural approach to direct practice in social work: A social constructionist perspective.* New York: Columbia University Press.

Chapter 16

Albrecht, G. (1992). *The disability business: Rehabilitation in America.* London: Sage.

American Anthropological Association. (1998, May 17).

American Anthropological Association statement on "race." Retrieved March 28, 2007, from http://www.aaa-net.org/stmts/racepp.htm

Americans with Disabilities Act of 1990, Pub. L No. 101-336, (1990).

Americans with Disabilities Amendments Act of 2008, Pub. L No. 110–325, (2008).

Australian Attorney General's Department. (1992). *Australian disability discrimination act of 1992*. Canberra, Australia: Author.

Blotzer, M. A., & Ruth, R. (1995). On sitting with uncertainty: Treatment considerations for persons with disabilities. In M. A. Blotzer & R. Ruth (Eds.), *Sometimes you just want to feel like a human being: Case studies of empowering psychotherapy with people with disabilities* (pp. 15–24). Baltimore, MD: Paul H. Brookes.

Brown, S. E. (1996). Deviants, invalids, and anthropologists: Cross-cultural perspectives on conditions of disability in one academic discipline. *Disability and Rehabilitation, 18*(5), 273–275.

Cacalli-Sforza, L. L. (2000). *Genes, peoples, and languages*. New York: Farrar, Straus and Giroux.

Callahan, J. (1989). *Don't worry, he won't get far on foot: The autobiography of a dangerous man*. New York: William Morrow.

Carrel, A. (1935). *Man, the unknown*. New York: Harper & Brothers.

Cohen, L. H. (1994). *Train go sorry: Inside a deaf world*. New York: Houghton Mifflin.

Colligan, S. (2004). Why the intersexed shouldn't be fixed: Insights from queer theory and disability studies. In B. Smith & B. Hutchinson (Eds.), *Gendering disability* (pp. 45–60). Piscataway, NJ: Rutgers University Press.

Council on Social Work Education. (1992). *Curriculum policy statement for baccalaureate and master's degree programs in social work education*. Alexandria, VA: Author.

Council on Social Work Education. (2008). *Educational policy and accreditation standards*. Alexandria, VA: Author.

DePoy, E., & Gilson, S. (2004). *Rethinking disability: Principles for professional and social change*. Belmont, CA: Brooks/Cole.

DREDF. (2000). *Laws for the welfare of disabled persons*. Retrieved June 23, 2007, from http://www.dredf.org/international/jordan.html

Erickson, W., & Lee, C. (2008). *2007 Disability status report: United States*. Ithaca, NY: Cornell University Rehabilitation Research and Training Center on Disability Demographics and Statistics.

Fernandez, M., & Freer, R. (1996). Application of an integrated model for counseling persons with spinal cord injury across ethnicities. *SCI Psychosocial Process, 9*(1), 4–9.

Fernandez, M., & Marini, I. (1995). Cultural values orientation in counseling persons with spinal cord injury. *SCI Psychosocial Process, 8*(4), 150–155.

Fine, M., & Asch, A. (1993). Disability beyond stigma: Social interaction, discrimination, and activism. In M. Nagler (Ed.), *Perspectives on disability: Text and readings on disability* (2nd ed.). (pp. 61–74). Palo Alto, CA: Health Markets Research.

Foster, M., & Sharp, R. (2002). Race, ethnicity, and genomics: Social classifications as proxies of biological heterogeneity. *Genome Research, 12* (6), 844–850.

Foucault, M. (2006). *History of madness* (J. Murphy & J. Khaifa, trans.). London: Routledge.

Garland-Thomson, R. (2002). Integrating disability, transforming feminist theory. *NWSA Journal, 14*(2), 1–32.

Garscha, W., & Kuretsidis-Haider, C. (1997, September). *War crimes trials in Austria*. Presented at the 21st annual conference of the German Studies Association, Washington, DC.

Ghana Review International. (2002). *Constitution of the republic of Ghana*. Retrieved June 25, 2007, from http://www.ghanareview.com/Gconst.html

Groce, N. (1999). Disability in cross-cultural perspective: Rethinking disability. *The Lancet, 354,* 756–757.

Hawking, S. (n.d.). *Prof. Stephen Hawkings disability advice*. Retrieved November 13, 2009, from http://www.hawking.org.uk/index.php/disability

Human Rights Watch. (2003). *Ill equipped: U.S. prisons and offenders with mental illness*. Retrieved June 9, 2008, from http://www.hrw.org/en/reports/2003/10/21/ill-equipped

IDEAnet. (2003a). *France*. Retrieved June 11, 2007, from http://www.ideanet.org/content.cfm?id=5B5D75&searchIT=1

IDEAnet. (2003b). *United Kingdom*. Retrieved June 14, 2007, from http://www.ideanet.org/content.cfm?id=5B5F72&searchIT=1

IDEAnet. (2003c). *Russian Federation*. Retrieved June 23, 2007, from http://www.ideanet.org/content.cfm?id=5B5F76&searchIT=1

IDEAnet. (2004a). *Chile*. Retrieved June 23, 2007, from http://www.ideanet.org/content.cfm?id=535F&searchI T=1

IDEAnet. (2004b). *Bolivia*. Retrieved June 23, 2007, from http://www.ideanet.org/content.cfm?id=5254&searchIT=1

IDEAnet. (2005). *India*. Retrieved June 22, 2007, from http://www.ideanet.org/content.cfm?id=585871 &searchIT=1

IDEAnet. (2007). *International disability rights monitor: Argentina 2004*. Retrieved June 14, 2007, from http://www.ideanet.org/content.cfm?id=525B

IDEAnet. (2009). *International disability rights monitor publications*. Retrieved November 13, 2009, from http://www.ideanet.org/content.cfm?id=5F55& searchIT=1

Johnson, A. G. (2006). *Privilege, power, and difference* (2nd ed.). New York: McGraw-Hill.

Kluckholm, F., & Strodtbeck, F. (1961). *Variations in value orientations*. Evanston, IL: Row Peterson.

Krieger, N. (2005). *If "race" is the answer, what is the question? On "race," racism, and health: A social epidemiologist's perspective*. Retrieved September 17, 2005, from http://raceandgenomics.ssrc.org/Krieger?

Lewis, V. A. (2006). *Beyond victims and villains: Contemporary plays by disabled playwrights*. New York: Theatre Communications Group.

Lifton, R. J. (1986). *Medical killing and the psychology of genocide*. New York: The Holocaust History Project. Retrieved November 13, 2009, from http://www.holocaust-history.org/lifton/contents.shtml

Lloyd, M. (1992). Does she boil eggs? Toward a feminist model of disability. *Disability, Handicap and Society*, 7(3), 207–221.

Longmore, P. K. (2003). *Why I burned my book and other essays on disability*. Philadelphia, PA: Temple University.

Longres, J. F. (2000). *Human behavior in the social environment* (3rd ed.). Itasca, IL: F.D. Peacock.

Lukin, J. (2006). Black disability studies. *Temple University Faculty Herald*, 36(4). Retrieved March 28, 2007, from http://www.temple.edu/instituteondisabilities/programs/ds/facultyherald2.htm

Mackelprang, R. W. (2002). Social work practice with persons with disabilities. In S. Gilson, E. DePoy, H. MacDuffie, & K. Meyershon (Eds.), In *Integrating disability content in social work education: A curriculum resource* (pp. 9–14). Alexandria, VA: Council on Social Work Education.

Mackelprang, R. W., & Salsgiver, R. O. (2009). *Disability: A diversity model in human service practice*. Chicago, IL: Lyceum Books.

Marx, K., & Engles, F. (1948). *Manifesto of the Communist Party*. New York: International Publishers.

Mashaw, J., & Reno, V. P. (Eds.). (1996). *Balancing security and opportunity: The challenge of disability income policy*. Washington, DC: National Academy of Social Insurance.

McGoldrick, M. (1982). Ethnicity and family therapy. In M. McGoldrick, J. Pearce, & J. Giordano (Eds.), *Ethnicity and family therapy* (pp. 3–30). New York: Guilford Press.

McGoldrick, M., Pearce, J., & Giordano, J. (1982.). *Ethnicity and family therapy*. New York: Guilford Press.

McNeil, J. (2001). Americans with disabilities. *Current Population Reports: Household studies, 1997*. Retrieved from http://www.census.gov/prod/2001pubs/p70-73.pdf

McRuer, R. (2006). *Crip theory: Cultural signs of queerness and disability*. New York: New York University Press.

Meyerson, L. (1990). The social psychology of physical disability: 1948 and 1988. In M. Nagler (Ed.), *Perspectives on disability: Text and readings on disability* (pp. 13–23). Palo Alto, CA: Health Markets Research.

Miles, M. (2002). *Community and individual responses to disablement in south Asian histories: Old traditions, new myths?* Stockholm-Johanneshov, Sweden: Independent Living Institute.

Mont, D. (2007). *Measuring disability prevalence*. (SP Discussion Paper #0706). Washington, DC: The World Bank.

Morris, J. (1992). Personal and political: A feminist perspective on researching physical disability. *Disability, Handicap and Society*, 7(2), 152–166.

Nagi, S. Z. (1969). *Disability and rehabilitation*. Columbus, OH: Ohio State University Press.

National Association of Social Workers. (2006). *Indicators for the achievement of the NASW standards for cultural competence in social work practice.* Washington, DC: Author.

National Association of Social Workers. (2008). *Code of ethics.* Washington, DC: Author.

National Association of Social Workers. (2009). Policy on disabilities. In *Social work speaks: NASW policy statements* (8th ed.). (pp. 247–350). Washington, DC: NASW Press.

Onken, S. J., & Mackelprang, R. W. (1997). *Building on shared experiences: Teaching disability and sexual minority content and practice.* Paper presented at the Annual Program Meeting, Council on Social Work Education, Chicago, IL.

Peterson, C. J. (2005). A progressive law with weak enforcement? An empirical study of Hong Kong's disability law. *Disability Studies Quarterly, 25*(4), 21.

Plato (1991). *The republic* (B. Jowett, Trans.). New York: Vintage Books.

Riddell, S., & Watson, N. (Eds.). (2003). *Disability, culture and identity.* London: Pearson.

Ridley, C. R., Baker, D. M., & Hill, C. L. (2001). Critical issues concerning cultural competence. *The Counseling Psychologist, 29*(6), 822–832.

Solomon, B. (1976). *Black empowerment: Social work in oppressed communities.* New York: Columbia University Press.

South Africa. (1996). *Constitution of South Africa.* Johannesburg: Author.

Snyder, S., & Mitchell, D. (2006). *Cultural locations of disability.* Chicago, IL: University of Chicago.

Szasz, T. (1977). *The theology of medicine.* Syracuse, NY: Syracuse University Press.

TenBroek, J., & Matson, F. W. (1959). *Hope deferred: Public welfare and the blind.* Berkeley: University of California Press.

United Nations. (2007). *Convention on the rights of persons with disabilities and optional protocol.* Retrieved from http://www.un.org/esa/socdev/enable/conventioninfo.htm

United Nations Radio. (2009, April 21). *Being albino: Tanzanian member of parliament speaks out.* Retrieved December 11, 2009, from http://www.unmultimedia.org/radio/english/detail/73272.html

Waldschmidt, A. (2006). Normalcy, bio-politics and disability: Some remarks on the German discourse. *Disability Studies Quarterly, 26*(2), 42.

Wiggam, A. E. (1924). *The fruit of the family tree.* Indianapolis, IN: Bobbs-Merrill.

Wilcox, S. (1989). *American deaf culture: An anthology.* Burtonsville, MD: Linstock.

Wright, B. (1983). *Physical disability—a psychological approach* (2nd ed.). New York: Harper & Row.

Chapter 17

AARP. (2001). *In the middle: A report on multicultural boomers coping with family and aging issues.* Washington DC: AARP.

Administration on Aging. (2009). *Aging statistics.* Retrieved May 6, 2010, from http://www.aoa.gov

Aging Services of California. (2010). http://www.aging.org

Alzheimer's Association, Northern California Chapter. (2009). *Media fact sheet—Greater San Francisco Bay Area.* Retrieved May 6, 2010, from www.alz.org/norcal/in_my_community_10872.asp

American Heart Association. (2009). *Heart disease and stroke statistics—2009 update.* Retrieved May 6, 2010, from www.american-heat.org

American Psychiatric Association. (1994). *Diagnostic and statistical manual of mental disorders.* Washington, DC: Author.

American Psychological Association. (2010). *Resolution on ageism.* Retrieved February 20, 2009, from http://www.apa.org

Anderson, G. F. & Horvath, J. (2004). The growing burden of chronic disease in America. *Public Health Reports, 119* (3), 263–270.

Asian Community Center. (2006). Unpublished data.

Associated Press. (2007). *McCain jokes to play down age as issue.* Retrieved December 23, 2009, from http://www.msnbc.msn.com/id/17686656/ns/politics-decision_08//

Austin, C. (2005). Not just another population. *Families in Society, 86*(4) Retrieved October 31, 2009 from https://www.familiesinsociety.org/new/SpecialIssue/OlderAdults/86_3/Pages/Articles.htm

Bouchardy, C., Rapiti, E., Blagojevic, S., Vlastos, A., & Vlastos, G. (2007, September 1). Older female cancer patients: Important causes and consequences of undertreatment. *Journal of Clinical Oncology, 25*(14), 1858–1869. Retrieved November 9, 2009, from http://www.cancernetwork.com

Braun, K., & Brown, C. (1998). Perceptions of dementia, caregiving, and help seeking among Asian and Pacific Islander Americans. *Health Social Work, 23*(4), 262–274.

Brunkard, J., Namulanda, G., & Ratard, R. (2008). *Hurricane Katrina deaths, Louisiana, 2005*. Disaster medicine and public health preparedness. American Medical Association.

Butler, R. (2008). Ageism. In E. Capezuti, E. Siegler, & M. Mezey (Eds.), *The encyclopedia of elder care: The comprehensive resource of geriatric and social care* (pp. 25–26) New York: Springer Publications.

Centers for Disease Control. (n.d.). *CDC's disaster planning goal: Protect vulnerable older adults*. Available at: http://www.cdc.gov/aging/pdf/disaster_planning_goal.pdf

Centers for Disease Control, National Center for Health Statistics. (2007). *The state of aging and health in America*. Available at: http://www.cdc.gov/aging/pdf/saha_exec_summary_2007.pdf

Centers for Disease Control. (2010). Office of Minority Health and Health Disparities. *About minority health*. Available at: http://cdc.gov/omhd/ahm/ahm.htm

CNN. (2005, September 13). *Nursing home owners face charges*. Available at: http://www.cnn.com/2005/US/09/13/katrina.impact/

Danner, D., Smith, C., Jessica, P., & Hudson, J. (2008). African Americans with memory loss: Findings from a community clinic in Lexington, Kentucky. *The Nursing Clinics of North America, 43*(3), 437–447.

Dyer, C. B., M. Regev, et al. (2008). SWIFT: A rapid triage tool for vulnerable older adults in disaster situations. *Disaster Medicine and Public Health Preparedness,* 2(Suppl. 1), S45–S50.

Federal Interagency Forum on Aging-Related Statistics. (2008). Retrieved May 7, 2010, from http://www.aoa.gov/agingstatsdotnet/Main_-Site/Data/2008_Documents/Population.aspx

Gurland, B. J., D. E. Wilder, R. Lantigua, et al. (1999). Rates of dementia in three ethnoracial groups. *International Journal of Geriatric Psychiatry, 14*(6), 481–493.

Insurance Institute for Highway Safety. Highway Loss Data Institute. (2010). *Older people*. Retrieved May 7, 2010, from http://iihs.org/research/qanda/olderpeople.html

International Longevity Center-USA. (2007). *Ageism in America. Executive summary*. Available at: http://Ilcusa/media/pdfs/AgeisminAmericaExecutiveSummary.pdf

Kinsella, K., & He, W. (2009). *An aging world. U.S. Department of the Census*. Retrieved January 19, 2009, from http://www.census.gov/prod/2009pubs/p95-09-1.pdf

Lawrence-Lightfoot, S. (2009). Later-life lessons: An interview with Sarah Lawrence-Lightfoot. *The Boston Globe,* January 5.

Lum, D. (2007). Skill development. In D. Lum (Ed.), *Culturally competent practice: A framework for understanding diverse groups and justice issue* (pp. 185–225). Belmont, CA: Thomson Learning Brooks/Cole.

Lum, D. (2011). Culturally competent practice. In D. Lum (Ed.), *Culturally competent practice: A framework for understanding diverse groups and social and economic justice issue* (pp. 3–47). Belmont, CA: Cengage Learning Brooks/Cole.

Masaki, K., White, L., Petrovitch, H., Ross, G. W., Curb, J., Abbott, R., et al. (1997). Frequency and characteristics of silent dementia among elderly Japanese-American men: The Honolulu-Asia Aging Study. *Journal of the American Medical Association,* ISSN: 0098-7484.

Olson, M. (1999). The heart still beats, but the brain doesn't answer: Perception and experience of old-age dementia in the Milwaukee Hmong community. *Theoretical Medicine, 20,* 85–95.

Pinquart, M., & Sorenson, S. (2003). Differences between caregivers and noncaregivers in psychological health and physical health: A meta-analysis. *Psychology & Aging, 18*(2), 250–267.

Pritchard, K. I. (2007). *Have we been guilty of ageism in the primary treatment of breast cancer?* Basingstoke: Nature Publishing Group.

Rawls, J. (1971). *A theory of justice*. Cambridge, MA: Harvard University Press.

Rogers, S., & Komisar, H. (2003). *Who needs long-term care? Fact Sheet, Long-Term Care Financing Project*. Washington, DC: Georgetown University Press.

Sharlach, A., Sirotnik, B., Beckman, S., Neiman, M., & Ruiz, C. (2003, January 31). *A profile of family caregivers: Results of the California statewide survey of caregivers*. Center for the Advanced Study of Aging Services.

Berkeley, CA: UC Berkeley Press. Available at: http://cssr.berkeley.edu/pdfs/FamCare-Profile_Exec.pdf

Stanford University School of Medicine. Chronic Disease Self-Management *Program*. Retrieved May 7, 2010, from, http://patienteducation.stanford.edu/programs/cdsmp.html

Tanabe, M. (n.d.). *Health & healthcare of Japanese-American elders*. Department of Geriartic Medicine, John A. Burns School of Medicine, University of Hawaii. Retrieved September 30, 2008, from http:// www.stanford.edu/group/ethnoger/japanese.html. Accessed on September 30, 2008.

Valcour, V., Maksa, K., Curb, D., & Blanchette, P. (2000, October 23). The detection of dementia in the primary care setting. Archives of Internal Medicine, 160. Retrieved September 30, 2008, from http://www.archinternmed.com

Wallace, S., & Smith, S. (2009, February). *Half a million older Californians living alone unable to make ends meet*. UCLA Health Policy Research Brief. Retrieved March 5, 2009, from http://www.healthpolicy.ucla.edu/pubs/files/Older_CAs_PB_0209.pdf

Wang, P., Tong, H., Liu, W., Long, S., Leung, L., Yau, E., et al. (2006). Working with Chinese American families. In G. Yeo & D. Gallagher-Thomson (Eds.), *Ethnicity and the dementias*. (pp. 172–188). London: Routlege.

White, L., Petrovitch, H., Ross, G.W., et al. (1996). Prevalence of dementia in older Japanese-American men in Hawaii: The Honolulu-Asia study. *Journal of the American Medical Association*, 276, 955–960.

Yeo, G., & Lieberman, M. (1993). Cases in the California ADDTC data bank by ethnicity. Unpublished data.

Chapter 18

Council on Social Work Education (CSWE). (2008). *Educational policy and accreditation standards*. Alexandria, VA: Author.

Cross, T. L., Bazron, B. J., Dennis, K. W., & Isaacs, M. R. (1989). *Toward a culturally competent system of care*. Washington, DC: Georgetown University Child Development Center.

Lum, D. (2004). *Social work practice and people of color: A process-stage approach* (5th ed.). Belmont, CA: Brooks/Cole–Thomson Learning.

Whaley, A. L., & Davis, K. E. (2007). Cultural competence and evidence-based practice in mental health services: A complementary perspective. *American Psychologist 62*(6), 563–574.

INDEX

CPSIA information can be obtained
at www.ICGtesting.com
Printed in the USA
FFOW04n0857170817
38898FF

9 780840 034434